FINANCIAL ACCOUNTING

About the author

Rod Monger, PhD is Adjunct Associate Professor of Accounting at the Hong Kong University of Science and Technology and Associate Professor at the American University of Iraq. He has also taught in Dubai, New York, Boston and Texas. His research interests focus on International Financial Reporting Standards and how they affect global capital markets.

Preface

What this book is about

The purpose of financial accounting is to report the financial results of businesses to parties who have a vested interest in the success or failure of that business. These include investors, investment advisers, creditors who lend money to the business, employees, customers, suppliers, governments and their regulators and the public at large.

Each of these groups has a specific need for information. Investors are interested in whether their money is productively invested. Creditors want to know if the money they have lent to the business can be repaid. Employees want assurances that the business will continue to operate successfully and that their jobs are secure. Customers want to know whether they can continue to depend on the business for their needs; suppliers whether they can guarantee continued sales. Governments and regulators, which have a responsibility to protect the public from unscrupulous business practices, are interested in whether the business is operated legally and responsibly. And finally, the public wants assurances that the business will continue to contribute to the community's economic success.

Financial accounting satisfies these needs by providing a set of financial reports called financial statements. Four standard financial statements are prepared and these are accompanied by a set of explanatory notes. These financial statements are the statement of financial position, statement of comprehensive income, statement of changes in equity and statement of cash flows. The purpose of this textbook is to explain what these financial statements contain, how they are prepared and what they mean.

The scene is the passenger lounge in a major international airport, one of many around the world. Three passengers – Chinese, American and German – are passing time before their flights and fall into a friendly conversation. They discover by coincidence that all three are accountants in their respective countries. Would these accountants understand each other when they talk about work? Let's listen in:

'The financial crisis has made this year very difficult,' says the Chinese. 'Revenues are down and uncollectible receivables have increased.'

'Yes,' says the American, 'the same is true for my company. Of course, the impact on cash flows has been terrible and the banks are not lending. We are very worried.'

'We have the same experience,' agrees the German. 'It also does not help that we have so many asset impairments.'

'At least that is not as much of a problem for us because we record those assets at cost and do not revalue,' responds the American.

'Yes, well, we revalue and that means that when values decline it affects our profit much more strongly,' says the German.

'Yes, yes,' says the Chinese. 'We revalue too and have the same problem.'

What's going on here? Clearly, when the three accountants discuss revenues, uncollectible receivables, cash flows and asset impairments – all of which you will know about by the end of this textbook – they clearly understand each other. They speak a common language. But when they discuss revaluation of assets, though each still understands what the others are saying, differences appear. The German and Chinese 'revalue' assets, the American does not.

Preparing the financial statements involves two major accounting activities. One activity – the accounting process – is universally used and understood throughout the world. The second – accounting standards – can vary between nations.

The accounting process is the method by which financial information is recorded and then classified into meaningful categories such as cash, equipment, materials, amounts owed to the business by customers for purchases, loans owed to creditors, sales to customers, salaries paid to employees and so forth. These categories are then reported in the financial statements. All modern financial accounting is based on this fundamental accounting process, which was invented hundreds of years ago.

The second major accounting activity is the use of accounting standards. Throughout the world governments, regulators and others require businesses to account for their financial activities in a specific way. While the accounting process is the same the world over, accounting standards vary from nation to nation. This is hardly surprising, since each nation wants to exercise its sovereign right over any commerce that takes place in that country.

However, this is changing. Over the past few decades, business has globalized. Major companies operate in many countries and increasingly obtain money from capital markets, private investors and lenders throughout the world. Thus, the flow of money between nations has increased significantly within the past few years. Not surprisingly, this trend towards globalization has been accompanied by efforts to create international accounting standards – a unified set of standards referred to as International Financial Reporting Standards or IFRS.

To date, some nations have completely adopted IFRS, while others have partially 'harmonized' their national standards to be more consistent with IFRS. Other countries continue to use their own national standards. The United Arab Emirates is completely compatible with IFRS for financial institutions, for example. The European Union's standards have only minor differences compared to IFRS. The United States still uses American standards, although it has committed to eventually converge with international standards.

While most accounting textbooks have, in the past, been based on national standards and particularly American accounting standards, this is one of a new generation to use international standards. However, since much of the book covers the accounting process, which is the same the world over, most students will see little difference compared to a textbook written under American standards, or any non-IFRS set of accounting standards. Any observable differences will be related to the accounting standards.

Any student who graduates and has a career in mainstream business must have an understanding of the accounting process and must be familiar with international accounting standards. A student who majors in marketing, operations, supply chain management, human resources or finance must also know these topics. An engineering student might argue that his or her task is engineering electrical components, for example, or an information technology specialist might say that his or her focus should be on developing applications. But machines are not engineered and software is not developed unless a contribution to financial results can be demonstrated. Modern businesses expect engineers, IT specialists and others to be able to articulate this contribution in the language that management understands and uses: financial accounting.

Organization of the book

This textbook has been divided into five parts.

Part I consists of three chapters. The first provides a general overview of major components that make up the financial accounting reporting system. Chapter 1 introduces the purpose, form and basic content of the four financial statements as well as the accounting process. Chapter 2 introduces International Financial Reporting Standards and how they are created. It also examines general concepts in accounting based on the Framework for the Preparation and Presentation of Financial Statements, which is a conceptual foundation for international standards. Chapter 3 expands our understanding of the financial statements. This chapter concludes with a look at the actual financial statements of Emirates Airline.

Part II covers the accounting process. In Chapter 4, we see how financial information is collected and then recorded. We also observe how this information is then classified into meaningful categories that correspond to what is reported in the financial statements. Chapter 5 continues the discussion of the accounting process by explaining how financial information is adjusted so that the financial results of the business are reported in the appropriate time period. Once the adjustment process is complete, the financial statements are then prepared and afterwards the accounting records are readied for future business. In Chapter 6, we learn how financial information flows are organized, particularly in large companies that use automated accounting software.

Part III discusses how we report financial position. In Chapter 7 we cover nonfinancial assets, which include inventories; property, plant and equipment; intangible assets; and investments. In Chapter 8, we examine financial assets and liabilities, which include cash, trade accounts receivables and payables, borrowings and bonds. And in Chapter 9 we learn about equity, which represents the investor's financial interest in the business.

Part IV covers the other three financial statements. Chapter 10 examines issues related to performance as reported by the statement of comprehensive income, and the statement of changes in equity. In Chapter 11, we discuss the statement of cash flows. Together, these two chapters explain how the financial position of the business changes from one time period to the next.

Part V concerns two important issues that arise after the financial statements are completed. The first is how we evaluate the information reported in these statements. In general, investors and others want to know whether the business is improving or deteriorating over time and they are also interested in comparing one company with competitors in the same industry. They want to know if the company can pay its obligations and is performing successfully. Techniques for obtaining answers to these questions are covered in Chapter 12. Finally, in Chapter 13, we examine assurance systems that answer one major question for people who use financial statements: How do we know that the information contained in those statements provides a 'true and fair view' of the financial results of the business?

Chapter features

Each chapter contains features that are designed to assist students with the task of learning financial accounting and relating it to actual business practice. Understanding these features should also help students know what is important and how best to organize their study of the material.

LEARNING OUTCOMES

Each chapter is organized around learning outcomes. A learning outcome identifies a specific task that you, as the student, should be able to perform when you complete your study of the topic. The task associated with each learning outcome will be at one of three levels. The first is rote learning, which means, for example, that you must learn the definition of asset or revenue, or you must know that cash is a current asset that appears on the statement of financial position. A learning outcome can be designed to help you apply a concept, for example how to calculate inventory value using the first-in, first-out method. Thirdly, a learning outcome could involve analysis. For example, you might be asked to determine the impact on profit of using the first-in, first-out method versus the average cost method of valuing inventories. The point is that learning will take place at all three levels – sometimes you will be memorizing, sometimes applying concepts and other times analysing what they mean. Each chapter concludes with a conclusion and a summary for each learning outcome within that chapter to help synthesize and consolidate the material covered.

ON YOUR OWN

After most learning outcomes, you will find a short practice section called 'On Your Own'. These include review questions to help you determine if you understand the material that has just been presented or would benefit from rereading it. In some cases practice questions are included. After reading the material for each learning outcome, take a breather and work through the On Your Own section before proceeding to the next.

TERMINOLOGY

Each chapter introduces new terms. These terms are shown in blue bold in the text when they are first defined. All key terms are listed at the end of the chapter and are also included in the glossary at the end of the book. When alternative terms are used in practice, these are included in the text and also as part of the glossary. For example, what Europeans refer to as 'ordinary shares', Americans call 'common stock'. In addition, self-study material at the end of each chapter contains a 'Terminology practice' section in fill-in-the-blank format. Online students will find that each chapter has a set of both multiple-choice and true-and-false questions that contain some items related to terminology.

GRAPHIC ILLUSTRATIONS

Different students learn in different ways. Some learn better by listening, some by doing and some by observing. In general, all students seem to understand material better when they can see a graphic illustration or diagram of the concepts being discussed. Plus, graphic illustrations help students to understand how the material currently being studied relates to other material presented throughout the textbook. Every effort has been made to present material graphically where doing so makes sense.

AUDITORY EXPLANATIONS

For those students who learn better by listening, some material in each chapter can be accessed through an auditory file on the textbook's website. These files can be downloaded onto your MP3 player, for example, and listened to while on the go, and they can be used to reinforce what you have read in the textbook.

EXTENDED EXAMPLES

Each chapter uses extended examples when it makes sense to do so, especially for key concepts. By working through a comprehensive example, students are better able to understand the accounting process. University graduates are rarely expected to perform bookkeeping functions, but at the same time some may be required at some point to supervise those who do. In some cases, a chapter works through the accounting for one time period and then asks the student to demonstrate his or her understanding by extending the example through the next time period.

REVIEW QUESTIONS

At the end of each chapter a set of review questions are included. These are an excellent place to start studying after reading the chapter, because they will quickly help you assess how well you understood the material presented.

APPLICATION EXERCISES AND PROBLEMS

Exercises and problems have been included at the end of each chapter. By far the best way to learn accounting is to work through examples. In some cases, exercises and problems are accompanied by forms or worksheets included on the textbook website.

CASE ANALYSIS

All chapters are accompanied by one or more case studies. Some of these cases span more than one chapter. For example, we will follow developments at Botswana Wild Safaris, LLC, owned by adventurer Tony Washford, in Chapters 7, 8 and 9. Cases provide you with an opportunity not only to analyse a complex business situation from an accounting perspective but also to observe how different accounting components are related. Other, more complex and thought-provoking cases have been made available to your instructor for use in graduate-level courses.

SUGGESTED READINGS

Some chapters include a brief list of optional suggested readings. Any student with an interest in a business career should find these readings interesting and informative.

WEB LINKS

Some chapters have a brief list of web links to help students expand their knowledge on topics covered in the chapter. These include links to accounting organizations, professional organizations, the larger accounting firms and others.

END NOTES

All references and explanatory material are included in an endnotes section at the end of each chapter to keep them from cluttering up the text. When possible, definitions are based on International Financial Reporting Standards. As already noted, this book is based on international accounting standards and part of the task at hand for the international accounting profession is to use terminology based on definitions provided in international standards.

CHAPTER QUIZ ONLINE

Each chapter also has both interactive multiple-choice and true-and-false questions online to provide the student with the ability to self-test their understanding of the chapter. Some of these questions have been created specifically for this textbook, while others have been adapted from professional accounting examinations.

The current business environment

Before you begin your study of financial accounting, I would like to 'set the stage' based on the current business environment. I wrote this textbook between 2007 and 2009. During most of that time, the world's financial markets and economies were in turmoil – the worst crisis since the Great Depression of the 1930s.

As I write these words, the economy is recovering, although most also agree that it will take a relatively long time for the situation to 'get back to normal'.

The accounting profession has not escaped a share of the blame for this financial crisis. Accusations have been made that certain accounting methods – specifically 'mark-to-market' – have created a distorted view of financial results. The accounting profession also suffered serious setbacks as the result of several recent scandals. Arthur Andersen had been among the largest and most respected accounting firms, but in 2002 the firm was convicted of illegal activities related to Enron, its client at the time. Enron, a major energy trader based in the United States, had engaged in fraudulent activities and misrepresented its financial results, subsequently going bankrupt.

Remember our earlier discussion about the financial information needs of investors, creditors, employees, suppliers, customers, governments, regulators and the public? All these groups were damaged in Enron's collapse. Loss estimates due to the Enron failure vary, but are often put at US$50 billion to $60 billion. Investors who owned shares that were trading at US$90 before the collapse saw their value decline to almost nothing. Employees lost their jobs and often their life savings. And Arthur Andersen, which was arguably a paragon in the accounting profession, went out of business, exiting the stage in shame.

From the accounting profession's perspective, that hurt. It hurt because the profession has the responsibility to help investors, creditors, employees, suppliers, customers, governments, regulators and the public at large understand the financial results of businesses like Enron. The organization that is responsible for setting international accounting standards – the International Accounting Standards Board or IASB – describes it this way:

> The objective of financial statements is to provide information about the financial position, performance and changes in financial position of an entity that is useful to a wide range of users in making economic decisions. Financial statements also show the results of the stewardship of management, or the accountability of management for the resources entrusted to it. Those users who wish to assess the stewardship or accountability of management do so in order that they may make economic decisions; these decisions may include, for example, whether to hold or sell their investment in the entity or whether to reappoint or replace the management.

During the time I was writing this textbook, I attended a class on corporate governance and specifically on the responsibilities of the board of directors in financial matters. The man who taught the course was on the board of three publicly traded companies and indeed was the single 'financial expert' on each board (one financial expert was required under local laws). Yet during the classroom discussion it became obvious that this highly placed individual did not have an adequate grasp of the financial matters that were affecting the companies he served, nor did he understand the causes and risks in the current crisis. Also, at the time, other publicly traded companies were in the news media because of major losses due to mismanagement of similar financial matters. It is very clear that real deficiencies in knowledge exist within the leadership of some of these companies, and that only puts an even greater burden on the accounting profession.

Finally, I want to point out that some people believe that accounting is missing the boat altogether. For example, here is what one observer, a sophisticated financial investment manager, has to say:

> (. . .), accounting methods not only summarize business information into irrelevant measures, but are also excruciatingly slow at doing so. In a world of instantaneous and continuous data... the annual financial statements are archaeological.[1]

You may be asking why the author of a textbook on financial accounting is so critical of the accounting profession. Here's the reason: for a student entering business today, given the financial crisis and the challenges that it presents, it is not enough to learn the terminology. It is not enough to be able to apply accounting concepts to specific problems. It is not enough to think analytically about how accounting should be applied to complex business situations.

I believe that you have a responsibility to evaluate critically every concept you are about to learn. And I also believe that you have a responsibility to use these concepts to evaluate critically every business decision, every company, every senior manager and every board member you encounter in your careers.

I want you to decide for yourself, as your understanding of financial accounting matures, whether *you think* that the accounting profession is doing its job. Is the accounting profession providing the information that investors, creditors and others need to make good decisions? Is the accounting profession adequately discharging its obligations? Is the accounting profession evolving adequately to meet the demands of a rapidly globalizing world? Or, as some say, is it 'archaeological'? And if the answer to this last question is 'yes', what are you going to do about it?

Endnote

1. Bookstaber, Richard (2007) *A Demon of Our Design: Markets, Hedge Funds, and the Perils of Financial Innovation*, Hoboken, NJ: John Wiley & Sons.

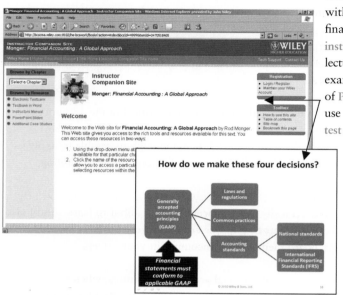

The instructor companion website provides you with all the resources you need to teach financial accounting: a comprehensive instructors' manual, including sample syllabi, lecture notes, case study teaching notes and exam questions for each chapter. There are a set of PowerPoint lecture slides that you can edit to use in your teaching, as well as a comprehensive test bank with over 1300 questions.

On the student companion site you will find several self-test quizzes for each chapter to test your understanding as you progress through the book. You can also access worked examples with audio to increase your knowledge of concepts, as well as web links and an online version of the glossary.

Understanding Financial Reports

INTRODUCTION TO PART I

This textbook covers financial accounting, which determines how a business reports its financial results to owners of the business, creditors who have lent money to the business and others. All these parties have a need to understand whether the business is financially sound and also whether it is successful. Financial results are reported in financial statements.

> The objective of financial statements is to provide information about the *financial position*, *performance* and *changes in financial position* of an entity that is useful to a wide range of users in making economic decisions.

> Financial statements also show the results of the stewardship of management, or the accountability of management for the resources entrusted to it. Those users who wish to assess the stewardship or accountability of management do so in order that they may make economic decisions; these decisions may include, for example, whether to hold or sell their investment in the entity or whether to reappoint or replace the management. (International Accounting Standards Board)

This textbook is organized into five parts, as illustrated in the following diagram.

In Part I we will learn about the financial statements: the statement of financial position, statement of comprehensive income, statement of changes in equity and statement of cash flows. Part I is divided into three chapters:

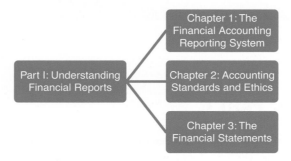

Chapter 1 introduces the financial accounting reporting system that is responsible for the financial statements. We will discuss who receives the financial statements, whom within the business is responsible for preparing the financial statements, what the financial statements contain, what the system is that generates the financial statements, the rules that govern how financial statements are prepared and finally how we can be sure that the information in the financial statements is reliable.

Chapter 2 covers accounting standards and ethics. Accounting standards are the rules that guide the preparation of financial statements. Although accounting standards vary between nations, international accounting standards have been created in recent years. Many countries now either use international standards or have increasingly 'harmonized' their national standards to be more consistent with international standards. This textbook is based on international accounting standards. In addition, Chapter 2 will explain the role that professional ethics play in financial accounting.

In Chapter 3 we will take an in-depth look at the four financial statements. We will see how financial information is classified. We will also see an actual set of financial statements as reported by Emirates Airline. Emirates is an official diminutive for the United Arab Emirates.

Part II covers the accounting process, which is the system that collects and summarizes financial information and prepares the financial statements. We will also see how large, modern companies organize accounting information systems to handle very large transaction volumes.

Part III examines several important issues related to financial position, as reported by the statement of financial position. In Part IV, we will learn how the performance of the business is reported in the statement of comprehensive income. We will also see how changes in financial position are reported in the remaining two financial statements: the statement of changes in equity and the statement of cash flows. Finally, in Part V, we will see how the information reported in the financial statements is used to evaluate the business. We will learn about the techniques used to perform this evaluation. And in the concluding chapter, we will learn about assurance systems, which provide a system of checks and balances to ensure that the information contained in the financial statements is reliable.

As you begin your exploration of financial accounting, I would like to offer these thoughts for your consideration.

This textbook would have been much simpler if it had been written based on the accounting practices of a single nation, like Australia, Brazil, China, France, Japan or the United Kingdom. Examples would have been in one currency and you would have fewer terms to learn. For example, you would not have to remember that common stock and ordinary shares mean the same thing. However, modern business is global and most students want a global perspective. Therefore, our task is laid: we must learn about multiple currencies and different terminology. Despite these differences, the process of accumulating accounting information is the same the world over, even if accounting standards differ. So learning a global perspective will require very little extra effort and offer a great deal of benefit.

The text uses many examples based on fictitious companies. If names in the textbook for these fictitious companies are the same as actual names of companies or individuals, that is purely the result of coincidence. However, the textbook relies on examples of several actual companies, particularly the airlines British Airways, Emirates and Lufthansa. When examples from these companies are used, actual information is often condensed for learning purposes. Readers should not rely on this information for any other purpose except as illustrations of points made in this textbook, and especially should not rely on this information to make investment and similar decisions.

Finally, years ago it used to be common for professors to tell students that accounting was 'the language of business'. This analogy is no longer in vogue, but I am proposing to resurrect it here. No matter what area of business you specialize in – marketing, supply chain management, operations, decision sciences, management, human resources, finance – accounting provides the vocabulary for understanding business and specifically for understanding a business or industry. Business is a financial undertaking. The language of accounting is financial.

If you have attempted to learn a foreign language, you know that a lot of tedious work goes into learning verb tenses or, in the case of a language like Cantonese, tones. Memorizing things by rote is not much fun. But it pays off because as your ability to understand the language comes together, you have access to a whole new world based on people who speak that foreign language. You understand things you would not otherwise have known about. You have opportunities that you would not otherwise have known existed. And you have a knowledge that is superior to people who do not speak that language.

It is the same with accounting. Fluency in financial accounting will enable you to access new worlds, you will understand things that you otherwise would not know, you will be presented with opportunities that you otherwise would not know about – and your knowledge of business will be superior to those who don't speak the language of accounting or don't speak it as fluently as you.

The financial accounting reporting system

1

LEARNING OUTCOMES

By the end of this chapter, you should be able to:

1. Describe the financial information needs of internal and external users.
2. Define a business entity and describe the three major forms of business organization.
3. Describe how financial information is reported to external users.
4. Explain the accounting process.
5. Define generally accepted accounting principles and explain their role in financial accounting.
6. Describe the assurance system for financial reporting.

LEARNING OUTCOME 1
DESCRIBE THE FINANCIAL INFORMATION NEEDS OF INTERNAL AND EXTERNAL USERS

1.1 What are the uses of accounting information?

1.2 Who are internal users and what are their financial information requirements?

1.3 Who are external users and what are their financial information requirements?

1.1 What are the uses of accounting information?

In 2008, *Forbes* magazine listed Warren Buffett as the world's richest man worth an estimated US$62 billion. Buffett has never worked in production, logistics, finance, marketing, sales or information technologies. Nor is he an accountant.

Buffett is an investor. Over his lifetime, he has accumulated ownership interests in many companies, including Coca-Cola, GEICO insurance, Wells Fargo Bank and the Washington Post. In 1965 he acquired Berkshire Hathaway, a textile company that he has since used as a holding company for other investments. By 2007, Berkshire Hathaway owned interests in 76 operating companies.

Buffett and his co-investors paid US$14.86 per Berkshire Hathaway share in 1965. Now those shares are trading for almost US$100 000. Berkshire Hathaway's value increased over twice as much as the stock market as a whole over the same time period (as measured by the Standard & Poor 500 Index, 1965–2007).

In 1950, Buffett enrolled at Columbia Business School, where he learned about 'value investing' from two professors, Benjamin Graham and David Dodd. Buffett was particularly influenced by Graham, who later wrote *The Intelligent Investor*, a book that explains value investing. Buffett, who worked with Graham for several years, later applied value investing concepts to his investment activities.

Value investing identifies companies whose shares are selling below the actual value of the company. This situation – when a company sells for less than its real value – can occur for different reasons. For example, investors may avoid companies in the luxury retail business during an economic downturn because they believe that prospects for growth are poor.

Value investors also avoid companies that are overvalued. For example, during the so-called dot-com bubble in the late 1990s, share prices of Internet companies soared to unrealistic levels as investors became excited about the commercial potential of the Internet. Later, the values of such companies declined significantly and in some cases they went out of business.

But what does this have to do with accounting? The answer is that Buffett and other investors use financial information to determine what a company is worth. They want information on the financial position of the company and its performance, as well as the factors that have caused the financial position to improve or deteriorate. Accounting accumulates and reports financial information. While Warren Buffett is not an accountant, he spends a significant amount of his time examining and analysing accounting information.

All accounting information is financial. Businesses also collect nonfinancial information. For example, a company maintains records on its employees including the number of people employed, their names, addresses, job titles and evaluations of their performance. A business may also collect and analyse information about customers such as their buying preferences or past order histories. A manufacturer may collect data on the amount of time a production machine is used and its output. However, this nonfinancial information is not maintained by accountants. The fact that we account for information that can be expressed in terms of money is referred to as the monetary unit assumption.

1.2 Who are internal users and what are their financial information requirements?

Accounting provides financial information to two groups of users: internal users and external users. Therefore, accounting is divided into two areas: managerial accounting and financial accounting.

- Managerial accounting accumulates and analyses financial information for internal users for planning, decision making and control.

FIGURE 1.1 MANAGERIAL VERSUS FINANCIAL ACCOUNTING

- Financial accounting accumulates and analyses financial information for external users who are interested in the performance and financial position of the business.

Each area addresses a different set of needs for financial information, as shown in Figure 1.1.

In accounting, a user is someone who uses accounting information. Internal users include managers, other employees and members of the board of directors. Normally, managerial accounting information is not provided to external users because it may reveal information that would put the company at a competitive disadvantage if it were known to outsiders. For example, a company may not want a competitor to know how much it pays for labour or materials used in production. Exceptions are made when an outsider has a 'need to know' the information. For example, an outside consultant is hired by the company to improve its production efficiency and needs information to analyse the company's operations. However, even this information is usually provided on the condition that the outsider will keep it confidential.

Managerial accounting information is used within the business for three main purposes:

- **Planning** – An example of planning is budgeting, which is the process of forecasting future financial needs based on what funds the company expects to collect as the result of sales and how much will be paid to purchase materials, for salaries and wages, and to acquire other resources.
- **Decision making** – Management may be considering whether to replace an older piece of equipment with a newer, more efficient model. Management accounting information would be needed to help evaluate the various alternatives available.
- **Control** – Management also uses accounting information to determine whether the business is operating according to its plans and identify situations when the business varies from those plans. For example, managerial accounting information might show that the business is spending more than predicted on wages and salaries for labour. After analysing this information, management concludes that employees are working inefficiently because they have not been adequately trained.

Figure 1.2 summarizes the information requirements of internal users.

FIGURE 1.2 USES OF FINANCIAL INFORMATION BY INTERNAL USERS

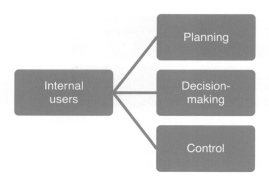

1.3 Who are external users and what are their financial information requirements?

In this textbook we will focus only on financial accounting, which provides information to external users. External users are third parties who have a stake or other vested interest in the business entity, and who are interested in the financial position of the business, its performance and changes in financial position. Figure 1.3 presents a list of different external users with a brief description of the financial information requirements for each.

Managers do not use financial accounting information to make internal decisions. However, they are concerned about how external users evaluate the business; and external users are interested in the financial position, performance and changes in financial position of the business. For that reason, managers and the board of directors pay particular attention to financial accounting reports. The reason is that they want to understand how an external user – especially investors like Warren Buffett and creditors like banks – view the company. Investors and creditors provide investment capital to the business, which is needed if the company is to prosper and grow.

Financial accounting reports information on events that occurred in the past. It does not predict the future. However, external users may use financial accounting information to make informed judgements about how the company will perform in the future. In contrast, managerial accounting information often uses estimates about the future. For example, to develop a budget, management may need to estimate the level of sales for the coming year or how much the company will have to pay for materials and labour.

Financial accounting also accounts for transactions that have occurred in the past. A transaction is an exchange of value between two parties. Until the fifteenth century, when the modern accounting process was invented, accounting mostly involved keeping detailed lists of trade goods. Ancient Egyptians and Mesopotamians used clay tablets to keep track of commodities like gold, silver, grain and olive oil in storehouses. In Peru, the Incans used *quipu*, a system of writing and accounting based on different coloured cords and knots. Archaeologists believe that the knots represented quantities of particular goods, including

FIGURE 1.3 EXTERNAL USERS AND THEIR INFORMATION REQUIREMENTS

Investors – Those who provide risk capital and their advisers. Their primary needs are for information to help them decide whether to buy, hold or sell equity securities in the company, and whether the company can pay dividends.

Employees – Employees and their representative groups who need information about the stability and the profitability of the business. Employees need financial information to be able to assess the company's ability to provide employment opportunities, and to pay compensation and retirement benefits.

Lenders – The major concern of lenders is whether their loans and the associated interest will be paid when due. Financial information is needed to understand whether the business entity can pay its debts, and if not, what assets are available to secure debts.

Suppliers and other trade creditors – Suppliers and other trade creditors, like lenders, are interested in whether amounts they are owed by the company will be paid.

Customers – Customers, especially those which are dependent on the business, are interested in the long-term viability of the entity.

Governments and their agencies – Governments and agencies need information for regulatory purposes, taxation and to develop national income and other statistics.

Public – The public needs financial information for a variety of purposes such as understanding the contributions to the local economy.

Source: Framework for the Preparation and Presentation of Financial Statements. Copyright © 2007 International Accounting Standards Committee Foundation. All rights reserved. No permission granted to reproduce or distribute.

subtotals and totals, as well as the locations of the goods. This allowed the Incans to keep track of commercial activity throughout their far-flung South American empire. With the introduction of money, accounting was increasingly used by civilizations like China, Greece and Rome to monitor government expenditure.

The double-entry accounting method – which modern accounting still uses today – was invented by Fra Luca Bartolomeo de Pacioli (1445–1517), an Italian mathematician and monk. Unlike ancient list keepers, the double-entry method accounts for transactions, which as we have seen is any exchange of value between two entities (we will discuss transactions in more detail in Chapter 4).

Figure 1.4 illustrates the financial information requirements of external users.

FIGURE 1.4 USES OF FINANCIAL INFORMATION BY EXTERNAL USERS

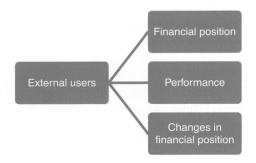

ON YOUR OWN

LEARNING OUTCOME REVIEW

1. Who are internal users and what uses do they make of accounting information?
2. List the types of external users and describe the information requirements of each.
3. For what does financial accounting account?
4. What uses do external users make of accounting information?
5. Why are internal users more interested in future-oriented financial information?
6. Why is future-oriented financial estimates typically not provided to external users?

LEARNING OUTCOME 2
DEFINE A BUSINESS ENTITY AND DESCRIBE THE THREE MAJOR FORMS OF BUSINESS ORGANIZATION

2.1   What is a business entity?

2.2   What are the three major forms of business organization?
      2.2.1   Limited liability companies
      2.2.2   Sole proprietorships
      2.2.3   Partnerships

2.1 What is a business entity?

An entity could be a business, customer, supplier, investor, creditor – any person or organization that enters into a transaction. The following case illustrates the different types of entities that can be involved in a transaction.

While a fine arts student at university, Li Jiazhen developed a passion for antique Chinese porcelain: vases, tea ware and similar items. With mainland China becoming more accessible to trade, many outstanding antique porcelain items were becoming available to the market.

Jiazhen began trading privately. His business grew and he eventually opened a retail shop in the Central District of Hong Kong, organized as Jiazhen Antique Porcelains Ltd. Jiazhen invested his small savings to begin the business. His parents also invested some money, becoming part owners of the business along with Jiazhen.

Jiazhen Antique Porcelains grew quickly and needed more capital to acquire additional porcelain to sell. Hong Kong China Bank provided a loan to the business, which was to be repaid over the next two years.

Because he was occupied in the shop, Jiazhen began to rely more and more on Shi Wenwei, who lived on the Chinese mainland, to procure antique porcelain items. Wenwei knew Jiazhen's taste very well, so she would acquire items and sell them to Jiazhen Antique Porcelains at a small mark-up to compensate for her effort. Jiazhen also hired Marie LeNestour, a young French woman whom he had studied with at university, to assist him in the shop.

Among the many customers who purchased porcelain from the shop, one in particular, Martin Strassberg, also developed an interest in antique Chinese porcelain and often purchased items of special interest.

From the brief case just presented, can you identify the different entities involved with Jiazhen Antique Porcelains Ltd? These entities are shown in Figure 1.5.

The business itself is one entity, and is also the entity we will focus on in this chapter. Jiazhen Antique Porcelains engages in transactions with Shi Wenwei, the supplier, as well as Marie LeNestour, the employee. And the business enters into transactions with a customer, Mark Strassberg. In addition, transactions occur between the business and Hong Kong China Bank.

But did you also list Jiazhen's parents and Jiazhen himself? As owners, the parents would be a separate entity engaging in transactions with Jiazhen Antique Porcelains. So too would Jiazhen. Even though Jiazhen seems to be one and the same as the business – he began the business, which is based on his interest in porcelain – he and Jiazhen Antique Porcelains are two separate entities, each of which engages in transactions with the other.

Transactions can be business or financial. In the Jiazhen Antique Porcelains example, business transactions include those with Martin Strassberg, Marie LeNestour and Shi Wenwei. Financial transactions, which involve only financial exchanges, include the investment by Li Jiazhen, Jiazhen's parents and the bank loan from Hong Kong China Bank.

FIGURE 1.5 JIAZHEN ANTIQUE PORCELAINS LTD AND OTHER ENTITIES

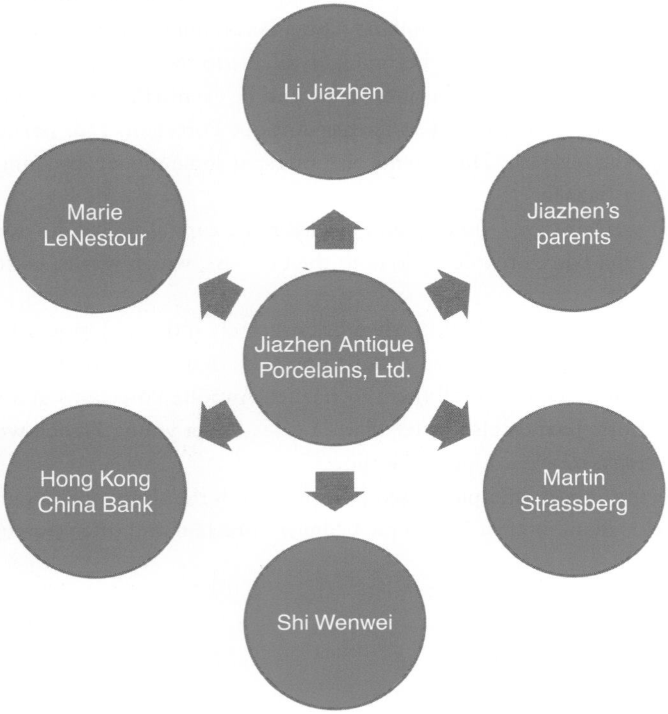

What form do these transactions take? Typical examples include the following:

- Martin Strassberg visits the shop and purchases a tea-ware set. A sale transaction has occurred. The business has exchanged the tea-ware set for money.
- Marie LeNestour works in the shop. The business gives Marie money in exchange for her services.
- Jiazhen's parents own part of the business. The business gives them part of the earnings from the business in exchange for the use of their money.
- Hong Kong China Bank has lent money to the business. The business gives the bank interest on the amount borrowed and eventually returns this amount to the bank in return for use of the bank's money for a period of time.
- Shi Wenwei supplies the business. The business gives Wenwei money in exchange for porcelain.
- Li Jiazhen is the manager and owner of the business. The business gives Jiazhen compensation for his managerial services and also part of the earnings as compensation for his ownership.

A business transaction can also be a barter transaction, an exchange that does not involve money. Suppose that Martin Strassberg offered to exchange some porcelain that he had bought in the past for some new items that have just arrived in the shop. Jiazhen agrees to the exchange.

When transactions occur, they are 'captured' by coding the financial information, the date the transaction occurred, who the transaction was with, what was exchanged and the financial amounts involved. In this way, business and financial transactions (including barter transactions) are recorded. Once recorded, the information captured is then summarized into meaningful categories. For example, Jiazhen might want to know: what amount was sold during a particular month. How much cash was received? How much money has the business paid Shi Wenwei for porcelain? How much did Martin Strassberg purchase? How much interest was paid to the bank? Is enough antique porcelain available to stock the shop properly? How much cash is available to pay the obligations of the business, including the loan to the bank?

In addition Jiazhen will also want to know that all this financial information is accurate and that transactions have been correctly recorded. Marie handles accounting for the business, and he trusts Marie. But how does he *verify* the information?

And finally, Jiazhen's parents and Jiazhen himself will want progress reports on the business. What is the current financial position? How has the financial position changed since the last report was prepared? Financial accounting addresses all these needs. Financial accounting 'is the system of recording and summarizing business and financial transactions and analyzing, verifying, and reporting the results; also: the principles and procedures of accounting.'[1]

In accounting, the identification of the business as a separate entity from other entities and from its owners is referred to as the entity concept. The entity concept is important, because once separate entities are correctly defined, then identifying transactions between those entities is easier. For example, Li Jiazhen and Jiazhen Antique Porcelains Ltd are two separate and distinct entities, as we have already discussed. Thus, any transactions between them must be accounted for.

Financial accounting applies not only to businesses but also individuals, governments, not-for-profit organizations like hospitals and art museums – any entity that engages in financial transactions. However, this textbook focuses only on accounting for business entities.

2.2 What are the three major forms of business organization?

In general, business entities can take one of three forms, as illustrated in Figure 1.6: a limited liability company, sole proprietorship or partnership.

FIGURE 1.6 MAJOR FORMS OF BUSINESS ORGANIZATION

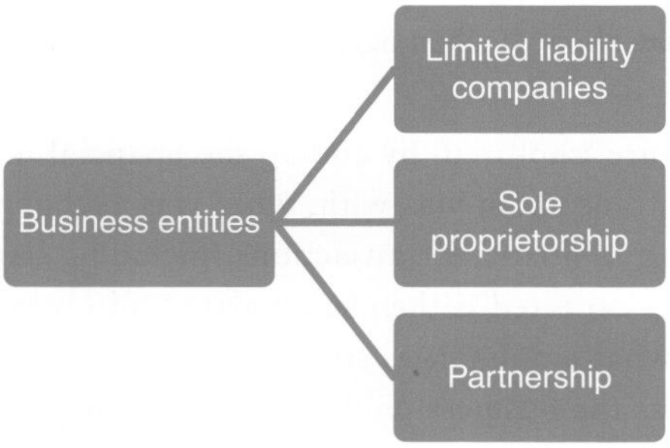

2.2.1 LIMITED LIABILITY COMPANY

A limited liability company is a legally independent entity established under the laws and regulations of the government in the jurisdiction where it is registered or incorporated. Figure 1.7 lists examples of different forms that legal liability companies can take depending on the country or region. Although the legal rights granted to

FIGURE 1.7 LIMITED LIABILITY COMPANIES IN DIFFERENT COUNTRIES

Country	Term	English translation	Abbreviation
Australia	Limited	Public limited company	LTD
Austria	Aktiengesellshaft	Stock corporation	AG
Brazil	Sociedade Anónima	Public limited company	SA
England	Public Limited Company	Public limited company	plc
European Union	Societas Europeaea	Public limited company	SE
France	Société Anonyme	Public limited company	SA
Germany	Aktiengesellshaft	Stock corporation	AG
Greece	Anonimi Etairia	Anonymous society	AE
Hong Kong	Limited	Private or public limited company	Ltd
India	Limited	Public limited company	Ltd
Italy	Società per Azioni	Stock corporation	SpA
Japan	Kabushiki kaisha	Business corporation	KK
Malaysia	Berhad	Stock corporation	Bhd
Russia	Otkrytoye aktsionernoye abshchestvo	Joint stock company	OAO
Singapore	Limited	Publicly listed	Ltd
Spain	Sociedad Anónima	Stock corporation	SA
Sweden	Aktiebolag	Limited company	AB
Switzerland	Aktiengesellshaft	Stock corporation	AG
United States	Corporation	Stock corporation	Inc.

the entity and its owners vary from jurisdiction to jurisdiction, limited liability companies can typically own assets, create debt obligations, enter into legal contracts and engage in business transactions on their own. When a limited liability company is created, we say that it has been registered or incorporated. Limited liability companies are sometimes referred to as corporations, joint stock companies or share-based entities.

Limited liability companies offer several advantages over the other two forms of business organization. For example, they continue to operate even though changes in ownership occur. These changes are accomplished through the purchase and sale of shares, which provide evidence of ownership of the limited liability company. Moreover, since the limited liability company continues business operations uninterrupted, obtaining the financial resources it needs for growth is much easier. Shareholders also have limited liability, as the name implies. A shareholder can lose the amount that he or she has invested, but cannot ordinarily be pursued by creditors for payment of debts that are the obligations of the limited liability company.

Some limited liability companies are publicly traded and all publicly traded companies are organized as limited liability companies. A publicly traded company is listed on an equity securities market (also known as stock exchange, stock market or bourse). Ownership of a large publicly traded company changes daily, as shares are frequently bought and sold on the world's stock exchanges. Figure 1.8 lists the world's ten largest exchanges along with the total value of shares traded in billions of US dollars.

Limited liability companies that are *not* publicly traded are privately held (or closely held). Some privately held companies are quite large. For example, Koch Industries (www.kochind.com) is in chemicals and other diversified businesses, with an estimated $90 billion in annual sales and 85 000 employees.[2] Small and medium-size enterprises (SMEs) can also be organized as limited liability companies, although most are privately held.

2.2.2 SOLE PROPRIETORSHIPS
Privately held businesses can also take the legal form of a sole proprietorship or partnership.

FIGURE 1.8 TEN LARGEST STOCK EXCHANGES

Exchange	Total Value of Share Trades (US$ trillion)
New York Stock Exchange	21.79
Nasdaq Stock Market	11.81
London Stock Exchange	7.57
Tokyo Stock Exchange	5.82
Euronext	3.85
Deutsche Boerse	2.74
BME Spanish Exchanges	1.93
Borsa Italiana	1.59
Swiss Exchange	1.40
Korea Stock Exchange	1.34

Source: World Federation of Exchanges, 2006 ranking.

A sole proprietorship is the simplest form of business organization and usually involves no legal registration. The owner (also known as a sole proprietor) conducts business under his or her own name. In some cases, government authorities have provisions that allow a sole proprietor to adopt a fictitious name for trade purposes. For example, Didier Bihayintore, a sole proprietor, may conduct business under the name Didier's Restaurant.

- The advantages of sole proprietorships are that they are simple and inexpensive to start since they require no registration, as already noted, and the cost of maintaining the business (for example accounting and legal fees) tends to be lower than for a limited liability company.
- The disadvantages are that raising capital is more difficult. Usually banks and other creditors lend capital to the sole proprietor rather than the business per se. This is because the business has no separate legal identity and therefore cannot engage in transactions or have legal obligations such as debt. Another disadvantage is that the sole proprietor has no protection from creditors, who can pursue the owner for the collection of all business debts.

2.2.3 PARTNERSHIPS

A partnership is an association of two or more persons or businesses as owners that conduct a business for profit. The owners are partners. Partnerships are created by a partnership agreement (a private legal contract) among the partners that specifies how profits and losses will be shared, other compensation to be received by partners, and the responsibilities of partners.

- The advantage of partnerships is that more than one person can contribute resources and expertise to the business, and also share the responsibilities for managing the enterprise.
- The disadvantages of partnerships are that individual partners are sometimes held accountable for obligations created by other partners for partnership purposes. In addition, individual partners are not protected from creditors. A creditor may seek repayment of a partnership loan from all other partners or any one partner. When ownership changes – when one partner leaves or a new partner is admitted – the partnership must be legally dissolved and a new partnership created to replace it.

Sole proprietorships and partnerships involve some differences in the owners' legal rights and responsibilities, especially when compared to the limited liability company business organization. The exact form of these three types of business varies from one government jurisdiction to the next. Hybrid forms of business organization often exist that have features of two forms. For example, investors may be able to create a limited liability company that has some characteristics of a partnership. While some variations also exist in how the ownership interests of sole proprietorships and partnerships are accounted for compared to limited liability companies, the accounting is generally the same.

This textbook focuses only on limited liability companies. We will use the terms business entity, business, company or corporation interchangeably to mean a limited liability company unless otherwise noted.

Summarizing the financial accounting reporting system

Figure 1.9 provides a graphical overview of the financial accounting reporting system that we have discussed so far. We know that financial accounting accounts for transactions between the business entity and other entities such as customers, suppliers, employees, investors and creditors. Accounting then reports

FIGURE 1.9 THE FINANCIAL ACCOUNTING REPORTING SYSTEM

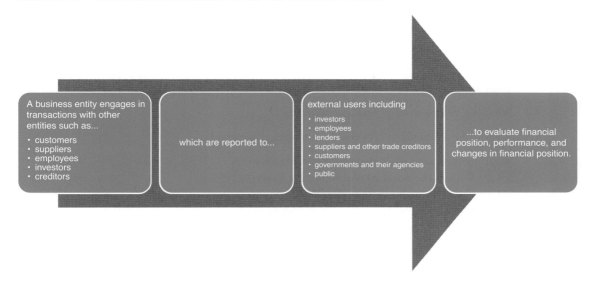

the financial results of these transactions to external users, including investors, employees, lenders, suppliers and other trade creditors, customers, governments and their agencies and the public. Notice from Figure 1.9 that an entity and an external user can sometimes be the same. From the reports they are supplied with, external users evaluate the financial position, performance and changes in financial position of the business entity. We will add other elements to the financial accounting reporting system throughout this chapter.

ON YOUR OWN

LEARNING OUTCOME REVIEW

1. Give examples of the types of entities that typically engage in transactions with a business entity.
2. In a previous example Didier Bihayintore, a sole proprietor, uses the trade name Didier's Restaurant. Are Didier Bihayintore and Didier's Restaurant the same business entity or separate business entities?
3. What is the difference between a business transaction, a financial transaction and a barter transaction?
4. What are the three forms of business organization? What are the advantages and disadvantages of each form?
5. What is the difference between a privately held and a publicly traded company? What forms of business organization can each take?

LEARNING OUTCOME 3
DESCRIBE HOW FINANCIAL INFORMATION IS REPORTED TO EXTERNAL USERS

3.1   What are general-purpose financial statements?

3.2   What is a complete set of financial statements?

3.3   What is the relationship between the financial statements?

3.4   What question does each financial statement answer?
    3.4.1   What is the financial position of the business?
    3.4.2   How did the business perform?
    3.4.3   What resources have the owners invested in the business?
    3.4.4   Where did the business obtain cash and how was it used?

3.1 What are general purpose financial statement?

Accounting information is reported in general-purpose financial statements that are 'intended to meet the needs of users who are not in a position to require an entity to prepare reports tailored to their specific needs'.[3] Sometimes accounting information is customized or tailored to the needs of specific users. For example, a government regulator may require a company to provide financial accounting information using its unique reporting format. Or a bank will ask a business that is requesting a loan to provide certain financial information on one of its application forms.

However, in accounting we assume that external users include a wide range of users. In other words, while some users may have a sophisticated understanding of business and be able to read and interpret accounting information, others will be less knowledgeable. Nevertheless, we also assume that users have a general understanding of business and accounting even though they may not be experts.

3.2 What is a complete set of financial statements?

A complete set of financial statements has five components, which include the:

- statement of financial position,
- statement of comprehensive income,
- statement of changes in equity,
- statement of cash flows, and
- notes to the financial statements.

The first four are actual statements that we will examine shortly. The fifth item is the notes that accompany the four statements. Notes provide information that is not included in the four financial statements, or they expand on information presented on the 'face' of the four financial statements. A note can relate to any one, or more than one, of the financial statements. Figure 1.10 shows a complete set of financial statements.

FIGURE 1.10 COMPLETE SET OF FINANCIAL STATEMENTS

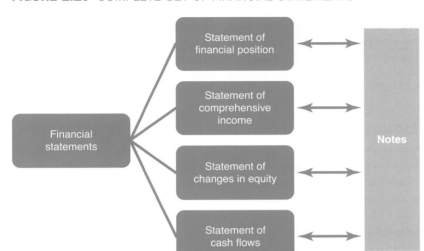

ONE SIZE FITS ALL

Suppose you are the owner of a business but are not involved in day-to-day operations; for this you have hired professional managers. What questions would you have about the business to assure yourself that the money you have invested in the business is being used wisely? Is this company the best investment for your money? Or could you sell this company and reinvest the proceeds into something else and be better off? Is this company 'underperforming' its potential; in other words, are the managers you hired doing an adequate job?

If you are a bank loan officer who is considering whether to provide a major loan to a company, what questions would you have? What confidence do you have that the company will be able to repay the loan? If the company cannot repay the loan, then what recourse does the bank have to recover the money that it lent to the business?

One question that arises is whether 'general-purpose' financial statements – a one size fits all approach – can adequately serve the diverse interests of different users. Proponents argue that management should have the flexibility to present financial information in a manner that they deem most appropriate. Critics argue that this latitude permits and even encourages managers to bias financial reports to serve their own vested interests, with the consequence of misleading users.

Under agency theory, both the board of directors and management are agents of the shareholders, who are principals. Thus, directors and managers have a fiduciary duty to shareholders. A fiduciary duty means that the agent, as a fiduciary, has a position of trust and confidence in relation to the principal. It requires, for example, that the fiduciary put the interests of the principal above his or her own interest. Fiduciary duty also requires full disclosure of any information in the fiduciary's possession if it affects the principals' interests, and also avoidance of conflicts of interest. In other words, the fiduciary is accountable to the principal.

This raises two issues. First, how is this accountability to be enforced? Second, how are conflicts of interest to be avoided? These questions address what is known as the 'agency problem'.

Accounting assumes that the interests of directors, managers and owners are congruent. Unfortunately, history offers many examples of situations in which these interests were not aligned, with the result that investors and other external users were poorly served. Thus, it is only prudent to recognize that in the wrong hands financial reports can be distorted and manipulated. Nonetheless, the approach of using general-purpose financial statements remains the most cost-effective solution for reporting financial information.

3.3 What is the relationship between the financial statements

Financial position is reported on the reporting date. This can be any date, but is usually the end of the year, quarter or month. A reporting period can span any amount of time, as already noted. The division of time into specific intervals such as a year, quarter or month is referred to in accounting as the time period assumption. Thus, the date of the statement of financial position will always be the same as the reporting date. That is why we sometimes say that the statement of financial position provides a 'snapshot' of the financial position of the business. The other three statements report what happened between reporting dates. Specifically, they report changes to the business entity's financial position. In general, the financial position changes because of what the business earns or because owners make more or fewer resources available to the business entity.

Figure 1.12 illustrates the relationship *between* the statement of financial position and the three statements that report changes in financial position.

You can see that Figure 1.12 shows three reporting dates: 31 December 2009, 31 December 2010 and 31 December 2011. It also shows the changes that occur during the period of 1 January 2010 *to* 31 December 2010 and 1 January 2011 *to* 31 December 2011.

Now let's examine how the financial statements answer each of the four questions.

3.4 What question does each financial statement answer?

Each of the four financial statements is designed to answer a different question for external users. The first question relates to the financial position of the business at a specific point in time, while the other three all concern changes to the financial position. These four questions and related financial statements are shown in Figure 1.11.

FIGURE 1.11 FOUR FINANCIAL STATEMENTS AND QUESTIONS

The following question . . .	. . . is answered by the . . .
What is the financial position of the business?	Statement of financial position
How did the business perform?	Statement of comprehensive income
What resources have the owners invested in the business?	Statement of changes in equity
Where did the business obtain cash and how was it used?	Statement of cash flows

FIGURE 1.12 RELATIONSHIP OF FINANCIAL STATEMENTS

REPORTING DATE 31 December 2009	1 January 2010 through 31 December 2010	REPORTING DATE 31 December 2010	1 January 2011 through 31 December 2011	REPORTING DATE 31 December 2011
Statement of financial position	Statement of comprehensive income	Statement of financial position	Statement of comprehensive income	Statement of financial position
	Statement of changes in equity		Statement of changes in equity	
	Statement of cash flows		Statement of cash flows	
Financial position	Changes in financial position	Financial position	Changes in financial position	Financial position

3.4.1 WHAT IS THE FINANCIAL POSITION OF THE BUSINESS?

The first question concerns what the business owns and what the business owes, and what the difference is between the two. What it owns, which are resources the business can use in the future, are assets. What it owes, which are obligations it must settle in the future, are liabilities. The difference is equity.

STUDY TIP

You will find that later chapters will be much easier to follow if you take a few minutes now to commit the names of the financial statements and their elements to memory. When you can comfortably answer these questions, continue with your reading.

1. What are the five components in a complete set of financial statements?
2. What question does each statement answer?
3. What are the three major elements in the statement of financial position?

These three elements of the statement of financial position are shown in Figure 1.13.

FIGURE 1.13 COMPLETE SET OF FINANCIAL STATEMENTS

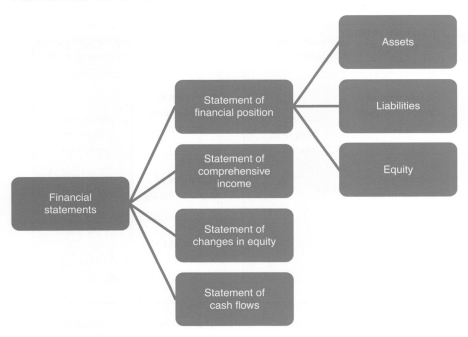

When we say that we report financial position, we mean the relationship of the assets, liabilities and equity of an entity, as reported in the statement of financial position.[4]

On 31 December 2009, Jiazhen Antique Porcelains Ltd has the following assets: HK$20 000 (Hong Kong dollars) in cash in the bank and trade accounts receivable for HK$10 000, which represents the amount owed by customers who have purchased porcelain but not yet paid for it. The business also has HK$20 000 of antique porcelain currently in the shop and being held for resale (referred to as inventories), HK$30 000 of equipment, and a small plot of land purchased for HK$70 000 with a view to building a warehouse in the future. Together these assets – which total HK$150 000 – can be summarized as follows:

Cash in bank	HK$20 000
Trade accounts receivable	10 000
Inventories	20 000
Equipment	30 000
Land	70 000
Total assets	HK$150 000

On the same date, Jiazhen Antique Porcelains Ltd has the following liabilities. It owes Shi Wenwei and other suppliers a total of HK$30 000 for porcelain that the business has received but not yet paid for (trade accounts payable). The business also owes Marie LeNestour HK$1000 in wages, which she has already earned but which have not been paid. The company also owes HK$40 000 to a bank for money bourowed. Jiazhen's business liabilities, which total HK$71 000, are listed as follows:

Trade accounts payable	HK$30 000
Wages payable	1 000
Loan payable	40 000
Total liabilities	HK$71 000

The difference is equity, which totals HK$79 000 (HK$150 000 – HK$71 000). But what is included in equity? Jiazhen Antique Porcelains Ltd's equity has two items: contributed capital and retained earnings. Contributed capital includes amounts that owners have put into the business, which total HK$50 000. The remainder of HK$29 000 (HK$79 000 – HK$50 000) is retained earnings, which include accumulated profits earned by the business in previous years. Jiazhen Antique Porcelains Ltd's equity is summarized as follows:

Contributed capital	HK$50 000
Retained earnings	29 000
Total equity	HK$79 000

All of these amounts for assets, liabilities and equity are the result of past transactions. The cash was obtained from past sales, the porcelain has already been purchased and Marie LeNestour, the employee, has already rendered her services, obligating the business to pay her. But also notice that all of these amounts will affect the business in the future. The cash in the bank can be used to buy more antique porcelain and pay employees. Customers will pay the trade accounts receivable with cash *in the future*. The inventories will be sold *in the future*. The wages owed must be paid in the future. The bank loan will be repaid *in the future*.

The statement of financial position for Jiazhen Antique Porcelains Ltd is shown in Figure 1.14.

First, notice that the heading of the statement of financial position in Figure 1.14 contains the name of the business entity being reported – in this case, Jiazhen Antique Porcelains Ltd. We know that this business is a limited liability company since it uses the suffix Ltd, which stands for Limited (see Figure 1.7). The heading also tells us that the reporting date of this statement is 31 December 2009. As already noted, the financial position of the business entity is presented for a single point in time – a snapshot. And finally, the heading tells us that amounts shown on this statement are denominated in Hong Kong dollars (HK$).

FIGURE 1.14 BASIC STATEMENT OF FINANCIAL POSITION

<table>
<tr><td colspan="4">Jiazhen Antique Porcelains, Ltd
Statement of Financial Position
31 December 2009
HK$</td></tr>
<tr><td>**ASSETS**</td><td></td><td>**LIABILITIES**</td><td></td></tr>
<tr><td>Cash in bank</td><td>20 000</td><td>Trade accounts payable</td><td>30 000</td></tr>
<tr><td>Trade accounts receivable</td><td>10 000</td><td>Wages payable</td><td>1 000</td></tr>
<tr><td>Inventories</td><td>20 000</td><td>Loan payable</td><td>40 000</td></tr>
<tr><td>Equipment</td><td>30 000</td><td>**TOTAL LIABILITIES**</td><td>71 000</td></tr>
<tr><td>Land</td><td>70 000</td><td></td><td></td></tr>
<tr><td></td><td></td><td>**EQUITY**</td><td></td></tr>
<tr><td></td><td></td><td>Contributed capital</td><td>50 000</td></tr>
<tr><td></td><td></td><td>Retained earnings</td><td>29 000</td></tr>
<tr><td></td><td></td><td>**TOTAL EQUITY**</td><td>79 000</td></tr>
<tr><td>**TOTAL ASSETS**</td><td>150 000</td><td>**TOTAL LIABILITIES AND EQUITY**</td><td>150 000</td></tr>
</table>

Notice also that the three elements on the statement of financial position are related through the accounting equation (also known as the balance sheet equation):

This equation tells us that the total resources (assets) of the business entity are equal to the total claims on the business from creditors (liabilities) and the ownership interest (equity). Within the schedule, we can see that the amounts for assets, liabilities and equity conform to the accounting equation:

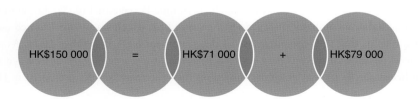

Figure 1.15 expands the statement of financial position to show not only the elements but the line items within each element, based on the Jiazhen Antique Porcelains example including amounts. A line item is the most detailed level of information included in a financial statement.

STUDY TIP

Keep memorizing! Knowing the relationships shown in Figure 1.15 will help later. For example:

- Contributed capital is part of equity, which appears in the statement of financial position.
- Trade accounts payable is part of liabilities, which appear in the statement of financial position.
- Inventories are part of assets, which appear in the statement of financial position.
- And so forth.

The statement of financial position for Jiazhen Antique Porcelains Ltd was presented in Figure 1.14 for 31 December 2009. Figure 1.16 shows the statement of financial position for 31 December 2010, one year later.

Compare the two statements of financial position, 31 December 2009 in Figure 1.14 and 31 December 2010 in Figure 1.16. You can see that the financial position has changed in several ways. Total assets have increased from HK$150 000 to HK$205 000; liabilities have decreased from HK$71 000 to HK$67 000; and equity has increased from HK$79 000 to HK$138 000. Within each of these categories, individual line items have changed as well. For example, cash in bank has increased from HK$20 000 to HK$35 000. Land has increased from HK$70 000 to HK$90 000, contributed capital has increased from HK$50 000 to HK$70 000 and retained earnings have increased from HK$29 000 to HK$63 000. And we can also see that a new item – a revaluation reserve for HK$5000 – has appeared in equity. But what explains these changes?

The answer is contained in the three remaining financial statements: the statement of comprehensive income, the statement of changes in equity and the statement of cash flows. These contain information that explains why the financial position of the business changed between reporting dates.

3.4.2 HOW DID THE BUSINESS PERFORM?

The statement of comprehensive income shown in Figure 1.17 answers the question of how the business performed for the period 1 January 2009 to 31 December 2009. We know this from the heading of the statement: *For the Year Ended 31 December 2009*.

The statement of comprehensive income has two categories: profit or loss and other comprehensive income. These elements are illustrated in Figure 1.18.

The first category – profit or loss – has two elements: revenue and expenses.

Revenue – also known as income or sales – is the inflow of economic benefits during the period arising from the entity's business activities.

FIGURE 1.15 STATEMENT OF FINANCIAL POSITION

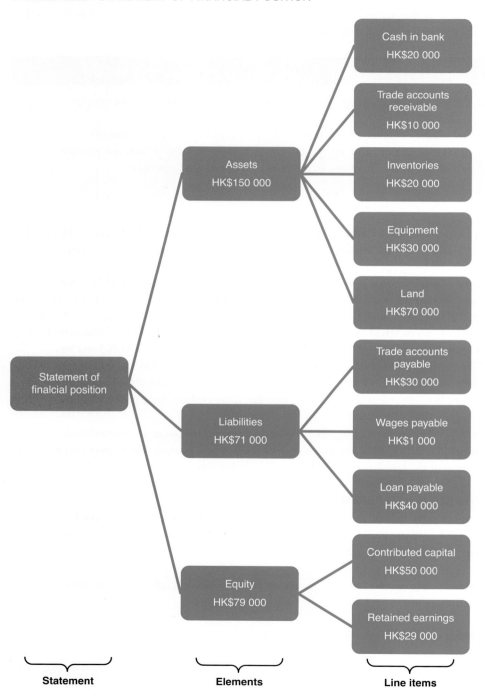

FIGURE 1.16 STATEMENT OF FINANCIAL POSITION, 31 DECEMBER 2010

Jiazhen Antique Porcelains Ltd
Statement of Financial Position
31 December 2010
HK$

ASSETS		LIABILITIES	
Cash in bank	35 000	Trade accounts payable	35 000
Trade accounts receivable	20 000	Wages payable	2 000
Inventories	25 000	Loan payable	30 000
Equipment	35 000	**TOTAL LIABILITIES**	67 000
Land	90 000		
		EQUITY	
		Contributed capital	70 000
		Revaluation reserve	5 000
		Retained earnings	63 000
		TOTAL EQUITY	138 000
TOTAL ASSETS	205 000	**TOTAL LIABILITIES AND EQUITY**	205 000

FIGURE 1.17 STATEMENT OF COMPREHENSIVE INCOME

Jiazhen Antique Porcelains Ltd
Statement of Comprehensive Income
For the Year Ended 31 December 2010
HK$

Revenue	200 000
Expenses	
Cost of porcelain sold	(90 000)
Wages expense	(38 000)
Rent expense	(31 000)
Total expenses	(159 000)
Profit or loss	41 000
Other comprehensive income	5 000
Total comprehensive income	46 000

FIGURE 1.18 STATEMENT OF COMPREHENSIVE INCOME

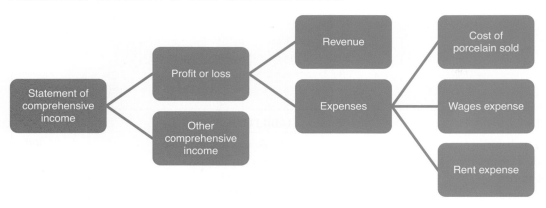

The statement of comprehensive income for Jiazhen Antique Porcelains tells us that revenue is HK$200 000. This means that the business sold porcelain for that total amount. For example, a customer purchases a porcelain tea-ware set for HK$2000. This transaction amount would be included in revenue on the statement of comprehensive income.

Expenses are outflows of economic benefits during the period arising from the entity's business activities.

In Figure 1.17, the statement of comprehensive income shows that Jiazhen Antique Porcelains had three expenses: the cost of the porcelain sold was HK$90 000, wages to compensate employees were HK$38 000 and rent on the shop space where the business is located was HK$31 000. Total expenses were HK$159 000.

Profit or loss is the difference between revenue and expenses.

Jiazhen Antique Porcelains's profit is HK$41 000 (HK$200 000 – HK$159 000). Because revenue exceeded expenses, the business was profitable.

When we refer to performance, we mean the relationship of the income and expenses of an entity as reported in the statement of comprehensive income.

Revenue, expenses and profit or loss are related in the income equation as follows:

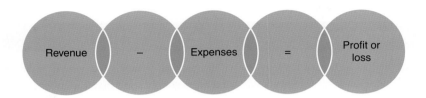

From the statement of comprehensive income in Figure 1.17, we can see that the income equation would be:

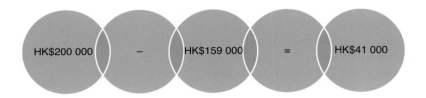

What if Jiazhen Antique Porcelains's expenses had exceeded its revenue? Figure 1.19 illustrates the statement of income for 2008 – the previous year – with a loss.

FIGURE 1.19 STATEMENT OF COMPREHENSIVE INCOME

Jiazhen Antique Porcelains Ltd Statement of Comprehensive Income For the Year Ended 31 December 2008 HK$	
Revenue	120 000
Expenses	
Cost of porcelain sold	(65 000)
Wages expense	(35 000)
Rent expense	(31 000)
Total expenses	(131 000)
Loss	(11 000)
Other comprehensive income	0
Total comprehensive income	(11 000)

Since revenue of HK$120 000 was less than expenses of HK$131 000, Jiazhen Antique Porcelains reported a loss of HK$11 000.

FOR YOUR INFORMATION

The expenses and the loss in Figure 1.19 are shown in brackets, which is one way to indicate a negative number in accounting. Financial statements will sometimes simply state that a number is to be added or subtracted. For example, the amounts in Figure 1.19 could have been presented as follows:

Revenue	HK$120 000
Less: Expenses	131 000
Loss	HK$11 000

In other cases, those who prepare financial statements assume that the reader knows whether a number is positive or negative given its context (for example, expenses are always subtracted from revenue). In this case, the same amounts would be presented as follows:

Revenue	HK$120 000
Expenses	131 000
Loss	HK$11 000

Because the result is labelled 'loss', the 11 000 is assumed to be negative.

Also note that the first number in a column of figures and the total (as well as any subtotals) are normally presented with the currency symbol. The exception is when amounts are presented in a schedule or statement that has the currency symbol in the heading. See Figure 1.19 for an example.

The second category of the statement of comprehensive income is other comprehensive income. In accounting, some types of income and expenses are not included in profit or loss but are separated into this second category. The reasons for this we will discuss later.

Jiazhen Antique Porcelains reports land of HK$70 000 at the end of 2009 (Figure 1.14), which increases to HK$90 000 by the end of 2010 (Figure 1.16). Assume that HK$5000 of this increase is due to an increase in the value of the existing land and the other HK$15 000 is additional land purchased. The HK$5000 increase in the value of the existing land is part of other comprehensive income. It is therefore reported in the second category on the statement of comprehensive income (Figure 1.17) and appears as a revaluation reserve on the statement of financial position at the end of 2010 (Figure 1.16).

The last amount on the statement of comprehensive income (Figure 1.17) is total comprehensive income of HK$46 000, which is the total of profit of HK$41 000 and other comprehensive income of HK$5000, as shown in this equation:

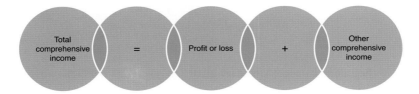

Substituting the amounts from Jiazhen Antique Porcelains' statement of comprehensive income:

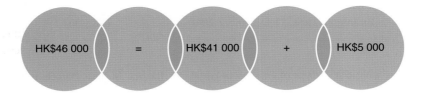

3.4.3 WHAT RESOURCES HAVE THE OWNERS INVESTED IN THE BUSINESS?

This question is answered by the statement of changes in equity. Recall that equity is the difference between assets and liabilities – what the business owns less what it owes. Equity has three basic elements: contributed capital, retained earnings and reserves.

In Figure 1.14, you can see that Jiazhen Antique Porcelains reported HK$50 000 in contributed capital for 31 December 2009. By the end of 31 December 2010 (Figure 1.16) this had increased to HK$70 000. Contributed capital represents the amount the owners have invested in the business. In this case, Jiazhen's parents increased the amount of money invested by HK$15 000 and Li Jiazhen invested an additional HK$5000 of his own money. This explains the total increase of HK$20 000 (HK$70 000 – HK$50 000).

During the same period, the business's retained earnings increased from HK$29 000 to HK$63 000. The difference is HK$34 000. Part of the difference is explained by the profit for the period reported in the statement of comprehensive income in Figure 1.17. In other words, the business earned HK$41 000 and this was 'retained', which means that it was not distributed to the owners.

However, if we add profit of HK$41 000 to the beginning retained earnings balance of only HK$29 000 the result is HK$70 000. Why is the ending retained earnings balance only HK$63 000? What is the HK$7000 difference? The answer is that this difference was distributed to the owners, Li Jiazhen and his parents. A distribution of retained earnings to owners is called a dividend. Finally, reserves increased by HK$5000 because of the revaluation of the land.

FIGURE 1.20 STATEMENT OF CHANGES IN EQUITY

Jiazhen Antique Porcelains Ltd Statement of Changes in Equity For the Year Ended 31 December 2010 HK$	
Beginning balance, 1 January 2010	79 000
Additional investment by owners	20 000
Profit	41 000
Increase in revaluation reserve	5 000
Dividend	(7 000)
Ending balance, 31 December 2010	138 000

Figure 1.20 illustrates a basic statement of changes in equity for Jiazhen Antique Porcelains for the year ended 31 December 2010.

Notice that the schedule begins with the beginning equity balance on 1 January 2010. This is the same as the ending balance for equity, which would be shown on the statement of financial position for 31 December 2009 (an ending balance of one period is the beginning balance for the next period). This amount is HK$79 000. We see that the ending balance on 31 December 2010 is HK$138 000. The statement of changes in equity (Figure 1.20) explains why this balance changed. The owners made an additional investment of HK$20 000, profit increased equity by HK$41 000 and land increased in value by HK$5000, all of which increased equity. Equity was decreased by HK$7000 because some earnings were distributed to the owners.

Figure 1.21 shows the statement of changes in equity in graphical form.

FIGURE 1.21 STATEMENT OF CHANGES IN EQUITY

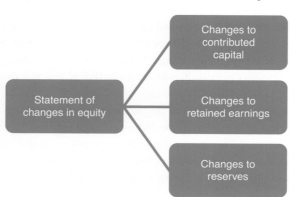

3.4.4 WHERE DID THE BUSINESS OBTAIN CASH AND HOW WAS IT USED?

This question is answered by the statement of cash flows. The purpose of the statement of cash flows is to explain the difference between the cash balance on the statement of financial position at the beginning of the period with the cash balance on the statement of financial position at the end of that period.

On 31 December 2009, Jiazhen Antique Porcelains's cash balance was HK$20 000 (Figure 1.14) and it had risen to HK$35 000 by 31 December 2010 (Figure 1.16). What caused it to change?

To answer this question, cash flows are separated into inflows and outflows of cash, also referred to as sources and uses of cash. Cash inflows and outflows are then each classified into three types of activities:

- Operating activities are cash flows related to the principal revenue-producing activities of the entity that do not qualify as investing or financing activities.
- Investing activities relate to the acquisition or disposal of major assets.
- Financing activities result in changes in the size and composition of the amount that owners have invested in the business and borrowings.

Each of these three activities can be a source and a use of cash. This is graphically shown in Figure 1.22 with an example from Jiazhen Antique Porcelains for each category.

The statement of cash flows is often considered to be the most important financial statement. Without a healthy cash flow, no business can survive. However, all four financial statements are important in order to have a complete understanding of the business.

Figure 1.23 presents the statement of cash flows for Jiazhen Antique Porcelains for the year ended 31 December 2010.

FIGURE 1.22 EXAMPLES OF CASH SOURCES AND USES BY ACTIVITY

	Source of cash	Use of cash
Operating activity	A piece of antique porcelain is sold to a customer who pays in cash.	A supplier is paid in cash.
Investing activity	The business purchases additional land.	The business sells land.
Financing activity	Cash is provided to the business by owners.	The business repays a loan to the bank.

FIGURE 1.23 STATEMENT OF CASH FLOWS

Jiazhen Antique Porcelains Ltd Statement of Cash Flows For the Year Ended 31 December 2010 HK$	
Operating activities	
Net cash from operating activities	32 000
Investing activities	
Net cash used for investing activities	(20 000)
Financing activities	
Net cash used for financing activities	3 000
Net decrease in cash	15 000
Cash balance, 1 January 2010	20 000
Cash balance, 31 December 2010	35 000

From this statement, we can see that the operating activities were a net source of cash of HK$32 000. We know that because the amount on the schedule is positive. A net source of cash from an activity increases the cash balance of the business. However, we can also see that investing activities were a net use of cash of HK$20 000. We know this because the number is negative. Finally, financing activities are a net source of cash of HK$3000.

When we combine these three activities we have a net increase in cash of HK$15 000 (HK$32 000 − HK$20 000 + HK$3000). We add this difference to the cash balance on 1 January 2010 of HK$20 000 to calculate the cash balance on 31 December 2010. This will be the amount shown on the statement of financial position. In other words, the purpose of the statement of cash flows is to explain why the amount of cash changed over the period.

Figure 1.24 expands the financial statements by adding the elements for the statement of cash flows.

INTERPRETING RESULTS

What story can we tell about Jiazhen Antique Porcelains Ltd based on the financial statements discussed in this chapter? Even without notes to the financial statements, we have a lot of information.

FIGURE 1.24 STATEMENT OF CASH FLOWS BY ELEMENTS

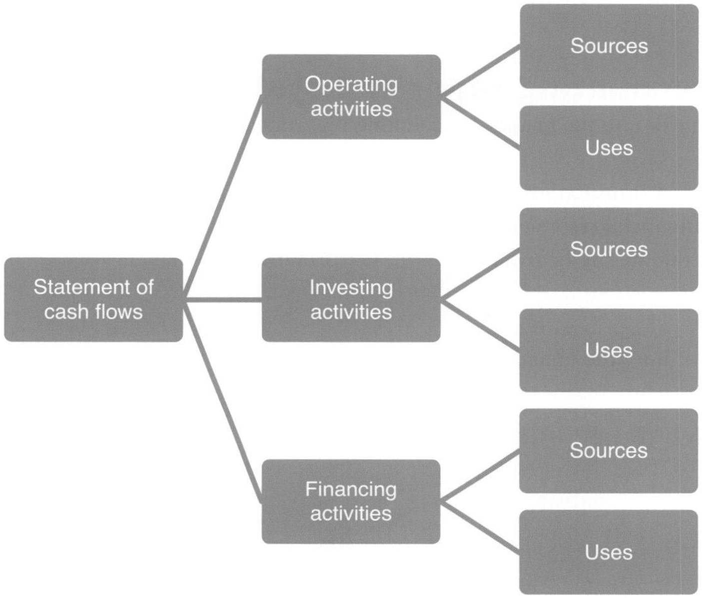

What is the financial position of the business? From the statement of financial position, we know that assets have increased, liabilities have decreased and equity has increased. We also know what changes have occurred in asset, liability and equity balances.

How did the business perform? From the statement of comprehensive income for 2010, we know that Jiazhen Antique Porcelains was profitable, since it reported a profit of HK$41 000 plus an increase in the value of land owned of HK$5000 shown in other comprehensive income.

What resources have the owners invested in the business? We know that the owners increased the amount of contributed capital by HK$20 000. And we also know that the profit of the business was retained except for HK$7000 paid to the owners as a dividend. From this we can tentatively conclude that since the business is now profitable and the investors are adding resources, they expect the business to prosper and grow in the future.

Finally, where did the business obtain cash and how was it used? The statement of cash flows tells us that Jiazhen Antique Porcelains's operating activities are 'cash flow positive'. This is not true for all businesses. We also know that the owners are increasing their investments in the business. Also, cash is being used for investment. The business has bought additional land in order to build a warehouse. These are usually positive signs, since investors are unlikely to invest in a business that is expected to be unsuccessful in the future.

You will see as we progress through this textbook how much more information about the business can be obtained from the financial statements. What we have here is only the basic story.

Extending the financial accounting reporting system

Let's pause to see how the financial statements fit into the financial accounting reporting system from Figure 1.9.

Figure 1.25 shows that the business engages in transactions with other entities. The financial results of these transactions are reported through the four financial statements and notes to external users. These external users interpret the financial statements to evaluate the financial position, performance and changes to financial position.

Now we turn our attention to the process of how the financial statements are prepared.

FIGURE 1.25 THE FINANCIAL ACCOUNTING REPORTING SYSTEM INCLUDING THE FINANCIAL STATEMENTS

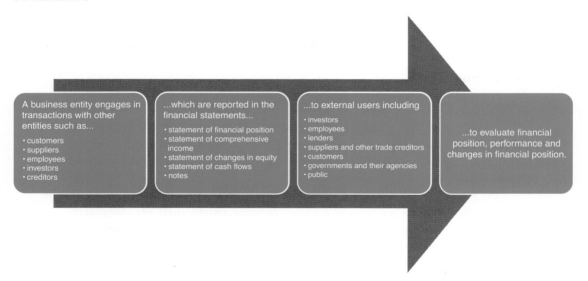

A business entity engages in transactions with other entities such as...
- customers
- suppliers
- employees
- investors
- creditors

...which are reported in the financial statements...
- statement of financial position
- statement of comprehensive income
- statement of changes in equity
- statement of cash flows
- notes

...to external users including
- investors
- employees
- lenders
- suppliers and other trade creditors
- customers
- governments and their agencies
- public

...to evaluate financial position, performance and changes in financial position.

ON YOUR OWN

LEARNING OUTCOME REVIEW

1. What are the five components in a complete set of financial statements?
2. What question does each financial statement answer?
3. What are the elements of each financial statement? Define each of these.
4. What purposes do the notes to the financial statement serve?

5. When we say that accounting generates 'general-purpose' financial statements, what are we assuming about the users?
6. What is financial position? What is performance?
7. Which financial statements report financial position? Which financial statements report changes in financial position? Which financial statements report performance?
8. What is the accounting equation?
9. What is a line item?
10. What is the difference between profit or loss and other comprehensive income?
11. What are the different ways to indicate that an amount on the financial statements is negative?

LEARNING OUTCOME PRACTICE

1. Trade accounts payable is reported as which of the following?
   a. A liability on the statement of financial position
   b. A liability on the statement of comprehensive income
   c. An asset on the statement of financial position
   d. An asset on the statement of comprehensive income

2. Equity would appear on which financial statement(s)?
   a. The statement of comprehensive income only
   b. The statement of financial position only
   c. The statement of comprehensive income and the statement of cash flows
   d. The statement of financial position and the statement of changes in equity

3. Expenses would appear on which financial statement(s)?
   a. The statement of comprehensive income only
   b. The statement of financial position only
   c. The statement of comprehensive income and the statement of cash flows
   d. The statement of financial position and the statement of changes in equity

4. If assets are $55 000 and equity is $25 000, how much are liabilities?
   a. $80 000
   b. $30 000
   c. ($30 000)
   d. Cannot be determined from the data given

5. Dividends appear on which financial statement(s)?
   a. The statement of comprehensive income only
   b. The statement of financial position only
   c. The statement of comprehensive income and the statement of changes in equity
   d. The statement of changes in equity only

LEARNING OUTCOME 4
EXPLAIN THE ACCOUNTING PROCESS

4.1   What is the accounting process?

4.2   How does the accounting process work?

4.1 What is the accounting process?

Recall that until Fra Pacioli invented the double-entry method, most accounting was simply keeping lists of storehouse goods. Now almost all businesses, large and small, use the double-entry method of accounting for transactions. But how does the double-entry system work? What is the process that businesses use to prepare the financial statements? And why is this method superior to just keeping lists the way the Incans and other ancient peoples did?

Let's say that you are a trader in ancient Egypt. You have lists kept by scribes of the olive oil and grain in your warehouse. You also have lists of the amount of money you are still owed by customers who have not yet paid.

In the 7th year of the reign of Ptolemy IV Philopator, Thoth, day 12 (or 27 October 216 BC), a valued customer enters your warehouse in Alexandria and purchases 400 amphorae of olive oil for 12 drachmas. You agree to let him pay for the olive oil next month. In fact, this customer often buys from you on credit and at any one time owes for several purchases. The customer puts the olive oil on his cart and leaves.

You keep a daily financial journal and record the transaction: 'Hrenamenpenaef purchased 400 amphorae of olive oil on 7th year of the reign of Ptolemy IV Philopator, Thoth, day 12 for 12 drachma and promised to pay next month.'

Later, this customer approaches you with a complaint. He asks you for an account: why do you think he owes the amount you claim? Finding your information about all the purchases is difficult because you have to go back and search all your journals for all the entries made for Hrenamenpenaef's purchases. Recall that he has several that are unpaid. Things get a lot more confusing if, for example, Hrenamenpenaef had made partial payment on some purchases.

The information would be more conveniently retrieved if you had made a notation in a *separate set of records* that listed all the transactions for Hrenamenpenaef. If you had done that, you would have set up a page with Hrenamenpenaef's name under 'trade accounts receivable'. Trade accounts receivable, as we already know, are amounts that customers owe you for purchases. So on this page you copy the information from your journal: '7th year of the reign of Ptolemy IV Philopator, Thoth, day 12, Hrenamenpenaef 12 drachma.'

> Now, when Hrenamenpenaef asks about his balance, you refer to the page that says 'trade accounts receivable' and see that among the other purchases that Hrenamenpenaef owes is the amount related to the transaction on 7th year of the reign of Ptolemy IV Philopator, Thoth, day 12. So you can say, 'Hrenamenpenaef, on Thoth, day 12 this year you purchased 400 amphorae of olive oil in my warehouse for 12 drachma.'
>
> Explaining that to him is difficult unless you have a system that relates the amount he owes to the purchases he made that created the obligation. This was the genius of Fra Pacioli – he realized that each transaction had two 'sides'. In a transaction, the business entity receives something and gives something and there must be a way to relate these two 'sides' to each other. You give Hrenamenpenaef olive oil and Hrenamenpenaef gives you his promise to pay you in the future.

Of course, double-entry accounting was not used in ancient Egypt. But by the late Renaissance period businesses had begun adopting the system. Pacioli had invented it not only so that financial information could be summarized in a meaningful way, but also because of accuracy. At that time, maintaining accounting records was a manual process and therefore cumbersome and error prone. To avoid these errors, Pacioli built a system of checks and balances into his accounting method to make sure, for example, that when information was copied from the financial journal to the trade accounts receivable page the amounts were not transposed or even accidentally omitted. Many clerks (or bookkeepers) were required to meticulously record, classify and summarize all this information.

Computers now make the task of recording and summarizing financial information immeasurably easier, and they have also greatly improved the accuracy and flexibility of reporting financial information. Modern accountants are therefore no longer burdened with the drudgery of manually recording and summarizing transactions, but rather focus on the interpretation and analysis of the results. While bookkeepers still enter some transactions into accounting systems, this task is increasingly handled by automation. For example, when a sale to a customer is entered into an electronic cash register in a retail store, that transaction is automatically entered into the business's accounting system.

Although large, global companies now use complex, computer-based accounting systems to cope with their high transaction volumes, the underlying accounting process is still the double-entry method invented by Pacioli hundreds of years ago. This means that *the double-entry method is well understood, universally accepted and used throughout the world*. Regardless of which country a company does business in, the accounting process is the same. It has been modernized, especially with computers. The accounting process has also proved exceptionally adaptable to the needs of large, complex businesses.

4.2 How does the accounting process work?

The accounting process involves four major steps, which we will examine in detail in Part II:

1.   Analyse and record transactions
2.   Adjust accounts
3.   Prepare the financial statements
4.   Close accounts

These four steps are illustrated graphically in Figure 1.26.

FIGURE 1.26 THE ACCOUNTING PROCESS

The accounting process is cyclical, in that the four steps all occur within a reporting period and then are repeated for the next reporting period, and so on. When transactions occur – as shown in Figure 1.26 – financial information from each transaction is analysed and then recorded in the accounting system. This process continues throughout the reporting period. At the end, accounts are 'adjusted' to ensure that financial results are reported in the appropriate reporting period. Then the financial statements are prepared.

FIGURE 1.27 THE FINANCIAL ACCOUNTING REPORTING SYSTEM

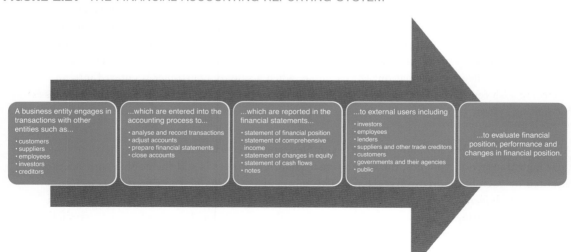

Once the financial statements are completed, the accounts are closed, which means that they are prepared for the next reporting period. In Part II of this textbook we will examine these four steps in the accounting process in detail, and will also see how they are accomplished in modern, computerized accounting systems.

Extending the financial accounting reporting system

The accounting process is an integral part of the financial accounting reporting system, as Figure 1.27 illustrates.

ON YOUR OWN

LEARNING OUTCOME REVIEW

1. What is the major advantage of the double-entry method of accounting?
2. What are the four steps in the accounting process?

LEARNING OUTCOME 5
DEFINE GENERALLY ACCEPTED ACCOUNTING PRINCIPLES AND EXPLAIN THEIR ROLE IN FINANCIAL ACCOUNTING

5.1 What decisions must be made in accounting for specific transactions?
    5.1.1 Should a transaction be included?
    5.1.2 What amount should be used to measure a transaction?
    5.1.3 How should financial results be reported in the financial statements?
    5.1.4 What additional information should be provided in the notes?

5.2 What are generally accepted accounting principles?

5.1 What decisions must be made in accounting for specific transactions?

Although the accounting process was invented centuries ago and is universally accepted today, questions about how to account for specific transactions still arise. Four major decisions have to be made about transactions: recognition, measurement, reporting and disclosure. These are summarized below along with the questions for each:

Decision	Question	
Recognition	1.	Should a transaction be included?
Measurement	2.	What amount should be used to measure a transaction?
Reporting	3.	How should financial results be reported in the financial statements?
Disclosure	4.	What additional information should be provided in the notes?

5.1.1 SHOULD A TRANSACTION BE INCLUDED?

Recognition refers to whether a financial item should be included on either the statement of financial position or statement of comprehensive income. To be recognized, any economic benefit associated with the item must flow to or from the business entity. We must also be able to measure the cost or value of the item reliably. Consider these two independent situations:

1. A customer enters Jiazhen's shop and says she wishes to purchase a porcelain vase that she has been admiring for HK$2400. She wants to take the porcelain with her and indicates that she will send payment in two weeks. This is a loyal customer whom Jiazhen trusts, so he agrees to her request. However, several weeks have passed and the woman has not paid for the vase. Should you include this sale transaction in Jiazhen Antique Porcelains's accounting records?
2. A customer enters Jiazhen's shop and indicates that he definitely plans to purchase a porcelain vase. However, he says that he will return in two weeks' time to select the vase he wants, pay for it and take it home. Again, would you include this in Jiazhen Antique Porcelains's accounting records?

In the first case, a sale of the vase did occur and you would account for the transaction. The fact that the woman has not yet paid for the item is not relevant to whether or not you recognize the sale. We still expect the economic benefit (cash) to flow to Jiazhen Antique Porcelains and we can reliably measure the benefit (HK$2400). In the second case, no transaction has occurred and you would not include this event in the accounting records. The customer has not completed the sale, nor do we know the price since no specific vase has been selected. Thus, we have no indication that the economic benefits will flow to the business, nor can we reliably measure cost or value.

5.1.2 WHAT AMOUNT SHOULD BE USED TO MEASURE A TRANSACTION?

Measurement determines what monetary amount will be recognized for a transaction. Consider this situation:

We know from the statement of financial position that Jiazhen Antique Porcelains had land for HK$70 000 on 31 December 2009 (Figure 1.14), and this was increased with an additional purchase to HK$90 000 by 31 December 2010 (Figure 1.16). Recall that the increase was HK$20 000. HK$15 000 of that increase was the purchase of additional land and that HK$5000 of the increase was from the increased value of the original land of HK$70 000, which increased to HK$75 000. Should you measure the land at the original cost of HK$70 000 or HK$75 000, its current value?

Since the business is located in Hong Kong, the answer is that you have a choice. You can elect to measure at 'historical cost', the amount originally paid for the land, or you can revalue it to its current market value. However, if the business were located in some other countries, this choice would not be available. You might be required, for example, to measure the land at its historical cost.

5.1.3 HOW SHOULD FINANCIAL RESULTS BE REPORTED IN THE FINANCIAL STATEMENTS?

Reporting means that transaction results are to be reported in the financial statements in a certain way. For example, let's assume that a business owes three amounts: $10 000 which must be repaid in the three months, $12 000 which must be repaid in six months and $50 000 which must be repaid in 18 months. We shall see later in the textbook, that the $10 000 and $12 000 can be combined but they must be reported separately from the $50 000 in the statement of financial position. Why? Because International Financial Reporting Standards require that these amounts be reported separately.

5.1.4 WHAT ADDITIONAL INFORMATION SHOULD BE PROVIDED IN THE NOTES?

Disclosure means that external users must be advised of a circumstance. This could be done, depending on the applicable accounting standards, by including an amount in the statement of financial position or statement of comprehensive income, or the disclosure may only be in the notes to the financial statements.

> Assume that Jiazhen has been sued by a customer who purchased an expensive porcelain bowl and later claimed that it was a fake. In this scenario, the case has not come to trial. The attorney for the business believes that it is unlikely that the customer will win the lawsuit or that Jiazhen Antique Porcelains will have to pay damages. Although no obligation to pay exists, there is some possibility that an award may have to be paid. Should external users be advised of this possibility?

Under International Financial Reporting Standards, the answer is yes. External users would probably be interested in knowing that the possibility of payment exists. In fact, this information could influence their decision to invest in the business. For that reason, we would disclose this information in the notes to the financial statements, but an amount would not be recognized in the statement of financial position or statement of comprehensive income.

But how can you *know* the answers to these and other questions that arise when accounting for specific transactions? The answer is that you must consult the accounting standards; when the standards contain no guidance, the generally accepted accounting principles in the country where the business is located apply.

5.2 What are generally accepted accounting principles?

Decisions about recognition, measurement, reporting and disclosure are based on generally accepted accounting principles or GAAP. Generally accepted accounting principles include laws, regulations and rules that govern accounting as well as commonly accepted practices. These principles are influenced by academic research, the opinions of industry groups, and companies and others who prepare financial statements. Generally accepted accounting principles are specific to nations and in some cases regions like the European Union.

Formal rules and regulations are referred to as accounting standards. Standards are almost always at a national level. Some countries have government organizations that are responsible for creating and enforcing accounting standards, which means that the standards become part of commercial law. In other countries, accounting standard setting is left to quasi-governmental organizations and in some cases to the accounting profession itself. In some countries, several organizations may have a role in developing accounting standards.

Since generally accepted accounting principles are nation based, a set of financial statements is prepared to conform to applicable GAAP. A Chinese company would use Chinese standards, an Australian company would use Australian standards and so forth. In some cases, a company may be required to prepare its financial statements in conformance with another country's accounting standards. An American company that does business in France, for example, may be required by French regulatory authorities to provide financial statements prepared to conform to French GAAP.

Three decades ago, recognizing that business was becoming more globalized, an international accounting standards-setting organization was established, the International Accounting Standards Board or IASB. This has created a significant movement to 'harmonize' accounting standards throughout the world. *Although nations still retain the final decision over accounting standards, some are opting to use international standards or standards that are very similar to international standards as their national standards.* This textbook is based on international standards, which are officially referred to as International Financial Reporting Standards or IFRS. We will examine accounting standards in more detail in Chapter 2.

Extending the financial accounting reporting system

Figure 1.28 shows the financial accounting reporting system with generally accepted accounting principles included:

FIGURE 1.28 THE FINANCIAL ACCOUNTING REPORTING SYSTEM INCLUDING GAAP

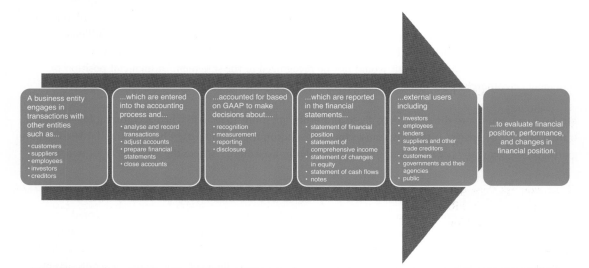

ON YOUR OWN

LEARNING OUTCOME REVIEW

1. What are the four major decisions that have to be made when accounting for transactions?
2. What are generally accepted accounting principles?

3. How do accounting standards and generally accepted accounting principles differ?
4. What is the International Accounting Standards Board?
5. What are International Financial Reporting Standards?

LEARNING OUTCOME 6
DESCRIBE THE ASSURANCE SYSTEM IN FINANCIAL REPORTING

6.1 How do users know that financial statements conform to GAAP?

6.2 Who within the business entity is responsible for financial reporting?

6.3 What role do professional ethics have in financial reporting?

6.1 How do users know that financial statements conform to GAAP?

Suppose you are an investor and you have been asked by Li Jiazhen to make a substantial investment in Jiazhen Antique Porcelains Ltd. In his presentation to you, Jiazhen claims that the demand for quality Chinese porcelains is very strong. If the business had more financial capital it could grow faster and earn much more profit.

To support his claims, he provides you with financial statements for the business from the past five years. They show that the business has become profitable and that sales are increasing rapidly. But how do you know that the financial statements are reliable? For that matter, how do you know what method was used to calculate sales or any other amounts included in the financial statements? Are porcelain inventories reported at cost or current value?

When you ask these questions, Jiazhen responds that he is required to use Hong Kong accounting standards which are based on IFRS. That tells you how the business *should* be accounting for transactions but it does not assure you that Hong Kong IFRS-based standards were *actually* used.

When you express this concern, Jiazhen responds that the financial statements have been independently audited and an unqualified audit opinion was given on the financial statements.

Now you have your answer. Businesses are often required by law or regulation to publish audited financial statements, especially if the company is publicly traded or is requesting a major loan from a creditor like a bank. An audit is a review by an independent professional accountant (usually a Certified Public Accountant or Chartered Accountant) to determine whether the financial statements were prepared in accordance with the applicable accounting standards. In Jiazhen Antique Porcelains's case, this would be Hong Kong

FIGURE 1.29 WORLD'S LARGEST ACCOUNTING FIRMS

Firm	Employees (thousands)	Revenues (US$ billions)	Rank
PricewaterhouseCoopers	156	$28	1
Deloitte Touche Tohmatsu	165	27	2
Ernst & Young	135	25	3
KPMG	137	23	4

IFRS-based standards. The auditor – the party conducting the audit – renders an opinion about whether the financial statements present a 'true and fair view' of the financial results of the entity.

Auditing is a major area of accounting practice, sometimes known as public accountancy. An auditor is a highly respected professional who provides assurances to external users of financial statements. Figure 1.29 shows a list of the world's largest public accounting firms based on 2008 fiscal year revenues. In Chapter 13, we will examine assurance systems designed to give users comfort that they can rely upon the financial statements of a business.

6.2 Who within the business entity is responsible for financial reporting?

Assurance systems also involve two other parties. The first is the board of directors who oversee the business on behalf of the investors and other external users. They are ultimately responsible for the financial statements and can be held accountable if the information contained in those financial statements is misleading or false. Thus, the financial accounting reporting system begins and ends with the board of directors.

The other party is management. The board of directors generally delegates the responsibility for preparing the financial statements to management. Though the board reviews and approves the financial statements before they are officially published to external users, and may review accounting policies and procedures, the accounting process is normally under the direction of the management team.

As part of their responsibility to prepare financial statements, management must establish accounting policies for the business. Accounting policies are formal and informal guidelines which determine how the business will account for financial transactions. Remember the choice that Jiazhen Antique Porcelains Ltd had to measure land at either cost or current value? Clearly, Jiazhen's accounting policy is to use current value since this is what appears on the company's statements of financial position.

In large companies, management needs assurances that the organization is working effectively towards the business's established goals and objectives. It also needs to know that organizational policies – including accounting policies – are being followed in accordance with management's wishes. For this, the business will have a system of internal control. Internal control provides reasonable assurances that the organization's objectives are being met with respect to 1) effectiveness and efficiency of operations, 2) reliability of financial reporting and 3) compliance with laws and regulations.

6.3 What role do professional ethics have in financial reporting?

Generally accepted accounting principles, oversight by the board of directors, management responsibility for preparing the financial statements, and independent audits are not enough. In order for the financial accounting reporting system to function effectively, one other element must be present: Professional ethics.

Despite the advantages of the limited liability company, a major disadvantage is that ownership and control are separated. We assume that managers conduct business in the interest of the owners. However, the separation of ownership and control creates opportunities for fraud and misrepresentation which unfortunately are an everyday occurrence in the business world.

In Chapter 2, we will discuss Enron, a US company that in a matter of months went from being considered one of the most successful and innovative businesses to bankruptcy. Investors, employees and others lost billions of US dollars. The scandal that followed forced Arthur Andersen, one of the largest and most respected public accounting firms at that time, out of business.

Did Enron's board of directors not provide the proper oversight for accounting? Did management inappropriately account for transactions? Did management not follow generally accepted accounting principles? Were the financial statements incorrectly prepared? Did the auditors fail to do their job in giving assurances to the external users that the financial statements truly and fairly presented the financial results of the business?

Almost any accounting standard can be circumvented whether by simply interpreting the rule in a different way or through outright fraud and misrepresentation. Thus, standards must be applied in the 'spirit' as well as the 'letter' of the law. This is why some accounting standards explicitly instruct preparers of financial statements to ignore the requirements in an accounting standard *if another method of accounting represents the financial results better.*

For now, we can note that without professional ethics, financial accounting cannot reach the goal of providing reliable information to external users. For that reason, professional ethics is a critical part of the overall financial accounting reporting system.

Extending the financial accounting reporting system

Figure 1.30 shows the financial accounting reporting system with components of the assurance system, including the auditors and board of directors.

FIGURE 1.30 THE FINANCIAL ACCOUNTING REPORTING SYSTEM WITH THE ASSURANCE SYSTEM

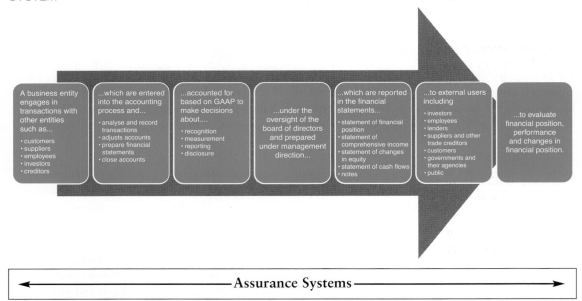

ON YOUR OWN

LEARNING OUTCOME REVIEW

1. How do external users know that the financial statements provide a true and fair view of the financial results of the business?
2. What is an independent audit? Who conducts an independent audit?
3. Who has the overall responsibility for overseeing financial reporting?
4. Who is responsible for preparing the financial statements?

Conclusion

Financial accounting is one of several major specialisms within the broader field of accounting. As a profession, accounting encompasses managerial accounting, which provides financial information for internal users for planning, decision making and control. The major objective of financial accounting is to generate general-purpose financial statements for external users who want to evaluate the financial position, performance and changes in financial position of the business entity.

Financial accounting is performed within the much larger and more complex financial accounting reporting system. Within this system, when business entities engage in transactions with other entities, those transactions are recognized by the accounting process. The transaction is analysed and, if appropriate, recorded. The financial statements are prepared from the resulting information. The accounting process is based on the double-entry method used throughout the world.

Specific accounting for transactions is handled somewhat differently from country to country depending on applicable generally accepted accounting principles. Formal accounting standards, which make up a large part of generally accepted accounting principles, are the rules that companies must follow. Standards cover most but not all situations that might be faced in accounting. Therefore, management may have to rely on other factors that influence generally accepted accounting principles, such as academic research and professional practice. Because business practices vary from region to region, some variations in generally accepted accounting practices are likely to persist.

However, globalization of business has created a growing need for international accounting standards. The International Accounting Standards Board (IASB), begun three decades ago, creates International Financial Reporting Standards (IFRS), which have already been adopted in many countries in whole or part. IFRS are particularly important for those companies listed on share exchanges, since these account for a large proportion of cross-border financial activity.

The financial accounting reporting system also has mechanisms to offer users assurances that the financial statements have been prepared in accordance with applicable GAAP and that they provide a true and fair view of financial results. Independent auditors examine the financial statements and render a professional opinion about whether this was achieved. The board of directors has responsibility for overseeing the financial reports. However, the financial accounting reporting system functions effectively only in an environment of acceptable professional ethics.

Since this textbook takes a global perspective, we will focus on the financial accounting reporting systems for large, multinational companies that are publicly traded. Invariably, these companies are organized as limited liability companies, one of the three major legal forms of business organization.

Summary
LEARNING OUTCOME 1
User Needs Explained

Accounting serves two broad categories of users. Internal users are served by managerial accounting, which produces financial information for planning, decision making and control. Internal users include managers, the board of directors and employees. Normally, managerial accounting information is not distributed to external users since it has competitive significance. Managerial accounting is not subject to generally accepted accounting principles or accounting standards. Rather, managerial accounting is a set of well-understood analytical tools such as cost-volume-profit analysis and variance analysis.

Financial accounting – the subject of this textbook – generates financial information for external users. External users include investors, employees, lenders, suppliers and other trade creditors, customers, governments and their agencies and the public. All have a financial stake in the business entity. Investors and creditors have money at risk because they have invested in or lent to the business. Employees earn wages and salaries and are therefore dependent on the business for their livelihood. Suppliers and customers may also be harmed if the business fails. The business is also part of the larger community and thus affects the welfare of the public. For example, the company's shares may be publicly traded or it may be a significant employer in a region.

LEARNING OUTCOME 2
Business Entities Defined

Business entities are organized as one of three forms: sole proprietorships, partnerships or limited liability companies. Each form offers advantages and disadvantages. For example, a sole proprietorship is easier to form and administer. But it may be difficult to raise capital for a sole proprietorship and it does not offer legal protection to its owners. A partnership is useful for combining the talents of two or more people. However, partnerships also do not offer legal protection to the owners.

The limited liability company offers significant advantages. It is legally treated as an autonomous entity and therefore continues to exist when the ownership changes. This allows the limited liability company to operate without interruption, including engaging in transactions to borrow capital. In addition, limited liability companies limit the risk to their investors. An investor can lose what he or she has invested but cannot normally be held accountable for the debts of the business. Only limited liability companies are publicly traded. This textbook focuses on financial accounting for limited liability companies.

LEARNING OUTCOME 3
Financial Reporting to External Users Described

The major objective of financial accounting is to produce four general-purpose financial statements for use by external users: the statement of financial position, statement of comprehensive income, statement of changes in equity and statement of cash flows. The first of these answers the question: *What is the financial position of the business?* The other three are related to changes in financial position. A complete set of financial statements also includes accompanying notes.

The statement of financial position is the only one of the four statements that is presented for a single point in time, the reporting date. It contains three major elements: assets, liabilities and equity. Assets are what the business owns and are expected to have future economic benefit. Liabilities are what the business owes and are expected to be settled in the future. The difference between assets and liabilities is equity, which includes contributed capital and retained earnings. Contributed capital is the amount that has been invested by the owners of the business. Retained earnings are past earnings that have not been distributed to the owners. Equity contains other elements that we will discuss in later chapters.

The statement of comprehensive income answers the question: *How did the business perform?* This statement presents financial information for the period of time ending with the reporting date. This time period can be for any length, but usually is for the year or quarter. The statement of comprehensive income includes revenue, which represents inflows of economic benefits received by the entity in the course of its ordinary activities. Expenses are outflows of economic benefits. The difference between the two is a profit, when that difference is positive, and otherwise a loss. The statement of comprehensive income also includes other comprehensive income, which we will discuss in later chapters.

The statement of changes in equity addresses the question: *What resources have the owners invested in the business?* First, an owner can invest directly by providing the business with additional capital. An investor can also withdraw his or her investment, thus reducing the amount of equity. The second major change in equity discussed in this chapter is retained earnings. Earnings belong to the owners of the business after it settles its liabilities. To the extent that these earnings are retained by the business and not distributed to the owners, they increase equity. When an owner receives a dividend distributing profit, equity is decreased. Again, other factors affect changes in equity and will be discussed in later chapters.

The fourth statement is the statement of cash flows, which answers the question: *Where did the business obtain cash and how was it used?* Transactions can be either a source or a use of cash. These sources and uses are divided into three categories: operating activities, which include cash related to the ordinary business activities of the business; investing activities related to the acquisition or disposal of major assets; and financing activities, which include changes in cash related to debt and equity transactions.

LEARNING OUTCOME 4
Accounting Process Explained

The accounting process – based on the double-entry method invented hundreds of years ago – analyses, records, adjusts and summarizes transactions to provide information for generating the financial statements. The same accounting process is used throughout the world with little variation. Accounting software for smaller computers as well as the large, complex software for multinational companies is all based on this double-entry accounting process.

LEARNING OUTCOME 5
Generally Accepted Accounting Principles Defined

Generally accepted accounting principles give guidance to managers and others who are responsible for preparing financial statements. Financial statements are developed in reference to particular generally accepted accounting principles. For example, financial statements may be prepared in accordance with US GAAP, European Union GAAP, Australian GAAP or IFRS. This also helps external users to understand how the financial statements were prepared. Generally accepted accounting principles include formal, written standards that are determined at the national level. Each country has its own accounting standards based on laws, regulations or rules regarding how companies – especially those that are publicly traded – should report financial results.

In recent years, the accounting standards in many countries have been 'harmonized' with International Financial Reporting Standards, which are established by the International Accounting Standards Board. This textbook is based on International Financial Reporting Standards. In addition, generally accepted accounting principles are influenced by other sources such as articles written by experts and common practice in an industry or geographic region.

LEARNING OUTCOME 6
Assurance System Described

External users often require companies to provide assurance that their financial statements are prepared in accordance with a particular set of generally accepted accounting principles. More importantly, they want to be confident that the financial statements reflect the economic substance of the business and fairly represent its financial position, performance and changes in financial position. One accepted method for providing this assurance is through an audit. Auditing is an accounting specialization within financial accounting. An auditor reviews the financial statements to give an opinion about whether they fairly present the financial results.

Auditors must be independent third parties. They are hired by the board of directors and report the audit findings, including the opinion, to the board of directors. The board then reviews the auditor's report. Then the financial statements, including the auditor's opinion, are released to external users. This is a formal process, particularly for publicly traded companies, as the financial statements often have consequences for external users. For example, better than expected financial results can cause the stock price to rise, whereas disappointing results may cause the stock price to fall.

The final component of the financial accounting reporting system is the role of ethics. For all the formal standards, centuries of accumulated accounting experience and assurances given by auditors, reliable financial reporting still depends on the good intentions of the board of directors and auditors. Some say that management and employees must be ethical. Others would extend that to customers, suppliers and others. But the viewpoint taken in this textbook is that the board of directors is ultimately responsible to external users for the quality of financial reporting. Auditors as independent third parties must also be ethical in order for the overall financial accounting reporting system to function as intended. In Chapter 2, we will explore these issues in detail.

REVIEW QUESTIONS

1. Who are the external users of financial reports? What are the information requirements of each? How do the needs of external users differ from those of internal users?
2. Describe the three forms of business organization. What are the advantages and disadvantages of each?

3. What must a complete set of general financial statements include? What question is answered by each financial statement? List and define the major elements in each financial statement. Give examples of specific line items included within each element of the statement of financial position and the statement of comprehensive income. [Example: Trade accounts receivable is an asset on the statement of financial position.]

4. What is the accounting process and what was its origin? Give a basic explanation of how the accounting process works.

5. What are generally accepted accounting principles? Describe the difference between generally accepted accounting principles and accounting standards. How are generally accepted accounting principles used in financial accounting? What are International Financial Reporting Standards?

6. Who is ultimately responsible for the financial statements? Who is responsible for preparing financial statements?

7. What is the assurance system? Describe the major parties that are involved in the assurance system and the role of each. What is the evidence that an external user can rely on the financial statements?

8. Explain why professional ethics must be part of the financial accounting reporting system in order for it to function properly.

Key terms

Accounting equation	Financing activities	Performance
Accounting policies	Financial position	Privately held
Accounting process	General-purpose financial	Profit
Accounting standards	statements	Profit or loss
Assets	Internal control	Publicly traded
Audit	Internal users	Recognition
Barter transaction	Inventories	Reporting date
Bourse	Investing activities	Reporting period
Business entity	Joint-stock companies	Revenue
Cash flows	Liabilities	Shares
Closely held	Limited liability company	Share-based entities
Corporations	Loss	Sole proprietorship
Disclosure	Managerial accounting	Sources and uses
Double-entry accounting	Monetary unit assumption	Statement of cash flows
Double-entry method	Notes	Statement of changes in equity
Equity securities market	Operating activities	Statement of comprehensive
Expenses	Ordinary share	income
External users	Other comprehensive income	Statement of financial position
Financial accounting	Partnership	Stock exchange

Stock market   Total comprehensive income   Trade accounts receivable
Time period assumption   Trade accounts payable   Transactions

Terminology practice

For each of the following, insert the correct term from the list of key terms preceding this section. Each key term can be used more than once.

1. The _____ is the division of time into specific time intervals such as a year, quarter or month.
2. When expenses exceed revenue, the business reports a _____, which is shown on the statement of _____.
3. _____ is the inflow of economic benefits from the ordinary activities of the business entity and is included in the statement of _____.
4. Evidence of ownership of a limited liability company takes the form of _____, also known as _____, _____ or _____.
5. _____ are what a business owes and are expected to be settled in the future.
6. Sources and uses of cash are known as _____.
7. Goods held for resale are _____ and are included as _____ on the statement of _____.
8. _____ are obligations to suppliers that are included on the statement of _____.
9. Formal, written guidelines for accounting developed at the national level are _____.
10. The _____ refers to the fact that we account for information that can be expressed in terms of money.
11. The accounting process uses the _____, which accounts for _____ between the business entity and other entities.
12. _____ accompany the financial statements and either explain information contained in the financial statements or provide additional information.
13. When a company's shares are not publicly traded, the company is _____ or _____.
14. Financial accounting provides information for _____. Managerial accounting provides information for _____.
15. When revenues exceed expenses, the business reports a _____, which is shown on the statement of _____.
16. _____ are obligations that customers have to the business, which are included in _____ on the statement of _____.
17. _____ are what a business owns and are expected to have economic benefits in the future.
18. The three forms of business organization are _____, _____ and _____.

19. Equity shares are traded on the _____, _____
    or _____.
20. _____ are an outflow of economic benefits from ordinary activities of the business
    entity and are included in the statement of _____.
21. The _____ is the date of the statement of financial position and a
    _____ is the time in between.
22. The _____ is assets = liabilities + equity. The _____, is revenues –
    expenses = profit or loss.
23. Three categories of cash sources and uses are _____, _____, and _____.
24. Profit and loss and other comprehensive income are added to calculate _____.
25. When the expenses are subtracted from revenues, the result is _____.

Application exercises

1. Place a tick in the appropriate boxes to indicate which financial statements the items in the left-hand
   column apply to.

	Statement of comprehensive income	Statement of financial position	Statement of changes in equity	Statement of cash flows
Assets				
Cash from investing activities				
Contributed capital including changes				
Trade accounts payable				
Retained earnings				
Revenue				
Cash from financing activities				
Expenses				
Trade accounts receivable				
Liabilities				
Wages payable				
Cash from operating activities				
Profit or loss				
Beginning equity balance				
Loan payable				
Ending equity balance				
Inventories				
Cash in bank				

2. Complete the items in the following diagram by writing in the appropriate name of the financial statement, financial statement element or item.

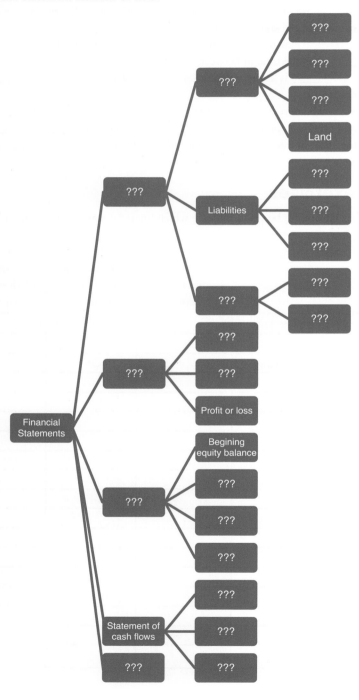

3. Complete the following schedule by supplying the missing information for each of the three companies:

	Company A	Company B	Company C
Revenue	£170 000	£55 000	?
Expenses	?	80 000	812 000
Profit (loss)	65 000	?	0
Assets	?	300 000	3 450 000
Liabilities	575 000	100 000	?
Equity	675 000	?	1 050 000

4. Complete the following schedule by supplying the missing information for each of the three companies:

	Company A	Company B	Company C
Statement of financial position 31 December 2010			
Assets	$15 000	$29 700	$938 000
Liabilities	14 000	?	505 000
Equity	?	?	?
Statement of financial position 31 December 2011			
Assets	$15 500	?	$1 100 000
Liabilities	?	17 000	660 000
Equity	2 000	11 000	?
Statement of comprehensive income for the year ended 31 December 2011			
Revenue	$3 500	?	?
Expenses	2 000	5 700	120 000
Profit (loss)	?	(3 700)	?
Dividends	?	0	223 000

5. Complete the following schedule by supplying the missing information for each of the four companies:

	Company A	Company B	Company C	Company D
Beginning equity balance	€750	€600	€1 900	€800
Sale of ordinary shares	0	75	?	50
Profit (loss)	200	100	300	?
Dividends	?	30	100	50
Ending equity balance	900	?	2 300	875

6. Complete the following schedule by supplying the missing information:

	Company A	Company B	Company C
Cash from (used by) operating activities	€6 000	?	(€510 000)
Cash from (used by) investing activities	?	(4 000)	150 000
Cash from (used by) financing activities	(500)	(7 500)	?
Net change in cash balance	2 500	?	(585 000)
Beginning cash balance	10 000	110 000	?
Ending cash balance	?	86 500	615 000

7. Based on the information below for Maize Industries LLC, construct a statement of financial position, statement of income, statement of changes in equity and statement of cash flows for the year ended 31 December 2010. Use appropriate headings for each statement.

Cash balance 31 December 2009	€700 000
Net increase in cash	5 610 000
Cash used for investing activities	4 790 000
Ordinary shares sold	200 000
Revenue	3 750 000
Liabilities	11 250 000
Equity balance 31 December 2009	5 550 000
Dividends paid	500 000
Cash from financing activities	2 000 000
Expenses	2 800 000

Case analysis

Shortly after Paolo Vencitti completed university, he went to work marketing electronic equipment. However, he did not find the job interesting. But soon an unusual opportunity presented itself. A woman in the town where he grew up was retiring. For many years she had made soap from natural ingredients in the area. She had created an excellent reputation for her fine soaps. Paolo would watch her make the soap and since boyhood was fascinated with the process. He also thought that consumers were more interested than ever in 'natural' products.

Paolo approached the woman to talk to her about his idea. Because his own funds were limited and he had no place to make the soap, he proposed that he rent her equipment and the small workshop on her property and continue her soap-making business. She liked the idea and agreed.

Paolo's parents were less enthusiastic, but they too eventually agreed that the idea had merit. The family's legal adviser set up a business entity named Italian Naturals SpA. Paolo invested € 20 000 from a small inheritance that he had received from his grandfather. In 2009, he began operations. He did most of the work himself, especially the soap making, since he knew that the product's quality was important.

Many clients who bought from the woman also bought from him and he was able to add a few new clients. A luxury bath shop in Rome carried the soap briefly and then lost interest. Paolo spent very little time on financial matters, thinking that if the soap sold well, money issues would take care of themselves. So at the end of the year when his accountant sent him the financial statements (see table), he was disappointed.

Paolo soon realized that if he were to expand the business and make it successful, he needed help. He called Matt Hopes, a Danish friend from school. After graduation, Matt had worked two years for a luxury brands manufacturer, then had taken time off to backpack in South America. After much discussion, the two agreed that Matt would join the business, investing the same amount that Paolo had initially invested. He would receive half the ownership of Italian Naturals SpA.

In 2010, Paolo and Matt worked hard to refine the soap-making process. They purchased different ingredients and experimented with new fragrances. When the financial statements were completed for 2010, they found that sales had increased, which was encouraging. However, they were a little surprised at some of the other amounts in the statements, thinking that they should have been better.

Nonetheless, Paolo and Matt continued their efforts throughout 2011. Both again focused on product quality and new, interesting fragrances, though Paolo began to spend more time trying to improve sales. For example, he began to approach shops in various towns and cities, with some success. He also convinced several luxury hotels to use the soap for guests and met with some success here. Nevertheless, it seemed that the more success he had with sales, the more the business ran short of cash. Finally, Paolo's parents offered to lend the company € 50 000.

Results for 2010 and 2011 are also shown in the table.

All amounts in euros	2009	2010	2011
Statement of Financial Position			
Assets			
Cash	5 000	3 500	1 500
Trade accounts receivable	3 000	11 500	12 000
Inventories	7 000	12 500	15 000
Supplies	4 200	11 000	11 000
Equipment	0	0	50 000
Total assets	**19 200**	**38 500**	**89 500**

(*Continued*)

All amounts in euros	2009	2010	2011
Statement of Comprehensive Income			
Revenue	18 000	22 000	34 500
Expenses:			
Cost of soap ingredients	6 500	7 000	8 500
Wages expense	12 000	14 000	18 000
Rent of soap-making equipment	6 000	6 000	6 000
Total expenses	24 500	27 000	32 500
Profit (loss)	(6 500)	(5 000)	2 000
Liabilities			
Trade accounts payable	4 000	7 000	6 500
Wages payable	1 700	3 000	2 500
Loans payable	–	–	50 000
Total liabilities	5 700	10 000	59 000
Equity			
Share capital	20 000	40 000	40 000
Retained earnings	(6 500)	(11 500)	(9 500)
Total equity	13 500	28 500	30 500
Total liabilities and equity	19 200	38 500	89 500
Statement of Changes in Equity			
Equity balance, 1 January	0	13 500	28 500
Change in contributed capital	20 000	20 000	0
Profit (loss)	(6 500)	(5 000)	2 000
Equity balance, 31 December	13 500	28 500	30 500
Statement of Cash Flows			
Net cash from (used by) operations activities	(15 000)	(21 500)	(2 000)
Net cash from (used by) investing activities	0	0	(50 000)
Net cash from (used by) financing activities	20 000	20 000	50 000
Change in cash balance	5 000	(1 500)	(2 000)
Beginning cash, 1 January	0	5 000	3 500
Ending cash, 31 December	5 000	3 500	1 500

This case analysis can be done individually, though the best results will come from a team effort. The team should first read and become familiar with the information in the case. Then as a group, answer the following questions for 2009, then 2010 and finally 2011. Once the first set of questions has been completed, proceed to the second set of questions.

FIRST QUESTION SET

These are the four questions answered by the financial statements:

1. What is the financial position of the business?
2. How did the business perform?
3. What resources have the owners invested in the business?
4. Where did the business obtain cash and how was it used?

SECOND QUESTION SET

Based on your analysis of the financial statements just completed, the team should now answer these questions:

1. In 2009, did Paolo do a good job managing the business? What did he do well? What needed improvement? What specific recommendations would you have for Paolo related to the business in 2009?
2. In 2010, did Paolo and Matt do a good job managing the business? What did they do well? What needed improvement? Again, what specific recommendations would you have for Paolo and Matt related to the business in 2010?
3. In 2011, did Paolo and Matt do a good job managing the business? What did they do well? What needed improvement? Again, what specific recommendations would you have for Paolo and Matt related to the business in 2011?

End notes

1. http://www.merriam-webster.com/dictionary/accounting.
2. 'The Largest Private Companies', www.forbes.com, 9 November 2006.
3. IAS 1 Presentation of Financial Statements, International Accounting Standards Board.
4. IFRS, IAS 1 Presentation of Financial Statements.
5. Not all countries in the EU use the euro. Countries that use the euro are Andorra, Austria, Belgium, Finland, France, Germany, Greece, Ireland, Italy, Kosovo, Luxembourg, Monaco, Montenegro, the Netherlands, Portugal, San Moreno, Slovenia, Spain and Vatican City.

Suggested reading

Graham, Benjamin (1985) *The Intelligent Investor: A Book of Practical Counsel*, New York: Harper & Row.

Web links

- www.berkshirehathaway.com – Warren Buffett is chairman of this company.
- www.iasb.org – International Accounting Standards Board. This organization establishes International Financial Reporting Standards.

PUBLIC ACCOUNTING FIRMS

- Deloitte Touche Tohmatsu – www.deloitte.com
- Ernst & Young – www.ey.com
- KPMG – www.kpmg.com
- PricewaterhouseCoopers – www.pwc.com

STOCK EXCHANGES

- New York Stock Exchange – www.nyse.com
- Nasdaq – www.nasdaq.com
- London Stock Exchange – www.londonstockexchange.com
- Tokyo Stock Exchange – www.tse.or.jp/english
- NYSE Euronext – www.euronext.com
- Deutsche Boerse – www.deutsche-boerse.com
- BME Spanish Exchanges – www.bolsasymercados.es
- Borsa Italiana – www.borsaitaliana.it
- SIX Swiss Exchange – www.six-swiss-exchange.com
- KRX Korea Stock Exchange – www.kse.or.kr

APPENDIX: CURRENCIES

Over 200 official currencies are used throughout the world and examples are shown in Figure 1A.1 (for a full list of currency symbols, see http://xe.com/symbols.php). For simplicity, five major currencies will be used in most examples in this textbook: the euro (€), the US dollar ($), the British pound (£) and the Chinese Yuan and Japanese yen, both of which use ¥ as the currency symbol.

Multinational businesses must transact business in multiple currencies. The complication arises because currencies can change in relative value. The euro, for example, can rise or fall in value against the US dollar. This means that a business can experience a gain or loss.

Two situations are common. The first is that a company may buy or sell goods involving a foreign currency transaction. A foreign currency transaction is a transaction denominated in or requiring settlement in a foreign currency. A foreign currency is *a currency other than the functional currency of the entity*, where functional currency is *the currency of the primary economic environment in which the business entity operates; usually where the business generates and spends the most cash*. For example, a company purchases goods from overseas and must pay for those goods in the currency of the foreign seller. In this case, the company will have to pay in the foreign currency. The current exchange rate, called the 'spot rate', is used to determine how much that foreign currency will cost at the time of payment.

Second, if a multinational company has overseas operations, then accounting records may be maintained in the local currency. Cash may also be kept in a bank overseas that is denominated in that foreign currency.

FIGURE 1A.1 CURRENCIES AND SYMBOLS

Geographic area	Currency	Symbol
Australia	Australian dollar	$
Brazil	Brazilian real	R$
Canada	Canadian dollar	$
China, People's Republic of	Yuan	¥
Denmark	Danish kroner	kr
Egypt	Egyptian pound	£
European Union	Euro	€[5]
Hong Kong	Hong Kong dollar	$
India	Indian rupee	Rs
Japan	Japanese yen	¥
Kazakhstan	Kazakhstani tenge	T
Mexico	Mexican peso	$
Russia	Rouble	*pyg*
Saudi Arabia	Saudi Arabian riyal	SRls
Singapore	Singaporean dollar	$
South Africa	Rand	R
Sweden	Kronor	SEK
Taiwan	New dollar	NS$
United Arab Emirates	UAE dirham	AED
United Kingdom	British pound	£
United States	Dollar	$

When the company wishes to combine these accounting records with the accounting records in the home country (which are of course denominated in the home country's currency), the foreign currency must be translated in terms of the home country's currency. For example, a French company maintains manufacturing facilities in Egypt. The Egyptian operations will maintain all records in Egyptian pounds, while the home office will use euros. That means that when accounting records are combined for the entire business, the Egyptian pounds must be converted to euros.

Either situation means that the 'foreign' currency must be converted into the 'functional' currency, which is basically the currency of the country where the company is headquartered. Currency exchange rates can be calculated in two ways. A direct exchange rate calculates the number of local currency units for one foreign currency unit:

$$\text{Direct exchange rate} = \text{functional currency units} / \text{foreign currency units}$$

An indirect exchange rate calculates the number of foreign currency units for one local currency unit:

$$\text{Indirect exchange rate} = \text{foreign currency units} / \text{functional currency unit}$$

Some currencies trade freely against another, so prices can go up and down as market forces dictate. However, some currencies are 'pegged' to other currencies, usually because of the country's economic policy. The US dollar has been considered a strong, stable currency in the past. Therefore, countries that depend heavily on trade with the US will often synchronize their currency with the US dollar. The Chinese yuan and the United Arab Emirates AED are examples. When the US dollar moves up in price, so do the pegged currencies of these two countries.

Accounting standards and ethics

2

LEARNING OUTCOMES

By the end of this chapter, you should be able to:

1. Explain how accounting standards are established.
2. Explain the Framework for the Preparation and Presentation of Financial Statements.
3. Discuss the general features of accounting in the Framework.
4. Define measurement concepts in the financial statements.
5. Explain the role of profesional ethics in accounting.

ENRON

In 2001, US-based Enron filed for bankruptcy after a 15-year history. Until just months before its failure, Enron was praised by the media, investors and analysts as being one of the most successful growth companies based on innovation in trading energy futures. The company's management created a very aggressive corporate culture in which employee performance was the primary focus. Those employees with high rankings were awarded generous bonuses and promotions, while those with the lowest rankings were often terminated. By 2000, Enron had sales of US$100 billion and profits had increased by 40% over the past three years.

During the summer of 2001, the company's chief executive officer, Jeffrey Skilling, resigned for 'personal reasons'. Then several irregularities at the company began to come to light. The company admitted that it had overstated 1997 profits and the public was made aware that significant obligations had not been disclosed. Banks and others who had lent money to Enron grew nervous and it became increasingly difficult for the company to obtain the money that it needed for daily operations. This caused a crisis so that in mid-November the company was forced to declare bankruptcy. By January 2002, government authorities in the United States had suspended trading of Enron shares.

Investors, creditors, employees, suppliers and others – the external users – lost billions of US dollars. For the accounting profession, an additional calamity occurred. The public accountant that audited Enron, Arthur Andersen LLP, also failed. At that time Arthur Andersen was one of the largest and most respected public audit firms. It hired top university graduates and had a reputation for encouraging its employees to 'think straight and talk straight'. By 2001, Arthur Andersen had offices in over 80 countries, 85 000 employees and $9 billion in revenues.

In June 2002, it was the first audit firm in history to be legally convicted of a felony (a major criminal offence). It had been investigated because it had presumably destroyed important documents related to Enron's affairs and also had given advice that was inappropriate for a public accountant to give. In 2002, Arthur Andersen surrendered its licence to practise as a public accountancy firm in the United States and was effectively disbanded.

Enron was only one scandal, albeit one of the largest. But it poses very serious questions about the extent to which external users can rely on financial statements. Arthur Andersen, as we know from Chapter 1, had the responsibility of auditing Enron's financial statements and providing an opinion on whether they fairly presented financial results. It did that. Yet it was clear that Enron had been having difficulties and engaging in unacceptable financial reporting practices before 2001. Why were external users kept in the dark about these problems? Did Enron not comply with generally accepted accounting principles? If not, did Arthur Andersen alert external users? Some people accused Arthur Andersen of collaborating with Enron inappropriately in order to mislead investors and others.

The collapse of Enron resulted in a number of new regulations for publicly traded companies to enhance the protection of investors and others who might be harmed by fraud and misrepresentation. Sadly, while this may have improved the situation somewhat, other scandals followed Enron and continue to occur. Reliability of financial reports is assured only when all elements of the financial accounting reporting system are working effectively. That includes the judicious application of accounting standards in a way that upholds professional ethics.

LEARNING OUTCOME 1
EXPLAIN HOW ACCOUNTING STANDARDS ARE ESTABLISHED

1.1   Who establishes accounting standards?

1.2   What are rules-based versus principles-based standards?

1.3   Who sets International Financial Reporting Standards?

1.4   What is the International Accounting Standards Board?

1.5   How does the International Accounting Standards Board set standards?

PricewaterhouseCoopers, one of the world's largest accounting firms, periodically surveys the financial reporting needs of investors and investment professionals. The firm's 2007 report[1] concludes that financial statements based on generally accepted accounting principles remain the 'bedrock' of financial analysis for this community.

1.1 Who sets accounting standards?

Accounting standards are established by each nation. That only makes sense because each country wants control over commercial activities in its own jurisdiction. For that reason, differences in accounting standards are likely to continue:

> 'Financial statements are prepared for external users by many entities around the world. Although such financial statements may appear similar from country to country, there are differences which have probably been caused by a variety of social, economic and legal circumstances and by different countries having in mind the needs of different users of financial statements when setting national requirements.'

Framework for the Preparation and Presentation of Financial Statements.
Copyright © 2007 International Accounting Standards Committee Foundation.
All rights reserved. No permission granted to reproduce or distribute.

However, economic globalization has increasingly created pressures to 'converge' accounting standards throughout the world. Events ultimately led to the founding of the International Accounting Standards Board, which is now an active and widely accepted authoritative source of accounting standards. In recent years, the influence of international standards has led some nations to reorganize their standard-setting organizations and practices to facilitate further convergence on International Financial Reporting Standards (IFRS). But, as already noted, accounting standards continue to be determined at the national level. Figure 2.1 illustrates the relationship of national standard setting to International Financial Reporting Standards.

FIGURE 2.1 EXAMPLES OF NATIONAL STANDARDS CONVERGED WITH IFRS

Notice in Figure 2.1 that nations like China, Japan and the United States have accounting standards specific to each respective country. These national standards have been converged with IFRS to various degrees. For example, Chinese standards almost completely conform to international standards. United States' standards still have differences, though authorities are working with the International Accounting Standards Board to converge American standards. In the European Union, each member nation has final control over the standard-setting process, but standards are coordinated. Appendix A contains an overview of national standard-setting practices in several countries and regions and discusses convergence efforts in each.

1.2 What are rules-based versus principles-based standards?

Different nations take one of two approaches to standard setting. Some accounting standards, such as those in the United States, are rules based. Rules-based standards provide specific guidelines for those who prepare financial statements. To avoid confusion, rules-based standards must be clear and understandable in their application and enforcement, and they must also be comprehensive, to avoid gaps that fail to provide guidance in all circumstances. Critics believe that management often has an incentive to apply rules-based standards by the 'letter of the law' rather than in the 'spirit of the law' as a means of circumventing certain requirements.

Principles-based standards, used in IFRS, focus on broad objectives that leave room for interpretation. Principles-based standards are therefore thought to avoid the issue of 'getting around the rules' and can be applied in different jurisdictions, each of which can have its own implementation of the standard in a way that satisfies local laws and culture. Under principles-based standards, those who prepare financial statements are expected to comply with the standard, or if not, explain why they departed from it ('comply or explain'). However, critics believe that principles-based standards leave some uncertainty about whether a company is in compliance or not, and that management has too much latitude in their application.

1.3 Who sets International Financial Reporting Standards?

The International Accounting Standards Board sets international accounting standards. Initially, the International Accounting Standards Committee (IASC) was created in 1973 in response to a growing recognition by diverse organizations like the World Bank, International Monetary Fund, International Organization of Securities Commissions, United Nations, Organization for Economic Cooperation and Development and Basel Committee on Banking Supervision that convergence of national accounting standards was required. As demands for international standards intensified, the IASC was reorganized in 2001 into the International Accounting Standards Board (IASB). The IASC Foundation was created, based in the US, to oversee the activities of the IASB (www.iasb.org), which operates from London.

IFRS International Financial Reporting Standards (IFRS) are Standards and Interpretations adopted by the IASB. These include International Financial Reporting Standards (IFRS), provided by the IASB, as well as International Accounting Standards (IAS) from the International Accounting Standards Committee. The IASB has adopted these IAS and retained their IAS designations, although some were later modified or replaced. IFRS also include Interpretations by the International Financial Reporting Interpretations Committee (IFRIC) and the former Standing Interpretations Committee that operated under the IASC.

1.4 What is the International Accounting Standards Board?

The International Accounting Standards Board (IASB) has the following three objectives:

IFRS The objectives of the IASB are:

(a) To develop, in the public interest, a single set of high quality, understandable and enforceable global accounting standards that require high quality, transparent and comparable information in financial statements and other financial reporting to help participants in the various capital markets of the world and other users of the information to make economic decisions;

(b) To promote the use and rigorous application of those standards; and

(c) To work actively with national standard-setters to bring about convergence of national accounting standards and IFRSs to high quality solutions.

The IASB is composed of several interlocking organizations, as shown in Figure 2.2.

- *International Accounting Standards Committee Foundation.* The Foundation is an independent body composed of 22 trustees that oversees the IASB and its activities. Funding is based on four principles:
  1) Support should be broad based and include major participants in the world's capital markets, including official institutions to ensure diversification and continuity.
  2) Funding should be compelling in the sense that use of standards becomes difficult without also providing support.
  3) Support should be open ended and sustained, such that the independence of the IASC Foundation would not be compromised.
  4) Funding should be shared by the major economies of the world in proportion to their respective gross domestic products.
- *International Accounting Standards Board.* Standard setting is primarily the responsibility of the IASB, which is comprised of 14 board members – each with one vote – appointed by Foundation trustees. Members are selected, according to the IASC Foundation constitution, for the 'best available combination of technical skills and background experience on relevant international business and market conditions'.

FIGURE 2.2 STRUCTURE OF THE IASB AND RELATED ORGANIZATIONS

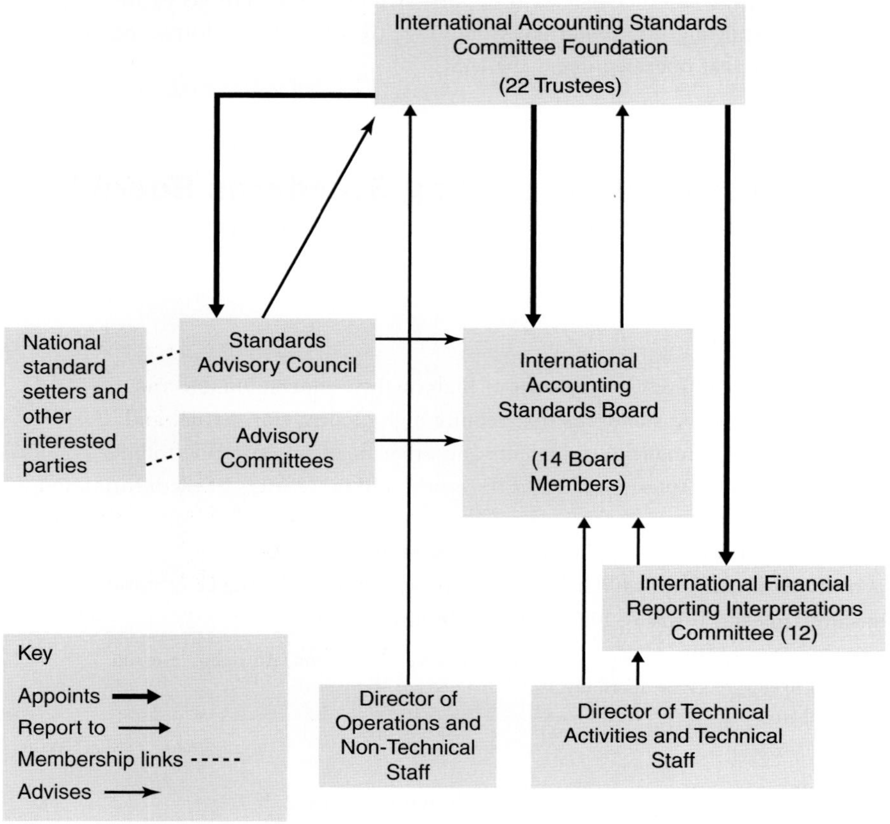

Source: www.iasb.org

- International Financial Reporting Interpretations Committee (IFRIC). **The Committee handles** situations where no authoritative guidance is available. For example, Committee interpretations address newly identified financial reporting issues not yet addressed by the IASB, and issues where unsatisfactory or conflicting interpretations have developed or seem likely to develop in the absence of authoritative guidance. As already noted, Committee interpretations are part of IFRS.
- *Standards Advisory Council.* The Council provides advice on the IASB agenda, project timetables and priorities, and on the practical application and implementation of existing standards. Members are drawn from user groups, financial statement preparers, financial analysts, academics, auditors, regulators and professional accounting bodies. The Council plays an active role in the promotion and adoption of international standards throughout the world.

1.5 How does the IASB set standards?

Figure 2.3 shows the six stages employed by the IASB to set accounting standards.

FIGURE 2.3 SIX STANDARD-SETTING STAGES

1. *Setting the agenda:* The IASB considers the following criteria when setting its agenda:
   a. The relevance to users of the information and the reliability of information that could be provided.
   b. Existing guidance available.
   c. The possibility of increasing convergence.
   d. The quality of the standard to be developed.
   e. Resource constraints.
2. *Project planning:* The IASB can decide whether it wishes to work alone on a specific project or jointly with another standard setter. In some cases the IASB may establish a working group. The Director of Technical Activities and the Director of Research select a project team and appoint a project manager, who draws up a project plan.
3. *Development and publication of a discussion paper:* a discussion paper typically includes a comprehensive overview of the issue, possible approaches to addressing the issue, preliminary views of the authors or the IASB, and an invitation to comment. Normally 120 days is allowed for comment.
4. *Development and publication of exposure draft:* a mandatory exposure draft is published setting out the proposed standard, or an amendment to an existing standard. The IASB invites comments typically for a period of 120 days, although for shorter periods in some cases.
5. *Development and publication of a standard:* after resolving issues that arise in the exposure draft, the IASB has the option of publishing a second exposure draft or issuing the actual standard.
6. *Procedures after a standard is issued:* IASB members and staff hold regular meetings with interested parties after issuing a standard to understand any unanticipated issues that may arise related to practical implementation or the standard's potential impact.

International accounting standards are developed based on three requirements:

- *Transparency and accessibility.* The IASB considers topics on its agenda based on consultations with constituents and research conducted with IASB staff. Comment letters from interested organizations, IASB meeting observer notes, IASB decisions and other materials are made available through the organization's website (www.iasb.org) and other media.
- *Extensive consultation and responsiveness.* The IASB solicits views and suggestions by inviting public comment on discussion papers and exposure drafts. The IASB may also arrange public hearings and working sessions. Comments from interested parties are summarized, analysed and considered by the staff, who makes recommendations to the IASB.
- *Accountability.* The IASB uses the 'comply or explain' approach. If the IASB omits a nonmandatory step, it is required by the organization's constitution to state its reasons. Figure 2.4 provides an overview of the mandatory versus nonmandatory steps in the IASB standard-setting process.

FIGURE 2.4 MANDATORY AND NONMANDATORY STEPS IN THE IASB
STANDARD-SETTING PROCESS

Mandatory	Nonmandatory
1. Develop and pursue the IASB technical agenda	1. Publish a discussion document (e.g. discussion paper)
2. Prepare and issue standards and exposure drafts, each of which is to include any dissenting opinions	2. Establish working groups or other types of specialist advisory groups
3. Establish procedures for reviewing comments made within a reasonable period on documents published for comment	3. Hold public hearings
	4. Undertake field tests (both in developed countries and in emerging markets)
4. Consult the SAC on major projects, agenda decisions and work priorities	
5. Publish basis for conclusions, with standards and exposure drafts	

ON YOUR OWN

LEARNING OUTCOME REVIEW

1. Why would nations want to have control over the accounting standard-setting process?
2. Compare and contrast the rules-based and principles-based approaches to setting accounting standards.
3. Which approach was used for IFRS: rules-based or principles-based standards?
4. What do IFRS include?
5. What are the objectives of the International Accounting Standards Board?
6. What is the structure of the IASB and related organizations? What is the role of each IASB-related organization?
7. Describe the six standard-setting stages used by the IASB.
8. What are the mandatory steps in the IASB standard-setting process? What are the nonmandatory steps?
9. What are the three requirements for setting international accounting standards?

LEARNING OUTCOME PRACTICE

1. IFRS include all of the following except:
   a. IFRS from the International Accounting Standards Board
   b. Decisions by the Standards Advisory Committee
   c. IAS from the International Accounting Standards Committee
   d. Interpretations by the International Financial Reporting Interpretations Committee (IFRIC)

2. The advantages of the principles-based approach to setting accounting standards do not include:
   a. Specific guidance for those who prepare financial statements
   b. Focusing on objectives for those who prepare financial statements
   c. Implementation that can be applied in different jurisdictions to satisfy local laws and culture
   d. Avoids gaps that fail to provide guidance in all circumstances

3. The requirements for setting international accounting standards do include which of the following:
   1. Transparency and accessibility
   2. Accountability
   3. Public acceptability
   4. Extensive consultation and responsiveness

   a. 1 and 2 only
   b. 1, 2, and 3 only
   c. 1, 2, and 4 only
   d. 1, 2, 3, and 4

LEARNING OUTCOME 2
EXPLAIN THE FRAMEWORK FOR THE PREPARATION AND PRESENTATION OF FINANCIAL STATEMENTS

2.1 What are the three levels of authoritative guidance?

2.2 What are the underlying assumptions in the Framework?

2.3 What are the qualitative characteristics of financial statements?

2.4 What are the constraints on relevant and reliable information?

The Framework for the Preparation and Presentation of Financial Statements (Framework) was created by the International Accounting Standards Board, although it is not an accounting standard per se. The Framework is intended to set out the concepts that underlie the preparation and presentation of financial statements to external users in a way that assists the IASB itself and national standard-setting bodies when developing accounting standards. It also provides assistance to those who prepare financial statements, auditors who must form an opinion about whether financial statements conform to International Financial Reporting Standards and users who must interpret the information in financial statements.

2.1 What are the three levels of authoritative guidance?

The Framework identifies three levels of authoritative guidance, as shown in Figure 2.5.

FIGURE 2.5 THREE LEVELS OF AUTHORITATIVE GUIDANCE

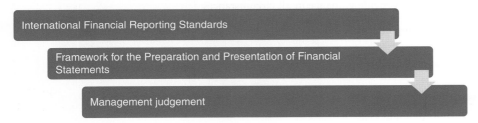

International Financial Reporting Standards

Framework for the Preparation and Presentation of Financial Statements

Management judgement

When attempting to resolve an accounting issue, the first level of guidance is specific International Reporting Financial Standards. Current IFRS at the time this book went to press are listed in Appendix B of this chapter, along with a brief description of each standard.

Secondly, if an issue is not specifically addressed by IFRS, then the next source of guidance would be the Framework. This includes definitions, qualitative characteristics of information and constraints on relevant and reliable information.

Thirdly, if the Framework provides no guidance, management must use its own judgement. In any event, the Framework requires that financial statements be presented in a way that conveys 'a true and fair view' of financial results.

According to the Framework, the objective of financial statements is to provide information about the financial position, performance and changes in financial position of a reporting entity that is useful to a wide range of users in making economic decisions. It identifies a reporting entity as any entity that has users who rely on its financial statements and notes as their major source of financial information. The external users identified in the Framework are those listed in Figure 1.3–investors, employees, lenders, suppliers and trade creditors, customers, governments and their agencies, and the public. The Framework applies to all commercial, industrial and business reporting entities, whether in the private or public sector.

2.2 What are the underlying assumptions in the Framework?

The Framework identifies two underlying assumptions: accrual basis and going concern.

Financial statements are prepared on the accrual basis of accounting, meaning that the effects of transactions are reported when they occur, which is not necessarily when cash is received or paid. For example, it is common for an employee to provide service to the employer and be paid later. A customer may pay a business entity in advance of receiving a good or service. In these cases, accrual accounting

FIGURE 2.6 UNDERLYING ASSUMPTIONS

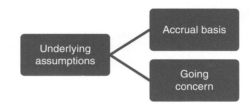

classifies these transactions in the period in which the employee renders the service and when the customer receives the good or service. Payment of cash or receipt of cash is not relevant. We will learn about accrual accounting in depth in Part II of this textbook.

The second underlying assumption in the Framework is going concern. The term going concern refers to the assumption that a business entity will continue operating without threat of liquidation in the foreseeable future. We assume that businesses prepare their financial statements on a going concern basis unless there is the intention to liquidate the business or management is being forced to liquidate the business. Liquidation refers to the process by which a business entity is brought to an end, which often means that assets must be sold for below value. If management intends to or must liquidate the business, then it must disclose that information. In addition, the financial statements would not be prepared on a going concern basis. For example, management may use liquidation values for assets.

Figure 2.6 graphically illustrates the two underlying assumptions in the Framework.

2.3 What are the qualitative characteristics of financial statements?

A qualitative characteristic is an attribute that makes information provided in financial statements useful to users. Four qualitative characteristics are identified in the Framework: understandability, relevance, reliability and comparability.

- Understandability: Users are assumed to have a reasonable knowledge of business, economic activities and financial accounting, and will study the information with reasonable diligence to comprehend its meaning. However, this does not imply that complex information should be excluded from financial statements just because some users might not be able to understand it.
- Relevance: Information is relevant when it makes a difference to users' decisions, either by helping them evaluate the effects of past, present or future transactions or other events on future cash flows (predictive value), or by confirming or correcting their previous evaluations (confirmatory value). Relevance is also affected by materiality (discussed below).
- Reliability: Information is free from material error and faithfully represents what it purports to represent. Thus, information should be presented in a way that emphasizes substance over form. The information should also be presented to provide a faithful representation of the transactions it is supposed to

Example: a business may sell an asset such as an aircraft and then continue to enjoy the future economic benefits of that asset through a rental or lease arrangement. In this case, reporting only the sale of the aircraft without disclosing information about the lease arrangement may not faithfully represent the transaction entered into.

represent. Thus, financial information must also have neutrality, which means that it is free from bias and does not influence a decision or judgement in order to achieve a predetermined result or outcome. Prudence is the degree of caution exercised in judgements about uncertainties such that assets or income are not overstated and liabilities and expenses are not understated in reporting information. However, this does not mean that assets or income should be deliberately understated, or that liabilities or expenses should be deliberately overstated, because doing so would not be neutral and therefore would not have the quality of reliability. Finally, reliability requires completeness, since omission of information can cause other information to be false or misleading, and thus unreliable (see example in shaded box).

- Comparability provides the ability for users to identify trends (similarities and differences) over time in a business entity's financial position and performance, and also between the financial statements of different entities, in order to evaluate their relative financial position, performance and changes in financial position. Comparability encompasses the concept of consistency, which refers to the use of the same set of accounting policies and procedures from period to period within an entity and between entities.

Figure 2.7 graphically illustrates the four qualitative characteristics of financial statements and the attributes that affect each characteristic.

2.4 What are the constraints on relevant and reliable information?

The Framework identifies four constraints on relevant and reliable information:

- Timeliness refers to whether the information is available to users before it loses its capacity to influence decisions.
- Balance between benefits and cost means that the benefits of reporting information should justify the cost associated with providing and using it.
- Balance between qualitative characteristics refers to the trade-off between qualitative characteristics when necessary, which is based on professional judgement about the relative importance of information.
- As already noted, the information should present a true and fair view, sometimes referred to as fair presentation. The Framework does not provide an explicit definition of true and fair view and it is therefore a matter of professional judgement.

Figure 2.8 graphically illustrates the four constraints on relevant and reliable information.

FIGURE 2.7 QUALITATIVE CHARACTERISTICS OF FINANCIAL STATEMENTS

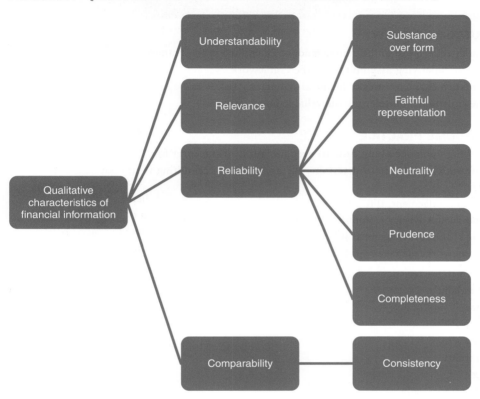

FIGURE 2.8 CONSTRAINTS ON RELEVANT AND RELIABLE INFORMATION

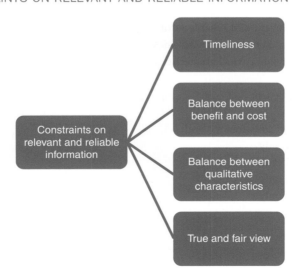

ON YOUR OWN

LEARNING OUTCOME REVIEW

1. What are the three levels of authoritative guidance identified in the Framework?
2. Explain the two underlying assumptions in the Framework.
3. List the qualitative characteristics of financial statements and describe each of them.
4. What are the constraints on relevant and reliable information?

LEARNING OUTCOME PRACTICE

1. Someone seeking guidance about how to prepare, audit or interpret financial statements would follow which sequence to determine the appropriate accounting treatment of a transaction?
   a. Management judgement, IFRS, Framework
   b. IFRS, Standard Advisory Committee pronouncement, Framework
   c. Framework, IFRS, management judgement
   d. IFRS, Framework, management judgement

2. The qualitative characteristics of financial statements include which of the following?
   1. Understandability
   2. Relevance
   3. Neutrality
   4. Reliability
   5. Comparability
   6. Prudence
      a. 1, 2, 3 and 5 only
      b. 1, 2, 4 and 5 only
      c. 1, 2, 4 and 6 only
      d. 2, 3, 4 and 6 only

3. The constraints on relevant and reliable information include which of the following?
   1. Balance between qualitative characteristics
   2. Completeness of qualitative characteristics
   3. True and fair view
   4. Balance between benefit and cost
   5. Timeliness
   6. Comparability and consistency
      a. 1, 2, 3 and 5 only
      b. 1, 3, 4 and 5 only
      c. 2, 3, 4 and 6 only
      d. 1, 3, 4 and 6 only

LEARNING OUTCOME 3
DISCUSS THE GENERAL FEATURES OF ACCOUNTING IN THE FRAMEWORK

3.1   What are fair presentation and compliance?

3.2   What are materiality and aggregation?

3.3   What is offsetting?

3.4   What is the frequency of reporting?

3.5   What is comparative information?

3.6   What is consistency of presentation?

3.1 What are fair presentation and compliance?

Financial statements should present the financial position, financial performance and cash flows of the business entity fairly. This means faithful representation of the effects of transactions. And it also means that the resulting financial statements as a whole are fairly presented. In addition, a reporting entity can claim that it has complied with IFRS *only* if it has comformed with all IFRS requirements. Then the reporting entity should make an *explicit and unreserved statement* in the notes to the financial statements that it has complied (see the example from Emirates airline).

Emirates Airline
From Note 2 Summaries of Significant Accounting Policies
Notes to the financial statements for the year ended 31 March 2007

The financial statements have been prepared in accordance with and comply with International Financial Reporting Standards (IFRS).

3.2 What are materiality and aggregation?

Materiality refers to the size of an item in comparison to the whole.

The sale of a €3 toy by a business that sells €100 million annually is likely to regard this transaction as immaterial. However, a sale of €5 million by the same company would probably be regarded as material.

IFRS 'Information is material if its omission or misstatement could influence the economic decisions of users taken on the basis of the financial statements.'

If an item is immaterial, then it is small enough when compared to the whole so that financial statement users would not be interested. Materiality helps determine how to aggregate information in the financial statements.

Continuing the preceding example, if €65 million of the €100 million in sales were to a single customer, then this information is likely to be of interest to an investor or creditor. Why? The reason is that if this customer ceased buying, the business would suffer a major reduction in sales. Therefore, to include this customer with all others would be inappropriate aggregation of the information given its materiality.

3.3 What is offsetting?

A reporting entity is not allowed to offset assets and liabilities.

Leung Information Systems Ltd sells computer outsourcing services to Arildsson Engineering Ltd. Arildsson currently owes Leung €150 000 for services already performed by Leung but for which it has not paid. In addition, Leung is planning to build a new computer facility and has hired Arildsson for €100 000 to design the electrical systems. Arildsson has already completed the design and delivered it to Leung, although Leung has not yet paid for the design services.

Thus, Arildsson owes €150 000 to Leung and is owed €100 000 by Leung. The difference is €50 000. However, Aridlsson would report the two items separately and not the net amount (difference) as a single item.

3.4 What is the frequency of reporting?

IFRS requires reporting entities to present a complete set of financial statements at least annually. The business can present financial statements for a shorter period (for example for two years or a quarter, respectively) as long as it meets its obligation to present once each year.

3.5 What is comparative information?

When the reporting entity presents financial statements, IFRS requires comparable information for the previous period to be included as a basis for comparison. For example, if the financial statements are presented for 2009, results from 2008 would also be included. If financial statements are presented for second quarter 2009, results from second quarter 2008 would also be reported.

3.6 What is consistency of presentation?

Businesses are to present financial statement information consistently over time. This means that the manner of presentation and the classification of financial information must be the same from period to period.

ON YOUR OWN

LEARNING OUTCOME REVIEW

1. How frequently are businesses required to report under IFRS?
2. What information must be included in the financial statements to achieve comparability under IFRS?
3. How does a business achieve consistency in financial reporting?
4. How does a business determine materiality?
5. Under what circumstances can a reporting entity claim to have complied with IFRS?

LEARNING OUTCOME PRACTICE

1. Which concept requires the effects of transactions and other events to be reported in the period to which they relate?
   a. Going concern
   b. Timeliness
   c. Accrual basis
   d. Relevance

2. What is the concept that the omission or misstatement of information could influence users' decisions?
   a. Relevance
   b. Understandability
   c. Reliability
   d. Materiality

LEARNING OUTCOME 4
DEFINE MEASUREMENT CONCEPTS IN FINANCIAL STATEMENTS

Financial accounting uses several different measurement bases which include:

- *Historical cost* – Assets are recorded for an amount of cash or cash equivalents paid or the fair value of the consideration given to acquire them at the time of their acquisition. Liabilities are measured by the amount of proceeds received in exchange for the obligation or in some circumstances, at the amounts of cash or cash equivalents expected to be paid to satisfy the liability in the normal course of business.
- *Fair value* – The amount for which an asset could be exchanged or a liability settled between knowledgeable, willing parties in an arm's-length transaction.
- *Current cost* – The amount of cash or cash equivalents that would have to be paid if the same or an equivalent asset was currently acquired. The amount of cash or cash equivalents that would be required to currently settle an obligation.
- *Realizable value* – The amount of cash or cash equivalents that could currently be obtained by selling an asset in an orderly disposal.
- *Present value* – A current estimate of the present discounted value of the future net cash flows in the normal course of business.

LEARNING OUTCOME 5
EXPLAIN THE ROLE OF PROFESSIONAL ETHICS
IN ACCOUNTING

5.1   What are professional ethics?

5.2   What are ethical codes?
     5.2.1   Business entity
     5.2.2   Accounting firm
     5.2.3   Professional organization

5.1 What are professional ethics?

Ethics can be defined as a theory or system of moral values or a set of principles of 'right' conduct. Some people describe ethics in broader terms, as a branch of philosophy that deals not only with human conduct but the 'good life' – the life worth living as opposed to moral conduct. Within the broader discipline of ethics we find applied ethics, which concerns how ethical theory is applied to real-world situations.

FIGURE 2.9 ETHICS TAXONOMY

Business ethics is a field within applied ethics and concerns how ethical theories and principles are applied in the business environment. Professional ethics is a specialism within the broader field of business ethics and accounting ethics would be part of professional ethics. Figure 2.9 illustrates this basic taxonomy.

One issue within professional ethics is whether professionals, including accountants, are able to make independent judgements about their work. Independent judgement can be contrasted to personal judgement, which may include decisions involving likes and dislikes based on emotion. Professional ethical judgements are made in reference to specific provisions of professional ethical codes or broader codes of business ethics. Specific provisions may be subjective and not easily measured. For example, professional ethical codes often call for accountants to have integrity or to exhibit 'professional behaviour'.

An important implication of independent judgement is that a professional accountant's responsibility is not exclusively to his or her employer or client. Consider the following case.

Cynthia Cooper was an employee of WorldCom, a major communications company that disclosed a US$3.8 billion accounting fraud in 2002, just months after the Enron collapse (see Suggested Reading). In the course of discharging her duties, Cooper found accounting irregularities that ultimately led to the discovery of the fraud. At one point she discussed her concerns about these irregularities with WorldCom's auditing firm, Arthur Andersen (which was also Enron's auditing firm). She was subsequently told by the chief financial officer not to discuss these questionable practices with Arthur Andersen or anyone else.

Source: 'WorldCom's Whistle-Blower Tells Her Story', *USA Today*, February 14, 2008.

What would someone like Cynthia Cooper be ethically obliged to do in a situation like this? Does she owe complete loyalty to her employer? Her professional training tells her that what she is observing is not appropriate and may even involve fraud and misrepresentation. In these cases, the professional may then be faced with an ethical dilemma. To whom exactly does she have an obligation? And how can that obligation be ethically discharged?

5.2 What are ethical codes?

Accounting standards and ethical codes come from different sources. Accounting standards, as we know, are set by the International Accounting Standards Board and national or regional standard-setting organizations. Normally, standards setters do not have ethical codes (sometimes referred to as conduct codes). Instead, these are normally established by professional organizations and employers. Although professional ethical codes often share similarities, they vary from organization to organization. The following presents examples of three different types of ethical and conduct codes.

These different types of codes are shown in Figure 2.10.

BUSINESS ENTITY'S CODE OF ETHICS

At the core of Figure 2.10 is the code of ethics established by the business entity. Codes will vary from company to company. As an example, excerpts from the British Airways Code of Conduct and Ethics follow.

FIGURE 2.10 BUSINESS AND PROFESSIONAL ETHICAL CODES

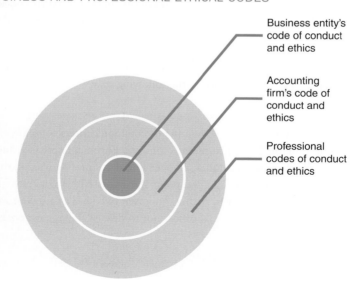

Business entity's code of conduct and ethics

Accounting firm's code of conduct and ethics

Professional codes of conduct and ethics

Conflicts of Interest — A 'conflict of interest' occurs when an individual's private interest interferes or appears to interfere with the interests of the Company. As a matter of Company policy, employees must not leave conflicts of interest unresolved unless approved by the Company. In particular, employees must never use or attempt to use their position at the Company to obtain any improper personal benefit for themselves, for their families, or for any other person.

Misuse of Opportunities and Information — Employees owe a duty to the Company to advance the Company's business interests when appropriate. Employees are prohibited from taking (or directing to a third party) a business opportunity that is discovered through the use of corporate property, information or position, unless the Company has already been offered the opportunity and turned it down. More generally, employees are prohibited from using corporate property, information or position for personal gain and from competing with the Company.

Confidentiality — In carrying out the Company's business, employees often learn confidential or proprietary information about the Company, its customers, suppliers, or joint venture parties. Employees must maintain the confidentiality of all information so entrusted to them, except when disclosure is authorised or legally mandated. Confidential or proprietary information of our Company, and of other companies, includes any non-public information that would be harmful to the relevant company or useful or helpful to competitors if disclosed.

Fair Dealing — We do not seek competitive advantages through illegal or unethical business practices. Each employee should endeavour to deal fairly with the Company's customers, service providers, suppliers, competitors and employees. No employee should take unfair advantage of anyone through manipulation, concealment, abuse of privileged information, misrepresentation of material facts, or any unfair dealing practice.

Protection and Proper Use of Company Assets — All employees should protect the Company's assets and ensure their efficient use. All Company assets should be used only for legitimate business purposes.

Compliance with Laws, Rules and Regulations — It is the Company's policy to comply with all applicable laws, rules and regulations. It is the personal responsibility of each employee to adhere to the standards and restrictions imposed by those laws, rules and regulations.

The British Airways Code of Conduct and Ethics is not specific to accountants, but applies to all employees within the company.

ACCOUNTING FIRM'S CODE OF CONDUCT AND ETHICS

When a business engages the service of a public accounting firm, that firm's code becomes a part of the overall professional ethics environment.

PricewaterhouseCoopers (PwC) is a network of firms that is one of the world's largest accounting and professional services providers, with more than 146 000 employees in 150 countries. PwC describes the need for a code of conduct as follows:

> We conduct our business within the framework of applicable professional standards, laws, and regulations together with PwC policies and standards. However, we also acknowledge that these standards, laws, regulations and policies do not govern all types of behavior. As a result, we also have a Code of Conduct for all PwC people and firms.

PwC communicates to all employees that ethical behaviour is required even in cases where the Code of Conduct offers no guidance:

> While the Code provides a broad range of guidance about the standards of integrity and business conduct, no code can address every situation that individuals are likely to encounter. As a result, this Code is not a substitute for our responsibility and accountability to exercise good judgement and obtain guidance on proper business conduct.

Part of PwC's Code of Conduct is a Framework for Ethical Decision Making:

> As a guide in deciding on a course of action, follow these steps and ask yourself these questions:

> Recognize the Event, Decision or Issue. Are you being asked to do something that you think might be wrong? Are you aware of potentially illegal or unethical conduct on the part of others at PwC or a client? Are you trying to make a decision and are you unsure about the ethical course of action?

> Think Before You Act. Summarize and clarify your issue. Ask yourself, why the dilemma? Consider the options and consequences. Consider who may be affected. Consult others.

> Decide on a Course of Action. Determine your responsibility. Review all relevant facts and information. Refer to applicable PwC policies or professional standards. Assess the risks and how you could reduce them. Contemplate the best course of action. Consult others.

> Test Your Decision. Review the 'Ethics Questions to Consider' (see below). Apply PwC's values to your decision. Make sure you have considered PwC policies, laws and professional standards. Consult others – enlist their opinion of your planned action.

> Proceed with Confidence. Communicate decision and rationale to stakeholders. Reflect upon what was learned. Share your success stories with others.

Ethics Questions to Consider:

1. *Is it against PwC or professional standards?*
2. *Does it feel right?*
3. *Is it legal?*
4. *Will it reflect negatively on you or PwC?*
5. *Who else could be affected by this (others in PwC, clients, you, etc.)?*
6. *Would you be embarrassed if others knew you took this course of action?*
7. *Is there an alternative that does not pose an ethical conflict?*
8. *How would it look in the newspapers?*
9. *What would a reasonable person think?*
10. *Can you sleep at night?*

PROFESSIONAL CODE OF CONDUCT AND ETHICS

Accountants often seek professional certification from industry organizations. In Hong Kong, for example, individuals who wish to practise as professional accountants can become a member of the Hong Kong Institute of Certified Public Accountants (HKICPA). This involves passing a competence exam as well as meeting other criteria. As a member of the Hong Kong Institute of Certified Public Accountants, an individual is required to abide by the Code of Ethics for Professional Accountants.

This code is similar in many ways to ethical codes in other professional accounting organizations, such as the Association of Chartered Certified Accountants (ACCA), the American Institute of Certified Accountants (AICPA), Chartered Accountants (CA), Institute of Management Accountants (IMA) and other organizations. For example, an accountant working for PricewaterhouseCoopers who is a member of the HKICPA would be responsible under both the PwC Code of Conduct and the HKICPA Code of Ethics for Professional Accountants. Fundamental principles from the HKICPA Code include:

Integrity — A professional accountant should be straightforward and honest in all professional and business relationships.

Objectivity — A professional accountant should not allow bias, conflict of interest or undue influence on others to override professional or business judgements.

Professional Competence and Due Care — A professional accountant has a continuing duty to maintain professional knowledge and skill at the level required to ensure that a client or employer receives competent professional service based on current developments in practice, legislation and techniques. A professional accountant should act diligently and in accordance with applicable technical and professional standards when providing professional services.

Confidentiality — A professional accountant should respect the confidentiality of information acquired as a result of professional and business relationships and should not disclose any such information to third parties without proper and specific authority unless there is a legal or professional right or duty to disclose. Confidential information acquired as a result of professional and business relationships should not be used for the personal advantage of the professional accountant or third parties.

Professional Behavior — A professional accountant should comply with relevant laws and regulations and should avoid any action that discredits the profession.

Conclusion

The globalization of capital markets that trade both equity securities and debt securities, as well as the growth of free trade between nations, has driven the need for international accounting standards. The requirement for efficient and cost-effective access to capital has encouraged many nations to improve the transparency and reliability of financial information, especially for publicly traded companies, by moving towards convergence with international accounting standards.

The Framework for the Preparation and Presentation of Financial Statements establishes the basic guidelines for reporting entities. The Framework requires the use of accrual basis accounting and the going concern assumption if applicable. It identifies four qualitative characteristics of decision-useful information: understandability, relevance, reliability and comparability. Constraints on relevant and reliable information include timeliness, balance between benefit and cost, balance regarding the relative importance of information and presentation of a 'true and fair view'.

Although many nations have moved and continue to move towards IFRS, few accept it verbatim. Most review IFRS as promulgated by the International Accounting Standards Board, then each creates an IFRS-equivalent standard that considers national and regional needs. Many nations also continue independent standard-setting activity for privately held companies, and for small and medium-sized businesses.

Summary
LEARNING OUTCOME 1
Accounting Standard-Setting Explained

Most accounting standards are set at the national level by government, quasi-government and private organizations. The exact standard-setting process varies from country to country. National standards typically reflect variations in law and culture. The International Accounting Standards Board was created to set international accounting standards, which are collectively referred to as International Financial Reporting Standards. Globalization of business and particularly financial markets has created pressure to converge accounting standards so that users throughout the world can better understand financial statements. National standards are converged with international standards to varying degrees. Some countries have adopted IFRS in their entirety, some use IFRS with minor modifications and others have not converged their standards at all.

Accounting standards can be rules based or principles based. International accounting standards are principle based, which means that they focus on broad objectives. This permits flexibility so that standards can be implemented in a way that satisfies local laws and culture.

LEARNING OUTCOME 2
Framework Explained

Those who set standards and those who prepare, audit or interpret financial statements have three levels of authoritative guidance. The first is specific requirements set out in International Financial Reporting Standards. The second level of guidance is the Framework for the Preparation and Presentation of Financial Statements and the third is management judgement.

The Framework contains definitions, underlying assumptions, qualitative characteristics of financial statements, and constraints on relevant and reliable information that underlie all IFRS. Financial statements are prepared based on two assumptions: accrual basis and going concern. The accrual basis requires that financial information be classified in the reporting period that it affects, not the period in which cash was received or paid. The going concern concept assumes that the reporting entity will not be liquidated in the foreseeable future.

Four qualitative characteristics that make financial statements useful to users include understandability, relevance, reliability and comparability. Understandability means that users have a reasonable knowledge of business, economic activities and financial accounting and will study information diligently. Relevance is whether information will make a difference to a user's decision. Reliability means that information is free from material error and faithfully represents what it purports to represent. Comparability is the ability to compare a reporting entity's financial results to other entities' financial results.

The Framework also addresses constraints on relevant and reliable information. These include timeliness, the balance between benefit and cost, the balance between qualitative characteristics and finally, the injunction that the financial statements must present a 'true and fair view' of the financial results of the reporting entity.

LEARNING OUTCOME 3
General Features of Framework Discussed

The Framework also contains general features that all financial statements should have. Not only should financial statements be presented based on the accrual basis and going concern assumptions, they must also fairly present financial information. Financial statements must be in complete compliance in order for a reporting entity to claim that it conforms to IFRS.

Material items must be considered when preparing financial statements. A material item is one that could influence the economic decisions of financial statement users. Materiality is also important for determining the best way to aggregate financial information when it is presented.

Financial information is not offset. IFRS also requires that at least one past period's information be included in the financial statements for comparison. Finally, financial statements must be prepared in a way that is consistent, meaning that information is presented in the same way from period to period.

LEARNING OUTCOME 4
Measurement Concepts Defined

Accounting uses several different measurement bases which include historical cost, current cost, realizable value, present value and fair value. The required method for a particular type of transaction is prescribed by accounting standards.

LEARNING OUTCOME 5
Role of Professional Ethics Explained

Professional ethics is a form of applied ethics that applies ethical theory to business issues. Professional ethics involves independent judgement, which may be based on subjective qualities such as integrity and honesty. Ethically, a professional does not necessarily owe complete loyalty to an employer or client, but may have to resolve situations where a conflict of interest is involved and afterwards take appropriate action. Employers and professional organizations typically have a code of ethics or code of conduct to guide employees in ethical decision making.

REVIEW QUESTIONS

1. What are the primary factors driving the convergence of national and regional accounting standards with international accounting standards?
2. What are rules-based standards? What are principles-based standards? What are the advantages and disadvantages of each?
3. What is the International Accounting Standards Committee Foundation, and what purposes does it serve?
4. What are the responsibilities of the International Accounting Standards Board? International Financial Reporting Interpretations Committee? Standards Advisory Council?
5. What are the IASB's six standard-setting stages? What are the three requirements for setting IFRS?

Key Terms

Accrual basis
Applied ethics
Balance between benefit and cost
Balance between qualitative characteristics
Business ethics
Codes of conduct
Comparability
Completeness
Consistency
Current cost
Ethical codes
Fair value
Faithful representation
Going concern
Historical cost
International Accounting Standards (IAS)
International Accounting Standards Board (IASB)
International Financial Reporting Interpretations
    Committee (IFRIC)

International Financial Reporting Standards (IFRS)
Liquidation
Materiality
Neutrality
Offsetting
Present value
Principles-based standards
Professional ethics
Prudence
Qualitative characteristic
Realizable value
Relevance
Reliability
Rules-based standards
Substance over form
Timeliness
True and fair view
Understandability

Terminology practice

For each of the following, insert the correct term from the preceding list of key terms. Each key term can be used more than once.

1. _____ concerns how ethical theory is applied to real-world situations.
2. _____ is required for information to be reliable, since omission of information can cause it to be false or misleading.
3. _____ concerns how ethical theories and principles are applied in the business environment.
4. _____ refers to the process by which a business entity is brought to an end.
5. _____ means that information is free from bias and does not influence a decision or judgement in order to achieve a predetermined result or outcome.
6. _____ refers to the use of the same set of accounting policies and procedures from period to period within an entity and between entities.
7. A _____ is an attribute that makes information provided in financial statements useful to users.
8. _____ standards focus on broad objectives that leave room for interpretation, while _____ standards provide specific guidelines.
9. _____ is when information makes a difference to users' decisions.
10. _____ accounting classifies the effects of transactions in the reporting period in which they occur, not necessarily when cash is received or paid.

11. Employers and professional organizations set out rules of appropriate ethical behaviour in _____ or _____ .

12. _____ concerns how professionals make independent judgements on business ethics.

13. _____ means that the omission or misstatement of information could influence the economic decisions of users taken on the basis of the financial statements.

14. _____ is the amount for which an asset could be exchanged or a liability settled between knowledgeable, willing parties in an arm's-length transaction.

15. _____ include all standards and interpretations adopted by the International Accounting Standards Board, including IFRS, IAS and interpretations by IFRIC.

16. _____ is the assumption that a business entity will continue operating without threat of liquidation in the foreseeable future.

17. Reliable information should be presented in a way that emphasizes substance over form and to provide a _____ of the transactions that it is supposed to represent.

18. _____ means that users are assumed to have a reasonable knowledge of business, economic activities and financial accounting and will study the information with reasonable diligence to comprehend its meaning.

19. _____ provides the ability for users to identify trends over time in a business entity's financial position and performance.

20. _____ means that information is free from material error and faithfully represents what it is supposed to represent.

21. _____ refers to whether information is available to users before it loses its capacity to influence decisions.

22. _____ is the amount of cash or cash equivalents that could currently be obtained by selling an asset in an orderly disposal.

23. _____ is the amount of cash or cash equivalents that would have to be paid if the same or an equivalent asset was currently acquired – or the amount of cash or cash equivalents that would be required to currently settle an obligation.

24. _____ is a measurement basis in which assets are recorded for an amount of cash or cash equivalents paid or the fair value of the consideration given to acquire them at the time of their acquisition. Liabilities are measured by the amount of proceeds received in exchange for the obligation or in some circumstances, at the amounts of cash or cash equivalents expected to be paid to satisfy the liability in the normal course of business.

25. _____ is a current estimate of the present discounted value of the future net cash flows in the normal course of business.

Case analysis
PRACTICE CASE 1

A significant number of entities and countries around the world have adopted International Financial Reporting Standards (IFRS) as their basis for financial reporting, often regarding these as a means to improve the quality of information on corporate performance. However, when the advantages of a common set of global reporting standards are recognized, there are a number of implementation challenges at the international and national levels if the objective of an improved and converged reporting system is to be achieved. [ACCA adapted]

REQUIRED:

Discuss the implementation challenges faced by the International Accounting Standards Board (IASB) if there is to be a successful move to International Financial Reporting Standards.

PRACTICE CASE 2

At a recent conference on corporate social responsibility, one speaker (Professor Cheung) argued that professional codes of ethics for accountants were not as useful as some have claimed because 'they assume professional accountants to be rules-driven, when in fact most professionals are more driven by principles that guide and underpin all aspects of professional behaviour, including professional ethics.' When quizzed from the audience about his views on the usefulness of professional codes of ethics, Professor Cheung suggested that the costs of writing, implementing, disseminating and monitoring ethical codes outweighed their usefulness. He said that as long as professional accountants personally observe the highest values of probity and integrity, there is no need for detailed codes of ethics. [ACCA adapted]

REQUIRED:

(a) Critically evaluate Professor Cheung's views on codes of professional ethics. Use examples of ethical codes, where appropriate, to illustrate your answer.

(b) With reference to Professor Cheung's comments, explain what is meant by 'integrity' and assess its importance as an underlying principle in corporate governance.

End note

1. *Corporate Reporting: Is It What Investment Professionals Expect?* PricewaterhouseCoopers, November 2007.

Suggested reading

Cooper, Cynthia (2008) *Extraordinary Circumstances: The Journey of a Corporate Whistle-blower*, Hoboken, NJ: John Wiley & Sons, Inc.

Hauser, Mark D. (2006) *Moral Minds: How Nature Designed Our Universal Sense of Right and Wrong*, New York: HarperCollins.

APPENDIX A: NATIONAL STANDARDS AND IFRS CONVERGENCE

European Union

The 27 countries that comprise the European Union together account for 30.2% of gross world product, according to the International Monetary Fund (2006). Each of the member nations retains control over accounting standards. However, through the European Union they cooperate to adopt IFRS, so that now all publicly traded companies in European Union capital markets are required to use IFRS as adopted by the European Union in certain circumstances.

This convergence was seen as important internally within the European Union as well as in the European Union's relationship with the rest of the world. The European Parliament and Council of the European Union promulgated Regulation (EC) No 1606/2002, dealing with the application of international accounting standards, which articulated the reasons for using IFRS as follows:

> This Regulation aims at contributing to the efficient and cost-effective functioning of the capital market. The protection of investors and the maintenance of confidence in the financial markets is also an important aspect of the completion of the internal market in this area. This Regulation reinforces the freedom of movement of capital in the internal market and helps to enable Community companies to compete on an equal footing for financial resources available in the Community capital markets as well as in world capital markets.

> Furthermore, it is important that the financial reporting standards applied by Community companies participating in financial markets are accepted internationally and are truly global standards. This implies an increasing convergence of accounting standards currently used internationally with the ultimate objective of achieving a single set of global accounting standards.

Regulation (EC) No 1606/2002 mandated that international standards developed by the IASB should be made 'obligatory for use by all publicly traded Community companies' wherever possible. However, this was subject to several general conditions: Their application must result in a true and fair view of the financial position and performance of an enterprise; must be conducive to the European public good; must meet basic criteria for usefulness to users; and must meet the criteria of understandability, relevance, reliability and comparability.

Adoption of IFRS by the European Union is therefore not automatic. The Council reviews new standards to determine whether the criteria already noted have been met. They are assisted by the Accounting Regulatory Committee, comprising representatives from European Union member countries, which provides the Council with opinions on Commission proposals to adopt or endorse any particular international accounting standard. According to Regulation (EC) No 1606/2002, 'the Commission should take into account the importance of avoiding competitive disadvantages for European companies operating in the global marketplace, and, to the maximum possible extent, the views expressed by the delegations in the Accounting Regulatory Commission'.

An accounting technical committee also provides support and expertise to the Commission in assessing international accounting standards. This role is fulfilled by the European Financial Reporting Advisory Group, which operates through a 12-member Technical Expert Group.

France

In 1998, the Comité de la Réglementation Comptable (CRC), or Accounting Regulation Committee, was created by law as the organization responsible for approving new accounting standards. The CRC is under the jurisdiction of the Ministry of Economy and Finance, and has 15 members that include representatives from the Conseil National de la Comptabilité (National Accounting Board), Autorité des Marches Financiers (Financial Markets Authority), Ordre des Experts-Comptables (Institute of Public Accountants) and the Compagnie Nationale des Commissaires aux Comptes (National Institute of Statutory Auditors). Two judges from France's highest courts are also members.

Rulings and recommendations are issued by the Conseil National de la Comptabilité (www.minefi.gouv.fr/directions_services/CNCompta/) and are then reviewed and converted into binding regulations by the CRC. The Conseil National de la Comptabilité has 58 members, including accounting professionals, employers, trade unions, government officials and others.

French accounting standards are embedded in law and are heavily influenced by the tax code. France introduced a national uniform accounting code – the Plan Comptable Général – in 1947 (later revised), which requires companies to use a national uniform chart of accounts. Sources of law,[1] hierarchically structured, are as follows:

- European Directives
- Code de Commerce (including accounting for all commercial entities and rules for consolidated accounts)
- Decrees and regulations, such as those now issued by the CRC
- Jurisprudence
- Interpretations and recommendations by the Compagnie Nationale des Commissaires aux Comptes and Ordre des Experts-Comptables

All companies must follow French statutory requirements, although the law now allows companies to use IFRS for its consolidated financial statements.

United Kingdom

Legal revisions in 1989 created the United Kingdom Financial Reporting Council (FRC) as the accounting standard setter (see http://frc.org.uk). The FRC has responsibility over six other groups: Accounting Standards Board, Auditing Practices Board, Board for Actuarial Standards, Professional Oversight Board, Financial Reporting Review Panel and Accountancy Investigation and Discipline Board.

The Accounting Standards Board (ASB) establishes and improves financial accounting and reporting standards. ASB's objectives include developing guiding principles, issuing new accounting standards and amending existing standards, and 'working with the International Accounting Standards Board (IASB), with national standards-setters and relevant European Union (EU) institutions to encourage high quality in the IASB's standards and their adoption in the EU' (see http://frc.org.uk).

Germany

Germany had no financial accounting standards organization until 1998, when laws were amended to permit the Ministry of Justice to recognize a private national standard-setting body. This became the Deutsches Rechnungslegungs Standards Committee EV (Accounting Standards Committee of Germany) or the ASCG (www.drsc.de). One objective of the ASCG is 'to improve the quality of accounting and financial reporting and to drive forward convergence of the national standards with internationally accepted accounting and financial reporting standards, in the public interest'. Another objective is to cooperate with and represent Germany to the IASB and other international standard-setting bodies.

The ASCG has an Executive Board that oversees the activities of the organization, a General Assembly representing the members, the German Accounting Standards Board (GASB), which is responsible for accomplishing the objectives of the ASCG, and an Accounting Interpretations Committee to work with the International Financial Reporting Interpretations Committee (IFRIC) of the IASB.

Italy

In 2001, a new standards setter was established in Italy: the Italian Accounting Committee or Organismo Italiano di Conabilità (OIC). The 15-person board of directors includes representatives from organizations such as the Italian National Council of Accountants, National Association of Banks, National Confederation of Commerce (Confcommercio), Association of Italian Auditors (Assirevi), Italian Government Accountants, Italian Stock Exchange and others. The OIC is responsible for issuing accounting principles for financial statements where international standards provide no guidance, and for not-for-profit and government entities. It also provides support for the application of international accounting standards in Italy, coordinating with European Union activities.

As an EU member, Italian companies listed on an EU securities market began using IFRS. In 2005, the Italian Council of Ministers approved a legislative decree requiring, among other provisions, that listed companies, issuers of financial instruments distributed to the public, banks, stock brokerages, fund management companies and regulated financial institutions must use IFRS beginning in 2006. Subsidiaries and companies associated with the aforementioned companies have the option to use IFRS beginning in 2005. For small companies, IFRS are not permitted.

United States

Standards are primarily developed by the Financial Accounting Standards Board (FASB), under the influence of two other organizations: the Securities and Exchange Commission (SEC) and the Public Companies Accounting Oversight Board (PCAOB).

FINANCIAL ACCOUNTING STANDARDS BOARD

Most US accounting standards are promulgated by the FASB (www.fasb.org), which was established in 1973 as the successor to the Accounting Principles Board (established in 1959). Accounting Principles Board standards remain in effect unless subsequently altered by the FASB.

The FASB is a private industry organization, supported by the Financial Accounting Foundation, a nonprofit organization that provides financial support and oversight to the FASB and the Financial Accounting Standards Advisory Council (FASAC). The Financial Accounting Foundation also oversees the Governmental Accounting Standards Board (GASB) and the Governmental Accounting Standards Advisory Council (GASAC). The Financial Accounting Foundation is in turn supported by a number of constituent organizations such as the American Accounting Association, American Institute of Certified Public Accountants, CFA Institute, Institute of Management Accountants and others. The Foundation also appoints members to the FASB.

The FASB's standard-setting process is similar to the IASB's. The Board identifies issues by monitoring published reports, legislation and regulations; and through liaisons with other organizations such as the Accounting Standards Executive Committee (AcSEC) and the Auditing Standards Board of the American Institute of Certified Public Accountants.

The FASB sets its own technical agenda. Staff are assigned to research issues and present results at FASB meetings, which are open to the public. All proposed standards and interpretations are first issued as an Exposure Draft for public comment. Comments are then considered by the FASB when developing the final version of the standard. These include:

- *Statements of Financial Accounting Standards (SFAS)*. These are the primary standards promulgated by the FASB. The FASB has issued 159 SFAS to date.
- *Statements of Concepts*. The Board also issues statements, which are intended to provide constituents with concepts as tools for solving problems. 'The framework defined in the Statements of Concepts helps the Board identify the right questions to ask in structuring technical projects and contributes to a consistent approach over time' (www.fasb.org). The same process used to develop a SFAS applies to Statements of Concepts.
- *Emerging Issues Task Force (EITF)*. This group has representatives from public accounting firms, large companies and other users of financial statements. In addition, the chief accountant of the US Securities and Exchange Commission attends meetings that are held at least four times annually. A consensus on an issue by the EITF suggests that no action is needed by the FASB and the position becomes part of US generally accepted accounting principles. Lack of a consensus indicates that action by the FASB may be required.

In addition, the FASB has issued 48 interpretations, as well as numerous Financial Staff Positions (FSP) and Technical Bulletins. The FASAC consults on technical issues on matters likely to require the attention of the FASB. The more than 30 advisory members represent financial statement preparers, auditors and users of financial information.

US SECURITIES AND EXCHANGE COMMISSION

The US Securities and Exchange Commission (SEC; www.sec.gov) is the government agency with the statutory authority to establish financial accounting and reporting standards for publicly held companies. The SEC was created by the national Securities Exchange Act of 1934, which charged it with the responsibility of protecting the public interest. The SEC has delegated authority for accounting standards setting to the FASB, presumably as long as its actions are in the public interest.

PUBLIC COMPANY ACCOUNTING OVERSIGHT BOARD

In recent years high-profile corporate scandals in companies such as Enron and WorldCom have caused major financial losses for investors, employees and others. In response, the US Congress passed the Sarbanes–Oxley Act of 2002, which had a large impact on both the US and international communities in terms of regulating corporate governance, financial accounting and auditing. Among its provisions, the Sarbanes–Oxley Act established a quasi-public agency, the Public Company Accounting Oversight Board (PCAOB; www.pcaob.org), which was charged with overseeing, regulating, inspecting and disciplining accounting firms in their roles as auditors of public companies. PCAOB's power was also extended to matters such as financial disclosure, internal control assessment, corporate governance and auditor independence.

GLOBAL PERSPECTIVE

In 2002, the IASB and FASB issued a memorandum of understanding setting out the two organizations' intentions to converge international and US accounting standards by 2005. In 2007, the FASB offered the following assessment of progress (www.fasb.org):

> *the FASB expects to make significant progress toward international convergence in the next few years. However, because of the volume of differences and the complex nature of some issues, the FASB anticipates that many differences between US and international standards will persist well beyond 2005. (By 2005, all EU-listed public companies are being required by the European Union to prepare their consolidated financial statements using IASB Standards.)*

Canada

The primary accounting standards setter in Canada is the Accounting Standards Board (AcSB), also Conseil des normes comptables (www.acsbcanada.org). AcSB's activities are guided by the Accounting Standards Oversight Council (AcSOC), which appoints members of the AcSB, provides strategic direction and sets priorities (www.acsoc.ca). Membership includes senior representatives from business, finance, government, academia, the accounting and legal professions, regulators and the financial analyst communities. The AcSOC also oversees the accounting standards for the public sector.

The AcSB is responsible for establishing accounting and reporting standards for Canadian companies and not-for-profit organizations. The AcSB works with the Emerging Issues Committee (EIC), which provides guidance on new and emerging accounting issues that cannot be addressed quickly enough by the normal standard-setting process.

The AcSB has set out a comprehensive timetable for public companies to converge with IFRS by 2011. An IFRS Advisory Committee provides input to standard-setting for Canadian public companies regarding the adoption of IFRS. The AcSB also provides support to Canadian representatives on IASB working groups, which usually consists of providing an advisory group comprised of individuals with relevant experience and knowledge on the topic under consideration. This advisory group provides information on the Canadian business environment as it relates to the issues being considered by the IASB working group (e.g. typical transactions, tax effects, regulatory issues).

When deciding on whether to consider a new standard, six of the nine AcSB members must vote in favour of the project. However, the AcSB gives particular attention to international standards (www.acsbcanada.org):

> *A decision to take on a global convergence project is somewhat abbreviated, relies on the work of other standard-setters, and focuses on whether global convergence on a particular topic in accordance with decisions made by another standard setter is an appropriate setup. The strategy to adopt IFRSs for Canadian publicly accountable enterprises has narrowed the decision-making discussion even further. For projects on the IASB's work plan, the question is whether there is any reason for the AcSB not to adopt the new standards the IASB is producing at the same time as the IASB. On selected topic for which improvements in current Canadian GAAP are considered important, the question is whether to import a better IASB standard on the topic in the short term rather than waiting for its adoption in several years' time. If the improvement under consideration emanates from the FASB, the question is whether it helps to maintain existing convergence on a common North American standard and is not in conflict with the IFRS convergence strategy.*

The AcSB further comments:

> *The increased extent to which the AcSB has been emphasizing global convergence since the mid-1990s, initially through convergence with US GAAP and latterly through convergence with IFRSs, has meant that the AcSB has increasingly adopted the technical decisions of other standards setters. This has not meant blind copying. All key decisions are reviewed by the AcSB in light of Canadian circumstances, which sometimes lead to modifications necessary to deal with different business conditions or avoid inconsistencies within Canadian GAAP.*

Mexico

Since 1993 with the implementation of the North American Free Trade Agreement and with pressures from major competitors like China, Mexico has been under pressure to internationalize its accounting practices. Beginning in 1995, Mexican authorities began requiring that international standards be used in situations where Mexican accounting standards had no guidance to offer. Because of close economic ties with the United States, Mexico has relied to some extent on US standards, although in recent years it has paid more attention to the specific requirements of the Mexican economy and to international standards.

In 2001, the Mexican Board for Research and Development of Standards for Financial Information (Consejo Mexicano para la Investigación y Desarrollo de Normas de Información Financiera or CINIF) was established to replace the efforts of earlier standard setters. The CINIF is an independent nonprofit entity to conduct research and related activities for setting national accounting standards, and to develop and issue accounting standards consistent with international accounting standards. Within the CINIF, the Centro de Investigación y Desarrollo or CID was created to be in charge of developing accounting standards.

Japan

Major changes were made to accounting standards setting in Japan when the Accounting Standards Board of Japan (ASBJ), a private-sector organization, was created in 2001 (see http://www.asb.or.jp/index_e.php). The ASBJ was developed in response to two trends. In its own words:

> the Board has been developing accounting standards under two major forces: response to the reforms of the business law systems in Japan (i.e., amendments to the Corporate Law and the Securities Exchange Law); and response to the demands for the global convergence of accounting standards.[2]

Founders included the Japanese Institute of Certified Public Accountants, Japan Federation of Economic Organizations, Tokyo Stock Exchange and the Japanese Bankers Association. Oversight is provided by the Financial Accounting Standards Foundation, which handles strategic issues, budgeting, fundraising and selection of members to serve on the ASBJ.

The ASBJ has the sole responsibility for developing accounting standards and providing implementation guidance, assisted by a number of technical committees that focus on topics such as stock options, financial instruments, fixed asset accounting, lease accounting, business combinations, inventories, related party disclosures and so forth. In addition, a standing committee addresses international issues. This committee is organized into working groups, one of which focuses on ASBJ and IASB convergence. In 2007, these two standard-setting organizations agreed to remove all differences by mid-2011. The ASBJ summarized its basic policy as follows:

> In developing Japanese accounting standards, it is a policy of the Board to seek consensus among constituents, such as enterprises, investors, auditors and analysts and thereby respond adequately and expeditiously to changes in environment surrounding business accounting, both in Japan and overseas, continuously adopting 'fairness,' 'transparency,' and 'independence' as its fundamental principles and considering global standards as an important factor.[3]

CONVERGENCE NOT EQUAL TO IDENTICAL

Synchronizing national accounting standards with IASB standards is only one task. In addition, international standards are also forcing nations, especially major trading partners, to coordinate with each other. For example, the Accounting Standards Board of Japan noted that it, and other nations, would be required by 2009 to prepare consolidated statements in accordance with 'IFRS as adopted by the European Union or its equivalent standards' when its companies trade their securities on an EU-regulated market. Notice that this recognizes that international accounting standards as adopted by the European Council may not be precisely the same as the promulgated IASB standard.

In 2005, Japan met with accounting standard setters from China and the Republic of Korea to discuss issues related to international convergence of accounting standards and obstacles encountered. In a Memorandum of Understanding from that meeting, the standard setters succinctly summarized the position of most of the world's nations with respect to international accounting standards as follows:

> *First, the three parties (Japan, China and Republic of Korea) recognize that the international convergence of accounting standards is the irreversible trend under the economic globalization; and the three countries support the efforts by the IASB to develop a single set of high-quality and globally-accepted accounting standards. In the meantime, the parties believe that convergence is not equal to identical. The international convergence of accounting standards shall be a market-driven gradual process and this process shall be two-way interactions between national accounting standards setters and the IASB, giving special considerations to special local environments.*[4]

Hong Kong and China

Hong Kong's accounting standards are the responsibility of the Hong Kong Institute of Certified Public Accountants (www.hkicpa.org). The Institute has broad responsibility not only for standard setting in accounting and auditing, but also for advising on legislation, technical services for members and professional interest groups, and other activities.

The Institute issues Hong Kong Accounting Standards, Statements of Accounting Practice and Interpretations, collectively referred to as Hong Kong Financial Reporting Standards. The Institute has established separate standards for small and medium-sized businesses under the SME Financial Reporting Framework and Financial Reporting Standard.

As part of China ('one nation, two systems'), the Institute also works with officials in the government of the People's Republic of China. In its Fifth Long-Range Plan 2007–2011, the Institute identifies the following objective: 'Cooperate with China Accounting Standards Committee with a view to bringing about full convergence of mainland standards with international standards.'

In the People's Republic of China, accounting standards are under the control of the Ministry of Finance (www.mof.gov.cn). In recent years, the Chinese government has done much to make its markets more competitive, to privatize state-owned industries and, as just noted, to revise accounting standards towards convergence with international standards.

Chinese accounting standards are based on the Accounting Standard for Business Enterprises, a conceptual framework issued by the Ministry of Finance in 1992. Within the Ministry of Finance, Accounting

Regulatory Department is the Chinese Accounting Standards Committee (CASC), which advises on accounting standards. The Committee was organized in 1988 and then reorganized as the 'second' CASC in 2003 under the Ministry's Accounting Regulatory Department.

The Committee has 20 members, selected from relevant government agencies, academics, accounting professional organizations, intermediaries and businesses.

The CASC has a four-stage standard-setting process:

1. *Initiating a new project.* The Accounting Regulatory Department sets priorities for new standards based on Chinese economic development needs, and then solicits comments from the CASC and other parties. The draft document is also submitted to Ministry of Finance officials for approval. The CASC then establishes a project research team.
2. *Drafting of exposure draft.* A drafting team prepares a discussion paper based on research and field investigation, and then consults the CASC.
3. *Soliciting public comments.* An exposure draft is distributed to both public and government entities for comments, which are incorporated into the draft standard.
4. *Releasing the accounting standard.* Once leaders in the Ministry of Finance have approved the standard, it is released for implementation.

In 2005, as the result of a meeting with the IASB, the CASC agreed that converging Chinese accounting standards with equivalent IFRS was a fundamental goal of the Chinese standard-setting programme. However, in the same meeting the IASB acknowledged that 'the convergence to IFRSs will take time and how to converge with IFRSs is a matter for China to determine'.[5]

According to the China Accounting Standards Committee:

> In the 21st Century, globalization of the economy and the capital market is inevitable in the development of the world economy. Accounting information, as commercial language that is internationally accepted, is playing increasingly important role. Control over accounting matters and the prevention of accounting risks have become a critical issue of economic development. The China Accounting Standards Committee will continue to perform its consulting role in the process of setting accounting standards, to assist the accounting standards setting body in establishing and improving the Chinese accounting standards, to participate actively in the international convergence process and contribute to the socialist market economy with Chinese characteristics.

Republic of Korea

In 2000, Korean law (dealing with audit and reporting requirements for large joint-stock companies) gave responsibility for Korean Financial Accounting Standards to the newly established Korea Accounting Institute (KAI). Although the law does not require that IFRS be adopted, Korean Financial Accounting Standards are largely consistent with international standards. While some differences exist, efforts have been underway to reduce these.

Singapore

Under the Singapore Companies Act, the Council on Corporate Disclosure and Governance, part of the Singapore Government, is empowered to prescribe accounting standards for companies incorporated in Singapore as well as foreign companies doing business in Singapore (www.asc.gov.sg). Standard setting is closely tied to IASB standard-setting activities. According to the Council, 'The policy intention is to adopt International Financial Reporting Standards (IFRSs) and International Accounting Standards (IASs) issued by the International Accounting Standards Board (IASB).'

When the IASB issues an exposure draft, the Council issues an equivalent exposure draft for public comment. Comments and feedback are gathered from industry associations, governmental bodies, listed companies, banks, securities firms and academic institutions, as well as other interested parties. When the IASB issues its final Standard or Interpretation, the CCDG, through various committees, determines whether to adopt the Standard or Interpretation in full or in part in Singapore.

GLOBAL PERSPECTIVE

The World Bank provides Reports on the Observance of Standards and Codes (ROSC); see http://www.worldbank.org/ifa/rosc_aa.html#ctry. Briefs are provided by country, and give useful background on the progress with the adoption of accounting and auditing standards.

India

Accounting standards in India are the statutory responsibility of the Institute of Chartered Accountants of India (ICAI; www.icai.org). The Council has 40 members, 32 of whom are elected by members with the remaining eight appointed by the Indian government to represent the Comptroller and Auditor General of India, Central Board of Direct Taxes, Department of Company Affairs and other stakeholders. The ICAI also determines qualifications for membership and provides the examination scheme for qualifying members to practise in the profession. It also maintains the registry of qualified practitioners.

In 2007, the ICAI announced a plan to converge Indian Accounting Standards with IFRS to be effective from April 1, 2011. All listed companies, banks, insurance companies and large companies would be required to use the new standards. However, the ICAI also noted that it would make modifications to IFRS where necessary to reflect 'Indian conditions'.

In 2006, the President of ICAI had the following observation when the professional organization announced that it was studying the full adoption of IFRS:

> In the globalised economic scenario, several multinational companies are establishing subsidiaries in India and many Indian companies are forming subsidiaries abroad. Flow of investment in the international scene clearly indicates that the stakeholders are spread across the globe. As the geographical barriers are vanishing, e-commerce is enlarging, and as raising of capital in foreign

markets is increasing, the need for examining the issues relating to convergence of Indian
Accounting Standards with International Accounting Standards is assuming greater significance.
We are in touch with the IASB in this regard besides considering this issue internally.

ACCOUNTING STANDARDS FOR ISLAMIC INSTITUTIONS

Recent years have seen a considerable growth of Islamic financial institutions, especially in predominantly Muslim countries in the Middle East and the Asia-Pacific region. Islamic financial institutions and companies are operated in a manner that is compliant with Islamic religious law, the Shari'a. Although the Shari'a is complex and not easily summarized, major tenets include:

- A prohibition on charging or receiving interest.
- Matching risk and reward, for example banks share in the profits and losses of business ventures that they finance.
- Making money from money is forbidden; if a bank or other institution finances the purchase of a piece of equipment, for example, it must at some point own and possess that equipment.
- Transactions may not involve uncertainty, risk or speculation because of their potential to create conflicts between parties to a contract.
- Certain commerce is forbidden, for example alcoholic beverages and gambling.

The International Monetary Fund estimated that total Islamic assets were US$250 billion in 2005, growing at an estimated 15% per year. In addition, approximately 20% of the world's people are Muslims, representing a potentially large market for Shari'a-compliant products and services. Sukuk, securities that are often characterized as Islamic bonds, have done particularly well.

Because Shari'a derives from ancient religious sources, Islamic jurists or scholars are required to interpret whether a specific transaction is Shari'a compliant. Shari'a boards are appointed to oversee this process in Islamic businesses. The Shari'a board meets to discuss and evaluate specific transactions, ethical or other issues, and is the final word with respect to compliance. Shari'a boards do not replace a board of directors, which functions separately.

The pressures of modern commerce have created a need in the Islamic world to have a set of standards available for use by Shari'a boards and others. The Accounting and Auditing Organization for Islamic Financial Institutions (AAOIFI) was created to be a standards setter for both accounting and auditing (www.aaoifi.com).

AAOIFI is supported by almost 200 Islamic institutions, including central banks, particularly in the Gulf Cooperation Council countries (Bahrain, Kuwait, Oman, Qatar, Saudi Arabia and the United Arab Emirates). Islamic standards have been adopted in the Kingdom of Bahrain, Dubai International Financial Centre, Jordan, Lebanon, Qatar, Sudan and Syria. The relevant authorities in Australia, Indonesia, Malaysia, Pakistan, Kingdom of Saudi Arabia and South Africa have issued guidelines that are based on AAOIFI standards and pronouncements.

Australia

Accounting standard setting in Australia for both the private and public sectors is handled by the Australian Accounting Standards Board (AASB). This organization was established under the 1999 Corporate Law Economic Reform Program Act. The AASB is governed by the Financial Reporting Council (FRC), comprised of key stakeholders from the business community, professional accounting bodies, governments and regulatory agencies. FRC members are appointed by the Australian Treasury.

The FRC advises the Australian government on accounting standards and the development of international accounting standards. It provides broad strategic direction to the AASB, as well as directions, advice and feedback on matters of general policy. The FRC also approves priorities, business plans, budget and staffing arrangements, although it is unable to influence the technical deliberations of the AASB or the content of accounting standards.

South Africa

Standard setting in South Africa is handled by the Accounting Practices Board within the South African Institute of Chartered Accountants (SAICA; www.saica.co.za). In 2003, SAICA decided to issue the text of IFRS as part of South African generally accepted accounting principles. Beginning in 2007, the two sets of standards (with the exception of IFRS 1, which applies to first-time adopters of IFRS) are completely converged. SAICA uses a dual number system to indicate both the IFRS number and the South African number.

However, recognizing that IFRS places a burden on small and medium-sized businesses, the Accounting Practices Board announced in 2007 that it was adopting the IASB proposed International Financial Reporting Standard for SMEs.

Russia

Russian accounting standards are the responsibility of the Ministry of Finance of the Russian Federation, Council for Audit Activities, except for financial institutions, which fall under the supervision of the Central Bank of the Russian Federation. In the late 1990s, the Ministry of Finance instituted revisions to move towards international accounting standards, as did the Central Bank. However, major differences between Russian Accounting Standards and IAS remain:

> *The main difference between Russian Accounting Standards (RAS) and IAS for banks and credit institutions is that income and expenses are accounted for on a cash basis under RAS. Income is recognized when cash (or other consideration) is received and expenses are recorded at the date the payment is made, with some exceptions. Services paid for are recorded in the statement of income on receipt of formal supporting documents confirming that services have been received.*[6]

In 2004, the Duma (Russian parliament) gave tentative approval to a bill requiring companies with more than one subsidiary to publish financial statements that conform to IFRS within six months of their financial year end. However, the bill did not pass.

What is Russia's current status regarding international accounting standards? In 2007, the Russian Collegium of Auditors (a national professional organization), which is represented on the Ministry of Finance's Council for Audit Activities, submitted a self-assessment to the International Federation of Accountants (IFAC; www.ifac.org), a worldwide professional organization. Here were the responses to questions regarding the adoption of international accounting standards:

Does the law/regulation require the use of International Financial Reporting Standards and other pronouncements issued by the International Accounting Standards Board? Select the answer that is most appropriate.

Answer: *The law/regulation contains the main principles of the IFRSs.*

Is information publicly available about IFRSs and other IASB pronouncements that have been established into law/regulation including: IFRSs and other IASB pronouncements that have been established into law/regulation; whether the IFRS or IASB pronouncement established into law/regulation is the version in effect as at September 30, 2005; the effective date set by law/regulation where it differs from the IFRS or IASB pronouncement; the differences between IFRSs and IASB pronouncements and what was established into law/regulation; and the reasons for the differences?

Answer: *No.*

Are the IFRSs and other IASB pronouncements translated into national language?

Answer: *No and English is not an official language or is not widely spoken.*

Brazil

In 2007, the Securities and Exchange Commission of Brazil – the Commissão de Valores Mobiliários (www.cvm.gov.br) – announced that all publicly listed companies would be required to publish their financial statements using IFRS from the beginning of 2010. In the interim, use of IFRS is optional. In addition, the Central Bank of Brazil announced that any bank, domestic or foreign, required by law or regulation to publish financial statements in Brazil would also be required to use IFRS beginning with the year ended December 31, 2010.

A new accounting standards organization, the Comitê de Pronunciamentos Contábeis (CPC) or Committee for Accounting Pronouncements, was formed in 2006 with the mandate to converge Brazilian accounting standards towards IFRS. Founding members included the association of Brazilian listed companies, association for analysts, the stock exchange (BOVESPA), the Federal Council of Accounting, the Institute of Independent Auditors (IBRACON) and the accounting research foundation representing academics.

The CPC is responsible for studying, preparing and issuing technical pronouncements, guidelines and interpretations. In addition, it will centralize and standardize accounting standards to establish a single set of standards for Brazil according to international standards. The CPC described the benefits as follows (www.cvm.gov.br):

> The adoption of a single set of accounting standards, recognized internationally, will facilitate the decision-making process of investors, contributing to the strength of the capital market in Brazil. It will attract more capital to the country and the reduction of the costs, to the extent that the perceived risk is lower, in addition to stimulating the growth of investments and transnational trade. Another benefit for companies is the reduction in the costs of preparation of financial statements to meet different criteria, as occurs today.

APPENDIX END NOTES

1. Jones, Chris & Samar-Fauchon, Marie-Dominique (2001) *European Comparison: UK & France*, Deloitte & Touche.
2. *Medium-Term Operating Policy*, Accounting Standard Board of Japan, June 15, 2001.
3. *Ibid.*
4. *Memorandum of Understanding (MoU) of the 5th Three Countries' Accounting Standard Setters' Meeting between China, Japan and Republic of Korea*, September 7, 2005, Xi'an, P.R. China.
5. *Bold steps toward convergence of Chinese accounting standards and international standards*, IASB, Press release, November 14, 2005.
6. Deloitte, Touche Tohmatsu, 2007.

APPENDIX B: SUMMARIES OF IFRS

IFRS 1 First-time Adoption of International Financial Reporting Standards. This Standard applies the first time a reporting entity prepares financial statements using IFRS.

IFRS 2 Share-Based Payment. This IFRS requires a reporting entity to recognize share-based transactions, which includes any transaction that involves shares or share options in exchange for goods and services.

IFRS 3 Business Combinations. This IFRS concerns situations where one entity obtains control of one or more other businesses, and consolidation of financial reports is required.

IFRS 4 Insurance Contracts. IFRS 4 requires that insurers identify and explain amounts arising from insurance contracts in their financial statements and notes, and helps the users of their financial statements understand the amount, timing and uncertainty of future cash flows related to these contracts.

IFRS 5 Non-current Assets Held for Sale or Discontinued Operations. IFRS 5 concerns the reporting of assets held for sale and also discontinued operations.

IFRS 6 Exploration for and Evaluation of Mineral Resources. This IFRS concerns the accounting for expenditures incurred to explore for mineral resources like petroleum, natural gas or metal ore before the technical feasibility and commercial viability of extracting the mineral resources have been decided.

IFRS 7 Financial Instruments: Disclosures. Business entities must disclose information about the significance of financial instruments to the business's financial position and performance, and the associated risk exposure.

IFRS 8 Operating Segments. Operating segments are components of a business entity that meet certain criteria, and usually include product and service categories, geographical areas and major customers. This IFRS requires that operating segments be reported for assets and liabilities, and profit and loss. The business is required to report segment information to users of financial statements on the same basis that internal managers use to evaluate segment performance and allocate assets.

IAS 1 Presentation of Financial Statements. This Standard requires the presentation of financial statements in a manner that allows users to compare them with the business's financial statements from previous years, and with other entities' financial statements.

IAS 2 Inventories. Inventories are to be measured at the lower of cost or net realizable value. Net realizable value is the estimated selling price less estimated completion and sale costs, in the normal course of business. Either the weighted average or first-in, first-out (FIFO) cost formula must be used to allocate costs between inventory and cost of sales.

IAS 7 Cash Flow Statements. The cash flow statement reports cash flows by operating activities, financing activities and investing activities, as well as cash flows related to foreign currencies. IAS 7 allows operating activities to be reported using either the direct method, which discloses major classes of cash receipts and payments, or the indirect method, which adjusts profit or loss by the effects of noncash transactions and certain deferrals. The cash flow statement must reconcile with the cash balances reported on the statement of financial position for the beginning of the period with the cash balance in the statement of financial position at the end of the period.

IAS 8 Accounting Policies, Changes in Accounting Estimates and Errors. Accounting policies, which are the rules and practices applied by an entity in preparing and presenting financial statements, must comply when an applicable IFRS exists. However, management is otherwise free to develop its own accounting policies, although they must be applied consistently and result in relevant and reliable information.

IAS 10 Events After the Statement of Financial Position Date. Events after the statement of financial position date occur between the statement of financial position date and the date on which the financial statements are authorized for issuance. IAS 10 identifies two categories: (a) adjusting events, which relate to conditions that existed on or before the statement of financial position date, and (b) nonadjusting events, which relate to conditions that existed after the statement of financial position date, and prescribes the treatment under each.

IAS 11 Construction Contracts. A construction contract is a contract specifically negotiated for the construction of an asset or a combination of assets that are closely interrelated or interdependent in terms of their design, technology and function or their ultimate purpose or use. Because construction contracts are usually long term, the issue is in which period to recognize revenue and expenses.

IAS 12 Income Taxes. When transactions and other events occur that result in the recognition of a profit or loss, any related tax consequences must be recognized in the same period whether or not the tax is actually paid in that period.

IAS 16 Property, Plant and Equipment. IAS 16 requires that property, plant and equipment be recorded at cost and then depreciated over its useful life. Management may adopt either the cost model or the revaluation model. Under the cost model, the asset's original cost remains unchanged except for accumulated depreciation and accumulated impairment adjustments. Under the revaluation model, the asset can be adjusted to its fair value if that can be reliably measured.

IAS 17 Leases. IAS 17 defines two types of leases. A finance lease transfers substantially all the risks and rewards of ownership, and an operating lease does not. Under operating leases, the lessee recognizes lease payments as they are incurred, and likewise the lessor recognizes lease revenue as earned. Under a finance lease, the lessee capitalizes an amount equal to the fair value of the leased property or, if lower, the discounted amount of minimum lease payments.

IAS 18 Revenue. This Standard applies to the sale of goods; rendering of services; and interest, royalties and dividends. Revenue is measured by the fair value of the consideration received or receivable, where fair value is defined as the amount for which an asset could be exchanged, or a liability settled, between knowledgeable, willing parties in an arm's-length transaction.

IAS 19 Employee Benefits. Employee benefits include all forms of consideration given by the reporting entity in exchange for services rendered by employees. These include short-term employee benefits (other than termination benefits), which fall within 12 months after the end of the period in which the employees render the related services, post-employment benefits, which are payable after the completion of employment, and termination benefits, which result from the entity's decision to terminate an employee before the normal retirement date, or the employee's decision to accept voluntary termination.

IAS 20 Accounting for Government Grants and Disclosure of Government Assistance. Government grants include resource transfers from government in return for past or future compliance with certain conditions relating to the operating activities of the business entity. Among other requirements, government grants are recognized only when there is reasonable assurance that the entity will comply with the conditions related to the grant, and that the grant will be received. Government assistance is an economic benefit provided by government to a business entity or class of entities.

IAS 21 The Effects of Changes in Foreign Exchange Rates. Two types of foreign activities are addressed in this Standard: 1) transactions denominated in foreign currencies and 2) foreign operations. A functional currency is the currency of the primary economic environment in which the entity operates, usually where the business generates and spends the most cash, although other criteria apply; foreign currency is any currency other than the functional currency. Two major issues are which exchange rates to use and how to report the effects of changes in foreign currency exchange rates in the financial statements.

IAS 23 Borrowing Costs. Borrowing costs include interest and other costs incurred to borrow funds. In general, borrowing costs should be recognized as an expense in the period incurred. However, management may elect to capitalize borrowing costs directly attributable to the acquisition, construction or production of a qualifying asset. A qualifying asset is one that takes substantial time to get ready for its intended use or sale, for example construction of a new manufacturing facility, or a cargo vessel being built for a customer.

IAS 24 Related Party Disclosures. This Standard mandates certain disclosures for related parties and for transactions and outstanding balances with related parties. A related party transaction is a transfer of resources, services or obligations between related parties, whether or not a price is charged.

IAS 26 Accounting and Reporting by Retirement Benefit Plans. Retirement benefits plans must have the following disclosures made in the financial statements: 1) a statement of changes in net assets available for benefits, 2) a summary of significant accounting policies, and 3) a description of the plan and the effect of any changes in the plan during the period.

IAS 27 Consolidated and Separate Financial Statements. Consolidated financial statements are required for groups, which include a parent business entity and all its subsidiaries. A subsidiary is an entity controlled by another entity. Control is the power to govern the financial and operating policies of an entity so as to obtain benefits from its activities. Consolidated financial statements present the parent and subsidiaries as if they were a single economic entity. Amounts for the minority interests in profit or loss and the net assets of the consolidated entity are calculated for each subsidiary. Minority interests, sometimes referred to as the noncontrolling interests, are those shareholders other than the parent.

IAS 28 Investments in Associates. This Standard requires use of the equity method of accounting for investments in other companies, which is applied if the investor has significant influence. Significant influence is the power to participate in the financial and operating policy decisions of the investee, but does not qualify as control, which is generally regarded as 20% or more of the voting power in a company.

IAS 29 Financial Reporting in Hyperinflationary Economies. Businesses that have a functional currency that is hyperinflationary are required to restate the previous financial statements in terms of the measuring unit currency at the statement of financial position date.

IAS 31 Interests in Joint Ventures. A joint venture is a contractual arrangement whereby two or more parties undertake an economic activity under joint control.

IAS 32 Financial Instruments: Presentation. This Standard concerns accounting for financial instruments such as derivatives and requires that they be classified as financial assets, financial liabilities or equity instruments. A financial instrument is any contract that gives rise to a financial asset of one entity and a financial liability or equity instrument of another entity. An equity instrument is a contract that grants a residual interest in the assets of an entity after deducting all liabilities.

IAS 33 Earnings per Share. This Standard requires that reporting entities present both a basic and diluted earnings per share on the face of the statement of income for continuing operations and, if applicable, discontinued operations.

IAS 34 Interim Financial Reporting. IAS 34 applies when business entities are either required to or voluntarily provide financial reports for an interim period. An interim period is shorter than one year, in practice normally quarterly or monthly.

IAS 36 Impairment of Assets. At each reporting date assets must be assessed to determine if their recoverable amounts are below the carrying amount of the asset on the statement of financial position. If so, then the asset is said to be impaired. If impaired, then the carrying amount of the asset is reduced and a loss recognized.

IAS 37 Provisions, Contingent Liabilities and Contingent Assets. This Standard provides accounting for provisions, contingent liabilities and contingent assets. A provision is a liability that has either an uncertain timing or amount. A contingent liability is a possible obligation that arises from past events, and the existence of which depends on the occurrence of uncertain future events not wholly within the control of the business entity; or a present obligation that arises from past events but is not recognized because an outflow of resources to settle the obligation is not probable, or the amount of the obligation cannot be reliably measured. A contingent asset is a possible asset that arises from past events and whose existence is based on the occurrence of a future uncertain event not wholly under the control of the business entity. Contingent assets are not recognized.

IAS 38 Intangible Assets. An intangible asset is an identifiable nonmonetary asset without physical substance that arises from contractual or legal rights. Recognition can occur only if it is probable that future economic benefits will flow from the asset to the business entity and the cost of the intangible asset can be reliably measured. If an intangible asset is acquired separately (e.g. purchased from a third party) or in a business combination, the recognition criteria are satisfied. This Standard does not permit internally generated goodwill or intangible assets arising from internal research expenditures to be recognized as assets.

IAS 39 Financial Instruments: Recognition and Measurement. IAS 39 requires that a financial asset or liability be recognized only when the reporting entity becomes a party to the financial contract. Initial recognition is at fair value. After initial recognition, financial assets are classified into one of the following four categories: financial assets at fair value through profit and loss; held-to-maturity investments; loans and receivables; and available-for-sale financial assets.

IAS 40 Investment Property. Investment property, which includes land or buildings or both, is held by the owner or a lessee under a finance lease to earn rentals or for capital appreciation, or both. It does not include: (a) property used for production or supply of goods or services, or for administrative purposes, or (b) for sale in the ordinary course of business. Investment property is capitalized only when (a) it is probable that future economic benefits from the property will flow to the entity; and (b) the property's cost can be reliably measured. After acquisition, the Standard permits management to use either the cost model to account for the property (IAS 16) or the fair value model, which recognizes changes in fair value in profit or loss.

IAS 41 Agriculture. This Standard prescribes accounting for agricultural activity up to the time of harvest.

The financial statements

3

LEARNING OUTCOMES

By the end of this chapter, you should be able to:

1. Explain the notes to the financial statements.
2. Describe financial position as reported by the statement of financial position.
3. Describe performance as reported by the statement of comprehensive income.
4. Explain the relationship between the statement of financial position and the statement of comprehensive income.
5. Explain the difference between expenditure, cost and expense.

Introducing the annual report

An annual report is a document published by companies to provide useful financial, operational and other information, and it frequently includes the financial statements. Annual reports are not part of the financial statements, but do provide a context for understanding the financial statements and notes.

The question is: How much value does the annual report provide? A survey of investment professionals'[1] views on the usefulness of financial reports had the following to say about financial statements:

> Without exception, active portfolio managers and analysts view financial statements as just one piece, albeit a critical piece, of the mosaic of information they can use in their evaluations of companies' economic potential.

However, when asked about their views on information presented outside the financial statements, those surveyed were divided. Some felt that this information was management's effort to 'spin' the company's performance (that is, provide a positive interpretation of the results), while others felt that it was a valid attempt to overcome any deficiencies in reporting under accounting standards.

The survey notes that while some nonfinancial information is valued by investors and analysts, in general they do not rate highly contextual information presented by management in the annual report, although they are not particularly concerned by this. Why?

> First, analysts and investors do not expect to be able to rely on this type of information for management information. Respondents commonly observed that human nature leads those

reviewing their own performance to emphasize the positive. There is a perception that management will almost invariably use the management discussion and analysis as a public relations tool rather than an opportunity for candid performance analysis.

Second, many contend that much of the contextual data that management might present has a limited shelf life. Given the production time required, the annual report does not necessarily contain the latest market data, and is not viewed as an adequate dissemination channel for time-sensitive information.

Finally, an honest appraisal of market conditions by management is helpful for investors and analysts, but a company offers only one perspective.

The Framework for the Preparation and Presentation of Financial Statements makes it clear that while financial statements may be accompanied by supplementary material, this does not extend to some features found in the typical annual report.

IFRS 'Financial statements form part of the process of financial reporting. A complete set of financial statements normally includes a statement of financial position, a statement of income, a statement of changes in financial position, and those notes and other statements and explanatory material that are an integral part of the financial statements. They may also include supplementary schedules and information based on or derived from, and expected to be read with, such statements. Such schedules and supplementary information may deal, for example, with financial information about industrial and geographical segments and disclosures about the effects of changing prices. Financial statements do not, however, include such items as reports by directors, statements by the chairman, discussion and analysis by management and similar items that may be included in a financial or annual report.'

In this chapter, we will begin with an overview of an annual report to better understand how companies typically present their view outside the financial statements, and then narrow our scope to the requirements for the presentation of financial statements, including notes, under IFRS:

- *Chairman's Statement*. This is an introductory letter from the chairman of the board that appears at the beginning of the annual report to set the tone.
- *Key Results*. Key data is often presented in annual reports for those users who want a 'quick read' of the company's performance. While some of this information – revenue, operating profit, profit before tax and net assets – is drawn from the financial statements, other nonaccounting information is also included – in this case, operating statistics such as passengers carried for an airline.
- *Director's Report and Business Review*. This includes the board's review, which typically describes the company's principal activities, strategic developments and investments, regulation, competition, key performance indicators, development and performance of the business, customers, suppliers, employees

When students read actual financial statements for the first time or two, they often confuse information like management's discretionary presentation of key results presented by British Airways – see earlier – with the actual financial statements. To make sure that you are looking at the financial statements, look at the heading, which will say statement of financial position, statement of income, statement of changes in equity or statement of cash flows. Second, from this chapter you should be familiar enough with the contents of each financial statement to recognize whether it is the genuine article or not.

and corporate responsibility. It also contains the board's assessment of the principal risks and uncertainties faced by the business and returns to the shareholders. A section on corporate governance addresses such issues as board and management compensation.

- *Independent Auditors' Report.* Capital market regulations and laws require that publicly traded companies have an independent auditor examine their financial records and render an opinion about whether they conform to applicable accounting standards. We will discuss the role of the auditor in Chapter 13, Assurance Systems. While an independent auditor's report may be required by a regulator or creditor, it is not required by accounting standards.

In fact, none of the annual report features discussed above are part of the financial statements. While many companies include the financial statements in the annual report, some present them separately. Still other reporting entities refer users to regulatory reports that contain the financial statements.

FINDING FINANCIAL STATEMENTS

Most companies have the last two to five years of financial statements on their website, usually as part of the annual report in an interactive or PDF format. These can usually be found by searching under 'Investor Relations' or a similar tab. Under 'Investor Relations', a tab for 'Financial Reports' or 'Annual Reports' will normally appear. Companies organize these differently, but with a bit of exploration you can find the report quite easily.

With consumer-oriented companies like retailers, airlines, banks or mobile telecommunications, the task may be more challenging. The reason is that these companies want their customers to focus on their products and services. If a tab for 'Investor Relations' does not appear on the home page, try 'About Us' and then look for one that says 'Investor Relations', 'Financial Information' or something similar. Also try the 'Site Map' feature.

Recall that a complete set of financial statements includes the statement of financial position, statement of comprehensive income, statement of changes in equity and statement of cash flows, as well as the notes that apply to all four financial statements. These are graphically illustrated in Figure 3.1.

FIGURE 3.1 COMPLETE SET OF FINANCIAL STATEMENTS

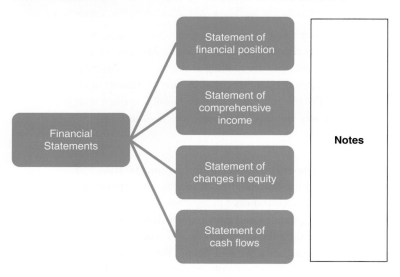

In this chapter, we will examine the financial statements in greater detail to see what line items make up each element. Accounting standards sometimes require that line items be reported; other titles for line items are created by management and therefore may be unique to a particular business. In fact, once you begin to examine actual financial statements, you find that considerable variation exists between the titles and other terminology from company to company. In some cases, titles and terminology are common to the industry. For example, in airline financial statements revenue is typically classified by 'passenger revenue' and 'cargo revenue'.

At the end of the chapter, the financial statements and notes of Emirates Airline will be presented, which have been prepared using International Financial Reporting Standards. Providing an actual set of financial statements at this point has three advantages. First, you will have seen an example of a set of actual financial statements. Secondly, examining Emirates Airline's financial statements will give you the opportunity to test what you have learned about financial accounting so far. And thirdly, as you progress through this textbook, you will have an example to refer to when we learn about reporting financial position, performance and changes in financial position.

LEARNING OUTCOME 1
EXPLAIN THE NOTES TO THE FINANCIAL STATEMENTS

Notes that accompany the financial statements serve several functions. The first is to disclose summaries of significant accounting policies used by the reporting entity. For example, the reporting entity must provide information about the measurement bases such as historical cost, current cost, net realizable value or fair value used in preparing the financial statements.

The notes should also contain information about any management judgements made in applying accounting policies when they have had a significant effect on financial statement amounts. Notes must also include information on any uncertainties regarding amounts of assets and liabilities at the statement of financial position date.

The second function of notes is to disclose any information required by IFRS, but not included on the face of the financial statements. The third function is to provide any additional information that is relevant to the understanding of the financial statements.

IAS 1 Presentation of Financial Statements outlines the following order for the presentation of notes:

1. a statement of compliance with IFRS,
2. a summary of significant accounting policies,
3. supporting information for items presented on the face of the financial statements,
4. other disclosures such as contingent liabilities and nonfinancial disclosures.

For example, the entity must include the domicile and legal form of the entity, the country of incorporation and address of its registered office or place of business. And the entity must provide a description of its operations and principal activities.

LEARNING OUTCOME 2
DESCRIBE FINANCIAL POSITION AS REPORTED BY THE STATEMENT OF FINANCIAL POSITION

2.1 What are assets?
    2.1.1. What are current assets?
    2.1.2. What are noncurrent assets?

2.2 What are liabilities?
    2.2.1. What are current liabilities?
    2.2.2. What are noncurrent liabilities?

2.3 What is equity?
    2.3.1. What is contributed capital?
    2.3.2. What are retained earnings?
    2.3.3. What are reserves?

2.4 What is an example of an actual statement of financial position, including related notes?

2.5 What is noncontrolling interest?

2.1 What are assets?

Recall that financial position is the relationship of the assets, liabilities and equity of an entity as reported in the statement of financial position. In Chapter 1, we were introduced to assets, liabilities and equity – the three elements in the statement of financial position. In the following, we will examine each in greater detail. Our discussion will be based on a fictitious company, Gulf Research LLC.

> Gulf Research LLC is based in Dubai. This international firm provides a broad range of services for the petroleum industry, including project management, drilling, reservoir testing and well analysis. Some of these services require large investments in equipment.

Figure 3.2 shows the statement of financial position of Gulf Research LLC at 31 December 2009.

Notice that the basic accounting equation still applies (total assets = total equity + liabilities). However, within each of these elements – assets, liabilities and equity – we now have more details.

THINGS TO LOOK OUT FOR

Accountants sometimes use a double underline to indicate the total for a column of figures. In Figure 3.2, *Total Assets* is double underlined, as is *Total Equity and Liabilities*. Subtotals (for example *Total Equity* and *Total Liabilities*) are indicated by a single underline of the amount. Also, notice that the currency symbol in Figure 3.2 is in the heading. The currency symbol is sometimes shown with the first number at the head of a column, and with subtotals and totals.

Recall that an asset is something that a business owns that has economic benefit in the future (see IFRS box).

IFRS An asset is 'a resource: (a) controlled by an entity as a result of past events; and (b) from which future economic benefits are expected to flow to the entity.'

Copyright © 2007 International Accounting Standards Committee Foundation. All rights reserved. No permission granted to reproduce or distribute.

FIGURE 3.2 STATEMENT OF FINANCIAL POSITION

Gulf Research LLC Statement of Financial Position 31 December 2009 € Euros thousands		
ASSETS		
Noncurrent assets		
Property, plant and equipment	600 000	
Intangible assets	100 000	
Investments in associates	500 000	
Financial assets	320 000	1 520 000
Current assets		
Cash and cash equivalents	90 000	
Investments in financial assets	40 000	
Trade accounts receivable	95 000	
Prepaid insurance	20 000	
Inventories	60 000	305 000
TOTAL ASSETS		**1 825 000**
Equity		
Capital	275 000	
Retained earnings	515 000	
Reserves	25 000	815 000
Noncurrent liabilities		
Borrowings	550 000	
Mortgage payable	200 000	750 000
Current liabilities		
Trade accounts payable	60 000	
Short-term note payable	150 000	
Current portion of noncurrent borrowings	50 000	260 000
Total liabilities		1 010 000
TOTAL EQUITY AND LIABILITIES		**1 825 000**

FIGURE 3.3 CURRENT AND NONCURRENT ASSETS

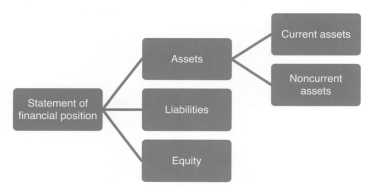

Assets are classified as either current or noncurrent, as illustrated in Figure 3.3.

2.1.1 WHAT ARE CURRENT ASSETS?

The definition of a current asset is shown in the IFRS box.

> **IFRS** 'An entity shall classify an asset as current when:
>
> (a) it expects to realize the asset or intends to sell or consume it in its normal operating cycle;
> (b) it holds the asset primarily for the purpose of trading;
> (c) it expects to realize the asset within twelve months after the reporting period;
> (d) that asset is cash or a cash equivalent...
>
> An entity shall classify all other assets as non-current.'
>

Generally speaking, a current asset (also referred to as a short-term asset) is an asset like a trade accounts receivable or inventories that is expected to be converted to cash or a cash equivalent (realized) within the normal operating cycle (see IFRS box).

> **IFRS** An operating cycle is 'the time between the acquisition of assets for processing and their realization in cash or cash equivalents'.
>

Most operating cycles are shorter than one year and businesses therefore typically use 12 months after the reporting period as their guideline for classifying an asset as current or noncurrent. Also notice that cash or cash equivalents (see the IFRS box for definitions) are current assets.

As you can see from the definition, cash is money that is either on hand or in the bank (demand deposit). When a business has cash with no immediate use for it, then it may invest the money for additional income, which usually takes the form of interest. These investments meet the definition of cash equivalents (see IFRS box) when they can be readily converted to a known amount of cash.

Figure 3.2 shows that Gulf Research has €305 000 in current assets. This total includes cash and cash equivalents, investments in financial assets, trade accounts receivable, prepaid insurance and inventories.

- Investment in financial assets refers to investments that Gulf Research has in shares of other companies, bonds and debt owed to Gulf Research by others. While these are being held for the short term (less than one year) and are thus classified as a current asset, they do not meet the definition for a cash equivalent and so are reported as a separate line item.
- Trade accounts receivable represent the business's right to collect cash in the future based on the customer's promises to pay for goods and services purchased before the reporting date.
- Prepaid insurance is one form of prepaid expense. Prepaid expenses are goods or services that are paid for before they are used. Thus they are an asset because the economic benefit will be used in the future. Most prepaid expenses are current assets, although it is possible to have a noncurrent prepaid expense.
- Inventories are 'assets: (a) held for sale in the ordinary course of business; (b) in the process of production for such sales; or (c) in the form of materials or supplies to be consumed in the production process or in the rendering of services'.

Figure 3.4 illustrates current asset line items graphically, based on the Gulf Research example.

2.1.2 WHAT ARE NONCURRENT ASSETS?

Noncurrent assets (or long-term assets) are assets that do not meet the definition for current assets. The statement of financial position for Gulf Research (Figure 3.2) includes property, plant and equipment, intangible assets, investments in associates, and financial assets.

- Property, plant and equipment (also capital assets or fixed assets) refer to assets used in the production of goods and services, rental to others or for administrative purposes, and are expected to be used for more than one period. Office buildings, manufacturing facilities and equipment are examples.

FIGURE 3.4 CURRENT ASSET COMPONENTS

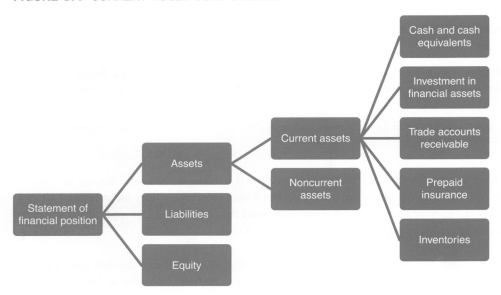

- Intangible assets are assets with no physical substance. Examples include copyrights, patents, brands and customer lists.
- Gulf Research also has an investment in associates. This represents the company's ownership of part of another business over which it has significant influence.
- Finally, Gulf Research reports financial assets of €320 000. These may be shares of other companies, bonds, debt owed to Gulf Research by others and any other financial instrument – except that these assets are long term.

Noncurrent assets total €1 520 000. When this amount is added to current assets of €305 000, total assets equal €1 825 000. Figure 3.5 adds noncurrent asset line items based on the Gulf Research example.

2.2 What are liabilities?

Recall that a liability is an obligation of the business that will have to be settled in the future. The definition is shown in the IFRS box.

IFRS A liability is 'a present obligation of the entity arising from past events, the settlement of which is expected to result in an outflow from the entity of resources embodying economic benefits'.

FIGURE 3.5 NONCURRENT ASSET COMPONENTS

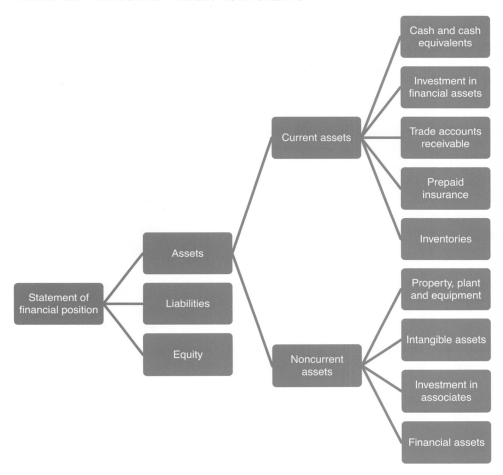

Many liabilities arise from legal obligations such as a binding contract or statutory requirements (for example tax laws). However, an obligation could also be created by normal business practice. For example, a business may decide to repair goods that it sold if a defect became apparent after the warranty period expired. Thus while not legally required to make the repairs, the intention to make them creates an obligation. However, liabilities do not arise based on future events like the intention to acquire an asset such as equipment, unless the company has entered into an irrevocable agreement to purchase the equipment.

The settlement of a liability can occur in several different ways. It can be settled by paying cash, transferring other assets, providing services, replacing one obligation with another, or converting the obligation to equity. Liabilities are created by past transactions or events. Even when payment will be made in the future, the obligation to do so is created by a past event. For example, a company may have promised rebates on products it sold to customers who will be paid in the future, but the obligation to pay the rebate was created by the sale of the product to the customer, a past transaction.

2.2.1 WHAT ARE CURRENT LIABILITIES?

Liabilities are also classified as either current or noncurrent. The definitions of current liability and noncurrent liability are shown in the IFRS box.

IFRS 'An entity shall classify a liability as current when:

(a) It expects to settle the liability in the normal operating cycle;
(b) It holds the liability primarily for the purpose of trading;
(c) The liability is due to be settled within twelve months after the reporting period; or
(d) The entity does not have an unconditional right to defter settlement of the liability for at least twelve months after the reporting period.

An entity shall classify all other liabilities as non-current.'

Figure 3.6 illustrates the statement of financial position, with liabilities categorized into current liabilities and noncurrent liabilities.

The statement of financial position in Figure 3.2 shows that Gulf Research has three current liabilities: the first is €60 000 for trade accounts payable, short-term note payable and current portion of noncurrent loans:

- A trade account payable is the amount the business owes to its suppliers. This liability was created when the business purchased goods or services on account and gave its promise to pay in the future.
- The short-term note payable for €150 000 represents an amount that the business owes on a note – money that it borrowed and that must be repaid in the short term.

FIGURE 3.6 CURRENT LIABILITY COMPONENTS

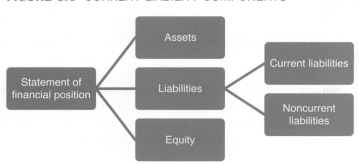

FIGURE 3.7 CURRENT LIABILITY COMPONENTS

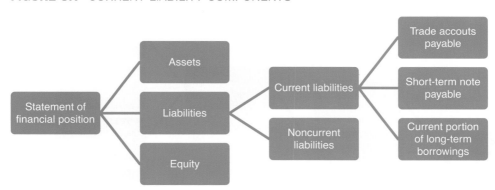

- The current portion of noncurrent borrowings represents an amount that the business must pay within the next 12 months on long-term borrowings. In other words, in the past the business borrowed an amount of money that it was obligated to repay over a period of more than 12 months. In each year, the business is required to repay some amount of this money in instalments. The current instalment due within 12 months would be reclassified as current. In Figure 3.2 you can see in noncurrent liabilities that Gulf Research has borrowings of €550 000. Total borrowings are €600 000 (€50 000 current + €550 000 noncurrent), of which €50 000 must be settled within 12 months.

When we then add €60 000 for trade accounts payable, €150 000 for the short-term note payable and €550 000 for the current portion of noncurrent borrowings, the total is €260 000 for current liabilities. Figure 3.7 graphically illustrates current liability line items based on the Gulf Research example.

WORKING CAPITAL

Why are assets and liabilities classified as current and noncurrent? The answer is that it is important to know what resources are available to the business in the short term or within the next year. If those resources are insufficient, this is a more immediate threat to the business than, say, a shortage of financial resources that is expected to occur two or three years into the future.

Short-term resources are measured by working capital, which is the difference between current assets and current liabilities. The formula is:

WORKING CAPITAL = CURRENT ASSETS − CURRENT LIABILITIES

For Gulf Research, working capital is €45 000, calculated:

WORKING CAPITAL = €305 000 − €260 000
€45 000 = €305 000 − €260 000

FIGURE 3.8 NONCURRENT LIABILITY COMPONENTS

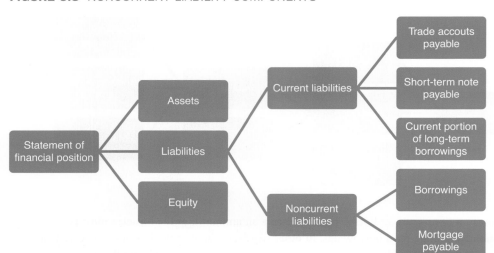

2.2.2 WHAT ARE NONCURRENT LIABILITIES?

A noncurrent liability (or long-term liability) is a liability that does not meet the definition for current liability. Gulf Research has two noncurrent liabilities: borrowings of €550 000 and a mortgage payable of €200 000 (Figure 3.2). A mortgage is a form of debt for the purchase of real estate; normally the real estate is pledged as security for the debt. If the debt is not paid, the creditor who lent the money may take possession of the property and sell it. The proceeds would be used to settle the debt. Presumably in Gulf Research's case, this mortgage payable was used to finance a building or other real estate in the property, plant and equipment asset category.

Together these two items total €750 000. Noncurrent and current liabilities are added together to equal total liabilities of €1 010 000. Figure 3.8 illustrates the statement of financial position with the line items for noncurrent liabilities included.

2.3 What is equity?

Equity is the third major element of the statement of financial position. The definition of equity is shown in the IFRS box.

IFRS	Equity is 'the residual interest in the assets of the entity after deducting all its liabilities'.

Copyright © 2007 International Accounting Standards Committee Foundation. All rights reserved. No permission granted to reproduce or distribute.

FIGURE 3.9 EQUITY ELEMENTS

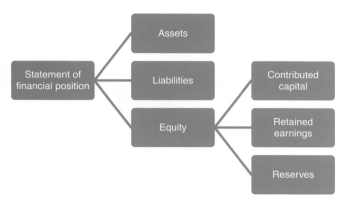

Equity is the residual interest in the entity, calculated by subtracting liabilities from assets. The amount of equity therefore depends on the measurement of assets and liabilities. However, equity can be classified into different components. The most common categories are contributed capital, retained earnings and other reserves. Figure 3.9 graphically illustrates this division of equity.

2.3.1 WHAT IS CONTRIBUTED CAPITAL?

Contributed capital (also capital or paid-in capital) is the amount that the owners have invested in the business. As we know, investors are given shares as evidence of their ownership. Contributed capital can be increased by selling additional shares to investors, and decreased when the business buys back its own shares from investors. Figure 3.2 shows that Gulf Research has capital totaling €275 000.

2.3.2 WHAT ARE RETAINED EARNINGS?

Retained earnings represent accumulated past earnings that have not been distributed to owners. Recall from Chapter 1 that profit is added to and dividends are subtracted from equity. This is normally done through retained earnings. Of course, a loss would be subtracted from retained earnings.

2.3.3 WHAT ARE RESERVES?

Reserves are created for different reasons. Management may create reserves for a variety of legal, statutory or other reasons. A reserve can be created by appropriating a portion of retained earnings. For example, the board may set aside a portion of retained earnings as a reserve for an amount that the business expects to pay to managers and employees as bonuses. Reserves can also be established through other comprehensive income. For example, a reserve could relate to the revaluation of an asset.

Figure 3.2 shows that Gulf Research has retained earnings of €515 000 and reserves of €25 000. Added to contributed capital these equal €815 000, which is the total equity balance. Equity and total liabilities tally to €1 825 000.

To summarize the statement of financial position for the Gulf Research example, Figure 3.10 shows all line items in all elements as they were discussed in this chapter.

FIGURE 3.10 STATEMENT OF FINANCIAL POSITION – ELEMENTS AND LINE ITEMS

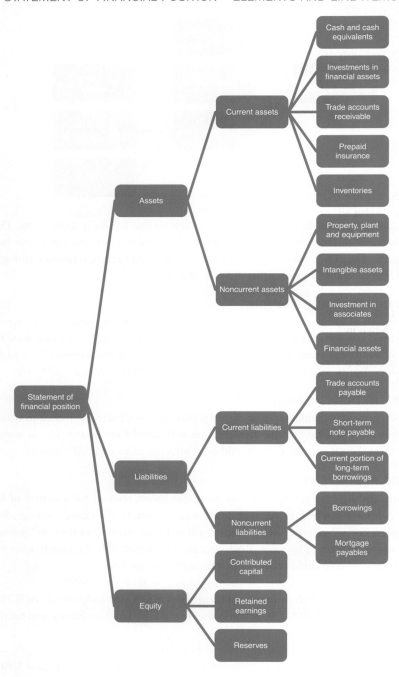

2.4 What is an example of an actual statement of financial position, including related notes?

Figure 3.11 shows Emirates Airline's statement of financial position at 31 March 2007, along with related notes.

We know from the heading that Emirates' annual reporting year ends on 31 March, not 31 December of each year. We can also see that all the amounts on the statement of financial position are reported in 'AED '000'. AED is the monetary symbol for the United Arab Emirates dirham and '000 means that all amounts are in thousands.

Now, let's take a closer look at each category on the statement of financial position.

EMIRATES AIRLINE, CURRENT ASSETS

The current assets section of Emirates Airline's statement of financial position (Figure 3.11) has been extracted and is shown in Figure 3.12.

The inventories account is familiar to us now. We can see that inventories increased from AED 479 569 000 in 2006 to AED 541 124 000 for year-end 2007. However, if we want more information, the 'Notes' column refers us to Note 15 (see the appendix to this chapter). Note 15 gives us the detail of each year's inventory amount in four classifications: engineering, in-flight consumables, consumer goods and other.

Advance lease rental is a prepaid expense. This means that amounts have been paid in advance to lease (or rent) equipment or other assets.

Trade and other receivables should also be familiar as well as cash and bank balances. We can also see four categories of investments held by Emirates Airline: available for sale financial assets: held-to-maturity investments loans and receivables, and derivative financial instruments. These are all basically financial investments.

EMIRATES AIRLINE, CURRENT LIABILITIES

The current liabilities section of Emirates Airline's statement of financial position (Figure 3.11) has been extracted and is shown in Figure 3.13.

Trade and other payables should be familiar (these are another title for trade accounts payable and notes payable). The title 'income tax liabilities' means that Emirates Airline owes taxes in these amounts. Borrowings (bonds and notes payable) and lease liabilities are amounts owed on short-term loans and the current portion (within the next 12 months) of any leases. We can obtain details on these obligations in

FIGURE 3.11 EMIRATES AIRLINE'S STATEMENT OF FINANCIAL POSITION

Emirates Airline Consolidated Statement of Financial Position at 31 March 2007			
	Notes	2007 AED '000	2006 AED '000
ASSETS			
Noncurrent assets			
Property, plant and equipment	9	17 173 958	13 534 875
Intangible assets	10	841 394	669 671
Investment in associated companies			
and joint ventures	11	435 344	268 293
Advance lease rentals	12	230 955	257 638
Available-for-sale financial assets	13	1 940 619	100 179
Held-to-maturity investments	13	397 811	349 344
Loans and receivables	14	341 228	450 863
Derivative financial instruments	31	1 168 779	1 387 001
		22 530 088	17 017 864
Current assets			
Inventories	15	541 124	479 569
Trade and other receivables	16	5 420 320	4 154 002
Held-to-maturity investments	13	136 730	183 650
Derivative financial instruments	31	206 617	359 457
Cash and bank balances	29	9 123 245	9 199 004
		15 428 036	14 375 682
Total assets		37 958 124	31 393 546
EQUITY AND LIABILITIES			
Capital and reserves			
Capital	17	801 214	801 214
Other reserves	18	1 155 717	1 600 145
Retained earnings		11 083 428	8 387 012
Attributable to Emirates' owner		13 040 359	10 788 371
Minority interest		129 599	130 180
Total equity		13 169 958	10 918 551
Noncurrent liabilities			
Borrowings and lease liabilities	19	12 409 330	9 097 330
Provisions	23	454 372	377 176
Deferred credits	24	700 634	795 547

Deferred tax liabilities	25	50 642	–
Trade and other payables	26	84 191	125 723
Derivative financial instruments	31	510 841	220 161
		14 210 010	10 615 937
Current liabilities			
Trade and other payables	26	9 303 772	7 454 635
Income tax liabilities		158 926	103 436
Borrowings and lease liabilities	19	929 139	2 149 224
Deferred credits	24	177 825	151 707
Derivative financial instruments	31	8 504	56
		10 578 156	9 859 058
Total liabilities		24 788 166	20 474 995
Total equity and liabilities		37 958 124	31 393 546

FIGURE 3.12 EMIRATES AIRLINE, CURRENT ASSETS

	Notes	2007 AED '000	2006 AED '000
Current assets			
Inventories	15	541 124	479 569
Trade and other receivables	16	5 420 320	4 154 002
Held-to-maturity investments	13	136 730	183 650
Derivative financial instruments	31	206 617	359 457
Cash and bank balances	29	9 123 245	9 199 004
		15 428 036	14 375 682

FIGURE 3.13 EMIRATES AIRLINE, CURRENT LIABILITIES

	Notes	2007 AED '000	2006 AED '000
Current liabilities			
Trade and other payables	26	9 303 772	7 454 635
Income tax liabilities		158 926	103 436
Borrowings and lease liabilities	19	929 139	2 149 224
Deferred credits	24	177 825	151 707
Derivative financial instruments	31	8 504	56
		10 578 156	9 859 058

Note 19. Emirates also owes amounts related to financial instruments (see IFRS box) and has other obligations listed as deferred credits (we will discuss these in a later chapter).

EMIRATES AIRLINE, WORKING CAPITAL

We can now calculate the working capital for both 2006 and 2007 for Emirates Airline. Recall that:

$$\text{WORKING CAPITAL} = \text{CURRENT ASSETS} - \text{CURRENT LIABILITIES}$$

For 2006, the calculation would be:

$$\text{WORKING CAPITAL} = \text{AED } 14\ 375\ 682\ 000 - \text{AED } 9\ 859\ 058\ 000$$
$$\text{WORKING CAPITAL} = \text{AED } 4\ 516\ 624\ 000$$

For 2007, the calculation would be:

$$\text{WORKING CAPITAL} = \text{AED } 15\ 428\ 036\ 000 - \text{AED } 10\ 578\ 156\ 000$$
$$\text{WORKING CAPITAL} = \text{AED } 4\ 849\ 880\ 000$$

We can see that working capital increased by AED 333 256 000. We will learn more about how to evaluate this change in working capital in a later chapter.

EMIRATES AIRLINE, NONCURRENT ASSETS

The noncurrent assets section of Emirates Airline's statement of financial position (Figure 3.11) has been extracted and is shown in Figure 3.14.

We have already discussed property, plant and equipment, intangible assets, investment in associates, loans and receivables and financial assets. The new item is advance lease rentals, which represent payments made in advance on leases (see IFRS box) on aircraft and other equipment.

FIGURE 3.14 EMIRATES AIRLINE, NONCURRENT ASSETS

	Notes	2007 AED '000	2006 AED '000
Noncurrent assets			
Property, plant and equipment	9	17 173 958	13 534 875
Intangible assets	10	841 394	669 671
Investment in associated companies and joint ventures	11	435 344	268 293
Advance lease rentals	12	230 955	257 638
Available-for-sale financial assets	13	1 940 619	100 179
Held-to-maturity investments	13	397 811	349 344
Loans and receivables	14	341 228	450 863
Derivative financial instruments	31	1 168 779	1 387 001
		22 530 088	17 017 864

EMIRATES AIRLINE, NONCURRENT LIABILITIES

The noncurrent liabilities section of Emirates Airline's statement of financial position (Figure 3.11) has been extracted and is shown in Figure 3.15.

In noncurrent liabilities, Emirates has borrowings and lease liabilities, deferred credits, deferred tax liabilities, trade and other payables, and amounts owing related to financial instruments. These liabilities are

FIGURE 3.15 EMIRATES AIRLINE, NONCURRENT LIABILITIES

	Notes	2007 AED '000	2006 AED '000
Noncurrent liabilities			
Borrowings and lease liabilities	19	12 409 330	9 097 330
Provisions	23	454 372	377 176
Deferred credits	24	700 634	795 547
Deferred tax liabilities	25	50 642	–
Trade and other payables	26	84 191	125 723
Derivative financial instruments	31	510 841	220 161
		14 210 010	10 615 937

all long term, meaning that they are obligations that must be settled more than 12 months in the future. The only item we have not seen before is provisions (see IFRS box).

IFRS A provision is 'a liability of uncertain timing or amount'.

EMIRATES AIRLINE, EQUITY

The equity section of Emirates Airline's statement of financial position (Figure 3.16) has been extracted and is shown in Figure 3.16.

FIGURE 3.16 EMIRATES AIRLINE, EQUITY

	Notes	2007 AED '000	2006 AED '000
Capital and reserves			
Capital	17	801 214	801 214
Other reserves	18	1 155 717	1 600 145
Retained earnings		11 083 428	8 387 012
Attributable to Emirates' owner		13 040 359	10 788 371
Minority interest		129 599	130 180
Total equity		13 169 958	10 918 551

2.5 What is a noncontrolling interest?

Notice also that the heading indicates that the statement of financial position is consolidated. Consolidated means that all the companies in a group, which includes the parent and its subsidiaries, are combined into a single set of financial statements (see IFRS box).

IFRS

- A parent is 'an entity that has one or more subsidiaries'.
- A subsidiary is 'an entity including an unincorporated entity, such as a partnership, that is controlled by another entity (known as the parent)'.
- A group is 'a parent and all its subsidiaries'. Therefore, consolidated financial statements are 'the financial statements of a group presented as those of a single economic entity'.

What this means is that several companies have been combined and presented as one business entity. But what companies? If we wanted the answer to that question, we could refer to Note 11, Investment in Subsidiaries, Associated Companies and Joint Ventures in Emirates Airline's financial statements, included as an appendix to this chapter.

Note 11 lists six principal subsidiaries (associated companies and joint ventures are not consolidated): Marine & Mercantile International LLC; Emirates Leisure Retail LLC; Emirates Leisure Retail Holding LLC; Emirates Hotel LLC; Emirates Hotel (Australia) Pty Ltd; and Emirates Flight Catering Company LLC. For each of these subsidiaries, we can see the percentage of equity owned by Emirates Airline, the principal activities of the subsidiary and where the company is incorporated. Graphically, the relationship between parent and subsidiaries is shown in Figure 3.17.

In Figure 3.17 subsidiaries are on the bottom row. The financial results of these subsidiaries have been combined with Emirates Airline – the parent company – to create the consolidated financial statements that we are now examining.

Notice also that the statement of financial position includes comparative financial information for both 2006 and 2007. Though this financial statement is reporting the results for 2007, we know from Chapter 2 that IFRS requires that at least one previous reporting period be included for comparison purposes.

Notice that the other two items are listed as 'Attributable to Emirates' owner' and 'Minority interest'. Recall that in Note 11, we saw that three subsidiaries – Marine & Mercantile International LLC, Emirates Leisure Retail LLC and Emirates Flight Catering Company LLC – are *partially owned* by Emirates. Owners of these companies other than Emirates are referred to as the noncontrolling interest (or minority interest).

> **IFRS** A non-controlling interest is 'the equity in a subsidiary not attributable, directly or indirectly to a parent'.
>

Based on the information provided in Note 11 of Emirates Airline (see appendix), Figure 3.18 shows the noncontrolling interest in each of the six principal subsidiaries.

We can see from Figure 3.18 that three companies do not have a noncontrolling interest because they are wholly owned subsidiaries: Emirates Leisure Retail Holding LLC, Emirates Hotel LLC and Emirates Hotel (Australia) Pty Ltd. Three subsidiaries have a noncontrolling interest: Marine & Mercantile

FIGURE 3.17 EMIRATES NON-CONTROLLING INTERESTS

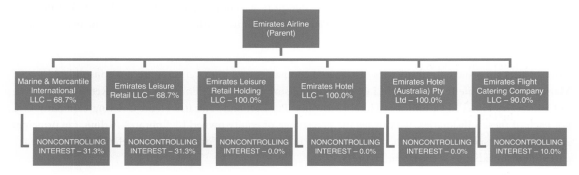

International LLC (31.3%), Emirates Leisure LLC (31.3%) and Emirates Flight Catering Company LLC (10%).

When consolidated financial statements are presented, an amount representing the minority interest's share of equity must be calculated and deducted from equity. The remainder of the equity is attributable to Emirates' owner. On Emirates' statement of financial position for 2007 we can add the amount attributable to Emirates' owner of AED 13 040 359 000 and the minority interest of AED 129 599 000 to calculate AED 13 169 958 000, which is total equity.

ON YOUR OWN

LEARNING OUTCOMES REVIEW

1. What criteria must an asset meet to be classified as a current asset? What criteria must an asset meet to be classified as a noncurrent asset?
2. What is an operating cycle?
3. To what does the term short term refer? To what does long term refer?
4. What is a trade accounts receivable? What is a trade accounts payable? How is each classified on the statement of financial position?
5. What are inventories? How are they classified on the statement of financial position?
6. What are property, plant and equipment? How are they classified on the statement of financial position?
7. What is an intangible asset?
8. To what does the term current portion of noncurrent borrowings refer?
9. What is contributed capital? How is it classified on the statement of financial position?
10. Define reserves. How are reserves classified on the statement of financial position?
11. Define retained earnings.
12. What are consolidated financial statements?

13. Define parent. Define subsidiary.
14. What is a minority interest?

LEARNING OUTCOME PRACTICE

1. Which of the following is not an asset?
   a. Cash
   b. Trade accounts payable
   c. Inventories
   d. Property, plant and equipment

2. Which of the following is not a current liability?
   a. Prepaid expense
   b. Current portion of borrowings
   c. Trade accounts payable
   d. Lease payable

3. Retained earnings is part of which of the following?
   a. Assets
   b. Liabilities
   c. Equity
   d. Revenue

4. Which of the following should be classified as current liabilities?
   1) Trade accounts receivables
   2) Sales tax payable
   3) Trade accounts payables
   4) Contributed capital
      a. 1 and 2
      b. 2 and 3
      c. 3 and 4
      d. 2 and 4
   ACCA adapted

5. On 1 March 2010 Andrew took out a loan for $50 000. The loan is to be repaid in five equal annual instalments, with the first repayment falling due on 1 March 2011. How should the balance on the loan be reported on Andrew's year-end statement of financial position as at 30 April 2009?
   a. $50 000 as a current liability
   b. $50 000 as a noncurrent liability
   c. $10 000 as a current liability and $40 000 as a noncurrent liability
   d. $40 000 as a current liability and $10 000 as a noncurrent liability
   ACCA adapted

LEARNING OUTCOME 3
DESCRIBE PERFORMANCE AS REPORTED BY THE
STATEMENT OF COMPREHENSIVE INCOME

3.1   What is performance?

3.2   What is the difference between income, revenue and gains?

3.3   What is the difference between cost of sales and other types of expenses?

3.4   What is an example of an actual statement of comprensive income?

3.1 What is performance?

Performance is the relationship of the income and expenses of an entity as reported in the statement of comprehensive income. Recall that the statement of comprehensive income contains two major components: profit or loss and other comprehensive income (see IFRS box).

> **IFRS**   Profit or loss is 'the total of income less expenses, excluding the components of other comprehensive income'.
>
> Other comprehensive income includes 'items of income and expense (including reclassification adjustments) that are not recognized in profit or loss as required or permitted by other IFRSs'.
>
> Copyright © 2007 International Accounting Standards Committee Foundation. All rights reserved. No permission granted to reproduce or distribute.

Figure 3.18 shows the statement of comprehensive income for Gulf Research LLC for the year ended 31 December 2009, which we will use as our example.

We can see from Figure 3.18 that profit is €500 000 and other comprehensive income is €55 000 for total comprehensive income of €555 000.

3.2 What is the difference between income, revenue and gains?

Reporting profit or loss and other comprehensive income involves three concepts related to the *increase* of economic benefits to the business entity: income, revenue and gains.

FIGURE 3.18 STATEMENT OF COMPREHENSIVE INCOME

Gulf Research LLC		
Statement of Comprehensive Income		
For the Year Ended 31 December 2009		
€(Euros)		
Revenue		2 500 000
Cost of sales		(1 200 000)
Gross profit		1 300 000
Operating expenses		
Selling expenses	(200 000)	
Administrative expenses	(500 000)	(700 000)
Operating profit		600 000
Other income and expenses		200 000
Profit before interest and taxes		800 000
Interest expense		(100 000)
Profit before taxes		700 000
Tax expense		(200 000)
PROFIT		500 000
Other comprehensive income		
Revaluation of equipment		55 000
TOTAL COMPREHENSIVE INCOME		555 000

In other words, income refers to an inflow of economic benefits that is reported in profit or loss or an inflow of economic benefits reported in other comprehensive income. When income is reported in profit or loss and is from the ordinary activities of the business, then it is referred to as revenue.

Revenue is referred to by different names, including sales, fees, interest, dividends, royalties and rent, all of which increase the flow of economic benefits to the business.

Gains are income. A gain may result in revenue if it arises in the course of ordinary activities. However, a gain can also result from an increase in the inflow of economic benefits to the business but not meet the definition of revenue. For example, the sale of equipment for more than the amount reported in the statement of financial position would result in a gain but be classified as revenue.

Vega Communications Ltd owned computing equipment that is recorded at $150 000 in its accounting records. Because this equipment was being replaced with a newer, more efficient computer, Vega sold the old equipment, receiving $200 000. Therefore, Vega had a $50 000 gain on the sale of the equipment ($200 000 – $150 000). This gain is reported in profit or loss but not as revenue.

Some gains are reported in other comprehensive income. Notice that in Figure 3.18 Gulf Research reports a revaluation of equipment of € 55 000. When the equipment increased in value by this amount, a gain occurred even through the equipment has not been sold.

Gulf Research owns oilfield equipment used to deliver its services. Over the past year, the demand for this equipment has been far in excess of the ability of manufacturers to supply new equipment. As a result, the market value of existing equipment has increased significantly.

Gulf Research hires a specialist in oilfield equipment to estimate the value its equipment. At 31 December 2008 (the previous year) this equipment was recorded in the property, plant and equipment account for € 245 000 and has now increased in value to € 300 000 – a difference of € 55 000. This revaluation amount is *not* recognized in profit or loss but in other comprehensive income (see Figure 3.18).

Figure 3.19 illustrates the relationship between income, revenue and gains.

3.3 What is the difference between cost of sales and other types of expenses?

Reporting profit or loss and other comprehensive income involves two concepts related to the *decrease* of economic benefits to the business entity: expenses and losses.

FIGURE 3.19 INCOME, REVENUE AND GAINS

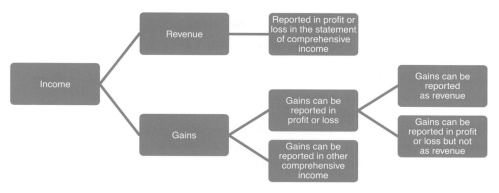

Losses are decreases in economic benefits that meet the definition of expenses. The terms 'expense' and 'loss' are interchangeable: an expense or loss could be reported in profit or loss or other comprehensive income. For example, a business may suffer major financial damage to its facilities from fire. In this case, we would normally say that a loss has occurred, and this loss would appear in profit or loss but not as part of ordinary activities.

However, in practice an expense usually refers to an item in profit or loss reported as part of the ordinary activities of the business. The term 'losses' is used for items reported in profit or loss but *not* as part of ordinary activities. Some losses are reported in other comprehensive income. Figure 3.20 illustrates how the terms expenses and losses are commonly used in practice.

FIGURE 3.20 EXPENSES AND LOSSES

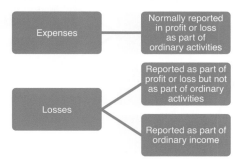

When reporting expenses associated with ordinary activities, businesses often classify expenses into the following line items:

- Cost of sales refers to an expense that is related to a good or service sold by the company during the reporting period.
- Operating expenses are those expenses that are not related to the good or service sold and are either:
  1. Selling expenses, which include sales, marketing, advertising and distribution costs.
  2. Administrative expenses, which include general administrative costs. Examples would be those expenses associated with the finance department and the human resources department.
- Financing expense (or interest expense) is the amount of interest and other financing costs – usually interest expense on debt – paid to banks and other creditors for borrowing money.
- Tax expense (or income tax expense) includes government taxes on the income for the period.

When cost of sales is subtracted from revenue, the result is gross profit (or gross margin).

$$\text{REVENUE} - \text{COST OF SALES} = \text{GROSS PROFIT}$$

Figure 3.21 graphically illustrates the classification of expenses related to the ordinary activities of the business.

COST OF SALES

For a service or sales business, the cost of sales includes amounts paid for labour and supplies directly related to the production of the service or sale. For merchandising and manufacturing businesses, the cost of sales is typically referred to as the cost of goods sold, which includes the costs of the physical item being sold or manufactured.

FIGURE 3.21 EXPENSE CLASSIFICATION

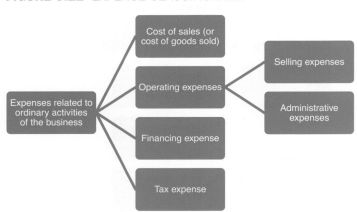

'Big box' retailers like French-based Carrefour and US-based Wal-Mart purchase merchandise from a manufacturer or wholesaler and sell it. The amounts these companies spend become part of the cost of sales once the merchandise is sold. For example, Carrefour may purchase consumer electronic devices from a Chinese manufacturer totalling ¥100 000 000 (yuan). This amount would appear as part of the cost of sales on the statement of comprehensive income as those devices are sold to customers.

Manufacturers such as Dell Computer and Toyota also sell physical merchandise, but they manufacture these goods themselves. All costs associated with the manufacture of computers and printers at Dell, and automobiles and trucks at Toyota, become part of the cost of sales once the manufactured goods are sold. At Dell, for example, these costs might include computer chips, plastic casings and wire, and also salaries and wages for workers to assemble laptop computers.

In Figure 3.19, we can see that Gulf Research's cost of sales is reported as a single amount: €1 200 000. When this is subtracted from revenue of €2 500 000 the result is €1 300 000, which is gross profit.

OTHER EXPENSES

Operating expenses are the next item on Gulf Research's statement of comprehensive income. This includes selling expenses of €200 000 and administrative expenses of €500 000. When added together, the result is total operating expenses of €700 000. This amount is subtracted from gross profit to calculate operating profit. This is the profit from the business's ordinary operations before other income and expenses, finance expense and tax expense are deducted.

In Figure 3.19, Gulf Research then reports other income and expenses of €200 000 and, since this amount is positive, it is added to operating profit. This result of this calculation is profit before interest and taxes. Then interest expense is deducted from profit before interest and taxes to give profit before taxes. And finally, tax expense is deducted to calculate profit or loss. Since this amount is positive, Gulf Research has earned a profit.

We can now summarize both income and expenses classifications as reported on the statement of comprehensive income with the illustration in Figure 3.22.

3.4 What is an example of an actual statement of comprehensive income?

Figure 3.23 presents Emirates Airline's consolidated statement of comprehensive income for the year ended 31 March 2007.

Compared to other large companies, Emirates Airlines presents a relatively simple statement of comprehensive income, although the company presents all information required by IFRS. A single amount is presented for revenue, although by referring to Note 4 we can view detail on sources of revenue: passenger, cargo, courier, excess baggage and so forth. Operating costs are also presented as a single

FIGURE 3.22 STATEMENT OF COMPREHENSIVE INCOME CLASSIFICATIONS

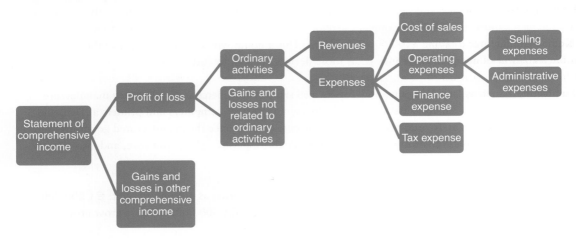

FIGURE 3.23 EMIRATES AIRLINE STATEMENT OF COMPREHENSIVE INCOME

		2007	2006
Emirates Airline Consolidated Statement of Comprehensive Income for the year ended 31 March 2007			
	Notes	AED '000	AED '000
Revenue	4	28 642 701	22 307 539
Other operating income	5	530 420	350 451
Operating costs	6	(25 834 248)	(20 005 699)
Operating profit		**3 338 873**	**2 652 291**
Finance costs – net	7	(87 790)	(58 364)
Share of results in associated companies and joint ventures	11	75 225	55 007
Profit before income tax		**3 326 308**	**2 648 934**
Income tax expense	8	(162 581)	(87 608)
Profit for the year		**3 163 727**	**2 561 326**
Profit attributable to minority interest		67 311	86 327
Profit attributable to Emirates' owner		3 096 416	2 474 999
Other comprehensive income[2]		**1 155 717**	**1 600 145**
Other comprehensive income attributable to minority interest		62 288	45 853
Other comprehensive income attributable to Emirates' owner		1 093 429	1 554 562

amount in Figure 3.23, but again, detail is available in Note 6, where we can observe that in both 2006 and 2007 the largest cost was fuel and oil, with employee costs coming in second.

Notice that the statement of comprehensive income also contains a line item for 'share of results in associated companies and joint ventures'. These amounts represent Emirates Airlines' share of the profit or loss from companies in which it owns an interest (see Note 11). And finally, the profit for the year is divided between Emirates Airline and the minority (noncontrolling) interest.

ON YOUR OWN

LEARNING OUTCOME REVIEW
1. Define cost of sales. Define operating expense.
2. What are the components of operating expense?
3. What other expenses are part of profit or loss?
4. How is gross profit calculated?
5. Describe the difference between profit or loss and other comprehensive income.

LEARNING OUTCOME PRACTICE
1. Canel Company had $950 000 in profit for the recent accounting period. Income tax expense was $225 000. Interest expense was $100 000. Sales were $2 500 000 and cost of sales was 40% of sales. Administrative expenses were $75 000. What were the sales and marketing expenses?
   a. $25 000
   b. $150 000
   c. $1 025 000
   d. Cannot be determined from the information given

2. Al Taya Corporation reported revenue of £1 250 000 for 2009. Tax expense was £145 000 and operating expenses were £850 000. Which of the following is true?
   a. The company had a profit of £255 000
   b. The company had a profit of £1 105 000
   c. The company had a profit of £400 000
   d. The company had a loss of £255 000

3. Al Taya Corporation reported revenue of £1 250 000 for 2009. Tax expense was £145 000 and operating expenses were £850 000. What was operating profit?
   a. £255 000
   b. £400 000
   c. £655 000
   d. The company had an operating loss

4. The cost of an automobile purchased from the manufacturer by an automobile dealership for resale to a customer and then sold would be in which expense category on the statement of comprehensive income?
   a. Operating expenses
   b. Selling expenses
   c. Administrative expenses
   d. Cost of sales

5. Where would the company president's salary typically appear on the statement of comprehensive income?
   a. Cost of sales
   b. Operating expenses
   c. Selling expense
   d. Other income and expenses

LEARNING OUTCOMES PROBLEM

Construct a statement of comprehensive income in good form for Dayan Ltd for the month of October 2010 from the following information:

Income taxes	¥5 803
Financing expense	1 172
Revenue	315 654
Administrative expenses	30 000
Selling expenses	26 733
Cost of sales	183 658

LEARNING OUTCOME 4
EXPLAIN THE RELATIONSHIP BETWEEN THE STATEMENT OF FINANCIAL POSITION AND THE STATEMENT OF COMPREHENSIVE INCOME

Now we can go one step further to reach a more complete understanding of the relationship between the statement of financial position and statement of comprehensive income. Figure 3.24 illustrates in a single diagram how they are interrelated.

The basic accounting equation is at the top of the diagram. We know that equity is comprised of contributed capital, retained earnings and reserves, shown on the next level. We also know that the ending retained earnings balance is calculated by adding profit to the beginning retained earnings balance and then subtracting dividends. Finally, we know from the statement of comprehensive income that profit or loss is calculated as the difference between revenue less expenses, which are shown on the bottom layer.

FIGURE 3.24 EXPANDED ACCOUNTING EQUATION

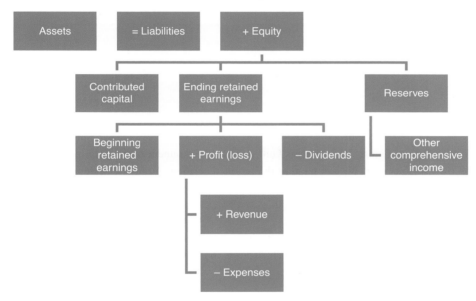

Why is this diagram important? The answer is that this expanded accounting equation allows us to analyse how the statement of comprehensive income affects the statement financial of position. For example:

Question: What is the effect on equity of selling more shares to investors?
Answer: Increases to contributed capital increase equity.

Question: What is the effect on equity of an increase in expenses?
Answer: If expenses increase, profit or loss (revenue less expenses) will also decrease. If profit or loss decreases, then retained earnings will decrease and therefore so will equity.

Question: What is the effect on equity of an increase in dividends to owners?
Answer: Dividends are deducted from retained earnings. So if dividends increase, retained earnings will decrease, which means that equity will also decrease.

Question: What is the effect on equity of an increase in revenue?

Answer: An increase in revenue will increase profit or loss, which increases retained earnings, and that in turn increases equity.

Recall that retained earnings are increased by profit (or decreased by losses) and also decreased by dividends. Profit is added to the *beginning* retained earnings balance and dividends subtracted to calculate the retained earnings balance at the end of the reporting period. The retained earnings amount that appears on the statement of financial position is the *ending* balance, as the following shows.

> BEGINNING RETAINED EARNINGS
> ADD: PROFIT
> LESS: DIVIDENDS
> = ENDING RETAINED EARNINGS

To better illustrate this relationship, Figure 3.25 presents Gulf Research's statement of financial position as of 31 December 2008 – the previous year. We can see that the retained earnings number is €365 000. This ending 2008 number is the same as the beginning balance for 2009. During 2009, Gulf Research's net income was €500 000 and dividends paid were €350 000.

In Figure 3.11 Gulf Research's 2009 statement of financial position shows ending retained earnings of €515 000, which means that during 2009 this number went from €365 000 to €515 000. This is because

FIGURE 3.25 GULF RESEARCH'S STATEMENT OF FINANCIAL POSITION AT 31 DECEMBER 2008

Gulf Research LLC Statement of Financial Position 31 December 2008 € (Euros)		
Assets		
Noncurrent assets		
Property, plant and equipment		525 000
Intangible assets		110 000
Investments in other companies		500 000
Other noncurrent assets		320 000
Total noncurrent assets		1 455 000

Current assets		
Cash and cash equivalents	290 000	
Trade receivable	77 000	
Prepaid insurance	3 000	
Inventories	55 000	425 000
TOTAL ASSETS		**1 880 000**
Equity		
Contributed capital		525 000
Retained earnings		365 000
Reserves		25 000
Total equity		415 000
Noncurrent liabilities		700 000
Current liabilities		
Accounts payable	45 000	
Salaries payable	50 000	
Note payable	170 000	265 000
Total liabilities		965 000
TOTAL LIABILITIES AND EQUITY		**1 880 000**

net income (€500 000) is added to beginning retained earnings and then dividends (€350 000) are subtracted to calculate ending retained earnings. Figure 3.26 shows this calculation. Notice that other comprehensive income does not affect retained earnings.

This interrelationship between income, dividends and retained earnings is shown graphically in Figure 3.27.

Assets on the statement of financial position at 31 December 2009 (on the left-hand side of Figure 3.27) become expenses on the statement of comprehensive income, and liabilities become revenue. (This does not mean that all assets necessarily become expenses or that all liabilities become revenue.) These expenses and revenue are reported on the statement of comprehensive income for the year ended 31 December 2010, and the difference (revenue less

FIGURE 3.26 RETAINED EARNINGS CALCULATION

Beginning retained earnings, 31 December 2008	€365 000
Add: 2009 Net Income	500 000
Subtotal	€865 000
Less: 2009 Dividends	(350 000)
Ending retained earnings, 31 December 2009	€515 000

FIGURE 3.27 RELATIONSHIP BETWEEN THE STATEMENT OF FINANCIAL POSITION AND STATEMENT OF COMPREHENSIVE INCOME

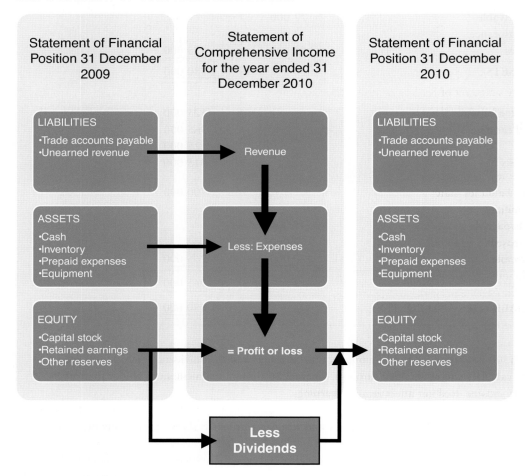

expenses) is profit or loss. This profit or loss is added to and dividends are subtracted from retained earnings shown in the 31 December 2009 statement of financial position to give the ending retained earnings balance on the 31 December 2010 statement of financial position (on the right-hand side of Figure 3-27).

ON YOUR OWN

LEARNING OUTCOME REVIEW

1. When revenue increases, what is the effect on equity?
2. When expenses decrease, what is the effect on equity?
3. When dividends increase, what is the effect on equity?
4. When a reserve is increased, what is the effect on equity?

LEARNING OUTCOME PRACTICE

1. A company has retained earnings of €855 000 and liabilities were €700 000 as of 30 June 2010, its fiscal year end. In fiscal 2011, profit was €175 000, dividends were €110 000 and liabilities increased by €45 000. Profit was €65 000 in fiscal 2012, dividends were €110 000 and liabilities decreased by €65 000; and in fiscal 2013 profit was €50 000, dividends were €40 000 and liabilities decreased by €75 000. Contributed capital remained the same. What is the retained earnings balance on the statement of financial position dated 30 June 2011?

2. A company has retained earnings of €855 000 and liabilities were €700 000 as of 30 June 2010, its fiscal year end. In fiscal 2011, profit was €175 000, dividends were €110 000 and liabilities increased by €45 000. Profit was €65 000 in fiscal 2012, dividends were €110 000 and liabilities decreased by €65 000; and in fiscal 2013 profit was €50 000, dividends were €40 000 and liabilities decreased by €75 000. Contributed capital remained the same. What is the liabilities balance on the statement of financial position dated 30 June 2011?

3. A company has retained earnings of €855 000 and liabilities were €700 000 as of 30 June 2010, its fiscal year end. In fiscal 2011, profit was €175 000, dividends were €110 000 and liabilities increased by €45 000. Profit was €65 000 in fiscal 2012, dividends were €110 000 and liabilities decreased by €65 000; and in fiscal 2013 profit was €50 000, dividends were €40 000 and liabilities decreased by €75 000. Contributed capital remained the same. By how much did total stockholders' equity increase or decrease during fiscal 2012?

4. A company has retained earnings of €855 000 and liabilities were €700 000 as of 30 June 2010, its fiscal year end. In fiscal 2011, profit was €175 000, dividends were €110 000 and liabilities increased by €45 000. Profit was €65 000 in fiscal 2012, dividends were €110 000 and liabilities decreased by €65 000; and in fiscal 2013 profit was €50 000, dividends were €40 000 and liabilities decreased by €75 000. Contributed capital remained the same. By how much did total assets increase or decrease during fiscal 2013?

5. Shown below is information for Gulf Research LLC for the year ended 31 December 2010. Use the 31 December 2009 statement of financial position shown in Figure 3.2 to construct the statement of comprehensive income for the year ended 2013 and the statement of financial position as of 31 December 2010 taking into account the following information. If no change occured, the line items remains the same.

Tax expense	€250 000
Financing expense	110 000
Increase in accounts payable	45 000
Gross profit	1 425 000
Increase in property, plant and equipment	200 000
Additional share capital sold	50 000
Decrease in trade accounts receivable	5 000
Dividends	400 000
Increase in inventories	10 000
Increase in short-term notes payable	30 000

Cost of sales	1 325 000
Selling expenses	220 000
Increase in cash and cash equivalents	135 000
Increase in salaries payable	20 000
Administrative expenses	300 000
Decrease in long-term borrowing	110 000
Decrease in mortgage payable	100 000
Decrease in investment in associates	230 000
Decrease in prepaid insurance	20 000

LEARNING OUTCOME 5
EXPLAIN THE DIFFERENCE BETWEEN EXPENDITURE, COST AND EXPENSES

5.1 What is expenditure?

5.2 What is a cost?

5.3 What is an expense?

To fully appreciate the interrelationship of the statement of comprehensive income and statement of financial position, we also need to consider the definitions of and differences between three terms: expenditure, cost and expense.

5.1 What is expenditure?

Expenditure refers to any outlay of cash or other consideration. We say 'the business's expenditure for supplies was €1200', which means that €1200 was spent on supplies. But this statement does not tell us whether we still have the supplies on hand and available for future use (so that the expenditure is classified as an asset on the statement of financial position) or whether they have already been consumed (so that the expenditure is classified as an expense on the statement of comprehensive income). The term expenditure also does not tell us whether an immediate cash outflow occurred. We may already have paid or only promised to pay in the future.

5.2 What is a cost?

A cost refers to the amount given to acquire an asset. If expenditure is made to acquire supplies, then the cost is the amount paid in cash to acquire those supplies – for example of €1200. However, the supplies could also be acquired on credit. Therefore, knowing that an asset cost €1200 does not tell us whether a cash outlay has occurred, nor does it tell us whether the supplies are still available for future use (an asset) or whether they have already been used (an expense).

A cost can be created by an estimate of future expenditures. For example, if the company sells €200 000 of electronic equipment in cash with a warranty to repair defects for one year after the sale, then an estimate of future expenditures related to those repairs is made – let's say €30 000. No immediate expenditure has been made, but the business has incurred a cost.

5.3 What is an expense?

We have already discussed expense earlier in the chapter. As we know, an expense refers to decreases in economic benefits. Because an expense is always reported on the statement of comprehensive income, it is a cost that has already been consumed – 'expired' – and therefore has no future value to the business. If we say 'supplies expense was €1200', then we know that supplies that cost €1200 have been consumed and are therefore no longer available for future use in the business. However, the term expense does not tell us whether payment has been made or not.

Figure 3.28 provides a graphical overview of the relationship between these terms.

Figure 3.28 shows how costs are expenditures that are either unexpired or expired. If unexpired, the cost is classified as an asset. If expired, the cost is classified as an expense. Also, as an asset is consumed, it too expires and therefore becomes an expense. Examples of costs that are classified as assets on the statement of financial position and later reclassified as expenses on the statement of comprehensive income because they have expired are shown in Figure 3.29.

Notice in particular 'inventories' and 'cost of goods sold' in the first item in Figure 3.29. Let's return to the example of Carrefour's cash purchase of consumer electronic devices from the Chinese supplier. This purchase is a cost. But in order to correctly classify this cost as an asset or an expense, we need to know whether it has expired. As long as the devices remain unsold, the cost appears on the statement of financial position as inventories (an asset). Once sold, the asset cost expires and becomes cost of sales (an expense) on the statement of comprehensive income. The diagram in Figure 3.30 shows this relationship.

The second line of Figure 3.29 shows that property, plant and equipment, which is an asset cost on the statement of financial position, expires to become depreciation expense on the statement of comprehensive

FIGURE 3.28 EXPENDITURE, COST AND EXPENSE

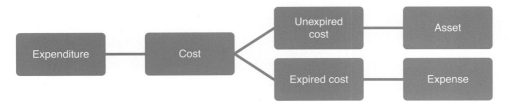

FIGURE 3.29 UNEXPIRED AND EXPIRED COSTS

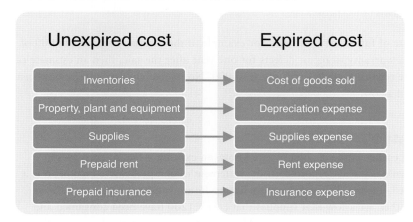

FIGURE 3.30 INVENTORIES VERSUS COST OF SALES

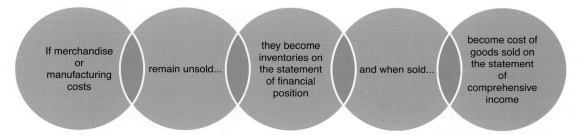

income. In other words, depreciation expense represents the amount of the cost for the property, plant and equipment that was consumed during the period. This is shown in Figure 3.31.

The same logic applies to supplies, prepaid rent, prepaid insurance and other costs that expire and are therefore reclassified from the statement of financial position to the statement of comprehensive income.

FIGURE 3.31 PROPERTY, PLANT AND EQUIPMENT VERSUS DEPRECIATION EXPENSE

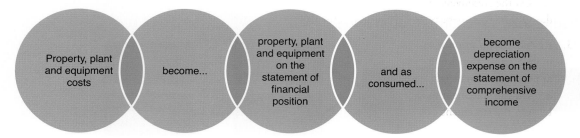

ON YOUR OWN

LEARNING OUTCOME REVIEW

1. What is expenditure? What is cost? What is expense?
2. Describe the difference between cost and expense.
3. On what financial statements does an expense appear?
4. On what financial statements does a cost appear?

LEARNING OUTCOME PRACTICE

1. A truck dealership purchases a truck for resale to a customer. Where does the cost of the truck appear in the financial statements if the truck has been sold?
   a. Cost of goods sold
   b. Inventories
   c. Property, plant and equipment
   d. Short-term investments

2. A truck dealership purchases a truck to use for delivery of parts. Where does the cost of this truck appear in the financial statements?
   a. Cost of goods sold
   b. Inventories
   c. Property, plant and equipment
   d. Short-term investment

3. A truck dealership purchases a truck to sell to a customer. Where does the cost of this truck appear in the financial statements if the truck has not been sold?
   a. Cost of goods sold
   b. Inventories
   c. Property, plant and equipment
   d. Short-term investment

4. Rashid Corporation purchased fuel for its delivery trucks that it used. Where does the cost of the fuel appear in the financial statements?
   a. On the statement of financial position as an asset
   b. On the statement of financial position as inventories
   c. On the statement of comprehensive income as sales expense
   d. On the statement of comprehensive income as cost of goods sold

5. Rashid Corporation purchased chemicals for use in the manufacturing of a cleaning solvent. After manufacture, the cleaning solvent was sold to customers. Where does the cost of the chemicals appear in the financial statements?
   a. On the statement of financial position as inventories
   b. On the statement of comprehensive income as cost of goods sold

    c.   On the statement of comprehensive income as a sales expense

    d.   On the statement of financial position as an asset

6.   Rashid Corporation purchased chemicals for use in manufacturing a cleaning solvent. After manufacture, the cleaning solvent remained unsold. Where does the cost of the chemicals appear in the financial statements?

    a.   On the statement of financial position as a liability

    b.   On the statement of financial position as inventories

    c.   On the statement of comprehensive income as a sales expense

    d.   On the statement of comprehensive income as revenue

7.   Rashid Corporation purchased supplies of £11 000 during the year. At the end of the year, only £1500 of these supplies remained on hand. What amount related to the total supplies purchased should appear on the statement of comprehensive income?

    a.   £1500

    b.   £9500

    c.   £0

    d.   £11 000

8.   Rashid Corporation purchased supplies of £11 000 during the year. At the end of the year, only £1500 of these supplies remained on hand. What amount related to the total supplies purchased should appear on the statement of financial position?

    a.   £1500

    b.   £9500

    c.   £11 000

    d.   £0

Conclusion

A complete set of financial statements includes a statement of financial position, statement of comprehensive income, statement of changes in equity and statement of cash flows as well as accompanying notes. In this chapter, we have focused on the statement of financial position and the statement of comprehensive income to understand in more detail the typical structure of each.

The major elements of the statement of financial position are assets, liabilities and equity. Assets and liabilities are both further classified as current or noncurrent. Current assets and liabilities are used to calculate working capital, which is the difference between the two amounts. Equity is classified into contributed capital, retained earnings and reserves. Contributed capital refers to the net amount invested by the owners of the business. Retaining earnings are accumulated earnings which have not been distributed to shareholders as dividends. Reserves are created at management's discretion or through specific IFRS requirements.

Summary
LEARNING OUTCOME 1
Notes Explained

Notes to the financial statement relate to any and all of the four financial statements. Notes contain information on significant accounting policies as well as how the reporting entity measures costs, which can include historical cost, current cost, net realizable value or fair value. Notes also contain information about any estimates made by management that would have a significant effect on the financial statements. Notes also disclose certain information required by IFRS and information that is relevant to understanding the financial statements.

LEARNING OUTCOME 2
Financial Position Described

Both assets and liabilities are classified as current and noncurrent. Within each category, specific titles for line items can vary depending on how management decides to communicate the financial results. Accounting standards typically do not mandate that specific title for accounts be used so long as they assist in providing a 'true and fair view' of the company's financial position. Thus minor variations can be observed. For example, trade accounts receivable is referred to in the Emirates Airline statement of financial position as 'trade and other receivables'.

A current asset or current liability is generally one that will be realized or settled respectively within 12 months of the reporting date. However, some businesses may have an operating cycle that is longer or shorter than one year, and management may elect to use this rather than the 12-month criterion for reporting current versus noncurrent items. Cash and cash equivalents are current assets. Any asset or liability not meeting the criteria for current is classified as noncurrent.

Working capital is the difference between current assets and current liabilities. If current assets exceed current liabilities, then working capital is positive. If current liabilities exceed current assets, then working capital is negative. Working capital is one measure used by management and external users to judge how able the business is to meet its short-term financial obligations.

Equity is classified in three ways. The first is contributed capital, which represents the net amount invested by owners. Retained earnings are accumulated earnings which have not been distributed to owners, and reserves are amounts set aside for specific purposes.

LEARNING OUTCOME 3
Performance Described

Expenses are classified into several major categories. The first is cost of sales (cost of goods sold for merchandisers and manufacturers). This represents the cost of producing the service or good that is sold to the customer. When the cost of sales or cost of goods sold is subtracted from revenue, the result is gross profit.

Operating expenses include selling and administrative expenses. Selling expenses include sales, marketing, advertising and distribution costs and administrative expenses include operating costs that cannot be directly associated with the production of goods or services. When operating expenses are subtracted from gross profit, the result is operating profit.

Finance expenses are costs associated with borrowing money. Since businesses can finance operations in different ways, finance costs could affect overall profitability. Interest on debt is included in finance expense, which is subtracted from operating income. However, dividends that compensate owners of the business for use of their capital are not deducted as finance expenses. Therefore, showing finance expenses separately allows users to evaluate the success of the business before and after finance expenses are taken into consideration.

Tax expense relates to income and other taxes paid to governments. After income tax is deducted, the result is a profit or a loss.

LEARNING OUTCOME 4
Relationship between Statement of Financial Position and Statement of Comprehensive Income Described

Profit for a reporting period increases retained earnings. If the business reports a loss, that will decrease retained earnings. Dividends are subtracted from retained earnings.

Reserves can be created at the discretion of the board and management and reserves can also be increased or decreased through other comprehensive income.

LEARNING OUTCOME 5
Difference between Expenditure, Costs and Expense Explained

When we say that a business had expenditure, we mean only that an outlay of cash or other resources has occurred. We cannot determine whether this expenditure has resulted in an asset or expense.

Expenditure results in a cost. However, a cost may also be created by an estimate of a future expenditure. For example, in accounting if we estimate that some traded accounts receivable will never be collected due to uncollectible accounts, that estimate is a cost that we understand when sales are made. We might say that our experience is that 5% of all sales made are uncollectible. However, the term cost still does not tell us whether an asset or expense has resulted.

Expense refers to a cost that has expired and thus expenses appear on the statement of comprehensive income. An expense refers to an item that has already been consumed. An unexpired cost appears on the statement of financial position as an asset. The term unexpired means that the item has not yet been consumed by the business.

REVIEW QUESTIONS

1. What are the elements of the expanded statement of financial position?
2. Explain the difference between current assets and noncurrent assets. What are examples of current assets? What are examples of noncurrent assets?
3. Explain the difference between current liabilities and noncurrent liabilities. What are examples of current liabilities? What are examples of noncurrent liabilities?
4. What is an operating cycle?
5. What are the components of equity?
6. What is a reserve? Provide examples. How are reserves created?
7. What are the categories and line items of the expanded statement of comprehensive income?
8. What is gross profit and how is it calculated? What is an alternative name for gross profit? What two types of businesses would calculate gross profit?
9. What is operating income and how is it calculated?
10. What is the difference between cost of sales and operating expenses?
11. What is expenditure? What is cost? What is expense? Explain the difference between these terms.
12. What is the difference between inventories and cost of sales?
13. How is a gain different from revenue?

Key terms

Administrative expenses
Annual Report
Assets
Capital
Capital assets
Cash
Cash equivalents
Consolidated
Contributed capital
Cost
Cost of goods sold
Cost of sales
Current assets
Current liabilities
Current portion of noncurrent borrowings
Equity
Expenditure

Expense
Financial statements
Financing expense
Fixed assets
Gross margin
Gross profit
Income tax expense
Intangible assets
Inventories
Investment in associates
Liabilities
Long-term asset
Long-term liabilities
Merchandise
Merchandise inventories
Minority interest
Mortgage

Noncontrolling interest

Noncurrent assets

Noncurrent liabilities

Operating cycle

Operating expenses

Operating income

Operating profit

Other comprehensive income

Paid-in capital

Parent

Performance

Prepaid expense

Profit or loss

Property, plant and equipment

Reserves

Retained earnings

Selling expenses

Short-term assets

Short-term liabilities

Subsidiary

Tax expense

Trade accounts payable

Trade accounts receivable

Terminology practice

For each of the following, insert the correct terms from the preceding list of key terms. Each key term can be used more than once.

1. A(n) _____ is a company that controls another company called the _____.

2. _____ are assets that the entity expects to realize or intends to sell or consume within 12 months or in its normal operating cycle.

3. _____ are present obligations of the entity arising from past events, the settlement of which is expected to result in an outflow from the entity of resources embodying economic benefits.

4. Assets with no physical substance are _____.

5. The cost of physical goods that a business owns and is holding for future sale to customers is classified as _____ and is sometimes referred to as *merchandise* or _____.

6. A(n) _____ is the amount the business owes to its suppliers created when the business purchased goods or services on account.

7. A _____ – also a noncontrolling interest – refers to owners of a subsidiary other than the _____.

8. The ownership of part of another business over which the entity has significant influence is classified as a(n) _____.

9. Working capital is calculated by subtracting _____ from _____.

10. Any outlay of cash or other consideration is a(n) _____.

11. _____ is calculated by subtracting operating expenses from gross profit.

12. Accumulated earnings of the business entity that have not been distributed to the owners are referred to as _____.

13. _____ – also _____ or _____ – represents the amount that owners have invested in the business.

14. Amounts paid to governments are classified as _____.

15. When a business has the right to collect cash in the future based on the customer's promises to pay for goods or services purchased before the reporting date this is referred to as _____.

16. _____ are resources controlled by an entity as a result of past events and from which future economic benefits are expected to flow to the entity.

17. A _____ represents a good or service that has been paid for in advance of its use.

18. _____ – also _____ – is calculated by subtracting cost of sales from revenue.

19. A(n) _____ is created by expenditure or an estimate of a future decrease in economic benefits to the business entity.

20. _____ is the total income less expenses of a business entity, excluding the components of other comprehensive income.

21. When an amount is owed on a noncurrent obligation within 12 months of the reporting date it would be classified as _____.

22. _____ refers to an expense that is related to goods produced or sold by a merchandiser or manufacturer.

23. A(n) _____ is a cost that has expired.

24. The residual interest in the assets of the entity after deducting all its liabilities is _____.

25. Interest on debt is classified as _____ on the statement of comprehensive income.

26. _____ – also referred to as _____ or _____ – are assets used in the production of goods or services, rental to others or for administrative purposes, and are expected to be used for more than one period.

27. A(n) _____ is a debt related to the purchase of real estate.

28. _____ includes items of income and expense that are not recognized in profit or loss.

Application exercises

1. For an accounting period, profit is $65 000 and dividends paid were $133 000. Beginning retained earnings were $200 000. How much are ending retained earnings?

2. Deborah's Bridal Shoppe Inc. reported the following figures for 2010. The business uses the calendar year for reporting purposes. Use the information provided to construct the statement of comprehensive income and statement of financial position. All figures are in US dollars. The tax on income is 30%. Any amount missing can be attributed to contributed capital.

Trade accounts payable	21 000	Dividends	100 000
Employee compensation	80 000	Sales revenue – alterations	70 000
Beginning retained earnings	85 000	Rent expense	36 000
Sales revenue – gowns	550 000	Cost of goods sold	247 500
Ending inventories	150 000	Short-term investments	17 000
Store fixtures and equipment	75 200	Trade accounts receivable	6000
Insurance expense	12 000	Cash	56 000
Advertising expense	23 000	Noncurrent note payable	60 000

3. Check the appropriate box to indicate to which financial statement line item described belongs.

	Cost of goods sold	Inventories	Property, Plant and Equipment	Short-term Investment
An office furniture retailer purchases furniture to sell to a customer. The furniture has been sold.				
An office furniture retailer purchases furniture for use in its reception area.				
An office furniture retailer purchases furniture to sell to a customer. The furniture has not been sold.				

4. Categorize the following financial account titles by which financial statements each would appear is by placing an X in the appropriate columns. If the item does not appear in either statement, leave the columns blank.

Item	Statement of Comprehensive Income	Statement of Financial Position
Repayments of borrowings		
Trade and other payables		
Trade accounts receivable		
Investment in own shares		
Operating income		
Noncurrent assets		
Notes payable		
Selling costs		
Tax expense		
Contributed capital		
Cash and cash equivalents		
Inventories		
Dividends		
Gross margin		
A cash purchase of property, plant and equipment		
Salary expenses		

Profit
Current liabilities
Interest expense
Beginning retained earnings

5. Care-Mart LLC reports all financial numbers in €thousands. Use the information presented below to construct a statement of comprehensive income and statement of financial position for 31 December 2011. Any amount missing can be attributed to paid-in capital. Round all calculations to the nearest Euro. The tax rate on income is 30%.

Proceeds from the disposal of assets	1 049
Cost of sales	240 391
Interest expense	1 171
Buildings and improvements	56 163
Trade accounts payable	25 373
Short-term notes payable	13 465
Taxes payable	1 340
Dividends paid	2 511
Purchase of Care-Mart common shares during 2011	3 469
Payment of long-term debt during 2011	2 724
Proceeds from issuance of long-term debt	7 691
Cash and cash equivalents	56 414
Property, plant and equipment	75 875
Land	16 643
Selling expenses	130 000
Other revenue	3 227
Sale of Care-Mart common shares	13 000
Payments for property, plant and equipment	14 563
Trade accounts receivable	32 662
Inventories	32 191
General and administrative expenses	36 733
Prepaid expenses	2 557
Merchandise sales	612 000
Fixtures and equipment	22 750
Transportation equipment	1 746
Long-term debt due within one year	4 595
Long-term debt	12 357
Beginning retained earnings	43 584

6. Following are the statement of comprehensive income and statement of financial position for Global Tire LLC. Fill in the missing numbers for each statement.

Statement of Comprehensive Income for the Years Ended 31 December ???
Dollars in millions

	2011	2010	2009
Sales	20 258	???	18 353
Cost of goods sold	???	15 887	???
Gross profit	3 252	3 836	???
Operating expenses	???	2 771	2 784
Operating income	262	???	773
Interest expense	???	???	450
Income before taxes	(224)	489	???
Taxes	???	250	???
Net income (loss)	(330)	???	115

Statement of Financial Position 31 December
Dollars in millions

	2011	2010
Assets		
Current assets		
Cash and cash equivalents	4 113	2 403
Accounts and notes receivable	2 973	3 158
Inventories	???	2 810
Prepaid expenses and other current assets	304	245
Total current assets	???	???
Intangible assets	851	???
Financial assets	155	102
Other assets	467	860
Properties and plants	5 377	5 231
Total assets	???	???
Liabilities		
Current liabilities		
Trade accounts payable	???	1,939
Employee benefits payable	905	1,773
Other current liabilities	839	???
Taxes payable	225	393
Notes payables and overdrafts	255	217
Long-term debt due within one year	405	448
Total current liabilities	???	5 441
Long-term debt	6 563	???

Employee benefits payable	4 965	3 828
Long-term taxes payable	333	304
Other long-term liabilities	1 260	1 217
Total liabilities	17 787	???
Stockholders' equity		
Common stock	178	177
Reserves	1 427	???
Retained earnings	(2 363)	(1 502)
Total shareholders' (deficit) equity	???	73
Total Liabilities and Shareholders' Equity	???	15 605

7. CNZ Group, a manufacturer of performance autos, reports all financial numbers in €millions. The company not only manufactures and sells autos but finances and leases them as well.

	2010	2009
Investments in other companies	60	94
Taxes payable – noncurrent	2 758	2 522
Reserves	1 911	1 971
Cash and cash equivalents	1 336	1 621
Intangible assets	815	643
Trade accounts receivables	2 258	2 135
Share capital	654	674
Trade accounts payables	3 737	3 544
Other assets – current	2 272	1 955
Current tax payable	666	831
Financial assets – current	3 134	2 654
Retained earnings	9 733	7 620
Financial liabilities – current	17 656	17 838
Property, plant and equipment	11 285	11 087
Inventories	6 794	6 527
Receivables from sales financing	17 865	17 202
Other current payable	567	462
Intangible assets	5 312	4 593
Other investments – noncurrent	401	1 178
Other assets – noncurrent	378	613
Pension liabilities – noncurrent	7 882	8 498
Other liabilities – noncurrent	1 932	1 659
Trade accounts receivables – noncurrent portion	5 178	5 455
Miscellaneous assets – noncurrent	744	772

Prepare a comparative statement of financial position for year-end 2010 and 2009 for CNZ Group. All amounts are £ British Pounds.

End notes

1. *Corporate Reporting: Is It What Investment Professionals Expect?* PricewaterhouseCoopers, November 2007.
2. Other comprehensive income was added to Emirates' statement of comprehensive income for the purposes of this textbook. When the 2007 financial statements were reported by Emirates Airline, other comprehensive income was not required to be included by IFRS.

APPENDIX: SELECTED NOTES TO EMIRATES AIRLINE CONSOLIDATED FINANCIAL STATEMENTS FOR THE YEAR ENDED 31 MARCH 2007

4. **Revenue**

	2007 AED'000	2006 AED'000
Services		
Passenger	21 677 143	16 370 146
Cargo	5 046 888	4 178 223
Courier	263 485	277 297
Excess baggage	217 153	173 810
Destination and leisure	182 953	146 718
Hotel operations	91 467	79 754
Mail	65 992	47 515
Training	62 900	69 217
Licensed engineering income	15 558	15 897
	27 623 539	**21 358 577**
Sale of goods	**1 019 162**	**948 962**
	28 642 701	22 307 539

5. **Other operating income**

   Other operating income includes an amount of AED 108.5 million (2006: AED 78.5 million) being collections from ancillary services provided in relation to transportation of passengers and cargo and a net foreign exchange gain of AED 99.9 million (2006: Nil).

6. **Operating costs**

	2007 AED'000	2006 AED'000
Fuel and oil	7 525 311	5 445 152
Employee (see (a) over)	4 024 328	3 187 108
Aircraft operating leases (see (b) over)	2 909 181	2 312 168
Sales and marketing	2 907 483	2 195 381
Handling (see (c) over)	1 751 697	1 406 250
In-flight catering and other operating costs	1 351 580	1 052 878
Depreciation (Note 9)	1 309 883	974 355

Overflying (see (c) over)	947 168	765 349
Cost of goods sold	547 927	541 846
Landing and parking (see (c) over)	534 754	436 904
Aircraft maintenance	499 630	373 401
Amortization (Note 10)	41 871	31 346
Corporate overheads (see (d) over)	1 483 435	1 283 561
	25 834 248	**20 005 699**

7. **Finance costs – net**

	2007 AED'000	2006 AED'000
Aircraft financing costs	(337 025)	(237 353)
Interest charges	(342 037)	(158 941)
Interest income	591 272	337 930
	(87 790)	**(58 364)**

8. **Income tax expense**

    The components of income tax expense are:

	2007 AED'000	2006 AED'000
Current tax	(111 939)	(87 608)
Deferred tax expense (Note 25)	(50 642)	–
	(162 581)	**(87 608)**

9. **Property, plant and equipment**

	Aircraft AED'000	Aircraft Engines and Parts AED'000	Land and Buildings AED'000	Other Property, Plant and Equipment AED'000	Capital Projects AED'000	Total AED'000
Cost						
1 April 2005	6 344 166	2 023 481	1 064 104	1 884 003	2 587 605	13 903 359
Additions	7 564	44 267	6 587	513 943	3 822 395	4 394 756
Transfers from capital projects	1 864 219	166 058	91 722	259 619	(2 445 993)	(64 375)
Disposals	(25 850)	(55 939)	(5 756)	(97 588)	(3 130)	(188 263)
31 March 2006	**8 190 099**	**2 177 867**	**1 156 657**	**2 559 977**	**3 960 877**	**18 045 477**
Depreciation						
1 April 2005	1 959 050	492 529	382 930	844 591	–	3 679 100
Charge for the year	416 874	134 211	53 913	369 357	–	974 355
Disposals	(25 850)	(20 249)	(658)	(96 096)	–	(142 853)
31 March 2006	**2 350 074**	**606 491**	**436 185**	**1 117 852**	**–**	**4 510 602**

(Continued)

Net book amount

31 March 2006	5 840 025	1 571 376	720 472	1 442 125	3 960 877	13 534 875
Cost						
1 April 2006	8 190 099	2 177 867	1 156 657	2 559 977	3 960 877	18 045 477
Additions	–	231 289	7 939	567 504	4 511 284	5 318 016
Currency translation differences	–	–	–	199	735	934
Transfers from capital projects	1 195 640	130 754	1 715 970	294 090	(3 336 454)	–
Disposals	(240 743)	(27 273)	(816)	(408 214)	(28 664)	(705 710)
31 March 2007	9 144 996	2 512 637	2 879 750	3 013 556	5 107 778	22 658 717
Depreciation						
1 April 2006	2 350 074	606 491	436 185	1 117 852	–	4 510 602
Charge for the year	533 787	153 869	125 693	496 534	–	1 309 883
Currency translation differences	–	–	–	79	–	79
Disposals	(163 094)	(15 789)	(702)	(156 220)	–	(335 805)
31 March 2007	2 720 767	744 571	561 176	1 458 245	–	5 484 759
Net book amount						
31 March 2007	6 424 229	1 768 066	2 318 574	1 555 311	5 107 778	17 173 958

10. Intangible assets

	Goodwill AED'000	Service rights AED'000	Computer software AED'000	Total AED'000
Cost				
1 April 2005	265 340	82 787	161 431	509 558
Additions	150 977	79 546	53 785	284 308
Disposals	–	–	(4 433)	(4 433)
31 March 2006	416 317	162 333	210 783	789 433
Amortization and impairment				
1 April 2005	6 738	4 185	79 423	90 346
Amortization for the year	–	7 396	23 950	31 346
Disposals	–	–	(1 930)	(1 930)
31 March 2006	6 738	11 581	101 443	119 762
Net book amount				
31 March 2006	409 579	150 752	109 340	669 671
Cost				
1 April 2006	416 317	162 333	210 783	789 433
Additions	150 350	–	70 420	220 770
Disposals (Note 33)	(7 176)	–	–	(7 176)

31 March 2007	559 491	162 333	281 203	1 003 027
Amortization and impairment				
1 April 2006	6 738	11 581	101 443	119 762
Amortization for the year	–	10 815	31 056	41 871
31 March 2007	6 738	22 396	132 499	161 633
Net book amount				
31 March 2007	552 753	139 937	148 704	841 394

11. Investment in subsidiaries, associated companies and joint ventures
   Principal subsidiaries

	Percentage of Equity Owned	Principal Activities	Country of Incorporation and Principal Operations
Maritime & Mercantile International LLC	68.7	Wholesale and retail of consumer goods	UAE
Emirates Leisure Retail LLC	68.7	Food and beverage operations	UAE
Emirates Leisure Retail Holding LLC	100.0	Holding company	UAE
Emirates Hotel LLC	100.0	Hotel operations	UAE
Emirates Hotel (Australia) Pty Ltd	100.0	Hotel operations	Australia
Emirates Flight Catering Company LLC	90.0	Catering services to airlines	UAE

Principal associated companies

	Percentage of Equity Owned	Principal Activities	Country of Incorporation and Principal Operations
SriLankan Airlines Limited	43.6	Air transportation, aircraft handling and catering	Sri Lanka

Joint ventures

	Percentage of Equity Owned	Principal Activities	Country of Incorporation and Principal Operations
Emirates-CAE Flight Training LLC	50.0	Flight simulator training	UAE
PTI Gulf Hotels LLC	51.0	Hotel operations	UAE

12. **Advance lease rentals**

	2007 AED'000	2006 AED'000
Balance brought forward	285 587	239 186
Additions / transfers during the year	–	72 307
Charge for the year	(26 811)	(25 906)
Balance carried forward	258 776	285 587
Advance lease rentals will be charged to the income statement as follows		
Within one year (Note 16)	27 821	27 949
Total over one year	230 955	257 638

Advance lease rentals are nonrefundable in the event of the related lease being terminated prior to its expiry.

13. **Other investments**
    (a) Available-for-sale financial assets

	2007 AED'000	2006 AED'000
Quoted	96 000	96 100
Unquoted	1 844 619	4 079
	1 940 619	**100 179**

Unquoted investments include:

	2007 AED'000	2006 AED'000
Capital guaranteed notes	1 840 540	–
Depository certificates	4 079	4 079
	1 844 619	**4 079**

Capital guaranteed notes are carried at fair value, the effective interest rate earned was 5.37% per annum. Depository certificates represent an investment in SITA Inc. and are without fixed maturity. The investment does not carry any voting rights and transfer is restricted. Therefore, the investment is measured at cost as the fair value cannot be reliably measured.

(b) Held-to-maturity investments

	2007 AED'000	2006 AED'000
Deposits with financial institutions:		
Current	136 730	183 650
Noncurrent	397 811	349 344
	534 541	**532 994**

The maturity dates fall into the following periods:

	2007 AED'000	2006 AED'000
Within 1 year	136 730	183 650
Between 1 and 2 years	397 811	136 730
Between 2 and 3 years	–	212 614

The effective interest rate earned was 5.63% (2006: 4.89%) per annum.
The carrying amounts of the investments approximate their fair value.

14. Loans and receivables

	2007 AED'000	2006 AED'000
Related parties (Note 32)	68 171	2 166
Other receivables	273 057	448 697
	341 228	**450 863**

The amounts are due as follows:

	2007 AED'000	2006 AED'000
Between 2 and 5 years	331 883	412 590
After 5 years	9 345	38 273
	341 228	**450 863**

15. Inventories

	2007 AED'000	2006 AED'000
Engineering	241 944	207 550
In-flight consumables	177 532	140 433
Consumer goods	65 749	85 495
Other	55 899	46 091
	541 124	**479 569**

16. Trade and other receivables

	2007 AED'000	2006 AED'000
Trade receivables	2 260 030	1 797 143
Related parties (Note 32)	150 621	23 630
Prepayments and deposits	1 231 053	876 043
Advance lease rentals (Note 12)	27 821	27 949

(Continued)

Operating lease deposits	738 992	717 981
Other receivables	1 353 031	1 162 119
	5 761 548	4 604 865
Less: Receivables over one year (Note 14)	(341 228)	(450 863)
	5 420 320	4 154 002

17. Capital

Capital represents the permanent capital provided by the Government of Dubai.

18. Other reserves

	Fair value reserve			
	Hedging Instruments AED'000	Other AED'000	Translation Reserve AED'000	Total AED'000
1 April 2005	**884 821**	**(3 900)**	**(18 161)**	**862 760**
Currency translation differences (Note 11)	–	–	(7 185)	(7 185)
Gain on fair value of cash flow hedges:				
– excluding associated companies	1 354 590	–	–	1 354 590
– associated companies	3 347	–	–	3 347
Transferred to income statement	(613 367)	–	–	(613 367)
31 March 2006	**1 629 391**	**(3 900)**	**(25 346)**	**1 600 145**
Currency translation differences	–	–	(11 753)	(11 753)
Loss on available-for-sale financial assets (Note 13)	–	(23 728)	–	(23 728)
Gain / (loss) on fair value of cash flow hedges:				
– excluding associated companies	358 302	–	–	358 302
– associated companies	(30 616)	–	–	(30 616)
Transferred to income statement	(736 633)	–	–	(736 633)
31 March 2007	**1 220 444**	**(27 628)**	**(37 099)**	**1 155 717**

19. Borrowings and lease liabilities

	2007 AED'000	2006 AED'000
Noncurrent		
Bonds (Note 20)	6 644 763	3 845 810
Term loans (Note 21)	951 588	765 661
Lease liabilities (Note 22)	4 812 979	4 485 859
	12 409 330	9 097 330

Current

Bonds (Note 20)	–	1 499 689
Term loans (Note 21)	119 583	55 402
Lease liabilities (Note 22)	809 546	583 811
Bank overdrafts (Note 29)	–	10 322
	929 129	**2 149 224**

23. Provisions

	End of Service Benefits AED'000	Frequent Flyer Programme AED'000	Total AED'000
Balance brought forward	317 862	59 314	377 176
Charge for the year	86 479	55 753	142 232
Payments made/benefits utilized during the year	(31 437)	(33 599)	(65 036)
Balance carried forward	372 904	81 468	454 372

The end of service benefit provision relates to employees who do not participate in the provident fund or the UAE government's pension fund.

In accordance with the provisions of IAS 19, management has carried out an exercise to assess the present value of its obligations at 31 March 2007, in respect of employees' end of service benefits payable under the relevant local regulations. The assessment assumed expected salary increases averaging 5% and a discount rate of 6% per annum. The present values of the obligations at 31 March 2007 were computed using the actuarial assumptions set out above.

24. Deferred credits

	2007 AED'000	2006 AED'000
Balance brought forward	947 254	581 658
Net additions during the year	91 209	449 663
Recognized during the year	(160 004)	(84 067)
Balance carried forward	878 459	947 254
Deferred credits will be recognized as follows:		
Within one year	177 825	151 707
Total over one year	700 634	795 547

25. Deferred tax liabilities

The movement in the deferred tax account during the year is as follows:

	2007 AED'000
Charge for the year	50 642
Balance carried forward	**50 642**

The charge for the year is on account of accelerated tax depreciation.

26. Trade and other payables

	2007 AED'000	2006 AED'000
Trade payables and accruals	5 199 273	4 158 735
Related parties (Note 32)	39 375	2 186
Passenger and cargo sales in advance	3 749 315	3 033 437
Dividend payable	400 000	386 000
	9 387 963	7 580 358
Less: Payables over one year	(84 191)	(125 723)
	9 303 772	7 454 635

29. Cash and cash equivalents

	2007 AED'000	2006 AED'000
Short term bank deposits and liquid funds	8 494 854	8 830 290
Cash and bank	628 391	368 714
Cash and bank balances	**9 123 245**	**9 199 004**
Bank overdrafts (Note 19)	–	(10 322)
	9 123 245	9 188 682
Less: Short term bank deposits over 3 months	(1 052 810)	(1 936 500)
	8 070 435	7 252 182

Cash and bank balances earned an effective interest rate of 5.61% (2006: 4.34%) per annum.

31. Financial instruments

(i) Interest rate risk

Emirates is exposed to interest rate fluctuations in the international financial market with respect to interest cost on its long term debt obligations and interest income on its cash surpluses.

The long term debt portfolio of Emirates has a combination of fixed and floating rate debt and lease liabilities. Emirates proactively manages interest rate exposure by using interest rate swaps and options as appropriate. A 1% increase in interest rates relating to the debt and operating lease liabilities will increase the charge to the income statement in the next financial year by AED 117.5 million (2006: AED

99.6 million). The effective interest rates per annum on aircraft related financing and term loans, bonds and bank overdrafts were 5.29% (2006: 4.43%), 6.11% (2006: 4.62%) and Nil (2006: 5.50%) respectively.

Emirates earns interest income on its cash surpluses. Emirates closely monitors interest rate trends and the related impact on interest income and manages interest rate exposure by entering into interest rate swaps and options.

Description	Term	AED'000
Cash flow hedge		
2007		
Interest rate swap asset	2007–2015	29 095
Interest rate swap liability	2007–2015	(3 833)
2006		
Interest rate swap asset	2006–2015	50 732
Interest rate swap liability	2006–2015	(4 374)

The notional principal amounts of the outstanding contracts at 31 March 2007 were AED 1168.9 million (2006: AED 1273.4 million).

The full fair value of the derivative instrument is classified as noncurrent if the remaining maturity of the hedged item is more than 12 months.

(ii) Currency risk

Emirates is exposed to exchange rate fluctuations between the UAE Dirham and other currencies which are generated from its revenue earning activities. Long term debt obligations are mainly denominated in UAE Dirham, the functional currency or in US Dollars to which the UAE Dirham is pegged. Emirates closely monitors currency rate trends and the related impact on revenues. Emirates proactively manages its currency exposure by using currency swaps, forwards and options, as appropriate, and matching foreign currency inflows and outflows.

Exchange rate hedges

Description	Term	AED'000
Cash flow hedge		
2007		
Currency swap and forward asset	2007–2017	19 705
Currency swap liability	2007–2008	(8 504)
Currency swap liability	2007–2017	(477 959)
2006		
Currency swap and forward asset	2006–2017	116 081
Currency swap liability	2006	(56)
Currency swap liability	2006–2011	(183 248)

(*Continued*)

Embedded derivatives

2007

Derivative asset	2007–2016	54 270
Derivative liability	2007–2015	(29 049)

2006

Derivative asset	2006–2016	60 258
Derivative liability	2006–2015	(32 539)

The notional principal amounts of the outstanding contracts at 31 March 2007 were AED 4694.5 million (2006: AED 3270.4 million).

Inflows on account of terminated currency derivatives amounting to AED 12.6 million (2006: AED 15.8 million) will enter into the determination of profit between 2007 and 2011.

A letter of credit for AED 129.3 million (2006: AED 21.9 million) has been placed as a collateral against the liability.

The full fair value of the derivative instrument is classified as noncurrent if the remaining maturity of the hedged item is more than 12 months.

(iii) Fuel price risk

The airline industry is exposed to fluctuations in the price of jet fuel. Emirates closely monitors the actual cost of fuel against forecasted cost. Emirates utilizes commodity futures and options to achieve a level of control over jet fuel costs so that profitability is not adversely affected. As a general principle, not more than the forecasted fuel consumption is hedged with percentage of cover being significantly higher in the near term than in latter periods.

Fuel price hedges

Description	Term	AED'000
Cash flow hedge		
2007		
Futures and options asset	2007–2008	206 617
Futures and options asset	2008–2011	1 065 709
2006		
Futures and options asset	2006–2007	359 457
Futures and options asset	2007–2010	1 159 930

The notional principal amounts of the outstanding contracts at 31 March 2007 were AED 14 086 million (2006: AED 11 817.8 million).

Inflows on account of terminated derivatives amounting to AED 441.2 million will enter into the determination of profit between 2007 and 2009 (2006: AED 98.1 million between 2006 and 2008).

In the event of the asset turning into a liability with the counter party, a letter of credit for AED 734.6 million has been pledged as collateral.

(iv) Credit risk

There are no significant concentrations of credit risk other than on derivative counterparties where transactions are limited to financial institutions possessing high credit quality and hence the risk of default is low.

The sale of passenger and cargo transportation is largely achieved through International Air Transport Association (IATA) approved sales agents. The credit risk associated with such sales agents is relatively small owing to a broad diversification.

Cash surpluses, held-to-maturity investments and available-for-sale financial assets are maintained with financial institutions possessing investment grade or higher credit quality. 13.6% (2006: 14.7%) of cash and bank balances and held-to-maturity investments are held with a financial institution under common control.

(v) Liquidity risk

Emirates proactively manages cash surpluses using a combination of short and long term investment programmes that ensure adequate liquidity to meet its short and long term obligations.

Preparing Financial Statements

INTRODUCTION TO PART II

In Part I, we were introduced to the four financial statements and to the financial accounting reporting system that generates them. Chapter 2 discussed generally accepted accounting principles, including accounting standards, which provide guidance for those who prepare financial statements. Recall that nations have different accounting standards. Thus, accounting standards are evolving all the time to meet the changing needs of modern business. And because business has become more global over the past few decades, we have also seen an international version of accounting standards.

But the system we use for the actual process of accounting – accumulating and summarizing financial information and preparing the financial statements – was created in the fifteenth century. The world's largest companies using sophisticated accounting software still account for financial transactions using this double-entry method which is our subject for Part III. This part is organized into three chapters, as shown in the following diagram:

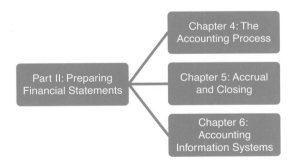

Chapter 4 covers the basic accounting process which accounts for transactions. We will see how transactions are analysed and then recorded in the company's accounting system. Then how this information is summarized in a manner that makes it easier to access and understand. In Chapter 5, we will see how accounting information is adjusted so that transactions are reported in the appropriate period.

We will observe at what point in the accounting process the financial statements are prepared. Chapter 5 will also explain how the accounting records must be prepared for the next business period.

Chapter 6 explains how the double-entry accounting process has been adapted to modern business. Global companies may have millions of transactions that must be accounted for and this is done using automated accounting software. But in many cases, the amount of transactions information is so large that it must be organized into flows of similar information.

The accounting process

4

Introduction

Even small and medium-size businesses must track a torrent of numbers, but large multinationals deal with a tsunami of financial information. All these numbers must somehow be collected, organized and condensed into the four financial statements. In this chapter, we will learn about the first step, which is analysing and recording financial information.

The accounting process is based on three basic concepts that will help keep all that is to follow in perspective:

- First, we account for business transactions, which are exchanges of value. What is exchanged can fall into three broad categories: cash, goods or services and promises. The financial statements report the cumulative effect of all transactions for a business entity.
- Second, all transactions are exchanges of *equal value*. What is received by the business in the transaction is equal to that which is given. This simple idea of accounting for both sides of a transaction is the root of the centuries-old double-entry method invented by Fra Luca Bartolomeo Pacioli which is still in use today.

- Third, numbers reported in financial statements are not per se a measure of value. For example, if a company reports ¥150 million in total assets on its statement of financial position, we cannot conclude that the company's assets are *worth* or have a *value* of ¥150 million. Accounting does not measure value. However, value may be taken into consideration and financial accounting information can offer important clues about the value of the business.

LEARNING OUTCOME 1
DESCRIBE THE FOUR MAJOR STEPS IN THE ACCOUNTING PROCESS

When financial transactions occur in a business, evidence of those transactions is provided to the accounting department. Accounting department refers to the organizational unit within the business entity responsible for accounting activities. Some companies may have several accounting units, but throughout this textbook we will use the term 'accounting department' in examples.

Each transaction is then processed through the accounting system in four major steps described below.

1. *Analyse and record transactions.* The first step is an ongoing activity that continues throughout the reporting period. Transactions are analysed based on information contained in source documents. This information is then recorded in the accounting system using a journal entry. Three basic reports are available once all the journal entries are recorded: the journal, the ledger and the trial balance.
2. *Adjust accounts.* Once all transactions for the reporting period are completed, adjusting entries are recorded. After adjustments have been made, the adjusted trial balance is generated.
3. *Prepare financial statements.* The adjusted trial balance is then used to prepare the financial statements.
4. *Close accounts.* Once financial statements have been completed, the accounting records are 'closed' and made ready for the next reporting period by recording closing entries. A post-closing trial balance is then generated, after which the accounting department can begin recording transactions for the next reporting period.

These four steps are shown graphically in Figure 4.1 along with the reports generated at each stage.

As you can see from Figure 4.1, we will discuss the first part of the accounting process in this chapter. The second part (which includes adjusting accounts, preparing financial statements and closing accounts) will be covered in Chapter 5.

FIGURE 4.1 THE ACCOUNTING PROCESS

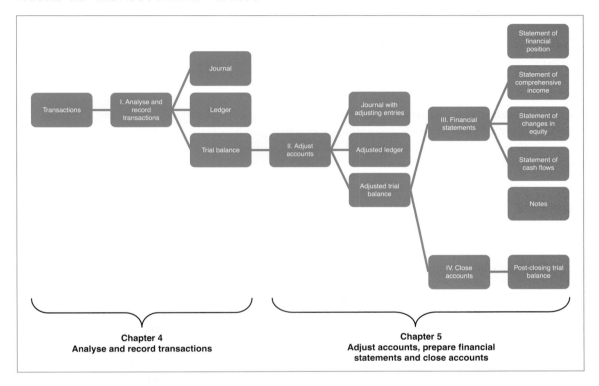

ON YOUR OWN

LEARNING OUTCOME REVIEW

1. What are the four major steps in the accounting process?
2. What is the sequence of the four major steps in the accounting process?

LEARNING OUTCOME 2
EXPLAIN HOW TRANSACTIONS ARE ANALYSED

The accounting process begins with transactions. As transactions occur, they are first analysed and then recorded. The analysis involves determining what the business has received and what it has given. By definition, as already noted, all accounting exchanges are of equal value. If the item received has a different value from what is given, then accounting normally assigns the value that was given to what is received.

A business purchases a plot of land for €100 000 cash. An appraisal (a professional estimate of value) determines that the market value of the land is €125 000. The land would be valued at the amount for the item given up in the transaction, which is €100 000. Thus, the land would appear on the statement of financial position at €100 000.

A transaction can involve an exchange of three types of items: goods and services, money and a promise. Promises usually take one of two forms: a promise to deliver goods or services or a promise to pay money in the future. Consider the diagram in Figure 4.2, which gives examples of transactions based on all possible combinations of these three categories.

FIGURE 4.2 TRANSACTION EXAMPLES BASED ON TYPES OF EXCHANGES

	Received in transaction		
Given in transaction	Good or service	Money	Promise
Good or service	Barter transaction – land is exchanged for equipment with no cash involved in the transaction	Cash sale to a customer for merchandise or a service (such as cleaning)	Credit sale to a customer for merchandise or a service (such as cleaning) – the customer promises to pay in the future (trade account receivable)
Money	Supplies are purchased in exchange for cash	A business buys (or sells) a foreign currency	The business pays a trade account payable – the promise to pay in the future is 'returned' in exchange for a cash payment
Promise	Supplies are purchased in exchange for a promise to pay in the future (trade account payable)	Money is borrowed from a bank receiving money in exchange for a promise to pay in the future	A new employee is hired – the employee promises to render services in the future in exchange for the business's promise to pay wages in the future

Figure 4.2 provides a framework for analysing what the business received and gave. Notice two things about the examples in this framework. First, promise-for-promise (the dark shaded boxes in the figure) transactions are usually not recorded. In the example given, an employee is hired and promises to render services in the future in exchange for the business's promise to pay wages to the employee in the future. A formal agreement may be reached between the new employee and company, but no exchange of value has occurred. Later, when the employee has rendered services and the business is obligated to pay, the transaction is recorded. This transaction is a service for promise (not promise for promise). In other words, the first step in the analysis is to determine whether a transaction should be recorded or not.

Second, consider a transaction where the business buys supplies on credit on 1 February 2009, which is a goods-for-promise transaction (see the light shaded box on the left-hand side). The business promises to pay on 28 February 2009. On 28 February, a second transaction occurs – a promise for money (see the light shaded box on the right-hand side). The business's promise is returned (the supplier no longer holds the business to its promise to pay) because the business has given the supplier cash to settle the debt (the trade account payable). In this example, two transactions have occurred at two different points in time, 1 February 2009 and 28 February 2009.

A second way to analyse a transaction is to determine which financial statement elements are affected. Only those elements on the statement of financial position – assets, liabilities and equity – and those on the statement of comprehensive income – revenue and expense – are normally involved. A transaction can occur between any two of these five elements. Examples of the different combinations are illustrated in Figure 4.3.

Four observations should be made about this chart. First, notice that revenue is not received but given (see box, Getting Revenue Right). Thus all transactions that involve receipt of revenue are marked 'not applicable'. Second, revenues and expenses are not exchanged, thus these items are also marked 'not applicable'. Third, an expense-for-equity transaction is possible but rare in practice. And fourth, a revenue-for-expense transaction is not possible. All other combinations can occur, although some are more common than others.

GETTING REVENUE RIGHT

Revenue is what a business gives up in a transaction, not what it receives. In a cash transaction for services rendered, the business receives cash and gives its services in exchange. Revenue represents the services provided. Think of revenue as an opportunity that has been forfeited. When the business renders a service, it gives up the opportunity to sell those services to anyone else. When it sells merchandise, the opportunity to sell that merchandise to someone else is lost.

What is received and given in a transaction is classified according to account titles. Typical account titles for assets, for example, include cash at bank; trade accounts receivable; inventories; property, plant and equipment; and so forth. Each account title belongs to a specific financial statement. So cash or trade

FIGURE 4.3 TRANSACTION EXAMPLES BASED ON FINANCIAL STATEMENT ELEMENTS

Given in transaction	Received in transaction				
	Asset	Liability	Equity	Revenue	Expense
Asset	Equipment is purchased for cash	A loan is settled (repaid) with cash	A business receives back shares in exchange for cash	Not applicable	Supplies used in the current reporting period are purchased for cash
Liability	Equipment is purchased on credit	A business refinances a loan that it was to pay back within one year for another loan that will be paid back over three years	A business receives back its shares in exchange for its promise to pay in the future. This could be a situation where an owner sells her shares to the company but is willing to wait a certain amount of time before receiving payment	Not applicable	A business receives an employee's services in exchange for a promise to pay in the future
Equity	A building is received in exchange for shares	A business receives shares in exchange for a loan to be paid to the owner in the future	A business can have different types of contributed capital. The business receives back one type of capital from an owner in exchange for another type of capital	Not applicable	A business purchases supplies in exchange for shares

Revenue	A cash sale	A maintenance company owes a supplier for cleaning materials and the supplier offers to discharge the debt if the maintenance company will clean its offices	Not applicable	Not applicable	Not applicable
Expense	An employee who has already rendered services is paid in cash	An employee who has already rendered services will be paid at the end of the month	A business receives supplies used in the current reporting period in exchange for shares	Not applicable	Not applicable

accounts receivable would never appear as an expense on the statement of comprehensive income – they are classified as an asset on the statement of financial position. Although some account titles are commonly used – such as cash at bank and trade accounts receivable – others are created at the discretion of management and used as the need arises.

A business makes a cash purchase of cleaning services, a service-for-money transaction. Thus, the business receives cleaning services (an expense) and gives cash at bank (an asset). Since expenses appear on the statement of comprehensive income and assets appear on the statement of financial position, both financial statements are affected.

In another example, a business buys production equipment on credit. This is an asset-for-liability transaction. The business receives equipment (an asset) and gives up a note payable (a liability). Since both assets and liabilities appear on the statement of financial position, only that financial statement would be affected. The statement of comprehensive income is not affected.

ON YOUR OWN

LEARNING OUTCOME REVIEW

1. What three types of items can be exchanged in a transaction?
2. Give examples of exchanges between good or services, money and promises.
3. Give examples of exchanges between financial statement elements.
4. Why is revenue 'given up' in a transaction? When revenue is given up, what can be received in exchange?

LEARNING OUTCOME 3
EXPLAIN HOW TRANSACTIONS ARE RECORDED

Journal entries record transactions. A journal entry is a method of coding a transaction so that the financial information can be processed by the accounting system. In the journal entry, what is received by the business is a debit and what is given in the transaction is a credit. We abbreviate debit as DR and credit as CR.

A small catering firm purchases a delivery van on 1 July 2009 for £15 000 cash. The business would record the transaction using the following journal entry.

Date	Account Titles	DR	CR
1 July 2009	Equipment – Delivery Van Cash	£15 000	£15 000
Purchased delivery van serial number 1-0200-90098-78424.			

Notice the following features of this entry:

- The journal entry always includes the date of the transaction so that the information it contains can be related to the appropriate reporting period. In the example above, the date will place this transaction in the 2009 reporting period.
- What was received or given in the transaction is classified by account titles. The debit account in this entry is 'Equipment – Delivery Van' and the credit account is 'Cash'.

- The amounts of the debit and credit are shown under the abbreviations DR and CR. In a journal entry, *debits must always equal credits.*
- Debits are listed first in the journal entry, with the debit amount shown in the left-hand column. Credits go below and in the right-hand column.
- In the bottom of the example above, an explanation is included in the journal entry: 'Purchased delivery van serial number 1-0200-90098-78424'. While the explanation often contains important information in practice, we will omit them from journal entries in examples throughout the remainder of this textbook.

Journal entries can be analysed to see what the effects will be on the financial statements. As we become more experienced with accounting, the analysis and conclusions that follow become almost second nature. The box below analyses the delivery van purchase transaction.

Transaction Analysis		
	DR	CR
What accounts are affected?	Equipment–Delivery van	Cash
Are accounts increased or decreased?	Increased	Decreased
What financial statement element is this?	Asset	Asset
What financial statement is affected?	Statement of financial position	Statement of financial position

What conclusions can we reach from this analysis? What we are looking for is the impact on particular financial statements. Knowing this allows us to determine what the effect is on financial position, performance and changes in financial position.

Based on the transaction analysis above, we can see that this was an asset-for-asset transaction. We also know that this entry increased and decreased assets by the same amount. Thus, consider the following questions based on this analysis:

Question: What was the net effect on assets?
Answer: No effect. Assets were increased and decreased by the same amount.

Question: What was the effect on liabilities?
Answer: Liabilities were not affected.

Question: What was the effect on equity?
Answer: Equity was not affected.

> Question: What was the effect on the statement of comprehensive income?
> Answer: Neither revenues nor expenses was affected. There was no impact on the statement of comprehensive income.

Now, let's change the example.

> Instead of paying for the delivery van with cash, the business paid the seller £5000 in cash and promised to pay the remainder within 30 days.

In this case, the business still debits 'Equipment – Delivery Van' for £15 000 as before, but now credits 'Cash' for £5000 and 'Note payable' for £10 000. Here is the journal entry:

Date	Account Titles	DR	CR
1 July 2009	Equipment – Delivery Van Cash Note payable	£15 000	 £5 000 10 000

This journal entry is different from the first because it involves credits to two accounts. Journal entries can have as many debits or credits as needed as long as *total debits equal total credits*. In this case, the total amount is still £15 000 on both sides of the transaction. Now let's try the analysis:

Transaction Analysis			
	DR	CR	CR
What accounts are affected?	Equipment	Cash	Note payable
Are accounts increased or decreased?	Increased	Decreased	Increased
What financial statement element is this?	Asset	Asset	Liability
What financial statement is affected?	Statement of financial position	Statement of financial position	Statement of financial position

What can we conclude from this analysis?

Question: What was the effect on assets?
Answer: Assets were increased. Equipment increased by £15 000 while cash was decreased by £5000, which means that the net increase in assets was £10 000.

Question: What was the effect on liabilities?
Answer: Liabilities increased by £10 000.

Question: What was the effect on equity?
Answer: No impact. The net increase in assets (£10 000) was equal to the net increase in liabilities (also £10 000) so the equity balance was not affected.

Question: What is the effect on the statement of comprehensive income?
Answer: No impact. Neither revenue nor expenses was affected.

HINT

The following three 'golden rules' may help you remember how to record transactions:

1. A debit comes in; a credit goes out.
2. A debit receives; a credit gives.
3. Debit expenses and assets; credit revenue and liabilities.

ON YOUR OWN

LEARNING OUTCOME REVIEW

1. What is the purpose of a journal entry?
2. List the five basic components of a complete journal entry.
3. How is a journal entry structured?

LEARNING OUTCOME 4
EXPLAIN WHAT SOURCE DOCUMENTS ARE AND THEIR IMPORTANCE IN THE ACCOUNTING PROCESS

Journal entries must be made from a verifiable source of information, usually either hard-copy source documents or electronic source records. A source document is the original record of a transaction.

Examples include customer invoices, supplier invoices, purchase orders, time cards, deposit slips, notes for loans, cash receipts, credit card receipts, cash register tapes and cancelled cheques.

- *Hard-copy source documents.* Source documents vary depending on the type of transaction. To record revenue, a retail outlet may use a register tape, which is the record of sales transactions printed by the cash register. If sales clerks write the sales receipts by hand, then copies of these receipts serve as the source documents. On the cost side, a company may purchase supplies and the supplier will provide an invoice, which becomes the source document.
- *Electronic source documents.* Increasingly, transactions have become paperless. For example, when a customer pays for merchandise at a retail store, the computer-based cash register can automatically record the journal entry to recognize the revenue for the sale. The same is true when a customer orders merchandise online using a credit card. Instead of a paper document, an electronic record of the order serves as the source 'document'. From this electronically generated order, the computer automatically generates the necessary journal entry to debit cash and credit revenue.

LEARNING OUTCOME 5
CONSTRUCT JOURNAL ENTRIES
TO RECORD TRANSACTIONS

Transactions, and therefore the journal entries that record them, take many forms. Therefore, our next task is to practise analysing and recording transactions, then reaching some conclusions about their impact on the financial statements. We will use Schwittay Consulting AG as our example.

Schwittay Consulting AG is a new business and in February 2009 opens an office in Berlin. The two owners previously worked for prestigious consulting firms, and have now decided to launch their own business together. Both are well established and have excellent access to the capital needed to start the firm. In addition, several clients have indicated their interest in using the new firm for their needs.

Chart of accounts

Each business develops a chart of accounts for its accounting system. A chart of accounts is a listing of all account titles authorized by the company. These accounts are used to summarize financial transaction information. An airline may have several sources of revenue, such as passenger revenue, cargo revenue and holiday tour revenue. Management may want to track how much sales are in each category. Therefore, account titles are set up for each source.

As Schwittay begins operations, one of the first accounting tasks is to establish its chart of accounts. Let's assume that the accountant hired by Schwittay established the chart of accounts shown in Figure 4.4.

FIGURE 4.4 CHART OF ACCOUNTS

Schwittay Consulting AG Chart of Accounts	
Elements	Account Titles
Revenue	Service revenue
	Interest revenue
Expenses	Salaries expense
	Interest expense
	Rent expense
	Supplies expense
	Insurance expense
	Improvements amortization
Assets	Cash
	Trade accounts receivable
	Prepaid rent
	Prepaid insurance
	Leasehold improvements
Liabilities	Trade accounts payable
	Salaries payable
	Interest payable
	Note payable
	Unearned service revenue
	Loan payable
Equity	Contributed capital
	Retained earnings
	Dividends

Notice that the chart of accounts lists only account titles and contains no financial information such as the account balances. In this case, the accounts are grouped by financial statement elements (revenues, expenses, assets, liabilities and equity). These account titles will be used when making journal entries.

Journal entries for February 2009
1 FEBRUARY 2009

On this date, the new owners met at the solicitor's office and signed the organization papers for their new business, which was organized as a limited liability company. Also on the same day each contributed capital of €10 000 in cash. The journal entry would be:

Date	Account Titles	DR	CR
1 Feb. 2009	Cash Contributed capital	€20 000	€20 000

Here is the analysis:

Transaction Analysis		
	DR	CR
What accounts are affected?	Cash	Contributed capital
Are accounts increased or decreased?	Increased	Increased
What financial statement element is this?	Asset	Equity
What financial statement is affected?	Statement of financial position	Statement of financial position

What can we conclude from this analysis?

Question: What was the effect on assets?
Answer: Assets were increased because cash was increased.

Question: What was the effect on liabilities?
Answer: None. No liability account was debited or credited.

Question: What was the effect on equity?
Answer: Equity was increased.

Question: What is the effect on the statement of comprehensive income?
Answer: No impact. Neither revenue nor expenses was affected.

1 FEBRUARY 2009

The owners borrowed €150 000 for furniture, equipment and other costs related to establishing the firm's new offices. The bank that provided the loan gave Schwittay three years to repay in equal annual instalments, and is charging 8% per annum interest. Payments are due on the anniversary date of the loan. Here's the journal entry:

Date	Account Titles	DR	CR
1 Feb. 2009	Cash	150 000	
	Loan payable		150 000

And now the analysis:

Transaction Analysis		
	DR	CR
What accounts are affected?	Cash	Loan payable
Are accounts increased or decreased?	Increased	Increased
What financial statement element is this?	Asset	Liability
What financial statement is affected?	Statement of financial position	Statement of financial position

What can we conclude from the analysis?

Question: What was the effect on assets?
Answer: Assets were increased because cash was increased.

Question:	What was the effect on liabilities?
Answer:	Liabilities were increased since the loan payable increased.
Question:	What was the effect on equity?
Answer:	Equity was not affected because the increase in assets and the increase in liabilities were the same. The difference between assets and liabilities was the same.
Question:	What is the effect on the statement of comprehensive income?
Answer:	No impact.

3 FEBRUARY 2009

On this date, a five-year lease for office space is signed with a rental rate of €4950 per month. Schwittay's owners are required to pay six months' rent in advance. The lease specifies that Schwittay may have possession of the space for operations on 1 March 2009. However, in order for construction workers to enter the space for renovations beforehand, the rental term is made effective from 1 February.

Date	Account Titles	DR	CR
3 Feb. 2009	Prepaid rent	€29 700	
	Cash		€29 700

Notice that prepaid rent is debited. This account is classified as an asset because the use of the space has not been consumed (or expired). Therefore, it has value to the company in the future.

Transaction Analysis		
	DR	CR
What accounts are affected?	Prepaid rent	Cash
Are accounts increased or decreased?	Increased	Decreased
What financial statement element is this?	Asset	Asset
What financial statement is affected?	Statement of financial position	Statement of financial position

What can we conclude from the analysis of this transaction?

Question: What was the effect on assets?
Answer: No impact. Assets were increased and decreased by the same amount.

Question: What was the effect on liabilities?
Answer: None. Liability accounts were not affected.

Question: What was the effect on equity?
Answer: None. Equity was not affected.

Question: What is the effect on the statement of comprehensive income?
Answer: None. Neither revenue nor expenses was affected.

5 FEBRUARY 2009

Schwittay's owners hire a contractor to renovate the office space for a total of €69 000. These improvements are expected to last for five years, the term of the lease. One third of the total amount is to be paid in advance, a further third when the job is half completed, and the final payment is due on completion of all work.

Date	Account Titles	DR	CR
5 Feb. 2009	Leasehold improvements Cash Note payable	€69 000	€23 000 46 000

First, the analysis:

Transaction Analysis			
	DR	CR	CR
What accounts are affected?	Leasehold improvements	Cash	Note payable
Are accounts increased or decreased?	Increased	Decreased	Increased
What financial statement element is this?	Asset	Asset	Liability
What financial statement is affected?	Statement of financial position	Statement of financial position	Statement of financial position

What can we conclude from the analysis?

Question: What was the effect on assets?
Answer: The net increase in assets is €46 000. The debit to improvements of €69 000 increases assets, but this is offset by the decrease in cash of €23 000.

Question: What was the effect on liabilities?
Answer: The note payable is increased for €46 000.

Question: What was the effect on equity?
Answer: Equity is not affected. The net increase in assets is €46 000, which is offset by the increase in liabilities for the same amount. The difference between assets and liabilities did not change.

Question: What is the effect on the statement of comprehensive income?
Answer: None.

7 FEBRUARY 2009

Under the terms of the office lease, Schwittay is required to carry insurance indemnifying the landlord against accidents and injury. The insurance provider requires advance payment of the €12 060 annual premium. Coverage begins on 1 March when the company moves into its new offices.

Date	Account Titles	DR	CR
7 Feb. 2009	Prepaid insurance	€12 060	
	Cash		€12 060

First, the analysis:

Transaction Analysis		
	DR	CR
What accounts are affected?	Prepaid insurance	Cash
Are accounts increased or decreased?	Asset	Asset
What financial statement element is this?	Increased	Decreased
What financial statement is affected?	Statement of financial position	Statement of financial position

What can we conclude from the analysis?

Question: What was the effect on assets?
Answer: Net assets are not affected because the increase in prepaid insurance is offset by the decrease in cash.

Question: What was the effect on liabilities?
Answer: No impact.

Question: What was the effect on equity?
Answer: Equity is not affected. Neither net assets nor liabilities changed.

Question: What is the effect on the statement of comprehensive income?
Answer: No impact.

15 FEBRUARY 2009

Schwittay's owners concluded a work agreement with a major client. The firm will undertake a project that is expected to last for one year. The total price of the project has been set at € 804 000. An advance of € 201 000 has been made to Schwittay. The remainder will be made in three instalments on 15 June 2009, 15 November 2009 and 15 February 2010. The journal entry to record the first instalment, which was paid when the agreement was signed, would be:

Date	Account Titles	DR	CR
15 Feb. 2009	Cash Unearned service revenue	€ 201 000	€ 201 000

First, the analysis:

Transaction Analysis		
	DR	CR
What accounts are affected?	Cash	Unearned service revenue
Are accounts increased or decreased?	Increased	Increased
What financial statement element is this?	Asset	Liability
What financial statement is affected?	Statement of financial position	Statement of financial position

In this case, unearned service revenue is credited. This represents Schwittay's promise to deliver its services in the future. The fact that Schwittay received partial payment in advance has created the need to recognize this liability.

What can we conclude from the analysis?

Question: What was the effect on assets?
Answer: Assets increased.

Question: What was the effect on liabilities?
Answer: Liabilities increased.

Question: What was the effect on equity?
Answer: Equity was not affected since assets and liabilities increased by the same amount.

Question: What was the effect on the statement of comprehensive income?
Answer: No impact. Neither revenue or expenses was affected.

15 FEBRUARY 2009

On the same day, Schwittay's owners hired three individuals to provide consulting services. Each employee would receive an annual salary of €108 000, to be paid monthly on the first day of the month following the month in which the work was done. All three began work immediately. In this case, no journal entry was recorded. This is a promise-for-promise transaction.

16 FEBRUARY 2009

The owners had been working on a small project for a client during the first half of the month, which was completed and delivered. No formal work agreement had been signed nor was any payment previously received. The client paid Schwittay's total fee of €13 500 in cash.

Date	Account Titles	DR	CR
16 Feb. 2009	Cash	€13 500	
	Service revenue		€13 500

First, notice that this journal entry is the first that has involved an account on the statement of comprehensive income. Now, the analysis:

Transaction Analysis		
	DR	CR
What accounts are affected?	Cash	Service revenue
Are accounts increased or decreased?	Increased	Increased
What financial statement element is this?	Asset	Revenue
What financial statement is affected?	Statement of financial position	Statement of comprehensive income

What can we conclude from the analysis?

Question: What was the effect on assets?
Answer: Assets increased.

Question: What was the effect on liabilities?
Answer: No impact.

Question: What was the effect on equity?
Answer: Equity increased by an amount equal to the increase in the asset.

Question: What is the effect on the statement of comprehensive income?
Answer: The net impact was positive since service revenue increased.

17 FEBRUARY 2009

Another client contacted Schwittay's owners and asked for a short engagement that should be completed within 10–12 days. The client would pay €20 000. Schwittay began work immediately. Again, a journal entry was not recorded at this point. This was a promise-for-promise exchange.

20 FEBRUARY 2009

The company purchased €3350 in supplies on account.

Date	Account Titles	DR	CR
20 Feb. 2009	Supplies Trade accounts payable	€3 350	€3 350

First, the analysis:

Transaction Analysis		
	DR	CR

What accounts are affected?
Are accounts increased
  or decreased?
What financial statement element is this?
What financial statement is affected?
	Supplies
	Increased
	
	Asset
	Statement of financial
	  position
		Trade accounts payables
		Increased
		
		Liability
		Statement of financial
		  position

What can we conclude from the analysis of this transaction?

Question: What was the effect on assets?
Answer: Assets increased.

Question: What was the effect on liabilities?
Answer: Liabilities increased.

Question: What was the effect on equity?
Answer: Equity was not affected because the increase in assets and increase in liabilities was the same. The difference between assets and liabilities was therefore the same.

Question: What was the effect on the statement of comprehensive income?
Answer: No impact.

23 FEBRUARY 2009

The renovations contractor reported that she had completed half of the work and wished to be paid the second payment.

Date	Account Titles	DR	CR
23 Feb. 2009	Note payable Cash	€23 000	€23 000

First, the analysis:

Transaction Analysis		
	DR	CR
What accounts are affected?	Note payable	Cash
Are accounts increased or decreased?	Decreased	Decreased
What financial statement element is this?	Liability	Asset
What financial statement is affected?	Statement of financial position	Statement of financial position

What can we conclude from the analysis?

Question: What was the effect on assets?
Answer: Assets decreased.

Question: What was the effect on liabilities?
Answer: Liabilities decreased.

Question: What was the effect on equity?
Answer: Equity was not affected since the decrease in liabilities was offset by the decrease in assets. The difference between assets and liabilities was therefore the same.

Question: What was the effect on the statement of comprehensive income?
Answer: No impact.

28 FEBRUARY 2009
Schwittay paid for the supplies purchased on 20 February 2009.

Date	Account Titles	DR	CR
28 Feb. 2009	Trade accounts payable Cash	€3 350	€3 350

First, the analysis:

Transaction Analysis		
	DR	CR
What accounts are affected?	Trade accounts payable	Cash
Are accounts increased or decreased?	Decreased	Decreased
What financial statement element is this?	Liability	Asset
What financial statement is affected?	Statement of financial position	Statement of financial position

What can we conclude from the analysis?

Question: What was the effect on assets?
Answer: Assets decreased.

Question: What was the effect on liabilities?
Answer: Liabilities decreased.

Question: What was the effect on equity?
Answer: Equity was not affected since the decrease in liabilities was offset by the decrease in assets. The difference between assets and liabilities was therefore the same.

Question: What was the effect on the statement of comprehensive income?
Answer: No impact.

28 FEBRUARY 2009

Schwittay earned €1250 in interest on the cash in its bank account during February.

Date	Account Titles	DR	CR
28 Feb. 2009	Cash	€1 250	
	Interest revenue		€1 250

First, the analysis:

Transaction Analysis		
	DR	CR
What accounts are affected?	Cash	Interest revenue
Are accounts increased or decreased?	Increased	Increased
What financial statement element is this?	Asset	Revenue
What financial statement is affected?	Statement of financial position	Statement of comprehensive income

What can we conclude from the analysis?

Question: What was the effect on assets?
Answer: Assets were increased.

Question: What was the effect on liabilities?
Answer: No effect.

Question: What was the effect on equity?
Answer: Equity increased.

Question: What was the effect on the statement of comprehensive income?
Answer: Revenue increased, which increased profit.

This was Schwittay's last transaction for the month of February.

FIGURE 4.5 ANALYSE AND RECORD TRANSACTIONS

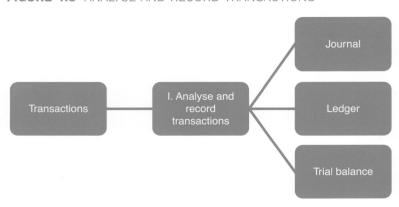

Once all transactions have been recorded for a reporting period, three reports are generated: the journal, the ledger and the trial balance. To review where we are in the accounting process, Figure 4.5 shows that portion of the accounting process related to analysing and recording transactions and the three reports.

LEARNING OUTCOME 6
DESCRIBE THE JOURNAL AND EXPLAIN ITS ROLE IN THE ACCOUNTING PROCESS

The first report is the journal. A journal lists all journal entries in chronological order. The journal is sometimes referred to as the 'book of original entry' or the 'book of prime entry'. It provides a useful record of transactions in the order entered, and thus has sometimes been described as the financial 'diary' of the business.

In manual accounting systems, the journal was literally a bound paper volume. In modern computer systems, it takes the form of an electronic database into which journal entries are entered and stored. This provides much greater flexibility than a manual system, since the information can be reorganized and reported at will. Computer-based accounting systems often still generate the journal, which is the listing of all journal entries in chronological order.

Figure 4.6 illustrates Schwittay Consulting AG's transactions as they would appear in the journal.

FIGURE 4.6 SCHWITTAY'S JOURNAL

Date	Account Titles	DR	CR
	Schwittay Consulting AG Journal € (Euros)		
1 Feb. 2009	Cash	20 000	
	Contributed capital		20 000
1 Feb. 2009	Cash	150 000	
	Loan payable		150 000
3 Feb. 2009	Prepaid rent	29 700	
	Cash		29 700
3 Feb. 2009	Leasehold improvements	69 000	
	Cash		23 000
	Note payable		46 000
7 Feb. 2009	Prepaid insurance	12 060	
	Cash		12 060
15 Feb. 2009	Cash	201 000	
	Unearned service revenue		201 000
16 Feb. 2009	Cash	13 500	
	Service revenue		13 500
20 Feb. 2009	Supplies	3 350	
	Trade accounts payable		3 350
23 Feb. 2009	Note payable	23 000	
	Cash		23 000
28 Feb. 2009	Trade accounts payable	3 350	
	Cash		3 350
28 Feb. 2009	Cash	1 250	
	Interest revenue		1 250

ON YOUR OWN

LEARNING OUTCOME REVIEW

1. Describe the journal.
2. What information is available in the journal?
3. What is the journal most likely to be used for?

LEARNING OUTCOME 7
DESCRIBE THE LEDGER AND EXPLAIN ITS ROLE IN THE ACCOUNTING PROCESS

The second report (see Figure 4.1) is the ledger. A ledger summarizes the information that has already been entered into the journal by account titles. This is because the chronological information provided by the journal is of limited usefulness for knowing the total amount in an account. For example, if you wanted to know how much cash the business has, you would check the balance in the cash ledger account. The journal would not be of much assistance since you would need to review all entries on all dates to calculate the cash balance.

We post debits and credits from the journal to the ledger. In manual systems, this is a physical process. The ledger is a second set of records in which each account has a separate page. As you might imagine, manually posting debits and credits was time consuming, cumbersome and error prone. Computer-based accounting systems make the process of generating a ledger far easier by simply reformatting the information already entered into the journal database into a ledger format.

We now take each line item in Schwittay's journal (Figure 4.6) and post it to the ledger, reorganizing all information and subtotalling it by account title. The ledger accounts at the end of February are shown in Figure 4.7.

FIGURE 4.7 SCHWITTAY'S LEDGER

Schwittay Consulting AG Ledger 28 February 2009 € (Euros)		
Date	DR	CR
SERVICE REVENUE		
Beginning balance, 1 Feb. 2009		0
16 Feb. 2009		13 500
Ending balance, 28 Feb. 2009		13 500
INTEREST REVENUE		
Beginning balance, 1 Feb. 2009		0
28 Feb. 2009		1 250
Ending balance, 28 Feb. 2009		1 250

SALARIES EXPENSE		
Beginning balance, 1 Feb. 2009	0	
Ending balance, 28 Feb. 2009	0	
INTEREST EXPENSE		
Beginning balance, 1 Feb. 2009	0	
Ending balance, 28 Feb. 2009	0	
RENT EXPENSE		
Beginning balance, 2. Feb. 2009	0	
Ending balance, 28 Feb. 2009	0	
SUPPLIES EXPENSE		
Beginning balance, 1 Feb. 2009	0	
Ending balance, 28 Feb. 2009	0	
INSURANCE EXPENSE		
Beginning balance, 1 Feb. 2009	0	
Ending balance, 28 Feb. 2009	0	
IMPROVEMENTS AMORTIZATION		
Beginning balance, 1 Feb. 2009	0	
Ending balance, 28 Feb. 2009	0	
CASH		
Beginning balance, 2 Feb. 2009	0	
2 Feb. 2009	20 000	
2 Feb. 2009	150 000	
3 Feb. 2009		29 700
3 Feb. 2009		23 000
7 Feb. 2009		12 060
15 Feb. 2009	201 000	
16 Feb. 2009	13 500	
23 Feb. 2009		23 000
28 Feb. 2009		3 350
28 Feb. 2009	1 250	
Ending balance, 28 Feb. 2009	294 640	

(*Continued*)

FIGURE 4.7 *(CONTINUED)*

Date	DR	CR
Schwittay Consulting AG Ledger 28 February 2009 € Euros		
TRADE ACCOUNTS RECEIVABLE		
Beginning balance, 2 Feb. 2009	0	
Ending balance, 28 Feb. 2009	0	
SUPPLIES		
Beginning balance, 2 Feb. 2009	0	
20 Feb. 2009	3 350	
Ending balance, 28 Feb. 2009	3 350	
PREPAID RENT		
Beginning balance, 2 Feb. 2009	0	
3 Feb. 2009	29 700	
Ending balance, 28 Feb. 2009	29 700	
PREPAID INSURANCE		
Beginning balance, 2 Feb. 2009		
7 Feb. 2009	12 060	
Ending balance, 28 Feb. 2009	12 060	
LEASEHOLD IMPROVEMENTS		
Beginning balance, 2 Feb. 2009		0
3 Feb. 2009	69 000	
Ending balance, 28 Feb. 2009	69 000	
TRADE ACCOUNTS PAYABLE		
Beginning balance, 2 Feb. 2009		
3 Feb. 2009		46 000
20 Feb. 2009		3 350
23 Feb. 2009	23 000	
28 Feb. 2009	3 350	
Ending balance, 28 Feb. 2009		23 000

SALARIES PAYABLE		
Beginning balance, 2 Feb. 2009		0
Ending balance, 28 Feb. 2009		0

INTEREST PAYABLE		
Beginning balance, 2 Feb. 2009		0
Ending balance, 28 Feb. 2009		0

UNEARNED SERVICE REVENUE		
Beginning balance, 2 Feb. 2009		
15 Feb. 2009		201 000
Ending balance, 28 Feb. 2009		201 000

LOAN PAYABLE		
Beginning balance, 2 Feb. 2009		0
2 Feb. 2009		150 000
Ending balance, 28 Feb. 2009		150 000

SHARE CAPITAL		
Beginning balance, 2 Feb. 2009		0
2 Feb. 2009		20 000
Ending balance, 28 Feb. 2009		20 000

RETAINED EARNINGS		
Beginning balance, 2 Feb. 2009		0
Ending balance, 28 Feb. 2009		0

DIVIDENDS		
Beginning balance, 2 Feb. 2009		0
Ending balance, 28 Feb. 2009		0

At this point, we can begin to ask some interesting questions about the business:

Question: What amount of services did Schwittay Consulting AG sell in February?
Answer: €13 500, which is the ending balance from the service revenue account.

Question: How much have the owners invested in the business?
Answer: €20 000, which is the ending balance in the contributed capital account.

Question: What amount of supplies is on hand?
Answer: €3350, which is the ending balance in the supplies account.

Question: How much cash does the company have on hand?
Answer: €294 640, which is the ending balance in the cash account.

A ledger contains the detail in each account, and thus is a complete record of all transactions that have affected that account. Notice, for example, that Schwittay ends the month with €294 640 in cash. We can see from the detail in the cash ledger account that ten different transactions affected this balance, either increasing (debits) or decreasing (credits) the balance.

Some accounts from the chart of accounts were not affected because no journal entries were recorded during the period, for example salaries expense. In others like supplies, only one entry has been posted so the ending balance in the account reflects only that entry.

A ledger account has a net debit balance when the total debits are greater than total credits, and a net credit balance when total credits are greater than total debits. Only one total is calculated for the account – debit or credit – depending on which is appropriate.

> **DEBITS > CREDITS = NET DEBIT BALANCE**

> **DEBITS < CREDITS = NET CREDIT BALANCE**

ON YOUR OWN

LEARNING OUTCOME REVIEW

1. What is a ledger?
2. What information is available in a ledger?
3. The ledger account for trade accounts receivable has a beginning balance of €1113. The following debits are posted during the month: €125, €517 and €362. The following credits are posted during the month: €600 and €744. What is the ending balance in the trade receivables account?
4. The ledger account for trade accounts payable has a beginning balance of €1113. The following debits are posted during the month: €125, €517 and €362. The following credits are posted during the month: €600 and €744. What is the ending balance in the trade receivables account?

LEARNING OUTCOME 8
DESCRIBE THE TRIAL BALANCE AND EXPLAIN ITS ROLE IN THE ACCOUNTING PROCESS

The third report is the trial balance. The trial balance is a listing of all ledger accounts and the net balance in each account. Like the ledger, the trial balance is generated as a report from the journal entries database. Figure 4.8 shows the trial balance for Schwittay Consulting for the month of February 2009.

FIGURE 4.8 SCHWITTAY'S TRIAL BALANCE

Schwittay Consulting AG Trial Balance 28 February 2009 € (Euros)		
Account Titles	DR	CR
Service revenue		13 500
Interest revenue		1 250
Salaries expense		
Rent expense		
Supplies expense		
Interest expense		
Cash	294 640	
Trade accounts receivable		
Supplies	3 350	
Prepaid rent	29 700	
Prepaid insurance	12 060	
Leasehold improvements	69 000	
Trade accounts payable		23 000
Interest payable		
Unearned service revenue		201 000
Loan payable		150 000
Contributed capital		20 000
Retained earnings		
Dividends		
	408 750	408 750

Notice first that only the net balance in each ledger account is shown in the trial balance. When the debit and credit columns for the entire trial balance are added, the totals for each must equal the other – in this case €408 750. In manual accounting systems, this was important because it helped confirm that journal entries were posted to the ledger correctly. However, computer-based accounting systems have eliminated the need for this cross-check. The trial balance is now typically used by management to informally review the balances and prepare for the next step, which is to make adjusting entries. Notice also the difference between a chart of accounts and a trial balance. Both contain a list of account titles, but the trial balance also has the net balance in each account.

Trial balance errors

In manual accounting systems, the process of recording journal entries in the journal, then posting to the ledger and tallying totals in individual accounts, was error prone. It was also time consuming and frustrating to find the source of an error once it was discovered and to make corrections. Automated accounting systems have virtually eliminated this need for error checking. Nonetheless, professional accounting exams sometimes ask questions related to how the trial balance aids with error detection and correction.

For example, if one side of a journal entry is omitted (referred to as an error of single entry), then the debt and credit totals in the trial balance will not be equal. Or if the credit side of the journal entry is mistakenly posted as a debit (also an error of single entry), this too would cause the debit and credit totals to be unequal.

Another common error is the transposition of digits within an amount (an error of transposition). For example, a journal entry debits cash and credits trade accounts receivable for €875, except that the debit is mistakenly recorded for €857, and the credit is recorded correctly. This too would cause an out-of-balance condition.

Where the trial balance will not be of any assistance is when a journal entry is mistakenly omitted (an error of omission) or entered twice (an error of commission). In both these instances, the debit–credit equality would be maintained in the trial balance and no indication that a problem exists would be evident.

ON YOUR OWN

LEARNING REVIEW POINTS

1. What is a trial balance? What purpose does a trial balance serve in a manual system?
2. Explain the difference between a trial balance and a ledger.

LEARNING OUTCOME 9
EXPLAIN NORMAL BALANCES AND DESCRIBE HOW NORMAL BALANCES ARE USED TO ANALYSE ACCOUNTING INFORMATION

In the analysis of accounts, you may already have noticed that a debit always *increases* an asset and expenses. A debit *decreases* liabilities and revenue. A debit also increases dividends. A credit has the opposite effect. A credit *decreases* an asset and revenue, but *increases* a liability, equity or expense. A credit also decreases dividends.

Each element on the statement of financial position and the statement of comprehensive income has a 'normal balance', which is a debit or credit depending on the element. The elements and the normal balances are shown in Figure 4.9.

FIGURE 4.9 NORMAL BALANCES BY ELEMENT

Category	Normal balance
Revenue	Credit
Expenses	Debit
Profit	Credit
Loss	Debit
Assets	Debit
Liabilities	Credit
Equity	Credit
Dividend	Debit

Notice in Figure 4.9 that dividends also have a debit normal balance. A balance is normal debit if a debit increases the account balance and normal credit if a credit increases the account balance. This can be summarized as follows:

NORMAL DEBIT BALANCE IS INCREASED BY A DEBIT.

NORMAL DEBIT BALANCE IS DECREASED BY A CREDIT.

NORMAL CREDIT BALANCE IS INCREASED BY A CREDIT.

NORMAL CREDIT BALANCE IS DECREASED BY A DEBIT.

In other words, a debit increases a debit and decreases a credit. And a credit increases a credit and decreases a debit. Another way to say this is 'likes increase, opposites decrease'.

This information can be quite useful. If you want to increase revenue, for example, you know that the normal balance for revenue is a credit, and you must therefore credit revenue. For assets, since the normal balance is a debit, assets are increased with a debit. However, if you are selling an asset and therefore want to remove it from the accounting records, you want to decrease the asset account. That means assets must be credited.

Normal balances also help us understand how the statement of comprehensive income and the statement of financial position relate to each other. Recall the expanded accounting equation from Chapter 3. This figure is reproduced in Figure 4.10 but with the normal balances indicated for each component of the equation.

On the first level, we can see the basic accounting equation (assets = liabilities + equity), where assets are normal debit, and equal assets plus liabilities, which are both normal credit. On the next level,

FIGURE 4.10 NORMAL BALANCES IN THE EXPANDED ACCOUNTING EQUATION

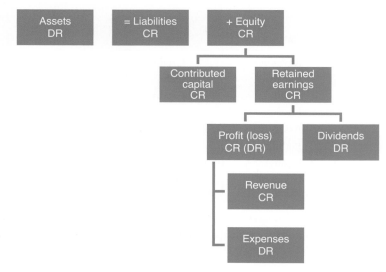

equity is made up of contributed capital and retained earnings, both of which also have a normal credit balance.

On the next level we already know that profit increases retained earnings and dividends decrease retained earnings. Since the retained earnings account is a normal credit balance, profit would also be a credit. If a business has a loss that would be a net debit balance, which would decrease retained earnings. However, dividends are increased by a debit, since dividends is a normal debit balance, although that debit will decrease retained earnings.

Using the same logic, a credit that increases revenue (normal credit) would increase profit (normal credit), which in turn increases retained earnings (normal credit), which increases equity (normal credit). But a debit that increases dividends (normal debit) decreases net income (normal credit), which decreases retained earnings (normal credit), which decreases equity (normal credit).

WHAT TO LOOK OUT FOR

Multiple-choice questions can be confusing when you are asked what the effect of a particular transaction will be on an account balance. Try this: in the margin of the exam paper, record the journal entry that the question refers to and then read the correct answer from your journal entry. As an example, consider the following multiple-choice question adapted from one of the ACCA professional accounting exam items:

Which of the following is the correct journal entry to record a cash purchase of supplies for $300 from Fuji?

    a. Debit Supplies $300   Credit Fuji $300
    b. Debit Fuji $300   Credit Supplies $300
    c. Debit Supplies $300   Credit Cash $300
    d. Debit Cash $300   Credit Supplies $300

In the margin, you would make the following journal entry:

Account Titles	DR	CR
Supplies	$300	
Cash		$300

It's easy to see that the debit is supplies and the credit is cash. All that remains to do is select the correct answer, which is c.

ON YOUR OWN

LEARNING OUTCOME REVIEW
1. Which financial statement elements have a normal debit balance?
2. Which financial statement elements have a normal credit balance?

Conclusion

Business entities account for business transactions. During a reporting period, these transactions are analysed and then, if appropriate, recorded in the journal. The information to record the transaction is taken from a source document, which provides evidence that a valid transaction has occurred.

When the reporting period is ended and all transactions have been recorded, three reports are available: the journal, which provides a chronological history of all recorded transactions; the ledger, which summarizes the journal detail by account; and the trial balance, which provides a summary of the net debit or credit balance in each account.

In the next chapter, we will examine the remainder of the accounting process. The next step is to adjust ledger accounts to convert them to the accrual basis of accounting. Afterwards, an adjusted trial balance is generated, which is used to prepare the financial statements. The last step in the accounting process is to close temporary accounts and make them ready to record transactions for the subsequent reporting period.

When transactions are recorded they change the financial statements in different ways. This is an important issue for managers and external users. The reason is that the amounts reported on the financial statements of a publicly traded business can affect its share price. For example, a higher profit may cause the share price to trade at a higher amount on the stock exchange.

Also, in some cases management compensation depends on share price. The higher the profit or share price, the more compensation managers will receive. The reason for this arrangement is to motivate managers to achieve better performance. The result is that publicly traded companies are under considerable pressure from investors and others to report higher earnings. As a result, the temptation for managers to record a transaction erroneously can be great.

Summary

LEARNING OUTCOME 1
Accounting Process Described

The accounting process has four major steps: analyse and record transactions, adjust accounts, prepare financial statements and close accounts. In this chapter, only the first step has been described.

LEARNING OUTCOME 2
Transactions Analysis Explained

The accounting process begins when a transaction between the business entity and another entity occurs. Evidence of the transaction comes from a source document, which can be either hard copy or soft copy. Each transaction is analysed to determine whether it should be recorded; promise-for-promise transactions are typically not recorded. If the transaction is to be recorded, then it is further analysed to determine what has been received by the business and what has been given, coded as debits and credits respectively.

LEARNING OUTCOME 3
Transactions Recorded

Throughout the reporting period, the task of recording transactions continues. Once all transactions for the reporting period have been recorded, the accounting process is ready to begin the second step, which is adjusting entries. However, before the adjusting entries are made, three interim reports are normally available: the journal, the ledger and the trial balance.

LEARNING OUTCOME 4
Source Documents Explained

Transactions are recorded from hard copy or electronic source documents that provide evidence that the transaction is valid.

LEARNING OUTCOME 5
Journal Entries Constructed

A journal entry codes transaction information into a form that can be processed by the accounting system. Each journal entry has four components. The first is the date, which must be accurate in order for the transaction to be included in the appropriate reporting period. Second is the account titles, which determine the financial statements that will be affected. The choice of account titles comes from the chart of accounts. The third component is the amounts of the debits and credits. Debits and credits must be equal in each journal entry. The fourth component is the explanation of the journal entry.

LEARNING OUTCOME 6
Journal Explained

The journal is sometimes referred to as the books of original or prime entry. Journal entries are recorded in the journal in chronological order. The journal serves three functions. First, it provides a historical record of business transactions. Second, the information is posted to the ledger and thus ledger accounts are constructed from debits and credits recorded in the journal.

Third, the journal cross-references the source document from which the transaction information was taken. Thus, an accountant who wishes to verify that the correct amount was charged to a customer might look up the transaction in the customer's account in the ledger, from that identify the transaction of interest, then find the transaction recorded in the journal. From this, the accountant could then determine the source document that he or she needs to consult in order to answer the question.

LEARNING OUTCOME 7
Ledger Explained

After journal entries have been entered into the journal, debits and credits are then posted to the ledger. The ledger is organized in account title order. Each ledger account contains the details of all journal entries that have affected that account and the current balance in the account. The ledger is the primary source of information about accounts.

LEARNING OUTCOME 8
Trial Balance Explained

The trial balance is a list of all account titles as of a particular date, with the net debit or credit balance in each account. In manual accounting systems, the trial balance served an important purpose, which was ensuring that journal entries were recorded and posted correctly (although the trial balance cannot identify all errors). Modern computer-based accounting systems have rendered this error-identification function largely obsolete since the computer now handles posting. However, many businesses still use trial balances as a 'draft' of the financial statements before their actual preparation.

LEARNING OUTCOME 9
Normal Balances Explained

Each financial statement element has either a normal debit or normal credit amount. Assets, expenses and dividends have normal debit balances. Revenue, liabilities and equity accounts have normal credit balances.

REVIEW QUESTIONS

1. What is a source document? Give examples. Why is a source document important?
2. Describe the accounting process, listing all steps and reports generated at each stage.
3. How is a transaction analysed and then recorded as a journal entry? What are the components of a journal entry?
4. What is the chart of accounts? Why do companies create and maintain a formal chart of accounts?
5. What is the difference between a journal, a ledger and a trial balance? Describe what each contains and how it is organized. What purpose does each serve in the accounting process?
6. At what stage in the accounting process are the financial statements prepared? Where is the information to generate the financial statements obtained?
7. What is a normal balance? What is the normal balance of revenues? Expenses? Profit? Loss? Assets? Liabilities? Equity? Dividends?

Key terms

Adjusted trial balance

Adjusting entries

Chart of accounts

Closing entries

Credit (CR)

Debit (DR)

Journal

Journal entry

Ledger

Normal balance

Post-closing trial balance

Posting

Record

Source document

Trial balance

Terminology practice

For each of the following statements, insert the correct term from the preceding list of key terms. Each key term can be used more than once.

1. Transactions are recorded in the _____ based on information from a _____.
2. A _____ is a formal list of account titles authorized by the business entity.
3. Debits and credits are summarized by account titles by _____ to the _____.
4. The _____ is a method accounting uses to code a _____.
5. What is given in transaction is recorded as a _____ while what is received is recorded as a _____.
6. When rent has been paid but not used it is referred to as _____ which is an asset on the statement of financial position.
7. A listing of accounts with the net balances of each is the _____.

Application exercises

1. What is the journal entry on 21 November 2013 to record payment of £10 000 by a client for work that had been completed in the previous accounting period?
2. What is the journal entry on 21 November 2013 to record payment of £10 000 by a client for work that had been completed in November but for which the revenue has already been recognized?
3. What is the journal entry on 21 November 2013 to record payment of £10 000 by a client for work that had been completed in November but for which the revenue has not already been recognized?
4. Jeffrey's trial balance at 30 September 2010 is shown below. [ACCA adapted]

	DR	CR
Capital at 1 October 2009		$32 285
Inventory at 1 October 2009	$12 560	
Trade accounts receivable	12 880	
Trade accounts payable		6 561
Cash	4 754	
Sales		90 935
Purchases	72 674	
Carriage inwards	974	
Wages	4 684	
Rent	3 200	
Stationery	3 200	
Travel	749	
Telephone	853	
General expenses	753	
Dividends	12 500	
	129 781	**129 781**

The value of Jeffrey's inventory at 30 September 2010 was $11 875.

Jeffrey has discovered the following errors in the postings:

   (i)   An invoice for carriage inwards was posted to the rent account. The invoice was for $264.
   (ii) A credit sale invoice for $560 was posted as $650.
   (iii) The telephone bill for 30 September 2010 has not been included. The bill is for $297.

Required:

   (a) Indicate which of the balances in the trial balance will be changed by the correction of the errors, and calculate the corrected balances.
   (b) Based on the corrected trial balance, calculate the gross profit and the profit for the year to 30 September 2010.

Case analysis
Li Designs LLC

Mai Li is a talented graphic designer and Rick's good friend. After university, Rick went to work for a medium-sized accounting firm and Mai went to work for a large, respected design firm. On 1 April 2010, after only six months on the job, Mai left and began her own design business. Several clients had expressed an interest in working with her directly and promised to follow her if she formed her own firm, which she named Li Designs LLC.

The business grew rapidly. In three short months, she rented loft office space in London, hired four employees and bought office and computer equipment. There have been some travel expenses as she and employees went to meet clients and discuss projects. Mai and her new employees have been spending long hours in the office to handle the workload and to deal with new clients wanting to use the firm's services. Everything happened very quickly and now she is having difficulty.

Mai calls her friend Rick and asks if he can meet her for coffee. The next day they get together and, once they have caught up on all that's been happening, Rick asks Mai what the problem is. She is clearly worried. The bank has called, says Mai, to tell her that the business account is overdrawn. She does not know what has happened to the money. She invested £5000 into the business, her meagre savings, and her parents invested another £5000. Their conversation continues as follows.

Mai: 'I thought I was doing so well. I have been busy working, working. Now the rent on the loft and salaries are due and I don't even have the money. When I paid my employees the other day, their cheques were returned for lack of sufficient funds. One quit! I was so embarrassed! I need him to help me with an important assignment. He says he will come back but he has bills to pay and must have his cheque on time. I don't know what to do!

'What is worse now is that my Aunt Ni has already lent me £7000. That's a fortune for her. She is not a wealthy woman but she believes in what I am doing. Yet even with that money, I can barely make ends meet. And I am not getting any profit to live on. I took some money from the business just to meet my personal expenses, but I cannot continue to work with no money.'

Rick: 'Mai, aren't you charging your clients enough money to cover your expenses and make a profit?'

Mai: 'Yes, of course! They like my work. They will pay me a lot of money, which is why I left the company I worked for. I wish now I hadn't left.'

Rick: 'What do you mean, your clients will pay you a lot of money? Aren't they paying you now?'

Mai: 'Yes. I mean, no. Yes and no. Some have paid. Some have agreed to pay. Some have paid me in advance. Others will pay as we complete the work. We have completed some, but everything is so confused that I cannot figure out how much they owe. They say I must send them an invoice to be paid. Frankly, I have no idea who owes me what. I cannot tell my customers that. What is worse is that I owe money to people the business buys supplies from. Some say I must pay cash or they will not sell to us.'

Rick: 'Mai, tell me something. Why did you write pay cheques to your employees if you did not have enough money in the bank?'

Mai: 'I had enough money! I called the bank that morning and asked how much money was in the account. There was not a lot, but enough for the cheques.'

Rick: 'You called the bank that morning? Mai, do you reconcile your bank account each month?'

Mai: 'What? What is reconcile? I'm a graphic artist and that's what I spend my time doing – being creative for my clients. I don't have time to reconcile accounts, whatever that is.'

Rick: 'Ah. I think I'm beginning to see the problem. Tell me, Mai, what else is bothering you?'

Mai: 'A big problem. One of my clients wants me to do the design work for a major new product. It's such an opportunity. But I need to buy four new computers and other equipment, which will be expensive. I need to hire new people. I need to travel to see this client too. I don't have the money to do these things. I cannot go back to my family for more money. So I went to the bank and asked if I could borrow some money.'

Rick: 'What did the bank say?'

Mai: 'They said that it is possible but I must give them financial statements on the business. Rick, what are financial statements?'

Rick: 'Well, I guess you will soon find out. Mai, do you have all the financial records of the business, such as the statements sent by the bank each month, invoices from suppliers, receipts from purchases, bills to clients and all that?'

Mai: 'I don't know. Any paper I get I put into cardboard boxes in the back office. There are a lot of boxes.'

Rick: 'I see. OK, here's what we're going to do. Let's go to the office and I'll take the boxes and start sorting through them and figuring things out. Let's first work out how much money you have and where you stand. Then we will prepare your financial statements so you can get the loan and start that assignment.'

After Rick leaves the café, he thinks back to their college days. Mai was never particularly interested in money. It seems to Rick that she was always trying to figure out how to pay her tuition fees at university. When he gets back to his office with the boxes full of Mai's financial records, he begins to sort through them. Nothing is filed. Everything has merely been tossed into the boxes, just as Mai said.

Mai is his best friend and she's very talented. He's determined to help her in any way he can. So Rick picks up the phone and calls you. You are his new junior employee. He asks you to go through the boxes, put things in order, and set up Li Design LLC's accounting records.

Mai's Cardboard Boxes

After sorting through Mai's boxes, you sort all the paperwork into two stacks, both shown in the case appendix. The first contains Li Designs LLC's bank statements since Mai opened the business. The second includes all other source documents.

Rick's Follow-up Discussion with Mai

Because you want to be sure of the information and because some information is missing, you ask Rick to call Mai to verify some issues. Here are the notes from their discussion:

1. Mai received share capital for the money she invested in Li Designs LLC.
2. Qing and John Li are Mai's parents. They invested in the company and also received share capital.
3. Worthington Clothiers, Thames Holdings LLC and Rawashdeh Hoteliers are clients. All advances from clients are recognized evenly over the time that Li Designs works on the project. The terms are in the client agreements. All work on client projects has been completed on time.
4. The £6300 cheque to Whitehall Properties represents £2100 for a deposit for the loft office, which will be refunded at the end of the three-year lease term. Another £2100 is for the first month's rent and the remaining £2100 is for the last month's rent at the end of the lease. Mai says that she has lost the copy of the lease that the landlord provided to her.
5. Office furniture is expected to last for three years and to have no value at the end of that time. The Dell computer is expected to last two years with no value at the end.
6. Marvin Wycherly, Jane Foo, Tom Johnson and David Weeks are contract employees. Taxes and other deductions are not subtracted from their pay.
7. All payments to MasterCard are for travel expenses.
8. Massey Insurance provides liability insurance to businesses. In this case, Li Designs was required by the landlord, Worthington Properties, to have insurance on the contents of the office as well as accident insurance if, for example, an employee or visitor injured themselves.
9. The £1300 commission paid on June 4 was an administrative expense related to recruiting employees.
10. Mai said that the company had completed a rush project for a client (Evangello of Santorini) on 30 June. The work was done on an oral agreement but it has been completed and a bill demanding payment of £26 000 was recently sent to the client, who is expected to pay in a week or so. The client paid a £5000 advance on 25 May.

After reviewing the documents that Mai has accumulated and you have sorted, Rick first created a chart of accounts for Li Designs LLC.

Li Designs LLC Chart Of Accounts	
Category	Account Title
Revenue	Service revenue
Expenses	Salaries and wages expense
	Rent expense
	Supplies expense
	Travel expense
	Insurance expense

	Administrative expense
	Office maintenance expense
	Depreciation expense
	Interest expense
	Bank service expenses
Assets	Cash
	Trade accounts receivable
	Supplies
	Prepaid insurance
	Prepaid rent
	Travel advances
	Improvement
	Equipment
	Accumulated depreciation – equipment
Liabilities	Trade accounts payable
	Salaries and wages payable
	Notes payable
	Unearned service revenue
Equity	Share capital
	Retained earnings

Rick decides that his goal is to create a current set of financial statements so that Mai can determine exactly where the business stands and so that she can give them to the bank to enable her to borrow the money she needs to continue operations.

Required: Record all journal entries based on the information contained in the source documents in the cardboard box. Then post your journal entries to the ledger and create a trial balance.

Bank Statements

City Bank of London *Bank Statement for Li Design LLC* *30 April 2010*		
Date	Deposit/Payee	Amount
	Beginning balance	£0
09 Apr	Deposit – Mai Li	5 000
09 Apr	Deposit – Qing and John Li	5 000

(Continued)

Date	Deposit/Payee	Amount
10 Apr	Deposit – Advance from Worthington Clothiers	12 000
14 Apr	Cheque – Whitehall Properties	−6 300
17 Apr	Cheque – Brooks Office Furnishings LLC	−9 540
20 Apr	Deposit – Thames Holdings LLC	13 400
22 Apr	Cheque – Marvin Wycherly	−512
25 Apr	Knightsbridge Stationery	−1 033
28 Apr	Dell Corporation	−2 640
29 Apr	Cheque – Marvin Wycherly	−512
30 Apr	Cheque – MasterCard	−200
30 Apr	Bank service charge	−11
	Ending balance	14 652

	City Bank of London *Bank Statement for Li Design LLC* *31 May 2010*	
Date	Deposit/Payee	Amount
	Beginning balance	14 652
01 May	Cheque – Whitehall Properties	−2 100
03 May	Cheque – Knightsbridge Stationery	−474
06 May	Cheque – Marvin Wycherly	−512
06 May	Cheque – Jane Foo	−730
07 May	London Computer Supplies	−244
10 May	Deposit – Rawashdeh Hotelier	5 000
11 May	Cheque – Aces Office Maintenance	−130
13 May	Cheque – Marvin Wycherly	−512
13 May	Cheque – Jane Foo	−730
18 May	Cheque – Chelsea Computer Supplies	−245
20 May	Cheque – Marvin Wycherly	−512
20 May	Cheque – Jane Foo	−730
21 May	Cheque – Knightsbridge Stationery	−802
25 May	Deposit – Evangellos of Santorini	5 000
25 May	Cheque – Travel advance to Jane Foo	−1 000
27 May	Cheque – Marvin Wycherly	−512
27 May	Cheque – Jane Foo	−730
29 May	Cheque – MasterCard	−800
31 May	Bank service charge	−14
	Ending balance	13 875

Date	Deposit/Payee	Amount
	City Bank of London *Bank Statement* *for Li Design LLC* *30 June 2010*	
	Beginning balance	13 875
01 Jun	Massey Insurance LLC	−5 400
02 Jun	Whitehall Properties	−2 100
03 Jun	Cheque – Marvin Wycherly	−512
03 Jun	Cheque – Jane Foo	−730
04 Jun	Cheque – Mathias Recruitment Agency	−1 300
10 Jun	Cheque – Marvin Wycherly	−512
10 Jun	Cheque – Jane Foo	−730
10 Jun	Cheque – Tom Johnson	−320
10 Jun	Cheque – David Weeks	−700
11 Jun	Cheque – Aces Office Maintenance	−130
13 Jun	Cheque – Soho Delivery Service	−34
13 Jun	Cheque – Federal Express	−60
17 Jun	Cheque – Marvin Wycherly	−512
17 Jun	Cheque – Jane Foo	−730
17 Jun	Cheque – Tom Johnson	−320
17 Jun	Cheque – David Weeks	−700
18 Jun	Deposit – Ni Li	7 000
20 Jun	Cheque – Knightsbridge Stationery	−1 113
24 Jun	Cheque – Marvin Wycherly	−512
24 Jun	Cheque – Jane Foo	−730
24 Jun	Cheque – Tom Johnson	−320
24 Jun	Cheque – David Weeks	−700
25 Jun	Cheque – Mai Li	−500
29 Jun	Cheque – MasterCard	−700
30 Jun	Cheque – Jane Foo – travel reimbursement	−268
30 Jun	Cheque – London Computer Supplies	−1 320
30 Jun	Insufficient funds charge	−90
30 Jun	Bank service charge	−18
	Ending balance	(186)

Source Documents

Travel Expense Report Jane Foo 30 June 2010	
Item	**Balance**
Airline charges	£520
Hotels	650
Meals	98
Total expenditures	1268
Less advances	(1000)
Amount owed	£268

Supplies Count	
Month	**Ending Balance**
April	£200
May	£770
June	£2040

Li Designs LLC Client Agreement	
Client: Worthington Clothiers	Date: 10 April 2010
Description: Design services for clothing line Total Amount: £36 000 Payment Terms: £12 000 advance with remainder to be paid monthly as work is completed over six months between 1 April and 30 September 2010.	

Invoice *Dell Corporation*	
28 April 2010	
Computer equipment Paid in full	£2640
TOTAL	£2640

Invoice	
Knightsbridge Stationery	
3 May 2010	
Various supplies	£948
Amount paid (reminder on account)	(474)
TOTAL	£474

Invoice	
London Computer Supplies	
30 June 2010	
Supplies	£1320
Paid in full	(1320)
TOTAL	£0

Li Designs LLC	
Client Agreement	
Client: Thomas Holdings LLC	Date: 20 April 2010
Description: Designs for office space Total Amount: £13 400	
Payment Terms: Paid in advance. Half of the work to be completed by 30 May and the remainder by 15 June.	

Invoice	
Brooks Office Furnishings LLC	
17 April 2010	
£9540	Li Designs LLC Office furniture, equipment Paid in full on delivery

Li Designs LLC	
Client Agreement	
Client: Rawashdeh Hoteliers	Date: 10 May 2010
Description: Design for executive suite Total Amount: £7500 Payment Terms: £5000 paid in advance. Work to be completed by 30 May 2010.	

Agreement
Ace Office Maintenance
11 May 2010
Li Designs LLC. Daily cleaning of office £130 monthly Due 11th each month, payable in advance

Purchase Receipt	
Chelsea Computer Supplies	
18 May 2010	
Paper, cartridges Paid in full	
TOTAL	£245

Invoice	
Knightsbridge Stationery	
25 April 2010	
Various supplies Paid in full	£1033
TOTAL	£1033

Invoice *Knightsbridge Stationery*	
21 May 2010	
Various supplies Paid in full	£802
TOTAL	£802

Invoice *Knightsbridge Stationery*	
20 June 2010	
Various supplies Paid in full	£1113
TOTAL	£1113

MasterCard Statement Li Designs LLC 25 April 2010		
Date	Item	Amount
Balance		£0
12 April 2010	British Airways	890
12 April 2010	Rotana Hotels	410
25 April 2010	Finance charge	26
	TOTAL DUE	£1326
	MINIMUM DUE	£200

MasterCard Statement Li Designs LLC 25 May 2010		
Date	Item	Amount
	Balance	£1326
10 May 2010	British Airways	1245
12 May 2010	Marriott Suites	855
13 May 2010	Less: Payments	(200)
25 May 2010	Finance charge	38
	TOTAL DUE	£3264
	MINIMUM DUE	£800

MasterCard Statement Li Designs LLC 25 June 2010		
Date	Item	Amount
10 June 2010 25 June 2010	Balance Less: Payments Finance charge	£3264 (800) 29
	TOTAL DUE MINIMUM DUE	£2493 £700

Invoice *London Computer Supplies*	
	07 May 2010
Supplies Paid in full	£244 (244)
Amount owed	£0

Accrual and closing

5

LEARNING OUTCOMES

At the completion of this chapter, students should be able to:

1. Describe the difference between cash-basis and accrual accounting.
2. Describe the four types of adjusting entries.
3. Demonstrate how adjusting entries are recorded.
4. Describe the four closing entries and explain the purpose of each.
5. Prepare financial statements using the extended trial balance worksheet.

Introducing shenanigans

Unfortunately, as we have already seen in Chapter 2 on accounting standards and ethics, managers and others sometimes engage in fraud and misrepresentation. Howard Schilit (see Suggested Reading) describes the most common methods, which he calls 'financial shenanigans' and defines as 'actions or omissions intended to hide or distort the real financial performance or financial condition of the entity'.

Some of Schilit's seven shenanigans involve reporting revenue that does not exist or failing to report a liability that does exist.

All other shenanigans involve recording revenue or expenses in the inappropriate reporting period. This includes:

- Recording revenue too soon.
- Shifting current expenses to a later reporting period.

Both of these shenanigans would cause profit to be higher in the current reporting period. However, publicly traded companies in particular are under pressure to demonstrate steady, smooth earnings growth, not just higher growth. Thus management may be tempted to postpone profits inappropriately to a later period if doing so accomplishes this objective. This is commonly done by:

- Shifting current revenue to a later reporting period.
- Shifting future expenses to the current reporting period.

FIGURE 5.1 FOUR SHENANIGANS TO SHIFT PROFIT

	Current Period Profits are Increased by…	Current Period Profits are Decreased by…
Revenue	Shifting future revenue to current reporting period	Shifting current revenue to future reporting period
Expenses	Shifting current expenses to future reporting period	Shifting future expenses to current reporting period
Impact on current reporting period's profit	Overstates profit	Understates profit

Figure 5.1 illustrates these four shenanigans.

Notice that when profit is shifted to the current period, the current reporting period's profit is overstated. When profit is shifted to a future period, current profit in the current reporting period is understated. Over time, profit may be the same because all revenue and expenses are classified into the statement of comprehensive income. But revenue, expenses and profits *for any given reporting period* are incorrectly reported.

Whether revenue and expenses are reported in the appropriate period is not only an issue for fraud and misrepresentation, it prevents users from having a full understanding of the business's performance over time. Consider the following simple example:

Iluh, who lives in Bali, wanted to earn money over the next three months before leaving for university. She observed that tourists on the beach near her home liked fresh fruit. So Iluh began to go to the local market early in the morning and purchase papayas and mangoes to sell on the beach. Business was brisk.

The first month she used some savings to buy a folding table for 2400 IDR (Indonesian rupiahs) to sell from on the beach. Business seemed good during the first month, but the sun was hot, so Iluh bought an umbrella the second month for 1600 IDR. She also bought a folding chair for 600 IDR and a cooler for ice to keep the fruit cool for 400 IDR.

At the end of the three months, just before she left for university, Iluh sold all the equipment she had purchased for 4000 IDR to a neighbour who wanted to continue the business – 1800 IDR for the folding table and the other 2200 for the equipment acquired in the second month.

If we account for Iluh's business over the three months on the basis of the cash she received for selling fruit less the cash she paid for acquiring the fruit and the equipment, the calculation of her income (in Indonesian rupiahs) would be as follows:

	First Month	Second Month	Third Month	Three-Month Total
Revenue	6 000	10 000	20 000	36 000
Cost of fruit	(4 000)	(6 000)	(12 000)	(22 000)
Cost of folding table	(2 400)	0	0	(2 400)
Cost of other equipment	0	(3 000)	0	(3 000)
Sale of equipment	0	0	4 000	4 000
Totals	(400)	1 000	12 000	12 600

These amounts show that Iluh had a loss for the first month, which would not have been very encouraging. Even during the second month she only earned 1000 IDR, which was not much profit for her efforts. But in the final month her profit increased substantially to 12 000. Part of this income was due to the 4000 IDR sale of equipment to Maria, her neighbour who wanted to continue the business.

Iluh made a total income of 12 600 IDR over the summer. However, had she used accrual accounting her reported results each month would have been different, and perhaps more encouraging in the first and second months. Accrual accounting records the effects of transactions when they occur rather than when cash is received or paid. Under accrual accounting, Iluh's profit statement would have been:

	First Month	Second Month	Third Month	Three-Month Total
Revenue	6 000	10 000	20 000	36 000
Cost of fruit	(4 000)	(6 000)	(12 000)	(22 000)
Cost of folding table	(200)	(200)	(200)	(600)
Cost of other equipment	0	(400)	(400)	(800)
Totals	1 800	3 400	7 400	12 600

The cost of the folding table was originally 2400 IDR and she received 1800 IDR when she sold it to Maria. That means that only 600 IDR (2400 IDR – 1800 IDR) of the asset cost was consumed. When this amount is allocated over the three months, the cost of the folding table for each month was 200 IDR (600 IDR ÷ 3 months). If we calculate the other equipment, then Iluh consumed only 800 IDR (3000 IDR – 2200 IDR). This would be allocated to the second and third months only since it was not acquired until the second month. So the amount for each of these two months would be 400 IDR.

Notice that the 4000 IDR sale of the equipment is not included in this schedule. That is because it has already been calculated into the allocated cost of the folding table and other equipment. In other words, the schedule includes only that portion of the cost that expired. But also notice that the total profit over all three months is the same (last column on the right), at 12 600 IDR. The difference is that the pattern of the profit is reported differently. Now, in the first month the schedule shows a profit and this increases in the second and third month. Why does the equipment cost allocation approach provide a better method of accounting? The answer is that the cost of the equipment is now matched to the sales revenue that it helped generate.

This matching of revenue and costs to the period affected is accrual accounting. Recall from Chapter 2 that businesses are required to use accrual accounting. Accrual accounting means that the transaction is recorded in the reporting period in which it occurs, not when cash is received or paid.

LEARNING OUTCOME 1
DESCRIBE THE DIFFERENCE BETWEEN CASH-BASIS AND ACCRUAL ACCOUNTING

Although accounting standards require entities to report financial results based on accrual accounting, some businesses continue to use cash-basis accounting. Cash-basis accounting means that revenue is recorded when cash is received and expenses are recorded when cash is paid. The reasons are that the business does not have major trade accounts receivable or payable and few, if any, major assets. Typically, these businesses make only cash sales and pay all expenses in cash.

In these cases accrual accounting would not significantly change the amount of profit reported from period to period when compared to cash-basis accounting. Also, these businesses may be privately held and the owners may not want to incur the additional cost of maintaining accounting records on the accrual basis. However, if a business is publicly held or seeks major loan financing from a creditor such as a bank, accrual accounting must be used.

Consider this example, which compares journal entries made under cash-basis versus accrual accounting.

Esposito Bakery purchases a delivery van for £15 000 cash on 1 July 2009. The journal entry using cash-basis accounting would be:

Date	Account Titles	DR	CR
1 July 2009	Delivery van expense Cash	€15 000	€15 000

Notice that the debit is recorded in Delivery van expense, which appears on the statement of comprehensive income. No part of the cost is allocated to future reporting periods, which are also expected to benefit from the use of the van. However, if this entry had been made under accrual accounting, it would have been:

Date	Account Titles	DR	CR
1 July 2009	Equipment – Delivery van	€15 000	
	Cash		€15 000

This accrual entry records the delivery van's cost in the statement of financial position which means that it is expected to have benefits for future periods.

Let's expand the last example to demonstrate accrual accounting further by examining three senarios related to supplies. Suppose Esposito buys supplies for €500 cash on 27 December 2009. The business takes delivery of the supplies, which are used immediately for a project that is currently in progress. That means that on 31 December 2009 the supplies have no future relevance to the business. In this scenario, Esposito would debit Supplies expense, which appears on the statement of comprehensive income:

Date	Account Titles	DR	CR
27 Dec. 2009	Supplies expense	€500	
	Cash		€500

In the second senario, suppose that instead of using the supplies immediately, the business puts the supplies in storage for future use. When the business takes delivery of the supplies, it is not clear when the supplies will be used. On the reporting date (31 December 2009) the supplies remain unused. In this case, the debit is recorded as Supplies, an asset account that will appear on the statement of financial position.

Date	Account Titles	DR	CR
27 Dec. 2009	Supplies	€500	
	Cash		€500

Now, in the third scenario, suppose that the supplies are received on 27 December 2009, as in the second scenario above. The business does not know when the supplies will be used so they are recorded as Supplies, an asset on the statement of financial position. On 30 December 2009, half the supplies are used for a catering job. The supplies that are used would be classified as Supplies expense on the statement of comprehensive income. Those that remain for future use should be classified as Supplies on the statement of financial position. Therefore, Esposito must make an adjustment to move half of the amount in Supplies to Supplies expense. The entry would be:

Date	Account Titles	DR	CR
29 Dec. 2009	Supplies expense	€250	
	Supplies		€250

Think about how the last scenario would appear in the ledger accounts. When the supplies are acquired, the entry would appear as follows:

Supplies		
Date	DR	CR
27 Dec. 2009	€5 000	

Cash		
Date	DR	CR
27 Dec. 2009		€5 000

Supplies Expense		
Date	DR	CR

On 29 December, when the journal entry is to reclassify half of the supplies into supplies expense, the ledger accounts would be:

Supplies		
Date	DR	CR
27 Dec. 2009	€5 000	
29 Dec. 2009		€2 500
Balance	€2 500	

Cash		
Date	DR	CR
27 Dec. 2009		€5 000

Supplies expense		
Date	DR	CR
29 Dec. 2009	€2 500	
Balance	€2 500	

Notice that the balance in the Supplies account is now a net debit of €2 500. This represents the one-half of the supplies that had been acquired on 27 December that remain on hand at the end of the year that will be consumed in the future. The Supplies Expense account also has a net debit balance of €2 500 but this represents the one-half of the supplies that were consumed in 2009. We say that portion of the cost 'expired' and so therefore it must be 'expensed'.

Graphically, this process of reclassifying supplies from the statement of financial position as they are consumed (or expensed) to the statement of comprehensive income is shown in Figure 5.2.

FIGURE 5.2 EXPENSING SUPPLIES

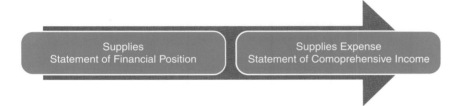

LEARNING OUTCOME 2
DESCRIBE THE FOUR TYPES OF ADJUSTING ENTRIES

2.1 What unrecorded transactions need to be recognized?
    2.1.1 How is unrecorded revenue accrued?
    2.1.2 How are unrecorded expenses accrued?

2.2 What assets and liabilities need to be reclassified to expense and revenue?
    2.2.1 How is unearned revenue recognized as revenue?
    2.2.2 How are prepaid expenses recognized as expenses?

After all transactions for the reporting period have been recorded, the next step is to adjust the accounts. Adjusting entries are journal entries that convert the accounting records to the accrual basis. These can be divided into two categories: those that relate to the *recognition* of previously unrecorded items; and those that had previously been recognized as unearned revenue (liabilities) or a prepaid expense (asset), which now need to be *reclassified* as revenue and expense respectively. Each category has two items each – one related to revenue and the other to expense. Together these represent four types of adjusting entries, as depicted in Figure 5.3.

FIGURE 5.3 FOUR TYPES OF ADJUSTING ENTRIES

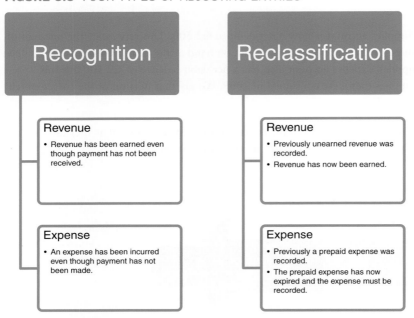

In this section we will examine each of these four types of adjusting entries.

2.1 What unrecorded transactions need to be recognized?

Two of the four adjusting entries are required because situations arise at the end of the reporting period in which transactions that should be recognized have not been recognized. One of these adjusting entries is related to unrecorded revenue and the second to unrecorded expenses.

2.1.1 HOW IS UNRECORDED REVENUE ACCRUED?

Suppose that Esposito Bakery is preparing financial reports at the end of the second quarter 2009. As sales were made throughout the period, journal entries were recorded. However, while making adjustments the accountant asks the owner if any additional sales should be recorded for the period.

The owner responds that a customer came into the store on 30 June and bought a number of pastries for a late afternoon business meeting. Because this was a repeat customer, the bakery allowed him to charge the items and pay later. He spent €75 and took the pastries with him.

In this case, the bakery is entitled to recognize the revenue in the current reporting period because the transaction occurred on 30 June. Therefore, an adjusting entry must be made to accrue the revenue:

Date	Account Titles	DR	CR
30 June 2009	Trade accounts receivable Service revenue	€75	€75

Why is this journal entry an adjustment instead of a routine entry to record the sale? There is no difference in the form of the journal entry. However, it may take time for a business to process all sales entries. Perhaps a company division in Angola has delivered equipment just before the end of the reporting period, but it takes several days for the paperwork to reach the African region accounting office in Cairo. In situations like this, the accounts must be adjusted.

HINT

Adjusting entries *must* meet two criteria:

1. They do *not* involve cash. Business transactions may include cash; adjusting entries may not.
2. Both the statement of comprehensive income and the statement of financial position must be affected. In the example above, service revenue appears on the statement of comprehensive income, and trade accounts receivable on the statement of financial position.

ON YOUR OWN

LEARNING OUTCOME REVIEW

1. Explain the circumstances that create the need to make an adjusting entry to accrue revenue.
2. What are the two tests that an adjusting entry must meet?

LEARNING OUTCOME PRACTICE

1. Able Cleaning Service Ltd prepares financial reports monthly. On 30 July 2009, the supervisor informs the accounting office that he has received a request from a customer, Nestor Almadar, for €550 in cleaning services to be performed on 2 August 2009. The customer will pay for the service when it is completed. What is the appropriate journal entry?

		DR	CR
a.	Trade accounts receivable	550	
	Service revenue		550
b.	Trade accounts receivable	550	
	Unearned revenue		550
c.	Cash	550	
	Service revenue		550
d.	No entry is made		

2. Able Cleaning Service Ltd prepares financial reports monthly. On 30 July 2009, the supervisor informs the accounting office that his crew completed work for a customer, Nestor Almadar, that morning for €550 in cleaning. The customer is to be sent an invoice and will pay in 10 days. What is the appropriate journal entry?

		DR	CR
a.	Trade accounts receivable	550	
	Service revenue		550
b.	Trade accounts receivable	550	
	Unearned revenue		550
c.	Cash	550	
	Service revenue		550
d.	No entry is made		

3. Able Cleaning Service Ltd prepares financial reports monthly. On 30 July 2009, the supervisor informs the accounting office that his crew completed work for a customer, Nestor Almadar, that morning for €550 in cleaning service and that the supervisor has the customer's cheque with him and will bring it to the office at lunchtime. What is the appropriate journal entry?

		DR	CR
a.	Trade accounts receivable	550	
	Service revenue		550
b.	Trade accounts receivable	550	
	Unearned revenue		550
c.	Cash	550	
	Service revenue		550
d.	No entry is made		

2.1.2 HOW ARE UNRECORDED EXPENSES ACCRUED?

The second type of adjusting entry accrues an expense that has been incurred but not yet recorded.

Esposito Bakery pays its employees every Friday. The baker earns €250 per week and works Monday to Friday. In June 2009, the end of the reporting period falls on a Tuesday. That means that on 30 June 2009, the reporting date, the baker has not been paid for Monday and Tuesday (29 June and 30 June), nor has the expense related to his labour been recorded. The following adjusting entry would be recorded:

Date	Account Titles	DR	CR
30 June 2009	Wages expense Wages payable	€100	€100

Again, notice that no entry is made to cash. Also, both the statement of comprehensive income and statement of financial position are affected. Both criteria for an adjusting entry are met.

Adjusting Entry Test		
Does the entry involve cash?	No	Passes test
Does the entry involve the statement of financial position and the statement of comprehensive income?	Yes	Passes test

ON YOUR OWN

LEARNING OUTCOME REVIEW

1. Explain the circumstances that create the need to make an adjusting entry to accrue expenses.

LEARNING OUTCOME PRACTICE

1. A company accrues salaries for the week just ended that will be paid at the end of the month. The debit in the journal entry would be to which financial statement category?
    a. Assets
    b. Liabilities
    c. Expenses
    d. Revenues

2. Able Cleaning Service Ltd prepares financial reports monthly. On 30 July 2009, the supervisor informs the accounting office that his crew completed work that morning for a customer, Nestor Almadar, who had paid for the job. The amount owed to employees who have already been paid for the work done was €225. What is the appropriate journal entry for the work performed by the employees?

		DR	CR
a.	Wage expense	225	
	Cash		225
b.	Prepaid wages	225	
	Cash		225
c.	Wage expense	225	
	Wages payable		225
d.	Prepaid wages	225	
	Wages payable		225

3. Able Cleaning Service Ltd prepares financial reports monthly. On 30 July 2009, the supervisor informs the accounting office that his crew completed work that morning for a customer, Nestor Almadar, who had paid for the job. The amount owed to employees totaled €225, which will be paid in approximately one week as part of their bi-monthly pay cheque. What is the appropriate journal entry for the work performed by the employees?

		DR	CR
a.	Wage expense	225	
	Cash		225
b.	Prepaid wages	225	
	Cash		225
c.	Wage expense	225	
	Wages payable		225
d.	Prepaid wages	225	
	Wages payable		225

Now, let's examine the two types of adjusting entries that relate to a reclassification of revenue or expense into the appropriate reporting period.

HINT

Both reclassification adjusting entries involve a previous transaction that has already been recorded. Previously, cash had been received before the goods or services were delivered to the customer, which resulted in a credit to unearned revenue (liability). Or cash had been paid for a cost that had not yet been consumed, resulting in a prepaid expense (asset). Both unearned revenue and prepaid expenses appear on the statement of financial position. However, an adjusting entry to reclassify these items from the statement of financial position to the statement of comprehensive income is now required. Why? Because the unearned revenue has now been earned and the prepaid expense has now expired.

2.2 What assets and liabilities need to be reclassified to expense and revenue?

The remaining two adjusting entries relate to transactions that have already been recorded but were recognized as either a liability (unearned revenue) or an asset (prepaid). During the reporting period the liability was settled or the asset consumed. Thus, the liability or asset must be reclassified as revenue or expense respectively.

2.2.1 HOW IS UNEARNED REVENUE RECOGNIZED AS REVENUE?

Since Esposito Bakery has a reputation for the best wedding cakes, orders must be placed in advance and full payment made at the time of the order. A wedding cake averages €200.

On 30 December 2009, a bride orders a cake, paying cash for a wedding on 15 February 2010. Should Esposito Bakery recognize the sales revenue in 2009 or 2010? The answer is that the revenue should be recognized in 2010 because that is when the cake will be delivered to the customer.

However, the bakery received €200 cash in 2009. Obviously, the debit must go to the Cash account, but if revenue cannot be credited in 2009, then what account should be credited? The answer is that an obligation to deliver the cake in 2010 must be recognized. The appropriate account to credit is unearned revenue, which is a liability on the statement of financial position.

Unearned revenue is a liability account used to record revenue that has not yet been earned and for which the customer has already paid.

Esposito would make the following journal entry at the time the customer paid for the cake:

Date	Account Titles	DR	CR
30 Dec. 2009	Cash	€200	
	Unearned revenue		€200

Notice that this is *not* an adjusting entry but rather a business transaction. The bakery will record the adjusting entry on 15 February 2010 when the cake is actually delivered and the revenue earned. The adjusting entry on that date will be:

Date	Account Titles	DR	CR
15 Feb. 2010	Unearned revenue	€200	
	Sales revenue		€200

Let's perform the check.

Adjusting Entry Check		
Does the entry involve cash?	No	Passes test
Does the entry involve the statement of financial position and the statement of comprehensive income?	Yes	Passes test

The preceding adjusting entry recognizes that the business's obligation to deliver the cake has been discharged and therefore the liability should be removed from the statement of financial position. The revenue is recognized and will appear on the statement of comprehensive income.

ON YOUR OWN

LEARNING OUTCOME REVIEW

1. Explain what circumstances cause an adjusting entry for unearned revenue to be recorded.
2. How is accrued revenue different from unearned revenue?
3. Which adjusting entry increases assets? Accrued revenue or unearned revenue?
4. Which adjusting entry decreases liabilities? Accrued revenue or unearned revenue?
5. Which adjusting entry increases profit? Accrued revenue or unearned revenue?
6. Which adjusting entry increases equity? Accrued revenue or unearned revenue?

LEARNING OUTCOME PRACTICE

1. Baity, a limited liability company, receives rent for subletting part of its office premises to a number of tenants. In the year ended 31 December 2009, Baity received cash of $318 600 from its tenants. Details of rent in advance and in arrears at the beginning and end of 2009 are as follows:

	31 December 2009	31 December 2008
Rent received in advance	428 400	24 600
Rent owing by tenants	18 300	16 900

All rent owing was subsequently received. What figure for rental income should be included in the statement of income of Baity for 2009?

a. $341 000
b. $336 400
c. $300 800
d. $316 200

ACCA adapted

2. A company sublets part of its office accommodation. In the year ended 30 June 2009 cash received from tenants was $83 700. Details of rent in arrears and in advance at the beginning and end of the year were:

	In Arrears	In Advance
30 June 2008	$3800	$2400
30 June 2009	$4700	$3000

All arrears of rent were subsequently received. What figure for rental income should be included in the company's statement of income for the year ended 30 June 2009?

a. $84 000
b. $83 400
c. $80 600
d. $85 800

ACCA adapted

2.2.2 HOW ARE PREPAID EXPENSES RECOGNIZED AS EXPENSES?

On 1 January 2009, Esposito Bakery paid €24 000 to the landlord for one year's rent on bakery facilities in advance. The following journal entry recorded the rent:

Date	Account Titles	DR	CR
1 Jan. 2009	Prepaid rent	€24 000	
	Cash		€24 000

Again, notice that this is *not* an adjusting entry but rather a business transaction recording an asset that represents rent paid in advance but unused. On 30 June 2009, the reporting date, Esposito must reclassify part of this asset as an expense. Why? The reason is that part of the asset has expired, or has been used.

Since Esposito paid rent for twelve months in advance and six months have lapsed, half of the asset would be reclassified as expense. The *adjusting entry* would be:

Date	Account Titles	DR	CR
30 June 2009	Rent expense Prepaid rent	€12 000	€12 000

Let's perform the check.

Adjusting Entry Check		
Does the entry involve cash?	No	Passes test
Does the entry involve the statement of financial position and the statement of comprehensive income?	Yes	Passes test

Other common prepaid expenses include insurance and wages. Remember that in general any item referred to as an expense appears on the statement of comprehensive income. However, a prepaid expense is an asset on the statement of financial position. A prepaid expense becomes an expense only when it expires.

ON YOUR OWN

LEARNING OUTCOME PRACTICE

1. What is the journal entry to record the prepayment of rent for the next three months in the amount of $33 000 on 1 June 2012?
2. What is the adjusting entry related to the prepayment of rent in Item 1 above for the month of June 2012?
3. What is the adjusting entry related to the prepayment of rent in Item 1 above for the month of September 2012?
4. A company has a supplies balance in its trial balance for 1 May 2012 for $45 000. A physical count reveals that $22 000 remains at the end of the month. What is the adjusting entry related to supplies for May?
5. A company has a supplies balance in its trial balance for 1 May 2012 for $45 000. Records indicate that $27 000 of the supplies were used during the month of May. What is the adjusting entry related to supplies for May?

6. In September 2010 Alison paid $7800 for rent for the four months from 1 October 2010. What should be reported on Alison's statement of financial position at 30 November 2010?
   a. An accrual of $3900
   b. An accrual of $1950
   c. A prepayment of $3900
   d. A prepayment of $1950
   ACCA adapted

7. A company prepares its financial statements on 30 April each year. Rent is paid quarterly in advance on 1 January, 1 April, 1 July and 1 October. The annual rent is $84 000 annually until 30 June 2012. Then the rent was increased to $96 000 per year. What rent expense and end-of-year prepayment should be included in the financial statements for the year ended 30 April 2013?

	Expense	Prepayment
a.	$93 000	$8 000
b.	$93 000	$16 000
c.	$94 000	$8 000
d.	$94 000	$16 000

   ACCA adapted

LEARNING OUTCOME 3
DEMONSTRATE HOW ADJUSTING ENTRIES ARE RECORDED

Now let's apply what we know about the four types of adjusting entries by continuing the Schwittay Consulting example begun in Chapter 4.

Recall from Chapter 4 that Schwittay Consulting began a short-term project for a client on 17 February 2009 that was expected to last only 10–12 days. At the end of February, the partner responsible for the assignment advises the accounting department that the project was completed on 27 February, that a request for payment of €20 000 has been sent to the client, and that payment should be received some time in March.

When this assignment was begun, no cash had been received so no journal entry was recorded. However, in order for the financial statements to be accurate, they must show that Schwittay has already earned the €20 000 in revenue and is entitled to payment. Therefore, the following accrual entry would be made to adjust the accounting records:

Date	Account Titles	DR	CR
28 Feb. 2009	Trade accounts receivable	€20 000	
	Service revenue		€20 000

At the end of the period, Schwittay must also determine whether expenses have been incurred that have not yet been recorded for the reporting period.

Recall that on 15 February, Schwittay hired three employees who began work immediately. No journal entry had been made at the time because no recordable transaction had occurred. However, at the end of February Schwittay had incurred half a month's salary for each of the three employees, which would not be paid until 1 March. Since each employee receives €108 000 annually, half a month's salary for one employee would be €4500. For three employees, the total is €13 500. Therefore, the adjusting entry would be:

Date	Account Titles	DR	CR
28 Feb. 2009	Salaries expense	€13 500	
	Salaries payable		€13 500

Another adjusting entry must be made to record interest expense that has accrued on the loan that Schwittay concluded on 1 February for €150 000. Even though interest is paid in annual instalments, an expense has been incurred for the time the loan has been outstanding during the month of February. The interest rate is 8% per annum, so the interest expense for one month is €1000 (€150 000 × .08 × 1/12). The adjusting entry would be:

Date	Account Titles	DR	CR
28 Feb. 2009	Interest expense	€1 000	
	Interest payable		€1 000

Schwittay Consulting was awarded a contract on 15 February for a total amount of €804 000, which was to be delivered over one year. However, the company also received a cash advance of €201 000.

This required a journal entry debiting cash and crediting unearned service revenue to be recorded. This was the business transaction entry. Now, Schwittay must record the adjusting entry. By the end of February, the firm had earned €33 500 (€804 000 ÷ 12 months × 1/2 for half the month of February). The adjusting entry to accrue the expense would be:

Date	Account Titles	DR	CR
28 Feb. 2009	Unearned service revenue	€33 500	
	Service revenue		€33 500

On 3 February, Schwittay Consulting paid €29 700 to the landlord for rent on office space for one year in advance. This amount was recorded in prepaid rent, an asset account. In order that the workers could begin renovations immediately, the lease began in February. In this case, one month of the lease has expired by the end of February, requiring an adjustment of €2475. The adjusting entry would be:

Date	Account Titles	DR	CR
28 Feb. 2009	Rent expense	€2 475	
	Prepaid rent		€2 475

Now, assume that Schwittay checks its stock of supplies and finds that only €2000 of the original amount remains. That means that €1350 (€3350 − 2000) was consumed, and so that portion of the cost has expired. The adjusting entry would be:

Date	Account Titles	DR	CR
28 Feb. 2009	Supplies expense	€1 350	
	Supplies		€1 350

Notice that no adjusting entry is made for the prepaid insurance because coverage does not begin until 1 March and thus none of the asset cost has expired by the reporting date (28 February 2009).

The ledger after all adjusting entries have been recorded at the end of the reporting period would appear as shown in Figure 5.4.

FIGURE 5.4 LEDGER ACCOUNTS AFTER POSTING ADJUSTING ENTRIES

Schwittay Consulting AG Adjusted Ledger 28 February 2009		
Date	DR	CR
SERVICE REVENUE		
Beginning balance, 1 Feb. 2009		0
16 Feb. 2009		13 500
28 Feb. 2009 Adjusting entry		20 000
28 Feb. 2009 Adjusting entry		33 500
Ending balance, 28 Feb. 2009		67 000
INTEREST REVENUE		
Beginning balance, 1 Feb. 2009		0
28 Feb. 2009		1 250
Ending balance, 28 Feb. 2009		1 250
SALARIES EXPENSE		
Beginning balance, 1 Feb. 2009	0	
28 Feb. 2009 Adjusting entry	13 500	
Ending balance, 28 Feb. 2009	13 500	
INTEREST EXPENSE		
Beginning balance, 1 Feb. 2009	0	
28 Feb. 2009 Adjusting entry	1 000	
Ending balance, 28 Feb. 2009	1 000	
RENT EXPENSE		
Beginning balance, 1 Feb. 2009	0	
28 Feb. 2009 Adjusting entry	2 475	
Ending balance, 28 Feb. 2009	2 475	
SUPPLIES EXPENSE		
Beginning balance, 1 Feb. 2009	0	
28 Feb. 2009 Adjusting entry	1 350	
Ending balance, 28 Feb. 2009	1 350	

INSURANCE EXPENSE		
Beginning balance, 1 Feb. 2009	0	
28 Feb. 2009 Adjusting entry	1 000	
Ending balance, 28 Feb. 2009	1 000	

IMPROVEMENTS AMORTIZATION		
Beginning balance, 1 Feb. 2009	0	
Ending balance, 28 Feb. 2009	0	

CASH		
Beginning balance, 1 Feb. 2009	0	
1 Feb. 2009	20 000	
1 Feb. 2009	150 000	
3 Feb. 2009		29 700
3 Feb. 2009		23 000
7 Feb. 2009		12 060
15 Feb. 2009	201 000	
16 Feb. 2009	13 500	
23 Feb. 2009		23 000
28 Feb. 2009		3 350
28 Feb. 2009	1 250	
Ending balance, 28 Feb. 2009	294 640	

TRADE ACCOUNTS RECEIVABLE		
Beginning balance, 1 Feb. 2009	0	
28 Feb. 2009 Adjusting entry	20 000	
Ending balance, 28 Feb. 2009	20 000	

SUPPLIES		
Beginning balance, 1 Feb. 2009	0	
20 Feb. 2009	3 350	
28 Feb. 2009 Adjusting entry		1 350
Ending balance, 28 Feb. 2009	2 000	

PREPAID RENT		
Beginning balance, 1 Feb. 2009	0	
3 Feb. 2009	29 700	
28 Feb. 2009 Adjusting entry		2 475
Ending balance, 28 Feb. 2009	27 225	

(*Continued*)

FIGURE 5.4 *(CONTINUED)*

Date	DR	CR
Schwittay Consulting AG Adjusted Ledger 28 February 2009		
PREPAID INSURANCE		
Beginning balance, 1 Feb. 2009	0	
7 Feb. 2009	12 060	
Ending balance, 28 Feb. 2009	12 060	
LEASEHOLD IMPROVEMENTS		
Beginning balance, 1 Feb. 2009		0
3 Feb. 2009	69 000	
Ending balance, 28 Feb. 2009	69 000	
TRADE ACCOUNTS PAYABLE		
Beginning balance, 1 Feb. 2009		0
3 Feb. 2009		46 000
20 Feb. 2009		3 350
23 Feb. 2009	23 000	
28 Feb. 2009	3 350	
Ending balance, 28 Feb. 2009		23 000
SALARIES PAYABLE		
Beginning balance, 1 Feb. 2009		0
28 Feb. 2009 Adjusting entry		13 500
Ending balance, 28 Feb. 2009		13 500
INTEREST PAYABLE		
Beginning balance, 1 Feb. 2009		0
28 Feb. 2009		1 000
Ending balance, 28 Feb. 2009		1 000
UNEARNED SERVICE REVENUE		
Beginning balance, 1 Feb. 2009		0
15 Feb. 2009		201 000
28 Feb. 2009 Adjusting entry	33 500	
Ending balance, 28 Feb. 2009		167 500

LOAN PAYABLE		
Beginning balance, 1 Feb. 2009		0
1 Feb. 2009		<u>150 000</u>
Ending balance, 28 Feb. 2009		150 000
CONTRIBUTED CAPITAL		
Beginning balance, 1 Feb. 2009		0
1 Feb. 2009		<u>20 000</u>
Ending balance, 28 Feb. 2009		20 000
RETAINED EARNINGS		
Beginning balance, 1 Feb. 2009		0
Ending balance, 28 Feb. 2009		0
DIVIDENDS		
Beginning balance, 1 Feb. 2009		0
Ending balance, 28 Feb. 2009		0

Figure 5.5 presents the adjusted trial balance. Recall that the trial balance shows only the net debit or net credit balance in each ledger account.

FIGURE 5.5 ADJUSTED TRIAL BALANCE

Schwittay Consulting AG Adjusted Trial Balance 28 February 2009 € Euros		
Account Titles	**DR**	**CR**
Service revenue		67 000
Interest revenue		1 250
Salaries expense	13 500	
Interest expense	1 000	
Rent expense	2 475	
Supplies expense	1 350	
Insurance expense		
Improvements amortization		
Cash	294 640	
Trade accounts receivables	20 000	

FIGURE 5.5 (*CONTINUED*)

Schwittay Consulting AG Adjusted Trial Balance 28 February 2009 € Euros		
Account Titles	DR	CR
Supplies	2 000	
Prepaid rent	27 225	
Prepaid insurance	12 060	
Leasehold improvements	69 000	
Trade accounts payable		23 000
Salaries payable		13 500
Interest payable		1 000
Unearned service revenue		167 500
Loan payable		150 000
Contributed capital		20 000
Retained earnings		
Dividends		
	443 250	443 250

FIGURE 5.6 THE ACCOUNTING PROCESS

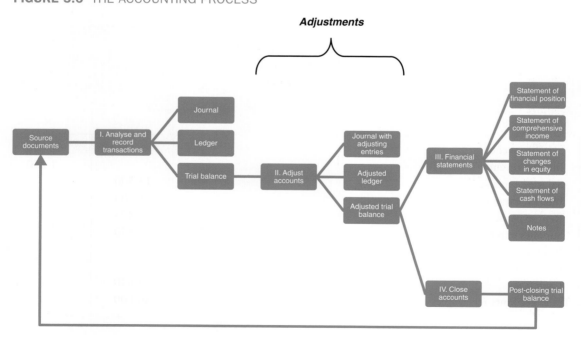

Before continuing to the next step in the accounting process, let's stop and take stock of where we are. Figure 5.6 is the graphical illustration of the accounting process that we first saw in Chapter 4.

We began with the trial balance and recorded adjusting entries at the end of the reporting period. This allowed us to generate three reports: the adjusted journal, which now includes the adjusting as well as the journal entries; the adjusted ledger; and the adjusted trial balance. The adjusted trial balance is used in the third major step in the accounting process, which is to prepare the financial statements.

Accounts shown in the adjusted trial balance are used to format the financial statements. The statement of financial position and statement of comprehensive income for Schwittay Consulting are shown below.

Statement of financial position

Schwittay Consulting AG Statement of financial position 28 February 2009 € Euros		
Account Titles	DR	CR
Assets		
Current assets		
Cash	294 640	
Trade accounts receivables	20 000	
Supplies	2 000	
Prepaid rent	27 225	
Prepaid insurance	12 060	355 925
Leasehold improvements		69 000
Total assets		**424 925**
Liabilities		
Current liabilities		
Trade accounts payable	23 000	
Salaries payable	13 500	
Interest payable	1 000	
Unearned service revenue	167 500	205 000
Loan payable		150 000
Total liabilities		355 000
Equity		
Contributed capital		20 000
Retained earnings		49 925
Total equity		69 925
Total liabilities and equity		**424 925**

Statement of comprehensive income

<table>
<tr><td colspan="3" align="center">Schwittay Consulting AG
Statement of Income
For the Month Ended 28 February 2009
€ Euros</td></tr>
<tr><th>Account Titles</th><th>DR</th><th>CR</th></tr>
<tr><td>Revenue</td><td></td><td></td></tr>
<tr><td>   Service revenue</td><td>67 000</td><td></td></tr>
<tr><td>   Interest revenue</td><td>1 250</td><td>68 250</td></tr>
<tr><td>Less: Expenses</td><td></td><td></td></tr>
<tr><td>   Salaries expense</td><td>13 500</td><td></td></tr>
<tr><td>   Rent expense</td><td>2 475</td><td></td></tr>
<tr><td>   Supplies expense</td><td>1 350</td><td></td></tr>
<tr><td>   Interest expense</td><td>1 000</td><td>18 325</td></tr>
<tr><td>**Profit**</td><td></td><td>**49 925**</td></tr>
</table>

LEARNING OUTCOME 4
DESCRIBE THE FOUR CLOSING ENTRIES AND EXPLAIN THE PURPOSE OF EACH

Once the financial statements have been prepared, the ledger accounts can be closed and prepared for the next reporting period. This is the fourth and final step in the accounting process. The purpose of closing entries is to reset all statement of comprehensive income accounts and the dividend account to zero. Taken together, these accounts are referred to as temporary accounts (or nominal accounts). Statement of financial position accounts are permanent accounts (or real accounts), which are not reset to zero. Temporary accounts are closed; permanent accounts are *not* closed.

Why are temporary accounts closed? The answer is that temporary accounts accumulate the changes in financial position over a reporting period. These changes include all items in the statement of comprehensive income and dividends. At the end of the reporting period these amounts are transferred to retained earnings, which is part of equity on the statement of financial position.

During July 2010, Ryuusei Paper Mills KK records a total of ¥12 400 000 in revenue. The ledger account would have this balance at the end of the month:

Ryuusei Paper Mills KK Ledger 31 July 2010 ¥ Japanese yen		
Date	DR	CR
REVENUE		
31 July 2010 Balance		¥12 400 000

What would happen if this account was not set to zero at the end of July?

In August 2010, the next month, Ryuusei records ¥11 500 000 in revenue. The journal entries to record this revenue are entered and appear in the ledger account. However, because the account balance from July was not cleared, the August amounts increase the July balance further. At the end of August the ledger account would appear as follows:

Ryuusei Paper Mills KK Ledger 31 July 2010 ¥ Japanese yen		
Date	DR	CR
REVENUE		
31 July 2010 Balance		¥12 400 000
Revenue entries for August		11 500 000
31 Aug. 2010 Balance		¥23 900 00

The ¥23 900 000 balance is inaccurate because it includes amounts from both July and August. The balance should only show the amount for August transactions at the end of August. That means that the balance for July must be removed before August transactions are recorded, which is what the closing entry accomplishes.

We close revenues, expenses and dividends at the end of the reporting period done with *four* closing entries, which are as follows:

1. Close revenue to income summary.
2. Close expenses to income summary.
3. Close income summary to retained earnings.
4. Close dividends to retained earnings.

Figure 5.7 illustrates how temporary accounts are closed to permanent accounts; specifically, retained earnings.

FIGURE 5.7 ACCOUNTS BEFORE CLOSING

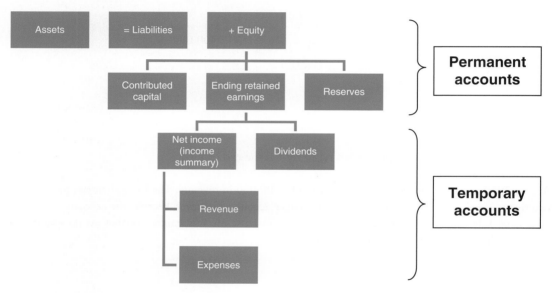

Notice in Figure 5.7 that all temporary balances are closed to retained earnings. Dividends are closed *directly* to retained earnings. However, revenue and expenses are first closed to an income summary account in order to measure income. Then the income summary account is closed to retained earnings.

Entry 1: Close Revenue

The first entry closes revenue to the income summary account. For Schwittay Consulting AG this entry would be:

Date	Account Titles	DR	CR
28 Feb. 2009	Service revenue	€67 000	
	Interest revenue	1 250	
	Income summary		€68 250

FIGURE 5.8 CLOSING REVENUE TO INCOME SUMMARY

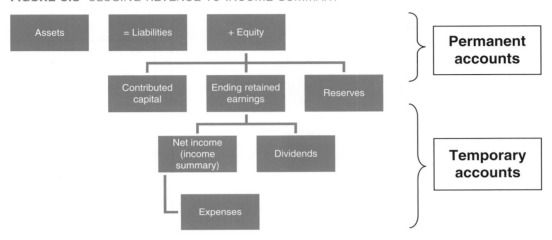

The balances come from the adjusted trial balance in Figure 5.5. Notice that the two revenue accounts are debited. This is because the balance in these accounts is a credit. In order to remove this balance, the account must be debited. Figure 5.8 shows how this entry removes revenue from the expanded accounting equation.

Entry 2: Close expenses

The second entry close expenses to the income summary account.

Date	Account Titles	DR	CR
28 Feb. 2009	Income summary	18 325	
	Salaries expense		13 500
	Rent expense		2 475
	Supplies expense		1 350
	Interest expense		1 000

Figure 5.9 shows how this entry removes expenses from the expanded accounting equations.

At this point, the income summary account in the ledger would appear as follows:

Income summary account	
	€68 250
€18 325	
	€49 925

FIGURE 5.9 CLOSING EXPENSES TO INCOME SUMMARY

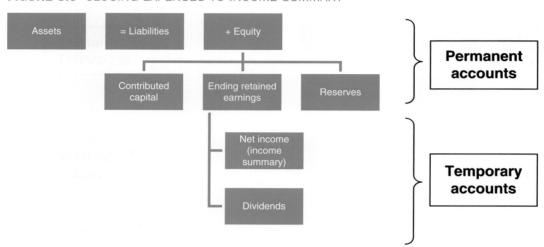

The balance of €49 925 is equal to the profit or loss shown on the statement of comprehensive income. Notice that other comprehensive income items are *not* closed.

Entry 3: Close income summary to retained earnings

The next step is to close the balance in the income summary account with a net credit of €49 925 (€68 250 − 18 325). Income summary must be debited to clear the account balance, and the credit goes to retained earnings. The closing entry would be:

Date	Account Titles	DR	CR
28 Feb. 2009	Income summary Retained earnings	€49 925	€49 925

The income summary ledger account would now have no remaining balance and would appear as follows:

Income summary account	
	€68 250
€18 325	
49 925	
−	−

FIGURE 5.10 CLOSING INCOME SUMMARY TO RETAINED EARNINGS

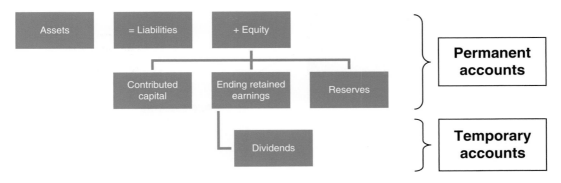

Figure 5.10 shows that the income summary account has been closed to retained earnings.

Entry 4: Close dividends to retained earnings

The fourth entry closes dividends directly to retained earnings. Remember that the normal balance in retained earnings is a credit and the normal balance in dividends is a debit. Therefore, dividends are subtracted from retained earnings. However, no closing entry is needed for February because a dividend was not paid. Figure 5.11 shows the permanent accounts after all temporary accounts have been closed.

FIGURE 5.11 COMPLETED CLOSING PROCESS

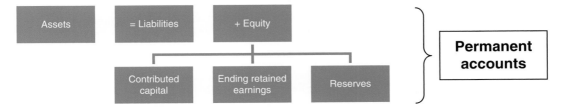

As you can see from Figure 5.11, only permanent accounts remain. All temporary account balances are zero. Accounts have now been prepared to receive journal entries for the subsequent reporting period. The accounting process is actually a cycle that repeats itself each reporting period, as graphically illustrated in Figure 5.12.

Figure 5.13 shows Schwittay's post-closing ledger after closing entries have been recorded.

Again, notice that all temporary accounts – revenue, expenses and dividends – are now zero, although no entry was made for dividends in the month of February. Permanent accounts – those on the statement of financial position – remain. The post-closing trial balance is shown in Figure 5.14.

FIGURE 5.12 THE CYCLICAL ACCOUNTING PROCESS

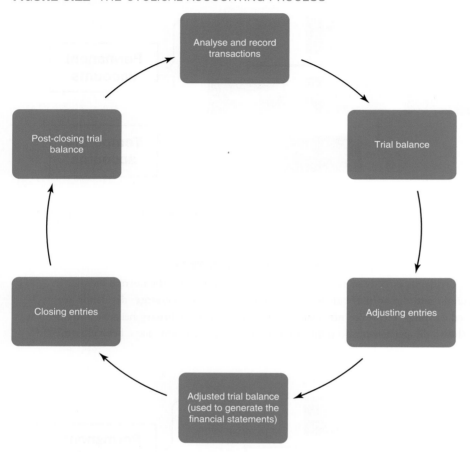

FIGURE 5.13 LEDGER ACCOUNTS AFTER CLOSING

Date	DR	CR
Schwittay Consulting AG Post-Closing Ledger 28 February 2009 € Euros		
SERVICE REVENUE		
Beginning balance, 1 Feb. 2009		0
16 Feb. 2009		13 500
28 Feb. 2009 Adjusting entry		20 000
28 Feb. 2009 Adjusting entry		33 500

28 Feb. 2009 Closing entry	<u>67 000</u>	
Ending balance, 28 Feb. 2009		0
INTEREST REVENUE		
Beginning balance, 1 Feb. 2009		0
12–28 Feb. 2009		1 250
28 Feb. 2009 Closing entry	<u>1 250</u>	
Ending balance, 28 Feb. 2009		0
SALARIES EXPENSE		
Beginning balance, 1 Feb. 2009	0	
28 Feb. 2009 Adjusting entry	13 500	
28 Feb. 2009 Closing entry		13 500
Ending balance, 28 Feb. 2009	0	
INTEREST EXPENSE		
Beginning balance, 1 Feb. 2009		
28 Feb. 2009 Adjusting entry	1 000	
28 Feb. 2009 Closing entry		<u>1 000</u>
Ending balance, 28 Feb. 2009	0	
RENT EXPENSE		
Beginning balance, 1 Feb. 2009	0	
28 Feb. 2009 Adjusting entry	2 475	
28 Feb. 2009 Closing entry		<u>2 475</u>
Ending balance, 28 Feb. 2009	0	
SUPPLIES EXPENSE		
Beginning balance, 1 Feb. 2009	0	
28 Feb. 2009 Adjusting entry	1 350	
28 Feb. 2009 Closing entry		1 350
Ending balance, 28 Feb. 2009	0	
INSURANCE EXPENSE		
Beginning balance, 1 Feb. 2009	0	
Ending balance, 28 Feb. 2009	0	
IMPROVEMENT AMORTIZATION		
Beginning balance, 1 Feb. 2009	0	
Ending balance, 28 Feb. 2009	0	

(*Continued*)

FIGURE 5.13 (*CONTINUED*)

Date	DR	CR
Schwittay Consulting AG Post-Closing Ledger 28 February 2009 € Euros		
CASH		
Beginning balance, 1 Feb. 2009	0	
1 Feb. 2009	20 000	
1 Feb. 2009	150 000	
3 Feb. 2009		29 700
3 Feb. 2009		23 000
7 Feb. 2009		12 060
15 Feb. 2009	201 000	
16 Feb. 2009	13 500	
23 Feb. 2009		23 000
28 Feb. 2009		3 350
28 Feb. 2009	1 250	
Ending balance, 28 Feb. 2009	294 640	
TRADE ACCOUNTS RECEIVABLE		
Beginning balance, 1 Feb. 2009	0	
28 Feb. 2009 Adjusting entry	20 000	
Ending balance, 28 Feb. 2009	20 000	
SUPPLIES		
Beginning balance, 1 Feb. 2009	0	
20 Feb. 2009	3 350	
28 Feb. 2009 Adjusting entry		1 350
Ending balance, 28 Feb. 2009	2 200	
PREPAID RENT		
Beginning balance, 1 Feb. 2009	0	
3 Feb. 2009	29 700	
28 Feb. 2009 Adjusting entry		2 475
Ending balance, 28 Feb. 2009	27 225	
PREPAID INSURANCE		
Beginning balance, 1 Feb. 2009	0	
7 Feb. 2009	12 060	
Ending balance, 28 Feb. 2009	12 060	

LEASEHOLD IMPROVEMENTS		
Beginning balance, 1 Feb. 2009		0
3 Feb. 2009	69 000	
Ending balance, 28 Feb. 2009	69 000	

TRADE ACCOUNTS PAYABLE		
Beginning balance, 1 Feb. 2009		0
3 Feb. 2009		46 000
20 Feb. 2009		3 350
23 Feb. 2009	23 000	
28 Feb. 2009 Adjusting entry	3 350	
Ending balance, 28 Feb. 2009		23 000

SALARIES PAYABLE		
Beginning balance, 1 Feb. 2009		0
28 Feb. 2009 Adjusting entry		13 500
Ending balance, 28 Feb. 2009		13 500

INTEREST PAYABLE		
Beginning balance, 1 Feb. 2009		0
28 Feb. 2009 Adjusting entry		1 000
Ending balance, 28 Feb. 2009		1 000

UNEARNED SERVICE REVENUE		
Beginning balance, 1 Feb. 2009		0
15 Feb. 2009		201 000
28 Feb. 2009 Adjusting entry	33 500	
Ending balance, 28 Feb. 2009		167 500

LOAN PAYABLE		
Beginning balance, 1 Feb. 2009		0
1 Feb. 2009		150 000
Ending balance, 28 Feb. 2009		150 000

CONTRIBUTED CAPITAL		
Beginning balance, 1 Feb. 2009		0
1 Feb. 2009		20 000
Ending balance, 28 Feb. 2009		20 000

(*Continued*)

FIGURE 5.13 (*CONTINUED*)

Date	DR	CR
Schwittay Consulting AG Post-Closing Ledger 28 February 2009 € Euros		
RETAINED EARNINGS		
Beginning balance, 1 Feb. 2009		0
28 Feb. 2009 Closing entry		68 250
28 Feb. 2009 Closing entry	18 325	
Ending balance, 28 Feb. 2009		49 925
DIVIDENDS		
Beginning balance, 1 Feb. 2009		0
Ending balance, 28 Feb. 2009		0

FIGURE 5.14 POST-CLOSING TRIAL BALANCE

Account Titles	DR	CR
Schwittay Consulting AG Post-Closing Ledger Trial Balance 28 February 2009		
Service revenue		0
Interest revenue	0	
Salaries expense	0	
Interest expense	0	
Rent expense	0	
Supplies expense	0	
Insurance expense	0	
Improvements amortization	0	
Cash	294 640	
Trade accounts receivable	20 000	
Supplies	2 000	
Prepaid rent	27 225	
Prepaid insurance	12 060	
Leasehold improvements	69 000	
Trade accounts payable		23 000

Salaries payable		13 500
Interest payable		1 000
Unearned service revenue		167 500
Loan payable		150 000
Contributed capital		20 000
Retained earnings		49 925
Dividends		
	424 925	**424 925**

The post-closing trial balance is the final step at the end of the accounting process. At this point, the ledger accounts are ready for the next reporting period.

ON YOUR OWN

LEARNING OUTCOME REVIEW

1. What is a temporary account? What is a permanent account?
2. Which accounts are closed – temporary or permanent?
3. Explain the four closing entries.

LEARNING OUTCOME PRACTICE

1. The adjusted trial balance for 30 September 2009 showed dividends of €500 just before closing. What is the closing entry?
2. The adjusted trial balance for 30 September 2009 showed revenues of €72 500 just before closing. What is the closing entry?
3. The adjusted trial balance for 30 September 2009 showed expenses of €84 200 just before closing. What is the closing entry?
4. Based on items 1, 2 and 3 above, what is the entry to close income summary to retained earnings?
5. Indicate whether each of the following accounts is temporary or permanent:

Account	Temporary	Permanent
Cash		
Revenue		
Trade accounts payable		
Share capital		
Reserves		
Expenses		
Dividends		
Trade accounts receivable		
Accumulated depreciation		
Depreciation expense		

HINT

We have examined three types of entries that are recorded in the journal:

1. Journal entries
2. Adjusting entries
3. Closing entries

All three of these entries use the same form, however each is made for a different reason. A journal entry records a transaction. An adjusting entry converts the ledger accounts to the accrual basis. And closing entries transfer temporary accounts to retained earnings.

REVIEW

COMPREHENSIVE REVIEW: SCHWITTAY CONSULTING AG
JOURNAL ENTRIES FOR MARCH 2009

Following are the transactions and adjusting events for *March* – the next month – for Schwittay Consulting. Record the journal entries, post the ledger and construct the trial balance. Then apply the appropriate adjusting entries, update the ledger and the adjusted trial balance. Then construct the statement of financial position, statement of comprehensive income and statement of changes in equity. Finally, record the closing entries, update the ledger and show the post-closing trial balance for the end of the March reporting period.

1 March 2009

The company pays employees for February.

Date	Account Titles	DR	CR
1 March 2009	Salaries payable	€13 500	
	Cash		€13 500

3 March 2009

The client whose revenue was recognized on 28 February makes the €20 000 payment.

Date	Account Titles	DR	CR
3 March 2009	Cash	€20 000	
	Trade accounts receivable		€20 000

5 March 2009

Because of the amount of administrative work involved with the current workload, the owners hire two assistants. They start immediately and each is paid €48 000 per year. They will also be paid on the first of each month for work done in the previous month.

No journal entry required on this date.

7 March 2009

Schwittay Consulting completes work on a project and delivers it to the client along with an invoice for €17 000.

Date	Account Titles	DR	CR
7 March 2009	Trade accounts receivable	€17 000	
	Service revenue		€17 000

10 March 2009

A minor project is completed for €7500 and delivered. The client pays immediately.

Date	Account Titles	DR	CR
10 March 2009	Cash	€7 500	
	Service revenue		€7 500

21 March 2009

The company purchases €4 240 in supplies on account.

Date	Account Titles	DR	CR
21 March 2009	Supplies	€4 240	
	Trade accounts payable		€4 240

22 March 2009

Schwittay signs a contract with a client and work begins immediately. The total amount of the contract is €10 000 for work that is expected to take three months is paid in advance.

Date	Account Titles	DR	CR
22 March 2009	Cash Unearned service revenue	€10 000	€10 000

26 March 2009

Supplies purchased on 21 March are paid in full.

Date	Account Titles	DR	CR
26 March 2009	Trade accounts payable Cash	€4 240	€4 240

28 March 2009

The client whose work was delivered on 7 March pays half of the amount owed.

Date	Account Titles	DR	CR
28 March 2009	Cash Trade accounts receivable	€8 500	€8 500

28 March 2009

The bank credits the company's account with €1180 for interest earned on the cash balance for March.

Date	Account Titles	DR	CR
28 March 2009	Cash Interest revenue	€1 180	€1 180

31 March 2009

The company pays a cash dividend of €20 000.

Date	Account Titles	DR	CR
31 March 2009	Dividends Cash	€20 000	 €20 000

Figure 5.15 presents the ledger accounts after the transactions have been entered.

FIGURE 5.15 MARCH 2009 LEDGER ACCOUNTS

Schwittay Consulting AG Ledger 31 March 2009 € Euros		
Date	DR	CR
SERVICE REVENUE		
Beginning balance, 1 March 2009		0
7 March 2009		17 000
10 March 2009		7 500
Ending balance, 31 March 2009		24 500
INTEREST REVENUE		
Beginning balance, 1 March 2009		0
28 March 2009		1 180
Ending balance, 31 March 2009		1 180
SALARIES EXPENSE		
Ending balance, 31 March 2009	0	
INTEREST EXPENSE		
Ending balance, 31 March 2009	0	
RENT EXPENSE		
Ending balance, 31 March 2009	0	
SUPPLIES EXPENSE		
Ending balance, 31 March 2009	0	

(*Continued*)

FIGURE 5.15 *(CONTINUED)*

Date	DR	CR
Schwittay Consulting AG *Ledger 31 March 2009* *€ Euros*		
INSURANCE EXPENSE		
Ending balance, 31 March 2009	0	
IMPROVEMENT AMORTIZATION		
Ending balance, 31 March 2009	0	
CASH		
Beginning balance, 1 March 2009	294 640	
1 March 2009		13 500
1 March 2009		23 000
3 March 2009	20 000	
10 March 2009	7 500	
22 March 2009	10 000	
26 March 2009		4 240
28 March 2009	8 500	
28 March 2009	1 180	
31 March 2009		20 000
Ending balance, 31 March 2009	281 080	
TRADE ACCOUNTS RECEIVABLE		
Beginning balance, 1 March 2009	20 000	
3 March 2009		20 000
7 March 2009	17 000	
28 March 2009		8 500
Ending balance, 31 March 2009	8 500	
SUPPLIES		
Beginning balance, 1 March 2009	2 000	
21 March 2009	4 240	
Ending balance, 31 March 2009	6 240	
PREPAID RENT		
Ending balance, 31 March 2009	27 225	

PREPAID INSURANCE		
Ending balance, 31 March 2009	12 060	

LEASEHOLD IMPROVEMENTS		
Ending balance, 31 March 2009	69 000	

TRADE ACCOUNTS PAYABLE		
Beginning balance, 1 March 2009		23 000
1 March 2009	23 000	
21 March 2009		4 240
22 March 2009	4 240	
Ending balance, 31 March 2009		0

SALARIES PAYABLE		
Beginning balance, 1 March 2009		13 500
1 March 2009	13 500	
Ending balance, 31 March 2009		0

INTEREST PAYABLE		
Beginning balance, 1 March 2009		1 000
Ending balance, 31 March 2009		1 000

UNEARNED SERVICE REVENUE		
Beginning balance, 1 March 2009		167 500
22 March 2009		10 000
Ending balance, 31 March 2009		177 500

LOAN PAYABLE		
Ending balance, 31 March 2009		150 000

CONTRIBUTED CAPITAL		
Ending balance, 31 March 2009		20 000

RETAINED EARNINGS		
Ending balance, 31 March 2009		49 925

DIVIDENDS		
Beginning balance, 1 March 2009	0	
31 March 2009	20 000	
Ending balance, 31 March 2009	20 000	

Figure 5.16 shows the trial balance once March transactions have been entered.

FIGURE 5.16 TRIAL BALANCE

Accounting Titles	DR	CR
Schwitty Consulting AG Trial Balance 31 March 2009		
Service revenue		24 500
Interest revenue		1 180
Salaries expense		
Interest expense		
Rent expense		
Supplies expense		
Insurance expense		
Improvements amortization		
Cash	281 080	
Trade accounts receivable	8 500	
Supplies	6 240	
Prepaid rent	27 225	
Prepaid insurance	12 060	
Leasehold improvements	69 000	
Trade accounts payable		
Salaries payable		
Interest payable		1 000
Unearned service revenue		177 500
Loan payable		150 000
Contributed capital		20 000
Retained earnings		49 925
Dividends	20 000	
	424 105	424 105

REVIEW

ADJUSTING ENTRIES FOR MARCH 2009
31 March 2009

Revenue earned on the contract that began on February 15 is recognized for March. The total revenue for the one year contract was for €804 000, of which €201 000 had been paid, creating an obligation that was booked as unearned service revenue. €33 500 of this obligation had been recognized as earned revenue in February, leaving a balance in the unearned service revenue account of €167 500. The following entry to recognize a full month's revenue earned in March, further reduces that balance.

Date	Account Titles	DR	CR
31 March 2009	Unearned service revenue Service revenue	€67 000	€67 000

31 March 2009

Rent expense for March is recognized.

Date	Account Titles	DR	CR
31 March 2009	Rent expense Prepaid rent	€2 475	€2 475

31 March 2009

Insurance expense for March is recognized. One month's portion of the annual premium is €1005 (12 060 ÷ 12).

Date	Account Titles	DR	CR
31 March 2009	Insurance expense Prepaid insurance	€1 005	€1 005

31 March 2009

Salaries are accrued. The three professional employees earned €9000 each (€108 000 ÷ 12). The total for all three would be €27 000. The two administrative assistants each earned €3355 (48 000 ÷ 12 months × 26/31 days worked in March) for a total of €6710. Total compensation for all employees was €33 710 (27 000 + 6710).

Date	Account Titles	DR	CR
31 March 2009	Salaries expense Salaries payable	€33 710	€33 710

31 March 2009

Supplies amounting to €4740 have been used during March.

Date	Account Titles	DR	CR
31 March 2009	Supplies expense Supplies	€4 740	€4 740

31 March 2009

Interest on the €150 000 loan is accrued.

Date	Account Titles	DR	CR
31 March 2009	Interest expense Interest payable	€1 000	€1 000

31 March 2009

Leasehold improvements must be amortized. The total cost was €69 000 and the improvements will be amortized over the lease the, which is five years. One month's expense is €1150 (€69 000 ÷ 60 months).

Date	Account Titles	DR	CR
31 March 2009	Improvement amortization Leasehold improvements	€1 150	€1 150

Figure 5.17 shows the ledger accounts after adjustments have been made for March.

FIGURE 5.17 MARCH 2009 ADJUSTED LEDGER ACCOUNTS

Schwittay Consulting AG Adjusted Ledger 31 March 2009		
Date	DR	CR
SERVICE REVENUE		
Beginning balance, 1 March 2009		0
7 March 2009		17 000
10 March 2009		7 500
31 March 2009 Adjusting entry		67 000
Ending balance, 31 March 2009		91 500
INTEREST REVENUE		
Beginning balance, 1 March 2009		0
28 March 2009		1 180
Ending balance, 31 March 2009		1 180
SALARIES EXPENSE		
Pre-adjustment balance, 31 March 2009	0	
31 March 2009 Adjusting entry	33 710	
Ending balance, 31 March 2009	33 710	
INTEREST EXPENSE		
Pre-adjustment balance, 31 March 2009	0	
31 March 2009 Adjusting entry	1 000	
Ending balance, 31 March 2009	1 000	
RENT EXPENSE		
Pre-adjustment, 31 March 2009	0	
31 March 2009 Adjusting entry	2 475	
Ending balance, 31 March 2009	2 475	
SUPPLIES EXPENSE		
Pre-adjustment balance, 31 March 2009	0	
31 March 2009 Adjusting entry	4 740	
Ending balance, 31 March 2009	4 740	

(Continued)

FIGURE 5.17 (*CONTINUED*)

Date	DR	CR
Schwittay Consulting AG Adjusted Ledger 31 March 2009		
INSURANCE EXPENSE		
Pre-adjustment balance, 31 March 2009	0	
31 March 2009 Adjusting entry	1 005	
Ending balance, 31 March 2009	1 005	
IMPROVEMENTS AMORTIZATION		
Pre-adjustment balance, 31 March 2009	0	
31 March 2009 Adjusting entry	1 150	
Ending balance, 31 March 2009	1 150	
CASH		
Beginning balance, 1 March 2009	294 640	
1 March 2009		13 500
1 March 2009		23 000
3 March 2009	20 000	
10 March 2009	7 500	
22 March 2009	10 000	
26 March 2009		4 240
28 March 2009	8 500	
28 March 2009	1 180	
31 March 2009		20 000
Ending balance, 31 March 2009	281 080	
TRADE ACCOUNTS RECEIVABLE		
Beginning balance, 1 March 2009	20 000	
3 March 2009		20 000
7 March 2009	17 000	
31 March 2009		8 500
Ending balance, 31 March 2009	8 500	
SUPPLIES		
Beginning balance, 1 March 2009	2 000	
21 March 2009	4 240	
31 March 2009 Adjusting entry		4 740
Ending balance, 31 March 2009	1 500	

PREPAID RENT		
Pre-adjustment balance, 31 March 2009	27 225	
31 March 2009 Adjusting entry		2 475
Ending balance, 31 March 2009	24 750	

PREPAID INSURANCE		
Pre-adjustment balance, 31 March 2009	12 060	
31 March 2009 Adjusting entry		1 005
Ending balance, 31 March 2009	11 055	

LEASEHOLD IMPROVEMENTS		
Ending balance, 31 March 2009	69 000	
31 March 2009 Adjusting entry		1 150
Ending balance, 31 March 2009	67 850	

TRADE ACCOUNTS PAYABLE		
Beginning balance, 1 March 2009		23 000
1 March 2009	23 000	
21 March 2009		4 240
22 March 2009	4 240	
Ending balance, 31 March 2009		0

SALARIES PAYABLE		
Beginning balance, 1 March 2009		13 500
1 March 2009	13 500	
31 March 2009 Adjusting entry		33 710
Ending balance, 31 March 2009		33 710

INTEREST PAYABLE		
Beginning balance, 1 March 2009		1000
31 March 2009 Adjusting entry		1000
Ending balance, 31 March 2009		2 000

UNEARNED SERVICE REVENUE		
Beginning balance, 1 March 2009		167 500
22 March 2009		10 000
31 March 2009 Adjusting entry	67 000	
Ending balance, 31 March 2009		110 500

LOAN PAYABLE		
Ending balance, 31 March 2009		150 000

(Continued)

FIGURE 5.17 (*CONTINUED*)

Date	DR	CR
Schwittay Consulting AG Adjusted Ledger 31 March 2009		
CONTRIBUTED CAPITAL		
Ending balance, 31 March 2009		20 000
RETAINED EARNINGS		
Ending balance, 31 March 2009		49 925
DIVIDENDS		
Beginning balance, 31 March 2009		0
31 March 2009	20 000	
Ending balance, 31 March 2009	20 000	

Figure 5.18 shows the adjusted trial balance once March transactions have been entered.

FIGURE 5.18 MARCH 2009 ADJUSTED TRIAL BALANCE

Account Titles	DR	CR
Schwittay Consulting AG Adjusted Trial Balance 31 MARCH 2009 € Euros		
Service revenue		91 500
Interest revenue		1 180
Salaries expense	33 710	
Interest expense	1 000	
Rent expense	2 475	
Supplies expense	4 740	
Insurance expense	1 005	
Improvements amortization	1 150	
Cash	281 080	
Trade accounts receivable	8 500	
Supplies	1 500	
Prepaid rent	24 750	

Prepaid insurance		11 055	
Leasehold improvements		67 850	
Trade accounts payable			
Salaries payable			33 710
Interest payable			2 000
Unearned service revenue			110 500
Loan payable			150 000
Contributed capital			20 000
Retained earnings			49 925
Dividends		20 000	
		458 815	458 815

LEARNING OUTCOME 5
PREPARE FINANCIAL STATEMENTS USING THE EXTENDED TRIAL BALANCE WORKSHEET

The adjusted trial balance is, as we already know, used to create the financial statements. To facilitate this process, an extended trial balance is used. An extended trial balance is a worksheet that has columns for statement of financial position and statement of comprehensive income line items. Figure 5.19 shows the trial balance from Figure 5.18 in the extended form.

FIGURE 5.19 EXTENDED TRIAL BALANCE

<table>
<tr><td colspan="7" align="center">Schwittay Consulting AG
Extended Trial Balance
31 March 2009
€ Euros</td></tr>
<tr><td rowspan="2">Account Titles</td><td colspan="2" align="center">Adjusted Trial Balance</td><td colspan="2" align="center">Balance Sheet</td><td colspan="2" align="center">Statement of Comprehensive Income</td></tr>
<tr><td>DR</td><td>CR</td><td>DR</td><td>CR</td><td>DR</td><td>CR</td></tr>
<tr><td>Service revenue</td><td></td><td>91 500</td><td></td><td></td><td></td><td>91 500</td></tr>
<tr><td>Interest revenue</td><td></td><td>1 180</td><td></td><td></td><td></td><td>1 180</td></tr>
<tr><td>Salaries expense</td><td>33 710</td><td></td><td></td><td></td><td>33 710</td><td></td></tr>
<tr><td>Interest expense</td><td>1 000</td><td></td><td></td><td></td><td>1 000</td><td></td></tr>
</table>

(*Continued*)

FIGURE 5.19 (CONTINUED)

Account Titles	Adjusted Trial Balance DR	Adjusted Trial Balance CR	Statement of Financial Position DR	Statement of Financial Position CR	Statement of Comprehensive Income DR	Statement of Comprehensive Income CR
Rent expense	2 475				2 475	
Supplies expense	4 740				4 740	
Insurance expense	1 005				1 005	
Improvement amortization	1 150				1 150	
Cash	281 080		281 080			
Trade accounts receivable	8 500		8 500			
Supplies	1 500		1 500			
Prepaid rent	24 750		24 750			
Prepaid insurance	11 055		11 055			
Leasehold improvements	67 850		67 850			
Trade accounts payable						
Salaries payable		33 710		33 710		
Interest payable		2 000		2 000		
Unearned service revenue		110 500		110 500		
Loan payable		150 000		150 000		
Contributed capital		20 000		20 000		
Retained earnings		49 925		49 925		
Dividends	20 000		20 000			
Totals	458 815	458 815	414 735	366 135	44 080	92 680
Profit				48 600	48 600	
Worksheet totals	458 815	458 815	414 735	414 735	92 680	92 680

Table header:

Schwittay Consulting AG
Extended Trial Balance
31 March 2009
€ Euros

Notice that the difference between the total debits and credits for the statement of comprehensive income is the amount of the profit of €48 600 for the reporting period. This is shown in the debit column because this amount of profit would be needed to set the two columns equal to each other. The offsetting amount is shown in the statement of financial position credit column.

ON YOUR OWN

LEARNING OUTCOME PRACTICE

1. When completing an extended trial balance that includes balances for depreciation expense and accumulated depreciation, into which columns should these balances be extended?

    Depreciation Expense   **Accumulated Depreciation**
    a. Statement of comprehensive income debit   Statement of comprehensive income credit
    b. Statement of financial position credit   Statement of financial position debit
    c. Statement of comprehensive income debit   Statement of financial position credit
    d. Statement of financial position debit   Statement of comprehensive income credit
    ACCA adapted

2. Heather is completing her extended trial balance. Into which columns should she extend the balance to close profit?

    Statement of Comprehensive Income   **Statement of Financial Position**
    a. Debit   Credit
    b. Credit   Debit
    c. Debit   Debit
    d. Credit   Credit
    ACCA adapted

3. Totals in an extended trial balance were:

Statement of Comprehensive Income Columns		Statement of Financial Position Columns	
Debit	Credit	Debit	Credit
$129 685	$136 894	$149 212	$142 003

    What is the profit for the period?
    a. A loss of $7209
    b. A loss of $12 318
    c. A profit of $7209
    d. A profit of $12 318
    ACCA adapted

Preparing the Financial Statements

Continuing the Schwittay Consulting example, we can use the figures from the extended trial balance (Figure 5.19) to construct the financial statements.

STATEMENT OF COMPREHENSIVE INCOME

Schwittay Consulting AG Statement of Comprehensive Income For the Month Ended 31 March 2009 € Euros		
Account Titles	DR	CR
Beginning balance, 1 March 2009		0
Revenue		
Service revenue	91 500	
Interest revenue	1 180	92 680
Less: Expenses		
Salaries expense	33 710	
Interest expense	1 000	
Rent expense	2 475	
Supplies expense	1 350	
Insurance expense	1 005	
Improvements amortization	1 150	44 080
Profit		**48 600**

STATEMENT OF FINANCIAL POSITION

Schwittay Consulting AG Statement of Financial Position 31 March 2009		
Account Titles	DR	CR
Assets		
Current assets		
Cash	281 080	
Trade accounts receivable	8 500	
Supplies	1 500	
Prepaid rent	24 750	
Prepaid insurance	11 055	326 885
Leasehold improvements		67 850
Total assets		**394 735**

Liabilities		
Current liabilities		
Trade Accounts payable	23 000	
Salaries payable	33 710	
Interest payable	2 000	
Unearned service revenue	110 500	146 210
Loan payable		150 000
Total liabilities		296 210
Equity		
Contributed capital		20 000
Retained earnings		78 525
Total equity		98 525
Total liabilities and equity		**394 735**

Once the financial statements are prepared, closing entries can be recorded.

ENTRY 1: CLOSE REVENUE TO INCOME SUMMARY

Date	Account Titles	DR	CR
31 March 2009	Service revenue	€91 500	
	Investment revenue	1 180	
	Income summary		€92 680

ENTRY 2: CLOSE EXPENSES TO INCOME SUMMARY

Date	Account Titles	DR	CR
31 March 2009	Income summary	€44 080	
	Salaries expense		33 710
	Interest expense		1 000
	Rent expense		2 475
	Supplies expense		4 740
	Insurance expense		1 005
	Leasehold improvements amortization		1 150

ENTRY 3: CLOSE INCOME SUMMARY TO RETAINED EARNINGS

Date	Account Titles	DR	CR
31 March 2009	Income summary Retained earnings	€48 600	€48 600

ENTRY 4: CLOSE DIVIDENDS DIRECTLY TO RETAINED EARNINGS

Date	Account Titles	DR	CR
31 March 2009	Retained earnings Dividends	€20 000	€20 000

After closing entries have been recorded, the ledger accounts will appear as shown in Figure 5.20.

FIGURE 5.20 MARCH 2009 POST-CLOSING LEDGER ACCOUNTS

Schwittay Consulting AG Post-Closing Ledger 31 March 2009 € Euros		
Date	**DR**	**CR**
SERVICE REVENUE		
Beginning balance, 1 March 2009		0
7 March 2009		17 000
10 March 2009		7 500
31 March 2009 Adjusting entry		67 000
31 March 2009 Closing entry	91 500	
Ending balance, 31 March 2009		0

INTEREST REVENUE		
Beginning balance, 1 March 2009		0
28 March 2009		1 180
31 March 2009 Closing entry	1 180	
Ending balance, 31 March 2009		0
SALARIES EXPENSE		
Pre-adjustment balance, 31 March 2009	0	
31 March 2009 Adjusting entry	33 710	
31 March 2009 Closing entry		33 710
Ending balance, 31 March 2009	0	
INTEREST EXPENSE		
Pre-adjustment balance, 31 March 2009	0	
31 March 2009 Adjusting entry	1 000	
31 March 2009 Closing entry		1 000
Ending balance, 31 March 2009	0	
RENT EXPENSE		
Pre-adjustment, 31 March 2009	0	
31 March 2009 Adjusting entry	2 475	
31 March 2009 Closing entry		2 475
Ending balance, 31 March 2009	0	
SUPPLIES EXPENSE		
Pre-adjustment balance, 31 March 2009	0	
31 March 2009 Adjusting entry	4 740	
31 March 2009 Closing entry		4 740
Ending balance, 31 March 2009	0	
INSURANCE EXPENSE		
Pre-adjustment balance, 31 March 2009	0	
31 March 2009 Adjusting entry	1 005	
31 March 2009 Closing entry		1 005
Ending balance, 31 March 2009	0	

(*Continued*)

FIGURE 5.20 *(CONTINUED)*

Date	DR	CR
Schwittay Consulting AG Post-Closing Ledger 31 March 2009 € Euros		
IMPROVEMENTS AMORTIZATION		
Pre-adjustment balance, 31 March 2009	0	
31 March 2009 Adjusting entry	1 150	
31 March 2009 Closing entry		1 150
Ending balance, 31 March 2009	0	
CASH		
Beginning balance, 1 March 2009	294 640	
1 March 2009		13 500
1 March 2009		23 000
3 March 2009	20 000	
10 March 2009	7 500	
22 March 2009	10 000	
26 March 2009		4 240
28 March 2009	8 500	
28 March 2009	1 180	
31 March 2009		20 000
Ending balance, 31 March 2009	281 080	
TRADE ACCOUNTS RECEIVABLE		
Beginning balance, 1 March 2009	20 000	
1 March 2009		20 000
7 March 2009	17 000	
31 March 2009		8 500
Ending balance, 31 March 2009	8 500	
SUPPLIES		
Beginning balance, 1 March 2009	2 000	
21 March 2009	4 240	
31 March 2009 Adjusting entry		4 740
Ending balance, 31 March 2009	1 500	

PREPAID RENT		
Pre-adjustment balance, 31 March 2009	27 225	
31 March 2009 Adjusting entry		2 475
Ending balance, 31 March 2009	24 750	

PREPAID INSURANCE		
Pre-adjustment balance, 31 March 2009	12 060	
31 March 2009 Adjusting entry		1 005
Ending balance, 31 March 2009	11 055	

LEASEHOLD IMPROVEMENTS		
Pre-closing balance, 31 March 2009	69 000	
31 March 2009 Adjusting entry		1 150
Ending balance, 31 March 2009	67 850	

TRADE ACCOUNTS PAYABLE		
Beginning balance, 1 March 2009		23 000
1 March 2009	23 000	
21 March 2009		4 240
22 March 2009	4 240	
Ending balance, 31 March 2009		0

SALARIES PAYABLE		
Beginning balance, 1 March 2009		13 500
1 March 2009	13 500	
31 March 2009 Adjusting entry		33 710
Ending balance, 31 March 2009		33 710

INTEREST PAYABLE		
Ending balance, 31 March 2009		2 000

UNEARNED SERVICE REVENUE		
Beginning balance, 1 March 2009		167 500
22 March 2009		10 000
31 March 2009 Adjusting entry	67 000	
Ending balance, 31 March 2009		110 500

(*Continued*)

FIGURE 5.20 *(CONTINUED)*

Date	DR	CR
Schwittay Consulting AG Post-Closing Ledger 31 March 2009 € Euros		
LOAN PAYABLE		
Ending balance, 31 March 2009		150 000
CONTRIBUTED CAPITAL		
Ending balance, 31 March 2009		20 000
RETAINED EARNINGS		
Pre-closing balance, 31 March 2009		49 925
31 March 2009 Closing entry		92 680
31 March 2009 Closing entry	44 080	
31 March 2009 Closing entry	20 000	
Ending balance, 31 March 2009		78 525
DIVIDENDS		
Beginning balance, 1 March 2009	0	
31 March 2009	20 000	
31 March 2009 Closing entry		20 000
Ending balance, 31 March 2009	0	

Finally, the post-closing trial balance is shown in Figure 5.21.

Schwittay Consulting is now ready to begin accumulating financial information for April 2009, the next reporting period.

Conclusion

In Chapter 4, we examined the first of four steps in the accounting process -- analyse and record journal entries. In this chapter, we covered the activities that occur at the end of the reporting period after all journal entries have been recorded. Ledger accounts are adjusted and an adjusted trial balance is generated. This adjusted trial balance is used to prepare the financial statements. Then closing entries are recorded and a post-closing trial balance is generated. At that point, the accounting records are ready to receive journal entries for transactions in the subsequent reporting period.

FIGURE 5.21 MARCH 2009 POST-CLOSING TRIAL BALANCE

Schwittay Consulting AG Post-Closing Trial Balance 31 March 2009		
Account Titles	DR	CR
Service revenue		0
Interest revenue		0
Salaries expense	0	
Interest expense	0	
Rent expense	0	
Supplies expense	0	
Insurance expense	0	
Improvements amortization	0	
Cash	281 080	
Trade accounts receivable	8 500	
Supplies	1 500	
Prepaid rent	24 750	
Prepaid insurance	11 055	
Leasehold improvements	67 850	
Trade accounts payable		0
Salaries payable		33 710
Interest payable		2 000
Unearned service revenue		110 500
Loan payable		150 000
Contributed capital		20 000
Retained earnings		78 525
Dividends	0	
	394 735	394 735

Adjusting entries are required to report financial information in the appropriate reporting period. Two of the four adjusting entries are accruals of transactions that should be reported in the current accounting period, but have not yet been recorded. For these we recognize the unrecorded revenue that has already been earned or the unrecorded expense that has already been incurred.

The second pair of the four adjusting entries relate to business transactions recorded in the past that must now be adjusted to reflect in the current time period. For unearned revenue, cash was received for a good to be delivered or a service to be provided in the future. Thus, the receipt of cash caused the original business transaction to be recorded and a liability recognized. The adjusting entry removes the liability and records the fact that the revenue has been earned.

A pre-paid cost represents a business transaction previously recorded because cash was paid in advance to acquire a good or service, which is an asset before it is consumed. Now an adjusting entry is required to show that the prepaid expense has wholly or partially expired.

Once financial statements have been constructed, closing entries are recorded. Closing entries remove the balances in temporary accounts to the retained earnings reserve, thus converting them to permanent balances.

Summary
LEARNING OUTCOME 1
Cash Versus Accrual Accounting Explained

Accrual accounting is required by most accounting standards and is used by almost all businesses. All publicly traded businesses use accrual accounting. Accrual accounting records transactions based on when their effects occur, not when cash related to the transaction is received or paid. This requires that adjustments be made to some ledger accounts after all transactions have been recorded for the reporting period.

The revenue principle and the matching principle guide accrual accounting. The revenue principle requires that revenue be recorded in the reporting period in which delivery of the good or service was made. The matching principle requires that the expenses that generated that revenue be recorded in the same reporting period as the revenue.

While accounting standards require that business entities use accrual accounting, some continue to use cash-basis accounting. Businesses that use cash-basis accounting are privately held and tend to be smaller. In addition, they typically have few trade accounts receivable and payable, and few major assets. Their rationale for using cash-basis accounting is that the financial results of the business would not be significantly different than if they were reported under accrual accounting. If the owners and creditors of the business do not require accrual accounting, then it may make more sense to use cash-basis accounting for its simplicity and lower costs.

Under cash-basis accounting, revenue is recorded when cash is received from the customer and expenses are recorded when cash is paid to suppliers. Thus, every journal entry involves either a debit or a credit to the cash account. It also means that no difference exists between the statement of comprehensive income and the statement of cash flows – they are the same. However, in practice some businesses use a hybrid of cash-basis and accrual accounting.

LEARNING OUTCOME 2
Adjusting Entries Explained

Accrual accounting is implemented through adjusting entries. Typically at the end of the reporting period, four different types of adjusting entries will be made. Two relate to the recognition of revenue and expenses. For example, the business may have earned revenue on sales of goods or services that have not yet been recorded. The other two adjusting entries relate to the reclassification of a liability obligation into revenue or an asset into an expense.

Adjusting entries must meet two criteria. First, they cannot involve cash. Only journal entries can involve cash. Second, the adjusting entry affects both the statement of financial position and the statement of comprehensive income. If only one or the other is involved, then the entry is not an adjusting entry.

LEARNING OUTCOME 3
Adjusting Entries Recorded

The first two types of adjusting entries *accrue* revenue or expense. The first is the recognition of revenue that has been earned but not yet recorded. The need for this type of adjusting entry arises because revenue earned has not been recorded. At the end of the reporting period these situations require that the revenue be accrued.

Likewise, at the end of the reporting period an expense may be incurred but not yet recorded. These too must be accrued.

The second two types of adjusting entries *reclassify* a liability (credit) to revenue (credit) and an asset (debit) to an expense (debit). Notice that the normal balances for each type are the same. Both a liability and revenue have a credit normal balance, while both an asset and an expense have a debit normal balance. Also notice that these entries, like all adjusting entries, involve both the statement of financial position and the statement of comprehensive income.

Reclassification adjusting entries follow a journal entry that was recorded in the past. In the case of reclassification to revenue, the original journal entry recorded unearned revenue because a customer paid in advance of delivery. When delivery is made and the revenue earned, the adjusting entry must be made to reclassify unearned revenue (a liability on the statement of financial position) to revenue (on the statement of comprehensive income).

Reclassification adjusting entries involving expense follow a previous journal entry to record a prepaid expense. This asset was recorded because the business paid an expense in advance. When the prepaid expense expires. Then an adjusting entry must be made to reclassify the asset (on the statement of financial position) to an expense (on the statement of comprehensive income).

LEARNING OUTCOMES 4 AND 5
Closing Entries Explained and Financial Statement Prepared

Financial statements are constructed from the adjusted trial balance that is generated after adjusting entries have been recorded and before closing entries are made. The extended trial balance is a worksheet for calculating the statement of financial position and the statement of comprehensive income. This worksheet starts with the adjusted trial balance accounts and also has columns for the statement of financial position and the statement of comprehensive income.

Once the financial statements have been constructed, temporary accounts are closed into the permanent accounts – specifically the retained earnings reserve. Temporary accounts include all accounts on the statement of comprehensive income and dividends. Permanent accounts are those that appear on the statement of financial position.

The first closing entry transfers the revenue balance into the income summary account which is an account used only during the closing process to measure profit or loss. The second closing entry transfers the balances in all expense accounts to the income summary account. At this point, the income summary account balance is equal to the profit or loss for the reporting period. The third closing entry transfers the balance in the income summary account to retained earnings. And finally, the fourth closing entry transfers any balance in the dividend account directly to retained earnings.

Once the closing process is finished, a post-closing trial balance can be generated. At this point, the accounting process is complete for the reporting period and journal entries for the next reporting period can be recorded.

REVIEW QUESTIONS

1. Why are adjusting entries made at the end of the reporting period? What are the four types of adjusting entries? Explain each type and provide an example. What are the two criteria that every adjusting entry must meet?
2. What is the difference between a temporary and permanent account? Which accounts are temporary accounts? Which accounts are permanent accounts?
3. Which accounts – temporary or permanent – are closed and show a balance of zero on the post-closing trial balance? Which accounts – temporary or permanent – have a balance in the post-closing trial balance?
4. Why are temporary accounts closed? Why are permanent accounts not closed?
5. What are the four closing entries?

Key terms

Accrual

Accrue

Adjusting entries

Closing entries

Extended trial balance

Nominal accounts

Permanent accounts

Real accounts

Temporary accounts

Unearned revenue

Terminology practice

For each of the following statements, insert the correct term from the preceding list of key terms. Each key term can be used more than once.

1. Entries that remove balances in temporary accounts to the retained earnings reserve are called _____.

2. _____ (also referred to as _____) include the statement of financial position accounts.

3. _____ is the process of classifying debits and credits into the appropriate reporting period.

4. _____ (also referred to as _____) include the statement of comprehensive income accounts and the dividend account.

5. _____ are not closed. _____ are closed at the end of the reporting period.

6. When revenue should be recognized in the current reporting period but it has not been recorded, then we must _____ the revenue. The same is true with expenses that have been incurred but not yet recorded.

7. A worksheet version of the adjusted trial balance called a(n) _____ can be used to construct the financial statements.

8. Entries that convert accounts to accrual basis are called _____.

Application exercises

1. On 31 March 2010, for the Bayan Café was preparing to make adjusting entries in order to prepare the quarterly financial statements. 31 March 2010 falls on a Wednesday. Based on the following information, what adjusting entries should the account record?

   a. On 15 February that same year, Bayan Café had borrowed $70 000 from the bank. The interest rate on the loan was 8% per annum. No payments are made on the loan until 15 July 2010 when the loan is due in full.

   b. Four employees work for the Bayan Café and are paid at the rate of $300 per week each. The work week is from Sunday until Friday. The Café is closed Saturday. Employees are paid on the Monday following of the following week.

   c. The Bayan Café paid rent in advance for six months on 1 December 2009 in the amount of $10 800.

   d. On 30 March 2010, the Café received an order from a customer to cater a birthday party on 2 March 2010. The customer paid half of the total amount of $1 500 in cash. Though the cash was deposited in the bank, no journal entry has been made in the accounting records.

   e. The manager of the Bayan Café estimates that the catering job (Item d) will incur expenses of $1 700.

   f. On 31 March, the Café was hired to cater a business breakfast. The price for the job was $3,330. Because the job was rush and requested by the customer at the last minute, no invoice has yet been sent for payment.

   g. The Bayan Café had purchased one year's coverage from an insurance provider that went into effect on 15 March 2010. The provider has yet to send an invoice for the $14 000 annual insurance premium.

2. Following is the extended trial balance worksheet for Al Awad Systems, Inc.

	Al Awad Systems, Inc. Extended Trial Balance 30 September 2011 £ British Pounds					
Account titles	Adjusted Trial Balance		Statement of Financial Position		Statement of Comprehensive Income	
	DR	CR	DR	CR	DR	CR
Cash and cash equivalents	2 310					
Trade accounts receivable	1 260					
Inventories	770					
Prepaid insurance	1 330					
Property, plant and equipment	4 620					
Accumulated depreciation		1 680				
Other assets	6 930					
Trade accounts payable		5 390				
Income taxes payable		420				
Other liabilities		1540				
Ordinary shares		3 430				
Beginning retained earnings		3 150				
Dividends	1190					
Sales revenue		28 700				
Cost of sales	17 500					
Operating expenses	7 000					
Income tax expense	1 400					
Totals	44 310	44 310				
Profit						
Worksheet totals	44 310	44 310				

Required:

1. Complete the extended worksheet.
2. Prepare the statement of comprehensive income.
3. Prepare the statement of financial position.

3. The June month end adjusted trial balance for Christophe Ceramics SA is as follows:

Christophe Ceramics SA Adjusted Trial Balance 30 June 2014 € Euros		
Account Titles	DR	CR
Sales revenue		635 000
Cost of sales	250 000	
Selling expenses	70 000	
Administrative expenses	110 000	
Interest expense	25 000	
Cash	500 000	
Trade accounts receivable	130 000	
Inventories	200 000	
Trade accounts payable		140 000
Borrowings		230 000
Capital stock		200 000
Retained earnings		150 000
Dividends	70 000	
Totals	**1 355 000**	**1 355 000**

Record the closing entries.

Case analysis
Li Designs LLC (Continued)

This is a continuation of the case analysis begun in Chapter 4 for Li Designs LLC. Remember that Mai, a talented designer, had begun Li Designs. Even though she was quite successful at attracting clients, the business seemed to have continual problems. She turned to Rick, an accountant and a friend she met at university. After consulting with Mai, Rick realized that Mai's financial records needed to be accounted for properly.

Rick asked you, an employee, to examine source documents and other records that Mai kept in cardboard boxes. In Chapter 4, you were to create a chart of accounts and then analyse and record the transactions. Having done that, you must now complete the accounting process for the April, May and June reporting periods.

Complete the accounting work for Li Designs by making the required adjusting entries, generating the adjusted trial balance. From this, construct the financial statements (you may omit the statement of cash flows). Then record the closing entries and generate the post-closing trial balance.

Suggested reading

Schilit, Howard M. (1993) *Financial Shenanigans: How to Detect Accounting Gimmicks and Fraud in Financial Reports*, New York: McGraw-Hill.

Accounting information systems

6

LEARNING OUTCOMES

By the end of this chapter, you should be able to:

1. Define the accounting information system and describe its components.
2. Describe the sales and cash receipts cycle.
3. Describe the purchases and cash disbursements cycle.
4. Describe the employee compensation, fixed assets and inventories and conversion cycles.
5. Define the audit trail.

Introducing accounting information systems

The first applications for computers in business were in accounting. Since those early days, automated accounting systems have become quite common. Even small businesses can readily accommodate their accounting needs with inexpensive software packages that operate on personal computers. Some of these systems are quite sophisticated.

However, in large multinational companies the requirements are quite different. Accounting information is processed by complex software packages capable of handling high transaction volumes. In fact, transaction volumes are often so large that specialized accounting subsystems are required. Thus, the overall accounting system in large companies typically comprises several separate software modules, each of which addresses a specialized area of accounting.

Furthermore, accounting systems in large companies do not operate in isolation. Computer automation and communications technologies have allowed companies to integrate information systems electronically for different business functions. This allows the business to share data between different organizational functions such as production, marketing, sales, human resources, finance and accounting. Information sharing has significant benefits for the business because it increases efficiency and provides a more complete understanding of the business as a whole. Figure 6.1 illustrates how different organizational functions interact in the overall business information system.

The top left quadrant of Figure 6.1 relates to the enterprise resource planning (ERP) system, of which financial accounting is one component. Others include manufacturing and human resource management. For

FIGURE 6.1 BUSINESS INFORMATION SYSTEMS

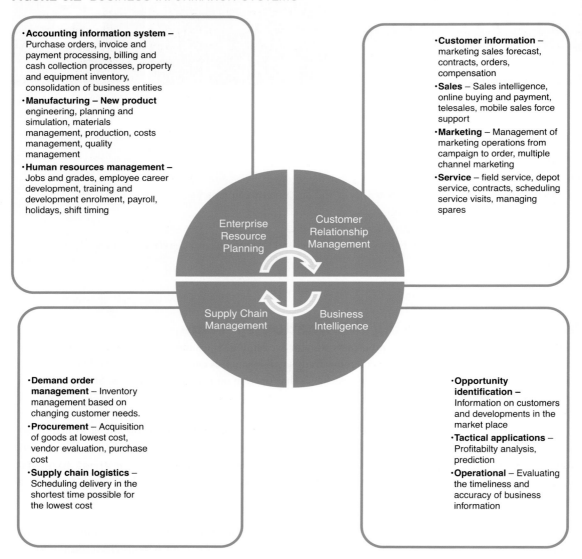

- **Accounting information system –** Purchase orders, invoice and payment processing, billing and cash collection processes, property and equipment inventory, consolidation of business entities
- **Manufacturing – New product** engineering, planning and simulation, materials management, production, costs management, quality management
- **Human resources management –** Jobs and grades, employee career development, training and development enrolment, payroll, holidays, shift timing

- **Customer information –** marketing sales forecast, contracts, orders, compensation
- **Sales** – Sales intelligence, online buying and payment, telesales, mobile sales force support
- **Marketing** – Management of marketing operations from campaign to order, multiple channel marketing
- **Service** – field service, depot service, contracts, scheduling service visits, managing spares

Enterprise Resource Planning

Customer Relationship Management

Supply Chain Management

Business Intelligence

- **Demand order management** – Inventory management based on changing customer needs.
- **Procurement** – Acquisition of goods at lowest cost, vendor evaluation, purchase cost
- **Supply chain logistics –** Scheduling delivery in the shortest time possible for the lowest cost

- **Opportunity identification –** Information on customers and developments in the market place
- **Tactical applications –** Profitabilty analysis, prediction
- **Operational** – Evaluating the timeliness and accuracy of business information

example, human resource management maintains records on employee pay rates and benefits. This information is used to account for payroll.

The top right quadrant of Figure 6.1 relates to the customer relationship management (CRM) system, which concerns the customer, marketing, sales and service. For example, information on a sale to a particular customer would be updated in the customer's sales history for future reference by sales and marketing staff. This would give them an idea about the products and services that the customer might demand in the future and therefore provide clues about how to market to the customer. Sales information is also needed by the accounting function to record sales revenue, cost of sales and trade accounts receivable. Thus, it makes sense to integrate or share information between both ERP and CRM systems.

The same reasoning applies to supply chain management (SCM) and business intelligence systems (BIS). SCM involves the acquisition of goods for resale, and materials and components to be used in manufacturing. The operational issues might include determining which vendors offer the best terms and prices. SCM systems would also update vendor records when purchases are made so that the purchasing function has a complete history from which to work. However, information on purchases is also needed by the accounting function in order to record inventory costs and related trade accounts payable.

In some companies these information systems are closely integrated. Consider, for example, a company that sells its products online either to consumers or business to business. A customer may directly order and pay for products online. The order would act as a trigger (an event that begins a process), which would cause a number of subsequent events to occur in the company's information systems. Without any human intervention, sales and service information for that customer would be updated in the CRM. The shipping department would be instructed to pull the item from inventory and ship it to the customer. Inventory records would be updated, and this in turn may affect the production schedule in manufacturing. But also, at the same time, the ERP would record automated journal entries for the sale and the receipt of funds from the customer's credit card company.

However, our interest is in the financial accounting component of ERP. In large companies, this single financial accounting component is actually a complex accounting information system. An accounting information system (AIS) is the overall accounting system maintained by a business entity, including computerized software modules that handle the accounting process that we discussed in Chapters 4 and 5. However, the accounting information system also includes the business's accounting policies and procedures as well as the human organizations that handle accounting activities.

LEARNING OUTCOME 1
DEFINE THE ACCOUNTING INFORMATION SYSTEM AND DESCRIBE ITS COMPONENTS

1.1   What are accounting cycles?

1.2   What are special journals, subsidiary ledgers and the general ledger?

1.3   What is an account coding structure?

1.1 What are accounting cycles?

Because the volume of transactions can be quite large, similar transactions are often grouped together and handled by dedicated computerized accounting modules. These groupings are referred to as accounting cycles. Common cycles include sales and cash receipts, purchases and cash disbursement, employee compensation, fixed assets and inventory. These are illustrated graphically in Figure 6.2.

FIGURE 6.2 ACCOUNTING CYCLES

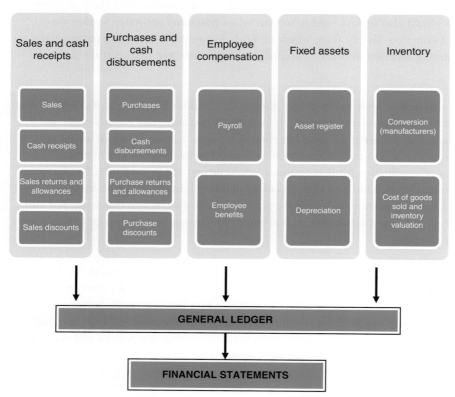

1.2 What are special journals, subsidiary ledgers and the general ledger?

In Chapter 4 we discussed how transactions were recorded in the journal and posted to the ledger. In complex accounting information systems, specialized journals and subsidiary ledgers are used for each accounting cycle. The information contained in these special journals is summarized and then flows into the general ledger, as shown in Figure 6.2. A general ledger is the 'master' ledger for the business. The relationship between the specialized journals, subsidiary ledgers and general ledger is illustrated in Figure 6.3.

FIGURE 6.3 SPECIAL JOURNALS, SUBSIDIARY LEDGERS AND THE GENERAL LEDGER

A special journal (sometimes referred to as a daybook) records only like entries. For example, credit card companies like MasterCard or American Express receive millions of customer payments each day. Each payment is a separate transaction, but recording a separate journal entry for each transaction would not be cost effective.

The solution is to combine these cash receipt transactions into a special journal. The credit goes to trade accounts receivable for different customers. Cash is always debited. The special journal is then totalled and this amount is recorded with one journal entry into a general ledger. The general ledger is the combined set of ledger accounts, as we discussed in Chapters 4 and 5. But the business will still need detailed information about what each customer paid and how much. This information is maintained in a subsidiary ledger (also subledger). The subsidiary ledger prevents the general ledger from being burdened with too much detail.

In the remainder of this chapter we will examine the major accounting cycles shown in Figure 6.2 and typical accounting subsystems within each cycle, using Sydney-based Melbourne Medical Equipment LLC. This fictitious company manufactures and sells various types of medical equipment, including X-ray machines, blood pressure devices, EKG devices and other diagnostic equipment.

In addition to maintaining financial records by the chart of accounts, Melbourne Medical Equipment wants to identify financial information by several divisions, including manufacturing, sales, financial and leasing in addition to the overall company. The business also wants to track financial results by product and customer. As a result, the accounting uses the account code structure shown in Figure 6.4.

1.3 What is an account code structure?

An account code structure allows each transaction to be coded in a way that makes the information easier for computers to process. An account code structure is also more precise and less confusing than account titles used in a basic chart of accounts. It also permits a business to refine accounting information. For example, a coding structure can be used to break information down by geographic areas, divisions, products, customers and other categories. Melbourne's coding structure (Figure 6.4) contains four tables: division, account, products and customers.

FIGURE 6.4 ACCOUNT CODE STRUCTURE

Division Codes

Code	Description
01	Headquarters
02	Manufacturing
03	Sales
04	Financial
05	Leasing

Account Codes

Code	Description
100	**Revenue**
110	Service revenue
120	Sales revenue
130	Sales returns and allowances
140	Sales discounts
200	**Expenses**
210	Cost of sales
220	Selling expenses
230	Administrative expenses
240	Research and development expenses
250	Interest expense
260	Tax expense
300	**Assets**
310	Cash
320	Trade accounts receivable
330	Prepaid advertising
340	Supplies
350	Inventories
360	Short-term investments
370	Property, plant and equipment
380	Intangible assets
390	Long-term investments
400	**Liabilities**
410	Trade accounts payable
420	Interest payable
430	Taxes payable
440	Short-term notes payable
450	Salaries payable

FIGURE 6.4 (CONTINUED)

Code	Description
460	Mortgages payable
470	Long-term borrowings
500	**Equity**
510	Capital stock
520	Retained earnings
530	Dividends

Product Codes

Code	Description
1000	X-ray machines
2000	Blood pressure devices
3300	EKG devices
4400	Diagnostic equipment

Customer Codes

Code	Description
10100	Brisbane City Clinic
10200	Melbourne Hospital
10300	Perth Hospital System
10400	Sydney Doctors' Group

In each journal entry, account titles for both debits and credits are coded using the following code structure sequence:

Division ➡ Account ➡ Product ➡ Customer

Suppose that the Melbourne Sales Division sold EKG devices to the Brisbane City Clinic for A$35 000 on 30 June 2009. The journal entry using this coding structure would be:

Date	Division	Account	Product	Customer	Account Title	DR	CR
30 June 2009	03	310	3300	10100	Cash	A$35 000	
	03	120	3300	10100	Sales revenue		A$35 000

In the division table, we can see that 03 is the code for Sales. Account code 310 is Cash and 120 is Sales Revenue. In the product table, 3300 is EKG equipment and in the customer table, 10100 is for the Brisbane City Clinic.

ON YOUR OWN

LEARNING OUTCOME REVIEW

1. Compare and contrast the accounting information system with the accounting process discussed in Chapters 4 and 5.
2. Compare and contrast a general journal entry and a special journal entry. How are they similar? How are they different? Why are special journal entries used in accounting?
3. Compare and contrast a general ledger and a subsidiary ledger. How are they similar? How are they different? Why are subsidiary ledgers used in accounting?
4. Compare and contrast a chart of accounts with an account code structure. How are they similar? How are they different?

LEARNING OUTCOME PRACTICE

1. What would be the appropriate account code for the credit side of the journal entry when cash is received from Sydney Doctors' Group to Melbourne Sales on the trade accounts receivable that was recorded for a purchase of blood pressure devices? See Figure 6.4.
   a. 04-3100-4400-10200
   b. 03-3100-4400-10400
   c. 03-3200-4400-10400
   d. 3300-3100-4400-03

2. What would be the appropriate account code for the debit side of the journal entry when cash is received from Sydney Doctors' Group to Melbourne Sales on the trade receivable that was recorded for a purchase of blood pressure devices? See Figure 6.4.
   a. 04-3100-4400-10200
   b. 03-3100-4400-10400
   c. 03-3200-4400-10400
   d. 3300-3100-4400-03

Now, using Melbourne Medical Equipment as our example, let's examine each of the accounting cycles. Each cycle contains one or more subsystems. For example, the sales and cash receipts cycle (see Figure 6.2) includes the sales, cash receipts, sales returns and allowances, and sales discount subsystems. Each of these subsystems will be illustrated using a simplified flowchart.

Flowcharts in this chapter are based on three basic symbols, shown in Figure 6.5. An elliptical symbol represents a trigger event that begins a process, a rectangle indicates a process within the subsystem and the rectangular symbol with the curved bottom line represents a document.

FIGURE 6.5 BASIC FLOWCHART SYMBOLS

| Trigger | Process | Document |

LEARNING OUTCOME 2
DESCRIBE THE SALES AND CASH RECEIPTS CYCLE

2.1   What is the sales subsystem?

2.2   What is the cash receipts subsystem?

2.3   What is the sales returns and allowances subsystem?

2.4   What is the sales discounts subsystem?

2.5   What modes of payment are used in sales transactions?

The sales and cash receipts cycle has four subsystems: sales, cash receipts, sales returns and allowances, and sales discounts. We will examine each separately below.

2.1 What is the sales subsystem?

Figure 6.6 shows a flowchart of Melbourne Medical Equipment's sales subsystem.

The sales subsystem begins when a customer places an order to purchase equipment. The source document for this is the customer purchase order. In Melbourne's case, we will assume that customer purchase orders are received as hard copy. However, in some businesses this document could be soft copy. For example, a retail customer might order through the Internet. In this case the purchase order would be electronic (soft copy) rather than on paper. In general, transactions are being received electronically more often (see box).

ELECTRONIC TRANSACTIONS

With EDI (electronic data interchange), data is exchanged electronically, replacing hard-copy documents like purchase orders, invoices, shipping notices and bills of lading. Likewise, money can be transferred electronically using EFT (electronic funds transfer), eliminating the need for hard-copy cheques.

EDI, POS (point of sale) and EFT systems, coupled with technologies like RFID (radio frequency identification devices), have enabled companies significantly to reduce processing costs and errors, as well as the amount of time needed to handle transactions. However, from an accounting viewpoint, electronic transactions processing must abide by the same requirements as hard-copy-based systems, namely that transactions must be able to be validated from source documents (even if in electronic form) and an audit trail maintained.

FIGURE 6.6 SALES SUBSYSTEM

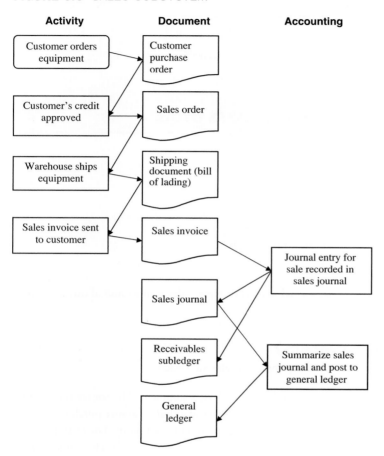

Before the equipment is shipped, a sales order is prepared. A sales order is an internal document that verifies that the appropriate internal approvals have been given. For example, an approval may be needed from the credit department to confirm that credit has been extended to the customer in cases where the sale has been made on account. The sales order is sent to the warehouse, which ships the equipment to the customer.

When the order is shipped, a sales invoice is generated. A sales invoice is a bill to the customer showing the date, what equipment was shipped, the quantity and the total amount owed to the company. The sales invoice is also sent to the accounting department, which records the journal entry for the sale. This also establishes the trade accounts receivable. This entry may be combined with similar transactions and recorded through a sales journal. The sales journal total would then be recorded in the general ledger.

However, the business still needs detailed information on all customer trade account receivable balances. This information is available through the trade accounts receivable subsidiary ledger, which contains an

FIGURE 6.7 GENERAL AND SUBSIDIARY LEDGERS

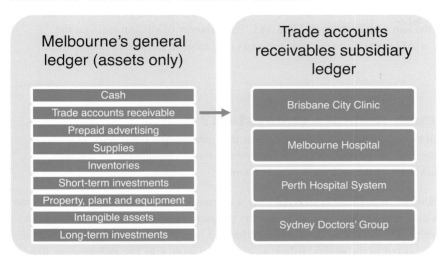

account for each customer. Figure 6.7 illustrates how the receivables subsidiary ledger relates to the general ledger account balance.

Detail would be available for each customer in the trade accounts receivable subsidiary ledger. Figure 6.8 shows an example of how the receivables ledger account might appear at the end of the July 2009 reporting period for Brisbane City Clinic in Melbourne's receivables subsidiary ledger.

FIGURE 6.8 TRADE ACCOUNTS RECEIVABLE SUBSIDIARY LEDGER

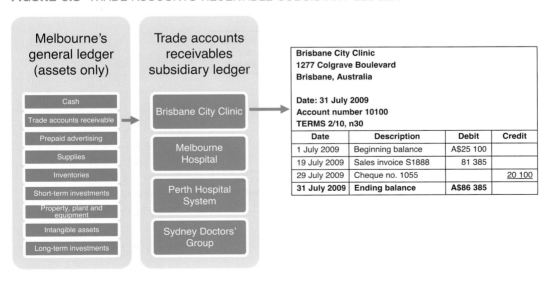

The receivables account begins with an unpaid balance of A$25 100. In July Brisbane made one purchase, which was recorded from sales invoice S1888 for A$81 385. Brisbane also made one payment of A$20 100. This left a balance owing at the end of July 2009 of A$86 385. The balances of all customers on the receivables subsidiary ledger would equal the total trade accounts receivable in the general ledger trade accounts receivable account.

2.2 What is the cash receipts subsystem?

The second subsystem within the sales and cash receipts cycle is the cash receipts subsystem. This subsystem deals with the collection of the trade accounts receivable balances established by the sales subsystem. Figure 6.9 is a flowchart of the cash receipts subsystem.

The cash receipts process begins when payment is received from a customer. The payment is deposited in the bank and is also placed on a cash receipts list. This list is used by the accounting department to record the journal entry for the cash receipt. This would be done through the cash receipts journal. The total from the cash receipts journal would be posted to the general ledger, as shown in Figure 6.9. The cash receipts would

FIGURE 6.9 CASH RECEIPTS SUBSYSTEM

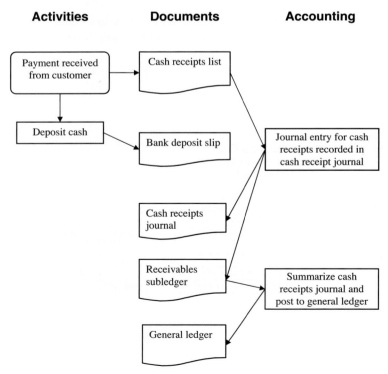

also appear on the receivables subledger. In Figure 6.8, we can see from the subledger account for Brisbane City Clinic that a payment for A$20 100 was received on 29 July 2009.

2.3 What is the sales returns and allowances subsystem?

Customers return goods to the seller for various reasons. They may have ordered more merchandise than they need, the business may have shipped the wrong colour merchandise to the customer or a customer may complain that the goods they received were defective. In these cases, businesses may take the merchandise back from the customer and credit the customer's trade accounts receivable, or the business may provide a credit to the customer. Together these are referred to as sales returns and allowances. Figure 6.10 shows the flowchart for sales returns and allowances.

The sales returns and allowance process begins when a customer requests a return or allowance. If granted by the business, a credit memo is prepared authorizing the customer's account to be credited. The

FIGURE 6.10 SALES RETURNS AND ALLOWANCES FLOWCHART

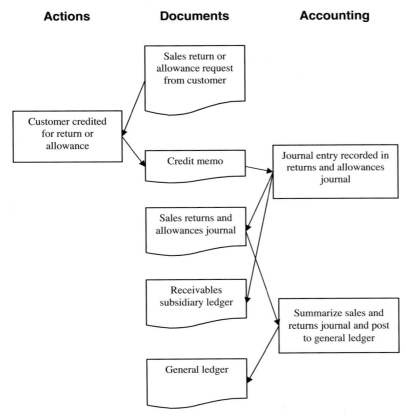

accounting department records the credit memo in the sales and returns journal. This information also appears in the receivables subsidiary ledger in the customer's account.

Brisbane City Clinic returns two EKG machines purchased for a total of A$4400 to Melbourne Medical Equipment. When these are received by Melbourne's warehouse on 30 July 2009, a credit memo is prepared and the following journal entry is made in the sales and return journal:

Date	Division	Account	Product	Customer	Account Title	DR	CR
30 July 2009	03	130	3300	10100	Sales returns and allowances	A$4 400	
	03	320	3300	10100	Trade accounts receivable		A$4 400

The information would appear as follows in the customer's accounts in the receivables subsidiary ledger:

Brisbane City Clinic
1277 Colgrave Boulevard
Brisbane, Australia
Date: 31 July 2009
Account number 10100
TERMS 3/12, n30

Date	Description	Debit	Credit
1 July 2009	Beginning balance	A$24 500	
19 July 2009	Sales invoice S1888	81 385	
29 July 2009	Cheque no. 1055		20 100
30 July 2009	Credit memo – returns and allowances		4 400
31 July 2009	**Ending balance**	A$81 385	

2.4 What is the sales discounts subsystem?

A business may offer a customer a discount on the amount owed if it is paid within a specified time period. For example, the customer may be required to pay within 30 days but will receive a 2% discount if payment is made within 12 days. This would be expressed as *2/12, net 30*. Net 30 means that the amount owed will be overdue if not paid within 30 days. However, if payment is received within 12 days, the customer may reduce the amount paid by 2%. Terms of 3/7, net 20 mean that payment is required within 20 days but a 3% discount will be provided if payment is received within 7 days.

Brisbane owes Melbourne Medical Equipment A$81 385 on terms 3/12, net 30. Brisbane pays this invoice on 30 July 2009. Since the invoice is dated 19 July, Brisbane is entitled to the discount. The discount would be A$2441 (rounded), which Brisbane would deduct from its payment. Thus, Melbourne would receive a check for A$78 944. The journal entry to record the payment when received on 30 July 2009 would be:

Date	Division	Account	Product	Customer	Account Title	DR	CR
	03	140	3300	10100	Sales discount	A$2 441	
30 July 2009	03	310	3300	10100	Cash	78 944	
	03	320	3300	10100	Trade accounts receivable		A$81 385

The customer's account would appear as follows in the receivables subsidiary ledger:

Brisbane City Clinic
1277 Colgrave Boulevard
Brisbane, Australia

Date: 31 July 2009
Account number 10100
TERMS 3/12, n30

Date	Description	Debit	Credit
1 July 2009	Beginning balance	A$24 500	
19 July 2009	Sales invoice S1888	81 385	
29 July 2009	Cheque no. 1055		20 100
30 July 2009	Credit memo – returns and allowances		4 400
31 July 2009	Payment received		81 385
31 July 2009	Ending balance	A$0	

We can see by examining this account that Brisbane now has no balance outstanding.

The sales returns and allowance and sales discount accounts both have a debit normal balance. Also, they are both contra accounts to revenue, which has a credit normal balance. A contra account is an account that offsets another account and is classified with that account in the financial statements. Thus, sales would appear as follows in the statement of comprehensive income for the month ended July 2009:

Sales revenue	$81 385
Less:	
Sales returns and allowances	(4 400)
Sales discounts	(2 441)
Net sales	**$74 544**

Notice that when sales returns and allowances and sales discounts are subtracted from total revenue, the result is net sales. We use the term gross sales to refer to total revenues before sales returns and allowances and sales discounts are deducted.

2.5 What modes of payment are used in sales transactions?

Businesses usually require that commercial customers like Brisbane City Clinic pay in one of two ways. The first is payment on an invoice payment basis, which is the method Melbourne is using. In this case, the customer is expected to pay each invoice separately. With the second, the customer is requested to pay on a statement. Typically, the customer is sent a statement each month that shows all amounts owing and the customer then returns payment for the total.

Credit cards are also a common mode of payment, although more typically for retail customers. Two types of credit cards are used. The first is internally owned by the company making the sale; the second is owned by a third party like Visa, MasterCard, Discover or American Express. Credit cards owned by the seller are a specific form of trade accounts receivable.

Suppose a customer named Elaine Harris has a credit card account with Excelsior Boutique, which extends credit to its select clientele. On 13 October 2010 Elaine purchases clothing for £880, charging the entire amount to her credit card. Because the credit card in this example is internal, the journal entry to record the sale would be as follows:

Date	Account Titles	DR	CR
13 Oct. 2010	Trade accounts receivable – Elaine Harris	£880	
	Sales revenue		£880

At this point, the credit card sale is treated like any other trade account receivable. Normally, retail credit cards are billed by monthly statement, which combines all current charges with any previous unpaid balance.

When a business uses a third-party credit card provider, the receivable from the customer is collected by the credit card provider, not the merchandise seller. Let's assume that Excelsior uses Visa and MasterCard instead of an internally owned card. When Elaine makes the purchase with Visa, the journal entry would be as follows:

Date	Account Titles	DR	CR
13 Oct. 2010	Trade accounts receivable – Visa	£880	
	Sales revenue		£880

Notice that the receivable is from Visa, not Elaine Harris. Normally, the third-party credit card company pays the seller soon after the purchase has been made. However, it will also charge the seller a fee for handling the transaction. Let's assume that Visa charges 2.5%. When payment is received, the fee will be deducted from the gross sale amount. The journal entry for payment made by Visa two days later would be as follows:

Date	Account Titles	DR	CR
15 Oct. 2010	Cash	£858	
	Credit card fees	22	
	Trade accounts receivable – Visa		£880

Visa deducts its fee and remits £858, and the difference is recorded as credit card fees, which is an expense that would appear on the statement of comprehensive income. The amount shown in the above journal entry would typically be included with other payments made in the same general time frame.

ON YOUR OWN

LEARNING OUTCOME REVIEW

1. Explain what the following documents are and how they are used in the sales and cash receipts cycle: customer purchase order, sales order and sales invoice.
2. What is the difference between a sales return and a sales allowance? Why would a business use one or the other?
3. What is a contra account?
4. Compare and contrast invoice payment with the statement method of paying for sales.
5. What is the difference between gross sales and net sales? How is each calculated?

LEARNING OUTCOME PRACTICE

1. A company sells $25 000 in merchandise to a customer on terms 2/8, net 30 on 29 October 2012. The customer pays on 7 November 2012 in full. What is the journal entry to record the payment?

2. A company sells $25 000 in merchandise to a customer on terms 2/8, net 30 on 29 October 2012. The customer pays on 5 November 2012 in full. What is the journal entry to record the payment?

3. Achillios Industries extends credit to its customers on terms 4/12, net 25. On 11 December 2014 a customer purchases €210 799 in merchandise. On 25 December 2014 payment is received by Achillios. The journal entry to record the payment would contain:
   a. €8431.96 credit to sales discount
   b. No entry to sales discount or sales returns and allowances
   c. €8431.96 credit to sales returns and allowances
   d. €8431.96 debit to sales returns and allowances

4. Lorenz-Wilhelm Steel receives an order for €3 324 885 from a construction company on 15 August 2013 on terms 3/10, net 30. On 17 August 2013, the customer returns merchandise for €215 300. The customer sends payment via EFT on 25 August 2013. What amount of sales discount is given, if any?
   a. €0
   b. €93 287.55
   c. €99 746.55
   d. €332 488.50

5. Tekko Fabrics reported $1 455 000 in revenues for fiscal 2011. Sales returns and allowances were $23 400, sales discounts $57 200, purchase discounts $77 990 and purchase returns and allowances $49 222. What were net sales?
   a. $1 374 400
   b. $1 247 188
   c. $1 327 788
   d. $1 353 610

LEARNING OUTCOME 3
DESCRIBE THE PURCHASES AND CASH DISBURSEMENTS CYCLE

3.1 What is the purchases subsystem?

3.2 What is the cash disbursements subsystem?

3.3 What is the purchases returns and allowances subsystem?

3.4 What are purchase discounts?

The purchases and cash disbursements cycle involves the acquisition of goods and services for use by the business. In this chapter we will examine four subsystems: purchases, cash disbursements, purchases returns and allowances, and purchase discounts.

3.1 What is the purchases subsystem?

Figure 6.11 shows the flowchart for the purchases subsystem.

FIGURE 6.11 PURCHASES SUBSYSTEM

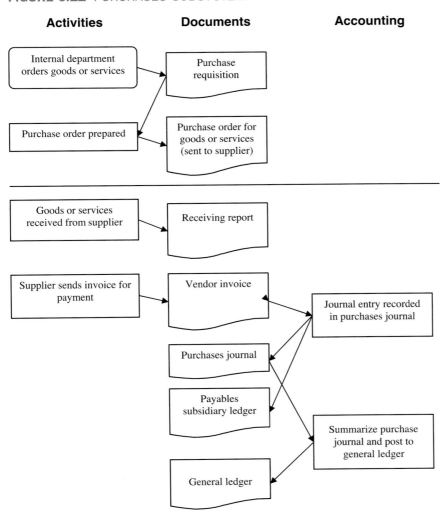

The purchase process begins when a department or function within the business needs to purchase goods or services. The department would prepare a purchase requisition, which is a request for the purchase. A purchase requisition is an internal document. This request is then processed by a central purchase department responsible for maintaining relationships with suppliers. The purchase department prepares and submits a purchase order to the supplier.

As we can see in Figure 6.11, the process is resumed when the supplier actually ships the goods or supplies the services requested. The receipt of these goods or services is documented using a receiving report. At this point, the supplier will also send an invoice for payment, which from the business's perspective is called a vendor invoice. The vendor invoice is the source document from which the accounting department records the trade accounts payable using a purchase journal. The trade accounts payable information also appears on the payables subsidiary ledger, which contains accounts for all suppliers. The total amount for the purchase journal is then posted to the general ledger.

3.2 What is the cash disbursements subsystem?

Figure 6.12 shows the flowchart for the cash disbursements subsystem.

The cash disbursements subsystem begins when the payment to a supplier becomes due. Suppliers typically offer credit terms. For example, a supplier may offer 30 days to pay. To conserve cash, the business will hold payment until this due date and then make payment.

Payment usually takes the form of either a cheque or electronic funds transfer to the supplier. Notice that a remittance advice accompanies the payment to advise the supplier which invoice or account is being paid.

FIGURE 6.12 CASH DISBURSEMENTS FLOWCHART

Actions	Documents	Accounting
Cash disbursement processed	Cheque or electronic funds transfer sent to vendor with remittance advice	Journal entry recorded in cash disbursements journal
	Cash disbursements journal	
	Payables subsidiary ledger	Summarize cash disbursements journal and post to general ledger
	General ledger	

The payment is a reduction to the cash balance, requiring that a journal entry be made to debit trade accounts payable and credit cash. The accounting department records this entry in the cash disbursements journal and the information appears in the payables subsidiary ledger. Also, a summary of the cash disbursements journal is posted to the general ledger.

3.3 What is the purchase returns and allowances subsystem?

The purchase returns and allowances account records situations when the business returns merchandise to the supplier or requests an allowance. The flowchart for this process is shown in Figure 6.13.

The business returns goods to a supplier requesting credit. When the supplier grants the request, a debit memo is received. As Figure 6.13 shows, this is recorded in the purchase returns and allowance journal.

FIGURE 6.13 PURCHASE RETURNS AND ALLOWANCE FLOWCHART

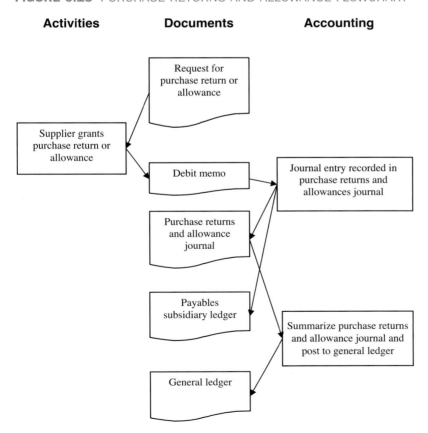

Morioka Foods returns canned goods to its supplier, Asia Imports Ltd, for a total of ¥50 000 on 7 December 2012 because the order sent was incorrect. Morioka records the following journal entry to the purchase returns and allowance journal:

Date	Account Titles	DR	CR
17 Dec. 2012	Purchase returns and allowances Merchandise inventory	¥50 000	¥50 000

Then a summary of the purchase returns and allowance journal is posted to the general ledger. The journal entry is posted to the payables subsidiary ledger, so that the trade accounts payable account to Asia Imports might appear as follows:

Supplier: Asia Imports Ltd Account SD 95933 – TERMS 3/15, n30 31 December 2012			
Date	Description	Debit	Credit
1 Dec. 2012	Beginning balance		¥0
3 Dec. 2012	Purchase invoice P2012-1802		528 660
14 Dec. 2012	Purchase invoice P2012-1995		120 510
20 Dec. 2012	Payment – Cheque no. 12-884	528 660	
17 Dec. 2012	Debit memo – returns and allowances	50 000	
19 Dec. 2012	Payment – Cheque no. 12-1012	70 550	
31 Dec. 2012	**Ending balance**	¥0	

3.4 What are purchase discounts?

A purchase discount is offered by a supplier for timely payment. From the business's perspective, paying on time and taking the discount is usually financially advantageous. Notice in the payables account for Asia Imports that no discount was taken on the purchase dated 3 December 2012. Asia Imports allows Morioka to receive a 3% discount if payment is made within 15 days. But Morioka paid on 20 December 2012, after the time for the discount period expired.

Morioka Foods purchases merchandise for ¥120 510 on 14 December 2012. On 17 December, ¥50 000 of this was returned to Asia Imports, leaving a balance of ¥70 510 owing. Morioka pays this balance on 19 December 2012. Since payment is made within the discount period, Morioka takes the discount, which is ¥2117 (rounded). The journal entry to record payment would be:

Date	Account Titles	DR	CR
19 Dec. 2012	Trade accounts payable	¥70 510	
	Purchase discount		¥2 117
	Cash		68 433

Both purchase discounts and purchase returns and allowances are contra accounts to purchases. Thus, purchase discounts and purchase returns and allowances are subtracted from purchases to calculate **net purchases**. For Morioka Foods, this would appear as follows for December 2012:

Purchases	¥649 170
Less:	
Purchase returns and allowances	(50 000)
Purchase discounts	(2 117)
Net purchases	**¥597 053**

ON YOUR OWN

LEARNING OUTCOME REVIEW

1. Explain what the following documents are and how they are used in the purchases and cash disbursements cycle: purchase requisition, purchase order, receiving report, vendor invoice and remittance advice.
2. What is the difference between a purchase return and a purchase allowance? Why would a business use one or the other?

LEARNING OUTCOME PRACTICE

1. Which document should accompany a payment made to a supplier?
   a. Sales invoice
   b. Remittance advice
   c. Purchase invoice
   d. Purchase requisition

2. Which of the following is correct when recording a discount received from a supplier?
   a. Debit trade accounts payable; credit cash
   b. Debit trade accounts receivable; credit cash
   c. Debit trade accounts payable; credit discount received
   d. Debit trade accounts receivable; credit discount received

3. The sequence of events to account for a purchase on credit for a contract cleaning company would be which of the following?
   a. record purchase in purchase journal, prepare purchase requisition, receive vendor invoice, prepare purchase order, summarize purchase journal and post to general ledger
   b. receive vendor invoice, record purchase in purchase journal, summarize purchase journal and post to general ledger, prepare purchase order, prepare purchase requisition
   c. prepare purchase requisition, receive vendor invoice, record purchase in purchase journal, summarize purchase journal and post to general ledger, prepare purchase order
   d. prepare purchase requisition, prepare purchase order, receive vendor invoice, record purchase in purchase journal, summarize purchase journal and post to general ledger

4. What document provides proof of payment in a business transaction?
   a. Debit note
   b. Invoice
   c. Cheque
   d. Claim

5. Manish buys goods on credit from Lisa but finds that some of them are faulty. What document would Manish return to Lisa with the faulty goods?
   a. Statement
   b. Debit note
   c. Sales invoice
   d. Purchase invoice
   ACCA adapted

6. Jonathan sends a debit note to one of his suppliers. In which of Jonathan's books of prime entry would this be recorded?
   a. Sales
   b. Purchases
   c. Sales returns
   d. Purchase returns
   ACCA adapted

LEARNING OUTCOME 4
DESCRIBE THE EMPLOYEE COMPENSATION, FIXED ASSETS AND INVENTORIES AND CONVERSION CYCLES

4.1 What is the employee compensation cycle?

4.2 What is the fixed assets cycle?

4.3 What is the inventories and conversion cycle?

4.1 What is the employee compensation cycle?

Accounting for labour, whether salaried or contract employees, is a major accounting task in organizations. In countries without taxation, trade unions, pension funds and other benefits, payment of compensation to employees can be straightforward. However, in many nations, businesses either voluntarily provide benefits or are legally required to provide benefits that complicate payroll accounting. Figure 6.14 shows an overview of the general functions that make up a basic payroll system.

FIGURE 6.14 PAYROLL SYSTEM

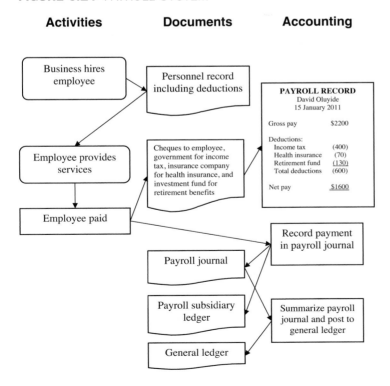

In Figure 6.14, we can see that the payroll process begins when the employee is hired. Personnel keeps records on the employee, which could include, for example, how much taxes the employee pays, cost for health insurance and deductions for retirement fund. These amounts are withheld from the employee's pay cheque.

Businesses usually pay employees on a weekly, bi-monthly or monthly basis. Payment is made through the payroll subsystem and the employee receives a pay cheque (or electronic funds transfer). We can see in Figure 6.14 that David Oluyide receives a cheque for $1600 accompanied by a remittance advice. His gross pay is $2200 for the period before deductions. From that Melbourne Medical Equipment has deducted taxes of $400, health insurance premiums of $70 and a contribution to David Oluyide's retirement fund for $130, leaving $1600 as net pay.

In many companies, employees receive other benefits besides cash payments for their services. Typical benefits include contributions by the employer to income after the employee retires from active employment, referred to as post-retirement benefits. Employers in some cases also provide medical and dental benefits, vacation time, leave days for sickness and personal business, contributions to educational tuition, child care and so forth.

4.2 What is the fixed assets cycle?

The fixed assets subsystem processes records on noncurrent assets like property, plant and equipment. Part of the function of the fixed assets subsystem is to maintain an asset register, which is a listing of the assets with information like the asset's identity (serial number, location and description), original cost and date of purchase. This information is needed to verify periodically that the assets are still in the company's possession.

The cost is required to calculate depreciation expense and any gain or loss that results from later disposal of the asset. When the business disposes of an asset by abandoning it or selling it to another party, it would be removed from the asset register. The fixed assets subsystem also automatically generates journal entries to record depreciation expense.

4.3 What is the inventories and conversion cycle?

Another cycle used by merchandising firms and manufacturers relates to inventory. The inventory subsystem maintains records on purchases of merchandise and shipments of inventory items. It also calculates the appropriate amount of cost of goods sold and the inventory value at the end of the reporting period.

When a company manufactures goods, inventory costs are accumulated through the conversion cycle. The conversion subsystem is that part of the accounting information system that handles the process of acquiring the materials and labour necessary to manufacture the goods, and the subsequent conversion of these resources into finished goods inventories. Finished goods inventories include all items on which production

FIGURE 6.15 OVERVIEW OF CONVERSION PROCESS

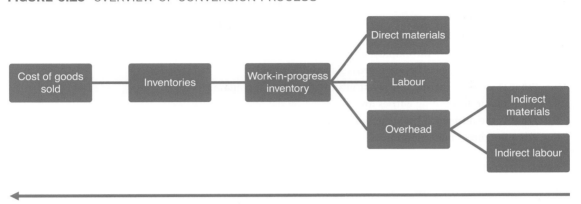

has been completed and that are ready for sale. Figure 6.15 provides a graphic overview of the conversion process.

The conversion process involves the acquisition of three major categories of costs: direct materials, direct labour and manufacturing overhead.

Direct materials are goods that go into the product itself. So for Dell Computer, this might include plastic parts, wire, circuits and other items needed to produce laptop computers. These are acquired through the purchases subsystem, which we have already discussed. As the materials arrive, they are typically stored in a materials store, which is a warehouse or storeroom for managing materials.

When the materials are needed, the production department requisitions the items needed from the materials storehouse. The related costs are then moved to work-in-process inventories, which are goods on which production has begun but not been completed by the end of the reporting period.

Direct labour includes those costs related to the conversion of the materials into product. Salaries and wages are paid through the payroll, which is part of the payroll cycle. These costs are also assigned to work-in-progress based on the amount of time employees spent on the production of each item.

The third component is overhead (also manufacturing overhead or indirect costs) associated with production. Overhead costs might include cleaning supplies related to the manufacturing facility, for example, or they could include the salary for the plant manager or security guards. Thus indirect costs typically come from both the purchases subsystem and payroll in the payroll cycle. These costs have no direct association with a particular job. Therefore, they are accumulated with other manufacturing costs in a separate manufacturing overhead account and then assigned to jobs on some allocation scheme.

As work in process is completed, costs are reclassified as finished goods inventories, which are available for sale to customers. Finally, when the goods are sold, the costs are reclassified to cost of goods sold.

ON YOUR OWN

LEARNING OUTCOME REVIEW

1. What activities does the employee compensation cycle address?
2. What is the difference between gross pay and net pay?
3. What is an asset register and what information does it contain?
4. What major accounting entries are generated by the fixed assets cycle?
5. What is the difference between work in progress and finished goods?
6. What are direct materials, direct labour and overhead?

LEARNING OUTCOME PRACTICE

1. Sophie has the following information about a recently acquired noncurrent asset that was financed by taking out a loan.

   (i)   serial number

   (ii)   cost

   (iii)   provider of loan

   (iv)   date of purchase

   What information will Sophie enter in the asset register?

   a. i, ii and iii

   b. ii, iii and iv

   c. i, ii and iv

   d. i, iii and iv

   ACCA adapted

2. Which of the following are reasons for maintaining a noncurrent asset register?

   (i)   To calculate the total balance outstanding on loans raised to buy noncurrent assets

   (ii)   To help in carrying out the physical verification of noncurrent assets

   (iii)   To calculate the profit and loss on disposal of noncurrent assets

       a. i, ii and iii

       b. i and ii only

       c. i and iii only

       d. ii and iii only

   ACCA adapted

3. Which of the following is/are correct?

   (i)   The noncurrent asset register is part of the double-entry system

   (ii)   A noncurrent asset register is required in every organization's accounting system

   (iii)   Assets should be removed from the noncurrent asset register when they have been fully depreciated

       a. i only

       b. ii only

       c. iii only

       d. None of the statements

   ACCA adapted

LEARNING OUTCOME 5
EXPLAIN THE AUDIT TRAIL

An audit trail provides links that allow a transaction to be traced through an accounting system from the source document all the way to the final account balance that appears on the financial statements. In other words, any account balance on a financial statement – for example cash on the statement of financial position – can be traced to all the specific transactions that are affected in that balance (see Figure 6.16).

FIGURE 6.16 AUDIT TRAIL

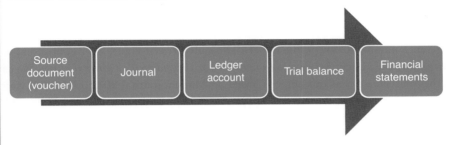

Audit trails are used for manual as well as computerized accounting systems. The following example shows how an audit trail would work in an automated system.

Suppose that Medical Sales LLC sold EKG equipment to Perth Hospital System on 14 August 2012 for Chinese ¥219 500. In an automated system, the journal entry might look something like the computer screen shown in Figure 6.17.

FIGURE 6.17 AUTOMATED JOURNAL ENTRY – COMPUTER SCREEN

Journal – Sales Invoices 14 August 2012		Reference no. S3342	
Journal	Sales invoice	Conversion	
Date	14 Aug. 2012	Currency	Chinese ¥
Description	Sales invoices for equipment	Date	14 Aug. 2012
Source	Manual journal 2012-12-10023		
Line	Account	Debit	Credit
1	03-310-3300-10300	219 000	
2	03-120-3300-10300		219 000
		219 000	219 000

This automated journal entry is much the same as the basic journal entry we used throughout Chapters 3 and 4, including the date as well as the debits and credits, but with two differences. First, account codes replace titles like 'cash' and 'revenue'. In Line 1 in Figure 6.17 we see that account code 310 is debited. Reference to the account code structure for Melbourne (Figure 6.4) tells us that this is the cash account. On the second line, the account code 120 is credited, representing sales revenue.

Another difference is that the currency is shown as Chinese Yuan in Figure 6.17, which we can see on the right-hand side of the computer screen. Thus, this is a foreign currency transaction, a sale that is denominated in a foreign currency. Because Melbourne is an Australian company and maintains its accounting records in Australian dollars, the Chinese Yuan would need to be converted. The computer system would do this automatically using the spot exchange rate on 14 August 2012, which is the date of the transaction.

Also notice the reference number S3342 in the upper right-hand area of Figure 6.17. This number is assigned automatically by the system as a *unique identifier for this particular journal entry*. We can also see by looking at the Source field that this entry is based on **Manual journal 2012-12-10023**, which tells us that the source document for this transaction is a hard-copy sales invoice that has been filed and thus can be retrieved with this Code (2012–12–10023). These reference numbers and other identifiers that cross-reference source documents to journal entries in ledger accounts are needed to establish an audit trail.

Figure 6.18 is the cash ledger account as it would appear in an automated accounting information system.

Notice that the journal entry in Figure 6.17 with reference number S3342 for AUS $219 000 is posted on the third line item in the Cash ledger account shown in Figure 6.18. If we are examining this account and

FIGURE 6.18 LEDGER ACCOUNT DETAIL – 8010 CASH

Account Details – 8010 Cash				
Reference	Class	Date	Debit	Credit
Balance		01 Aug. 2012	1 660 000	
P6489	Trade payable	14 Aug. 2012		45 000
S3342	Sales invoice	14 Aug. 2012	219 000	
S3356	Sales invoice	15 Aug. 2012	145 000	
P6501	Trade payable	18 Aug. 2012		70 000
PR3390	Payroll disbursement	25 Aug. 2012		340 000
		Cumulative balance	1 569 000	

wish to know the source of the AUS $219 000, we may want to go one step further to see the source document, which we can do by retrieving journal entry S3342 (see Figure 6.17). From that, we then know to reference Manual journal 2012-12-10023. This reference to the manual journal should allow us to locate the source document in the company's filing system.

ON YOUR OWN

LEARNING OUTCOME REVIEW
1. Define audit trail.
2. What purposes do audit trails serve?

Conclusion

At the heart of every accounting information system is the double-entry accounting process that we discussed in Chapters 4 and 5. This involves analysing and recording transactions, adjusting them so that they conform to the accrual basis of accounting, preparing the financial statements and then closing temporary accounts.

In large companies the accounting process is embedded within an accounting information system that is automated. Because of the high volume of transactions in these large companies, the accounting information system is subdivided into cycles and the cycles are subdivided into subsystems. The most common cycles include sales and cash receipts, purchases and cash disbursements, employee compensation, fixed assets and inventories. Firms like Oracle and SAP sell accounting software to large companies so that different subsystems can be purchased or leased depending on the client's accounting requirements. The subsystems are integrated so that information from the sales subsystem, for example, works with the cash receipts subsystem, or the fixed assets subsystem works with the general ledger.

These subsystems are not only integrated within the accounting information system but the business's overall information systems environment. Thus, the accounting information system can share information with the manufacturing and human resources management components within the enterprise resource planning system. These in turn can share information across the organization to the supply chain management, customer relationship management and business intelligence systems.

Summary
LEARNING OUTCOME 1
Accounting Information System Defined

An accounting information system is the overall accounting system maintained by a business. It includes not only the accounting software that processes journal entries and generates the journal, ledger and trial balances, but also the people who are responsible for the accounting function. The accounting information system also encompasses the accounting policies and procedures of the business. The accounting information system is typically part of the enterprise resource planning system in large companies.

Accounting information systems are subdivided into cycles. A cycle handles transactions of a similar nature, such as sales and cash receipts, purchases and cash disbursements, employee compensation, fixed assets and inventories. Because of the very large volumes of certain types of transactions, a company may use special journals that combine like transactions into a single special journal entry. The result is that a summary number for this group of transactions is recorded in the general journal and appears in summary form in the general ledger. Detailed information, such as the balance for each customer's trade account receivable, is maintained in a subsidiary ledger.

In large companies with many functions – sales, marketing, production, logistics, finance – and divisions, accounting is more complex. Most companies need access to accounting information by function, division, product, customer and so forth. In these companies, a chart of accounts takes the form of an account code structure, which is made up of different tables of codes. These can be combined to extract specific accounting information.

LEARNING OUTCOME 2
Sales and Cash Receipts Cycle Described

The sales and cash receipts cycle involves four different subsystems: sales, cash receipts, sales returns and allowances, and sales discounts. Sales involves the process of receiving an order from a customer, authorizing the sale including obtaining credit approval, shipping the goods and then invoicing the customer for the amount owed. In accounting, the result is that the sales and trade accounts receivable transaction is recorded. Cash receipts involve customers' payments of their trade accounts receivable balances. Cash is received and deposited with the bank. In accounting, the cash receipt is recorded against the customer's trade account receivable.

The trade accounts receivable balance is also affected by returns and allowances and sales discounts. In some cases, a customer may return merchandise because it is defective or the incorrect merchandise was shipped. In other cases, a customer may be given an allowance to compensate for damaged merchandise. Finally, based on the business's credit terms, a customer may be rewarded for timely payment of the amount owed on the trade account receivable balance by providing a sales discount.

LEARNING OUTCOME 3
Purchases and Cash Disbursements Cycle Described

The purchases and cash disbursements cycle begins with the purchases subsystem, which handles the acquisition of goods and services for the business. Accounting typically becomes involved when the vendor invoices the business for the goods or services it has provided. These invoices become the source documents for the journal entries recorded in the purchase journal. Purchase journals are summarized and posted to the general ledger. All resulting trade accounts payable are listed in a payables subsidiary ledger.

The second subsystem is cash disbursements, which relate to the amounts owed to vendors. When cash payments are made, a journal entry is recorded through the cash disbursements journal. Summary amounts of these journals are posted to the general ledger. Payments would also appear in the payables subsidiary ledger, providing information on each vendor's resulting balance.

The amount owed through trade accounts payable is affected by any purchase returns, allowances and discounts. These are normally recorded by accounting based on debit memos, which advise that the amount owed by the business has been reduced.

LEARNING OUTCOME 4
Other Cycles Described

Other cycles included in accounting information systems include payroll and employee benefits, fixed assets and conversion. The payroll and employee benefits cycle encompasses all accounting activities for hiring and compensating employees, including compensation other than cash payments for services and benefits provided after retirement from employment.

The fixed asset cycle involves the acquisition of and accounting for long-term depreciable assets, including property, plant and equipment and intangible assets. This includes the depreciation and amortization of these assets.

The inventories cycle relates to merchandising and manufacturing companies. Since merchandising companies are not engaged in manufacturing, the major tasks are accounting for the acquisition cost of goods and then allocating these costs between inventories on the statement of financial position and cost of goods sold, depending on whether the goods are unsold or sold respectively.

For manufacturing firms, the inventories cycle is more complex. It also involves accounting for all costs that become part of the production process. These are classified into direct materials, direct labour and overhead, which include indirect materials and indirect labour. While goods are being produced, these items are classified as work in progress; once they are completed they are classified as finished goods. This finished goods amount must then be allocated between inventories on the statement of financial position and cost of goods sold, depending on whether the goods are unsold or sold respectively.

LEARNING OUTCOME 5
Audit Trail Explained

An audit trail is a method of linking source documents and journal entries recorded in the journal to the ledger and then to the balance as reported in the financial statements. Audit trails are an important tool for investigating and verifying the source of accounting information. Audit trails are particularly useful to auditors.

REVIEW QUESTIONS

1. Define an accounting information system. How does an accounting information system differ from the accounting process?
2. What are the cycles typically found in large accounting systems?
3. Define account coding structures and explain how they function.
4. What is a special journal? How and why are special journals used? What are examples of typical special journals?
5. What is a subsidiary ledger? How and why are subsidiary ledgers used? What are examples of typical subsidiary ledgers?
6. For each cycle in the accounting information system (sales and cash receipts, purchases and cash disbursements and payroll), describe the sequence of events. What documents are typically used in each cycle?
7. Describe the major functions of the fixed assets cycle.
8. Describe the major functions of the inventories and conversion cycle.
9. Define the audit trail and describe how an audit trail is created. What is the purpose of an audit trail?

Key terms

Asset register
Audit trail
Bill of lading
Cash disbursements journal
Cash receipts journal
Contra account
Conversion cycle
Credit memo
Customer purchase order
Daybook
Debit memo
Direct material
Finished goods
Fixed assets cycle
General ledger
Gross pay
Gross sales
Indirect costs
Indirect labour
Indirect materials
Invoice
Net pay

Net sales
Overhead
Payables subsidiary ledger
Purchase discounts
Purchase invoice
Purchase journal
Purchase order
Purchase requisition
Purchase returns and allowances
Receivables subsidiary ledger
Receiving report
Remittance advice
Sales discount
Sales invoice
Sales order
Sales returns and allowances
Special journals
Statement
Subsidiary ledger
Vendor invoice
Work in process

Terminology practice

For each of the following statements, insert the correct term from the key terms list. Each key term can be used more than once.

1. Similar transactions are recorded using _____, also referred to as _____.

2. To find all items that have affected a customer's account, you would examine the _____. For all items that have affected an account that the business owes, you would examine the _____.

3. When _____ and _____ are subtracted from gross sales, the result is _____.

4. The _____ allows a transaction to be traced from the source document through the accounting system to the financial statement.

5. A(n) _____ is a bill for goods or services.

6. Cheques sent in payment of a good or service are accompanied by a(n) _____.

7. A(n) _____ provides detailed information on a particular general ledger account.

8. A customer makes a request to purchase goods or services by submitting a(n) _____. When this is received by the business, an internal document called a(n) _____ is prepared.

9. A bill for goods or services that has been received from a supplier is referred to as a(n) _____.

10. In the conversion process, _____ and _____ are included in overhead.

11. When a customer requests an allowance for defective goods, a(n) _____ is issued. When a business requests that a supplier provide an allowance for defective goods, a(n) _____ is recorded.

12. When a good or service is received by a business, an internal document called a(n) _____ is prepared.

13. _____ are reductions are offered by a business to a customer if the customer pays within a specified time period.

14. A _____ offsets another account.

15. A list of noncurrent assets including information like original cost, date purchased and serial number can be found on the _____, which is part of the _____.

16. When production of goods has begun but has not been completed at the reporting date, we classify related costs in _____. If production has been completed at the reporting date, these costs are classified as _____.

17. A(n) _____ is a summary of all account activity for a period of time and is used to request payment from the customer.

18. When _____ and _____ are subtracted from gross purchases, the result is _____.

19. The amount an employee receives in his or her pay cheque is _____. This is calculated by deducting _____ from _____.

20. A department within a company uses a(n) _____ to submit a request to purchase goods. The next step is to prepare a _____ that is forwarded to the supplier.

21. _____ are reductions offered by a supplier if the business pays within a specified time period.

Application exercises

1. In the sales subsystem flowchart shown below, fill in the missing items with the activity, document or accounting from the following terms: sales invoice, sales journal posted to general ledger, sales order, bill of lading, sales journal, sales invoice sent to customer, customer purchase order, customer's credit approved, receivable sub-ledger.

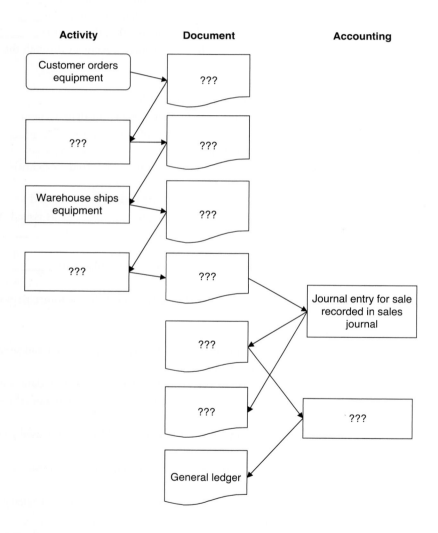

2. In the cash receipts subsystem flowchart shown below, fill in the missing items with the activity, document or accounting from the following terms: bank deposit slip, journal entry for cash receipts recorded in cash receipts journal, cash receipts list, summary of cash receipts posted to general ledger, payment received from customer, general ledger, deposit cash.

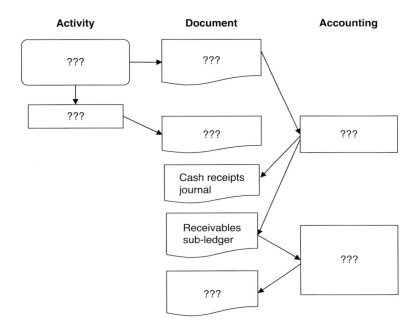

3. In the sales returns and allowances subsystem flowchart shown below, fill in the missing items with the activity, document or accounting from the following terms: sales returns and allowances journal, summary of sales and returns journal posted to general ledger, credit memo, receivables subsidiary ledger, sales return or allowance request from customer, customer credited for return or allowance.

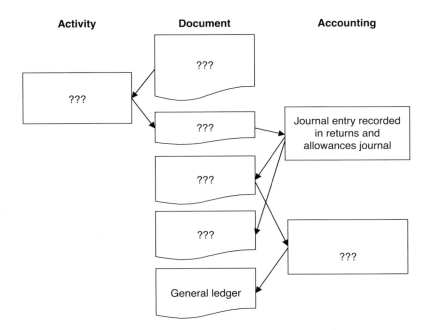

4. In the purchases subsystem flowchart shown below, fill in the missing items with the activity, document or accounting from the following terms: payables journal, vendor invoice, journal entry recorded in purchases journal, receiving report, purchase requisition, goods or services received from supplier, purchase order for goods or services sent to supplier.

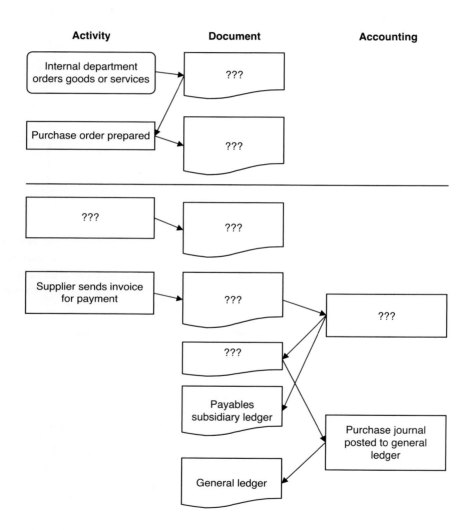

5. In the cash disbursements subsystem flowchart shown below, fill in the missing items with the activity, document or accounting from the following terms: payables subsidiary ledger, summary of cash disbursements journal posted to general ledger, cash disbursement processed, cash disbursements journal, journal entry recorded in cash disbursements journal.

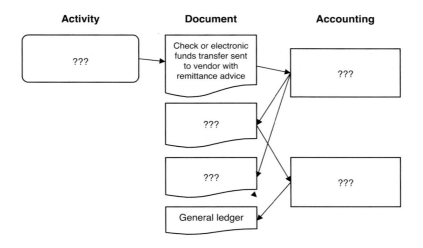

6. In the purchase returns and allowances subsystem flowchart shown below, fill in the missing items with the activity, document or accounting from the following terms: debit memo, request for purchase return or allowance, general ledger, supplier grants purchase return or allowance, journal entry recorded in purchase returns and allowance journal, payables subsidiary ledger.

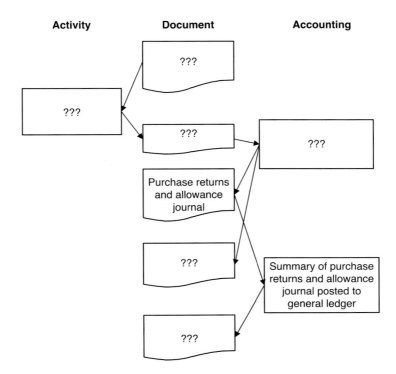

7. In the payroll subsystem flowchart shown below, fill in the missing items with the activity, document or accounting from the following terms: payroll subsidiary ledger, business hires employee, record payment in payroll journal, employee paid, payroll journal, personnel record including deductions, summarize payroll journal and post to general ledger.

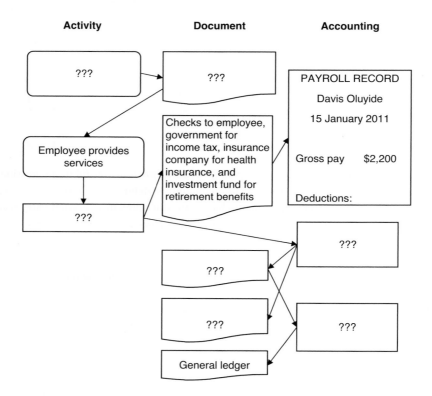

Comprehensive application exercises

Professional accounting examinations often test the exam taker's understanding of the accounting process and the financial statements by presenting errors and asking for the entries necessary to correct them. Following are two examples of problems that require you to correct errors.

1. At 30 November 2010, the balance in the receivables account for Elizabeth Cosmetics Corporation was €39 982. The company's accounting department then discovered the following errors:
   a. A sales invoice for €288 was not recoded.
   b. A payment of €1300 was accepted in full settlement of a balance of €1309. No entry was made to record the discount.
   c. A credit note issued to a credit customer for €120 was incorrectly treated as an invoice.
   d. An addition error on a customer's account understated the balance by €27.

e. A customer had lodged a payment of €325 directly to Elizabeth's bank account. Nor entry was recorded for the payment.

f. A sales invoice for €644 was mistakenly recorded for €466.

g. A customer's payment for €47 was recorded as a debit to the customer's account and a credit to cash.

Required:

Make the necessary entries to correct these errors. What amount should the receivables account be?

[ACCA adapted]

2. You are assisting in the preparation of the 31 December 2011 year-end accounts of Tofiq & Company. The balance on the trade payables account is £45 505. You have noted the following irregularities in the accounting records:

a. An invoice from a supplier for £739 has been entirely omitted.

b. A credit memo received from a supplier for £266 was entered as an invoice.

c. No entries have been made in respect of an agreement to offset a credit balance of £864 in the payables ledger against a debit balance in the receivables ledger.

d. Payments to a supplier totaling £1800 have not been recorded.

e. A payment of £17 500 was made to settle a balance of £17 585. The difference between the two amounts has not been recorded.

f. A payment of £340 to a supplier was recorded as £430.

Required:

Make the necessary entries to correct these errors. What amount should the payables account be?

[ACCA adapted]

Reporting Financial Position

PART III

INTRODUCTION TO PART III

In Part I, we were introduced to the four financial statements: the statement of financial position, statement of comprehensive income, statement of changes in equity and the statement of cash flows as well as the accompanying notes. We also learned about generally accepted accounting principles, including accounting standards that provide specific guidelines for preparing financial statements.

In Part II, we covered the accounting process: how transactions are recorded, posted to ledger accounts then summarized for use in the financial statements. In Chapter 6, we discussed how modern businesses organize accounting information flows in order to handle large transaction volumes.

Now, we begin a detailed examination of generally accepted accounting principles which determine how we account for specific types of transactions. As already noted, we will use IFRS for guidance. Part III covers accounting for financial position, which is reported by the statement of financial position. This part is organized into three chapters that examine different categories of the statement of financial position, as shown in the following diagram.

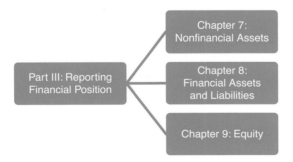

In Chapter 7, we will learn about major types of nonfinancial assets, including inventories; property, plant and equipment; intangible assets; and investment assets. In Chapter 8 we will examine financial assets and liabilities, including trade accounts, notes and bonds. Together these two chapters cover both assets and liabilities. Finally, in Chapter 9 we will discuss the major accounting issues related to equity.

Nonfinancial assets

LEARNING OUTCOMES

At the completion of this chapter, students should be able to:

1. Define capitalization.
2. Explain accounting practices for inventories.
3. Explain major accounting practices for property, plant and equipment.
4. Explain major accounting practices for intangible assets.
5. Explain major accounting practices for investment properties.

A SURFING PARABLE

Javad is a very intelligent young man whom you met at university some years ago. He has already had some successes as an entrepreneur. You respect his judgement in business. But Javad is also an avid surfer and he has been known to disappear from time to time in search of the 'big wave'. He always returns with great stories to tell about his adventures.

You have now been working for several years and have saved up about €55 000. Javad approaches and invites you to invest in a new enterprise he is planning. At Starbucks one evening, he describes how he has found an old, abandoned manufacturing plant that can be purchased inexpensively. 'My idea,' he says, 'is to manufacture surfboards. I have a lot of friends and contacts that would buy from me because I know how to design and build them for the best performance.' You agree to invest €50 000, almost all of your savings. Javad invests the same amount.

Javad establishes the company Javad Surfboards Ltd on 1 July 2009. You invest your €50 000. Later that day, Javad calls your mobile phone and says that the factory has been purchased for €75 000. He'll get in touch soon. Then he disappears for two months.

A month later, Javad calls your mobile enthusiastically describing the big waves he surfed in Tahiti. After some time you ask about the surfboard business. 'What's going on with that?' you ask, trying not to sound worried.

'Oh,' says Javad, 'the business. Well, it's not going to happen right away because I promised some friends I would spend a year with them travelling to some of the famous surf beaches around the world.'

'But what about the building?' you reply. 'What about my money?'

'Oh,' says Javad, 'the building and the money. Funny thing about that. Before I left for Tahiti I bought the factory as I told you. But of course nothing happened while I was gone. When I got back I found that the large company next door to the factory had been trying to locate me. They are expanding their facilities and offered three times what we paid for the old manufacturing plant. So I am trying to figure out whether to sell or hold the factory to see if the value goes up or whether just to wait until I get back in a year and open the surfboard business.'

What if, as an investor, you did not know Javad? Suppose you had to rely on the financial statements to evaluate the financial position, performance and changes in financial position of the business? Then what information would you have? Let's take a look at a basic statement of financial position and statement of comprehensive income for Javad Surfboards Ltd for the July 2009 reporting period (Figure 7.1).

FIGURE 7.1 STATEMENTS OF FINANCIAL POSITION AND COMPREHENSIVE INCOME

Statement of Financial Position 1 July 2009		Statement of Comprehensive Income for the Month Ended 31 July 2009		Statement of Financial Position 31 July 2009	
Assets		Revenue	0	Assets	
Cash	€25 000	Expenses	0	Cash	€25 000
Factory	75 000	Profit or loss	0	Factory	75 000
Total assets	€100 000			Total assets	€100 000
Liabilities	0			Liabilities	0
Equity				Equity	
Paid in capital	100 000			Paid in capital	100 000
Reserves	0			Reserves	0
Total equity	€100 000			Total equity	€100 000
Total liabilities and equity	€100 000			Total liabilities and equity	€100 000

You can see that there is not much to be optimistic about. Nothing happened in July. The capital that you provided to Javad Surfboards seems to be lying idle and not earning any return.

Or is it? Take a look at the financial statements again. They have been recalculated in Figure 7.2 assuming that the increase in the value of the factory is taken into account when measuring the

FIGURE 7.2 RECALCULATED FINANCIAL STATEMENTS

Statement of Financial Position 1 July 2009		Statement of Comprehensive Income for the Month Ended 31 July 2009		Statement of Financial Position 31 July 2009	
Assets		Revenue	0	Assets	
Cash	€25 000	Expenses	0	Cash	€25 000
Factory	75 000	Profit or loss	0	Factory	225 000
Total assets	€100 000	Other comprehensive			
		income	€150 000	Total assets	€250 000
		Total comprehensive			
		income	€150 000		
Liabilities	0			Liabilities	0
Equity				Equity	
Paid in capital	100 000			Paid in capital	100 000
Reserves	0			Reserves	150 000
Total equity	€100 000			Total equity	€250 000
Total liabilities				Total liabilities	
and equity	€100 000			and equity	€250 000

financial position of the business. The factory tripled in value, so it is now worth €225 000 (3 × €75 000).

The results are quite different. Notice that total comprehensive income is now €150 000 and investors' equity has increased to a total of €250 000. As an investor, this raises some serious questions. You have benefited considerably because of the increase in the business's value. But the value is no more than an amount shown on a financial statement. So, is this a good investment? Are you happy with Javad's performance as a manager? Can you conclude from these financial statements that the business has good prospects in the future? Would you invest with Javad again?

Financial statements do not give the answers to these questions, but instead provide the information that users need to obtain the answers. You might argue that all you need to evaluate the business is a statement of financial position on each reporting date. By comparing the statement of financial position for 31 July with the one from 1 July, you can see for yourself that the situation improved. But most users want more than that. They want to know *why* it improved, and to answer that we need a complete set of financial statements.

In Part III, we will examine the statement of financial position in greater detail. In this chapter we will learn more about nonfinancial assets, which generally include property, plant and equipment, as well as intangibles. In the next chapter, we will consider financial assets and liabilities, and in Chapter 9, the last in Part III, we will examine equity.

LEARNING OUTCOME 1
DEFINE CAPITALIZATION

A major issue with respect to assets is whether certain costs should be capitalized or expensed. When a cost is included as part of a tangible or intangible asset, we say that the cost is a capital expenditure – or that the cost has been 'capitalized'. It therefore becomes a capital asset or fixed asset, and is sometimes referred to as a depreciable asset. We know from Chapter 3 that a capitalized cost – one that appears on the statement of financial position – is 'unexpired', meaning that it is still capable of providing economic benefit to the business entity in the future. A cost that is expensed is referred to as revenue expenditure, which means that it is an expense and that therefore the cost has expired.

When a capital expenditure is incorrectly classified as revenue expenditure or vice versa, the result is that both the statement of financial position and the statement of income are misstated. If a capital expenditure is misclassified as revenue expenditure, assets are understated and expenses are overstated. Overstated expenses mean that profit is understated. If revenue expenditure is understated then profit will be overstated, and capital expenditure will also be overstated. These effects are shown in Figure 7.3.

FIGURE 7.3 OVERSTATING AND UNDERSTATING

Statement of Financial Position	Statement of Comprehensive Income	
If a capital expenditure is . . .	then the revenue expenditure is . . .	and profit is . . .
Understated	Overstated	Understated
Overstated	Understated	Overstated

Why is this issue of capital versus revenue expenditure an important issue as we examine nonfinancial assets in this chapter? The answer is that the chapter illustrates how capital costs are reclassified to the statement of financial position for three major nonfinancial assets: inventories; property, plant and equipment; and intangible assets.

ON YOUR OWN

LEARNING OUTCOMES REVIEW

1. What is a capital expenditure? Which financial statement does it appear on?
2. What is revenue expenditure? Which financial statement does it appear on?

LEARNING OUTCOME PRACTICE

1. A business's statement of comprehensive income for the year ended 31 December 2009 showed a profit of $83 600. It was later found that $13 500 was paid for the purchase of a motor van that had been debited to the motor expenses account. What would the profit be after adjusting for this error?
   a. $106 100
   b. $70 100
   c. $97 100
   d. $101 600
   ACCA adapted

2. If a capital expenditure is incorrectly classified as revenue expenditure, how will net profit and net assets be affected?

	Net profit	Net assets
a.	Understated	Understated
b.	Understated	Overstated
c.	Overstated	Overstated
d.	Overstated	Understated

   ACCA adapted

LEARNING OUTCOME 2
EXPLAIN ACCOUNTING PRACTICES FOR INVENTORIES

2.1 What costs should be included in inventories?

2.2 How are inventory costs allocated to cost of goods sold?
   2.2.1 What is specific identification?
   2.2.2 What are cost flow assumptions?
   First-in, first-out
   Average cost

2.3 How frequently are inventory costs updated?

2.4 What adjustments should be made when inventory values decline?

2.5 How do we evaluate inventories?

Inventories are goods held for resale to the business's customers (see IFRS box).

Inventories are created in two ways.

First, a merchandising company buys finished goods from a wholesaler or manufacturer. A finished good is one on which production has been completed. The merchandising company does not itself manufacture goods.

Secondly, a manufacturer produces goods by converting materials and labour into finished goods. Thus a manufacturer may have three types of inventory: materials that will be used in the production process, work in process, goods that have begun but not completed the production process, and finished goods. Normally, inventory costs are classified as current assets because the sale to the customer is expected within 12 months.

When finished goods are purchased for resale to customers, we say that the costs 'flow' through the accounting system. Figure 7.4 shows the flow of costs for a merchandiser.

FIGURE 7.4 MERCHANDISER'S FLOW OF GOODS COST

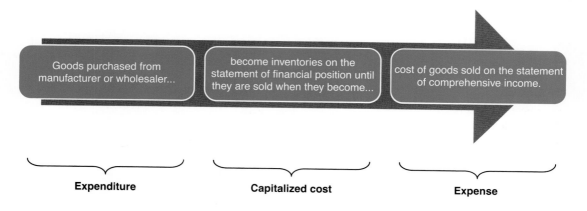

FIGURE 7.5 MANUFACTURER'S FLOW OF GOODS COSTS

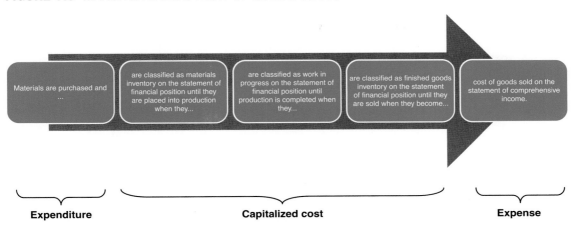

Notice in Figure 7.4 that purchases become inventories. Once they are sold, they are then reclassified to cost of goods sold. For manufacturers, the cost flow is similar but varies because materials and work-in-process inventories must be taken into account. Figure 7.5 illustrates the manufacturer's flow.

In this textbook, we will not focus on materials and work in process but only on finished goods inventories, whether for manufacturer or merchandiser.

2.1 What costs should be included in inventories?

The initial amount recorded for inventories is the cost of purchase, cost of conversion (manufacture) and other costs incurred to bring the inventories to their present location and condition. Inventory includes costs such as custom duties, sales taxes and transportation costs. Carriage-inwards (also transportation-in or freight-in) are costs to bring the goods to the current location.

Carriage-outwards costs (also transportation-out or freight-out costs) refer to the shipment of goods to customers and these are always included as part of sales expense, not inventory. Thus, carriage-outwards costs are revenue expenditure; they are not capitalized.

On 7 July 2011, Melbourne Medical Sales purchases new model magnetic resonance imaging (MRI) equipment for A$150 000 from Howe MRI Equipment Corporation in Boston, which it intends to offer for sale to customers. Melbourne pays A$7000 in shipping costs, A$3000 for sales taxes and another A$200 for customs handling. Howe offers terms of 2/15, n30. The journal entry to record the inventories cost would be as follows:

Date	Account Titles	DR	CR
7 July 2011	Inventories	A$160 000	
	Trade accounts payable – Howe		
	MRI Equipment Corporation		A$150 000
	Trade accounts payable – Pacific		
	Freight Company		7 000
	Cash – taxes and		3 200
	Customs duties		

On 9 July 2011, while unpacking the shipment, Melbourne discovers that one MRI unit with a cost of $2500 is defective and immediately returns it to Howe. The journal entry to record this transaction would be as follows:

Date	Account Titles	DR	CR
9 July 2011	Trade accounts payable – Howe	A$2 500	
	MRI Equipment Corporation		
	Purchase returns and allowances		A$2 500

This transaction leaves a balance of A$147 500 still owing in the trade payables – Howe MRI Equipment Corporation account.

Melbourne pays for the equipment on 21 July 2011, within the time allowed to qualify for the purchase discount, which is A$2950 (0.02 × $147 500). This is calculated as follows:

Original purchase amount	A$150 000
Less:	
Purchase returns and allowances	2 500
Purchase discount	2 950
Net purchase	A$142 050

The journal entry to record the payment would be as follows:

Date	Account Titles	DR	CR
21 July 2011	Trade accounts payable – Howe MRI Equipment Corporation	A$147 500	
	Purchase discount		A$2 950
	Cash		142 050

Now the calculation of the inventory cost can be summarized as follows:

Purchase amount	A$150 000
Add:	
Transportation in	7 000
Other costs	3 200
	A$160 200
Less:	
Purchase returns and allowances	2 500
Purchase discount	2 950
Net purchase	A$154 750

The preceding example illustrates how the purchase amount should be recorded. But businesses typically have some inventories still on hand from the previous reporting period and these are added to the purchases made in the current reporting period to calculate cost of goods available (see Figure 7.6).

You can see from Figure 7.6 that the cost of goods available must be separated into the ending inventories at the end of the reporting period and those inventory costs that will be expensed as cost of goods sold for the reporting period.

FIGURE 7.6 COST OF GOODS AVAILABLE

Melbourne's beginning inventory for the medical equipment was $72 000. This would be added to the net purchases from the preceding example to give the cost of goods available balance, which is $226 750. This calculation is summarized below:

Beginning inventories		$72 000
Purchase amount	150 000	
Add:		
Transportation in	7 000	
Other costs	3 200	
	$160 200	
Less:		
Purchase returns and allowances	2 500	
Purchase discount	2 950	
Net purchase		154 750
Cost of goods available		$226 750

ON YOUR OWN

LEARNING OUTCOME REVIEW

1. What costs should be included in inventories?
2. Are carriage-inwards costs capital expenditure or revenue expenditure?
3. Are carriage-outwards costs capital expenditure or revenue expenditure?
4. What is the cost of goods available? How is the cost of goods available calculated?

LEARNING OUTCOME PRACTICE

1. Which of the following costs should be included in the inventories of a manufacturing company?
   - i. Carriage inwards
   - ii. Carriage outwards
   - iii. Factory costs
   - iv. Administrative expenses
      - a. All four items
      - b. i, ii and iv
      - c. ii and iii only
      - d. i and iii only
   - ACCA adapted

2.2 How are inventory costs allocated to cost of goods sold?

While the first question addressed how to calculate the cost of goods available, the second question is how we determine which of these costs should be moved from inventories into cost of goods sold when the goods sell. Accounting uses two major methods to reclassify inventory costs: specific identification and cost flow assumption. If the latter is used, entities are allowed to choose one of two assumptions under IFRS: average cost or first-in, first-out. These are graphically illustrated in Figure 7.7.

FIGURE 7.7 TWO METHODS OF RECLASSIFYING INVENTORY COSTS

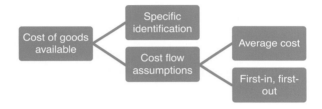

2.2.1 WHAT IS SPECIFIC IDENTIFICATION?

Specific identification means that the cost for each separate inventory item can be identified when the sale is made. Specific identification is used for items that are unique as opposed to commodities or items that are otherwise indistinguishable from each other (see IFRS box).

> **IFRS**
>
> 'The cost of inventories of items that are not normally interchangeable and goods or services produced [...] shall be assigned by using specific identification of their individual costs.'
>
> *IAS 2 Inventories*
>
> Copyright © 2007 International Accounting Standards Committee Foundation. All rights reserved. No permission granted to reproduce or distribute.

In recent years inexpensive computer processing coupled with technologies like bar codes and radio frequency identification (RFID) have made tracking low-value items cost effective. As a result, specific identification is increasingly applied to high-volume, low-cost inventories like groceries, discount store goods, inexpensive machine parts and many other items (see box).

MILKING INVENTORY COSTS

Computer control has led to improvements in operational inventory management such as ordering and delivery scheduled to be just in time for sale to the customer. This has also allowed for a reduction in the amount of inventory that must be carried in stock, which reduces carrying costs. In recent years, some retailers have begun reviving consignment sales, whereby ownership of the goods does not pass to the retailer. For example, a US grocery retailer sells milk, cheese and other products from a local dairy in its stores. Ownership of the goods remains with the dairy until a carton of milk, for example, is actually sold to the consumer. When the milk carton is scanned, two entries are recorded. One records the sale to the consumer and the second the purchase of the milk from the dairy. Therefore, the retailer has no inventory for accounting purposes.

Naik Jewellers, which retails fine jewellery, purchases a luxury watch from the manufacturer for resale on 15 February 2010 for £1857. The entry to record the acquisition would be:

Date	Account Titles	DR	CR
15 Feb. 2010	Inventories	£1 857	
	Cash		£1 857

Let's assume that the watch sold on account on 23 February 2010 for £3495. Under the specific identification method, Naik would *record two journal entries*: one to recognize the revenue and another to match the cost.

Recognize revenue

The entry to recognize the revenue would be as follows:

Date	Account Titles	DR	CR
23 Feb. 2010	Trade accounts receivable	£3 495	
	Sales revenue		£3 495

Match costs

The second entry matches the cost to the revenue, as follows:

Date	Account Titles	DR	CR
23 Feb. 2010	Cost of goods sold Inventories	£1 857	£1 857

This entry is recorded at the same time the revenue is recognized because Naik Jewellers can identify the cost associated with the specific watch that was sold.

WHAT TO LOOK OUT FOR

When a sale occurs, two entries must be made: the sales-side entry and the cost-side entry. The first recognizes revenue and the second matches the cost to the revenue. Students are sometimes confused when determining what amounts to use for each. The sales-side entry is always measured at the selling price – that is, the watch sold for £3495. The cost-side entry is measured at what the business paid for the inventory item – £1857 in the above example.

ON YOUR OWN

LEARNING OUTCOME PRACTICE

On 4 January 2009, Mirhadi Auto Sales LLC purchased three new vehicles for its inventories with the following manufacturer's invoice price: BMW Series 3 for €14 500; BMW Series 5 for €38 900; and BMW Series X3 for €27 200. On 1 February 2009 a customer purchased the Series 3 model for €29 800 cash. What are the journal entries to record both the sale side of the transaction and the cost side using the specific identification method?

2.2.2 WHAT ARE COST FLOW ASSUMPTIONS?

Some inventory items are interchangeable. In these cases, a cost flow assumption is used, which is the second method of assigning cost of goods available to cost of ending inventory and cost of goods sold. When specific identification is not appropriate, a cost flow assumption is used.

Under the cost flow approach, *an assumption* is made about the order in which the costs will be assigned to ending inventories and cost of goods sold. If the cost per item of all purchases over time were the same, then no cost flow assumption would be needed. However, the cost per unit often varies even when the items are interchangeable. The following example illustrates this point.

A food retailer purchases cases of canned tuna three times during September, as shown in Figure 7.8:

FIGURE 7.8 CANNED TUNA INVENTORY

Date	Quantity	Cost Per Case	Total Cost
Beginning inventory, 1 Sep. 2010	100	£18.10	£1 810
10 Sep. 2010	200	15.00	3 000
17 Sep. 2010	150	14.50	2 175
25 Sep. 2010	75	19.00	1 425
Totals	525		£8 410

The month begins with 100 cases of inventory at a cost of £18.10 per case for a total cost of £1810. This is the first inventory 'layer'. Then three purchases were made during September, each at a different cost per case. By the end of September, the retailer has 525 cases with a total amount of goods available for sale of £8410. As we can see, the cost per case has varied, perhaps because the retailer had purchased from different suppliers or the cost of canned tuna changed over time.

Suppose at the end of September 2010 only 120 cases remain in physical inventory. That means that 405 (525 – 120) have been sold. Now we must assign the total cost of goods available to the cost of goods sold and ending inventories. But what is the cost of the cases that sold: £18.10, £15.00, £14.50 or £19.00?

Management can choose one of the two cost flow assumptions to account for the inventories: first-in, first-out (FIFO) or average cost (AVCO). The FIFO cost flow assumption assigns the first or oldest costs to the cost of goods sold on the statement of comprehensive income and the last or newest costs to ending inventories. The AVCO cost flow assumption assigns the average cost of goods available to both cost of goods sold and ending inventories. No matter which method management chooses – FIFO or AVCO – the objective remains the same: to allocate the cost of goods available to cost of goods sold and ending inventory.

THINGS TO LOOK OUT FOR

The choice of FIFO or AVCO as the cost flow assumption is *not related to the physical flow of goods*. It just makes sense that the oldest goods would be *physically* moved out of the warehouse and sold first to prevent spoilage, deterioration and obsolescence. However, the management of physical inventory flows has nothing to do with the accounting for the goods. Whether FIFO or AVCO is chosen for financial reporting, the physical flow will almost always be FIFO.

First-In, First-Out (FIFO)

In the example presented in Figure 7.8 we know that 405 cases of canned tuna were sold out of the 525 purchased in September 2010, which means that 120 remain in inventory. Figure 7.9 shows the calculations for assigning cost of goods available to the cost of goods sold and the ending inventory.

FIGURE 7.9 ASSIGNING COST OF GOODS AVAILABLE

Category	Quantity	Cost
Cost of goods sold	405	£1 810.00 = 100 × £18.10 3 000.00 = 200 × £15.00 1 522.50 = 105 × £14.50 £6 332.50 405 Cost of goods sold
Ending inventory	120	£652.50 = 45 × £14.50 1 425.00 = 75 × £19.00 £2 077.50 120 Ending inventory
Goods available	**525**	£8 410.00 525

Under the FIFO method, the first costs are assigned to cost of goods sold. In Figure 7.8, the first layer of costs is the beginning inventory of 100 cases for a total of £1810. But this accounts for only part of the 405 cases sold. So we must move to the next oldest costs in the second layer.

From the second layer, we assign £3000 for the 200 cases purchased on 10 September to the cost of goods sold. At this point, we have accounted for 300 (100 + 200) of the 405 cases needed. So we must also use 105 cases from the third layer purchased on 17 September. The cost of these 105 cases is £1522.50 (105 × £14.50). We can now add the amounts assigned to cost of goods sold from each of the three layers to get £6332.50.

At this point we could take a short cut to calculate the ending inventory amount. We know that the total cost is £8410.00, of which £6332.50 has now been assigned to cost of goods sold. So the remaining amount of £2077.50 (£8410.00 – £6332.50) is assigned to ending inventory. However, this amount can be verified independently by calculating the layers that are assigned to ending inventory. Under FIFO, since the oldest costs are assigned to cost of goods sold, the most recent costs are assigned to ending inventory.

WHAT TO LOOK OUT FOR

It's easy to become confused when a problem asks you to calculate *ending inventory* under FIFO. The first reaction is to use the first or oldest costs to calculate the layers. But those belong to cost of goods sold. So when we say first-in, first-out, we always mean that the first or oldest costs are assigned to the cost of goods sold. The last or newest cost goes to ending inventories under FIFO. Be sure that you know what you are being asked to calculate: cost of goods sold or ending inventories.

Thus, to calculate ending inventory, we start with the last layer of cost, which is the 75 cases from the 25 September purchase of £1425.00. We then take that part of the third layer of cost that was not assigned to cost of goods sold. Of the 150 cases purchased on 17 September, 105 have been assigned to cost of goods sold, which means that the remaining 45 will be assigned to ending inventory for £652.50 (45 × £14.50). When these two amounts are added together, the result is £2077.50 – the same number that we calculated in our short cut by subtracting cost of goods sold from cost of goods available.

Average Cost (AVCO)

Under AVCO, an average cost per unit is calculated based on the total goods available using the following formula:

$$\text{Average cost per unit} = \frac{\text{Total cost of goods available}}{\text{Total number of goods available}}$$

Based on the example from Figure 7.8, the average cost would be calculated as follows:

$$\text{Average cost per unit} = \frac{£8410.00}{525}$$

$$£16.02 = \frac{£8410.00}{525}$$

Cost is then assigned as shown in Figure 7.10.

For cost of goods sold, the number of units sold is multiplied by the average cost to get £6488.10 (405 × £16.02). Ending inventory is calculated by multiplying the number of items in ending inventory by the average cost per unit to get £1922.40 (120 × £16.02). Together these two amounts total £8410.50.

FIGURE 7.10 ASSIGNING COST OF GOODS AVAILABLE

Category	Quantity	Cost
Cost of goods sold	405	£6 488.10 = 405 × £16.02 £6 488.10 405 Cost of goods sold
Ending inventory	120	£1 922.40 = 120 × £16.02 £1 922.40 120 Ending inventory
Goods available	525	£8 410.50 525 (rounding difference)

WHAT TO LOOK OUT FOR

Notice that the total calculated under AVCO when the amounts are assigned to cost or sales and ending inventories is £0.50 more than the total cost of goods available. This is due to a rounding difference, which often occurs in average cost calculations.

ON YOUR OWN

LEARNING OUTCOME REVIEW

1. What are the two inventory cost flow assumptions permitted under IFRS?
2. What is meant by FIFO?
3. Where are the first costs assigned under FIFO? To cost of goods sold or ending inventories?

LEARNING OUTCOME PRACTICE

1. Magliori Construction Inc. builds residential villas. The following schedule shows the beginning inventory for October 2011 for 2 × 4 wooden studs and the purchases made throughout the month. The company accounts for inventory monthly on a periodic basis.

Date	Quantity	Cost Per Plank
1 Oct. 2011	7800	$3.10
3 Oct. 2011	2000	3.10
7 Oct. 2011	3500	3.12
11 Oct. 2011	4000	3.15
16 Oct. 2011	1500	3.17
25 Oct. 2011	4400	3.18
30 Oct. 2011	1700	3.20

At the end of October, the warehouse counted the remaining inventory of wooden studs and found 8200 still in stock.

a) Under the AVCO method, calculate the cost of ending inventory.
b) Under the AVCO method, calculate the cost of goods sold.
c) What is the month-end entry to record cost of goods sold under AVCO?
d) Under the FIFO method, calculate the cost of ending inventory.
e) Under the FIFO method, calculate the cost of goods sold.
f) What is the month-end entry to record cost of goods sold under FIFO?

2.3 How frequently are inventory costs updated?

In the previous discussion of FIFO and AVCO cost flow assumptions, we have been using periodic inventory calculations. Periodic inventory means that the cost of goods available is assigned to cost of goods sold and ending inventory at the end of the reporting period. A second method is to update inventory costs continuously as sales and purchases of inventory are made, which is referred to as the perpetual inventory method. The following example for Colors of Portofino LLC demonstrates how this is done, first using perpetual FIFO and then perpetual AVCO.

COLORS OF PORTOFINO LLC

Perpetual Inventory using FIFO

Colors of Portofino LLC is a trendy Italian clothing retailer that caters to young consumers. While the company sells large lots of identical items – for example T-shirts in a particular colour – the styles and colours change frequently. Management is therefore interested in tracking sales and profitability on a daily basis so that appropriate decisions can be made about continuing a style or colour that is popular, or discontinuing something when it has proved unpopular.

The company's stores use point-of-sale terminals that continuously collect sales information that is sent to headquarters on a daily basis. During the evening, the accounting records are updated and reports are generated and available to management the next morning. Management has chosen to use FIFO as the cost flow assumption, but on a perpetual basis so that cost of goods sold is calculated and recorded as each sales entry is made. Sales and purchases are all in cash. Following are the purchases and sales that the company made in one week aggregated for all its retail stores.

	Item: T-Shirt			
	Style: M-633			
	Color: Orange			
Date	Transaction	Quantity	Cost Per Item	Price Per Item
12 Apr. 2010	Beginning inventory	54 000	€1.70	
	Sales	22 117		€6.50
13 Apr. 2010	Purchases	75 000	1.58	
	Sales	33 104		6.50
14 Apr. 2010	Sales	29 944		6.70
15 Apr. 2010	Sales	27 699		6.75
16 Apr. 2010	Purchases	45 000	1.72	
	Sales	34 800		6.70
17 Apr. 2010	Purchases	47 000	1.75	
	Sales	31 527		6.65
18 Apr. 2010	Sales	38 830		6.66

Following are the journal entries to record both the sales revenue and cost of goods sold as the week progresses. First, the journal entry on the first day of the week, 12 April, to record sales of €143 760.50 (22 117 × €6.50), would appear as follows:

Date	Account Titles	DR	CR
12 Apr. 2011	Cash	€143 760.50	
	Sales revenue		€143 760.50

At the same time, the cost of goods sold would be recorded. Since the only layer of inventory available at this point is the beginning inventory for €1.70 per unit, this is the cost used. Thus, the cost of goods sold would be calculated at €37 598.90 (22 117 × €1.70).

Date	Account Titles	DR	CR
12 Apr. 2011	Cost of goods sold	€37 598.90	
	Merchandise inventory		€37 598.90

The next entry records the transactions for 13 April. The first entry is a purchase of 75 000 T-shirts at €1.58 each, or a total of €118 500.00. This would be recorded in inventories.

Date	Account Titles	DR	CR
13 Apr. 2011	Merchandise inventory Cash	€118 500.00	€118 500.00

The next transaction on 13 April is a sale of 33 104 items at €6.50 each, for a total of €215 176.00.

Date	Account Titles	DR	CR
13 Apr. 2011	Cash Sales revenue	€215 176.00	€215 176.00

To record the cost of goods sold for the sale of 33 104 items, of which 31 883 (54 000 – 22 177) comes from the beginning inventory layer at €1.70 each and the other 1221 (33 104 – 31 883) comes from purchases made on 13 April at €1.58 each, the calculation is as follows:

$$
\begin{array}{ll}
31\ 883 \times €1.70 = & €54\ 201.10 \\
1221 \times €1.58 = & \underline{1\ 929.18} \\
\text{Total cost of goods sold} = & €56\ 130.28
\end{array}
$$

Date	Account Titles	DR	CR
13 Apr. 2011	Cost of goods sold Merchandise inventory	€56 130.28	€56 130.28

At this point 73 779 units (75 000–1221) remain from the 13 April purchase layer. On 14 April, the first transaction is a sale for €200 624.80 (29 944 items at €6.70 each).

Date	Account Titles	DR	CR
14 Apr. 2011	Cash Sales revenue	€200 624.80	€200 624.80

The cost of goods sold is calculated for 29 944 items, all of which are taken from the purchases made on 13 April at €1.58 each. At this point, 43 835 items remain of the 13 April purchase:

Date	Account Titles	DR	CR
14 Apr. 2011	Cost of goods sold	€47 311.52	
	Merchandise inventory		€47 311.52

The next entry records the sale of 27 699 items on 15 April at €6.75 each for a total of €186 968.50.

Date	Account Titles	DR	CR
15 Apr. 2011	Cash	€186 968.25	
	Sales revenue		€186 968.25

The cost of goods sold is for 27 699 items, all of which are taken from the purchases made on 13 April, at €1.58 each for a total of €43 764.42. At this point, 16 136 items remain of the 13 April purchase layer.

Date	Account Titles	DR	CR
15 Apr. 2011	Cost of goods sold	€43 764.42	
	Merchandise inventory		€43 764.42

On 16 April, 45 000 items are purchased at €1.72 each:

Date	Account Titles	DR	CR
16 Apr. 2011	Merchandise inventory	€77 400.00	
	Cash		€77 400.00

A sale is recorded for 34 800 items at €6.70 each.

Date	Account Titles	DR	CR
16 Apr. 2011	Cash	€233 160.00	
	Sales revenue		€233 160.00

The cost of goods sold is recorded for the sale of 34 800 items. 16 136 are taken from the purchases made on 13 April at €1.58 each and the other 28 634 are taken from purchases made on 16 April at €1.72 each. The calculation is:

$$16\ 136 \times €1.58 = \qquad €25\ 494.88$$
$$18\ 664 \times €1.72 = \qquad \underline{32\ 102.08}$$
$$\text{Total cost of goods sold} = €57\ 596.96$$

Date	Account Titles	DR	CR
17 Apr. 2011	Cost of goods sold Merchandise inventory	€57 596.96	€57 596.96

At this point 26 336 items remain of the 16 April purchase layer. On 17 April, a purchase of 47 000 items at €1.75 each is recorded.

Date	Account Titles	DR	CR
17 Apr. 2011	Merchandise inventory Cash	€82 250.00	€82 250.00

A sale is recorded for 31 527 items at €6.65 each:

Date	Account Titles	DR	CR
17 Apr. 2011	Cash Sales revenue	€209 654.55	€209 654.55

The cost of goods sold for 31 527 items is recorded, of which 26 336 are taken from the purchases made on 16 April at €1.72 each and the other 15 161 are taken from purchases made on 17 April at €1.77 each. The calculation is:

$$26\ 336 \times €1.72 = \qquad €45\ 297.92$$
$$5191 \times €1.75 = \qquad \underline{9\ 084.25}$$
$$\text{Total cost of goods sold} = €54\ 382.17$$

Date	Account Titles	DR	CR
17 Apr. 2011	Cost of goods sold Merchandise inventory	€54 382.17	€54 382.17

At this point 41 809 items remain of the 17 April purchase layer. The final sale for the week is on 18 April: 38 830 items at €6.66 each:

Date	Account Titles	DR	CR
18 Apr. 2011	Cash Sales revenue	€258 607.80	€258 607.80

Cost of goods sold is recorded for 38 830 items, all of which are taken from the purchases made on 17 April at €1.75 each:

Date	Account Titles	DR	CR
18 Apr. 2011	Cost of goods sold Merchandise inventory	€67 952.50	€67 952.50

At this point 2979 items remain of the 17 April purchase layer. This means that the ending inventory would be calculated by multiplying $2979 \times €1.75 = €5213.25$. Summarizing the calculations for cost of goods sold and ending inventory under the FIFO method, we would get the following:

Date	Sales Revenue	Cost of Goods Sold	Purchases
12 Apr. 2011	€143 760.50	€37 598.90	
13 Apr. 2011	215 176.00	56 130.28	€118 500.00
14 Apr. 2011	200 624.80	47 311.52	
15 Apr. 2011	186 958.25	43 764.42	
16 Apr. 2011	233 160.00	57 596.96	77 400.00
17 Apr. 2011	209 654.55	54 382.17	82 250.00
18 Apr. 2011	258 607.80	67 952.50	
Totals	€1 447 951.90	€364 736.75	€278 150.00

From these figures we can now summarize the transactions for the week:

Beginning inventory	€91 800.00
Purchases	278 150.00
Goods available	369 950.00
Less: Cost of goods sold	(364 736.75)
Ending inventory	€5 213.25

The ending inventory of €5213.25 reconciles with our previous calculation (2979 × €1.75 = €5213.25).

Perpetual Inventory using AVCO

Using the same fact pattern for Colors of Portofino LLC, we can calculate the cost of goods sold and inventory amounts using the perpetual inventory method under average cost.

Date	Account Titles	DR	CR
12 Apr. 2011	Cash	€143 760.50	
	Sales revenue		€143 760.50

To record sales of 22 117 items at €6.50 each.

Date	Account Titles	DR	CR
12 Apr. 2011	Cost of goods sold	€37 598.90	
	Merchandise inventory		€37 598.90

To record the cost of goods sold for the sale of 22 117 items at €1.70 each. This is the only layer available, so the cost of goods sold would be the same as under FIFO. At this point, 31 883 items are left in merchandise inventory:

Date	Account Titles	DR	CR
13 Apr. 2011	Merchandise inventory	€118 500.00	
	Cash		€118 500.00

To record the purchase of 75 000 items at €1.58 each. This entry is also the same as under FIFO. The status of the merchandise inventory after the 13 April purchase is as follows:

Date	Quantity	Cost per Item	Total Cost
12 Apr. 2011	31 883	€1.70	€54 201.10
13 Apr. 2011	75 000	€1.58	118 500.00
Totals	106 883		€172 701.50
Average cost per item €1.615 = €172 701.50 ÷ 106 883			

Date	Account Titles	DR	CR
13 Apr. 2011	Cash	€215 176.00	
	Sales revenue		€215 176.00

To record the sale of 33 104 items at €6.50 each.

Date	Account Titles	DR	CR
13 Apr. 2011	Cost of goods sold	€53 462.96	
	Merchandise inventory		€53 462.96

To record the cost of goods sold for the sale of 33 104 items using the average cost per item of €1.615 already calculated for a total of €53 462.96. At this point 73 779 units remain in merchandise inventory with an average cost of €1.615.

Date	Account Titles	DR	CR
14 Apr. 2011	Cash	€200 624.80	
	Sales revenue		€200 624.80

To record the sale of 29 944 items at €6.70 each.

Date	Account Titles	DR	CR
14 Apr. 2011	Cost of goods sold	€48 359.56	
	Merchandise inventory		€48 359.56

To record the cost of goods sold for the sale of 29 944 items. Since no purchases have been made since the last sale transaction, the average cost per item is still €1.615 and this would be the amount used to calculate cost of goods sold. At this point 43 835 items remain in merchandise inventory with an average cost of €1.615 each.

Date	Account Titles	DR	CR
15 Apr. 2011	Cash	€186 968.25	
	Sales revenue		€186 968.25

To record the sale of 27 699 items at €6.75 each.

Date	Account Titles	DR	CR
15 Apr. 2011	Cost of goods sold	€44 733.89	
	Merchandise inventory		€44 733.89

To record the cost of goods sold for the sale of 27 699 items with an average cost per item of €1.615 each. At this point 16 166 items remain in merchandise inventory.

Date	Account Titles	DR	CR
16 Apr. 2011	Merchandise inventory	€77 400.00	
	Cash		€77 400.00

To record the purchase of 45 000 items at €1.72 each.

The status of the merchandise inventory after the 16 April purchase is as follows:

Date	Quantity	Cost Per Item	Total Cost
Previous average	16 166	€1.615	€26 108.09
16 Apr. 2011	45 000	€1.72	77 400.00
Totals	61 166		€103 508.09
Average cost per item €1.692 = €103 508.09 ÷ 61 166			

The average cost per item has now risen to €1.692.

Date	Account Titles	DR	CR
16 Apr. 2011	Cash Sales revenue	€233 160.00	€233 160.00

To record the sale of 34 800 items at €6.70 each.

Date	Account Titles	DR	CR
17 Apr. 2011	Cost of goods sold Merchandise inventory	€58 881.60	€58 881.60

To record the cost of goods sold for the sale of 34 800 items based on the revised average cost per unit of €1.692. At this point 26 336 items remain in merchandise inventory.

Date	Account Titles	DR	CR
17 Apr. 2011	Merchandise inventory Cash	€82 250.00	€82 250.00

To record the purchase of 47 000 items at €1.75 each. The status of the merchandise inventory after the 17 April purchase is as follows:

Date	Quantity	Cost per Item	Total Cost
Previous average	26 336	€1.692	€44 560.51
17 Apr. 2011	47 000	€1.75	82 250.00
Totals	73 336		€126 810.51
Average cost per item €1.729171 = €126 810.51 ÷ 73 336			

Date	Account Titles	DR	CR
17 Apr. 2011	Cash Sales revenue	€209 654.55	€209 654.55

To record the sale of 31 527 items at €6.65 each.

Date	Account Titles	DR	CR
17 Apr. 2011	Cost of goods sold Merchandise inventory	€54 515.59	€54 515.59

To record the cost of goods sold for the sale of 31 527 items at an average cost of €1.729171 per item (this amount is carried out to a greater number of decimals to reduce rounding errors). At this point 41 809 items remain in merchandise inventory.

Date	Account Titles	DR	CR
18 Apr. 2011	Cash Sales revenue	€258 607.80	€258 607.80

To record the sale of 38 830 items at €6.66 each.

Date	Account Titles	DR	CR
18 Apr. 2011	Cost of goods sold Merchandise inventory	€67 143.72	€67 143.72

To record the cost of goods sold for the sale of 38 830 items at €1.729171 per item. At this point 2979 items remain in merchandise inventory. This means that the ending inventory would be calculated by multiplying 2979 × €1.729171 = €5151.20.

Summarizing the calculations for cost of goods sold and ending inventory under the average cost method, we would get the following:

Date	Sales Revenue	Cost of Goods Sold	Purchases
12 Apr. 2011	€143 760.50	€37 598.90	
13 Apr. 2011	215 176.00	53 462.96	€118 500.00
14 Apr. 2011	200 624.80	48 359.56	
15 Apr. 2011	186 968.25	44 733.89	
16 Apr. 2011	233 160.00	58 881.60	77 400.00
17 Apr. 2011	209 654.55	54 515.59	82 250.00
18 Apr. 2011	258 607.80	67 143.72	
Totals	€ 1 447 951.90	€ 364 696.20	€278 150.00

From these figures we can now summarize the transactions for the week:

Beginning inventory	€91 800.00
Purchases	278 150.00
Goods available	369 950.00
Less: Cost of goods sold	(364 696.20)
Ending inventory	€5 253.80

ON YOUR OWN

LEARNING OUTCOME REVIEW

1. Explain the difference between the perpetual and periodic inventory methods.
2. Is specific identification a perpetual or periodic inventory method?

2.4 What adjustments should be made when inventory values decline?

Following the acquisition of inventories and before the sale to a customer, inventories can decline in value because of damage, obsolescence or declining market prices. In these cases, the carrying amount of inventories may not be recoverable in the normal course of trade. As a result, the amount of inventories on the statement of financial position should be adjusted to lower of cost and net realizable value (see IFRS box).

> **IFRS**
>
> Net realizable value is the 'estimated selling price in the ordinary course of business less the estimated costs of completion and the estimated costs necessary to make the sale'.
>
> *IAS 2 Inventories*
>

LOWER OF COST AND NET REALIZABLE VALUE

The following is an example of how the lower of cost and net realizable method is applied.

Suppose that on 31 December 2010 Naik Jewellers has the following inventory of watches:

Model	Cost	Net Realizable Value	Lower of Cost and Net Realizable Value	Amount Below Cost
G742	£3495	£4500	£3495	–
G744	1810	1440	1440	£370
H1318	2315	2600	2315	–
A4150	2800	1500	1500	1300
P111	6117	7400	6177	–

Two watches have net realizable values that fall below their cost, and therefore an adjustment must be made to write down the inventories cost by £1670 (£370 + 1300). The journal entry would be as follows:

Date	Account Titles	DR	CR
31 Dec. 2010	Cost of goods sold	£1 670	
	Inventories		£1 670

If for some reason the net realizable value of the revalued watches subsequently increases, then the current period's cost of goods sold is reduced.

Suppose that net realizable value for model A4150 rises to £1800 from the current carrying amount of £1500. Then the journal entry would be as follows:

Date	Account Titles	DR	CR
31 Jan. 2011	Inventories	£300	
	Cost of goods sold		£300

ON YOUR OWN

LEARNING OUTCOME PRACTICE

1. A company values its inventory using the first-in, first-out (FIFO) method. On 1 May 2010 the company had 700 engines in inventory, valued at $190 each. During the year ended 30 April 2012 the following transactions took place:

2010

1 July	Purchased	500 engines	at $220 each
1 November	Sold	400 engines	for $160 000

2011

1 February	Purchased	300 engines	at $230 each
15 April	Sold	250 engines	for $125 000

What is the value of the company's closing inventory of engines on 30 April 2011?

a. $188 500
b. $195 500
c. $166 000
d. $106 000

ACCA adapted

2. Colin made a mistake in his calculations that resulted in the value of his closing inventory at 30 April 2009 being overstated by $900. The value was calculated correctly at 30 April 2010. What was the effect of the error on the profit reported in Colin's accounts for each of the two years?

	2009	**2010**
a.	Overstated by $900	not affected
b.	Overstated by $900	understated by $900
c.	Understated by $900	not affected
d.	Understated by $900	overstated by $900

ACCA adapted

3. Kieron is an antiques dealer. His inventory included a clock that cost $15 100. Kieron expects to spend $700 on repairing the clock, which will mean that he will be able to sell it for $26 000. At what value should the clock be included in Kieron's inventory?

a. $15 100
b. $15 800
c. $25 300
d. $26 000

ACCA adapted

4. The inventories value for the financial statements of Q for the year ended 31 December 2009 was based on an inventories count on 4 January 2010, which gave a total inventories value of $836 200. Between 31 December 2009 and 4 January 2010 the following transactions took place:

Purchases of goods	$8 600
Sales of goods (at cost)	14 000
Goods returned by Q to supplier	700

What adjusted figure should be included in the financial statements for inventories at 31 December 2009?

   a. $840 900
   b. $830 100
   c. $859 500
   d. $832 300

ACCA adapted

5. On 1 September 2010, a business had inventories of $380 000. During the month, sales totalled $650 000 and purchases $480 000. On 30 September 2010 a fire destroyed some of the inventories. The undamaged goods in inventories were valued at $220 000. The cost of goods sold for September was $500 000. Based on this information, what is the cost of the inventories destroyed in the fire?

   a. $185 000
   b. $140 000
   c. $405 000
   d. $360 000

ACCA adapted

2.5 How are inventories evaluated?

Each merchandising or manufacturing business needs some level of inventories on hand at all times. A manufacturer must keep some stock available to respond to orders, otherwise customers will go to competitors who can respond to their needs more quickly. However, in general businesses want to minimize inventories. The reason is that inventories tie up cash. If inventory levels can be reduced without negatively affecting sales, then cash is released for investment elsewhere. Businesses that are inventory intensive, like merchandisers and manufacturers, focus substantial effort on achieving these reductions.

From the accounting perspective, we measure the ability of a business to convert inventories to cash using two ratios: the inventories turnover ratio and days in inventory.

INVENTORIES TURNOVER RATIO

The inventories turnover ratio tells us for an average level of inventory what sales can be generated. The formula is as follows:

$$\text{Inventories turnover ratio} = \frac{\text{Sales}}{\text{Average inventories}}$$

Average inventories are computed by averaging the beginning inventories with the ending inventories for the period.

Heliard Coffees plc had the following statement of income for the year ended 31 December 2009.

Heliard Coffees plc Statement of Income For the year ended 31 December 2009 € Euro	
Sales revenue	€150 000
Cost of goods sold	70 000
Gross profit	80 000
Operating expenses	20 000
Interest expense	10 000
Profit before income tax	50 000
Income tax (20%)	10 000
Profit	€40 000

Inventories on 1 January 2009 were €29 000 and they were €27 500 on 31 December 2009. What is the inventories turnover ratio?

First, we calculate the average inventories:

$$\text{Average inventories} = \frac{\text{Beginning inventories} + \text{ending inventories}}{2}$$

$$\text{Average inventories} = \frac{€29\ 000 + €27\ 500}{2}$$

$$\text{Average inventories} = €28\ 250$$

$$\text{Inventories turnover ratio} = \frac{\text{Sales}}{\text{Average inventories}}$$

$$\text{Inventories turnover ratio} = \frac{€150,000}{€28\ 250}$$

$$\text{Inventories turnover ratio} = 5.31$$

HOW TO ANALYSE RATIOS

Two basic techniques can be used to analyse ratios: hold the denominator constant and vary the numerator; and hold the numerator constant and vary the denominator:

1. For the inventory turnover ratio, assume that the denominator remains the same. If you are an investor, do you want more sales or less? The answer is more, sales for a given level of inventories.
2. For the second approach, hold the numerator constant. Now, would you rather have more or less inventories for a given level of sales? The answer is less, for the same reason. You would like to be able to reduce your investment in inventory and free your cash for other productive uses.

Thus, for the inventories turnover ratio, businesses want a higher ratio rather than a lower one.

Let's assume that Heliard's major competitor is Starsky LLC. Following is Starsky's statement of income for the year ended 31 December 2009.

Sales revenue	€225 000
Cost of goods sold	100 000
Gross profit	125 000
Operating expenses	60 000
Profit	€65 000

Inventories on 1 January 2009 were €35 000 and they were €32 000 on 31 December 2009. What is Starsky's inventories turnover ratio?

First, we calculate the average inventories:

$$\text{Average inventories} = \frac{\text{Beginning inventories} + \text{ending inventories}}{2}$$

$$\text{Average inventories} = \frac{€35\ 000 + €32\ 000}{2}$$

$$\text{Average inventories} = €33\ 500$$

$$\text{Inventories turnover ratio} = \frac{€225\ 000}{€33\ 500}$$

$$\text{Inventories turnover ratio} = 6.72$$

We can now compare the two companies to see how they are performing on inventory management. Clearly, Starsky is doing better than Heliard, since its inventories turnover ratio is 6.72, which is higher than Heliard's 5.31.

Let's take it one step further and assume that you are the chief executive officer of Heliard. You call your inventories manager into your office and say: 'I was just comparing our inventories turnover ratio with Starsky's and see that they are doing significantly better. Can you explain why?'

The inventories manager answers that she only took the position a year ago on 1 January 2009. The inventories turnover ratio for 2008 was 4.40. Her response is: 'The ratio has improved to 5.31 from 4.40 since I took this position. Besides, the industry average is 4.60 so we are doing better than that. Further improvements are coming!'

What you observe in this exchange between you and your inventories manager is the three major ways in which ratios are used. The inventories turnover ratio was first used to compare performance with a specific competitor, second to compare with overall industry performance, and third to compare the performance of Heliard over time.

DAYS IN INVENTORY

The second ratio is days in inventory, which is calculated as follows:

$$\text{Days in inventory} = \frac{365}{\text{Inventories turnover ratio}}$$

As we can see, days in inventory is a way of expressing how quickly inventories turn into sales – the number of days in a year is divided by the inventories turnover ratio. Heliard's days in inventory would be as follows:

$$\text{Days in inventory} = \frac{365}{5.31}$$
$$\text{Days in inventory} = 68.7$$

Starsky's days in inventory would be:

$$\text{Days in inventory} = \frac{365}{6.72}$$
$$\text{Days in inventory} = 54.3$$

In this case, a business would want the ratio to be lower; in other words, it wants the number of days an item remains in inventory before it sells to be lower.

ON YOUR OWN

LEARNING OUTCOME REVIEW

1. Explain the two approaches for interpreting ratios.
2. What are the two key ratios used to evaluate inventories?

LEARNING OUTCOME PRACTICE

1. A company has beginning inventories of ¥1 500 000 and ending inventories of ¥1 400 000 for the reporting period. Gross profit is ¥4 000 000 and revenue is ¥10 000 000. Profit for the period is ¥1 000 000. What is the inventories turnover ratio?
   a. 1.45
   b. 6.9
   c. 4.14
   d. 0.24

2. A company has beginning inventories of ¥1 500 000 and ending inventories of ¥1 400 000 for the reporting period. Gross profit is ¥4 000 000 and revenue is ¥10 000 000. Profit for the period is ¥1 000 000. What are the days in inventory?
   a. 88.2
   b. 251.9
   c. 52.9
   d. 87.6

LEARNING OUTCOME 3
EXPLAIN ACCOUNTING FOR PROPERTY, PLANT AND EQUIPMENT

As already noted, property, plant and equipment (see IFRS box) are sometimes referred to as capital assets, fixed assets or depreciable assets.

IFRS Property, plant and equipment are 'tangible items that: (a) are held for use in the production or supply of goods or services, for rental to others, or for administrative purposes; and (b) are expected to be used during more than one period.'

Property, plant and equipment are often recorded by asset class. A class of property, plant and equipment is a group of assets of similar nature and use in the business's operations. Examples include land, buildings, production machinery, vessels, aircraft, motor vehicles and office equipment. If an asset is not used in production, for rental or for administration, then it is classified as an investment – not property, plant and equipment.

We will discuss four major issues related to property, plant and equipment.

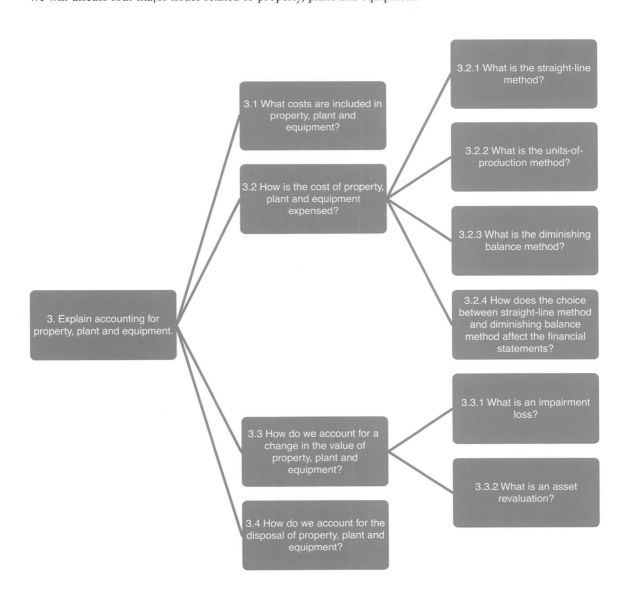

3.1 What costs are included in property, plant and equipment?

When property, plant and equipment are first acquired, they are recorded at cost (see IFRS box), which is the amount that is given in the transaction. This cost may or may not reflect what the asset is worth in the market place.

> **IFRS** '...property, plant and equipment that qualifies for recognition as an asset shall be measured at its cost.'
>

Your business wishes to purchase a van for delivery. You see a previously owned van advertised for £2000, but you know that vans of this type and age usually sell for about £8000. You visit the seller and learn that he needs to liquidate her business quickly and is therefore willing to sell the van for much less than it is worth. You purchase the van.

What is the cost of the van that you record in your accounting records? The answer is cost, which is measured by what you gave up in the transaction, or £2000. So you would debit equipment for this amount. The result is that when this van first appears in the accounts, it will be shown at £2000.

Cost includes purchase price, import duties, taxes and any other cost to bring the asset to the location and condition necessary for use as management intended. Any trade discounts or other rebates are deducted. Trade discounts and rebates are reductions to list price provided to valued customers or as incentives to purchase, respectively. In addition, if an estimate can be made for dismantling the equipment and restoring the site on which the item was located, then that estimated cost should be included as well.

Melbourne Medical Equipment purchases new production equipment for its manufacturing facilities on 1 January 2010 for A$387 111. Shipping costs are A$12 500 and custom duties are A$850. The company must also install new electrical capacity to accommodate the new equipment, and this will cost A$15 750. Installation costs will be A$7250. Training of its workers on the use of the equipment will cost A$1200. The equipment seller grants a 10% trade discount on the purchase. Finally, Melbourne's management estimates that the equipment will be used for three years, after which A$5 000 will be spent to restore the site where the equipment was located.

What amount should be recognized for the equipment cost? The calculation is as follows:

List price	A$387 111
Less: Trade discount	38 711
	A$348 400
Add:	
Shipping costs	12 500
Customs duties	850
Installation	7 250
Training	1 200
Site restoration	5 000
Total equipment cost	A$375 200

The journal entry to record the acquisition of the new equipment would be:

Date	Account Titles	DR	CR
1 Jan. 2009	Equipment Cash or trade accounts receivables	338 800	338 800

Since the property, plant and equipment will contribute economic benefits over *more than one* time period, the cost of the asset should be allocated to those periods in which it was used to conform to the accrual basis assumption. The process of allocating the costs is depreciation (see IFRS box).

IFRS

Depreciation is the 'systematic allocation of the depreciable amount of an asset over its useful life'. The depreciable amount is 'the cost of an asset less its residual value'.

Residual value is 'the estimated amount that an entity would currently obtain from disposal of an asset, after deducting the estimated costs of disposal, if the asset were already at the age and in the condition expected at the end of its useful life.'

IAS 16 Property, Plant and Equipment

The depreciable amount is calculated using the following formula:

Depreciable amount = Cost − residual value

Melbourne estimates that the equipment it has just acquired will have a residual value of $30 000 at the end of its four-year useful life. We can summarize the information about this equipment in the following table:

Melbourne Medical Equipment LLC Computer Equipment Acquired 1 January 2010	
Cost	A$375 200
Less: Residual value	30 000
Depreciable amount	A$345 200

The asset's useful life must also be estimated.

IFRS

Useful life is 'either: (a) the period over which an asset is expected to be available for use by an entity; or (b) the number of production or similar units expected to be obtained from the asset by the entity.'

IAS 16 Property, Plant and Equipment

Copyright © 2007 International Accounting Standards Committee Foundation. All rights reserved. No permission granted to reproduce or distribute.

The useful life is the period of time for which the asset is expected to be used by the business, not necessarily the actual physical life of the asset. Useful life can also be expressed in terms of estimated production hours, number of units produced or a similar measure. The depreciable amount is allocated over the useful life of the asset and the result – which is the depreciation expense – recognized in profit or loss.

ON YOUR OWN

LEARNING OUTCOME REVIEW
1. What conditions must be met in order to recognize an asset?
2. What are trade discounts and rebates?
3. What is residual value? What is the useful life?
4. How is the depreciable amount calculated?
5. Explain the difference between depreciable amount and asset cost.
6. Explain the difference between residual value and depreciable amount.

LEARNING OUTCOME PRACTICE

1. An asset cost ¥850 000. Its residual value is ¥150 000 and the useful life is estimated at eight years. What is the depreciable amount?
    a. ¥850 000
    b. ¥150 000
    c. ¥1 000 000
    d. ¥700 000

3.2 How is the cost of property, plant and equipment expensed?

IFRS do not specify a particular method of depreciating assets. The only guideline is that the depreciation method used should reflect the pattern of economic benefits derived from the asset over its useful life. However, several methods are commonly used in practice, and in this chapter we will discuss three: straight line, units of production and diminishing balance.

3.2.1 STRAIGHT-LINE METHOD

The straight-line method of depreciation expenses the depreciable amount evenly over the useful life of the asset. The formula is:

$$\text{Depreciation expense} = \frac{\text{Depreciable amount}}{\text{Useful life}}$$

$$\text{Depreciation expense} = \frac{\text{Cost} - \text{residual value}}{\text{Useful life}}$$

Based on the information for Melbourne's equipment (shown earlier in the chapter), the annual depreciation would be calculated as follows:

$$\text{Depreciation expense} = \frac{\text{A \$375 200} - 30\ 000}{4 \text{ years}}$$

$$\text{A \$86 300} = \frac{\text{A \$345 200}}{4 \text{ years}}$$

Once the amount of depreciation expense is calculated, an adjusting entry is recorded by debiting depreciation expense and crediting accumulated depreciation, as shown in the following:

Date	Account Titles	DR	CR
31 Dec. 2010	Depreciation expense Accumulated depreciation	$86 300	$86 300

Depreciation expense is the expired portion of the asset cost, and thus appears in the statement of comprehensive income. Expenses, including depreciation expense, are temporary accounts, which means that they are closed at the end of the reporting period. Accumulated depreciation is a contra-asset account. Because accumulated depreciation is a permanent account, the balance is not closed to retained earnings at the end of each reporting period. Therefore, accumulated depreciation measures the total of depreciation expense to date for the asset.

At the end of the first year, the equipment would be presented on Melbourne's 31 December 2009 statement of financial position as follows:

Equipment	A$375 200
Accumulated depreciation	(86 300)
Carrying amount	A$288 900

Notice that when the accumulated depreciation is subtracted from equipment, the result is the **carrying amount** (also book value or net book value). The following table shows the pattern of depreciation expense based on the straight-line method with accumulated depreciation and carrying amount for Melbourne's equipment.

Year	Depreciation Expense	Accumulated Depreciation	Carrying Amount
2010	A$86 300	A$86 300	A$288 900
2011	86 300	172 600	202 600
2012	86 300	258 900	116 300
2013	86 300	345 200	30 000

Notice that the depreciation expense is the same amount each year. However, the carrying amount (cost less accumulated depreciation) declines until at the end of the asset's useful life, the carrying amount is equal to the residual value.

3.2.2 UNITS-OF-PRODUCTION METHOD

The second method of allocating costs over the useful life of the asset is units of production. The units-of-production method allocates the depreciable amount based on the expected use or output of the asset. To calculate depreciation expense under the units-of-production method, the depreciable amount (cost – residual value) is divided by total activity. Activity can be machine hours, production quantity or another metric that measures the consumption of the asset.

Melbourne's new equipment is expected to operate for 120 000 machine hours over its useful life. The calculation of depreciation expense per machine hour would be as follows:

$$\text{Depreciation expense per machine hour} = \frac{\text{Depreciable amount}}{\text{Activity base}}$$

$$= \frac{\text{Cost} - \text{residual value}}{\text{Activity base}}$$

$$= \frac{\text{A\$375 200} - 30\ 000}{120\ 000\ \text{machine hours}}$$

$$= \frac{\text{A\$345 200}}{120\ 000}$$

$$= \text{A\$2.88}$$

Let's assume that over the next four years, the company actually operates the equipment as shown in the following table:

Year	Hours of Operation
2010	27 000
2011	21 000
2012	29 500
2013	25 000

For each hour of operation, the machine would be depreciated by A$2.88. In the first year, the depreciation expense would be $77 760 ($2.88 × 27 000 hours of operation). The remaining three years are calculated in the same way. The results are summarized in the following table:

Year	Depreciation Expense	Accumulated Depreciation	Carrying Amount
2010	A$77 760	A$77 760	A$297 440
2011	60 480	172 600	202 600
2012	84 960	257 560	117 640
2013	72 000	328 560	45 640

We can see that by the end of the asset's usual life (the fourth year), the carrying amount of the equipment is not equal to the residual value as it was with the straight-line method. This is because the amount of depreciation expense in any period depends on actual usage, which may or may not be the same as the predicted usage over the asset's useful life (120 000 hours in this example).

Managers often favour the units-of-production method because it synchronizes the amount of depreciation expense with revenue. Use of the equipment would typically increase as more units are produced and sold. Thus, as revenue increases, so does the amount of depreciation expense. When revenue decreases, depreciation expense also decreases, softening the impact on profit or loss. Therefore, the units-of-production method achieves a better matching of expenses to revenue.

3.2.3 DIMINISHING BALANCE METHOD

The diminishing balance method (also reducing balance method or declining balance method) shifts depreciation expense to earlier time periods in the asset's useful life. This results in a decreasing charge to depreciation expense over that useful life. Thus, the diminishing balance method is sometimes referred to as accelerated depreciation. The rate at which depreciation is accelerated can vary, but a typical application doubles the straight-line rate and is therefore called double-declining balance. We will use double-declining balance for our example below.

The first step is to calculate the depreciation rate. The useful life is divided into one, and the result is doubled as shown in the following equation:

$$\text{Double-declining depreciation rate} = \frac{1}{\text{Useful life}} \times 2$$

Melbourne's equipment has a four-year useful life, so the depreciation rate would be calculated as follows:

$$\text{Double-declining depreciation rate} = \frac{1}{4} \times 2$$

$$50\% = \frac{1}{4} \times 2$$

This rate is used to calculate the amount of depreciation expense for each year, as the following schedule shows:

Year	Carrying Amount at Beginning of Year	Double-Declining Rate %	Depreciation Expense	Accumulated Depreciation	Carrying Amount at End of Year
2010	A$375 200	50	A$187 600	A$187 600	A$187 600
2011	187 600	50	93 800	281 400	93 800
2012	93 800	50	46 900	328 300	46 900
2013	46 900	50	16 900	345 200	30 000

As we can see from the schedule, the carrying amount at the beginning of the year ($375 200 for 2010) is multiplied by the double-declining rate (50%) to calculate depreciation expense, which is $187 600. Notice that residual value is not deducted for this calculation. Accumulated depreciation for 2010 is deducted from the original cost to calculate the carrying amount on 31 December 2010, which is $187 600 ($375 200 – 187 600).

For 2011, the carrying amount at the end of 2010 is brought forward, and multiplied by 0.50 to give the 2011 depreciation expense of $93 800. This increases accumulated depreciation to $281 400 and leaves the carrying amount for the end of 2011 at $93 800. Then the calculations are repeated for the remainder of the asset's useful life.

Notice that in 2013 the carrying amount at the beginning of the year is $46 900 and when this is multiplied by 0.50 the result is $23 450. However, only $16 900 is charged to depreciation expense. The reason is that to charge more than this amount would cause the carrying amount to drop below the residual value of $30 000. Thus, in the last period management may adjust depreciation expense to achieve this end.

3.2.4 HOW DOES THE CHOICE BETWEEN STRAIGHT-LINE METHOD AND DIMINISHING BALANCE METHOD AFFECT THE FINANCIAL STATEMENTS?

Obviously, the straight-line and diminishing balance methods will produce different patterns of depreciation expense over the asset's useful life. Figure 7.11 compares the results of the two methods for the Melbourne Medical Equipment example.

Notice in Figure 7.11 that diminishing balance generates more depreciation expense in the first two years of the asset's useful life when compared to the straight-line depreciation method. However, in the last two years it generates less.

Why would a company choose an accelerated method like diminishing balance? One answer is that management believes that the diminishing balance more accurately reflects the flow of costs associated with the use of the equipment. In other words, more expense should be recognized on a new machine than an older one that is likely to be less productive.

FIGURE 7.11 MELBOURNE MEDICAL EQUIPMENT COMPARISON

Method	Year 1	Year 2	Year 3	Year 4
Straight line	$86 300	$86 300	$86 300	$86 300
Diminishing balance	187 600	93 800	46 900	16 900
Difference	($101 300)	(7 500)	39 400	69 400

However, in countries with business income tax, accelerated methods are sometimes accepted for tax reporting purposes even when straight-line and units-of-production methods may be used for financial reports. Earlier in the useful life of the asset, the straight-line method generates less depreciation expense, which causes profit to be higher. Using diminishing balance for tax reporting increases expenses and decreases profit, which in turn reduces taxes paid.

During the last two years, the situation is reversed, as Figure 7.11 shows. Diminishing balance generates less depreciation expense than straight line and the business now has an incentive to sell or trade the existing asset for new, more productive equipment. The diminishing balance method uses the new cost so that the accelerated depreciation scheme begins anew. In countries with tax systems that permit accelerated depreciation methods, the effect is to subsidize investment to spur productivity, which is a driver of economic growth.

Partial Years

Property, plant and equipment are usually depreciated only for that portion of the year that they are in service.

Now, let's assume that Melbourne uses the straight-line method and acquired the equipment in the foregoing example on 1 July 2010. Depreciation expense for one year under the straight-line method was calculated at $86 300, but since the equipment was in service for six months, only $43 150 would be recognized in the first year. The year-end adjusting entry would be as follows:

Date	Account Titles	DR	CR
31 Dec. 2010	Depreciation expense	$43 150	
	Accumulated depreciation		$43 150

Suppose that Melbourne uses diminishing declining balance and places the equipment into service on 25 November 2010. The adjusting entry would be $12 058 [(51 days remaining in the year ÷ 365) × $86 300]. So the adjusting entry would be:

Date	Account Titles	DR	CR
31 Dec. 2010	Depreciation expense	$12 058	
	Accumulated depreciation		$12 058

In both cases, the depreciation expense recorded in 2011 would be for a full year.

ON YOUR OWN

LEARNING OUTCOME REVIEW

1. Name the principal methods of allocating the depreciation amount over the useful life of property, plant and equipment.
2. What is the difference between depreciation expense and accumulated depreciation?
3. How is depreciation expense calculated under the straight-line method?
4. How is depreciation expense calculated under the units-of-production method?
5. How is depreciation expense calculated under the diminishing balance method?
6. Which depreciation method increases profit during the earliest years of the asset's useful life?
7. Which depreciation method results in the highest carrying amount for an asset during the earliest years of its useful life?
8. Which account is temporary: depreciation expense or accumulated depreciation?

LEARNING OUTCOME PRACTICE

1. On 1 July 2009 Tom bought a machine for $15 500. He depreciates machinery at a rate of 20% per annum on the reducing balance basis. A full year's depreciation is charged in the year an asset is purchased. His year end is 31 October. What is the depreciation charge on the machine for the year to 31 October 2009?
   a. $3100
   b. $2480
   c. $2232
   d. $1984
   ACCA adapted

2. A business purchased a car on 1 July 2010 for $20 000. It is to be depreciated at 20% per year on the straight-line basis, assuming a residual value at the end of five years of $4000, with a proportionate depreciation charge in the year of purchase. The $20 000 cost was correctly entered in the cash book but posted to the debit of the motor vehicles repairs account. How will the business's profit for the year ended 31 December 2010 be affected by the error?
   a. Understated by $18 400
   b. Understated by $16 800
   c. Understated by $18 000
   d. Overstated by $18 400
   ACCA adapted

WHO KNOWS?

When a business acquires an asset, estimates must be made for residual value and useful life. But how do managers know that a delivery truck, for example, will last five years and be worth €3000 at the end of its useful life? Or for that matter, how do managers know that the economic benefits of the truck will be consumed evenly over its useful life, making the choice of the straight-line method appropriate? Or that more economic benefit will be obtained earlier in the truck's useful life when the diminishing balance method is chosen?

They don't. The truck may experience heavier-than-expected use and wear out more quickly. A new, more efficient model may make it attractive to trade in the old truck earlier. An employee may mistreat the truck, causing rapid deterioration. All managers can do is make their best estimate, although a business may have some past experience that helps with the estimates. And in some cases, consultants may collate information on the residual values and useful lives of certain assets, on which management relies.

Residual value and useful life are just estimates, and management may realize during the asset's lifetime that a change in the estimates needs to be made.

Changing Depreciation Estimates

Useful life and residual value are based on estimates that may later prove to be inaccurate. Over time, a business may determine that its estimates need to be revised, which results in a change in accounting estimate (see IFRS box).

IFRS

'A change in accounting estimate is an adjustment to the carrying amount of an asset or a liability, or the amount of the periodic consumption of the asset, that results from the assessment of the present status of, and expected future benefits and obligations associated with, assets and liabilities. Changes in accounting estimates result from new information or new developments and, accordingly, are not corrections of errors.'

IAS 8 Accounting Policies, Changes in Accounting Estimates and Errors

When this happens, the depreciation expense is recalculated based on the carrying amount less the *revised* residual value and the *revised* remaining useful life.

Melbourne uses the straight-line method to depreciate its equipment. At the end of year two, the carrying value would be as follows:

Equipment	A$375 200
Accumulated depreciation	(172 600)
Carrying amount	A$202 600

Based on the original four-year estimate, two years remain on the equipment's useful life. But now, management estimates that the equipment will last another five years, although at the end of that time the residual value will only be $5000. What amount of depreciation expense should be recorded in 2012? The calculation would be as follows:

$$\text{Depreciation expense} = \frac{\$202\,600 - 5000}{5 \text{ years}}$$

$$\text{A }\$39\,520 = \frac{\$197\,600}{5 \text{ years}}$$

Figure 7.12 shows the depreciation schedule after estimates of residual value and useful life have been revised.

FIGURE 7.12 DEPRECIATION SCHEDULE AFTER CHANGE IN ESTIMATE

Year	Depreciation Expense	Accumulated Depreciation	Carrying Amount
2010	A$86 300	A$86 300	A$288 900
2011	86 300	172 600	202 600
2012	39 520	212 120	163 080
2013	39 520	251 640	123 560
2014	39 520	291 160	84 040
2015	39 520	330 680	44 520
2016	39 520	370 200	5 000

3.3 How do we account for a change in the value of property, plant and equipment?

Two situations can arise when the value of property, plant or equipment changes while the assets are still in use: a decline in value, which may result in an impairment loss; and an increase in value, which can result in a revaluation of the asset in the accounting records.

3.3.1 WHAT IS AN IMPAIRMENT LOSS?

Situations arise when an asset may decline in value for any variety of reasons. For example, equipment may become obsolete or may be damaged by fire or natural disaster. In these cases, we say that a property has an impairment loss (see IFRS box).

Each year, management must conduct tests to determine whether assets are impaired. This is done by comparing the carrying amount with the replacement cost of the asset. When this test indicates that impairment has occurred, then the asset carrying amount is reduced and a loss is recognized immediately on the statement of comprehensive income.

Elron Energy AG owns a coal-burning electric generating plant, the Highland Facility, which has a carrying amount of €72 000 000 (€85 000 000 cost − 13 000 000 accumulated depreciation). A new emissions law has been passed that will force the company to retrofit the facility with scrubbers in order to meet the new environmental requirements. This suggests that since the plant does not have this required equipment, its value may have declined. As a result, Elron's management conducted an impairment test.

The impairment test showed that as of 31 December 2010, the plant's replacement cost is €55 000 000. Since this is less than the carrying amount by €17 000 000 (€72 000 000 − 55 000 000), an impairment loss has occurred. This loss is recognized immediately by recording the following entry:

Date	Account Titles	DR	CR
31 Dec. 2010	Impairment loss − Highland Facility Accumulated impairment losses − Highland Facility	€17 000 000	€17 000 000

After recognition of an impairment loss, depreciation would be adjusted for the revised carrying amount, residual value and remaining useful life. If the recoverable amount of an asset with a past impairment loss subsequently rises, then the asset may be written up to the new recoverable amount, and the difference between the new recoverable amount and the carrying amount recognized in profit or loss.

Assume that during 2011, Elron again tests the Highland Facility for impairment, but now finds that the value in use has risen to €65 000 000. Elron would make the following entry:

Date	Account Titles	DR	CR
31 Dec. 2011	Accumulated impairment losses – Highland Facility	€10 000 000	
	Impairment gain – Highland Facility		€10 000 000

3.3.2 WHAT IS AN ASSET REVALUATION?

After an asset has been acquired, management has the option to continue carrying the property, plant and equipment at the original cost or, if the value of the asset increases, to revalue it. For management this would be a choice between the cost model and the revaluation model (see IFRS box).

The cost model means that the asset's original cost is not changed, while the revaluation model allows an increase to fair value (see IFRS box). Under the revaluation model, management is required to determine the fair value once per year.

Al Azzam Enterprises LLC, a speciality foods distributor, purchases an office building on the outskirts of Dubai for €2 500 000 in 2008. Rapid growth has meant that property values have been increasing rapidly. At the end of 2009, an appraiser estimates that the property value is now €3 200 000. Al Azzam's management has elected to use the revaluation model for all land and buildings. The following adjusting entry would be made:

Date	Account Titles	DR	CR
31 Dec. 2009	Office buildings Revaluation reserve − other comprehensive income	€700 000	€700 000

Notice that the credit in the journal entry shown above is directly to a revaluation reserve in equity. In other words, any gain that results from a revaluation of the property is not recognized in profit, or loss. However, the amount of the revaluation would appear in other comprehensive income on the statement of comprehensive income.

At the end of 2010 Al Azzam has the building appraised again, and finds that property values have decreased somewhat. The appraisal on the office building is now €2 800 000. Because a revaluation reserve has already been established for this asset, the decline in value would be offset against that. The journal entry would be as follows:

Date	Account Titles	DR	CR
31 Dec. 2010	Revaluation reserve − other comprehensive income Office buildings	€400 000	€400 000

Notice again that the transaction does not affect either profit or loss. Further declines in value would continue to be offset against any revaluation reserve until it is completely eliminated. Declines beyond that mean that the asset value has fallen below its original cost. Once the revaluation reserve is exhausted, the asset would be subject to impairment, which we have already discussed.

ON YOUR OWN

LEARNING OUTCOME REVIEW
1. To what does impairment refer?
2. How can a business determine whether an asset is impaired?

3. Define recoverable amount, fair value less costs to sell and value in use.
4. What are the two models for revaluing property, plant and equipment?

LEARNING OUTCOME PRACTICE

1. Under the revaluation model, how often should management determine the fair value of the asset?
   a. On the anniversary of the asset's acquisition
   b. Once per year
   c. On the first day of the reporting period
   d. Only when circumstances suggest that a revaluation may be necessary

2. A company originally purchased equipment at $45 000. Its carrying amount is now $25 000. The equipment is now valued at $47 000. The journal entry to adjust the asset value under the revaluation model would include a:
   a. Debit to accumulated depreciation for $2000
   b. Credit to accumulated depreciation for $2000
   c. Credit revaluation reserve for $2000
   d. Debit revaluation reserve for $2000

3.4 How do we account for the disposal of property, plant and equipment?

When a business disposes of property, plant and equipment, then all balances related to that asset are removed from the ledger accounts and a gain or loss is recognized based on the difference between the carrying amount of the asset and the amount received for the asset, if any.

Melbourne fully depreciates the equipment based on the schedule shown above for seven years, so that at the end of the equipment's useful life the carrying amount is A$5000 as shown in Figure 7.12. On 31 December 2016, Melbourne sells the equipment for $6500. The journal entry to record the disposal would be as follows:

Date	Account Titles	DR	CR
31 Dec. 2016	Cash	A$6 500	
	Accumulated depreciation	370 200	
	Equipment		A$375 200
	Gain on equipment disposal		1 500

Notice that the credit to the equipment account removes all cost associated with this particular item. A debit removes all related accumulated depreciation. The difference between these two balances is $5000, which is the carrying amount. We also debit cash for the $6500 received, which results in a credit difference of $1500. This is a gain on the disposal of the equipment.

WHAT TO LOOK OUT FOR

When making a journal entry to dispose of property, plant and equipment, students sometimes try to calculate the gain or loss first. This leads to confusion. Relax and let the journal entry do the work for you. First, debit and credit the asset account and the associated accumulated depreciation to remove the balances from the ledger accounts. Second, debit what you received for the equipment – usually cash. Now, calculate the difference just as we did for the preceding journal entry. If the difference is a credit, congratulations, you have a gain. A debit? Too bad, it's a loss. Test this method on the next example.

Suppose that the Melbourne equipment was sold for A$4500 instead of A$6500. Now the journal entry would be as follows:

Date	Account Titles	DR	CR
31 Dec. 2016	Cash Accumulated depreciation Loss on equipment disposal Equipment	A$4 500 370 200 500	A$375 200

In this example, the amount received is less than the carrying amount of the equipment given up in the exchange, so a debit resulted, which is a loss.

Trade-ins

Often businesses trade old equipment as part of the transaction with the seller when buying new equipment. The seller may offer a trade-in allowance.

Suppose that Melbourne's equipment in the previous example is traded in for new equipment with a list price of A$405 000. The dealer offers a A$15 000 trade-in allowance for the old equipment and Melbourne must pay the difference in cash. The journal entry to record this transaction would be:

Date	Account Titles	DR	CR
31 Dec. 2016	Equipment – new Accumulated depreciation Equipment – old Cash	A$395 000 370 200	 A$375 200 390 000

Notice that this entry removes the cost and accumulated depreciation for the old equipment, then records the amount of cash that Melbourne must pay to acquire the new equipment, which is A$390 000 (A$405 000 – 15 000 trade-in allowance). The difference is a net debit of A$395 000, which is recorded as the new equipment cost. The list price of A$405 000 is not relevant. The only significance of the A$15 000 trade-in allowance is to calculate the cash portion that Melbourne must pay.

ON YOUR OWN

LEARNING OUTCOME PRACTICE

1. A company bought a machine for use in his business on 1 January 2010. He gave the supplier a cheque for $11 750 and traded in an old machine. The supplier allowed him $4430 in part exchange for the old machine. The company depreciates machinery on the reducing basis at a rate of 20% per annum. The old machine had cost $12 000 and had accumulated depreciation of $5856.

    What is the depreciation charge on the new machine for the year ended 31 October 2010?

    a. $886
    b. $2350
    c. $4465
    d. $3578
    ACCA adapted

RIO TINTO

Rio Tinto is a leading worldwide company engaged in the business of finding, mining and processing the earth's mineral resources. Following is its explanation of accounting policies related to property, plant and equipment in its 2007 financial statement notes.

Depreciation of noncurrent assets

Property, plant and equipment is depreciated over its useful life, or over the remaining life of the mine if shorter. The major categories of property, plant and equipment are depreciated on units-of-production and/or straight-line basis as follows.

Units-of-production basis

For mining properties and leases and certain mining equipment, the economic benefits from the asset are consumed in a pattern which is linked to the production level. Except as noted below, such assets are depreciated on units-of-production basis.

Straight-line basis

Assets within operations for which production is not expected to fluctuate significantly from one year to another or which have a physical life shorter than the related mine are depreciated on a straight-line basis as follows:

Buildings 5 to 50 years
Plant and equipment 3 to 35 years
Power assets 25 to 100 years
Land Not depreciated

Residual values and useful lives are reviewed, and adjusted if appropriate, at each balance sheet date. Changes to the estimated residual values or useful lives are accounted for prospectively. In applying the units-of-production method, depreciation is normally calculated using the quantity of material extracted from the mine in the period as a percentage of the total quantity of material to be extracted in current and future periods based on proved and probable reserves and, for some mines, other mineral resources.

LEARNING OUTCOME 4
EXPLAIN ACCOUNTING PRACTICES FOR INTANGIBLE ASSETS

Assets with *physical substance*, such as inventories and property, plant and equipment, are referred to as tangible assets. However, some assets have no physical substance and are referred to as intangible assets. Intangible assets also exclude financial assets like investments in share capital and debt instruments. Common examples of intangibles include computer software, patents, copyrights, motion picture films, customer lists, franchises and marketing rights.

We will examine five issues related to intangible assets.

4.1 What costs are included in intangible assets?

4.2 How are intangible asset costs expensed?

4.3 How do we account for a change in the value of intangible assets?

4.4 How do we account for the disposal of an intangible asset?

4.5 What is goodwill and how do we account for it?

4.1 What costs are included in intangible assets?

Intangible assets are recognized at cost *if the asset is externally acquired*. The cost would include any directly attributable costs to bring the asset to its working condition, professional fees and costs of testing whether the asset is functioning properly.

Xiaoshan Metallurgy Company purchases an accounting software package for ¥700 000 on 3 September 2009. Legal fees were ¥8000. The software developer granted Xiaoshan a 10% trade discount. Costs for installation and testing were ¥30 000. These costs are summarized as follows:

Purchase price	¥700 000
Less: Trade discount	70 000
Add:	¥630 000
Legal fees	8 000
Installation and testing	30 000
Intangible asset cost	¥668 000

Xiaoshan would make the following journal entry to record the cost of the intangible asset.

Date	Account Titles	DR	CR
3 Sep. 2009	Intangible asset − Software	¥668 000	
	Cash (various)		¥668 000

4.2 How are intangible asset costs expensed?

Intangible assets can be acquired in one of two ways: from an outside entity and by internal development. For example, a pharmaceuticals company may acquire an already existing patent from another business entity. This could be a patent for a sinus medication that the business entity does not want to manufacture and market itself. In this case, as with all intangible assets acquired from an outside entity, the cost of the patent would be capitalized.

Alternatively, the pharmaceuticals company may elect to develop the patent internally. In this case, the decision whether to capitalize or expense the costs depends on the nature of the research and development activity (see IFRS box).

IFRS

'Research is original and planned investigation undertaken with the prospect of gaining new scientific or technical knowledge and understanding.'

'Development is the application of research findings or other knowledge to a plan or design for the production of new or substantially improved materials, devices, products, processes, systems or services before the start of commercial production or use.'

IAS 38 Intangible Assets

Copyright © 2007 International Accounting Standards Committee Foundation. All rights reserved. No permission granted to reproduce or distribute.

Research costs are always expensed (see IFRS box).

IFRS

'No intangible asset arising from research shall be recognized [as an asset]. Expenditure on research shall be recognized as an expense when it is incurred.'

IAS 38 Intangible Assets

Copyright © 2007 International Accounting Standards Committee Foundation. All rights reserved. No permission granted to reproduce or distribute.

Development costs can be capitalized as part of an intangible asset only when certain criteria are met. Basically, evidence must exist that the intangible asset can and will be developed into a commercially useable or saleable product.

AMORTIZATION

When acquired, an intangible asset is recorded at cost. After recognition, the business chooses either the cost model or the revaluation model to account for the intangible asset. Thus, the accounting is basically the same as for property, plant and equipment, with three differences. First, we amortize the cost of the intangible to time periods, rather than depreciating the asset cost as we do for property, plant and equipment. This is only a terminological difference; in fact, the definition of amortization is the same as depreciation: 'the systematic allocation of the depreciable amount of an asset over its useful life.'

The second difference is that intangible assets do not use an accumulated amortization account comparable to the accumulated depreciation account for property, plant and equipment. Instead, the credit in the amortization entry is recorded in the intangible asset account itself.

Chen Pharmaceuticals Ltd purchased a patent for ¥10 000 000 on 1 January 2006. The useful life of the patent was estimated to be eight years. Each year Chen would make the following adjusting entry to record amortization of the patent.

Date	Account Titles	DR	CR
1 Jan. 2009	Amortization expense	¥1 250 000	
	Patent		¥1 250 000

Amortization expense appears on the statement of comprehensive income, while patent, the intangible asset, appears on the statement of financial position.

The third difference is that intangible assets often have a limited legal life. If the patent's legal life is shorter than its useful life, the patent would be amortized over the legal life. If, however, the useful life is shorter than the patent's legal life, the useful life would be used to calculate amortization.

The patent that Chen Pharmaceuticals acquired (in the previous example) has a legal life of six years beginning 1 January 2007. Thus, when Chen purchased the patent two years later, only four years of legal life remained. Since this is less than the estimate useful life of eight years, Chen would amortize the patent over the four remaining years of its legal life at ¥2 500 000 per year (¥10 000 000 ÷ 4 years). The adjusting entry would be:

Date	Account Titles	DR	CR
1 Jan. 2009	Amortization expense	¥2 500 000	
	Patent		¥2 500 000

Residual value is assumed to be zero unless a commitment exists for a third party to buy the asset at the end of its useful life, or the residual value can be determined by reference to an active market.

4.3 How do we account for a change in the value of intangible assets?

Again, intangible assets are similar to property, plant and equipment in that they are subject to impairment tests each year. If the intangible asset is impaired, the impaired amount must be recognized immediately in profit or loss.

Also, the business entity can choose either the cost model or the revaluation model to account for the intangible asset after initial recognition:

- *Cost model.* Under the cost model, the intangible asset is carried at cost less any accumulated amortization and any accumulated impairment losses.
- *Revaluation model.* Under the revaluation model, the intangible asset is carried at fair value less any accumulated amortization and accumulated impairment losses since the date of revaluation. When an intangible asset increases because of a revaluation, the increase is credited directly to equity as a revaluation surplus in other comprehensive income. In other words, the increase is not recognized in profit. If an intangible asset decreases because of a revaluation, the decrease is first debited to any revaluation surplus in equity and then to profit or loss.

On 1 January 2011, two years after acquiring the patent, Chen Pharmaceuticals determined that the value of the patent was ¥7 000 000. The carrying amount of the patent at this date is ¥5 000 000 (¥10 000 000 − 5 000 000). Chen would therefore make the following revaluation entry:

Date	Account Titles	DR	CR
1 Jan. 2011	Patent Other comprehensive income − revaluation account	¥2 000 000	¥2 000 000

Notice that the balance in the patent account is now ¥7 000 000. The legal life of the asset has two years remaining. At the end of 2011, Chen would record the following entry for amortization expense:

Date	Account Titles	DR	CR
31 Dec. 2011	Amortization expense Patent	¥3 500 000	¥3 500 000

The ¥3 500 000 is calculated by taking the revalued patent amount of ¥7 000 000 and dividing it by the two remaining years (2011 and 2012). Thus the unamortized balance on 31 December 2011 is ¥3 500 000.

On 30 June 2012, Chen Pharmaceuticals has encountered legal problems with the patent and determines that the value has now declined to ¥1 000 000. This means that the following entry is required:

Date	Account Titles	DR	CR
30 June 2011	Other comprehensive income – revaluation account	¥2 000 000	
	Impairment loss	500 000	
	Patent		¥2 500 000

The patent is credited for ¥2 500 000, so that the carrying amount is now ¥1 000 000. The revaluation reserve in other comprehensive income is removed for the full amount and the remainder is recorded in profit or loss on the statement of comprehensive income.

A change in the value of an intangible asset is often difficult to determine. Most intangible assets are unique and do not trade on an active market. That means that value must be established in some other way, such as by appraisal.

4.4 How do we account for the disposal of an intangible asset?

When an intangible asset is disposed of, or no further economic benefits are expected, then it should be removed from the ledger accounts, and a gain or loss recognized as measured by the difference between the carrying amount and the net disposal proceeds.

4.5 Goodwill

Goodwill is an asset that represents the future economic benefits that arise from assets acquired when one business buys another. Goodwill is created when the amount paid for the acquired business exceeds the fair value of the net assets acquired.

Melbourne Medical Equipment LLC purchases Perth MedSystems LLC, a marketing firm for medical equipment with distribution channels in geographic areas where Melbourne wishes to expand rapidly. Melbourne plans to conduct all business in its own name in the future. Perth's asset and liability accounts are shown below along with fair values.

	Carrying Amount	Fair Value
Assets		
Current assets	A$340 000	A$340 000
Noncurrent assets	2 700 000	3 200 000
	A$3 040 000	A$3 540 000
Liabilities		
Current liabilities	$100 000	$100 000
Noncurrent liabilities	1 500 000	1 500 000
	A$1 600 000	A$1 600 000
Equity	$1 440 000	$1 940 000
Total liabilities and equity	A$3 040 000	A$3 540 000

Suppose that on 15 June 2009 Melbourne paid A$2 500 000 for Perth MedSystems. Notice that this is more than the carrying amount of the equity, and is in fact more than the equity when measured at fair value. The A$2 500 000 is assigned to the identifiable assets and liabilities (shown in the right-hand column), which net to A$1 940 000. But what is the difference of A$560 000 (A$2 500 000 – 1 940 000), which is the amount over net fair value of the identifiable assets paid for Perth MedSystems? This is recognized as goodwill.

Melbourne Medical Equipment would make the following journal entry to record the acquisition of Perth MedSystems' assets and liabilities:

Date	Account Titles	DR	CR
15 June 2009	Current assets	A$340 000	
	Noncurrent assets	3 200 000	
	Goodwill	560 000	
	Current liabilities		100 000
	Noncurrent liabilities		1500 000
	Cash		2500 000

Goodwill is classified as an intangible asset. However, unlike other intangible assets, it is not amortized, although it is subject to impairment.

WHAT TO LOOK OUT FOR

Students sometimes mistake goodwill for the good feeling that consumers and others have towards a company's products or its social activities, like contributing to education or improvement of the environment. However, this is not what accounting goodwill is. In accounting, goodwill is a technical term, and it means the excess amount that a business entity paid for another over the fair value of the net assets acquired.

LVMH: INTANGIBLE ASSETS

Intangible assets can sometimes be a major asset for a business. Moët Hennessy-Louis Vuitton (LVMH) is one of the premier luxury brand merchandising firms, with businesses in fashion and leather goods, perfumes and cosmetics, watches and jewellery and 'selective' retailing.

In 2007, consolidated net income was €2.3 billion and the company had €30.7 billion in assets, of which €20.3 billion were noncurrent assets. As the table below illustrates, a significant part of noncurrent assets were brands and other intangibles for almost €8 billion and goodwill for €4.8 billion. That means that intangible assets totalled €12.8 billion, which represented 42% (€12.8 billion ÷ 30.7 billion) of the total assets of the company.

Assets € millions	2007
Brands and other intangible assets − net	7 999
Goodwill − net	4 818
Property, plant and equipment − net	5 419
Investment in associates	129
Financial assets	823
Other noncurrent assets	586
Deferred tax	492
NONCURRENT ASSETS	20 266

ON YOUR OWN

LEARNING OUTCOME REVIEW

1. What are examples of intangible assets?
2. When an intangible asset is acquired externally, what is the appropriate accounting?
3. When an asset is developed internally, what is the appropriate accounting?
4. What is the difference between research and development?
5. How are research costs accounted for?
6. How are development costs accounted for?
7. What two models can a reporting entity use to account for changes to the value of intangible assets?
8. What is goodwill? How is it created?

LEARNING OUTCOME PRACTICE

1. Which of the following statements is/are correct?
   i. Capitalized development expenditure must be amortized over a period not exceeding five years.
   ii. Capitalized development costs are shown in the statement of financial position under the heading of noncurrent assets.
   iii. If certain criteria are met, research expenditure can be recognized as an intangible asset.
      a. ii only
      b. ii and iii
      c. i only
      d. i and iii
      ACCA adapted

2. At 31 December 2012, Manchester Software Systems Ltd had capitalized software costs of €900 000. The useful life was estimated at four years, with no residual value. Sales for 2013 were 10% of the total expected sales of the software. At the 2013 year-end, the software had a recoverable amount of €720 000. What amount should Manchester report as the net capitalized software on its 31 December 2013 statement of financial position?
      a. €648 000
      b. €675 000
      c. €720 000
      d. €810 000
      ACCA adapted

3. Netherland Company acquired a patent on 1 January 2011 for $112 500. This amount was to be amortized over 15 years with no residual value. In 2014, Netherland sued another company for infringement of its patent rights. Legal fees were $37 500, although no settlement was received. That year, Netherland sold the patent for $187 500. Assuming that no amortization expense was recognized in 2014, what amount would Netherland report in its 2014 statement of comprehensive income for gain on sale of patent?
      a. $37 500
      b. $60 000
      c. $67 500
      d. $107 500

4. Which of the following statements about intangible assets are correct?
   i. If certain criteria are met, research expenditure may be recognized as an intangible asset.
   ii. Goodwill may not be revalued upwards.
   iii. Internally generated goodwill should not be capitalized.
      a. ii and iii only
      b. i and iii only
      c. i and ii only

    d.   All three statements are correct

    ACCA adapted

5. Which of the following statements about intangible assets in company financial statements are correct according to international accounting standards?

    i.   Internally generated goodwill should not be capitalized.

    ii. Purchased goodwill should normally be amortized through the statement of comprehensive income.

    iii. Development expenditure may be capitalized if certain conditions are met.

        a.   i and iii only

        b.   i and ii only

        c.   ii and iii only

        d.   All three statements are correct

    ACCA adapted

LEARNING OUTCOME 5
EXPLAIN ACCOUNTING PRACTICES FOR INVESTMENT PROPERTIES

Assets, whether tangible or intangible, can be acquired for investment purposes rather than for resale to a customer or to use in production, for renting to a customer or to use in the business. For example, a business entity purchases a tract of land because management believes that it might make a good site for a new manufacturing plant, although management has no immediate plans to build a new facility. In cases like this, the asset is classified as investment property (see IFRS box).

IFRS

'Investment property is property (land or a building – or part of a building – or both) held (by the owner or by the lessee under a finance lease) to earn rentals or for capital appreciation or both; rather than for (a) use in the production or supply of goods or services or for administrative purposes; or (b) sale in the ordinary course of business.

IAS 40 Investment Property

Investment properties are recorded at their cost plus any related costs such as legal fees, property transfer taxes and real estate commissions. A significant difference between an asset classified as an investment property and a depreciable asset like property, plant and equipment or an intangible is that investment properties are not depreciated or amortized. However, if an investment asset is impaired, an impairment loss is recorded in profit or loss. Also, after the asset is acquired, the business can use either the cost model or fair value model for investment properties. Under the cost model, the asset is recorded at cost and remains unchanged unless impaired. And under the fair value model, the business recognizes any difference between the carrying amount of the investment property and its fair value in profit or loss (see IFRS box). Notice that the difference is not recognized in other comprehensive income, as would be the case with property, plant and equipment.

IFRS	'A gain or loss arising from a change in the fair value of investment property shall be recognized in profit or loss for the period in which it arises.'

On 2 July 2008 Stéphan Luc SA purchased an old office building in Paris for €8 000 000. The plan was eventually to raze the building and build a new corporate headquarters tower, but construction was not expected to begin until 2013.

In the meantime, Stéphan Luc rented the building to a number of small commercial tenants. When the building was acquired, Stéphan Luc incurred about €270 000 in directly attributable expenditure, mostly legal fees and estate agent commissions. The company would make the following entry to record the acquisition:

Date	Account Titles	DR	CR
2 July 2008	Investment property	€8 270 000	
	Cash		€8 270 000

On 31 December 2008, an appraiser values the building at €7 900 000. Stéphan Luc would make the following journal entry to recognize the impairment loss:

Date	Account Titles	DR	CR
31 Dec. 2008	Loss on investment property	€370 000	
	Investment property		€370 000

At the end of 2009, another appraisal shows that the property has recovered some of its value and now has a fair value of €8 100 000. The adjusting entry would be:

Date	Account Titles	DR	CR
31 Dec. 2009	Investment property	€200 000	
	Gain on investment property		€200 000

Notice that the gain is calculated based on the difference between the fair value and the carrying amount of €7 900 000 after it had been adjusted in 2008, not on the original cost of €8 270 000. At this point, the investment property's carrying amount is €8 100 000.

DISPOSAL OF INVESTMENT PROPERTY

When the business retires or disposes of an investment property, then the difference between the net disposal proceeds and the carrying amount is recognized in profit or loss.

Suppose that on 1 January 2010 Stéphan Luc decides to sell the office building, abandoning its plans to build a new office tower in that location. On this date the carrying amount of the existing building is €7 900 000

The building is sold for €9 700 000. However, Stéphan Luc must pay a real estate commission and other sales-related fees of €600 000. The journal entry to record the sales transaction would be as follows:

Date	Account Titles	DR	CR
1 Jan. 2010	Cash	€9 700 000	
	Gain on disposal of investment property		€1 200 000
	Investment property		7 900 000
	Cash		600 000

ON YOUR OWN

LEARNING OUTCOME REVIEW

1. How is an investment property different from property, plant and equipment?
2. Under IFRS, what are the two accounting methods businesses can choose for accounting for investment property?

LEARNING OUTCOME PRACTICE

1. Which of the following would not qualify as an investment property?
    a. Land
    b. Buildings
    c. Trademark
    d. Factory currently used in production
2. Which is inaccurate regarding the accounting for investment property?
    a. The carrying amount cannot be historical cost.
    b. Any difference between the fair value of an investment property and its carrying amount is recognized in profit or loss.
    c. Investment property can be revalued to fair value.
    d. Investment property is not depreciated.

Summary

In this chapter, we have examined accounting for major categories of nonfinancial assets, including inventories; property, plant and equipment; intangible assets; and investment properties. For each category, five basic decisions must be made. First, what amount is recorded when the asset is acquired? Second, if the asset declines in value after acquisition, what adjustment needs to be made in the carrying amount? Third, if the asset increases in value, what adjustment needs to be made in the carrying amount? Fourth, how is the asset cost allocated to expense? And fifth, how do we account for the disposal of the asset?

Figure 7.13 compares the answers to these questions for the nonfinancial assets we have discussed in this chapter.

LEARNING OUTCOME 1
Capitalization Explained

When a business incurs a cost, a decision must be made about whether to account for that cost as capital expenditure or revenue expenditure. When it is accounted for as capital expenditure, we say that we have capitalized the cost and it will therefore appear on the statement of financial position as an asset. This means that we expect the cost to have some future economic benefit to the business. However, if the cost has no future benefit, then it is accounted for as revenue expenditure, which means that it is not capitalized. Revenue expenditure is an expense that appears on the statement of comprehensive income for the reporting period.

FIGURE 7.13 SUMMARY OF ACCOUNTING FOR NON-FINANCIAL ASSETS

	Inventories	Property, Plant and Equipment	Intangible Assets	Investment Properties
Acquisition	Recorded at cost	Recorded at cost	Recorded at cost	Recorded at cost
Decline in value	Lower of cost or net realizable value method is used	Any impairment losses are recognized in profit or loss	Any impairment losses are recognized in profit or loss	Not applicable
Increase in value	Increases in value are not recognized	An increase in value can be recorded in other comprehensive income	An increase in value can be recorded in other comprehensive income	The difference between fair value and carrying amount is recognized in profit or loss
Allocation to expense	Not applicable	Depreciation	Amortization	Not applicable
Disposal	When sold, inventory costs are reclassified as cost of goods sold	A gain or loss is recognized on the difference between the amount received for the asset and its carrying amount	A gain or loss is recognized on the difference between the amount received for the asset and its carrying amount	A gain or loss is recognized on the difference between the amount received for the asset and its carrying amount

LEARNING OUTCOME 2
Accounting for Inventories Explained

Inventories are goods held for resale to customers. All costs incurred in acquiring the goods and bringing them to their present location and condition are capitalized in inventory. Inventories can take three forms: finished goods ready for sale to customers; work-in-process inventories, which are goods on which production has begun but not yet been completed; and materials and supplies that will be consumed in the production process. If inventories decline in value before sale to the customer, then the carrying value is reduced using the lower of cost and net realizable value.

Goods available for sale include beginning inventory for the reporting period plus net purchases. The cost of goods available for sale must be allocated between ending inventories and cost of goods sold. Allocation methods include: specific identification, which expenses the actual cost, and cost flow assumptions. The two major cost flow assumptions are first-in, first-out (FIFO) and average cost (AVCO). FIFO expenses the oldest costs first, leaving newer costs in inventory, while AVCO proportions the cost of goods available based on the average unit cost in the reporting period. Both cost flow assumptions may be applied using either the periodic or perpetual approach. Under the periodic approach the FIFO and AVCO calculations are made at the end of the reporting period, while under the perpetual approach the calculations are made as each inventory-related transaction occurs.

Profit or loss can vary depending on whether the FIFO or AVCO method is used. In a period of rising prices, FIFO will result in a lower cost of goods sold and therefore a higher profit when compared to AVCO. In a period of declining prices, AVCO will result a lower cost of goods sold and a higher profit when compared to FIFO.

Cash invested in inventories is not available for other uses in the business. Therefore, the performance of a business can depend partly on whether inventories are effectively managed. To help evaluate inventories, we use the inventories turnover ratio, which divides cost of goods sold by average inventories for the period, and days in inventory, which divides the days in the year (365) by the inventory turnover ratio.

LEARNING OUTCOME 3
Accounting for Property, Plant and Equipment Explained

Property, plant and equipment are tangible assets employed in production, rented to customers or used in administration over multiple periods. Property, plant and equipment are recorded at cost. All costs to bring the asset to the location and condition necessary for its intended use are capitalized.

As property, plant and equipment are consumed, the costs are depreciated or allocated to the periods in which the asset generates economic benefits for the business entity. Three common methods are used to depreciate the assets: straight line, units of production and declining balance. The straight-line method allocates an equal amount of depreciation expense over the useful life based on the depreciable amount (cost less residual value). Both useful life and residual value are estimates. The units-of-production method allocates the depreciable amount based on the use of the asset as measured by an activity base like machine hours, number of units produced and so forth. Declining balance, an accelerated method, depreciates the cost without considering residual value. The amount of depreciation expense in each period is based on a factor (two for double-declining balance) times the percentage of cost that would be depreciated under the straight-line method.

The choice of depreciation method will affect profit or loss differently. Diminishing balance will result in more depreciation expense in the early life of the asset, which increases expenses and decreases profit. However, later in the asset's life the amount of depreciation expense recorded in each period will decline below the amount that would be recorded under the straight-line method. The units-of-production method has no pattern of depreciation expense that can be predicted in advance. However, the units-of-production method tends to rise and fall with increases and decreases in sales, respectively, and can have a smoothing effect on profit and loss.

After acquisition of the asset, if an impairment loss occurs then the asset's carrying amount is reduced and the difference between the amounts of impairment is recognized in profit or loss.

Management may choose to account for property, plant and equipment under either the cost method or the revaluation method. Under the cost method, the asset's carrying amount is the original cost less accumulated depreciation and accumulated impairment losses. Under the revaluation method, if the asset's fair value increases, the asset's carrying amount can be increased, with the difference between the fair value of the asset and its carrying amount credited to other comprehensive income. If a revalued asset subsequently declines in value, then the decline is first recorded against the revaluation reserve in other comprehensive income. If the revaluation reserve is eliminated, then any additional decline in fair value is recorded in profit or loss.

LEARNING OUTCOME 4
Accounting for Intangible Assets Explained

Intangible assets have no physical substance. When an intangible asset is acquired from a third party, the cost of the intangible asset is capitalized. The intangible asset is also allocated to reporting periods using one of the methods described for property, plant and equipment (straight line, units of production or declining balance). However, the allocation is referred to as amortization rather than depreciation. The amortized amount is not accumulated in a contra account (which is the case with property, plant and equipment), but is credited directly to the intangible asset itself.

Impairment losses on intangible assets are recorded in profit or loss. Management may also account for an intangible asset by either the cost model or the revaluation model. Under the cost model, the intangible asset is carried at cost less accumulated amortization less accumulated impairment losses. Under the revaluation model, any increase in the value of the intangible asset is credited to other comprehensive income. Subsequent declines are first offset against the revaluation reserve in other comprehensive income. Once this reserve is eliminated, any further declines in value are recorded in profit or loss.

When an intangible asset is developed by the business entity, then research and development costs are accounted for separately. Research costs are not capitalized and instead are expensed in the period incurred. Development costs can be capitalized, but only if certain criteria are met regarding the future useability or saleability of the good or service being developed.

Goodwill is also an intangible asset. Goodwill is the amount a business entity pays for another business entity in excess of the net assets of the acquired entity. Goodwill cannot be internally generated within a business. Once recorded, goodwill is not amortized. However, any impairment loss is recorded in profit or loss for the period.

LEARNING OUTCOME 5
Accounting for Investment Property Explained

Assets can be held by a business entity for investment rather than resale to customers or use in production, rental or administration. An investment asset is recorded at cost. However, investment assets are not depreciated or amortized. Also, changes to the fair value of the asset compared to its carrying amount are recorded immediately in profit or loss.

REVIEW QUESTIONS

1. If a capital expenditure has been expensed before the cost has expired, what is the impact on profit or loss? If a capital expenditure has not been expensed once the cost has expired, what is the impact on profit or loss?
2. How do a manufacturer's or merchandiser's inventories differ from a service firm's?
3. What choices does management have for allocating the cost of goods available between ending inventories and cost of goods sold?
4. What costs are included in property, plant and equipment? How are these costs allocated to reporting periods? What accounting options does management have after acquisition of property, plant and equipment? What effect does the choice of depreciation have on profit or loss? How do we account for the disposal of property, plant and equipment?
5. Which intangible asset costs are capitalized? Which are expensed? How are capitalized intangible asset costs allocated to reporting periods? What is goodwill and how is it accounted for?
6. What is investment property? How is a gain or a loss on investment property accounted for?

Key terms

Accumulated depreciation

Amotization

Average cost method

Book value

Capital assets

Capital expenditure

Carrying amount

Consignment sales

Cost model

Cost of goods available

Days in inventory

Declining balance method

Depreciable amount

Depreciable asset

Depreciation

Development

Diminishing balance method

Fair value

Finished goods

First-in, first-out

Fixed asset

Goodwill

Impairment

Intangible assets

Inventories

Inventories turnover ratio

Investment property

Lower of cost and net realizable method

Materials

Net book value

Net realizable value

Periodic inventory method

Perpetual inventory method

Property, plant and equipment

Rebate

Reducing balance method

Research

Residual value

Revaluation model

Revenue expenditure

Specific identification

Straight-line method

Trade discounts

Units-of-production method

Useful life

Work in process

Terminology practice

For each of the following, insert the correct term from the preceding list of key terms. Each key term may be used more than once.

1. _____ is equal to beginning inventory plus net purchases for the reporting period.
2. _____ is either the period over which an asset is expected to be available for use by an entity or the number of production units expected to be obtained from the asset by the entity.
3. _____ is the original and planned investigation undertaken with the prospect of gaining new scientific or technical knowledge and understanding.
4. The _____ is calculated by dividing sales by average inventories.
5. _____ are tangible items that are held for use in production or supply of goods or services, for rental to others or for administrative purposes, and expected to be used during more than one period.
6. The method of allocating property, plant and equipment costs to a reporting period that expenses the depreciable amount in equal instalments is the _____.
7. The systematic allocation of the depreciable amount of an asset over its useful life is _____ for property, plant and equipment, and _____ for intangible assets.
8. The _____ is the amount at which an asset is recognized in the statement of financial position. This amount is sometimes referred to as _____ or _____.
9. The method of determining whether inventories have declined below the carrying amount is called the _____ .
10. The _____ method assigns the oldest costs to cost of goods sold and the most recent costs to ending inventories.
11. In _____ , ownership of the goods does not pass to the seller.
12. _____ is the amount for which an asset could be exchanged, or a liability settled between knowledgeable, willing parties in an arm's-length transaction.
13. _____ assets are not capitalized but expressed immediately.
14. _____ is the estimated amount that an entity would currently obtain from disposal of an asset, after deducting the estimated costs of disposal, if the asset were already at the age and in the condition expected at the end of its useful life.
15. The method of allocating property, plant and equipment costs to a reporting period that is based on use of the asset rather than time is the _____.
16. An _____ is an asset without physical substance.
17. The method of allocating property, plant and equipment costs to a reporting period that accelerates depreciation when compared to the straight-line method is _____ , also referred to as the _____ method or _____.
18. Assets held for sale in the ordinary course of business, in the process of production for such sale or in the form of materials and supplies to be consumed in production are _____ .
19. Under the _____ the cost of goods available is allocated between ending inventories and costs of goods sold at the end of the reporting period.

20. _____ is the application of research findings or other knowledge to a plan or design for the production of new or substantially improved materials, devices, products, processes, systems or services before the start of commercial production or use.

21. _____ is a land or building held to earn rentals or for capital appreciation or both rather than for use in the production or supply of goods or services or for administrative purposes, or sale in the ordinary course of business.

22. When property, plant and equipment and intangible assets decline in value below their carrying amounts, then a(n) _____ loss may need to be recorded.

23. The _____ calculates an average cost of inventory items for the reporting period and then allocates the cost of goods available based on the result.

24. The method of inventory used when goods or services produced are not normally interchangeable is the _____.

25. _____ is the estimated selling price in the ordinary course of business less the estimated selling costs of completion and the estimated costs necessary to make the sale.

26. _____ and _____ are reductions to the selling price provided by a seller to customers as an incentive to purchase.

27. A _____ – which are also referred to as _____, *fixed assets* or _____ – means that a cost has been capitalized.

28. _____ is calculated by dividing the number of days in the year by the inventories turnover ratio.

29. _____ are goods or services on which production has begun but not been completed.

30. The _____ calculates the amount of inventory costs allocated to cost of goods sold with each sale transaction.

31. _____ is an asset representing the future economic benefits arising from other assets being acquired in a business combination that are not individually identified and separately recognized.

Application exercises

1. Yen Electronics Corporation uses a periodic inventory system. The following information shows inventory transactions in June 2009 for its new e-book reader. At the end of June, 700 e-book units remained in inventory.

Date	Transaction	No. of Units	Unit Cost
1 June	Beginning inventories	1000	€85
15 June	Purchase	2200	90
20 June	Purchase	3100	100
25 June	Purchase	1900	110

Compute the amounts for ending inventory and cost of goods sold for June 2009 under both the FIFO and average cost inventory methods.

2. Radwan SpA uses a perpetual inventory system. The following information shows inventory transactions in the second quarter of 2009 for its weight training machine.

Date	Transaction	No. of Units	Unit Cost	Sales Price
1 March	Beginning inventories	55	$800	
12 March	Purchase	60	776	
15 April	Sale	80		1100
20 April	Purchase	70	750	
25 April	Sale	60		1050
5 May	Sale	10		1070
18 May	Purchase	200	765	

Compute the amounts for ending inventory and cost of goods sold for the second quarter of 2009 using both FIFO and average cost methods and record all journal entries for these transactions.

3. Compute the missing amounts in the following schedule. Each company is independent of the others.

	Company A	Company B	Company C
Revenue	$1700	$1600	???
Cost of goods sold	???	???	690
Profit or loss	???	(100)	120
Total goods available for sale	???	???	???
Purchases	1000	830	???
Ending inventories	300	210	150
Gross profit	???	???	???
Other expenses	550	800	810
Beginning inventories	200	???	170

4. On 1 January 2009, Mietal Resources Inc. purchased earth-moving equipment for $875 000. The equipment is rated for a total of 10 000 hours of operation. Actual hours of operation were 1850 in 2009, 2010 in 2010, 2200 in 2011 and 2100 in 2012. Transportation for the equipment cost $22 000. The equipment has an estimated useful life of four years with a $150 000 residual value. The company uses the double-diminishing balance method to allocate the asset's cost to income. Based on this information, complete the following schedule.

Date	Annual Depreciation Expense	Carrying Amount at Year End
31 December 2009		
31 December 2010		
31 December 2011		
31 December 2012		

5. On 1 January 2009, Mietal Resources Inc. purchased earth-moving equipment for $875 000. The equipment is rated for a total of 10 000 hours of operation. Actual hours of operation were 1850 in 2009, 2010 in 2010, 2200 in 2011 and 2100 in 2012. Transportation for the equipment cost $22 000. The equipment has an estimated useful life of four years with a $150 000 residual value. The company uses the straight-line method to allocate the asset's cost to income. Based on this information, complete the following schedule.

Date	Annual Depreciation Expense	Carrying Amount at Year End
31 December 2009		
31 December 2010		
31 December 2011		
31 December 2012		

6. On 1 January 2009, Mietal Resources Inc. purchased earth-moving equipment for $875 000. The equipment is rated for a total of 10 000 hours of operation. Actual hours of operation were 1850 in 2009, 2010 in 2010, 2200 in 2011 and 2100 in 2012. Transportation for the equipment cost $22 000. The equipment has an estimated useful life of four years with a $150 000 residual value. The company uses the units-of-production method to allocate the asset's cost to income. Based on this information, complete the following schedule.

Date	Annual Depreciation Expense	Carrying Amount at Year End
31 December 2009		
31 December 2010		
31 December 2011		
31 December 2012		

7. Compute the missing amounts in the schedule shown below under FIFO and AVCO.

	FIFO	AVCO
Revenue (2000 units sold at $22 per unit)		
Beginning inventories (500 units at $6 per unit)		
Purchases (2600 units at $6.50 per unit)		
Costs of goods available		
Ending inventories (900 units)		
Cost of goods sold		
Gross profit		
Other expenses	11 000	11 000
Profit or loss		

8. Prater Luxury Linens Ltd sells bed and bath linens. For the month of February 2011, the company had a beginning inventory of 1 250 linens with a unit cost of £18. On 3 February, an additional 550 sets of linens were purchased for £19 each. On 7 February, 600 sets were sold for €45 per set. On 14 February, Pater purchased another 400 sets at £18 per set and then sold 720 sets on 26 February for £45 per set.

   Required:
   1. Calculate the cost of goods sold and ending inventory for February under FIFO.
   2. Calculate the cost of goods sold and ending inventory for February under the average cost method.

9. Simon depreciates his machinery at a rate of 20% per annum on a reducing balance basis. He provides a full year's depreciation in the year an asset is acquired, and no depreciation expense is recorded in the year of disposal. At 1 November 2010, the cost of Simon's machinery was $140 900, and the carrying value was $94 570. During the year to 31 October 2011, a machine that had cost $35 000 and had been fully depreciated with $5000 residual value was traded in for a new machine. The price of the new machine was $50 000 and the trade-in value was $14 000. At 31 October 2011 the balance of the cost of the new machine was still outstanding.
   (a) Calculate the depreciation charge for machinery for the year to 31 October 2011.
   (b) Show the following ledger accounts for the year:
       (i) Machinery at cost
       (ii) Accumulated depreciation
   (c) Calculate the total depreciation expense to be reported in the statement of comprehensive income for the year to 31 October 2011 in respect of machinery.
   (d) State the balances to be reported in the statement of financial position as at 31 October 2011 as a result of these transactions. [ACCA adapted]

10. You work for a wholesale firm that distributes a single product. A trainee has prepared accounts for the month of October 2010. The accounts report a net loss of $35 580 and total net assets of $283 468. You have noted that:
   i. The statement of comprehensive income does not report a figure for gross profit.
   ii. The trainee has not included any value for closing inventory.
   iii. The trainee has included $57 600 for opening inventory. This was calculated on the first-in, first-out (FIFO) basis. There were 480 items, valued at $120 per item.
   Purchases during the month were:

Date	Number of Items	Cost Per Item ($)
October 9	1 140	145
October 15	1 310	150
October 24	620	155
	3 070	

Sales during the month were:

Date	Number of Items	Selling Price Per Item ($)
October 12	1 040	205
October 21	1 840	220
	2 880	

As well as purchases, the other costs deducted from sales to calculate net loss were:

Wages of staff	44 700
Premises expenses	42 750
Administrative expenses	13 620
Selling and marketing costs	17 890
Carriage inwards	3 750
Carriage outwards	4 120
Depreciation	11 250
	138 080

Required:

(a) Calculate:

    i.   The number of items in inventory at 31 October 2010.

    ii.   The value of inventory at 31 October 2010 on the FIFO basis.

(b) Using the revised inventory value calculated in (a), calculate:

    i.   Cost of sales for October 2010.

    ii.   Gross profit for October 2010.

    iii. Net profit for October 2010.

    iv. Net assets at 31 October 2010. [ACCA adapted]

Case analysis
BOTSWANA WILD SAFARIS LLC

Botswana Wild Safaris LLC is a comprehensive case that we will use in Parts III and IV of this textbook. In this chapter, we will see how Tony Washford, who recently purchased the company, accounts for nonfinancial assets over a three-year period – 2009, 2010 and 2011. In the next few chapters, we will see how he accounts for financial assets and liabilities (Chapter 8) and equity (Chapter 9). Casework in later chapters depends on information presented below.

South African Tony Washford had been leading groups on camera safaris into Botswana and the Okavango Delta for several years, working for various tour companies. Gerhardt Perst, his friend and the owner of Botswana Wild Safaris, asked if he were interested in buying the business because he wanted to retire to Cape Town and spend more time with his grandchildren.

Tony finally agreed to buy all of the ordinary shares in the business, and on 1 January 2009 the transaction was completed. On that date noncurrent assets on the statement of financial position was as follows:

	Botswana Wild Tours As at 1 January 2009 € Euros		
Noncurrent assets			
Storage and repair facility			
land		50 000	
buildings		125 000	
accumulated depreciation – facility		32 000	143 000
River campsite			
land		40 000	
building		160 000	
accumulated depreciation – campsite		44 800	155 200
Equipment		350 000	
Accumulated depreciation – equipment		130 000	220 000
Vehicles			
Cost		510 000	
Accumulated depreciation – vehicles		17 000	493 000
Intangible assets – software			19 000
Investment in property			35 000
Total noncurrent assets			**1 065 200**

Botswana Wild Safaris uses the calendar year end as its reporting date. The accounting records were last closed on 1 January 2009.

The storage and repair facility and the campsites were both being depreciated using the straight-line method, with an estimated life of 25 years. Residual value for the storage and repair buildings was €25 000 and the residual value for both the River and new campsite buildings is €20 000. The equipment has a five-year useful life with a €25 000 residual value, and is being depreciated using the straight-line method. The software originally cost €28 500 and has a three-year useful life, no residual value and is being amortized using the straight-line method.

NEW CAMPSITE

On 30 January 2009, Tony decided that he would acquire a second camp just outside one of the national parks. He purchased land with buildings for €150 000 in cash and began to organize the new permanent camp. Land represented 20% of this amount. A fence was long overdue for painting, which Tony had done for €1800 although the painting did not extend the useful life or enhance the functioning of the fence. Tony paid the invoice on 23 March 2009.

VEHICLES

Safari guests toured Botswana's national parks from three large Mercedes truck chassis that had been outfitted to Botswana Wild Tours' specifications. Each of these had cost €170 000 when purchased new, and each was expected to operate for a total of 300 000 kilometres. Botswana Wild Tours uses the units-of-production method for accounting for the vehicles, assuming €20 000 residual values for each. These three vehicles were depreciated at a rate of €0.50 per kilometre. In 2010, vehicle no. 3 was traded in for a new vehicle. The actual kilometres over which each vehicle was used follow:

Vehicle Kilometres Usage					
Year	Vehicle No. 1	Vehicle No. 2	Vehicle No. 3	New Vehicle	Totals
2009	22 000	25 500	24 500	–	72 000
2010	38 000	56 000	42 000	26 000	162 000
2011	33 000	52 000	0	74 000	159 000
Totals	93 000	133 500	66 500	100 000	393 000

NEW VEHICLE

On 30 September 2010 Tony traded in one of the vehicles for a newer model. The vehicle traded in had given the company difficulties during the summer season, and was nearing the end of its useful life anyway. This vehicle (no. 3) had 272 000 kilometres on the clock by the time of the trade-in. The dealer quoted €180 000 for the new vehicle, which had some additional luxury features that Tony hoped would appeal to upscale clients. The dealer gave Botswana Wild Tours a 5% trade discount on the new vehicle and a €20 000 trade-in allowance for the old vehicle. The useful life of the new vehicle was estimated at 300 000 kilometres and the residual value at €30 000.

NEW TENTS

Another major asset for Botswana Wild Tours were the tents used to house the clients at the campsites. Tony was dissatisfied with the ones the company currently owned because they had flaws that made sealing the doors difficult and therefore allowed insects and even small creatures into the tents, which annoyed guests. These were in fact a large source of complaints in the evaluations that clients completed after each tour.

Therefore, Tony found that other tour operators had the same experience with this particular brand of tents. After some calculations, Tony decided that in 2011, the tents would have to be replaced. On 31 December 2009, he determined that the tents were worthless and an impairment loss needed to be recognized.

On 1 January 2011 he replaced all the tents at a cost of €375 000, choosing better tents designed to appeal to wealthier clientele. Tony decided that the new tents would have a three-year useful life with a residual value of €50 000, and that he would use the straight-line method for depreciation. When the new tents were acquired, the old tents were to be donated to a welfare organization.

PROPERTY VALUES

On each reporting date, Tony had the investment land, the storage and repair facility and the campsites valued by a professional appraiser, who provided him with the following new valuations:

	2009	2010	2011
Storage and repair building	–	148 000	–
River campsite land	–	70 000	–
River campsite building	–	–	190 000
New campsite land	–	–	–
New campsite building	–	–	–
Investment in property	50 000	50 000	N/A

Tony elected to use the revaluation model for the storage and repair facility, campsites and investment property.

On 1 April 2011 Tony sold the property investments for $115 000. This substantially higher price was obtained because the property was on a river that had been dry for several years due to drought conditions in the Okavango Delta. Now, normal conditions had returned and the river filled again, making the property attractive.

REQUIRED:

Record all transactions and adjusting entries for 2009 to 2011 related to property, plant and equipment, and intangible assets. Construct the noncurrent section of the statement of financial position on the reporting dates.

Financial assets and liabilities

8

LEARNING OUTCOMES

By the end of this chapter, you should be able to:

1. Explain the accounting for cash and cash equivalents.
2. Explain how financial assets and liabilities are classified.
3. Apply the effective interest rate method.
4. Explain the accounting for trade accounts.
5. Explain the accounting for credit card receivables.
6. Explain the accounting for notes.
7. Explain the accounting for bonds.
8. Evaluate assets and liabilities.

The importance of financial instruments

In 2008–09, the global economy suffered the worst decline in almost 70 years – the first since the Great Depression of the 1930s. Millions of people throughout the world lost their jobs and the value of publicly traded companies declined significantly.

Authorities estimated at the time the crisis began that global financial assets, which include stocks, debt and bank deposits, totalled US$167 trillion. However, at the same time a form of sophisticated financial instrument was valued at over $477 trillion.[1] These sophisticated instruments are based on the value of an underlying factor such as a stock price, interest rate or index. In fact, in 2008 over $400 trillion in derivatives depended on a single index: the London Interbank Offer Rate (LIBOR).[2] When the underlying factor, like the LIBOR, moves unexpectedly, the effect on financial markets can be quite large and damaging.

In 2007, prices in the residential housing market in the United States declined, causing an increase in the number of homeowners who could not pay back loans on their homes. These loans were the underlying factor for some of the sophisticated financial instruments already described.

As the US housing market worsened, a chain reaction occurred that caused large losses in other global capital markets. The result was that many investment banks, commercial banks and other firms experienced huge losses and in some cases were forced into bankruptcy. These losses made it even harder for capital markets to provide the capital needed by companies and others. The result was that financial markets the world over experienced what was described as a 'meltdown' and ceased functioning effectively. Massive government bailout programmes followed to provide the necessary capital and stimulate the world economy to recover.

It also became obvious during this period that some companies were using these sophisticated instruments in ways that created major losses. In Autumn 2008 Hong Kong-based Citic Pacific's shares lost more than half their value and public trading of the shares was suspended. The reason was that the company had reported losses of Hong Kong $16.8 billion as of November 2008, with the possibility that even more could occur.

Citic Pacific's losses were caused by a derivative-based financial instrument. The company was under contract to buy an iron-ore mine in Australia for Hong Kong $1.6 billion. Citic Pacific was 'exposed' to the Australian dollar since the purchase of the iron-ore mine would be settled in Australian dollars if the value of the Australian dollar increased compared to the Hong Kong dollar. That would effectively have increased the purchase price of the iron-ore mine. Since Citic Pacific did not want this risk, it entered into a financial transaction in which another entity agreed to pay the company if the Australian dollar increased against the Hong Kong dollar.

In return, Citic Pacific apparently agreed to pay the other entity if the Australian dollar declined in value. Thus the other entity was betting that the Australian dollar would not go up and Citic Pacific was betting that the Australian dollar would not go down. Citic Pacific lost. The financial crisis that began in 2007 and became worse in 2008 caused the Australian dollar to drop 30% from a 25-year high. Citic Pacific was therefore obligated to pay the other entity for the decreased amount.

China's largest state-owned investment company, Citic Group, which owned Citic Pacific, was obliged to pay Hong Kong $11.6 billion to Citic Pacific to cover the losses and to assume responsibility for any future losses. Citic Pacific was investigated by the Hong Kong Securities and Futures Commission. Notice in this transaction that Citic Pacific suffered many times the losses that it would have incurred compared to the amount of the initial transaction.

Sophisticated financial instruments like the ones just discussed have only been invented since the 1970s (see Richard Bookstaber in Suggested Reading). In many cases, managers and others, including many boards of directors, have insufficient understanding of how these financial instruments work and how they can affect the financial position and performance of a business. Thus, we should learn at least the basic accounting issues involved in these financial instruments.

Introducing financial assets and liabilities

The statement of financial position of many companies now contains a large proportion of financial assets and liabilities. A financial asset is an asset that is cash, a cash equivalent, an equity instrument of another entity, a contractual right to receive cash or another financial asset, or a contract that will be settled in the entity's own equity instruments.

FIGURE 8.1 FINANCIAL ASSET AND LIABILITY CATEGORIES

A financial liability is a liability that is a contractual obligation to deliver cash or another financial asset or a contract that will be settled in the entity's own equity instruments. Examples include trade accounts payable and notes payable. If both a financial asset and a financial liability are involved in a transaction, it takes the form of a financial instrument.

Financial assets and liabilities can be divided into three major categories, as shown in Figure 8.1.

Each of these categories is discussed below.

LEARNING OUTCOME 1
EXPLAIN THE ACCOUNTING FOR CASH AND CASH EQUIVALENTS

1.1   What forms can cash and cash equivalents take?

1.2   How do we account for petty cash?

1.3   How do we reconcile cash?

1.1 What forms can cash and cash equivalents take?

As we already know, cash includes cash on hand and demand deposits. Cash on hand is usually in the form of currency, which includes coins and paper money that might be kept on the premises of the business as the result of sales, to give change to customers or for other reasons. A demand deposit is an account from which funds normally held at a commercial bank can be withdrawn without prior notice; most often in the form of a current account or savings account with cheque-writing privileges. A cash equivalent is a highly liquid investment that can be converted to a known amount of cash, normally within three months.

Cash may also take the following specialized forms:

- Restricted cash means that an amount has been set aside for a specific purpose. The business may have a large payment on a debt or a legal settlement that is due soon. Restricted cash may also represent a compensating balance.
- A compensating balance is a minimum balance that must be kept on hand at all times as part of a loan agreement with a lender. The restricted amount may be presented as a separate line item on the statement

of financial position to communicate to users that this cash is not available for the settlement of obligations.

- A business may for a variety of reasons overdraw the amount of cash it has in its bank account, which results in a bank overdraft. This means that the bank balance is negative or, put another way, that the balance in the ledger account is a credit instead of the normal debit balance.
- Finally, cash is sometimes kept in the form of petty cash. A petty cash (also imprest petty cash) fund refers to cash that is kept on hand in a business to pay small expenses such as postage, delivery charges, entertainment for clients and other miscellaneous expenses.

1.2 How do we account for petty cash?

Melbourne Medical sales staff often take visiting customers to lunch at a local restaurant that does not accept credit cards. So on 15 April 2010 the sales manager decides to create a petty cash fund of A$500 for lunches and for other miscellaneous expenses.

A petty cash fund is established by writing a cheque for cash. The money is then given to an employee, who acts as custodian and who is responsible for dispersing cash to sales staff as needed. Notes and coins are kept in a cash box along with vouchers and IOUs for money that employees have withdrawn.

A voucher is a written record as proof of expenditure or disbursement, such as a cash receipt provided by the restaurant. Because of the small amounts, approvals are not typically needed for petty cash expenditure. An IOU is typically a slip that shows that an employee has withdrawn cash but has not returned a voucher. The journal entry to establish the fund is as follows:

Date	Account Titles	DR	CR
15 Apr. 2010	Petty cash	A$500	
	Cash		A$500

Over the month, as employees use petty cash, they return the receipts for their purchases to the petty cash custodian, who stores them along with the remaining petty cash. On 30 April, the custodian determines that he must replenish the petty cash fund. He therefore provides all receipts to the accounting department, who issue a cheque to restore the petty cash balance to $500. Assume that the custodian has the following receipts:

Lunches	A$284
Postage	50

Miscellaneous		17
Total receipts		A$351

If A$351 has been spent, then A$149 should be remaining in petty cash. However, the custodian finds that there is A$152 remaining. In this case, the accounting department would write the replenishment cheque for A$348 (A$500 − 152) and would make the following journal entry:

Date	Account Titles	DR	CR
30 Apr. 2010	Entertainment expenses	A$284	
	Postage expense	50	
	Miscellaneous expense	17	
	Cash over and short		A$3
	Cash		348

Notice that the unexplained difference of A$3.00 is credited to a 'cash over and short' account. In this case an overage has occurred, which resulted in a credit to the account. A shortage would cause the account to be debited. At the end of the period, any balance in the cash over and short account is closed to miscellaneous expenses.

The petty cash fund can be reduced by simply returning a portion of the petty cash fund to cash. Let's assume that on 1 May 2010 the sales manager decides that a A$400 petty cash fund would be adequate, so A$100 is removed from the petty cash fund and deposited in the business's bank account. This transaction is recorded with the following journal entry:

Date	Account Titles	DR	CR
1 May 2010	Cash	A$100	
	Petty cash		A$100

1.3 How do we reconcile cash?

Cash is particularly difficult to control. Its portability, at least as currency, which is also difficult to trace, makes it an easy target for theft, fraud and loss through mishandling. Businesses that handle large quantities of cash – casinos, retail stores, restaurants – typically have specialized internal controls in place to ensure that cash is accounted for properly.

One of the most important controls related to cash is reconciliation of the cash balance as reported in the business entity's accounts with the cash balance in the bank. The bank will issue a bank statement that shows all activity on the entity's bank account for the month or some other period. The bank statement may be hard copy or electronic.

A reconciliation is necessary because of timing differences between the entity and the bank, which can be classified into two categories: cash-related transactions that have been recorded in the entity's accounting records but not recorded at the bank, and transactions that have occurred at the bank but have not yet been recorded by the entity.

TRANSACTIONS RECORDED BY THE ENTITY BUT NOT THE BANK

Transactions that have not been recorded by the bank are related to either the receipt of cash or payment.

- *Cash receipt.* As an example, a company receives a cash payment from a customer that it processes late on the afternoon of 31 August. This means that the journal entry that debits cash and credits accounts receivable is entered into the journal and posted to the ledger on that date. The customer's cheque is prepared for deposit at the bank, but this deposit does not occur until the morning of 1 September, which is the date the bank will use to record the deposit in the business entity's bank account.
- *Cash payment.* In this second example, a company pays an invoice to a supplier by preparing a cheque and mailing it on 31 August. The journal entry that debits accounts payable and credits cash is entered into the journal and posted to the ledger on that date. However, the supplier does not receive the cheque until 2 September. The cheque is deposited in the supplier's bank account and is then presented to the entity's bank for payment on 4 September.

TRANSACTIONS RECORDED BY THE BANK BUT NOT THE ENTITY

These transactions have been recorded by the bank and therefore they appear on the entity's bank statement. However, no entry has been made to the entity's accounts.

- *Cash deposits into the entity's account.* Some customers may arrange to make payments by directly depositing the money into the entity's bank account. Another example would be interest earned on the entity's bank balance, which is added to the account by the bank itself. When the bank statement is received from the bank, an entry must be made in the accounting records of the entity to record the transaction.
- *Cash deductions from the entity's account.* Examples of cash deductions include a cheque from a customer that had previously been credited to the entity's account, but that is now deducted because the customer's bank has refused to pay the cheque since the customer has insufficient funds in his account. Another example would be bank fees and other charges deducted from the account.

Once the entity is informed of transactions recorded by the bank but not the entity, a journal entry must be made to make the entity's cash account current. Figure 8.2 summarizes the cash reconciliation procedure.

FIGURE 8.2 CASH RECONCILIATION PROCEDURE

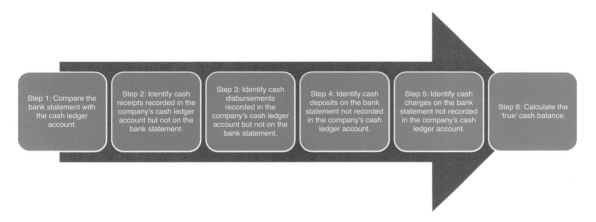

Suppose that a company ends the month of June with a balance of ¥432 414 in its cash account. On 7 July, the bank statement that shows all activity for the company's bank account for the month of November reports an ending cash balance of ¥451 700. When the company's cash account is compared with the bank statement, the following differences are noted:

Transactions recorded by the entity but not the bank

- Deposits in transit totalling ¥66 093 were recorded by the company on 30 June but not by the bank until 2 July.
- Cheques were written to suppliers and others totalling ¥34 119 and were recorded on 30 June but did not clear the bank until 5 July.

Transactions recorded by the bank but not the entity

- Electronic payments by customers made directly into the entity's bank account totalled ¥56 002 during November.
- A customer's cheque for ¥5500 was returned because of insufficient funds.
- The bank credited the entity's account with ¥2258 in interest earned on the average balance in the account.
- The bank charged the entity's account ¥1500 for various fees related to the processing of the electronic payments noted above.

The reconciliation of the cash account is shown below.

Cash Reconciliation			
Accounting Records		Bank Statement	
Cash balance before reconciliation	¥432 414	Ending balance on bank statement, 30 June	¥451 700
Add: Electronic deposits	56 002	Add: Deposits in transit	66 093
Bank interest	2 258	Less: Cheques in transit	34 119
Less: Returned cheque	5 500		
Bank fees	1 500		
Reconciled balance	¥483 674	Reconciled balance	¥483 674

Notice in the cash reconciliation schedule that the reconciled balance (sometimes referred to as the 'true balance') is ¥483 674, indicating that the reconciliation was accomplished. At this point, the company would need to make entries to correct the cash balance in the company's accounting records:

- Electronic deposits are recorded.

Date	Account Titles	DR	CR
30 June	Cash	56 002	
	Trade accounts receivable		56 002

- Bank interest is recorded.

Date	Account Titles	DR	CR
30 June	Cash	2 258	
	Interest revenue		2 258

- The returned cheque is recorded and trade accounts receivable is increased, showing that the customer's balance remains unpaid.

Date	Account Titles	DR	CR
30 June	Trade accounts receivable	5 500	
	Cash		5 500

- Bank fees are recorded.

Date	Account Titles	DR	CR
30 June	Bank fees expense	1 500	
	Cash		1 500

When these entries are posted to the ledger account, as shown below, the cash balance reflects the reconciled or true balance, and this would be the amount reported on the balance sheet dated 30 June.

Cash		
Account	DR	CR
Balance before reconciliation	¥432 414	
Electronic deposits	56 002	
Interest earned	2 258	
Returned cheque		5 500
Bank fees		1 500
Reconciled balance, 30 June	**¥483 674**	

ON YOUR OWN

LEARNING OUTCOME REVIEW

1. Define financial asset and financial liability.
2. What is cash? What is cash equivalent?
3. What is a demand deposit?
4. What is the time frame applied to determine whether an item is a cash equivalent, current financial investment or noncurrent financial investment?

5. Explain why cash is presented in the statement of financial position as restricted.
6. What is a bank overdraft?
7. Describe how petty cash is accounted for when the petty cash fund is first created, when the petty cash fund must be replenished and when the petty cash balance is reduced.
8. What is a voucher? What is an IOU?

LEARNING OUTCOME PRACTICE

1. Which of the following represents the correct amount in an imprest petty cash fund?
   a. Notes and coins in the cash box − vouchers − IOUs
   b. Notes and coins in the cash box + vouchers − IOUs
   c. Notes and coins in the cash box − vouchers + IOUs
   d. Notes and coins in the cash box + vouchers + IOUs
   ACCA adapted

2. A company's bank reconciliation statement shows outstanding amounts from customers paid of $3800. Cheques outstanding to suppliers were $3500. The cash ledger account has a net debit balance of $25 000. What is the balance on the bank statement?
   a. $25 000
   b. $24 700
   c. $25 300
   d. $32 300

3. According to Lettice Corporation's records, the bank account is overdrawn by $2600, yet the balance shown on the bank statement is only $1200 overdrawn. Assuming that no errors have been made by Lettice's accountants or the bank, what could account for this difference?
   a. Bank interest of $1400 was charged by the bank.
   b. Customer cheques totalling $1400 were deposited into the bank by Lettice.
   c. Cheques not yet presented to the bank for payment have been posted to the cash ledger account for $1400.
   d. A $1400 increase in Lettice's overdraft facility.
   ACCA adapted

4. Obake Ltd's cash ledger account shows a month end debit balance of $13 100. The company's bank statement, however, shows a different figure. Obake has identified four differences:
   • Bank charges of $950 have been deducted during the last quarter, but not yet entered in the cash account.
   • A cheque for $11 600 paid to a creditor has not been presented to the bank.
   • A customer's cheque for $6820 paid into the bank has not yet been cleared.
   • Obake had forgotten that an annual direct debt of $1020 was due, and this has been taken from the account.

   What is the balance of Obake's bank statement at the end of the month?
   a. $10 920
   b. $11 130

    c. $15 910

    d. $17 880

    ACCA adapted

5. Sigma's bank statement shows an overdrawn balance of $38 600 at 30 June 2010. A check against the company's cash account revealed the following differences:

- Bank charges of $200 have not been entered in the cash account.
- Items recorded on 30 June 2010 but credited by the bank in July $14 700.
- Cheque payment entered in cash account but not presented for payment at 30 June 2010 totalled $27 800.
- A cheque payment to a supplier of $4200 charged to the account in June 2010 was recorded in the cash account as a receipt.

Based on this information, what was the cash account balance before any adjustments?

    a. $43 100 overdrawn

    b. $16 900 overdrawn

    c. $60 300 overdrawn

    d. $34 100 overdrawn

    ACCA adapted

6. Tormé Publishing Ltd received the monthly bank statement for 31 August 2010. The statement shows an ending balance of €297 500. The statement lists a deposit of €15 000 during the month which as a payment made directly to the bank by electronic funds transfer. The bank also charged a service fee of €120 for August as well as a €90 fee for printed checks. In addition, two checks totaling €6 500 from customers were returned for non-payment due to insufficient funds.

Tormé's accountant reconciling the bank account noticed that two checks totaling €31 000 were outstanding and a deposit make on 31 August for €17 880 was still in transit. The cash ledger account has a balance of €289 140. However, the accountant noticed that a cash disbursement for €14 500 had been mistakenly recorded for €1 450 in the cash ledger account.

Required: Calculate the true cash balance for Tormé Publishing on 31 August 2010. Make the journal entries necessary as the result of the reconciliation.

LEARNING OUTCOME 2
EXPLAIN HOW FINANCIAL ASSETS AND LIABILITIES ARE CLASSIFIED

2.1 What are held-for-trading financial assets and liabilities?

2.2 What are held-to-maturity investments?

2.3   What are loans and receivables?

2.4   What are available-for-sale financial assets?

One way to classify financial assets and liabilities is by time horizon, as shown in Figure 8.3.

FIGURE 8.3 TIME CLASSIFICATION OF FINANCIAL ASSETS AND LIABILITIES

Time	Assets	Liabilities
Immediate	Cash	
0–3 months	Cash equivalent	
3–12 months	Current financial assets	Current financial liabilities
>12 months	Noncurrent financial assets	Noncurrent financial liabilities

Cash is available immediately and cash equivalents are usually available to the business entity within three months. Financial assets and liabilities are then classified as current or noncurrent. However, a second classification is used depending on the characteristics of the financial asset or liability. Four classifications are illustrated in Figure 8.4.

FIGURE 8.4 CLASSIFICATION OF FINANCIAL ASSETS AND LIABILITIES

Financial assets and liabilities			
Held-for-trading financial assets and liabilities	Held-to-maturity financial assets	Loans and receivables financial assets and liabilities	Available-for-sale financial assets

This classification is important, because it determines how we account for the financial asset or liability.

2.1 What are held-for-trading financial assets and liabilities?

Officially, held-for-trading financial assets and liabilities are referred to as 'at fair value through profit or loss' (see IFRS box).

IFRS A financial asset or financial liability at fair value through profit or loss is 'a financial asset or financial liability that meets either of the following conditions:

(a) It is classified as held for trading

(b) Upon initial recognition it is designated by the entity as at fair value through profit and loss.'

Basically, a financial asset or liability is held for trading if it is acquired primarily for the purpose of selling or repurchasing it in the near term. This could also include those that are part of a portfolio of financial investments managed for short-term profit. For example, a business purchases the shares of another business entity with the intention of selling them for a gain. Held for trading also includes some types of derivatives which are more sophisticated forms of financial instruments. Management must designate the financial asset or financial liability as 'at fair value through profit or loss'.

A held-for-trading security is recorded at cost. After acquisition, it is revalued to fair value. Recall that fair value is the amount for which an asset could be exchanged or a liability settled between knowledgeable, willing parties in an arm's-length transaction. Fair value is most easily and reliably established if an active market for the financial instrument exists. Any difference between the fair value and carrying amount of the financial asset or liability is recorded in profit or loss.

On 14 April 2012, the CFO of Wei Ling Ltd, a Hong Kong-based company, decides to invest ¥11 400 000 of the company's excess cash into the share capital of Pacific Enterprises Corporation. Pacific Enterprises is a publicly traded company. Wei Ling's management designates the investment as held for trading (at fair value through profit or loss). The entry to record the purchase would be as follows:

Date	Account Titles	DR	CR
14 Apr. 2012	Held-for-trading securities	¥11 400 000	
	Cash		¥11 400 000

By month end, the fair value based on the market for Pacific Enterprise's shares had declined to ¥11 100 000. The adjusting entry would be:

Date	Account Titles	DR	CR
30 Apr. 2012	Loss on held-for-trading securities Held-for-trading securities	¥300 000	¥300 000

The investment now has a carrying value of ¥11 100 000 (¥11 400 000 − 300 000). Notice also that the loss of ¥300 000 is recognized immediately in profit or loss.

At the end of May, the fair value of Pacific Enterprises' shares based on market price increased to ¥12 100 000. As a result, Wei Ling has a gain of ¥1 000 000, calculated by subtracting the carrying amount of the shares from the fair value (¥12 100 000 − 11 100 000). The gain is recognized as profit with the following adjusting entry at the end of May:

Date	Account Titles	DR	CR
31 May 2012	Held-for-trading securities Gain on held-for-trading securities	¥1 000 000	¥1 000 000

The carrying value of the investment on the statement of financial position is now ¥12 100 000.

2.2 What are held-to-maturity investments?

The second category of financial assets and liabilities are classified as held-to-maturity investments (see IFRS box).

IFRS Held-to-maturity investments are '. . . financial assets with fixed or determinable payments and a fixed maturity that an entity has the positive intention and ability to hold to maturity . . .'

Typical held-to-maturity investments would include bonds and corporate notes in which the business entity invests. These bonds and notes represent debts owed by other business entities with the promise to repay the amounts borrowed, usually with interest. Bonds and corporate notes are traded on exchanges in much the same way as shares are traded. We will discuss both bonds and corporate notes later in this chapter.

Wei Ling Ltd invests in corporate notes for ¥20 000 000. The note will pay the entire amount owed at the end of two years with 8% interest. The CFO classifies the investment as held to maturity because the payments are determinable with a fixed maturity date and the business intends to hold the note to maturity and has the ability to do so.

Held-to-maturity investments are measured at amortized cost using the effective interest method, which is also used for loans and receivables, discussed later in this chapter.

2.3 What are loans and receivables?

The third category of financial assets are loans and receivables (see IFRS box).

> **IFRS** Loans and receivables are '. . . financial assets with fixed or determinable payments that are not quoted in an active market . . .'
>

One of Wei Ling's customers asks to borrow ¥8 000 000 to expand operations. This is an attractive investment for Wei Ling because the customer will repay the note within six months at 14% interest. In addition, the expansion of the customer's operations will mean more business for Wei Ling in the future. This investment is classified as a loan and receivable because no active market exists for the note.

Notice that we are discussing loans and receivables only as financial assets and not financial liabilities. Loans and receivables, as investments, are also accounted for under amortized cost using the effective interest method which, again, we will discuss later in this chapter.

2.4 What are available-for-sale financial assets?

Financial assets can also be classified as available for sale (see IFRS box).

> **IFRS** Available-for-sale financial assets are 'designated as available for sale or are not classified as (a) loans and receivables, (b) held-to-maturity investments, or (c) financial assets at fair value through profit or loss.'
>

Available-for-sale financial assets are a 'miscellaneous' category. Any difference between the carrying amount of an available-for-sale financial asset and its fair value is recorded in other comprehensive income. When a business disposes of an available-for-sale financial asset, the cumulative gains and losses recognized in equity are then recognized in profit or loss.

All financial liabilities, other than those classified as a financial liability at fair value through profit or loss, are accounted for at amortized cost using the effective interest method.

Accounting for financial assets is summarized in Figure 8.5.

FIGURE 8.5 ACCOUNTING FOR FINANCIAL ASSETS AND LIABILITIES

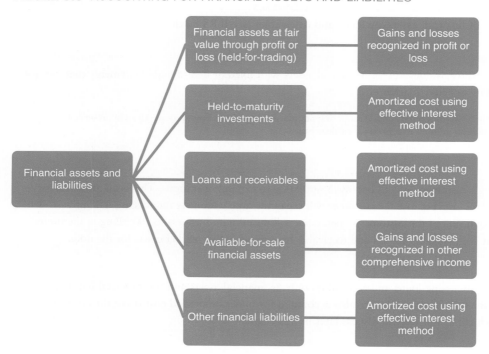

Accounting for financial liabilities is summarized in Figure 8.6.

FIGURE 8.6 ACCOUNTING FOR FINANCIAL LIABILITIES

ON YOUR OWN

LEARNING OUTCOME REVIEW

1. List the four categories of financial assets and liabilities.
2. What are the criteria for including a financial asset or liabilities as held for trading?
3. What are the criteria for including a financial asset as held to maturity?
4. What are the criteria for including a financial asset and liability as loans and receivables?
5. What are the criteria for including a financial asset as available for sale?
6. Which categories of financial assets or liabilities are accounted for using fair value through profit or loss?
7. Which categories of financial assets or liabilities are accounted for using the amortized cost using effective interest method?

LEARNING OUTCOME 3
APPLY THE EFFECTIVE INTEREST RATE METHOD

Under IFRS, the amortized cost of a financial asset or liability is the difference between the initial amounts recorded less principal payments received during the term of the financial instrument. The payments are first adjusted using the effective interest method.

EXAMPLE 1: NO INTEREST

On 1 January 2009, Melbourne Medical Sales sells equipment to a customer for A$150 000. The customer requests that a single payment be made to Melbourne at the end of three years. Moreover, an agreement is reached that the customer will not pay interest on the amount. From Melbourne's perspective this cost would qualify in the 'loan and receivable' category and therefore he accounted for using the amortized cost using effective interest rate method.

How should Melbourne account for this transaction?

Melbourne must first determine the fair value of the amount owed. This is done by discounting the amount to calculate its present value. The cash payment pattern is as follows:

	1 Jan. 2009	31 Dec. 2009	31 Dec. 2010	31 Dec. 2011
Interest payments	0	0	0	0
Principal payment	0	0	0	150 000
Total payments	0	0	0	$150 000

To discount the cash payments, Melbourne must apply a discount factor. Management determines that the appropriate discount factor is 6%. Using a financial calculator, data would be entered as follows:

N	i/Y	PMT	PV	FV
3	6	0	?	150 000

CPT PV = A$125 942.89

Based on this calculation, the financial asset, which is the amount owed by the customer, would be recorded as follows:

Date	Account Titles	DR	CR
1 Jan. 2009	Receivable from customer Discount Sales revenue	A$150 000.00	 A$24 057.11 125 942.89

Notice that the sale is recorded for the discounted amount of A$125 942.89 and the amount owing from the customer – the receivable from the customer – is recorded at the full amount. A discount account is established as a contra to the receivable with a credit of A$24 057.11. Since the contra has a credit balance, it offsets the receivable so that the carrying amount shown on the statement of financial position is $125 942.89. This would appear on the statement of financial position on 1 January 2009 as follows:

Receivable from customer	A$150 000.00
Less: Discount	24 057.11
Carrying amount	A$125 942.89

The discount account of A$24 057.11 must now be amortized over the three-year life of the financial asset using the effective interest method. The effective rate in this case would be the 6% discount factor, which is used to create the amortization schedule as follows:

Date	Beginning Balance	Interest Accrued	Interest Payment	Unamortized Discount	Ending Balance
1 Jan. 2009	–	–	–	A$24 057.11	A$125 942.89
31 Dec. 2009	A$125 942.89	A$7 556.57	0	16 500.54	133 499.46
31 Dec. 2010	133 499.46	8 009.97	0	8 490.57	141 509.32
31 Dec. 2011	141 509.32	8 490.57	0	0	150 000.00

Notice that to calculate the interest accrued, 6% is multiplied by the ending balance each year, which is brought forward as the beginning balance. At the end of each year, an adjusting entry would be made to amortize the discount amount and simultaneously accrue the interest earned on the receivable. For 31 December 2009, the entry would be as follows:

Date	Account Titles	DR	CR
31 Dec. 2009	Discount	A$16 500.54	
	Interest revenue		A$16 500.54

At the end of the three-year period, the discount amount has been fully amortized and the carrying amount of the receivable would be $150 000. The customer would at this point send the amount owed, and Melbourne would make the following journal entry:

Date	Account Titles	DR	CR
31 Dec. 2011	Cash	A$150 000.00	
	Receivable from customer		A$150 000.00

EXAMPLE 2: INTEREST ONLY PAYMENT WITH REPRESENTATIVE INTEREST RATE

Let's take a second example in which the customer agrees to pay 6% interest on the outstanding balance of the receivable each year, and this interest rate is the appropriate rate for a financial instrument of this type. Otherwise the terms of the receivable from the customer remain the same.

How should Melbourne account for this transaction?

In this example, the cash flow payments from the customer would be as follows:

	1 Jan. 2009	31 Dec. 2009	31 Dec. 2010	31 Dec. 2011
Interest payments	0	A$6 000	A$6 000	A$6 000
Principal payment	0	0	0	150 000
Total payments	0	0	0	A$156 000

At the end of each year, the customer would pay A$6000 (6% × A$150 000) and at the end of 2011 the customer would also return the principal amount. Since these cash payments are discounted at the same rate as the interest rate paid by the customer, the discounting will result in a present value of $150 000. Thus, the receivable from the customer is recorded at the principal amount as follows:

Date	Account Titles	DR	CR
1 Jan. 2009	Receivable from customer Sales revenue	A$150 000.00	A$150 000.00

At the end of both 2009 and 2010, the customer would pay the interest accrued for that year and the following journal entry would be made by Melbourne:

Date	Account Titles	DR	CR
31 Dec. 2009 and 31 Dec. 2010	Cash Interest revenue	A$6 000	A$6 000

And in the final year when the interest for 2011 is received with the principal payment, the following journal entry would be made:

Date	Account Titles	DR	CR
31 Dec. 2011	Cash Interest revenue Receivable from customer	$156 000	$6 000 150 000

EXAMPLE 3: INTEREST-ONLY PAYMENT WITH NONREPRESENTATIVE INTEREST RATE

In the third example, Melbourne's customer agrees to pay on the same terms as outlined in Example 2, including a 6% interest rate. However, this rate was given to the customer as a concession and is lower than the normal discount rate for financial instruments of this type, which management determines to be 8%.

How should Melbourne account for this transaction?

As with Example 1, Melbourne must first determine the fair value of the amount owed. The cash payment pattern is as follows:

	1 Jan. 2009	31 Dec. 2009	31 Dec. 2010	31 Dec. 2011
Interest payments	0	A$6 000	A$6 000	A$6 000
Principal payment	0	0	0	150 000
Total payments	0	0	0	A$156 000

To discount the cash payments, Melbourne must apply the 8% discount factor – not the nominal 6% paid by the customer. Using a financial calculator, data would be entered as follows:

N	i/Y	PMT	PV	FV
3	8	6000	?	150 000

CPT PV = A$134 537.42

Based on this calculation, the financial asset, which is the amount owed by the customer, would be recorded as follows:

Date	Account Titles	DR	CR
1 Jan. 2009	Receivable from customer	A$150 000.00	
	Discount		A$15 462.58
	Sales revenue		134 537.42

The sale is recorded for the discounted amount of A$134 537.42 and the amount owing from the customer is recorded at the full amount. The discount account is established at A$15 462.58. The discount amount must now be amortized over the three-year life of the financial asset using the effective interest method, which is 8%, as follows:

Date	Beginning Balance	Interest Accrued	Interest Payment	Unamortized Discount	Ending Balance
1 Jan. 2009	–	–	–	A$15 462.58	A$134 537.42
31 Dec. 2009	A$134 537.42	A$10 763.00	A$6 000.00	10 699.58	139 300.42
31 Dec. 2010	139 300.42	11 144.04	6 000.00	5 555,54	144 444.46
31 Dec. 2011	144 444.46	11 555.54*	6 000.00	0	150 000.00

* rounded

Notice that to calculate the interest accrued, 8% is multiplied by the ending balance each year, which is brought forward as the beginning balance. An interest payment of A$6000 is made each year, and the unamortized discount is calculated as the previous unamortized discount balance less the interest accrued plus the interest payment. The ending balance is the receivable balance of A$150 000 less the unamortized discount.

At the end of each year, an adjusting entry would be made to amortize the discount amount, allocate the payment of cash by the customer and simultaneously accrue the interest earned on the receivable. For 31 December 2009, the entry would be as follows:

Date	Account Titles	DR	CR
31 Dec. 2011	Discount	A$4 763.00	
	Cash	6 000.00	
	Interest revenue		A$10 763.00

At the end of the three-year period, the discount amount has been fully amortized and the carrying amount of the receivable would be $150 000. The customer would at this point send the amount owed, and Melbourne would make the following journal entry:

Date	Account Titles	DR	CR
31 Dec. 2011	Cash	A$150 000.00	
	Receivable from customer		A$150 000.00

LEARNING OUTCOME 4
EXPLAIN THE ACCOUNTING FOR TRADE ACCOUNTS

4.1 How is the effective interest rate method applied to trade accounts?

4.2 How do we account for uncollectible trade accounts receivable balances?

4.3 How do we account for the amount of uncollectible trade accounts receivable estimated?
   4.3.1 What is the percentage of sales method?
   4.3.2 What is the aged receivables method?
   4.3.3 How are estimates of uncollectible trade accounts receivable balances recorded?

4.4 What entries are recorded when a customer defaults?

Trade accounts include both trade accounts receivable and trade accounts payable.

4.1 How is the effective interest rate method applied to trade accounts?

The following example demonstrates how the amortized cost using the interest rate method would be applied to a trade accounts receivable.

Poonaki Industries LLC manufactures and sells engine components to large auto manufacturers. On 1 July 2009, the company sells £760 000 in radiators to one customer. The customer has three months to pay. Poonaki discounts trade receivables on a monthly basis and uses 14% as the discount rate. Using a financial calculator, data would be entered as follows:

N	i/Y	PMT	PV	FV
3	1.166	0	?	£760 000

Notice in this calculation that the number of periods (N) is three for the three months that the trade receivable will be outstanding. The discount rate (i/Y) is 1.166% (14% annually ÷ 12 months). The present value is £734 023.32. This makes the discount £25 976.68, a potentially material amount even though the trade receivable is outstanding for only three months. The journal entry to record the sale would be as follows:

Date	Account Titles	DR	CR
1 July 2009	Trade accounts receivable	£760 000.00	
	Discount		£25 976.68
	Sales revenue		734 023.32

The effective rate of 1.166% per month is then used to create the amortization schedule, as follows:

Date	Beginning Balance	Interest Accrued	Interest Payment	Unamortized Discount	Ending Balance
1 July 2009	–	–	–	£25 976.68	£734 023.32
31 July 2009	£734 023.32	£8 558.71	0	17 417.97	742 582.03
31 Aug. 2009	742 582.03	8 658.51	0	8 759.46	751 240.54
31 Sep. 2009	751 240.54	8 759.46	0	0	760 000.00

Notice that to calculate the interest revenue, the effective interest rate of 1.166% is multiplied by the ending balance each month, which is brought forward as the beginning balance for the next month. At the end of each month, an adjusting entry would be made to amortize the discount amount and simultaneously accrue the interest earned on the receivable. For 31 July 2009, the entry would be as follows:

Date	Account Titles	DR	CR
31 July 2009	Discount Interest revenue	£8 558.71	£8 558.71

For August 2009 the entry would be:

Date	Account Titles	DR	CR
31 Aug. 2009	Discount Interest revenue	£8 658.51	£8 658.51

For September 2009 the entry would be:

Date	Account Titles	DR	CR
31 Sep. 2009	Discount Interest revenue	£8 759.46	£8 759.46

At the end of the three-month period, once the discount amount has been fully amortized, the carrying amount of the receivable would be £760 000. The customer would at this point send the amount owed, and Poonaki would record the following journal entry:

Date	Account Titles	DR	CR
30 Sep. 2009	Cash Receivable from customer	£760 000.00	£760 000.00

Trade accounts payable are also accounted for using the effective interest method. Recall in the earlier example for trade accounts receivable that Poonaki Industries LLC had sold radiators to a customer. That customer, General Auto Ltd, would record a trade accounts payable for the amount owed to Poonaki.

General Auto Ltd purchased £760 000 in radiators from Poonaki Industries LLC on 1 July 2009. General Auto has three months to pay. General Auto uses 12% as its discount rate. Using a financial calculator, data would be entered as follows:

N	i/Y	PMT	PV	FV
3	1.0	0	?	£760 000

First, notice that the discount factor for Poonaki (14%) is not the same as that used by General Auto. Each company will have its own discount rate.

Also notice that in the calculation shown above, the number of periods (N) is three for the three months that the trade receivable will be outstanding. The discount rate (i/Y) is 1.0% (12% annually ÷ 12 months). The present value is £737 648.51. This makes the discount £22 351.49, a potentially material amount even though the trade receivable is outstanding for only three months. The journal entry to record the sale would be as follows:

Date	Account Titles	DR	CR
1 July 2009	Purchases	£737 648.51	
	Discount	22 351.49	
	Trade accounts payable		£760 000.00

The effective rate of 1.0% per month is then used to create the amortization schedule, as follows:

Date	Beginning Balance	Interest Accrued	Interest Payment	Unamortized Discount	Ending Balance
1 July 2009	–	–	–	£22 351.49	£737 648.51
31 July 2009	£737 648.51	£7 376.48	0	14 975.00	745 025.00
31 Aug. 2009	745 025.00	7 450.25	0	7 524.75	752 475.25
31 Sep. 2009	752 475.25	7 524.75	0	0	760 000.00

Notice that to calculate the interest expense, the effective interest rate of 1% is multiplied by the ending balance each month, which is brought forward as the beginning balance. At the end of each month, an adjusting entry would be made to amortize the discount amount and simultaneously accrue the interest expense on the payable. For 31 July 2009, the entry would be as follows:

Date	Account Titles	DR	CR
31 July 2009	Interest expense	£7 376.48	
	Discount		£7 376.48

For August 2009:

Date	Account Titles	DR	CR
31 Aug. 2009	Interest expense	£7 450.25	
	Discount		£7 450.25

For September 2009:

Date	Account Titles	DR	CR
30 Sep. 2009	Interest expense	£7 524.75	
	Discount		£7 524.75

Since 30 September is also the due date, General Auto makes payment and records the entry:

Date	Account Titles	DR	CR
30 Sep. 2009	Trade account payable	£760 000.00	
	Cash		£760 000.00

4.2 How do we account for uncollectible trade accounts receivable balances?

When a business has a substantial volume of trade accounts receivable, some uncollectible debts are inevitable and are simply a cost of doing business. Effective management of receivables involves establishing terms on which credit is extended to customers, discounts and procedures to ensure timely collection of amounts owed. This, of course, means making judgements about creditworthiness based on the business's experience with the customer's payment habits.

However, in some cases management recognizes that a customer cannot pay or is unlikely to pay the balance owed, and a decision is made to remove the obligation from trade accounts receivable. A customer may enter bankruptcy, in which the collection of the amount owed is unlikely because of insufficient assets. Bankruptcy is a legal procedure that provides protection from creditors while the business is either reorganized or liquidated. Or management may decide that attempting to collect the amount owed is not worth the administrative costs that must be incurred to obtain full or more likely partial payment.

If a business has few trade receivables, or if defaults by customers are rare, then it may simply write off the amount owed when the default occurs which is sometimes referred to as the direct write-off method. A default is nonpayment of an obligation. The amount owed is removed from trade receivables and recorded as an uncollectible accounts expense.

A medical clinic owes A$1800 to Melbourne Medical Equipment on a purchase it made in November 2012. Because of financial problems, the clinic files for bankruptcy protection. Since the clinic has few assets and even partial payment of the debt seems unlikely, Melbourne's management decides to write off the amount. The journal entry would be as follows:

Date	Account Titles	DR	CR
13 Jan. 2013	Uncollectible accounts expense Trade accounts receivable	A$1 800	A$1 800

If a customer whose debt has been written off subsequently pays all or part of the amount owed, then the entry is reversed and the amount collected is recorded.

The owners of the bankrupt clinic find that they are able to pay $500 to Melbourne on 15 February 2013. The journal entries to record this transaction would be as follows:

Date	Account Titles	DR	CR
15 Feb. 2013	Trade accounts receivable	$500	
	Uncollectible accounts expense		$500

Date	Account Titles	DR	CR
15 Feb. 2013	Cash	$500	
	Trade accounts receivable		$500

A business would use this approach only if defaults were infrequent and more likely because trade accounts receivable are not a major factor. For example, the business could sell on a cash-only basis. However, almost all larger companies have a significant amount of trade accounts receivable.

Also, accounting standards do not generally permit direct write-offs of uncollectible amounts. The reason is that the revenue that gave rise to the uncollectible accounts expense is not properly matched. Notice in the foregoing example that the revenue for the medical equipment was recognized in November 2012, while the related uncollectible accounts expense was recognized in January 2013. Thus a proper matching did not occur. As a result, *accounting standards mandate the use of the allowance method.*

Under the allowance method, an estimate of the amount of uncollectible receivables is recorded as an uncollectible expense when revenue is recognized. The offsetting credit is recorded in allowance for uncollectible accounts, a contra account to trade receivables. The allowance account is deducted from trade accounts receivable on the statement of financial position to give net receivables. We also say that this is the carrying amount of the receivables.

Melbourne has a trade accounts receivable balance of $5 447 000 and the company estimates that $350 000 will be uncollectible. This would appear on the statement of financial position in current assets as follows:

Trade accounts receivable	$5 447 000
Less: Allowance for uncollectible accounts	(350 000)
Accounts receivable, net	$5 097 000

Assets have normal debit balances, as we know. The allowance account is a credit, but we still regard it as part of assets because it is a contra to trade accounts receivable, which is an asset.

4.3 How is the amount of uncollectible trade accounts receivable estimated?

Businesses use one of two methods to estimate the amount of uncollectible accounts: percentage of sales and ageing of receivables.

4.3.1 WHAT IS THE PERCENTAGE OF SALES METHOD?

With the percentage of sales method, a business relies on its past experience to predict the amount of current credit sales that will be uncollectible.

Suppose Melbourne has found that on average about 1.5% of its credit sales are uncollectible. On 27 December 2012, the company records A$670 000 in credit sales and makes the following journal entries:

Date	Account Titles	DR	CR
27 Dec. 2012	Trade accounts receivable	A$670 000	
	Sales revenue		A$670 000

Date	Account Titles	DR	CR
27 Dec. 2012	Uncollectible accounts expense	A$10 050	
	Allowance for uncollectible accounts		A$10 050

The first entry records the sales on account. The second records the associated uncollectible accounts expense with the credit to the allowance for uncollectible accounts for A$10 050 ($670 000 × 1.5%).

Suppose that the allowance for uncollectible accounts ledger account has a A$2000 beginning credit balance before the adjusting entry for the estimate is made:

Allowance for Uncollectible Accounts		
	DR	CR
Beginning balance		A$2 000
27 Dec. 2012 Adjusting entry		10 050
Ending balance		A$12 050

Notice that the adjusting entry is made for the full amount of the estimate (A$10 050). When it is posted, the ending balance in the allowance account is A$12 050. In other words, the beginning balance is not considered when determining how much the adjustment will be.

An important point to bear in mind is that under the allowance method, the debit to uncollectible accounts expense occurs when the estimate of the uncollectible amount is made, which is when the revenue is recognized. Notice also that no account has defaulted at this point, we are only estimating that the A$10 050 will be uncollectible.

4.3.2 WHAT IS THE AGED RECEIVABLES METHOD?

Other companies estimate uncollectible amounts using the aged receivables method. As amounts owed are outstanding for longer, the likelihood of collecting the money from the customer decreases. This is only logical, since slow-paying customers often have financial difficulties and must concentrate cash resources on immediate business needs. An example of an aged receivables subledger follows:

	Aged Accounts Receivable Subledger 31 December 2012				
	AS $				
Customer	Amount Due	1–30 Days	31–60 Days	61–90 Days	Over 90 Days
CXC Healthcare	A$34 200	A$2 400	A$16 000	A$15 800	A$0
Denby Clinic	13 700	13 700	0	0	0
Kelso Clinic	56 200	0	0	24 200	32 000
Nanking Hospital	112 000	112 000	0	0	0
Totals	216 100	128 100	16 000	40 000	32 000
Estimated uncollectible percentage		1.5%	3.8%	7.1%	10.4%
Estimated uncollectible amount	A$8 696	A$1 920	A$608	A$2 840	A$3 328

Notice that each customer's total amount due is shown, and this number is then aged into 30-day increments. CXC Healthcare, for example, owes A$34 200, of which A$2400 represents purchases made within the last 30 days, another A$16 000 between 31 and 60 days, with the remaining A$15 800 between 61 and 90 days. At the bottom of the schedule, the total amount for each age category is calculated and then multiplied by an estimated uncollectible percentage to give the estimated uncollectible amount. The results are added across to give the total amount that the company estimates to be uncollectible (A$8696).

4.3.3 HOW ARE ESTIMATES OF UNCOLLECTIBLE TRADE ACCOUNTS RECEIVABLE BALANCES RECORDED?

The aged receivables method differs from the percentage sales method in how this estimate is recorded. Under the percentage sales method the entire amount of the estimated uncollectible amount is added to the allowance account. However, *under the aged receivables method the allowance account is adjusted for only that amount needed to make the ending balance in the account equal to the total estimated uncollectible amount.*

Suppose that the balance in the allowance for uncollectible accounts appeared as follows before any adjustment is made:

Allowance for Uncollectible Accounts		
	DR	CR
Beginning balance		A$2 000

We can see that the account has a beginning credit balance of A$2000, as in the previous example. Under the aged receivables method, we record only that amount necessary to make the account equal to the total estimated uncollectible amount. Because a credit balance of A$2000 already exists, only a A$6696 credit is needed for the account then to total A$8696. Therefore, the adjusting entry would be as follows:

Date	Account Titles	DR	CR
31 Dec. 2012	Uncollectible accounts expense	A$6 696	
	Allowance for uncollectible accounts		A$6 696

Once posted, the allowance for uncollectible accounts would appear as follows:

Allowance for Uncollectible Accounts		
	DR	CR
Beginning balance		A$2 000
31 Dec. 2012 adjustment		6 696
Ending balance		A$8 696

Why do we take the existing balance in the allowance account into consideration with the aged receivables method and not with the percentage sales method? Under aged receivables, we are making an estimate for all accounts receivable amounts currently outstanding. Under percentage of sales, we are making an estimate only for the additional amount of estimated uncollectible accounts caused by new sales.

Now, suppose that instead of having a credit balance in the allowance account before the adjustment is made, we observe a debit balance:

Allowance for Uncollectible Accounts		
	DR	CR
Beginning balance	A$2 000	

In this case, we would make the following adjusting entry under the aged receivables method:

Date	Account Titles	DR	CR
31 Dec. 2012	Uncollectible accounts expense Allowance for uncollectible accounts	A$10 696	A$10 696

When this entry is posted, the allowance for uncollectible accounts would appear as follows:

Allowance for Uncollectible Accounts		
	DR	CR
Beginning balance	A$2 000	
31 Dec. 2012 adjustment		10 696
Ending balance		A$8 696

We can see that the ending balance is A$8696. However, with a beginning debit balance, a credit of A$10 696 was needed to set the balance equal to the total amount for the uncollectible estimate. This is because the amount of the adjustment had to cover the beginning debit balance as well as the current estimated uncollectible amount.

Figure 8.7 presents a decision flow diagram that illustrates the accounting for the estimate of uncollectible accounts.

FIGURE 8.7 ESTIMATE OF UNCOLLECTIBLE AMOUNT

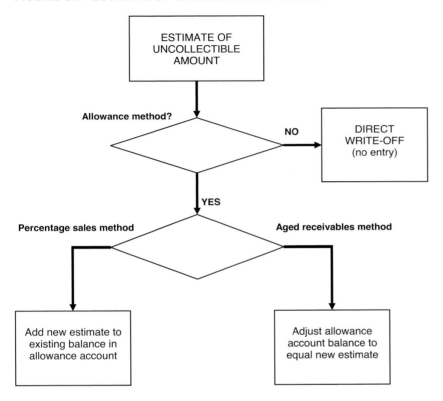

ON YOUR OWN

LEARNING OUTCOMES REVIEW

1. Into what category of financial assets and liabilities are trade receivables and trade payables classified?
2. What financial accounting method – fair value through profit or loss or amortized cost using effective interest method – applies to trade receivables and trade payables?
3. What is bankruptcy?
4. What is the allowance method of accounting for uncollectible accounts?
5. Define net receivables.
6. What are the two methods of estimating uncollectible accounts?
7. How is the adjusting entry for the percentage of sales method made to the allowance account? Is the balance in the allowance account considered or not when determining the amount of the adjusting entry?
8. How is the adjusting entry for the aged receivables method made to the allowance account? Is the balance in the allowance account considered or not when determining the amount of the adjusting entry?

LEARNING OUTCOME PRACTICE

1. On 30 June 2010 Apex Chemicals Ltd had a €24 522 credit balance in allowance for uncollectible accounts. The company uses the percentage of sales method to estimate uncollectible accounts. In the third quarter, Apex had the following credit sales: July €1 710 500; August €1 655 000; and September €1 670 000. During the same three months, defaults totalled €59 000; €27 500 and €26 000, respectively. The company uses 2.38% of sales to estimate uncollectible amounts.

    What journal entries were made related to these events? What was the balance in the allowance account on 20 September 2010?

2. Following is the aged receivables subledger for SOS Executive Trainers Inc. at 30 April 2012.

    a) Based on the information presented in the subledger, what is the estimated uncollectible amount for these accounts? Round all figures to the nearest dollar.

    b) What is the journal entry if the allowance account contains a $2200 debit balance to record the estimate?

    c) What is the journal entry if the allowance account contains a $1600 credit balance to record the estimate?

Aged Accounts Receivables Subledger 30 April 2012					
Customer	Amount Due	1–30 Days	31–60 Days	61–90 Days	Over 90 Days
Canon Enterprises	144 000	72 300	71 700	0	0
Dell Bluestone Company	456 522	29 500	176 000	160 022	91 000
Shubh Rathry Imaging Corporation	89 800	89 800	0	0	0
Skribble Stationery Ltd	520 400	212 000	198 400	110 000	0
Totals	1 210 722	403 600	446 100	270 022	91 000
Estimated uncollectible percentage		0.78%	2.11%	6.50%	9.85%
Estimated uncollectible amount					

4.4 What entries are recorded when a customer defaults?

When a customer defaults, a journal entry is made to remove the amount from trade accounts receivable, since the trade accounts receivable as an asset no longer exists. The defaulted amount is debited to the allowance account. In the example of the medical clinic that entered bankruptcy owing Melbourne Medical Equipment A$1800, the entry to record the default transaction would be:

Date	Account Titles	DR	CR
13 Jan. 2013	Allowance for uncollectible accounts Trade accounts receivable	A$1 800	A$1 800

Notice two points about this default transaction. First, the statement of income is not affected – there is no impact on profit. Second, although the allowance for uncollectible accounts and the accounts receivable balances (both statement of financial position accounts) have changed, net receivables have not changed, as we can see in the following comparison:

	Before Default Transaction	After Default Transaction
Trade accounts receivable	A$670 000	A$668 200
Less: Allowance for uncollectible accounts	10 050	8 250
Trade receivable, net	**A$659 950**	**A$659 950**

BMW GROUP: ALLOWANCE FOR IMPAIRMENT

In its 2007 financial statements, BMW Group, which manufactures BMW autos, reported the following for its trade receivables balance in the notes:

Trade receivables
Trade receivables amounting in total to euro 2672 million (2006: euro 2258 million) include euro 3 million due later than one year (2006: euro 21 million).

Allowance for impairment and credit risk

in euro million	31.12.2007	31.12.2006
Gross carrying amount	2717	2335
Allowance for impairment	45	77
Net carrying amount	**2672**	**2258**

As this example shows, the net trade accounts receivable remains unchanged. This is because the debit and credit in the default entry were made to two statements of financial position accounts that offset each other: trade receivable and its contra account, allowance for uncollectible accounts. Therefore, when an actual default occurs, these two accounts are affected, but the net trade receivable total is not – nor is current assets or total assets.

Summary: uncollectible accounts

Figure 8.8 summarizes the journal entries made by event and method and Figure 8.9 shows the adjustment to the allowance account by the method of estimating the uncollectible amount.

FIGURE 8.8 ENTRIES BY EVENT AND METHOD

Event	Direct Write-Off Method	Allowance Method
Estimate	No entry is made	Debit uncollectible accounts expense Credit allowance account
Default	Debit uncollectible accounts expense Credit accounts receivable	Debit allowance account Credit accounts receivable

FIGURE 8.9 CALCULATING ADJUSTMENTS BY METHOD OF ESTIMATING UNCOLLECTIBLE AMOUNTS

Prior Balance in Allowance Account	Percentage of Sales Method	Aged Receivables Method
Credit	Add estimate without adjustment for prior balance in allowance account	Subtract prior credit in allowance account from estimate
Debit	Add estimate without adjustment for prior balance in allowance account	Add prior credit in allowance account from estimate

ON YOUR OWN

LEARNING OUTCOMES PRACTICE

Use the following information for questions 1–3:

Arnbjorg Marine sells yachting equipment. On 4 September 2011, the company received notice that one of its customers has gone into bankruptcy owing Arnbjorg 125 000 kroner. Further investigation reveals that this customer has only an insignificant amount of assets, and a reasonable settlement of the debt seems unlikely. Arnbjorg's management instructs its accounting department to write the amount off.

1. If Arnbjorg uses the write-off method, what is the journal entry to record the default?
2. If Arnbjorg uses the allowance method and a 55 000 kroner debit already exists in the allowance account when the default occurs, what is the journal entry to record the default?
3. If Arnbjorg uses the allowance method and a 30 000 kroner credit already exists in the allowance account when the default occurs, what is the journal entry to record the default?

Use the following information for questions 4–5:
On 30 September 2011 Arnbjorg determines that its total sales for September were 1 770 000 kroner. Arnbjorg uses the percentage of sales method and estimates that uncollectible accounts will be 4.3%.

4. If a 55 000 kroner debit already exists in the allowance account, what would be the adjusting entry to record the uncollectible estimate?
5. If a 30 000 kroner credit already exists in the allowance account, what would be the adjusting entry to record the uncollectible estimate?

Use the following information for questions 6–7:
On 30 September 2011, Arnbjorg determines that its total sales for September were 1 770 000 kroner. Arnbjorg uses the aged receivables method and estimates that uncollectible accounts will be 22 900 kroner.

6. If a 55 000 kroner debit already exists in the allowance account, what would be the adjusting entry to record the uncollectible estimate?
7. If a 3000 kroner credit already exists in the allowance account, what would be the adjusting entry to record the uncollectible estimate?
8. At 1 June 2011, a company's allowance for receivables was $39 000. At year end on 30 June 2011, trade receivables totalled $517 000. It was decided to write off debts totalling $37 000 and to then adjust the allowance for receivables to the equivalent of 5% of the trade accounts receivable based on past experience. What figure should appear in the statement of income for the year ended 30 June 2011 for these items?
   a. $61 000
   b. $22 000
   c. $24 000
   d. $23 850
   ACCA adapted

GLOBAL PERSPECTIVE

Trade accounts receivables management has become quite sophisticated. For years, companies like Fair Isaac (www.fairisaac.com) have developed models based on statistical techniques to predict uncollectible amounts. These estimates have become quite accurate, so that companies are able to determine whether an account is likely to go delinquent and how much of the amount owed will be collected.

In addition, such companies provide analytical models that help determine how best to recover money owed on trade accounts receivable. A company that has had no success collecting a delinquent account will often refer the account to a collection agency or a solicitor. In some cases, the delinquent accounts are sold outright to the agency, and then the agency earns a profit on the spread between what it paid to the company to purchase the delinquent accounts and the amount it ultimately collects. Suppose that a company had €30 000 in uncollectible accounts, which it referred to an agency, and that the agency paid €22 000 for the accounts. The journal entry to record the sale of these trade account receivables, assuming the company used the allowance method, would be:

Date	Account Titles	DR	CR
30 Sep. 2011	Cash Allowance for uncollectible accounts	€22 000	€22 000

Another type of arrangement would be when a company refers accounts to an agency and accepts, say, half of any money the agency collects.

LEARNING OUTCOME 5
EXPLAIN THE ACCOUNTING FOR CREDIT CARD RECEIVABLES

5.1   How do we account for internal credit cards?

5.2   How do we account for third-party credit cards?

Retail sales are often made using credit cards. Credit cards can be either internal or obtained through a third-party provider like Visa, MasterCard, Discover and American Express.

5.1 How do we account for internal credit cards?

When a business issues its own credit cards to customers, this is simply a specialized form of trade receivables. Thus, the responsibility for maintaining related accounting records and cash collections remains with the business, just as with other trade receivables.

Suppose that Elaine Harris, a retail customer, has a credit card issued by Excelsior Boutique, which extends credit to select clientele. On 13 October 2010, Elaine purchases clothing for £880, charging the entire amount to her credit card. The journal entry to record the sale would be as follows:

Date	Account Titles	DR	CR
13 Oct. 2010	Credit card receivables – Elaine Harris	£880	
	Sales revenue		£880

Normally, retail credit cards are billed by monthly statement, which combines all current charges with any previous unpaid balance rather than sending an invoice for each purchase.

On 31 October 2010, Elaine makes full payment. The following journal entry would be recorded:

Date	Account Titles	DR	CR
31 Oct. 2010	Cash	£880	
	Credit card receivables – Elaine Harris		£880

Notice that the credit card receivable is accounted for in the same manner as any other trade receivable.

5.2 How do we account for third-party credit cards?

When a business relies on a third-party credit card provider, the receivable from the customer is collected by the credit card provider, not the seller. That means that the business does not have the responsibility for either maintaining credit card receivables accounting records or cash collection.

Let's assume that Excelsior Boutique uses Visa and MasterCard instead of an internally owned card and that Elaine made her purchase with Visa. The journal entry would be as follows:

Date	Account Titles	DR	CR
13 Oct. 2010	Trade receivable – Visa	£880	
	Sales revenue		£880

Notice that the receivable is from Visa, not Elaine Harris. Normally, the third-party credit card company will pay the seller soon after the transaction has occurred. However, the credit card service provider will also charge the seller a fee for handling the transaction. Let's assume that Visa charges Excelsior Boutique a 2.5% fee on the sales amount. When payment is received two days later, the fee will have been deducted. The journal entry would be as follows:

Date	Account Titles	DR	CR
15 Oct. 2010	Cash	£858	
	Credit card fees	22	
	Trade accounts receivable – Visa		£880

Visa deducts its fee and remits £858 and the difference is recorded as credit card fees, which is an expense that would appear on the statement of income. The amount shown in the above journal entry would typically be included with other payments made in the same general time frame.

LEARNING OUTCOME 6
EXPLAIN THE ACCOUNTING FOR NOTES

6.1   How do we account for interest-bearing notes?

6.2   How do we account for noninterest-bearing notes?

A note or promissory note is a formal contract entered into by two entities whereby one business - the issuer or maker of the note – agrees to pay the other a specified amount of money plus interest in exchange for either the loan of money or the purchase of goods or services. A note can be noninterest bearing. The time for payment to be made is the term of the note, and the interest rate is the stated rate. From the issuer's perspective, the note is a note payable; from the investor's perspective a note receivable. Some corporate notes, like bonds, are traded in markets, although notes are often between private parties such as the business and a bank, or the business and an employee or supplier. A note can be interest bearing or noninterest bearing.

6.1 How do we account for interest-bearing notes?

On 1 January 2009, Maksim LLC invested in a privately placed corporate note issued by Rio Telefonica, a telecommunications firm based in Rio de Janerio. The note was for 10 000 000 Brazilian reals for a three-year term. The stated interest is 8.75% and is to be paid annually, with the principal due in full on the maturity date. The market rate of interest for this type of financial instrument is 9.5%.

First, the cash flow for the note is discounted using the market rate of interest for a present value of 9 811 840 reals. Maksim's entry to record the investment in the note would be:

Date	Account Titles	DR	CR
1 Jan. 2009	Note receivable	10 000 000	
	Discount on note		188 160
	Cash		10 000 000

The discount account is a contra to the note receivable. Over the term of the note – three years – this will be amortized using the effective interest method, as shown in the following schedule.

Year	Beginning Balance	Effective Interest Rate	Note Amortization	Interest Received	Ending Balance
2009	9 811 840	9.5%	57 125	875 000	9 868 965
2010	9 868 965	9.5%	62 552	875 000	9 931 517
2011	9 931 517	9.5%	68 483*	875 000	10 000 000

* Rounded.

Based on this schedule, Maksim's journal entries would be:

Date	Account Titles	DR	CR
31 Dec. 2009	Cash	875 000	
	Discount on note	57 125	
	Interest revenue		932 125

For 2010:

Date	Account Titles	DR	CR
31 Dec. 2010	Cash	875 000	
	Discount on note	62 552	
	Interest revenue		937 552

For 2011:

Date	Account Titles	DR	CR
31 Dec. 2011	Cash	875 000	
	Discount on note	68 483	
	Interest revenue		943 483

On the maturity date, Rio Telefonica repays the note and Maksim would record the following entry:

Date	Account Titles	DR	CR
31 Dec. 2011	Cash	10 000 000	
	Note receivable		10 000 000

Note that the total interest revenue recorded over the three-year term is 2 436 840 reals, compared to the 2 625 000 reals (875 000 × 3) actually received. Because the note's stated rate was below the market rate of interest, interest revenue was increased.

Now let's have a look at the other side of the accounting, for Rio Telefonica.

First, the cash flow for the note is discounted using the market rate of interest for a present value of 9 811 840 reals. The entry to issue the note is as follows:

Date	Account Titles	DR	CR
1 Jan. 2009	Cash	10 000 000	
	Note payable		9 811 840
	Discount on note payable		188 160

The discount account is a contra to the note payable. Over the term of the note – three years – this will be amortized using the effective interest method, as shown in the following schedule:

Year	Amortized Cost Beginning Balance	Effective Interest Rate	Note Amortization	Interest Paid	Amortized Cost Ending Balance
2009	9 811 840	9.5%	57 125	875 000	9 868 965
2010	9 868 965	9.5%	62 552	875 000	9 931 517
2011	9 931 517	9.5%	68 483*	875 000	10 000 000

* Rounded.

Based on this schedule, journal entries would be recorded as follows:

Date	Account Titles	DR	CR
31 Dec. 2009	Interest expense	817 875	
	Discount on note payable	57 125	
	Cash		875 000

For 2010:

Date	Account Titles	DR	CR
31 Dec. 2010	Interest expense	812 448	
	Discount on note payable	62 552	
	Cash		875 000

For 2011:

Date	Account Titles	DR	CR
31 Dec. 2011	Interest expense	806 517	
	Discount on note payable	68 483	
	Cash		875 000

On the maturity date, Rio Telefonica repays the note, and the following entry is made:

Date	Account Titles	DR	CR
31 Dec. 2011	Note receivable	10 000 000	
	Cash		10 000 000

6.2 How do we account for noninterest-bearing notes?

Let's assume that on 1 January 2013 Maksim lent 70 000 reals to one of its customers without any stated interest. The note is a two-year term and the market rate of interest is 9.5%. Again, the future cash flow would first be discounted for a present value of 58 381 reals. The entry to record the note would be:

Date	Account Titles	DR	CR
1 Jan. 2013	Note receivable	58 381	
	Discount on note receivable	11 619	
	Cash		70 000

Over the two-year term of the note, the discount will be amortized as before, as shown in the following schedule:

Year	Amortized Cost Beginning Balance	Effective Interest Rate	Note Amortization	Interest Received	Amortized Cost Ending Balance
2013	58 381	9.5%	5 546	0	63 927
2014	63 927	9.5%	6 073	0	70 000

Based on this schedule, journal entries would be made as follows:

Date	Account Titles	DR	CR
31 Dec. 2013	Discount on note receivablee Interest revenue	5 546	5 546

For 2014:

Date	Account Titles	DR	CR
31 Dec. 2014	Discount on note receivablee Interest revenue	6 073	6 073

On the maturity date, the customer repays the note and Maksim records the following entry:

Date	Account Titles	DR	CR
31 Dec. 2014	Cash Note receivable	70 000	70 000

ON YOUR OWN

LEARNING OUTCOMES REVIEW

1. What is a promissory note?
2. Who is the issuer of a note?
3. How do notes receivable and notes payable differ from trade accounts receivable and trade accounts payable, respectively?
4. What is the stated rate on a note?
5. Why would the rate used to discount a note be different from the stated rate?
6. What is the financial accounting method used for notes receivable and notes payable?

LEARNING OUTCOME 7
EXPLAIN THE ACCOUNTING FOR BONDS

7.1   What are bonds and what are the types of bonds?

7.2   How do we account for bonds issued at par?

7.3   How do we account for bonds issued at a premium?

7.4   How do we account for bonds issued at a discount?

7.5   How do we account for noninterest-bearing bonds?

7.6   How do we account for a bond that is sold?

7.1 What are bonds and what are the types of bonds?

Bonds are normally used when large amounts of money are needed for the long term, which means that bond borrowing is frequently an alternative to increasing the equity investment in a business. A bond is a debt instrument in which a borrower, also known as the issuer, promises to repay an amount of money over time plus interest. Bonds have a stated value or face value, with each bond being denominated in increments of $1000, $5000 and so forth.

Typically, interest is paid periodically, with the principal being repaid by the issuer on the maturity date, or the date on which the issuer must repay the principal. Interest is calculated on the stated value, and is thus referred to as the stated interest rate, coupon rate or nominal interest rate. With some bonds, the principal is repaid in instalments over the term or life of the bond.

TYPES OF BONDS

The following are features of different types of bonds:

- Term bond: A bond on which the principal (the amount borrowed) is due on the maturity date.
- Serial bond: A bond on which the principal is paid in instalments over the term of the bond.
- Callable bond: The issuer has the right to purchase the bond from the investor at a certain call price.
- Secured bond: Also referred to as a debenture bond. Secured bonds are backed by a pledge of some asset such as real estate. The investor has a priority claim on the pledged asset in the event of liquidation.
- Unsecured bond: A bond that is sold on the cognizance of the issuer, with no claim against assets.
- Zero-interest bond: A bond that pays no interest but on which the investor earns a return by purchasing the bond at a discounted price.

Only large companies sell bonds in publicly traded bond markets. Bond issues are also complex to arrange and usually involve several advisers: finance specialists who advise the company on the amount of the stated interest to offer, accountants to determine what the impact will be on future financial statements, and attorneys to ensure that the bonds meet all legal and regulatory requirements.

Based on financial advice, a company may decide to offer 4% stated interest because 4% is the market rate of interest. In other words, investors can expect to receive 4% in the current market. But after the decision about what interest rate to offer on a bond is made, weeks may pass before the other financial and legal work is concluded and the bond is ready for the market. In the meantime, the bond market rate of interest may have changed. It may have increased or decreased.

> Bernardo Metals Ltd is planning to issue bonds in late April 2009 totalling $100 000 000 to finance work on a new iron-ore mine. The company's financial advisers and attorneys begin work on preparing the bond in early March when the market rate for bonds is 4%. Thus, Bernardo Metals offers 4% as its stated interest rate.
>
> During March, news of inflationary prices causes the market rate of interest in the bond market to rise to 4.5%. That means that the 4% rate offered by Bernardo Metals will not attract investors. Bernardo could change its bond to have a 4.5% rate, but that would take additional time and no guarantee exists that the market rate of interest will be 4.5% when the bond is revised.

So how does Bernardo Metals, or any other company issuing a new bond, handle this problem? The answer is that the bond is sold for an amount other than its face value. If the market rate of interest has increased over the stated rate, then the bond is sold for less or at a discount. If the market rate of interest decreases to lower than the stated rate on the bond, the bond can be sold for more or at a premium. If the market rate of interest is the same as the stated rate on the bond, then the bond will sell at par. Figure 8.10 graphically illustrates the relationship between the bond's stated interest rate and the market rate of interest.

FIGURE 8.10 STATED INTEREST VERSUS MARKET INTEREST

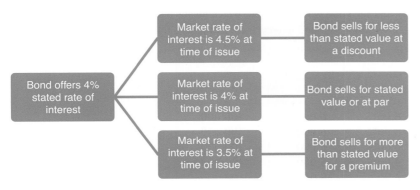

7.2 How do we account for bonds issued at par?

On 1 January 2012, the CFO of Wei Ling Ltd, a Hong Kong-based company with excess cash, purchases $100 000 in bonds issued by Pacific Enterprises Inc. based in San Diego, California. The bonds have a five-year term with a coupon rate of 6%. Interest is paid on the last day of each year. The journal entry to acquire the bonds is as follows:

Date	Account Titles	DR	CR
1 Jan. 2012	Bond investment	$100 000	
	Cash		$100 000

At the end of 2012, the entry to record interest revenue would be as follows:

Date	Account Titles	DR	CR
31 Dec. 2012	Cash	$6 000	
	Bond interest revenue		$6 000

This entry would be repeated in each of the subsequent four years: 2013, 2014, 2015 and 2016. However, on the last day of 2016 the issuer, Pacific Enterprises, repays the principal. The additional journal entry would be:

Date	Account Titles	DR	CR
31 Dec. 2016	Cash	$100 000	
	Bond investment		$100 000

In the example above, we would say that the bond was sold at par, which means that the investor paid an amount equal to the face value of the bond. If we amortize bond interest income, the schedule would appear as follows:

Year	Amortized Cost Beginning Balance $	Effective Interest Rate	Interest Received %	Amortized Cost Ending Balance $
2012	100 000	6.00%	6 000	100 000
2013	100 000	6.00%	6 000	100 000
2014	100 000	6.00%	6 000	100 000
2015	100 000	6.00%	6 000	100 000
2016	100 000	6.00%	6 000	100 000

Notice that the effective rate of interest is equal to the stated rate. This is because the bond was purchased at par.

Bonds can be privately placed with investors, or they can be sold into a bond market in a debt IPO (initial public offering). Thereafter they are traded much like equity securities: the price of the bond will rise and fall as market conditions, such as the market interest rate, decreases or increases. When the market interest rate increases, the price of existing bonds normally falls, while a market interest rate decrease will cause bond prices to rise. When the market price of the bond falls below the stated value, we say that the bond sells at a discount. When the market price is above the stated value, we say that the bond sells at a premium.

Let's say a bond sells for 98% of its stated value: we would say that the bond sold for 98, which would be a discount. If the bond sold at 4% above its stated value, we would say that it sold for 104.

7.3 How do we account for bonds issued at a premium?

Using the fact pattern from the previous example, suppose that the bond was purchased by Wei Ling for 104 rather than at par, which means that Wei Ling paid $104 000. The entry to acquire the bond would be:

Date	Account Titles	DR	CR
1 Jan. 2012	Bond investment Cash	$104 000	$104 000

The amortization schedule would be:

Year	Amortized Cost Beginning Balance $	Effective Interest Rate	Interest Received %	Bond Amortization	Amortized Cost Ending Balance $
2012	104 000	5.0742%	6 000	723	103 277
2013	103 277	5.0742%	6 000	759	102 518
2014	102 518	5.0742%	6 000	798	101 720
2015	101 720	5.0742%	6 000	839	100 881
2016	100 881	5.0742%	6 000	881	100 000

The cash flow pattern would be as follows:

2012	2013	2014	2015	2016
	+6000	+6000	+6000	+106 000

−104 000

When we solve for the internal rate of return (IRR) in a financial calculator, the result is 5.0742% which is the effective interest rate (see amortization schedule above).

Based on this schedule, journal entries would be made as follows:

Date	Account Titles	DR	CR
31 Dec. 2012	Cash	$6 000	
	Bond investment		$723
	Bond interest revenue		5 277

For 2013:

Date	Account Titles	DR	CR
31 Dec. 2013	Cash	$6 000	
	Bond investment		$759
	Bond interest revenue		5 241

For 2014:

Date	Account Titles	DR	CR
31 Dec. 2014	Cash	$6 000	
	Bond investment		$798
	Bond interest revenue		5 202

For 2015:

Date	Account Titles	DR	CR
31 Dec. 2015	Cash	$6 000	
	Bond investment		$839
	Bond interest revenue		5 161

For 2016:

Date	Account Titles	DR	CR
31 Dec. 2016	Cash	$6 000	
	Bond investment		$881
	Bond interest revenue		5 119

On the same date, Wei Ling would expect to receive payment of the principal from Pacific Enterprises. The entry would be:

Date	Account Titles	DR	CR
31 Dec. 2016	Cash	$100 000	
	Bond investment		$100 000

7.4 How do we account for bonds issued at a discount?

Again, let's assume the same fact pattern for Wei Ling's purchase of the Pacific Enterprises bond, except that the bond sold at a discount for 98. The entry to acquire the bond would be:

Date	Account Titles	DR	CR
1 Jan. 2012	Bond investment	$98 000	
	Cash		$98 000

The amortization schedule would now be:

Year	Amortized Cost Beginning Balance $	Effective Interest Rate	Interest Received %	Bond Amortization	Amortized Cost Ending Balance $
2012	98 000	6.48102%	6 000	351	98 351
2013	98 351	6.48102%	6 000	375	98 726
2014	98 726	6.48102%	6 000	398	99 124
2015	99 124	6.48102%	6 000	424	99 548
2016	99 548	6.48102%	6 000	452	100 000

Based on this schedule, journal entries would be recorded as follows:

Date	Account Titles	DR	CR
31 Dec. 2012	Cash	$6 000	
	Bond investment	351	
	Bond interest revenue		$6 351

For 2013:

Date	Account Titles	DR	CR
31 Dec. 2013	Cash	$6 000	
	Bond investment	375	
	Bond interest revenue		$6 375

For 2014:

Date	Account Titles	DR	CR
31 Dec. 2014	Cash	$6 000	
	Bond investment	398	
	Bond investment		$6 398

For 2015:

Date	Account Titles	DR	CR
31 Dec. 2015	Cash	$6 000	
	Bond investment	424	
	Bond investment		$6 424

For 2016:

Date	Account Titles	DR	CR
31 Dec. 2016	Cash	$6 000	
	Bond interest revenue	452	
	Bond investment		$6 452

On 1 January 2016, Wei Ling would expect to receive payment of the principal from Pacific Enterprises. The entry would be:

Date	Account Titles	DR	CR
31 Dec. 2016	Cash	$100 000	
	Bond investments		$100 000

7.5 How do we account for noninterest-bearing bonds?

Noninterest-bearing bonds pay no interest. Instead, the return to the investor is based on the difference between the stated amount on the bond paid at maturity, and the price paid when the bond is acquired.

Wei Ling purchases noninterest-bearing bonds issued by Pacific Enterprises for 94 on 1 January 2014. The bonds were originally issued on 1 January 2013 with a four-year term. Wei Ling purchases $150 000 of the bonds. The entry to record acquisition of the bonds would be:

Date	Account Titles	DR	CR
1 Jan. 2014	Bond investment	141 000	
	Cash		141 000

The amortization schedule would be as follows:

Year	Amortized Cost Beginning Balance	Effective Interest Rate	Bond Amortization	Amortized Cost Ending Balance
2014	126 000	5.984%	7 540	133 540
2015	133 540	5.984%	7 991	141 531
2016	141 531	5.984%	8 469	150 000

Based on this schedule, journal entries would be made as follows:

Date	Account Titles	DR	CR
31 Dec. 2014	Bond investment	7 540	
	Bond interest revenue		7 540

For 2015:

Date	Account Titles	DR	CR
31 Dec. 2015	Bond investment	7 991	
	Bond interest revenue		7 991

For 2016:

Date	Account Titles	DR	CR
31 Dec. 2016	Bond investment	8 469	
	Bond interest revenue		8 469

Over the remaining term, the bond's carrying value has been written up to its stated value. Thus, on the maturity date, Wei Ling would receive payment of the principal from Pacific Enterprises. The entry would be:

Date	Account Titles	DR	CR
31 Dec. 2016	Cash	150 000	
	Bond investment		150 000

7.6 How do we account for a bond that is sold?

When an investor sells a bond, the difference between the carrying amount of the asset and the sum of consideration received and any cumulative gains or losses that had been recognized directly in equity should be recognized in profit or loss.

Return to the example above in which Wei Ling purchased noninterest-bearing bonds from Pacific Enterprises. The bonds had a face value of $150 000 but were acquired at $141 000 with the following amortization schedule:

Year	Amortized Cost Beginning Balance	Effective Interest Rate	Bond Amortization $	Amortized Cost Ending Balance $
2014	126 000	5.984%	7 540	133 540
2015	133 540	5.984%	7 991	141 531
2016	141 531	5.984%	8 469	150 000

Now, suppose that Wei Ling decided to dispose of the bonds at year-end 2015 when, due to market circumstances, the price was 92, which means that the bonds are sold for $138 000. The entry to record the sale of the bonds would be:

Date	Account Titles	DR	CR
31 Dec. 2015	Cash	$138 000	
	Loss on sale of bonds		$3 531
	Carrying amount of bonds		141 531

For the issuer, the bond liability is removed when the obligation specified in the contact has been discharged, has been cancelled or has expired. Any gain or loss is calculated based on the difference between the carrying amount of the bond liability and the consideration paid.

On 15 February 2014, Mumbai-based Oberoi Services Ltd owes 100 000 000 rupees in bonds at face value. The carrying amount of these notes is 89 455 000 rupees after interest has been accrued to 15 February. Management decides to pay 70 000 000 rupees from cash and to issue a two-year note for the remainder, which the creditor has approved. The discounted value of the new note is 16 100 000 rupees. The entry to record the transaction would be as follows:

Date	Account Titles	DR	CR
15 Feb. 2014	Bonds payable	89 455 000	
	Gain on bonds	3 355 000	
	Cash		70 000 000
	Note payable		16 100 000

ON YOUR OWN

LEARNING OUTCOME REVIEW

1. Define a bond. How is a bond different from a note?
2. Who is the issuer of the bond: the party who owes the money or the creditor?
3. What does maturity date mean?
4. What is the stated interest rate or nominal interest rate?
5. Explain what a callable feature is on a bond.
6. Explain the difference between a term bond and a serial bond.
7. Explain the difference between a secured bond and an unsecured bond.
8. What does it mean that a bond is sold at par? At a premium? At a discount?
9. If the market rate of interest is above the stated rate of interest on a bond, will a premium or a discount result?
10. How is a premium or a discount on a bond accounted for?

LEARNING OUTCOME 8
EVALUATE ASSETS AND LIABILITIES

8.1 What is liquidity?
    8.1.1 What is working capital?
    8.1.2 What is the current ratio?
    8.1.3 What is the acid-test ratio?
    8.1.4 What is the cash ratio?
    8.1.5 What is the receivables turnover ratio?
    8.1.6 What is the average collectioin period?

8.2 What is solvency?

Several ratios evaluate the relationship between assets and liabilities, or between sales and profit on the statement of income and assets and liabilities.

Let's expand on our example of Heliard Coffees plc from Chapter 7. The following is the statement of income for the year ended 31 December 2009, and following that the statement of financial position for 2008 and 2009.

Heliard Coffees plc Statement of Income For the Year Ended 31 December 2009 € Euros	
	200 000
Sales revenue	€150 000
Cost of sales	70 000
Gross profit	80 000
Operating expenses	20 000
Interest expense	10 000
Profit before income tax	50 000
Income tax (20%)	10 000
Profit	€40 000

All of Heliard's sales are on credit.

Heliard Coffees plc Statement of Financial Position At 31 December 2009 € Euros		
Noncurrent assets	**2009**	**2008**
Property, plant and equipment	180 000	200 000
Less: Accumulated depreciation	(28 500)	(55 000)
	151 500	145 000
Investments at fair value	33 000	28 000
Goodwill	5 000	5 000
Total noncurrent assets	190 000	178 500
Current assets		
Inventories	29 000	27 500
Trade accounts receivable	28 000	28 500

(*Continued*)

FIGURE 5.13 *(CONTINUED)*

Heliard Coffees plc Statement of Financial Position At 31 December 2009 € Euros		
Marketable securities	9 500	7 000
Cash and cash equivalents	5 000	3 500
Total current assets	71 500	66 500
TOTAL ASSETS	**261 500**	**245 000**
Shareholders' equity		
Share capital	50 000	50 000
Share premium	35 000	35 000
Reserves	42 000	30 000
Total shareholders' equity	127 000	115 000
Noncurrent liabilities		
Borrowings	65 000	60 000
Total noncurrent liabilities	65 000	60 000
Current liabilities		
Notes payable	32 500	37 500
Accrued liabilities	22 000	20 000
Trade accounts payable	15 000	12 500
Total current liabilities	69 500	70 000
Total liabilities	**134 500**	**130 000**
TOTAL SHAREHOLDERS' EQUITY AND LIABILITIES	**261 500**	**245 000**

8.1 What is liquidity?

In other words, liquidity measures the business's ability to pay maturing obligations in the short term. Liquidity measures discussed in this chapter include working capital, current ratio, acid-test ratio, cash ratio, receivables turnover ratio and average collection period.

8.1.1 WHAT IS WORKING CAPITAL?

While technically not a ratio, working capital is often included in ratio analysis.

$$\text{Working capital} = \text{Current assets} - \text{Current liabilities}$$

Current assets are those assets that are expected to convert to cash within 12 months, while current liabilities are those obligations that are expected to be settled within 12 months. Thus, working capital measures the ability to meet current liabilities solely from current assets. The calculations for Heliard would be:

$$\text{Working capital} = \text{Current assets} - \text{Current liabilities}$$

For 2009:

$$\text{Working capital} = €71\,500 - 69\,500$$
$$€2000 = €71\,500 - 69\,500$$

For 2008:

$$\text{Working capital} = €66\,500 - 70\,000$$
$$(€3500) = €66\,500 - 70\,000$$

We can see that the working capital balance was positive in 2009 at 2000 and negative for 2008 at (€3 500).

8.1.2 WHAT IS THE CURRENT RATIO?

The current ratio also uses current assets and current liabilities, but in ratio form:

$$\text{Current ratio} = \frac{\text{Current assets}}{\text{Current liabilities}}$$

Heliard current ratios for the two years would be as follows.

For 2009:

$$\text{Current ratio} = \frac{€71\,500}{€69\,500}$$
$$1.03 = \frac{€71\,500}{€69\,500}$$

For 2008:

$$\text{Current ratio} = \frac{€66\,500}{€70\,000}$$
$$0.95 = \frac{€66\,500}{€70\,000}$$

Thus, Heliard has been able to improve its working capital position between 2008 and 2009. Both working capital and the current ratio give us insight into liquidity over the next 12 months.

8.1.3 WHAT IS THE ACID-TEST RATIO?

The acid-test ratio focuses on the ability of the business to meet its current liabilities from cash and cash equivalents, trade receivables and marketable securities.

$$\text{Acid-test ratio} = \frac{\text{Cash and cash equivalents} + \text{trade accounts receivable} + \text{marketable securities}}{\text{Current liabilities}}$$

Heliard's calculation for 2009 would be:

$$\text{Acid-test ratio} = \frac{€\,5000 + 28\,000 + 9500}{€\,69\,500}$$

$$0.61 = \frac{€\,42\,500}{€\,69\,500}$$

Heliard's calculation for 2008 would be:

$$\text{Acid-test ratio} = \frac{€\,3500 + 28\,500 + 7000}{€\,70\,500}$$

$$0.56 = \frac{€\,39\,000}{€\,70\,000}$$

Based on the acid-test ratio, the liquidity of Heliard has improved.

8.1.4 WHAT IS THE CASH RATIO?

The most stringent ratio is the cash ratio, which includes only cash and cash equivalents and marketable securities.

$$\text{Cash ratio} = \frac{\text{Cash and cash equivalents} + \text{marketable securities}}{\text{Current liabilities}}$$

Heliard's calculation for 2009 would be:

$$\text{Cash ratio} = \frac{€\,5000 + 9500}{€\,69\,500}$$

$$0.21 = \frac{€\,14\,500}{€\,69\,500}$$

Heliard's calculation for 2008 would be:

$$\text{Cash ratio} = \frac{€\,3500 + 7000}{€\,70\,000}$$

$$0.15 = \frac{€\,10\,500}{€\,70\,000}$$

This shows that Heliard's ability to meet current liabilities from readily available cash sources – cash, cash equivalents and marketable securities – has also improved between 2008 and 2009.

8.1.5 WHAT IS THE RECEIVABLES TURNOVER RATIO?

The receivables turnover ratio measures the relationship between receivables and net credit sales:

$$\text{Receivables turnover ratio} = \frac{\text{Net credit sales}}{\text{Average receivables}}$$

The 2009 average receivables would be calculated as the ending balance of trade receivables averaged with the beginning balance.

$$\text{Average receivables} = \frac{\text{Receivables beginning balance} + \text{receivables ending balance}}{2}$$

$$\text{Average receivables} = \frac{€28\,000 + 28\,500}{2}$$

$$€28\,250 = \frac{€28\,000 + 28\,500}{2}$$

$$\text{Receivables turnover ratio} = \frac{€150\,000}{€28\,250}$$

$$5.31 = \frac{€150\,000}{€28\,250}$$

What the receivables turnover ratio tells us is what level of credit sales the business was able to generate for a given level of trade accounts receivable (holding the denominator constant). Thus, we would normally want this ratio to be higher. Or we could say that for a given level of credit sales (holding the numerator constant), we want to see less cash tied up in trade receivables. A higher ratio is generally desirable and suggests that trade receivables are being measured effectively.

8.1.6 WHAT IS THE AVERAGE COLLECTION PERIOD?

The average collection period converts the receivables turnover ratio into the number of days in receivables:

$$\text{Average collection period} = \frac{365}{\text{Recivables turnover ratio}}$$

For Heliard, the calculation would be:

$$\text{Average collection period} = \frac{365}{5.31}$$

$$68.7 \text{ days} = \frac{365}{5.31}$$

Thus, we can see from this that on average each euro of credit sale remains in receivables for 68.7 days. Generally, a lower average collection period is better.

8.2 What is solvency?

Solvency ratios measure the ability of the business to meet its long-term obligations. In this chapter, we examine one ratio: the debt ratio. The debt ratio compares total liabilities to total assets:

$$\text{Debt ratio} = \frac{\text{Total liabilities}}{\text{Total assets}}$$

For 2009, Heliard's calculation would be as follows:

$$\text{Debt ratio} = \frac{€\,134\,500}{€\,261\,500}$$

$$0.52 = \frac{€\,134\,500}{€\,261\,500}$$

For 2008:

$$\text{Debt ratio} = \frac{€\,130\,000}{€\,245\,000}$$

$$0.53 = \frac{€\,130\,000}{€\,245\,000}$$

We can see from the difference between the two years that very little change occurred in solvency based on the debt ratio.

Summary

Financial assets and liabilities are a major share of the overall assets and liabilities in many businesses. Outside cash and cash equivalents, financial assets are classified into four categories: financial assets and liabilities at fair value through profit and loss; held-to-maturity investments; loans and receivables; and available-for-sale investments.

Financial assets and liabilities at fair value through profit and loss are those that are being held for trading. Held-to-maturity investments are financial assets with fixed or determinable payments, which the business intends to hold until maturity. Loans and receivables include financial assets and liabilities that have a fixed or determinable payment but are not traded on an active market. All other financial assets and financial liabilities not included in one of the three preceding categories are classified as available for sale. Held-to-maturity investments, loans and receivables are accounted for by the amortized cost using the effective interest method.

An issue with trade accounts receivable relates to nonpayment by customers. The business must make an estimate of the uncollectible amount when the sales occur, and record this in the allowance for uncollectible accounts. The allowance account is a contra to the trade receivables account. The estimate can be made using either the percentage-of-sale method or the aged receivables method. When the actual default occurs, the customer's balance is written off against the allowance for uncollectible accounts. As a result, defaults do not affect the statement of income, nor current assets, total assets or equity on the statement of financial position.

The growing use of complex financial instruments like derivatives, especially for hedging, has made them a common inclusion in the financial statements of multinational companies. Because they are based on the values of other factors like commodities indexes, interest rates and securities prices, the accounting can be complex and also is beyond the scope of this book.

LEARNING OUTCOME 1
Cash and Cash Equivalents Explained

Cash includes cash on hand and demand deposits, while cash equivalents are highly liquid investments that can be converted to a known amount of cash, normally within three months. Cash can be restricted in the sense that it is designated for a specific purpose. Banks and other creditors may require that the entity keep part of cash as a compensating balance. Cash can also be kept in a petty cash fund for minor and miscellaneous disbursement needs.

Because most cash is kept in commercial banks, an important procedure is the cash reconciliation, which ensures that the cash balance provided by the bank agrees with the cash balance in the entity's ledger account. The reconciliation is carried out by comparing the detail in the bank statement with the cash ledger account and noting differences. In some cases, the business may have cash receipts or disbursements that have been recorded but have not yet been processed by the bank. These are included in the reconciliation to calculate a 'true' cash balance.

However, in some cases the bank will have cash receipts and disbursements included in the company's bank account that have not been recorded on the company's ledger. These items must not only be included in the reconciliation but also must be recorded using journal entries.

LEARNING OUTCOME 2
Financial Assets and Liabilities Defined

Financial assets and liabilities are classified into four categories depending on the characteristics of the asset or liability and management's intention. The first category is 'a financial asset or financial liability at fair value through profit or loss', more commonly known as held for trading. The second category is held-to-maturity investments, which are financial assets with fixed or determinable payments and a fixed maturity. To be classified as held to maturity, management must have the intention and the ability to hold the financial asset to maturity.

Loans and receivables are the third category and include financial assets with fixed and determinable payments that are not quoted on an active market. The fourth category is available for sale, which includes financial assets not classified as either loans or receivables, held to maturity or at fair value through profit or loss.

LEARNING OUTCOME 3
Effective Interest Rate Method Applied

Held-to-maturity investments, loans and receivables and other financial liabilities not included in the four categories listed above are accounted for using amortized cost using the effective interest method. The amortized cost is the difference between the initial amount recorded for the financial asset or liability less principal payments received over the term. This difference is amortized based on the carrying amount of the financial asset or liability during each period.

LEARNING OUTCOME 4
Accounting for Trade Accounts Explained

Trade accounts receivable and trade accounts payable are debts created when a customer buys goods or services from a supplier. Trade receivables and payables are accounted for at amortized cost using the effective interest method.

With trade accounts receivable, an additional consideration is when a customer is delinquent on the amount owed or actually defaults. This may occur for a number of reasons, including bankruptcy of the customer. Based on experience with uncollectible amounts, businesses usually estimate the amount of uncollectible receivables they are likely to have when the sale is made. Businesses use either the percentage of sales method or the aged receivables method to make the estimate. Under the allowance method, when the estimate is calculated, an amount is recorded in the allowance for uncollectibles account and the amount is expensed immediately.

When a default occurs, the unpaid amount is then removed from trade accounts receivable with a credit and debited to the allowance for uncollectible account. Since the allowance for uncollectibles account is a contra-asset account, the journal entry to write off the defaulted amount affects only the statement of financial position. *The entry does not affect the statement of comprehensive income.*

LEARNING OUTCOME 5
Credit Card Accounting Receivables Explained

Many sales are made using credit cards. If the credit card is internal, which means that it is owned by the business making the sale, the customer's credit card account is a specialized form of a trade accounts receivable. In this case, we account for the credit card purchase in a manner that is similar to any trade account receivable.

However, businesses often use third-party credit card service providers like Visa and MasterCard. In these cases, the sale does not result in a receivable from the customer because the credit card service provider pays the business for what the customer has charged. Thus, the receivable belongs to the credit card service provider. The business may have a short waiting period before it is reimbursed by the credit card service provider, and the business must usually pay a service fee to the credit card service provider, which is recorded as a sales expense.

LEARNING OUTCOME 6
Accounting for Notes Explained

Notes are promissory notes whereby the issuer promises to pay a certain amount of money on the maturity date. For the issuer, the note is a note payable. The investor who is owed the money will record the note as a note receivable. Notes can be interest bearing or noninterest bearing. Both the issuer and the investor are required to use amortized cost using the effective interest method to account for the amount owed. Notes can be issued for trade purposes. In other words, a note may be used instead of a trade account payable to purchase goods or services. Notes can also be issued for nontrade purposes when a business lends money to an employee for personal reasons.

LEARNING OUTCOME 7
Bond Accounting Explained

Bonds are a form of debt for long-term financing. The bond issuer is the entity borrowing the money, while the investor is the entity lending the money. Bonds exist in many variations. Most have a stated interest rate and interest payments are made to the investor semi-annually or on some other schedule. For term bonds, the principal is paid on the maturity date. However, with serial bonds, principal is paid over the life of the bond. Bonds can also be callable, secured, unsecured or zero interest.

When bonds are issued, the stated interest rate may vary from the current bond market rate. When the bond market rate is above the stated rate, the bond will sell for a discount. When the bond market is below the stated rate, the bond will sell at a premium. The resulting discount or premium is amortized over the life of the bond using the effective interest method. In the cases of bonds that sell at a discount, this amortization increases the amount of interest expense recognized by the issuer. When the bond is sold at a premium, the amortization decreases the amount of interest expense.

The opposite is true for the investor. When the investor buys the bonds at a discount, the amortization of the premium will increase the interest revenue recognized. When the investor pays a premium to acquire bonds, the amortization of the premium will decrease the interest revenue recognized.

LEARNING OUTCOME 8
Assets and Liabilities Evaluated

Several ratios related to financial assets and liabilities are used to evaluate both liquidity and solvency. Liquidity refers to the availability of cash in the near future after deducting financial commitments over the same period. Solvency is the ability to pay obligations when they become due.

Liquidity measures include working capital, which is the difference between current assets and current liabilities. This is converted into the current ratio, which divides current assets by current liabilities. To provide a more rigorous measure of liquidity, an acid-test ratio is calculated. This calculates cash and cash equivalents, trade accounts receivable and marketable securities only as a percentage of current liabilities. These current assets would usually be converted to cash within three months or less. Even more rigorous is the cash ratio, which divides cash, cash equivalents and marketable securities by current liabilities. The business would normally be able to obtain cash needed for settlement of an obligation immediately or within a few days at most.

Both the current ratio and the acid-test ratio include trade accounts receivable. Thus, an important question is how long it takes for these receivables to be collected and converted to cash. The receivables turnover ratio is calculated by dividing net credit sales by average receivables. Then the receivables turnover ratio is divided into 365 to calculate the average collection period, which provides some information about how quickly receivables can be converted into cash.

Key terms

Acid-test ratio	IOU
Aged receivables method	Issuer
Allowance method	Liquidity
Amortized cost	Loans and receivables
Available-for-sale financial assets	Maturity date
Average collection period	Net receivables
Bank overdraft	Nominal interest rate
Bankruptcy	Note
Bank statement	Note payable
Bond	Note receivable
Callable bond	Percentage of sales method
Cash ratio	Petty cash
Compensating balance	Premium
Coupon rate	Promissory note
Current ratio	Receivables turnover ratio
Debt ratio	Restricted cash
Discount	Secured bond
Face value	Serial bond
Financial asset	Solvency
Financial asset or financial liability at fair value through profit or loss	Stated interest rate
	Term
Financial liability	Term bond
Held for trading	Unsecured bond
Held-to-maturity investments	Voucher
Imprest petty cash	Zero-interest bond

Terminology review

For each of the following statements, insert the correct term from the preceding list of key terms. Each key term may be used more than once.

1. The _____ or _____ is the amount used to calculate the interest due based on the face value of a note or bond.
2. A _____ is provided by a bank and shows all activity on the entity's bank account for some period of time.
3. _____ is a cash amount set aside for a specific purpose.
4. The _____ divides cash and cash equivalents + trade receivables + marketable securities by current liabilities.
5. _____ (also _____) refers to cash kept on hand to pay small expenses such as postage, delivery charges, entertainment for clients and other miscellaneous expenses.
6. _____ are financial assets or liabilities with fixed or determinable payments that are not quoted on an active market.
7. A _____ is a bond on which the principal is paid in instalments over the term of the bond.
8. _____ is the availability of cash in the near future after taking account of financial commitments over this period.
9. The _____ of accounting for uncollectible accounts records an estimated amount of uncollectible receivables as uncollectible expense when revenue is recognized.
10. The _____ is calculated by dividing current assets by current liabilities.
11. A _____ is a debt instrument in which the issuer promises to pay an amount of money over time plus a stated interest rate.
12. A _____ is a formal contract between two entities whereby the issuer agrees to pay a specified amount of money plus interest in exchange for either the loan of money or the purchase of goods or services.
13. A _____ is a written record as proof of an expenditure or disbursement.
14. The _____ estimates the amount of uncollectible accounts as a proportion of sales for the period.
15. _____ is the availability of cash over the longer term to meet financial commitments as they come due.
16. To calculate the _____, the receivables turnover ratio is divided into 365.
17. A _____ is a bond on which the principal is due on the maturity date.
18. A _____ is an asset that is cash, an equity instrument of another entity, a contractual right to receive cash or another financial asset.
19. _____ are financial assets with fixed or determinable payments and a fixed maturity that an entity has the positive intention and ability to hold to maturity.
20. _____ is a legal procedure that provides protection from creditors while the business is either reorganized or liquidated.

21. A _____ occurs in situations when a business overdraws the amount of cash it has in its bank account.

22. _____ is calculated by subtracting the allowance account for uncollectible accounts from trade accounts receivable.

23. A _____ is a bond that pays no interest but on which the investor earns a return by purchasing the bond at a discounted price.

24. A _____ results when the market price of the bond is below the stated value of the bond.

25. A _____ is a minimum cash balance that must be kept on hand at all times as part of a loan agreement with a lender.

26. _____ are financial assets other than cash or cash equivalent that are not classified as (a) loans and receivables, (b) held-to-maturity investments, or (c) financial assets at fair value through profit or loss.

27. _____ is the date on which the issuer must repay the principal.

28. A _____ results when the market price of a bond is above the stated value of the bond.

29. The _____ is calculated by dividing total liabilities by total assets.

30. The _____ is calculated by dividing net credit sales by average receivables.

31. The _____ estimates the amount of uncollectible receivables based on the likelihood of collection for the time the amounts have been outstanding.

32. A _____ is a liability that is a contractual obligation to deliver cash or another financial asset, or a contract that will be settled in the entity's own equity instruments.

33. _____ is the repayment period for a note or bond.

34. A _____ grants the issuer the right to purchase the bonds from investors, at a certain price.

35. A _____ is a financial asset or financial liability that is either classified as held for trading or on initial recognition is designated as at fair value through profit and loss.

36. A _____ is backed by a pledge of some asset such as real estate on which the investor has a priority claim in the event of liquidation.

37. The _____ divides cash and cash equivalents + marketable securities by current liabilities.

38. The _____ is the party who must repay the amount owed on a note.

Application exercises

1. Collier Publications Inc. purchases a forklift for use in its warehouse for €43 000 on 1 January 2009. The company has agreed to pay the seller in equal annual instalments over three years. The seller charges 8% interest on the loan, which is equal to the current market interest rate. How much is each annual payment?

2. Collier Publications Inc. purchases a forklift for use in its warehouse for €43 000 on 1 January 2009. The company has agreed to pay the seller in equal *monthly instalments* over three years. The seller charges 8% interest on the loan, which reflects the current market interest rate. How much is each annual payment?

3. On 1 January 2009, Premier Financial Ltd purchased equipment from Tam Banking Equipment Inc. Premier paid £130 000 in cash and signed a noninterest-bearing note for £550 000, due in full on 31 December 2011. The market rate of interest is 9%.
   a. Record Premier's journal entry related to the purchase of the equipment.
   b. Record the adjusting entries for 2009, 2010 and 2011.
   c. Record the journal entry for the payment of the note on 31 December 2011.

4. Based on the information provided in 3, assume that the note had a stated interest rate of 7% and that interest-only payments are paid semi-annually on 30 June and 31 December of each year.
   a. Record Premier's journal entry related to the purchase of the equipment.
   b. Record the adjusting entries for 2009, 2010 and 2011.
   c. Record the journal entry for the payment of the note on 31 December 2011.

5. Based on the information provided in 3, assume that the note had a stated interest rate of 7% and that the loan is fully amortizing. Payments are made semi-annually on 30 June and 31 December of each year.
   a. Record Premier's journal entry related to the purchase of the equipment.
   b. Record the adjusting entries for 2009, 2010 and 2011.
   c. Record the journal entry for the payment of the note on 31 December 2011.

6. Ren Motors Ltd, which manufactures energy-efficient 'smart' autos, issued ¥100 000 000 of 20-year bonds with a stated interest rate of 9% to be paid semi-annually on 30 June and 31 December. The bonds were issued on 1 January 2009 at 97. On 30 June 2012, Ren retired the bonds at 101. Record the journal entry for the issuance of the bonds, interest payment dates and retirement.

7. Restaurant Concepts Inc. issued $20 000 000 of 5-year bonds on 1 January 2008 with a stated interest rate of 7%. Interest is paid annually on 30 June. The market rate on this date was 6.5%.
   a. Compute the price that the bonds sold for.
   b. Record the journal entry for the issue.
   c. Record the journal entries on the interest payment dates.
   d. Record the repayment of the principal amount on the maturity date.

8. Restaurant Concepts Inc. issued $20 000 000 of 5-year bonds on 1 January 2008 with a stated interest rate of 7%. Interest is paid annually on 30 June. The market rate on this date was 7.75%.
   a. Compute the price that the bonds sold for.
   b. Record the journal entry for the issue.
   c. Record the journal entries on the interest payment dates.
   d. Record the repayment of the principal amount on the maturity date.

COMPREHENSIVE APPLICATION PROBLEMS

9. A trainee in your office has prepared draft accounts for a client for the year ended 31 March 2010, but has not dealt with the adjustments for accrued expenses, prepaid expenses, bad and doubtful debts and depreciation. Following the preparation of the statement of income, the trainee prepared

the statement of financial position shown below. You have been asked to complete the final accounts.

Draft Statement of Financial Position as at 31 March 2010 (Before Adjustments)		
Noncurrent assets		
Equipment at cost	$175 000	
Accumulated depreciation at 31 March 2009	(85 400)	89 600
Current assets		
Inventories	42 339	
Trade accounts receivable – Net	149 411	
Bank account	6 280	198 030
		287 630
Equity		201 070
Current liabilities		86 560
Trade payables		287 630

The trainee has given you the following information about the remaining adjustments:

i.   The last invoice received for electricity covered the three-month period to 31 January 2010. The invoice was for $6870.
ii. Rent of $28 500 for the six months to 30 June 2010 was paid in January.
iii. The trade receivables figure of $149 411 is stated after deducting the existing allowance for doubtful debts of $7900 from the trade accounts receivable balance of $157 311.
iv. The total trade accounts receivable balance of $157 311 includes a balance of $660, which has been outstanding for eight months. The company has decided to write off this balance.
v.   The client's policy is to allow for doubtful debts on the basis of the length of time the debt has been outstanding. The aged analysis of trade receivables at 31 March 2010 and the required allowance is shown below:

Age of Debt	Balance	Allowance Required
0–30 days	$125 275	Nil
31–60 days	27 200	20% of balances
Over 60 days	4 836	75% of balances
	157 311	

vi. Depreciation is to be provided at a rate of 20% per annum on the reducing balance basis.

Required:
   (a) Calculate the correct balance at 31 March 2010 for each of the following:
      a.   Accrued expenses
      b.   Prepaid expenses

c. Allowance for doubtful accounts

d. Accumulated depreciation

(b) Prepare the corrected statement of financial position as at 31 March 2010. [ACCA adapted]

10. You are preparing the year-end accounts for a client who buys and sells industrial machinery. You are dealing with bad debts and closing inventories:

(a) Bad and doubtful debts

Included in the trade receivables balance is an amount of $3574 that has been outstanding for just over a year. Your client has decided to write this balance off.

The allowance for doubtful debts is to be calculated as follows:

- 6% of balances that have been outstanding for between 30 and 59 days.
- 50% of balances that have been outstanding for 60 days or more.

At the end of the previous year the allowance for doubtful debts was $4516.

The trade receivables balances, including the irrecoverable balance of $3574, have been analysed as follows:

Age of Debt	
Less than 30 days	$35 591
30 days to 59 days	18 700
60 days and over	9 722
Total receivables	$65 013

At the year end, your client had three machines in inventories. Details of the machines are:

Machine Type	Packing Machine	Industrial Press	Forklift Truck
Cost	$5 890	$11 670	$3 926
Expected sales value	5 500	14 900	4 200
Expenses of sale	200	475	720

Required:

a. Briefly explain the difference between a bad debt and a doubtful debt.

b. Calculate the total charge to the statement of income for the year in respect of bad and doubtful debts and the value to be reported in the statement of financial position for trade receivables.

c. Briefly state the basic rule to be applied to the valuation of inventories.

d. Calculate the value of closing inventories to be reported in the statement of financial position. [ACCA adapted]

11. Wilson is preparing his bank reconciliation at 31 May 2011. His bank statement shows a balance of $228 cash at the bank. The balance on the bank account in his general ledger is $113 (credit). He has noted the following reasons for the difference:

(i) Cheque number 958602 was incorrectly recorded in Wilson's cashbook at $760. The cheque was correctly debited on the bank statement on 2 May as $670.

(ii) Bank charges of $428 were debited by the bank on 4 May.

(iii) A customer's cheque for $320 was returned by Wilson's bank in May as the customer had insufficient funds in his account. Wilson has not recorded the return of the cheque in his records.

(iv) The bank has incorrectly credited Wilson's account with interest of $220. This is interest on a deposit account held by Wilson personally. The bank had not corrected the error by 31 May.

(v) A deposit of $850 entered in Wilson's cashbook on 31 May was credited on the bank statement on 3 June.

(vi) Five cheques have not yet been presented at the bank. These are:

Cheque Number	$	
956784	625	See note (vii)
956892	326	
958452	469	
958541	122	
958668	87	
	1629	

(vii) Cheque number 956784 was lost in the post and was cancelled. Wilson has not recorded the cancellation of the cheque.

Required:

(a) Show Wilson's general ledger bank account including the necessary correcting entries.

(b) Prepare a reconciliation of the bank statement balance to the corrected general ledger balance.

(c) Indicate how the bank balance will be reported in Wilson's final accounts. [ACCA adapted]

Case Analysis
BOTSWANA WILD SAFARIS LLC

Botswana Wild Safaris LLC was introduced in Chapter 7. In this chapter we will continue the case by focusing on financial assets and liabilities. Recall that Tony Washford had purchased the company from Gerhardt Perst on 1 January 2009.

The following schedule shows the current assets of Botswana Wild Safaris on the date of acquisition (1 January 2009) and the three 31 December reporting dates:

€ Euros	Jan. 2009	31 Dec. 2009	31 Dec. 2010	31 Dec. 2011
Cash	110 000	214 200	807 000	1 160 500
Trade accounts receivable	615 000	424 000	365 000	410 000
Prepaid expenses	20 000	35 000	70 000	80 000
Other current assets	55 000	45 000	80 000	88 000

The trade account receivables are reported at the gross amount owed by customers, mostly tour operators that subcontracted safari trips to Botswana Wild Tours. After careful research, Tony found that his estimate of uncollectible expenses was 3% of total sales each year. In 2009 customers defaulted on €13 000, and in 2010 and 2011 defaults were €14 000 and €37 000, respectively. Sales in 2009 were €800 000; €1 110 000 in 2010; and €1460 000 in 2011.

Noncurrent liabilities

On the acquisition date, the company owed notes totalling €1 100 000 with 9% annual interest. These notes were due in full on 31 December 2009. On that same date, Tony borrowed €200 000 on a new note with the same interest rate, which was due in full on 31 December 2012. Also, on 31 December 2009, Tony privately placed a term bond issue with an insurance company. The bond face value was €700 000 with a stated interest rate of 6.5% paid annually. The bond was sold to the insurance company at par. The bond was due on 31 December 2014. The new note and the bond are accounted for using the effective interest method.

The following schedule shows the current liabilities of Botswana Wild Safaris on the date of acquisition (1 January 2009) and the three 31 December reporting dates:

	Jan. 2009	31 Dec. 2009	31 Dec. 2010	31 Dec. 2011
Trade accounts payable	160 000	128 200	330 000	270 000
Accrued liabilities	45 000	25 000	10 000	5 000
Other current liabilities	30 000	10 000	15 000	15 000

REQUIRED:

Record all transactions and adjusting entries for 2009 to 2011. Construct the current assets, current liabilities and noncurrent liabilities sections of the statement of financial position on the reporting dates.

End notes

1. *Mapping Global Capital Markets*, Fourth Annual Report, McKinsey Global Institute, January 2008.
2. *Global Financial Stability Report*, International Monetary Fund, October 2008.

Suggested reading

Bookstaber, Richard (2007) *A Demon of Our Design: Markets, Hedge Funds, and the Perils of Financial Innovation*, Hoboken, NJ: John Wiley & Sons.

Equity 9

Capital at risk

The third element of the statement of financial position is equity (see IFRS box).

Equity represents the economic interest that the owners have in the business entity. Once all the liabilities of the business are settled, the remainder of the assets belong to the investors. This is a critical point, because it means that once the obligations are discharged, the business has no other commitment to a creditor and certainly *no obligation to share profit.*

For example, a business borrows €100 000 at 6% interest for one year. At maturity, the principal is repaid along with the interest due for a total of €106 000, and no further obligation exists. All economic benefits that follow belong to the investors. However, if the €100 000 is obtained by selling additional ownership shares in the business, the capital is provided by an investor – not a creditor. No interest must be paid since the €100 000 is not a liability, but the investor will always be entitled to a proportional share of the equity.

On the other hand, the business entity is not required to pay an investor anything and, unless there is a contract to the contrary, the business is not required to return equity capital to investors. However, without an acceptable return for the use of their capital, investors will not invest. Therefore, the business entity has an incentive to provide a return to the investors.

If the business performs well, the investors are the ultimate beneficiaries after all creditors have been paid. If the business performs poorly, then the investors must absorb all losses. Even with losses, obligations to creditors must be settled. Thus, creditors have priority claims on the business ahead of equity investors. If a business is liquidated and its assets are distributed, creditors receive what is owed to them before equity owners are able to take any proceeds.

This relationship between creditors and investors – between debt and equity, respectively – is one of the most important concepts in business. Investors, whether individuals or institutions, vary with respect to the degree of risk they are willing to accept. Debt, by its nature, tends to be less risky, although this does not mean that debt is without risk or that someone who invests in debt instruments cannot lose his or her investment.

In general, less risky investments earn smaller returns. Thus, the higher the risk associated with the investment, the higher the return investors want. A risk-averse investor may be more interested in debt, knowing that the return is likely to be less than for equity but the likelihood of receiving the return is high, and the overall risk low. A risk-accepting investor purchases equity shares fully aware that, in general, the risk will be higher, but that the likelihood of receiving any return will be lower. However, that investor also knows that the potential return could be much higher.

Figure 9.1 illustrates these relationships between debt and equity as investment options.

FIGURE 9.1 DEBT VERSUS EQUITY

Investment	Return	Likelihood of Receiving Any Return	Risk
Debt	Fixed	Higher	Lower
Equity	Variable	Lower	Higher

Recall that equity has three elements: contributed capital, retained earnings and reserves. These are highlighted in the financial statements taxonomy shown in Figure 9.2.

In this chapter, we will examine each of these two equity components in detail. As a refresher, recall that a limited liability company is legally autonomous: it can engage in transactions, own assets and create debt obligations. Limited liability companies are owned by individuals and institutions, and the evidence of their ownership is share capital, which is why limited liability companies are referred to as share-based entities. Recall from Chapter 1 that limited liability companies are created by a government authority located in a particular jurisdiction. The

FIGURE 9.2 EQUITY ELEMENTS

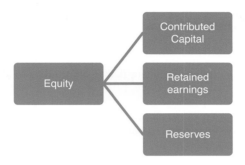

company's founders register the business with the authority, which grants legal status as a limited liability company. A founding slate of members or shareholders must usually be identified during the registration process.

LEARNING OUTCOME 1
EXPLAIN THE DIFFERENCE BETWEEN ORDINARY SHARES AND PREFERENCE SHARES

1.1   What are ordinary shares?

1.2   What are preference shares?

A share-based entity can have two general types of equity: ordinary shares and preference shares. Each type of share may have different classes. Whether a limited liability company chooses to have preference shares or classes of ordinary shares depends on the specific needs of that business and its owners. Many companies have neither preference shares nor share classes. Indeed, not all jurisdictional authorities permit preference shares and share classes. However, all limited liability companies must have at least one class of ordinary shares. Figure 9.3 shows an equity structure illustrating both preference shares and classes of ordinary shares.

FIGURE 9.3 EQUITY STRUCTURE WITH ORDINARY AND PREFERENCE SHARES

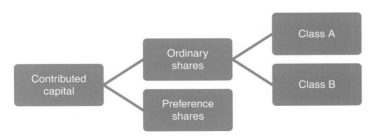

1.1 What are ordinary shares?

Ordinary shares (see IFRS box) represent the ownership interest of last resort – that group of shareholders who own the residual interest in the assets of the business entity.

IFRS An ordinary share is 'an equity instrument that is subordinate to all other classes of equity instruments'.

Ordinary shares are also known as common shares or common stock. Ordinary shareholders typically have voting rights to elect the board of directors who represent the shareholders' interests. Ordinary shareholders receive a distribution of profits from the business only if and when the board declares a dividend. If a share-based business is liquidated, the ordinary shareholders receive a distribution of the liquidation proceeds only after creditors and preference shareholders have been paid. Ordinary shares may have a pre-emptive right which means that shareholders have first right of refusal when additional shares are issued.

FIGURE 9.4 CLASSES OF STOCK

BERKSHIRE HATHAWAY INC.
1440 KIEWIT PLAZA
OMAHA, NEBRASKA 68131
TELEPHONE (402) 346-1400

WARREN E. BUFFETT, CHAIRMAN

Memo

From: Warren Buffett
Subject: Comparative Rights and Relative Prices of Berkshire Class A and Class B Stock

Comparison of Berkshire Hathaway Inc. Class A and Class B Common Stock

Berkshire Hathaway Inc. has two classes of common stock designated Class A and Class B. A share of Class B common stock has the rights of 1/30th of a share of Class A common stock except that a Class B share has 1/200th of the voting rights of a Class A share (rather than 1/30th of the vote). Each share of a Class A common stock is convertible at any time, at the holder's option, into 30 shares of Class B common stock. This conversion privilege does not extend in the opposite direction. That is, holders of Class B shares are not able to convert them into Class A shares. Both Class A & B shareholders are entitled to attend the Berkshire Hathaway Annual Meeting which is held the first Saturday in May.

In some cases, share-based businesses will have two or more classes of ordinary shares. Founders of a company may wish to increase the amount of contributed capital but also to retain control of the business. Thus, one class of shares may be reserved for the business's founders, who have a higher number of votes per share. For example, Berkshire Hathaway Inc.'s two classes of common stock are described in a publicly available memorandum from the company's chairman, Warren Buffett, as shown in Figure 9.4.

The convertibility feature mentioned in Figure 9.4 refers to the ability to exchange Class A stock for Class B stock. In other words, at the discretion of Class A owners, they can forfeit control of the business when, for example, they are ready to turn control over to Class B owners. A founding owner of a business may be ready to retire and allow his or her children to lead the business, for example. While the legal rights granted to each class of shares may differ, all shareholders must be treated equally within a class of shares. For example, if a dividend is declared for a particular share class, all shareholders in that class receive the dividend. No discrimination between shareholders within a class can occur.

1.2 What are preference shares?

Share-based entities can also have preference shares (or preferred shares). Features of preference shares vary. For example, most do not have voting rights. Some may have a convertible feature that allows the preference shares to be exchanged for ordinary shares at some point in the future. From an investor's point of view, preference shares offer two major advantages:

- First, the preference shareholders have priority over ordinary shareholders in the event of the business's liquidation, though preference shareholders are subordinate to creditors. Thus, creditors are paid first from any liquidation proceeds, then preference shareholders and finally ordinary shareholders.

- Second, preference shares have a stated dividend. Thus, preference shares provide a predictable return, such as interest that a creditor receives on debt. However, in addition the preference **shareholder** can benefit from any capital appreciation based on increases in share price.

From the business's perspective, preference shares provide another option for obtaining financial capital, since they appeal to investors who want both fixed income and the opportunity for capital appreciation.

GLOBAL PERSPECTIVE

Muslims comprise an estimated 20% of the world's population. Under Shari'a or Islamic law, preference shares are not permitted. The Shari'a, which governs many aspects of commercial dealings in Muslim life, prohibits separation of risk and reward. The Accounting and Auditing Organization for Islamic Financial Institutions (www.aaoifi.com) is a modern accounting standards setter. Among its pronouncements are Shari'a standards, which are the result of rulings by Islamic jurists who have the responsibility for interpreting Islamic religious law. According to Shari'a Standard No. 12 Sharika (Musharaka) and Modern Corporations, 'It is not permitted to issue preference shares, i.e., shares that have special financial characteristics that given them a priority at the date of liquidation of the company or at the date of distribution of profit.'

ON YOUR OWN

LEARNING OUTCOME REVIEW
1. Name the two major types of share capital.
2. What is the difference between ordinary shares and preference shares?
3. Do ordinary shares or preference shares have priority if the business is liquidated?

LEARNING OUTCOME 2
DEFINE AUTHORIZED SHARE CAPITAL, ISSUED SHARES, INVESTMENT IN OWN SHARES AND OUTSTANDING SHARES

2.1   What is authorized share capital?

2.2   How are shares issued?
    2.2.1   What is the difference between a private placement and public sale of shares?
    2.2.2   What is the difference between the primary versus secondary market?
    2.2.3   What are share-based payments?

2.3   What is investment in own shares?

2.4   What are outstanding shares?

2.1 What is authorized share capital?

As part of the registration process for a limited liability company, the jurisdictional authority grants permission for the company to have a certain number of authorized shares and a stated amount of authorized share capital. The number of authorized shares can be subsequently altered. In some jurisdictions, this requires the registration documents to be modified, while in others the business only needs to notify the jurisdictional authority that a resolution was passed by the board of directors increasing the amount of authorized share capital.

Authorized share capital is the amount of share capital that a share-based business can issue to owners, either by sale or grant. Shares also have a nominal value when authorized. The nominal value is the total currency amount of the authorized share capital divided. Nominal value can be divided by the number of shares authorized to calculate nominal value per share, also referred to as par value.

$$\text{Nominal value per share} = \frac{\text{Authorized share capital}}{\text{Number of shares authorized}}$$

A group of individuals wishes to form a business entity, to be called Christies Céramique SA, for the purpose of manufacturing fine dinnerware. The founders apply to the appropriate government authority where the business will be domiciled, which authorizes 10 000 000 ordinary shares with authorized share capital of €20 000 000. Thus, the nominal value of each share is calculated as follows:

$$\text{Nominal value per share} = \frac{€20\ 000\ 000}{10\ 000\ 000}$$

$$€2\ \text{per share} = \frac{€20\ 000\ 000}{10\ 000\ 000}$$

At the time shares are authorized, no accounting entry is recorded.

In addition to the registration with the government authority, share-based companies create a charter. A charter is an internal document, although it is sometimes filed with the government authority, that determines how the share-based business will be governed. For example, the charter may include provisions about how many directors will serve on the board, how they will be elected, and what issues require approval of the business's shareholders.

2.2 How are shares issued?

The board of directors can approve the issuance of shares up to the number authorized. Issued shares are those shares that are owned by investors. The individual or institution receiving the share is referred to as a member or shareholder, and is listed in the company's register of members, or shareholder register. This is the official list of shareholders at any point in time. Shares of publicly traded companies can be traded thousands of times daily on stock markets, so maintaining the register of members can be a formidable task. Nonetheless, the need for an accurate register is critical, as we will shortly see.

In some cases, members must vote to approve new share issuances. This is normally done at the general shareholders' meeting (or annual meeting), which is an annual gathering of members. General meetings provide members with an opportunity to hear management's views on business developments and financial results. Shareholders may have an opportunity to ask questions and raise concerns. In addition, the charter may require that members vote on certain issues such as the election of board members or to approve share issuances.

Between general meetings, the board may allot shares for issuance. Allotment is the process by which the board grants a right to receive shares, often subject to the vote of the membership. For example, the board may allot a certain number of shares for executive compensation. The board of directors may increase issued capital by allotting more shares up to the number of authorized shares. Once the allotted shares are issued, and consideration received, then they are referred to as allotted, called up and fully paid.

Shares can be issued by sale or by grant, and in some cases by a partial grant. A sale means that shares are issued to the investor for cash or other consideration such as real estate, shares of another business, or another asset. Issuance by grant means that shares are given to an individual or institution. Presumably, some consideration is received with a grant; for example, shares are issued to employees for job performance. In some cases, shares will be granted but the investor must pay some amount to receive the shares that is less than the share market value. These are referred to as share options; they grant the right, but not the obligation, to buy at a reduced price.

Recall that a nominal value is established when shares are authorized at registration. However, this amount does not necessarily reflect the real value of the shares, which is what the investor is willing to pay. When an active market for the shares exists, such as when the shares are publicly traded, then the real value is the market share price. However, for privately held companies, establishing a value for shares may be difficult. In any event, the amount that shares are issued for may differ from the nominal value. Thus, when a transaction to record an issuance occurs, the nominal value is recorded in the share capital account. Any amount over the nominal value is recorded in a separate share premium account.

Christies Céramique SA's board of directors votes to issue 50 000 shares with a nominal value of €2 each. These are sold to the founding investors on 20 October 2010 at €15 per share or €750 000 in total. The journal entry would be as follows:

Date	Account Titles	DR	CR
20 Oct. 2010	Cash	€750 000	
	Share capital		€100 000
	Share premium		650 000

The share capital account is credited for €100 000, which is calculated as the number of shares issued times the nominal value (50 000 × €2): The remainder of €650 000 is credited to the share premium account.

CAPITALIZATION

An active market exists if quoted prices are readily and regularly available that represent actual and regularly occurring market transactions on an arm's-length basis. Thus, the share's market price is the standard measure of a publicly traded company's value or capitalization. Capitalization refers to the value of the share-based entity as determined by market price.

If Christies, from the preceding example, were publicly traded, then the capitalization of the firm would be €750 000 (50 000 shares issued × €15). However, if the market price increases to €16, then the capitalization is €800 000 (50 000 × €16). Notice, however, that these changes to share price in the stock market have no impact on the accounting records of the business.

Over time, the real value of shares is likely to change, reflecting changes to the underlying worth of the company. This will, of course, change what investors are willing to pay for shares.

On 10 November 2010, Christies' board issued another 50 000 shares, which sold at €17 per share. The journal entry to record this transaction would be as follows:

Date	Account Titles	DR	CR
10 Nov. 2010	Cash	€850 000	
	Share capital		€100 000
	Share premium		750 000

Notice that the credit to share capital is the same as in the previous example's entry when the real value was €15 per share. Share capital is always recorded at nominal value, which for Christies is €2 per share.

2.2.1 WHAT IS THE DIFFERENCE BETWEEN A PRIVATE PLACEMENT AND A PUBLIC SALE OF SHARES?

If a company is privately held, then issuance takes the form of a private placement. This can be a sale of stock to the founders, as already described. Shares can also be sold to private investors, other businesses, and also venture capital firms that specialize in providing financing to privately held start-up and growth companies.

Jurisdictions often have strict limits on the number of potential investors who can be solicited to buy shares, or otherwise confine private placements to family members and previous business associates, for example. When a share-based business wants to sell shares to the public at large, the company must list on an equities market. This is a complex and costly process, normally guided by professionals such as investment bankers, attorneys, accountants and other specialists. Public listing also subjects the business to a much higher level of scrutiny by regulators and the investing public. Thus, offering shares for sale to the public is usually an option open only to companies with a credible history.

Shares are initially sold into a public equities market in an initial public offering or IPO. The IPO generates money for the business, as the following example illustrates.

Christies' board votes to 'take the company public' through an IPO. On 1 April 2011, Christies sells 500 000 shares at a market price of €24 per share. The journal entry to record this transaction would be as follows:

Date	Account Titles	DR	CR
1 Apr. 2010	Cash Share capital Share premium	€12 000 000	€1 000 000 11 000 000

2.2.2 WHAT IS THE DIFFERENCE BETWEEN THE PRIMARY VERSUS THE SECONDARY MARKET?

Christies sells its shares into the primary market, which results in the shares being listed on the equities market. After this primary sale, the listed shares will be traded between investors who buy and sell between themselves, which is the secondary market. The secondary market trades have no impact on the accounting records of the business. Figure 9.5 illustrates the difference between the primary and secondary markets.

FIGURE 9.5 PRIMARY VERSUS SECONDARY MARKETS

2.2.3 WHAT ARE SHARE-BASED PAYMENTS?

Although issuance of shares for cash is common, shares can be issued in exchange for any consideration. Shares are sometimes issued to make payments to acquire assets or to settle obligations in lieu of cash. For example, shares may be issued in exchange for real estate. Or a founder of a company may contribute an office building or even her existing company as part of the basis of a new business entity. In exchange, she would receive shares in the new business entity.

Shares may also be granted in other types of noncash transactions, or for an amount of cash that represents only a portion of the share's value. The most common example is when shares are granted to an executive or another employee as compensation. This could take the form of an outright grant with no cash involved. Or shares may be offered to employees as part of their compensation at below the market value. Following are some examples.

EXAMPLE 1: SHARES ISSUED IN EXCHANGE FOR REAL ESTATE

On 1 June 2011, Christies' board issues 40 000 shares to an investor in exchange for a building. The board retained a professional appraiser whose opinion of the building's value was €1 400 000. The journal entry to record the transaction would be:

Date	Account Titles	DR	CR
1 June 2011	Building Share capital Share premium	€1 400 000	 €80 000 1 320 000

Notice that the transaction is valued at the fair value of the asset received – the building. Share capital is recorded at €80 000 (40 000 shares issued × €2 nominal value) and the remainder is recorded in the share premium account.

EXAMPLE 2: SHARES ISSUED IN EXCHANGE FOR SHARES IN ANOTHER COMPANY

On 15 July 2011, Christies' board voted to acquire all the shares of a privately held family business, Frederick Stein AG, in exchange for 100 000 Christies shares. The shares are to be delivered on 15 September 2011, which is the acquisition date. Since the fair value of Frederick Stein AG cannot be reliably measured, Christies uses the market value of its own shares to record the transaction. On 15 September 2011 Christies' share price is €35 per share.

Date	Account Titles	DR	CR
15 Sep. 2011	Investment in Frederick Stein AG	€3 500 000	
	Share capital		€100 000
	Share premium		1 650 000
	Shares deliverable		1 750 000

Notice that half the shares – those issued on 15 September – are classified as share capital and share premium as before. The obligation to deliver the other 50 000 shares is recognized as a liability to be discharged on 1 October 2011. On 1 October 2011, Christies must now deliver the remaining 50 000 shares. However, by this date share price had risen to €40. Christies would therefore make the following journal entry:

Date	Account Titles	DR	CR
15 Sep. 2011	Investment in Frederick Stein AG	€250 000	
	Shares deliverable	1 750 00	
	Share capital		€100 000
	Share premium		1 950 000

EXAMPLE 3: SHARES ISSUED AS PART OF EMPLOYEE COMPENSATION

Jamila Shurpawala was hired as chief executive officer of Christies on 1 January 2011. The hiring agreement specified that she would have the option to purchase 2000 Christies shares for €10 per share once she had remained in the CEO position for one full year. On 31 December 2011, after one year on the job, Jamila exercised her option to purchase the shares. On this date, Christies' shares were trading for €45 each. The journal entry to record the transaction would be as follows.

Date	Account Titles	DR	CR
31 Dec. 2011	Employee compensation Share capital Shares premium	€90 000	 €4 000 86 000

A variant of the share option is a rights issue. A rights issue allows existing shareholders to purchase shares at a discounted price in proportion to their current shareholdings. In some jurisdictions, rights issues are a common feature when new shares are issued, because legally shareholders have a right of first refusal on new share issuances, referred to as pre-emptive rights.

2.3 What is investment in own shares?

Share-based entities frequently acquire their own shares by either purchasing the shares from private investors or through the public market. The business purchases its own shares for different reasons. For example, the business may acquire shares in preparation to grant those shares to an executive or other employee as compensation. A company may also purchase its own shares simply because they are a good investment, a point we will return to later in a case study of Brik's Restaurants plc. Another motive would be to amass shares to use in a bid to take over another company.

When a company invests in its own shares, they are classified as investment in own shares (also treasury shares). Investment in own shares is a contra account to equity. These shares are not deducted from the share capital account or the share premium account. When the purchase entry is recorded, unlike the issuance entry, no distinction is made between nominal and real value. The entity simply records the total amount paid for the shares in the investment in own shares account.

On 5 January 2011, Christies acquires 700 of its own shares, paying €16 per share. The journal entry would be as follows:

Date	Account Titles	DR	CR
5 Jan. 2011	Investment in own shares Cash	€11 200	 €11 200

On 10 January 2011, Christies purchases another 300 shares at €18 per share. The journal entry would be as follows:

Date	Account Titles	DR	CR
10 Jan. 2011	Investment in own shares Cash	€7 400	€7 400

2.4 What are outstanding shares?

The company is now in possession of 1000 shares, for which it paid a total of €18 600. When this amount in the investment in own shares account is deducted from issued shares, the result is outstanding shares. We can summarize the preceding share capital transactions for authorized, issued, investment in own shares and outstanding shares for Christies Céramique SA. as follows:

Category	Number of Shares	Amount
Authorized	20 000 000	n/a
Issued	742 000	€18 500 000
Treasury shares	(1 000)	(18 600)
Outstanding	741 000	€18 481 400

ON YOUR OWN

LEARNING OUTCOME REVIEW

1. What are authorized shares?
2. What is the nominal value or par value of a share? What is the real value?
3. What is a charter? What are examples of common provisions found in a charter?
4. What is an issued share? How is an issued share different from an authorized share?
5. To what does the term 'member' refer?
6. What is the register of members?
7. What is the purpose of the general shareholders' meeting?
8. Explain what a share premium account is.
9. What is a share-based payment? Give examples of the different forms a share-based payment can take.

10. Why would a company invest in its own shares? How is investment in own shares accounted for?
11. What are outstanding shares?

LEARNING OUTCOME PRACTICE

1. A company has 10 000 shares issued, the maximum number it is permitted to issue, and 1000 investment in own shares. Nominal value is €1.50 per share. Real value has always been €7 per share. What is the outstanding number of shares?
   a. 11 000
   b. 9000
   c. 10 000
   d. Not enough information to answer

2. A company has 10 000 shares issued, the maximum number it is permitted to issue, and 1000 investment in own shares. Nominal value is €1.50 per share. Real value has always been €7 per share. What is the authorized number of shares?
   a. 11 000
   b. 9000
   c. 10 000
   d. Not enough information to answer

3. A company has 10 000 shares issued, the maximum number it is permitted to issue, and 1000 investment in own shares. Nominal value is €1.50 per share. Real value has always been €7 per share. What is the amount of authorized share capital?
   a. €15 000
   b. €60 000
   c. €70 000
   d. Not enough information to answer

4. A company has 10 000 shares issued, the maximum number it is permitted to issue, and 1000 investment in own shares. Nominal value is €1.50 per share. Real value has always been €7 per share. What is the amount of issued share capital?
   a. €15 000
   b. €60 000
   c. €70 000
   d. Not enough information to answer

5. A company has 10 000 shares issued, the maximum number it is permitted to issue, and 1000 investment in own shares. Nominal value is €1.50 per share. Real value has always been €7 per share. What is the amount of share premium?
   a. €15 000
   b. €60 000
   c. €70 000
   d. Not enough information to answer

6. A limited liability company issued 50 000 ordinary shares with a nominal value of $0.25 each at a premium of $0.50 per share. The cash received was correctly recorded, but the full

amount was credited to the ordinary share capital. Which of the following journal entries is needed to correct this error?

		Debit	Credit
a.	Share premium account	$25 000	
	Share capital account		$25 000
b.	Share capital account	$25 000	
	Share premium account		$25 000
c.	Share capital account	$37 500	
	Share premium account		$37 500
d.	Share capital account	$25 000	
	Cash		$25 000

ACCA adapted

LEARNING OUTCOME 3
EXPLAIN THE ACCOUNTING FOR CASH DIVIDENDS, SCRIP ISSUES AND SHARE SPLITS

3.1 What is the process for paying dividends?
    3.1.1 What is the declaration date?
    3.1.2 What is the date of record?
    3.1.3 What is the payment date?

3.2 How do we account for preference dividends?
    3.2.1 What is a cumulative preference dividend?
    3.2.2 What is a participating feature for a preference share?

3.3 What are non cash dividends?
    3.3.1 What is a scrip issue?
    3.2.2 What are share splits?

3.1 What is the process for paying dividends?

Recall that a dividend is a distribution of profit to owners. Dividends take three major forms: cash payments, scrip dividends and share splits. Dividends are paid only on outstanding shares and must be declared by the board of directors in share-based businesses. A board may declare any amount of dividend on ordinary shares. As a practical matter, the board is usually advised by the company's chief financial officer and others on the amount of the dividend that should be paid to owners. The board then takes a decision about the dividend, and a formal dividend declaration is made, which is entered into the minutes of the board's meeting.

BREYDEN FOODS BOARD MEETING, 31 MARCH 2009

Chairman of the Board Marcus Breyden: The next item on the board's agenda is whether or not to declare a dividend. Maria, what is your recommendation for this quarter?

Chief Financial Officer Maria O'Brien: Marcus, I think we should declare a $0.70 per share dividend. Our cash position is strong, so there are no worries there. This is the amount we have paid for the last six quarters, so we would be consistent. We have no plans to issue new shares in the equities market for the next year, so no reason exists to increase the dividend to make our shares more attractive. So I recommend we stay the course.

Breyden: I agree. Are there any questions from other directors?

Board member Riad Jarjour: When will the dividend be paid?

O'Brien: I think 30 April. We usually pay at the end of the month following the quarter that the dividend is declared. It can be any date the board wishes, but this would be consistent with our past practice.

Breyden: Again, I agree that we want to be as consistent as possible.

O'Brien: Also, I just consulted my diary and see that 15 April is a Friday. Since that is the end of the work week for us, then I suggest we make that the date of record.

Breyden: Does anyone have any thoughts on that? (Pause) No? Then let's take a vote.

The board votes and passes the resolution to declare the dividend.

3.1.1 WHAT IS THE DECLARATION DATE?

Notice in the partial transcript from the Breyden board meeting that three dates are set by the board: the declaration date, the date of record and the payment date. The date on which the board declares the dividend is the declaration date. When the board declares the dividend, it becomes a legal obligation of the entity. At this point, the accounting function will make a journal entry to record this obligation.

The board of directors of Breyden Foods Inc. met on 31 March 2009 and declared a $0.70 dividend on each of the 100 000 outstanding ordinary shares. The journal entry to record this transaction would be:

Date	Account Titles	DR	CR
31 Mar. 2009	Dividends Dividend payable	$70 000	$70 000

3.1.2 WHAT IS THE DATE OF RECORD?

The board also set two other dates. The first is the date of record, which is the date that determines which shareholders will receive the dividend: these are the shareholders on the date of record. Recall that a share-based business maintains a register of members to determine who the legal owners of the shares are on a particular date. For publicly traded companies, once all equity market transactions for the date of record are settled to the register of members, this list becomes the official record from which dividends are paid. Once the date of record passes, the shares trade ex-dividend, which means that someone who purchases the shares will not receive the dividend that has already been declared.

3.1.3 WHAT IS THE PAYMENT DATE?

The second date is the payment date on which the payment is made.

Breyden's board also sets 15 April 2009 as the date of record. When all transactions are settled after trading on this date, the legal list of shareholders can be determined. The board sets the payment date at 30 April 2009, which means that the cash dividend is sent via cheque or electronic funds transfer on that date. The journal entry would be:

Date	Account Titles	DR	CR
30 Apr. 2009	Dividends payable Cash	$70 000	$70 000

Figure 9.6 summarizes the dividend declaration and payment process in graphical form.

FIGURE 9.6 DIVIDEND PROCESS

Recall that *dividends are not an expense* of the business. However, the dividend account is a temporary account, which is closed to retained earnings at the end of the accounting period.

3.2 How do we account for preference dividends?

The terms of a preference dividend are fixed at the date of issuance of the preference shares, either at a stated amount or as a percentage of nominal value.

For example, the preference dividend could be stated at €1.80 per share or as a percentage of the share's nominal value (see case study below). In order for a preference dividend to be a legal obligation of the business, the board of directors must still declare the dividend.

Breyden Foods has 8000 preference shares outstanding with a $50 nominal value and a 4% preference dividend. On 31 December 2010 the board declares the preference dividend, and at that time it becomes a legal obligation of the company. The accounting function therefore records the following journal entry:

Date	Account Titles	DR	CR
30 Apr. 2009	Dividend – preference shares Preference dividend payable	$16 000	$16 000

If a preference dividend is not declared by the board, then no legal obligation to pay the dividend exists. However, as a practical matter, not declaring and paying a preference dividend would raise substantial concerns from investors and capital markets about the business's financial situation.

Ordinary share dividends cannot be paid until preference shareholders receive their dividends. However, the amount that must first be paid to preference shareholders depends on whether the preference shares are cumulative or noncumulative.

3.2.1 WHAT IS A CUMULATIVE PREFERENCE DIVIDEND?

A cumulative preference dividend means that all past preference dividends that have not been declared and therefore have not been paid must be satisfied before any dividends can be declared and paid to ordinary shareholders. An undeclared cumulative preference dividend is referred to as in arrears.

Costa Blanca, SA has 10 000 cumulative preference shares outstanding, at a €40 nominal value with a 4% dividend. The annual dividend is therefore €1.60 per share or $16 000 per annum. In 2010, Costa Blanca's board decides not to pay this preference dividend because of a critical cash shortage, which means that the dividend is now in arrears.

In 2011, continuing problems with cash flow cause Costa Blanca's board again to withhold the preference dividend. The total amount of dividends in arrears is now €32 000 (2 years × $16 000).

In 2012, with improved business conditions, Costa Blanca's board decides to make €100 000 available in dividends to all shareholders. At this point, an additional €16 000 must be added to the €32 000 of preference dividends in arrears for a total of €48 000, which must be paid to preference shareholders before ordinary shareholders can receive a dividend distribution.

On 31 March 2012, Costa Blanca's board declares a €48 000 preference dividend and €52 000 in ordinary dividends. This is summarized below:

Total funds available for 2012 dividends		€100 000
2010 preference dividend in arrears	€16 000	
2011 preference dividend in arrears	16 000	
2012 current preference dividend	16 000	
Preference dividends to be paid		€48 000
Ordinary dividends to be paid		€52 000

Noncumulative preference shares do not provide for dividends in arrears. If the current preference dividend is not declared, the company has no obligation to pay the preference dividend in later periods – it is not in arrears – before current dividend distributions are made to preference and ordinary shareholders.

Assume that Costa Blanca's preference shares from the previous example are noncumulative rather than cumulative. At the 2012 board meeting when €100 000 is made available for dividends, the preference shareholders would receive only €16 000 and would not be entitled to the €32 000 in dividend payments for the previous two years. The ordinary shareholders would receive €84 000. This calculation is summarized below:

Total funds available for 2012 dividends		€100 000
2010 preference dividend in arrears	Noncumulative	
2011 preference dividend in arrears	Noncumulative	
2012 current preference dividend	16 000	
Preference dividends to be paid		€16 000
Ordinary dividends to be paid		$84 000

3.2.2 WHAT IS A PARTICIPATION FEATURE FOR A PREFERENCE SHARE?

When preference shares are authorized, the dividend is also designated as either participating or non-participating. Participating preference shares receive a share of dividend distributions over and above the preference dividend amount. Nonparticipating preference shares receive only the preference dividend.

Let's return to the example where Breyden Foods LLC has 8000 preference shares outstanding, at $50 nominal value with a 4% dividend. However, let's now assume that the preference shares are participating. Breyden's board declares the preference dividend and also declares a $1.50 dividend per share on ordinary shares. Each preference shareholder would therefore receive a dividend of $3.50 ($2 per share preference dividend plus $1.50 per share participating dividend).

3.3 What are noncash dividends?

In addition to cash distributions, dividends can take two other forms: scrip issue and share split, although share splits are not strictly a distribution of earnings.

3.3.1 WHAT IS A SCRIP ISSUE?

A scrip issue (also share dividend or bonus issue) means that additional shares are issued to members in some proportion to their current shareholdings. For example, for each five shares owned, a member may receive one additional share. Because the distribution must be given to all shareholders in a particular class, the proportion of each shareholder's interest in the total business does not change.

On 6 June 2009, the board of directors for Jeevan Herbal Products Ltd declares a 10% scrip issue. On that date Jeevan has 20 000 shares outstanding, which are owned by four shareholders. The real value of the shares is €38 and the nominal value is €5 each. The number of shares and the percentage ownership of the company before and after the scrip issue are shown in the schedule below:

	Before Scrip Issue		After Scrip Issue	
Shareholder	Number of Shares	Percentage Ownership	Number of Shares	Percentage Ownership
Aquil Jaidev	7 000	35.0%	7 700	35.0%
Vinod Mistry	5 500	27.5%	6 050	27.5%
Naveen Hotchandani	4 000	20.0%	4 400	20.0%
Junaid Lalchand	3 500	17.5%	3 850	17.5%
Total shares	**20 000**	**100.0%**	**22 000**	**100%**

When a scrip issue is declared, the amount equal to the fair value of the shares is transferred from the retained earnings reserve to share capital.

The journal entry to record the scrip issue for Jeevan is as follows:

Date	Account Titles	DR	CR
6 June 2009	Retained earnings Share capital Share premium	€76 000	€10 000 66 000

What motives would a board have for declaring a scrip issue instead of a cash dividend? Payment of a cash dividend is taxable to shareholders in taxable jurisdictions where a distribution of shares may not be. Also, the dividend does not require a cash outlay by the business. The fact that retained earnings *are reclassified to contributed capital* also makes clear that part of retained earnings is no longer available from which to pay cash dividends. Scrip issues are typical in growth companies, which usually reinvest earnings rather than distributing them to investors. Investors expect their return to come from the appreciation of the share value.

3.3.2 WHAT ARE SHARE SPLITS?

A share split is an increase in the number of shares based on a ratio that is determined by the board of directors. For example, the board may declare a 2-for-1 split, which means that every share will be replaced by two new shares. A 3-for-1 split would replace each share with three shares.

Jeevan Herbal Products Ltd currently has 22 000 ordinary shares issued with a nominal value of €5 each. The market price is €40 per share; thus, the market capitalization of Jeevan is €880 000. On 1 December 2009 the board declares a 4-for-1 share split. The result is that Jeevan has 88 000 shares issued at a nominal value of €1.25 per share. The market price adjusted for the split would be €10 per share, making the market capitalization €880 000, which is the same as before the share split took place.

Notice that *no accounting entry is made for a share split*. If preference shares are split, then the preference dividend would be adjusted accordingly. Thus, when a preference share that pays a €2 preference dividend is split 2 for 1, the resulting preference dividend would be €1 per share.

WHY DO COMPANIES SPLIT SHARES?

The reason normally given is that the share price is reduced, which makes shares more affordable, although most shares are bought and sold by large institutions on behalf of individual investors and the magnitude of these transactions makes the share price irrelevant. The more likely reason is that share splits, like share dividends, are a way for the board to signal their optimism about the business's future prospects to investors. However, no conclusive evidence exists that splits actually increase the total value of the shares.

ON YOUR OWN

LEARNING OUTCOME REVIEW

1. What are the three dates which boards of directors must consider when making dividend distributions?
2. When does a dividend become a legal obligation?
3. What is the importance of the date of record?
4. What is the difference between a dividend on ordinary shares and a preference dividend?
5. What is a cumulative versus noncumulative preference dividend?
6. When is a preference dividend in arrears?
7. What is the difference between a participating and nonparticipating dividend?
8. What is a scrip issue? What is the accounting for a scrip issue?
9. What is a share split? What is the accounting for a share split?
10. Explain the difference between a scrip issue and a share split. If two shares are granted for each share currently owned, would this be a scrip issue or a share split?

LEARNING OUTCOME 4
EXPLAIN HOW DEBT AND EQUITY ARE ACCOUNTED FOR DIFFERENTLY

A share-based company can raise capital by either borrowing – creating debt – or expanding equity – selling more shares to investors. In either case, the company must provide some return to those who invest their capital. Interest must be paid to creditors and dividends are paid to shareholders.

From an accounting perspective, a difference exists between the two options. Interest on borrowings is an *expense* of the business, and therefore appears on the statement of comprehensive income. Interest expense reduces profit. *Dividends are not an expense* but are rather a distribution of earnings. Recall from Chapter 5, Accrual and Closing, that dividends are closed directly to retained earnings. A dividend does not affect the current period's profit or loss. The difference in accounting between the two options is illustrated in the following example.

Minh Software Ltd was started by Minh Quan. Minh began the company from personal savings, but as sales grew rapidly he quickly reached the point where he needed to raise an additional ¥1 500 000 in capital. He is considering two options: borrowing from a commercial bank or issuing additional shares in the company. Currently, Minh Software has 300 000 shares outstanding, worth ¥15 per share.

Minh Software's 2009 actual statement of comprehensive income and the forecast for 2010 and 2011 are presented below, assuming that the company borrows the money at 7% annual interest.

	Actual	Forecast	
	2009	**2010**	**2011**
	Minh Software Ltd		
	Statements of Comprehensive Income		
	for the Years Ended		
Sales revenue	¥800 000	¥1 900 000	¥3 100 000
Expenses	600 000	850 000	1 200 000
Profit before interest expense	200 000	1 010 000	1 900 000
Interest expense	105 000	105 000	105 000
Profit	¥95 000	¥905 000	¥1 795 000
Shares outstanding	300 000	300 000	300 000
Profit per share	¥0.32	¥3.02	¥5.98

To raise the amount needed by selling additional shares, Minh Software would need to sell 100 000 shares for ¥15 each. Following are the statements of comprehensive income presented above but with the effect of the additional issued shares included, and the interest on the borrowings excluded.

| | Actual | Forecast | |
	2009	2010	2011
		Minh Software Ltd	
		Statements of Comprehensive Income	
		for the Years Ended	
Sales revenue	¥800 000	¥1 900 000	¥3 100 000
Expenses	600 000	850 000	1 200 000
Profit	¥200 000	¥1 010 000	¥1 900 000
Shares outstanding	400 000	400 000	400 000
Profit per share	¥0.50	¥2.52	¥4.75

Notice that with the debt the profit per each share is lower for 2009. At first it appears to be more attractive to avoid the interest expense and issue more shares. But as profit rises in 2010 and 2011, the additional profit that goes to each share declines when compared to the amount that would go to each share if the capital had been raised by borrowing.

Why is this? The answer is that all increases in earnings go to the shareholders and not creditors in the form of interest. Interest does not rise as profits rise. This example demonstrates the importance of being able to evaluate financial information, and the central importance of profit in that evaluation, as we will see in the next section.

LEARNING OUTCOME 5
CALCULATE EQUITY-RELATED RATIOS USED TO EVALUATE FINANCIAL POSITION

5.1   What is the dividend yield ratio?

5.2   What is earnings per share?

5.3   What is diluted earnings per share?

5.4   What is the price–earnings ratio?

5.5 What is book value per share?

5.6 What is the debt-to-equity ratio?

5.7 What is the debt ratio?

From the investor's perspective, increases in wealth come from two sources with respect to an equity investment: distribution of profits in the form of dividends, and capital appreciation, which is the increase in share price. The first is measured by the dividend yield ratio.

5.1 What is the dividend yield ratio?

The dividend yield ratio measures the amount of dividend paid to investors as a percentage of the share price. The formula is as follows:

$$\text{Dividend yield} = \frac{\text{Annual dividend}}{\text{Share price}}$$

A company pays a £3 per share dividend in 2008. The current share price is £20.

$$\text{Dividend yield} = \frac{£3}{£20}$$

$$15\% = \frac{£3}{£20}$$

Given the amount of capital an investor has tied up in a share, 15% is being returned in the form of a cash dividend.

Some investors prefer to invest for income, which means that they favour equity investments that consistently pay a dividend and therefore have a high dividend yield.

The share price of the business is linked with its profitability. If profit increases, all other factors being equal, we generally expect the share price to increase. If profit decreases, then we generally expect the share price to drop. This relationship is affected by other factors, however. We can say that earnings have an impact on the trading value of shares. Thus, we measure share-based performance using three ratios: earnings per share, diluted earnings per share and price–earnings ratio.

5.2 What is earnings per share?

Some investors are more interested in capital appreciation than income from dividends. Capital appreciation comes from increases in share price, and share price is closely associated with earnings. A major measure used by these and other investors is earnings per share or EPS. The formula for earnings per share is as follows:

$$\text{Earnings per share} = \frac{\text{Profit less preference dividends}}{\text{Average ordinary shares outstanding}}$$

The formula focuses on ordinary shareholders. Notice in the equation that preference dividends are deducted from profit before dividing by the ordinary shares outstanding. Recall that preference dividends are a fixed amount per share, and thus in that sense are similar to interest on debt. But interest on debt is an expense of the business and therefore is deducted to calculate profit, as we discussed in the preceding section. Dividends are not. Besides, a dividend is limited and profit is not otherwise available to preference shareholders, so we deduct the preference dividend from profit – the remainder belongs to the ordinary shareholders. So even though preference shareholders are legally owners of the business, because the preference dividend is fixed, we treat it the same way as interest on debt.

The denominator is based on a calculation of the average number of ordinary shares outstanding multiplied by the time they were outstanding as a proportion of the period. This would, of course, change as shares are issued or repurchased by the entity.

Bijan Manufacturing LLC reports $8 600 000 in profit for 2009. During the year, the company declared and paid a preference dividend of $2.70 per share on 100 000 shares outstanding. At the beginning of the year, Bijan had 750 000 ordinary shares outstanding, and on 31 December 2009 there were 850 000 shares outstanding. Earnings per share is calculated as follows:

$$\text{Earnings per share} = \frac{\$8\ 600\ 000 - 270\ 000}{[75\ 000 + 85\ 000] \div 2}$$

$$\text{Earnings per share} = \frac{\$8\ 330\ 000}{80\ 000}$$

$$\$10.41 = \frac{\$8\ 330\ 000}{800\ 000}$$

Notice that in the denominator for the earnings per share calculation, no preference shares are included.

5.3 What is diluted earnings per share?

Calculating only basic earnings per share does not give the investor the complete picture. Recall from Chapter 8, Financial Assets and Liabilities, that certain debt instruments like bonds have a convertible feature, which means that they can be converted into ordinary shares. If they do convert to ordinary shares, then the number of shares outstanding will increase, which will affect the earnings per share calculation – we say it will dilute earnings per share. Dilution refers to the effect that conversion of all convertible financial instruments has on earnings per share. The diluted earnings per share calculation is based on the assumption that all potential conversions into ordinary shares have been made, as the following example illustrates.

Returning to the Bijan example, let's now assume that the company also has 5000 convertible bonds with a stated value of $1000 and 6% interest, which can each be converted to 10 ordinary shares. That means that before conversion Bijan pays $300 000 per year in interest expense on the bonds (5000 × $1000 × 0.06) and that this amount is deducted to calculate profit (ignoring any tax effect). Therefore, if the bonds are converted, this interest expense would no longer exist. Thus, the interest amount is added back into the numerator on the diluted earnings per share calculation. Also, if the bonds were converted the number of shares outstanding would increase by 50 000 (5000 × 10). When these effects are taken into account, the calculation for diluted earnings per share would be as follows:

$$\text{Diluted earnings per share} = \frac{\$8\ 600\ 000 - 270\ 000 + 300\ 000}{[[750\ 000 + 850\ 000] \div 2] + 50\ 000}$$

$$\text{Earnings per share} = \frac{\$8\ 630\ 000}{850\ 000}$$

$$\$10.15 = \frac{\$8\ 630\ 000}{850\ 000}$$

What the investor would see is that earnings per share is $10.41, but if all bond holders converted into ordinary shares, the maximum dilution would be to $10.15.

5.4 What is the price–earnings ratio?

Share price is influenced by earnings as measured by earnings per share. Thus, if earnings per share increases, the share price is likely to increase as well. Other factors also have an influence on share price, so the relationship between earnings per share and share price is far from perfect. However, this relationship is measured by the price–earnings ratio (also PE ratio or multiple), which divides the share price by earnings per share. The formula is:

$$\text{Price–earnings ratio} = \frac{\text{Share price}}{\text{Earnings per share}}$$

In the preceding example, Bijan Manufacturing reports earnings per share of $10.41. Assume that the share price for Bijan is $156. The price–earnings ratio would be calculated as follows:

$$\text{Price–earnings ratio} = \frac{\$156.00}{\$10.41}$$

$$15 = \frac{\$156.00}{\$10.41}$$

Essentially, the equities market is willing to pay $15 for every $1 of profit. Now suppose that management is able to improve earnings per share to $11.50 and the price–earnings ratio remains at fifteen. That implies that the share price will rise based on the price–earnings ratio formula as calculated below:

$$\text{Price–earnings ratio} = \frac{\text{Share price}}{\text{Earnings per share}}$$

$$15 = \frac{\text{Share price}}{\$11.50}$$

Solving for share price:

$$\text{Share price} = \text{Price–earnings ratio} \times \text{Earnings per share}$$

$$\text{Share price} = 15 \times \$11.50$$

$$\$172.50 = 15 \times \$11.50$$

Thus, the share price should rise to $172.50.

The equities market generally values different industries (or sectors) at different price–earnings ratios. A high-technology, high-growth industry such as telecommunications services may have a higher price–earnings ratio than a mature, lower-growth industry like air transportation. Figure 9.7 has representative price–earnings ratios for several industries.

FIGURE 9.7 PRICE–EARNINGS RATIOS

Industry	Price–Earnings Ratio
Air transport	17
Banks	23
Environmental companies	28
Paper/forestry	19
Restaurants	24
Retail stores	19
Telecommunications services	41

The differences in price–earnings ratios reflect the expectations that the equities market has about future profitability.

5.5 What is book value per share?

This ratio calculates the amount of equity per ordinary shares. The formula is as follows:

$$\text{Book value per share} = \frac{\text{Equity} - \text{Preference shares amount}}{\text{Ordinary shares outstanding}}$$

We will continue the Heliard Coffees example from Chapter 8 based on the following information:

<table>
<tr><td colspan="2" align="center">Heliard Coffees plc
Statement of Income
for the Year Ended 31 December 2009
€ Euros</td></tr>
<tr><td>Sales revenue</td><td>€150 000</td></tr>
<tr><td>Cost of sales</td><td>70 000</td></tr>
<tr><td>Gross profit</td><td>80 000</td></tr>
<tr><td>Operating expenses</td><td>20 000</td></tr>
<tr><td>Interest expense</td><td>10 000</td></tr>
<tr><td>Profit before income tax</td><td>50 000</td></tr>
<tr><td>Income tax (20%)</td><td>10 000</td></tr>
<tr><td>Profit</td><td>€40 000</td></tr>
</table>

Recall that all of Heliard's sales are on credit.

<table>
<tr><td colspan="3" align="center">Heliard Coffees plc
Statement of Financial Position
At 31 December 2009
€ Euros</td></tr>
<tr><td>Noncurrent assets</td><td></td><td></td></tr>
<tr><td>Property, plant and equipment</td><td>180 000</td><td>200 000</td></tr>
<tr><td>Less: Accumulated depreciation</td><td>(28 500)</td><td>(55 000)</td></tr>
<tr><td></td><td>151 500</td><td>145 000</td></tr>
<tr><td>Investments at fair value</td><td>33 000</td><td>28 000</td></tr>
<tr><td>Goodwill</td><td>5 000</td><td>5 000</td></tr>
<tr><td>Total noncurrent assets</td><td>190 000</td><td>178 500</td></tr>
</table>

Current assets		
Inventories	29 000	27 500
Trade receivables	28 000	28 500
Marketable securities	9 500	7 000
Cash and cash equivalents	5 000	3 500
Total current assets	71 500	66 500
TOTAL ASSETS	**261 500**	**245 000**
Shareholders' equity		
Share capital	50 000	50 000
Share premium	35 000	35 000
Retained earnings	42 000	30 000
Total shareholders' equity	127 000	115 000
Noncurrent liabilities		
Borrowings	65 000	60 000
Total noncurrent liabilities	65 000	60 000
Current liabilities		
Notes payable	32 500	37 500
Accrued liabilities	22 000	20 000
Trade payable	15 000	12 500
Total current liabilities	69 500	70 000
Total liabilities	**134 500**	**130 000**
TOTAL SHAREHOLDERS' EQUITY AND LIABILITIES	**261 500**	**245 000**

Assume that 10 000 shares were issued and outstanding in both 2008 and 2009

For 2009, the book value per share calculation would be:

$$\text{Book value per share} = \frac{\text{€}127\,000 - 0}{10\,000}$$

$$\text{€}12.70 = \frac{\text{€}127\,000 - 0}{10\,000}$$

For 2008, the calculation would be:

$$\text{Book value per share} = \frac{\text{€}115\,000 - 0}{10\,000}$$

$$\text{€}11.50 = \frac{\text{€}115\,000 - 0}{10\,000}$$

5.6 What is the debt-to-equity ratio?

The debt-to-equity ratio measures the overall indebtedness of the business as a percentage of its total equity. A higher ratio means that more capital comes from creditors compared to equity investors.

$$\text{Debt to equity} = \frac{\text{Total liabilities}}{\text{Total equity}}$$

Heliard's calculation for 2009 is as follows:

$$\text{Debt to equity} = \frac{€134\,500}{€127\,000}$$

$$1.06 = \frac{€134\,500}{€127\,000}$$

Heliard's calculation for 2008 is as follows:

$$\text{Debt to equity} = \frac{€130\,000}{€115\,000}$$

$$1.13 = \frac{€130\,000}{€115\,000}$$

Thus, we can see from the calculation above that Heliard Coffees is relying less on debt as a percentage of total equity in 2009 than in 2008.

GOOD AND BAD RATIOS

Students like to come to a conclusion about whether a particular ratio is good or bad, or at least better or worse. In most cases it depends.

In the Heliard example above, the debt-to-equity ratio decreased between 2008 and 2009. Less debt per euro of equity is good, right? The answer is maybe. It depends on other factors. For example, can Heliard pay the level of debt it has now? This ratio does not answer that question. Also, maybe Heliard has too little debt. If the industry average is, for example, 2.0, then perhaps more debt would allow the number of shareholders to be reduced following a strategy similar to Brik's Restaurants, which we discuss later in this chapter. In fact, maybe Heliard wants to borrow more money to buy back some of its own equity shares. That happens all the time.

The point to remember when examining any ratio is that it provides only one piece of the overall picture to evaluate a company's financial standing. In Chapter 12, Comparability and Consistency, we will pull all the pieces of that puzzle together so that we can begin to make judgements about liquidity, solvency, and profitability – and see the business from the perspective of the investor and other external users. This evaluation is usually performed in the context of the industry, which is why investment analysts always begin by updating their knowledge of industry trends and ratios.

PUTTING NUMBERS INTO PRACTICE: BRIK'S RESTAURANTS LTD

Brik's Restaurants Ltd is a publicly listed company that creates restaurant concepts and then launches new chains of restaurants, both domestically and internationally. The company has been quite successful in creating new and popular themes. For example, it launched a highly successful Italian concept complete with waiters who sing opera (or at least attempt to do so). Other concepts have been launched based on family-oriented seafood restaurants and casual eateries where young professionals meet after work. The company has been very profitable and because restaurants are cash-oriented businesses, Brik's has built up a substantial balance of cash.

This cash has begun to create a problem, because management believes that the company is not growing fast enough because of its inability to hire the right number of capable managers. The chief financial officer has invested the cash in various debt and equity instruments. The return is acceptable but not exceptional. Management has also explored the possibility of entering other businesses, but does not wish to divert attention away from the core restaurant business.

Institutional investors have made their concerns known to the chief executive officer and several board members. They have expressed the view that the company should either find a way to invest the excess cash profitably, or return it to investors as a special, one-time dividend so that shareholders can invest elsewhere. Management has been seriously considering this option.

The accounting department has now made another proposal: to increase the market value of the company, its capitalization, by using excess cash to buy back Brik's own share capital. The chief executive officer is interested in the proposal and wants to see what impact this would have on the share price.

Brik's currently has €1.2 billion in cash, of which management wants to retain €400 million. Profit for the year just ended was €130 million. The company has 120 million outstanding shares, which are currently trading for €18.42. Assuming that the company uses the excess cash over €400 million to purchase its own shares, what would be the effect on the total market capitalization of the business?

With excess cash of €800 million (€1.2 billion – €400 million), Brik's could purchase 43 431 053 shares (€800 million ÷ €18.42 per share). That means that 76 568 947 shares remain outstanding.

(Brik has no preference shares) What would this mean for the share price? To calculate the effect, we must determine the price–earnings ratio which requires that we first calculate earnings per share.

$$\text{Earnings per share} = \frac{\text{Profit less preference dividends}}{\text{Ordinary shares outstanding}}$$

$$\text{Earnings per share} = \frac{\text{€}130\,000\,000 - 0}{120\,000\,000}$$

Notice that no preference dividends are involved.

$$\text{€}1.08 = \frac{\text{€}130\,000\,000 - 0}{120\,000\,000}$$

From earnings per share, the price–earnings ratio can now be determined.

$$\text{Price–earnings ratio} = \frac{\text{Share price}}{\text{Earnings per share}}$$

$$17 = \frac{\text{€}18.42}{\text{€}1.08}$$

We can now use the remaining outstanding shares to recalculate the earnings per share:

$$\text{€}1.70 = \frac{\text{€}130\,000\,000 - 0}{76\,568\,947}$$

From this we can conclude that the share price will rise if the price–earnings ratio remains constant. The calculation for the new share price would be as follows:

$$\text{Share price} = \text{Price–earnings ratio} \times \text{Earnings per share}$$

$$\text{Share price} = 17 \times \text{€}1.70$$

$$\text{€}28.90 = 17 \times \text{€}1.70$$

Thus, in this simple example we have seen the share price rise by €10.48 (€28.90 – 18.42). Although the overall market value of the company has not changed, the price of individual shares certainly has changed and as a result the wealth of the individual investors.

ON YOUR OWN

LEARING OUTCOME REVIEW

1. How is the dividend yield ratio calculated? What does the dividend yield ratio tell an investor? Which type of investor would be more interested in the dividend yield ratio: an investor for income or capital appreciation?
2. How are earnings per share calculated? What do earnings per share tell an investor?

3. Why are preference dividends subtracted from profit in the numerator of the earnings per share calculation?
4. What is dilution? What causes dilution? How are diluted earnings per share calculated? What do diluted earnings per share tell an investor that earnings per share do not?
5. How is the book value to share ratio calculated?
6. What does the debt-to-equity ratio measure? How is this ratio calculated?
7. Why can we say that there is no good or bad ratio when we look at that ratio in isolation?

Conclusion

In Part III, we have focused on the financial position of the business as reported by the statement of financial position. In Chapters 7 and 8, we explored assets and liabilities – tangible, intangible and financial. In doing so, we addressed the following accounting issues:

*   What costs or obligations are recognized as assets and liabilities? Which are included? Which are excluded?
*   How are these assets and liabilities to be measured at the time the assets are acquired and the obligations are created? And how are they subsequently measured?
*   How are assets and liabilities to be presented in the financial statements and what related information should be disclosed?

Why are these questions important? The reason is that the inclusion or exclusion of each asset and liability, and the amount, affects equity. Thus any material misstatement of an asset or liability provides misleading information to investors about their interest in the business.

Equity is the difference between assets and liabilities – the net assets of the business. Within equity, as we have seen in this chapter, different types of shareholders – preference and ordinary – have different claims on those net assets. Even within a share type, a business can have different classes of shareholders. All these shareholders receive their reward in one or both of two ways: either through distribution of profits through dividends or through capital appreciation.

Share-based payments are used in various transactions. Most commonly, shares are used as compensation to employees. Shares can also be issued to acquire assets and to settle obligations. Shares may be issued as part of a rights issue to honour shareholders' pre-emptive rights, or as a scrip issue or share split to increase share ownership among existing investors without an outlay of cash.

In Part IV, we move on to consider changes in financial position. What are the factors that cause financial position to improve or deteriorate? In Chapter 10 we will explore issues related to changes in equity, and in Chapter 11 we will analyse cash flows.

Summary

LEARNING OUTCOME 1
Ordinary and Preference Shares Explained

Share-based companies can have two types of share capital: ordinary shares and preference shares. Ordinary shares represent the residual interest in the business entity, which means that they are subordinate not only to creditors but also to preference shares. Dividends to ordinary shares are paid only when declared by the board of directors. Ordinary shares may or may not have a par value. Both ordinary and preference shares can have different classes. A class establishes the specific rights that shareholders in that class have. All shareholders within a class must be treated the same.

LEARNING OUTCOME 2
Authorized Share Capital, Issued Shares, Investment in Own Shares and Outstanding Shares Explained

When share-based entity is registered, authorized share capital is established. This is the amount of share capital that can be issued to investors. Share capital may be authorized at a nominal or par value. Shares are then issued to investors through sale or by grant. The issuance of shares depends on provisions in the business entity's charter. For example, in some cases shares may be issued only after a member vote. In these cases, the board may allot shares by approval of the shareholders.

Shares of privately held companies are privately placed. Shares of publicly traded companies can be either privately placed or sold in a public equities market. A company selling shares to the public for the first time is making an initial public offering, which is a primary market transaction. Once the shares are listed by the stock exchange, then the public can buy and sell the shares in the secondary market.

A company may repurchase its own shares that have been previously issued, making an investment in its own shares. When these shares are subtracted from issued shares, the result is outstanding shares. Dividends are paid based on shares outstanding.

LEARNING OUTCOME 3
Cash Dividends, Preference Dividends, Scrip Issues and Share Splits Explained

Accumulated earnings of the business entity are distributed to shareholders as dividends. Dividends take three basic forms: cash dividends, scrip issues and share splits. A scrip issue provides additional shares to existing shareholders rather than cash. The amount of the scrip issue dividend is reclassified from reserves into contributed capital. Cash dividends and scrip issues both reduce reserves. A share split awards a different number of shares to shareholders based on proportional holdings. No journal entry is required for a share split, thus neither contributed capital nor reserves is affected in total. None of these dividends changes the proportion of ownership by a specific shareholder.

Preference shares are paid a preference dividend, which is either a stated amount or percentage of par value. Like ordinary shares, preference shares may or may not have a par value. Preference dividends become a legal obligation of the business entity only when they are declared by the board of directors. A cumulative preference dividend means that dividends from a prior period are unpaid and the current preference dividend must be paid before ordinary shareholders can receive a dividend distribution. If preference shares are noncumulative, then an undeclared dividend from a previous year need not be paid before a distribution to ordinary shareholders. Preference shares can be participating, which means that they share in dividend distributions over and above the stated preference dividend. If the preference share is noncumulative, then it receives only the preference dividend and nothing more.

A dividend becomes a legal liability of the business entity on the date it is declared by the board of directors. The board establishes a date of record. All shareholders on the date of record receive the dividend. After the date of record, the shares trade ex-dividend, which means that those who purchased the shares after the date of record are not entitled to the dividend. The dividend is disbursed to shareholders on the payment date, which is also established by the board.

LEARNING OUTCOME 4
Debt Versus Equity Accounting Explained

The major difference in accounting for debt versus equity is that interest expense is an expense of the business and therefore is included with other expenses on the statement of comprehensive income. Interest expense reduces profit. Dividends paid to shareholders, whether on ordinary shares or preference shares, are not an expense of the business but are a distribution of earnings. Because interest expense reduces profit, it also decreases the amount of income taxes owed if those income taxes are based on profit. Dividends are not deductible for tax purposes.

LEARNING OUTCOME 5
Equity-Related Ratios Calculated

Analysis of dividends, earnings and share price is usually based on per share calculations. The reason is that the return from an investment must be measured in relation to the amount of that investment. Dividend performance, for example, is measured by the dividend yield ratio, which calculates the amount of the annual dividend divided by the share price.

Earnings performance is measured by earnings per share, which divides profit available to ordinary shareholders by the number of shares outstanding. However, earnings can be diluted if additional shares can be issued through convertible features of bonds or preference shares and for other reasons. For that reason, diluted earnings per share is also computed by assuming that all shares that could be issued have been issued. To evaluate the relationship between earnings and share price, the price–earnings ratio is calculated by dividing share price by earnings per share. Different industries and companies have different price–earnings ratios depending on investors' judgement of the future potential for earnings growth.

Solvency is the ability of the business entity to meet financial commitments as they come due. Common ratios to evaluate solvency include the debt-to-equity ratio and the debt ratio. The debt-to-equity ratio divides total liabilities by total equity to determine what proportion of claims are held by creditors compared to shareholders. The debt ratio divides total liabilities by total assets.

Key terms

Allotment	Outstanding shares
Annual meeting	Par value
Authorized share capital	Participating preference shares
Book value per share	Payment date
Bonus issue	Pre-emptive right
Capital appreciation	Preference dividend
Charter	Preference shares
Common shares	Preferred shares
Common stock	Price–earnings ratio (PE ratio)
Convertible feature	Primary market
Cumulative preference dividend	Real value
Date of record	Register of members
Debt-to-equity ratio	Right issue
Declaration date	Scrip issue
Diluted earnings per share	Secondary market
Dilution	Share-based entity
Dividend yield ratio	Share-based payments
Earnings per share (EPS)	Shareholder register
General shareholders' meeting	Share options
Investment in own shares	Share premium
Issued shares	Share price
Members	Share split
Nominal value	Treasury shares
Ordinary shares	

Terminology practice

1. A _____ gives shareholders the right of first refusal on new share issuances.
2. _____ is the total amount of shares that a limited liability company can issue.
3. The _____ is calculated by dividing share price by earnings per share.
4. _____ give preference shareholders the right to receive a share of dividends beyond the preference dividend.
5. The date that determines which shareholders will be paid a dividend is the _____.
6. When the number of treasury shares is subtracted from issued shares the result is _____ .
7. A _____ is the difference between the amount recorded when shares are issued over their nominal value.
8. The _____ is calculated by dividing the annual dividend by share price.
9. _____ is calculated by dividing profit less preference dividends by the average ordinary shares outstanding.

10. Shareholders are also referred to as _____ .

11. The _____ or _____ is an official listing of all current shareholders.

12. A _____ is stated but is not a legal obligation of the business entity until declared by the board of directors.

13. Ordinary shares are also referred to as _____ and _____.

14. A dividend becomes a legal obligation of the business entity on the _____.

15. _____ refers to increases in share value.

16. The _____ feature gives preference shareholders the right to receive dividends in arrears.

17. The _____ is calculated by dividing total liabilities by total equity.

18. The _____ is an internal document that determines how the a share-based business will be governed.

19. _____, also known as _____, are when a company invests in its own shares.

20. The annual gathering of members is referred to as the _____ or _____.

21. The total authorized value for share capital is the _____.

22. A _____ or _____ refers to a dividend distribution, which is given as additional shares issued to members in proportion to their current shareholdings.

23. _____ is calculated by dividing equity less preference shares by ordinary shares outstanding.

24. _____ is the effect that conversion of all convertible financial instruments has on earnings per share. The result is _____.

25. Debt is subordinate to _____ which are subordinate to _____.

26. When the board of directors does not declare a preference dividend, then that dividend is _____.

27. A debt instrument or preference share can be exchanged for an ordinary share if it has a _____.

28. A _____ occurs when the board of directors divides shares into a multiple (for example, two shares for each currently authorized share).

Application exercises

1. At 31 December 2010 the capital structure of Ambia, a limited liability company, was as follows:

1 000 000 ordinary shares of $1 each	$1 000 000
Share premium account	200 000
Revaluation reserve	100 000
Retained earnings	50 000

The authorized share capital of the company was $1 000 000. The directors of the company are considering the following proposals:

   i.   Making a bonus issue of one ordinary share for every two held, in order to raise $500 000 for the company.

   ii.   Paying a dividend of 10 cents per share.

   iii.   Increasing the revaluation reserve to $300 000 by revaluing goodwill from $800 000 to $1 100 000.

Required: Comment on the validity of these proposals. [ACCA adapted]

2.   The board of directors of Sailbird Inc. declared total dividends of $50 000 for 2009. The following shares were outstanding at that time:

Preference shares, noncumulative 6%,	
5000 shares, $8 par	$40 000
Ordinary shares, 50 000 shares, $10 par	$500 000

For the previous two years, no dividends had been paid for either 2007 or 2008. How much in dividends should be paid to preference shareholders and ordinary shareholders?

3.   The board of directors of Sailbird Inc. declared total dividends of $50 000 for 2009. The following shares were outstanding at that time:

Preference shares, cumulative 6%,	
5000 shares, $8 par	$40 000
Ordinary shares, 50 000 shares, $10 par	$500 000

For the previous two years, no dividends had been paid for either 2007 or 2008. How much in dividends are paid to preference shareholders and ordinary shareholders?

4.   Jerome Highland Corporation reported the following balances on its statement of financial position on 1 January 2009:

Ordinary shares, £1 par, authorized 100 000 shares	100 000
Ordinary share premium (£2 per share)	120 000
Retained earnings	580 000

The following transactions occurred during 2009.

i.   Issued a 100% share dividend when the market price was £4 per share.

ii.   Purchased 1200 treasury shares for £4600.

iii.   Declared and paid dividends of £18 000.

iv.   Reported profit of £32 000.

Required: Construct the equity section for Jerome Highland at 31 December 2009 after all the above listed transactions had been completed.

5.   A company issues 30 000 ordinary shares for cash on 30 April 2009 for $20 per share. On 30 November 2009, the company's board of directors declared a dividend of $0.30 per share, which was paid on 15 December 2009.

Required: Record the journal entries for the issuance of the shares, assuming that each share had a $12 par value. Also record the journal entries for the issuance of the shares, and the declaration and payment of the dividend.

6.   A company issues 30 000 ordinary shares on 30 April 2009 for $20 per share. On 30 November 2009, the company's board of directors declared a dividend of $0.30 per share, which was paid on 15 December 2009.

Required: Record the journal entries for the issuance of the shares, assuming that the shares had no par value. Also record the journal entries for the declaration and payment of the dividend.

7.   A company issues 30 000 ordinary shares on 30 April 2009 for $20 per share. On 1 October 2009 the company purchases 5000 of its own shares for $110 000 to hold as treasury shares. On 30 November 2009, the company's board of directors declared a dividend of $0.30 per share, which was paid on 15 December 2009.

Required: Record the journal entries for the issuance of the shares, assuming that the shares had no par value. Also record the journal entries for the declaration and payment of the dividend.

8.   A company reports the following amounts on its 31 December 2010 statement of financial position. Treasury shares had been acquired at £2.50 each.

Ordinary shares, £1 par, authorized 120 000 shares	£80 000
Ordinary share premium (£2 per share)	14 000
Retained earnings	180 000
Treasury shares	25 000

Required:

a)   How many treasury shares does the company have?

b)   How many unissued shares does the company have?

c)   How many outstanding shares does the company have?

d)   How many authorized shares does the company have?

e)   How many issued shares does the company have?

Case analysis
BOTSWANA WILD SAFARIS LLC

Botswana Wild Safaris LLC was introduced in Chapter 7. In this chapter we will continue the case by focusing on equity. Recall that Tony Washford had purchased the company from Gerhardt Perst on 1 January 2009. Use the information presented for Botswana Wild Safaris from both Chapters 7 and 8 in addition to the information presented below to complete the requirements of the case.

On the acquisition date, Botswana Wildlife Safaris had 30 000 no par shares outstanding, with €300 000 in total contributed capital. On 1 January 2010, the company issued another 20 000 shares to Tony for €200 000. On 1 January 2011, the company purchased 25 000 shares from Tony for a total of €300 000. Cash dividends of €50 000 were declared and paid on 30 June of both 2010 and 2011.

REQUIRED:

Record all transactions and adjusting entries for 2009 to 2011 related to items in equity and construct *complete statements of financial position* for all three reporting dates.

Reporting Changes in Financial Position

PART IV

INTRODUCTION TO PART IV

In Part III, we discussed in detail the statement of financial position, including nonfinancial assets, financial assets and liabilities and equity. In Part IV, we will focus on the other three financial statements that report performance and changes in financial position.

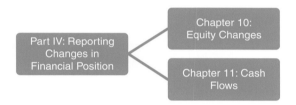

In Chapter 10, we will examine issues related to the statement of comprehensive income and the statement of changes in equity. The statements of comprehensive income affects financial position in two ways. First, profits increase and loses decrease the retained earnings balance, which is part of equity. Secondly, changes in other comprehensive income reported on the statement of comprehensive income are accumulated as reserves in equity. The statement of change in equity includes not only the effect on profit or loss and other comprehensive income, but also dividends distributed to shareholders and any changes to contributed capital such as the issuance of additional shares or their repurchase as treasury shares.

Chapter 11 focuses on the statement of cash flows. The statement of cash flows explains why the balance of cash and cash equivalents reported on the statement of financial position has changed between the beginning of the reporting period and the end.

Equity changes 10

LEARNING OUTCOMES

By the end of this chapter, you should be able to:

1. Explain what transactions change equity.
2. Describe the statement of comprehensive income.
3. Explain how revenue is recognized.
4. Explain when expenses are recognized.
5. Explain how gains and losses are included in other comprehensive income.
6. Describe the reporting requirements for the statement of changes in equity.
7. Explain how equity changes are evaluated.

LEARNING OUTCOME 1
EXPLAIN WHAT TRANSACTIONS CHANGE EQUITY

1.1 What transactions affect contributed capital?

1.2 What transactions affect retained earnings?

1.3 What transactions affect reserves?

1.4 How are investments in own shares reported?

As we know, equity contains three major elements: contributed capital, retained earnings and reserves. Changes to contributed capital are reported only in the statement of changes in equity, while changes to retained earnings and reserves are first reported in the statement of comprehensive income and the statement of changes in equity, and then are included in retained earnings and reserves in equity on the statement of financial position. Figure 10.1 illustrates this reporting for changes in contributed capital versus retained earnings and reserves.

Recall that not all transactions change equity. For example, if a business borrows €100 000, assets are increased (cash) as are liabilities (notes payable), but this transaction does not change the net assets (equity) balance. The transaction affects only assets and liabilities and does not change equity.

FIGURE 10.1 REPORTING CHANGES IN CONTRIBUTED CAPITAL VERSUS RETAINED EARNINGS AND OTHER RESERVES

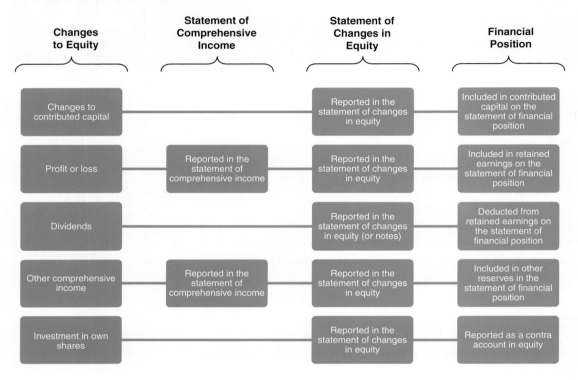

1.1 What transactions affect contributed capital?

Three major types of transactions increase or decrease contributed capital:

- Issuance of ordinary or preference shares
- Repurchase of own shares
- Scrip dividend

Each of these transactions was reviewed in Chapter 9. Contributed capital is increased when ordinary or preference shares are issued. It decreases when shares are repurchased to be retired or to be held as an investment in own shares. And finally, a scrip dividend is recorded as a reclassification of retained earnings to contributed capital. This increases contributed capital but decreases retained earnings by a like amount and therefore leaves the total equity balance unchanged. However, this reclassification of retained earnings to contributed capital affects the composition of equity and is reported in the statement of changes in equity. As Figure 10.1 shows, changes to contributed capital are reported on the statement of changes in equity and appear as part of contributed capital in the statement of financial position, but are not reported in the statement of comprehensive income.

Equity other than contributed capital includes retained earnings and other reserves.

1.2 What transactions affect retained earnings?

Two types of transactions increase or decrease retained earnings:

- Profit or loss
- Dividends

As we know, retained earnings are increased when revenues and expenses are closed to the income summary account and the income summary account is closed to retained earnings. However, when expenses exceed revenue for the reporting period, the entity has reported a loss and retained earnings are decreased when revenue and expense accounts are closed. As shown in Figure 10.1, profit or loss is reported on the statement of comprehensive income, the statement of changes in equity and then becomes part of retained earnings on the statement of financial position.

Retained earnings are reduced by a dividend distribution whether the dividend is paid in cash, scrip or property. Stock splits do not affect the retained earnings or any other account balance. Management has a choice about how to report dividends: either in the statement of changes in equity or the notes to the financial statements, as shown in Figure 10.1. Dividends are not included in the statement of comprehensive income.

1.3 What transactions affect reserves?

IFRS identify five specific transactions that increase or decrease other reserves through other comprehensive income:

1. Revaluations of property, plant and equipment and intangible assets.
2. Gains and losses related to available-for-sale financial assets.
3. Gains and losses related to certain types of employee benefits.
4. Gains and losses related to the translations of foreign currencies.
5. Gains and losses related to certain advanced financial transactions.

In this textbook we cover item 1 above, while items 2, 3, 4 and 5 are advanced topics. However, the important point is that reserves are affected by *specific IFRS requirements*, as listed above. We know from Chapter 7, Nonfinancial Assets, that an increase in the value of property, plant and equipment will cause reserves to increase if management uses the revaluation method. A subsequent decline in the value or disposal of that property, plant and equipment will cause reserves to decrease. As Figure 10.1 illustrates, items recognized as other comprehensive income such as a revaluation of property are reported on the statement of comprehensive income and the statement of changes in equity, and become part of other reserves in the statement of financial position.

1.4 How are investments in own shares reported?

Recall also that when a company invests in its own shares, these are recorded in a contra account to the equity section. Thus, investment in own shares will reduce equity. As shown in Figure 10.1, investments in own shares are reported on the statement of changes in equity and as a contra account to equity on the statement of financial position.

LEARNING OUTCOME 2
DESCRIBE THE STATEMENT OF COMPREHENSIVE INCOME

2.1 What information is included in the statement of comprehensive income?

2.2 What two formats can be used to report total comprehensive income?
    2.2.1 What are the requirements for a single statement presentation?
    2.2.2 What are the requirements for a two statement presentation?

We are now familiar with the statement of comprehensive income and know that it reports two major categories: profit or loss and other comprehensive income. These two categories added together equal total comprehensive income.

2.1 What information is included in the statement of comprehensive income?

Figure 10.2 shows the specific information to be reported in each category according to IFRS.

FIGURE 10.2 COMPONENTS OF TOTAL COMPREHENSIVE INCOME

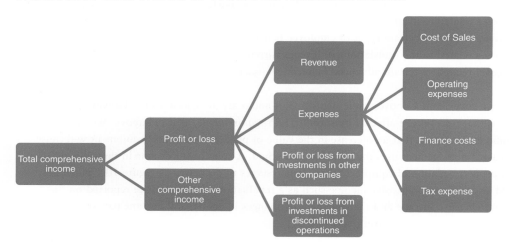

Other comprehensive income would also contain other comprehensive income from investments in other companies, just as profit or loss from investments in other companies is reported as part of overall profit and loss (Figure 10.1). Notice too that profit and loss includes a separate reporting line item for profit or loss that comes from operations that the company has discontinued. In addition, profit or loss and other comprehensive income is allocated between the parent company and noncontrolling interests.

2.2 What two formats can be used to report total comprehensive income?

Until 2009, IFRS required only a statement of income that reported profit or loss. Afterwards, reporting entities that use IFRS to prepare their financial statements are required to report other comprehensive income. Together, profit or loss and other comprehensive income equal total comprehensive income. IFRS offer two options for reporting total comprehensive income. The first option is a single statement of comprehensive income, which is the approach we have followed in this textbook. The second option permits the business entity to provide two statements: one reports only profit or loss and the second begins with profit or loss and then reports components of other comprehensive income.

2.2.1 WHAT ARE THE REQUIREMENTS FOR A SINGLE STATEMENT PRESENTATION?

The following statement of comprehensive income for Chang Mao Electrical Ltd illustrates the single statement presentation. In this statement, expenses have been organized by function.

Chang Mao Electrical Ltd Statement of Comprehensive Income for the Years Ended 31 December ¥ Millions		
	2009	2008
Revenue	380 000	360 000
Cost of sales	(245 000)	(235 000)
Gross profit	135 000	125 000
Other income	20 500	11 300
Distribution costs	(7 000)	(8 200)
Administrative expenses	(20 000)	(21 000)
Other expenses	(3 500)	(1 700)
Finance costs	(12 000)	(9 500)
Share of profit from investment in associates	32 500	32 100
Profit before tax	145 500	128 000
Income tax expense	(36 375)	(32 000)
Profit from continuing operations	109 125	96 000
Loss from discontinued operations	–	(36 500)

(Continued)

Chang Mao Electrical Ltd
Statement of Comprehensive Income
for the Years Ended 31 December
¥ Millions

	2009	2008
Profit	109 125	59 500
Other comprehensive income		
Currency translation differences on foreign operations	7 419	10 500
Available-for-sale financial assets	(38 000)	26 500
Cash flow hedges	1 600	4 000
Gains on revaluation of property	920	3 200
Actuarial gains (losses) on defined benefit pension plans	(650)	1 333
Share of comprehensive income of associates	11 400	(700)
Income tax relating to other comprehensive income	5 540	(9 000)
Other comprehensive income, net of tax	(11 771)	35 833
TOTAL COMPREHENSIVE INCOME	97 354	95 333
Profit attributable to		
Owners of the parent	87 300	47 600
Minority interest	21 825	11 900
	109 125	59 500
Total comprehensive income attributable to		
Owners of the parent	77 883	78 667
Minority interest	19 471	16 666
	97 354	95 333

Notice in this statement of comprehensive income that more information is presented than is required. Additional line items of information are included at management's discretion when their presentation is relevant to understanding the entity's financial performance. Information on expenses can be reported based on nature or function (see box).

STATEMENT OF INCOME FORMATS: NATURE AND FUNCTION

The reporting entity should also present an analysis of expenses based on either their nature or function. Examples of expenses reported by nature would include depreciation, materials purchases and employee benefits. The following example classifies expenses by nature:

Revenue		X
Other income		X
Changes in inventories of finished goods and work in process		
Raw materials and consumables used	X	
Employee benefits expense	X	

Depreciation and amortization expense	X
Other expenses	<u>X</u>
Total expenses	<u>(X)</u>
Profit	<u><u>X</u></u>

The second form classifies expenses by function. Examples include cost of sales, distribution costs and administrative expenses. The following form is an example of classifying by function:

Revenue	X
Cost of sales	(X)
Gross profit	X
Other income	X
Distribution costs	(X)
Administrative expenses	(X)
Other expenses	(X)
Profit	<u><u>X</u></u>

If the expenses are classified by function, then additional information on their nature should be disclosed, including depreciation and amortization, and employee benefits expense.

2.2.2 WHAT ARE THE REQUIREMENTS FOR A TWO STATEMENT PRESENTATION?

Under the second option, a business may use two statements: a statement of income, and a statement of comprehensive income that begins with profit or loss. The following example illustrates how expenses are organized by nature. The statement of income reports only those items reported through profit or loss.

Chang Mao Electrical Ltd Statement of Income for the Years Ended 31 December ¥ Millions		
	2009	2008
Revenue	380 000	360 000
Other income	20 500	11 300
Changes in inventories	(194 500)	(191 500)
Employee benefits expense	(43 500)	(42 000)
Depreciation and amortization expense	(18 000)	(13 000)
Impairment of property, plant and equipment	(7 000)	–
Other expenses	(6 000)	(6 400)
Finance costs	(18 500)	(22 500)
Share of profit of associates	<u>32 500</u>	<u>32 100</u>

(Continued)

Chang Mao Electrical Ltd Statement of Income for the Years Ended 31 December ¥ Millions		
	2009	**2008**
Profit before tax	145 500	128 000
Income tax expense	(36 375)	(32 000)
Profit from continuing operations	109 125	96 000
Loss from discontinued operations	(36 375)	(32 000)
Profit	**109 125**	59 500
Profit attributable to		
Owners of the parent	87 300	47 600
Minority interest	21 825	11 900
	109 125	59 500

The second statement is the statement of comprehensive income, which shows only items related to other comprehensive income but starts with profit or loss from the statement of income.

Chang Mao Electrical Ltd Statement of Comprehensive Income for the Years Ended 31 December ¥ Millions		
	2009	**2008**
Profit	109 125	59 500
Other comprehensive income		
Currency translation differences on foreign operations	7 419	10 500
Available-for-sale financial assets	(38 000)	26 500
Cash flow hedges	1 600	4 000
Gains on revaluation of property	920	3 200
Actuarial gains (losses) on defined benefit pension plans	(650)	1 333
Share of comprehensive income of associates	11 400	(700)
Income tax relating to other comprehensive income	5 540	(9 000)
Other comprehensive income, net of tax	(11 771)	35 833
TOTAL COMPREHENSIVE INCOME	**97 354**	**95 333**
Total comprehensive income attributable to		
Owners of the parent	77 883	78 667
Minority interest	19 471	16 666
	97 354	95 333

ON YOUR OWN

LEARNING OUTCOME REVIEW

1. What are the two choices management has for presenting total comprehensive income?

LEARNING OUTCOME 3
EXPLAIN HOW REVENUE IS RECOGNIZED

3.   Explain how to account for profit or loss.
    3.1   How is revenue recognized?
           3.1.1 When should revenue for goods be recognized?
           3.1.2 When should revenue for services be recognized?
           3.1.3 When should revenue from interest, royalties and dividends be recognized?

    3.2   How do we account for revenue taxes like the sales tax and VAT?

3.1 How is revenue recognized?

Recall that revenue relates to the inflow of economic benefits from ordinary business activities.

> **IFRS**   Revenue is 'the gross inflow of economic benefits during the period arising in the course of the ordinary activities of an entity when those inflows result in increases in equity, other than increases relating to contributions from equity participants'.
>

Revenue arises from the sale of goods, the rendering of services and the use by others of entity assets that yield interest, royalties and dividends.

Why is correct revenue recognition an important issue in financial accounting? The reason is that revenue is perhaps the most manipulated item in the financial statements along with expenses. Inappropriate recognition means that profit is either overstated or understated (see box).

SHENANIGANS

Recall from Chapter 5 that shenanigans are schemes or scams that manipulate financial information. Howard Schilit[1] observes that all accounting deceits involve one of two basic strategies: inflating current period earnings by inflating current period revenue and gains, or by deflating current period expenses; and deflating current period earnings and consequently deflating future periods' results by deflating current period revenue or inflating current period expenses. Many deceits involve assigning either revenue or expenses to the incorrect accounting period.

Schilit also details seven shenanigans or tactics that serve these two strategies. These are summarized as follows:

Shenanigan (tactic)	Accounts	Strategy
1. Recording revenue too soon	Revenue or gains	Inflate current period
2. Record bogus revenue	Revenue or gains	Inflate current period
3. Boosting income with one-time gains	Revenue or gains Expenses or losses	Inflate current period
4. Shifting current expenses to a later period	Expenses or losses	Inflate current period
5. Failing to record or improperly reducing liabilities	Revenue or gains Expenses or losses	Inflate current period
6. Shifting current revenue to a later period	Revenue or gains	Deflate current period
7. Shifting future expenses to the current period as a special charge	Expenses or losses	Deflate current period

Revenue is measured at the fair value of the consideration received or receivable. Recall that fair value is the amount for which the asset could be exchanged, or a liability settled, between knowledgeable, willing parties in an arm's-length transaction. If another asset is received in a revenue transaction, then that asset is measured at fair value.

On 16 November 2009, a small lumber company sells some plywood to a contractor. Rather than receiving cash, the lumber company agrees to accept a used truck in payment with a market value of $8500. This would be the fair value at which the transaction is recorded:

Date	Account Titles	DR	CR
16 Nov. 2009	Equipment – used truck	$8 500	
	Sales revenue		$8 500

When goods and services are exchanged for goods or services that are similar in nature, the exchange is not regarded as a revenue-generating transaction. Examples include an exchange of a commodity like crude oil in two locations between two companies.

When the inflow of cash or cash equivalents is deferred, then the fair value may be less than the nominal amount of the receivable. In these cases, the amount receivable must be discounted and the difference between the nominal and discounted amounts be recognized as interest revenue.

A farm machinery dealer sells a major combine to a farmer for £120 000 on 2 October 2009, but allows the farmer to pay the amount owed in one year's time. The prevailing rate of interest is 8.5% on similar transactions. Thus, the present value of the amount receivable by the dealer is £110 599 (£120 000 ÷ 1.085). The revenue entry would be:

Date	Account Titles	DR	CR
2 Oct. 2009	Trade accounts receivable Interest receivable Sales revenue	£110 599 9 401	 £120 000

3.1.1 WHEN SHOULD REVENUE FOR GOODS BE RECOGNIZED?

Revenue is recognized when it is earned. But how do we know when revenue is earned? We apply the following criteria:

- When ownership is transferred to the buyer.
- When the business no longer has control over the goods sold.
- When the amount of revenues and the costs associated with that revenue can be reliably measured.
- When it is probable that the economic benefits of the sale will flow to the business.

Most businesses regard these conditions as satisfied when the goods have been delivered to the customer. But this too raises issues. When the goods are shipped, the terms of shipment are typically specified between seller and buyer. Delivery depends on whether the goods are shipped FOB (freight on board or free on board) shipping point or destination (see box).

SHIPPING POINTS

FOB shipping point means that the buyer assumes ownership and responsibility for the goods when the seller turns them over to the carrier (shipping company).

FOB destination means that the buyer assumes ownership and thus responsibility when the carrier delivers the goods to the buyer.

A Japanese company in Shiga, Japan, sells four heavy-duty tractors to a construction company on 13 September. The tractors are shipped from Japan on 25 September FOB Dubai. They are received in Dubai on 17 October. When should the company recognize the revenue?

The answer is on 17 October, once it receives confirmation of delivery to the customer. This means that for the third quarter, the financial statements would not report revenue and the tractors would still be included in inventories of the seller even though the company is no longer in physical possession of the tractors.

Suppose instead that the tractors were shipped FOB Shiga, Japan. This means that delivery to the customer took place when the goods left the seller's premises in Japan on 25 September. Thus, the revenue would be recognized in the third quarter statement of income, but would be excluded from inventories on the statement of financial position.

3.1.2 WHEN SHOULD REVENUE FOR SERVICES BE RECOGNIZED?

The recognition of services depends on how complete the services are. Of course, revenues for services rendered in a single day, for example, would be recognized immediately. However, some services may continue for months and even years. In this case, we recognize service revenue based on the stage of completion at the reporting date. However, several conditions must be met: the amount of revenue, associated costs and stage of completion must be able to be reliably measured; and the economic benefits from the service revenue transaction must flow to the business entity.

EXAMPLE 1

A company requests its attorney to review a contract with a supplier. The company sends the contract to the attorney on 26 May, the attorney returns it to the company with her analysis and comments on 30 May, the attorney sends an invoice for payment on 3 June, and the company pays the invoice on 17 June. The company's cheque for payment clears the bank on 22 June. When should the attorney recognize the revenue related to this transaction?

The answer is 30 May, since rendering of the service had been completed on that date. In other words, the service was 100% complete by the end of May, the reporting date.

EXAMPLE 2

A Prague theatre company sells subscriptions to its annual season, which contains six plays. A season subscription is sold for €840 on 7 August 2012 and is paid in full. When a season's ticket is sold, the receipt of the cash would be recorded as follows:

Date	Account Titles	DR	CR
7 Aug. 2012	Cash	€840	
	Unearned subscription revenue		€840

No revenue is recognized because no delivery of services has occurred as of this date. However, as each play is presented, that portion of revenue is recognized in the corresponding accounting period. Suppose that the first performance is in September 2012, which would result in the following adjusting entry to recognize revenue for the month end:

Date	Account Titles	DR	CR
30 Sep. 2012	Unearned subscription revenue	140	
	Revenue		140

In this case, on the 30 September reporting date, the service was one sixth completed.

EXAMPLE 3

An engineering firm is engaged by a building contractor to work out specifications on a bridge. The total contract amount is fixed at \$720 000 and the engineering work is expected to take about six months. At the end of the January 2011, the first month, the engineering firm estimates that the work is 15% complete. The engineering firm would recognize \$108 000 in revenue (.15 × \$720 000). The journal entry would be:

Date	Account Titles	DR	CR
31 Jan. 2011	Trade accounts receivable	108 000	
	Service revenue		108 000

In some cases, revenue recognition is based on the passage of time, since there is no other reasonable basis for recognizing the revenue.

EXAMPLE 4

On 1 June 2009, a security firm is hired by a company to guard its warehouse facility on a flat-fee contract of Hong Kong $1 920 000 per annum. At the end of each quarter, the security firm bills the company for services rendered to date. However, the security firm closes its books monthly, and therefore must recognize the revenue earned. This would be done by recognizing an equal amount each month (HK$1 920 000 ÷ 12 months = HK$160 000). Each month, the following adjusting entry would be made to recognize revenue:

Date	Account Titles	DR	CR
30 June 2009	Trade accounts receivable Sales revenue	HK$160 000	HK$160 000

In cases where the outcome of a service transaction cannot be reliably measured, then revenue should be recognized only to the extent of the recoverable expenses.

3.1.3 WHEN SHOULD REVENUE FROM INTEREST, ROYALTIES AND DIVIDENDS BE RECOGNIZED?

Revenue can also be *earned* from interest, royalties and dividends:

* *Interest* is charged on amounts due to the business for cash lent to other parties.
* *Royalties* are charges for the use of long-term assets such as patents, trademarks, copyrights and software.
* *Dividends are revenue when the business owns shares of other businesses that pay the dividends.* This is unrelated to dividends paid by the business to its own shareholders.

Recognition is generally based on when the business is entitled to the economic benefits and when they can be reliably measured.

Guangchou Entertainment plc owns shares in Gộn Việt Nam Resorts. Gộn Việt Nam declares a dividend of ¥200 000 on 31 March 2009 with a payment date of 10 February 2009. Since the dividend has already been declared and is therefore a liability by Gộn Việt Nam and the amount is reliably measurable, Guangchou would recognize the dividend revenue on 31 March 2009.

3.2 How do we account for revenue taxes like the sales tax and VAT?

Many jurisdictions levy a tax on items being sold, whether to consumers or business-to-business customers. Some taxes, like the value added tax (VAT) in Europe (or goods and services tax in Australia), are embedded. A value added tax is assessed on the value added to goods and services. Part of the total price paid by the customer is actually a tax being collected for the government by the seller. A value added tax is embedded in the price.

On 13 October 2009 Elaine Harris makes a purchase at Excelsior Boutique for £880. This price contains a value added tax of £31. Assuming that the purchase was for cash, the journal entry would be:

Date	Account Titles	DR	CR
13 Oct. 2010	Cash	£880	
	VAT payable		£31
	Sales revenue		849

Notice that the Excelsior Boutique is collecting the tax on behalf of the tax authority and that at some time must forward all taxes collected to the tax collection office. For this single purchase, the entry to remit the amount collected to the tax authority, assuming that payment is made at the end of each month, would be as follows:

Date	Account Titles	DR	CR
31 Oct. 2010	VAT payable	£31	
	Cash		£31

A sales tax is levied on the total value of the exchange when goods or services are sold. Thus, sales taxes are added to the price charged to the customer at the point of sale.

Ahmed Kayali visits Discount Outlet, an electronics retailer, where he purchases merchandise for $880 on 3 February 2010. Sales tax of 8.25% is added to the purchase price at the point of sale. Ahmed therefore pays an additional $72.80 ($880 × 8.25%) in sales taxes, or a total of $952.60. The journal entry would be as follows:

Date	Account Titles	DR	CR
3 Feb. 2010	Cash	$952.60	
	Sales tax payable		$72.60
	Sales revenue		880.00

Discount Outlet remits sales taxes collected to the tax authority at the end of the month. The journal entry for this single transaction would be as follows:

Date	Account Titles	DR	CR
28 Feb. 2010	Cash	$72.70	
	Sales tax payable		$72.60

ON YOUR OWN

LEARNING OUTCOME REVIEW

1. What are the two major components of total comprehensive income?
2. What is the difference between income and profit or loss?
3. Define revenue. What is the difference between revenue and income?
4. What are royalties?
5. When is revenue recognized for the sale of goods? For rendering of services? For interest, royalties and dividends? How is revenue measured?
6. What is FOB shipping point? What is FOB destination?
7. Why is revenue such a critical issue for accounting?

LEARNING OUTCOME PRACTICE

1. Hisham Ltd acquired a truck for €75 000 in 2007. In 2009, the company acquired two pieces of computer equipment from Lanzhou Electronics that had a fair value of €72 000. Hisham

worked out an arrangement whereby Lanzhou would take the truck in exchange for the computer equipment with no cash changing hands. The truck had a market value of €68 000. Accumulated depreciation on the truck was €25 000 at the time of the exchange. How much revenue should Lanzhou recognize?

a. €75 000
b. €72 000
c. €68 000
d. €50 000

2. Which of the following conditions does not have to be met in order for revenue to be recognized for goods?

a. The amount of revenue must be able to be measured reliably.
b. It is probable that the economic benefits of the transaction will flow to the entity.
c. The business no longer has control over the goods.
d. The costs associated with the revenue must have already been incurred.

3. Goods are shipped from Paris to Brussels on 12 November 2009 on terms FOB shipping point. The customer is invoiced for the goods on 15 November 2009. The goods arrive in Brussels and are received by the buyer on 14 November 2009. The customer issues a cheque for full payment on 21 November 2009. When should revenue be recognized by the seller in Paris?

a. 12 November 2009
b. 14 November 2009
c. 15 November 2009
d. 21 November 2009

4. Goods are shipped from Paris to Brussels on 12 November 2009 on terms FOB destination. The customer is invoiced for the goods on 15 November 2009. The goods arrive in Brussels and are received by the buyer on 14 November 2009. The customer issues a cheque for full payment on 21 November 2009. When should revenue be recognized by the seller in Paris?

a. 12 November 2009
b. 14 November 2009
c. 15 November 2009
d. 21 November 2009

5. Which of the following conditions does not have to be met in order for revenue to be recognized for services?

a. The amount of revenue must be able to be measured reliably.
b. Services must be substantially complete.
c. Costs incurred and to be incurred related to the transaction must be able to be measured reliably.
d. It is probable that the economic benefits of the transaction will flow to the entity.

6. Roldo Cosmetics plc owns 10% of the capital stock in Vittorio Ltd. On 29 December 2009, Vittorio declares €200 000 dividends, which are paid on 7 January 2010. On 28 December 2010, Vittorio's board declares a dividend of €250 000, which will be paid 5 January 2011. How much dividend revenue should Roldo recognize in 2010?

   a. €200 000
   b. €250 000
   c. €450 000
   d. Nil

LEARNING OUTCOME 4
EXPLAIN WHEN EXPENSES ARE RECOGNIZED

Expenses are recognized for one of four reasons:

- Costs are matched to revenue on the basis of a direct association between the cost incurred and the earning of specific revenue.
- Asset costs are systematically allocated such as depreciation of property, plant and equipment and amortization of intangible assets.
- When expenditure produces no future economic benefit that would qualify as recognition of an asset on the statement of financial position.
- When a liability is incurred *without* the recognition of an asset. For example, employees have rendered services for which the business has not paid.

When costs and revenues are matched, expenses are recognized simultaneously with either a decrease in assets or an increase in liabilities, as the following example illustrates.

Lakshmanan Services Ltd pays employees a total of 12 500 in cash rupees on Friday, 6 February 2009 for construction work during the week. The journal entry would be:

Date	Account Titles	DR	CR
6 Feb. 2009	Wage expense	12 500	
	Cash		12 500

This expense is recognized by decreasing an asset. However, if Lakshmanan pays at the end of the month, the journal entry to record wage expense would have been:

Date	Account Titles	DR	CR
6 Feb. 2009	Wage expense Wages payable	12 500	12 500

In this case, the expense is recognized simultaneously with the increase in a liability.

LEARNING OUTCOME 5
EXPLAIN WHY GAINS AND LOSSES ARE INCLUDED IN OTHER COMPREHENSIVE INCOME

All items related to revenue or expenses are recognized in profit or loss unless IFRS requires or permits the item to be reported in other comprehensive income. When an item is included in other comprehensive income, we say that it is recognized *directly in equity* and therefore does not appear in profit or loss. For example, an asset can be revalued to a higher, current market value.

Assume that a company purchases land as an investment for £10 000 000. After one year, the market value has risen to £11 000 000, an increase of £1 000 000. The £11 000 000 is the realizable value (see box).

IFRS Realizable value is 'the amount of cash or cash equivalent that could currently be obtained by selling an asset in an orderly disposal'.

Realization means that a transaction has been completed or consummated. In this example, realization has not occurred. Realization occurs *when the property is actually sold* and the economic benefit secured for the reporting entity. The gain is reported in profit and loss only when it has been realized. Items recognized in other comprehensive income are not realized and thus are *not* reported in profit or loss.

In this textbook we focus only on the revaluation of property, plant and equipment and intangible assets.

Hanoi-based Phuong Development Ltd acquired land for 8.5 billion VND (Viet Nam đồng) on 30 June 2009, anticipating expansion of one of its apartment blocks located next door. However, construction would not begin until 2013. On 31 December 2009 Phuong had the property appraised at 9.25 billion VND. Because the company uses the revaluation method to account for property, the following entry was made:

Date	Account Titles	DR	CR
31 Dec. 2009	Land Revaluation reserve – other comprehensive income	750 000 000	750 000 000

The 750 million VND credit appears as other comprehensive income and is reported on the statement of comprehensive income. Since this amount bypasses profit or loss, we say that it is recognized directly in equity as a revaluation reserve.

Figure 10.3 illustrates the difference in an item recognized in profit or loss versus an item recognized directly in equity through other comprehensive income.

FIGURE 10.3 RECOGNITION IN PROFIT OR LOSS VERSUS OTHER COMPREHENSIVE INCOME

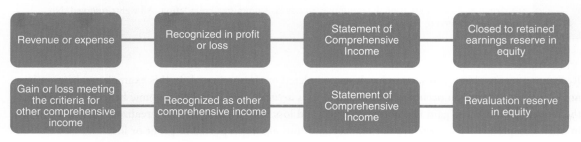

The difference as shown in Figure 10.3 is that revenue and expenses are recognized in profit or loss. Profit and loss is reported on the statement of comprehensive income. We know from Part II that these are temporary accounts that are *closed* to retained earnings. An amount recognized directly in other comprehensive income is not a temporary account but *a change to a permanent account in equity*, even though it appears on the statement of comprehensive income.

On 31 December 2010, Phuong Development Ltd again appraises the land it bought on 30 June 2009. The appraisal shows that the land value has declined to 8.75 billion VND because of an economic downturn. Phuong would then make the following entry:

Date	Account Titles	DR	CR
31 Dec. 2010	Revaluation reserve – other comprehensive income Land	500 000 000	500 000 000

Phuong's land has declined less than the previous revaluation upwards. This decline is therefore debited to the revaluation reserve. The 500 000 000 VND would appear on the statement of comprehensive income. It also reduces the amount of the revaluation reserve in equity to 8 750 000 000 VND, which is the land's current value.

During 2011, the land decreases to 8 000 000 000 VND according to the appraiser. Under the revaluation method, Phuong must again adjust the carrying amount and would make the following entry:

Date	Account Titles	DR	CR
31 Dec. 2011	Revaluation reserve – other comprehensive income Impairment loss Land	250 000 000 500 000 000	750 000 000

The decline in the value of the land from its carrying amount is 750 million VND (8 750 000 000 VND – 8 000 000 000 VND). Notice that the land declined in value more than the amount in the revaluation reserve. Thus, the revaluation reserve is debited for 250 000 000 VND. The remainder of the decline in value is debited for 500 000 000 VND to impairment loss and is therefore part of profit or loss.

Figure 10.4 provides a decision diagram that illustrates how revaluations that subsequently decline in value are recognized in other comprehensive income and profit or loss.

FIGURE 10.4 DECISION DIAGRAM FOR REVALUATIONS

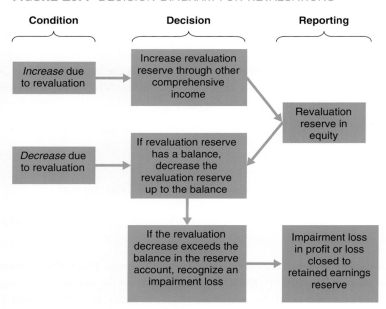

ON YOUR OWN

LEARNING REVIEW PRACTICE

1. A company buys a building that increases in value over one year. The company then sells the property for cash for an amount higher than its carrying amount, which is duly recorded in the accounting records. Which of the following statements is correct?
   a. The company has only realized a gain
   b. The company has recognized but not realized a gain
   c. A gain has been neither recognized nor realized
   d. A gain has been both recognized and realized

2. A company buys a building that increases in value over the five-year holding period. The increase is recorded under the revaluation method. The company does not sell the property. Which is correct?
   a. The company has only realized a gain
   b. The company has recognized but not realized a gain
   c. A gain has neither been realized nor recognized
   d. A gain has been both recognized and realized

LEARNING OUTCOME 6
DESCRIBE THE REPORTING REQUIREMENTS FOR THE STATEMENT OF CHANGES IN EQUITY

The statement of changes in equity brings together *all* changes to equity accounts. For each component of equity, the beginning and ending amounts are shown with reconciliations for profit or loss, each item of other comprehensive income and transactions with owners. In addition, amounts attributable to the parent and noncontrolling interests must be shown separately. The following example illustrates the format for the statement of changes in equity.

	Share Capital	Retained Earnings	Translation of Foreign Operations	Available-for Sale Financial Assets	Cash Flow Hedges	Revaluation Surplus	Total	Noncontrolling Interest	Total Equity
				Chang Mao Electrical Ltd Statement of Changes in Equity for the Years Ended 31 December 2009 ¥ Millions					
Balance at 1 January 2008	550 000	117 500	(5 000)	1 800	2 000	–	666 300	166 575	832 875
Changes in equity for 2008									
Dividends	–	(20 000)	–	–	–	–	(20 000)	–	(20 000)
Total comprehensive income for the year	–	55 000	7 500	26 500	1 800	1 020	91 820	19 800	111 620
Balance at 31 December 2008	550 000	152 500	2 500	28 300	3 800	1 020	738 120	186 375	924 495
Changes in equity for 2009									
Issue of share capital	50 000	–	–	–	–	–	50 000	–	50 000
Dividends	–	(20 000)	–	–	–	–	(20 000)	–	(20 000)
Total comprehensive income for the year	–	95 000	3 000	(17 400)	(500)	850	80 950	20 200	101 150
Balance at 31 December 2009	600 000	227 500	5 500	10 900	3 300	1 870	849 070	206 575	1 055 645

GLOBAL PERSPECTIVE

PricewaterhouseCoopers conducts a periodic survey of investment professionals on issues related to corporate reporting. In the 2007 version, respondents reported that the statement of income was highly important for assessing the operational performance of a business. In fact, these professionals said that they wanted even more detail than is currently provided.

Specifically, they want to be able to assess whether any increases in revenues or income are sustainable, and whether they come from growth from the existing business or from acquisition of other businesses. They also want to be able to separate the effect of volume gains from price rises.

The respondents believed that current methodologies used to recognize revenues are overly complex and often leave them unclear about how accounting standards have been implemented by companies. The result is that some lack confidence that they are comparing companies on an equitable basis.

Methods of categorizing costs also cause frustration. Respondents said that cost categories are often too broad and that more detail is needed. However, the respondents supported the move by the IASB to mandate cost reporting 'by nature', for example labour and depreciation as opposed to cost of sales.

LEARNING OUTCOME 7
EXPLAIN HOW EQUITY CHANGES ARE EVALUATED

7.1 What profitability ratios are related to equity changes?
    7.1.1 How do we calculate the gross profit ratio?
    7.1.2 How do we calculate the profit margin ratio?
    7.1.3 How do we calculate return on assets?
    7.1.4 How do we calculate return on investment?

7.2 How does the times interest earned ratio measure solvency?

7.1 What profitability ratios are related to equity changes?

Four ratios to evaluate profitability are commonly used: gross profit ratio, profit ratio, return on assets and return on investment. We will continue using Heliard Coffees plc for our example. The statement of financial position and the statement of comprehensive income are shown below.

Heliard Coffees plc Statement of Financial Position At 31 December € Euros		
	2009	**2008**
Noncurrent assets		
Property, plant and equipment	180 000	200 000
Less: Accumulated depreciation	(28 500)	(55 000)
	151 500	145 000
Investments at fair value	33 000	28 000
Goodwill	5 000	5 000
Total noncurrent assets	190 000	178 500
Current assets		
Inventories	29 000	27 500
Trade accounts receivable	28 000	28 500
Marketable securities	9 500	7 000
Cash and cash equivalents	5 000	3 500
Total current assets	71 500	66 500
TOTAL ASSETS	261 500	245 000
Shareholders' equity		
Share capital	50 000	50 000
Share premium	35 000	35 000
Reserves	42 000	30 000
Total shareholders' equity	127 000	115 000
Noncurrent liabilities		
Borrowings	65 000	60 000
Total noncurrent liabilities	65 000	60 000
Current liabilities		
Notes payable	32 500	37 500
Accrued liabilities	22 000	20 000
Trade accounts payable	15 000	12 500
Total current liabilities	69 500	70 000
Total liabilities	134 500	130 000
TOTAL SHAREHOLDERS' EQUITY AND LIABILITIES	261 500	245 000

The statement of income for Heliard Coffees plc is shown below.

The two profitability ratios both use net sales in the denominator. However, the gross profit ratio measures gross profit as a percentage of net sales, while the net profit ratio uses profit as a percentage of net sales.

Heliard Coffees plc
Statement of Income
for the Year Ended
31 December 2009
€ Euros

Sales revenue	€ 150 000
Cost of sales	70 000
Gross profit	80 000
Operating expenses	20 000
Interest expense	10 000
Profit before income tax	50 000
Income tax (20%)	10 000
Profit	€ 40 000

7.1.1 HOW DO WE CALCULATE THE GROSS PROFIT RATIO?

The gross profit ratio measures gross profit as a percentage of net sales. Recall that gross profit is calculated by subtracting cost of goods sold or cost of sales from net sales. Thus, gross profit is the profit before operating expenses, finance expenses and tax expenses are deducted. Therefore gross profit tells us the amount of profit after deducting only those expenses that are directly attributable to the production of the goods or services. The gross profit ratio expresses that number as a percentage. The calculation is:

$$\text{Gross profit ratio} = \frac{\text{Gross profit}}{\text{Net sales}}$$

For Heliard Coffees plc we substitute:

$$\text{Gross profit ratio} = \frac{€\,80\,000}{€\,150\,000}$$

$$0.53 = \frac{€\,80\,000}{€\,150\,000}$$

7.1.2 HOW DO WE CALCULATE THE PROFIT MARGIN RATIO?

The profit margin ratio is calculated by dividing profit (after all expenses have been deducted) by net sales.

$$\text{Profit margin ratio} = \frac{\text{Profit}}{\text{Net sales}}$$

For Heliard Coffees we substitute:

$$\text{Profit margin ratio} = \frac{€40\ 000}{€150\ 000}$$

$$0.27 = \frac{€40\ 000}{€150\ 000}$$

7.1.3 HOW DO WE CALCULATE RETURN ON ASSETS?

The return on assets ratio measures the amount of profit that was generated as a percentage of the average total assets.

$$\text{Return on assets} = \frac{\text{Profit}}{\text{Average total assets}}$$

Heliard's calculation for 2009 is as follows.

First, average total assets must be calculated:

$$\text{Average total assets} = \frac{€261\ 500 + €245\ 000}{2}$$

$$€253\ 250 = \frac{€261\ 500 + €245\ 000}{2}$$

And then the return on assets:

$$\text{Return on assets} = \frac{€40\ 000}{€253\ 250}$$

$$15.8\% = \frac{€40\ 000}{€253\ 250}$$

Since we do not have the total assets balance for the beginning of 2008, the return on assets ratio for 2008 cannot be calculated.

7.1.4 HOW DO WE CALCULATE RETURN ON INVESTMENT?

The return on investment ratio measures the performance of the firm without taking into account the method of financing.

$$\text{Return on investment} = \frac{\text{Profit} + \text{interest expense } (1 - \text{tax rate})}{\text{Average noncurrent liabilities} + \text{equity}}$$

First for 2009, average noncurrent liabilities plus equity is calculated:

$$\text{Average noncurrent liabilities} + \text{equity} = \frac{[€65\ 000\ +\ €127\ 000]\ +\ [€60\ 000\ +\ €115\ 000]}{2}$$

$$\text{Average noncurrent liabilities} + \text{equity} = \frac{[€19\ 000]\ +\ €175\ 000]}{2}$$

$$€183\ 000 = \frac{[€191\ 000]\ +\ €175\ 000]}{2}$$

Then **return on investment** is calculated:

$$\text{Return on investment} = \frac{€40\ 000\ +\ €10\ 000\ (1\ -\ 0.20)}{€183\ 000}$$

$$\text{Return on investment} = \frac{€40\ 000\ +\ €8\ 000}{€183\ 000}$$

$$26.2\% = \frac{€48\ 000}{€183\ 000}$$

The return on investment formula adds back in the after-tax interest expense (after-tax because interest is deducted from profit before tax is calculated – at 20% in the Heliard example). This allows the investor to judge profit performance as it would be whether the company's activities are financed by either debt or equity.

7.2 What solvency ratios are related to equity changes?

The times interest earned ratio provides a measure of the business's ability to pay interest expense compared to pre-interest, pre-tax earnings divided by interest expense.

$$\text{Times interest earned} = \frac{\text{Profit}\ +\ \text{interest expense}\ +\ \text{tax expense}}{\text{Interest expense}}$$

The calculation of the times interest earned ratio for Heliard would be:

$$\text{Times interest earned} = \frac{€40\ 000\ +\ €10\ 000\ +\ €10\ 000}{€10\ 000}$$

$$\text{Times interest earned} = \frac{€60\ 000}{€10\ 000}$$

$$6.0 = \frac{€60\ 000}{€10\ 000}$$

But what do these ratios mean? And how are they used? Let's compare the four ratios computed above with Chiu Coffee Houses Ltd, a competitor to Heliard Coffees plc, which has the following statement of comprehensive income for the same reporting period.

Chiu Coffee Houses Ltd Statement of Income for the Year Ended 31 December 2009 € Euros	
Sales revenue	€270 000
Cost of sales	125 000
Gross profit	145 000
Operating expenses	45 000
Interest expense	26 250
Profit before income tax	73 750
Income tax (20%)	14 750
Profit	€59 000

Here are the calculations for Chiu Coffee Houses' gross profit ratio:

$$\text{Gross profit ratio} = \frac{\text{Gross profit}}{\text{Net sales}}$$

$$\text{Gross profit ratio} = \frac{€145\,000}{€270\,000}$$

$$0.54 = \frac{€145\,000}{€270\,000}$$

And the profit ratio:

$$\text{Profit margin ratio} = \frac{\text{Profit}}{\text{Net sales}}$$

$$\text{Profit margin ratio} = \frac{€59\,000}{€270\,000}$$

$$0.22 = \frac{€59\,000}{€270\,000}$$

What we can see from this comparison between Heliard and Chiu is that the amount of profit that Chiu's management is able to obtain from net sales as measured by the profit margin ratio is less than Heliard's (0.22 versus 0.27). But the question we now must address is why. Is Chiu paying too much for coffee compared to Heliard? The answer is no, because the gross margin ratio is 0.54 for Chiu versus 0.53 for Heliard. There is no significant difference. So that means that the operating expenses, interest expense and tax expense must account for the difference.

We can now calculate the times interest earned ratio for Chiu Coffee Houses.

$$\text{Times interest earned} = \frac{€59\,000 + €26\,250 + €14\,750}{€26\,250}$$

$$\text{Times interest earned} = \frac{€100\,000}{€26\,250}$$

$$3.8 = \frac{€100\,000}{€26\,250}$$

The times interest earned ratio tells us that Chiu has 3.8 times its interest expense in pre-interest, pre-tax profit compared to Heliard's times interest earned ratio of 6.0. Thus, the amount of debt that Chiu is carrying does in fact cause its profit margin ratio to be lower, although this may not be the entire explanation.

ON YOUR OWN

LEARNING OUTCOME REVIEW

1. How is the times interest earned ratio calculated? What does the times interest earned ratio measure?
2. How is the gross profit ratio calculated? What does the gross profit ratio measure?
3. How is the profit margin ratio calculated? What does the profit margin ratio measure?
4. What is the difference between the gross profit ratio and the profit margin ratio?
5. How is return on assets calculated? What does return on assets measure?
6. How is return on investments calculated? What does return on investments measure?

Conclusion

In this chapter, we have examined changes in financial position. A change in financial position occurs for one of the following reasons:

- Contributed capital is increased by the issuance of shares for another asset such as cash, shares of another business, real estate or another asset or reduction to a liability. Contributed capital is decreased by the company's purchase of its own shares.

- Equity other than contributed capital is increased or decreased by profit or loss, respectively. In addition, a dividend involving the distribution of cash or another asset would decrease equity. Increases and decreases also come from items recognized as part of other comprehensive income. These include revaluations of property, plant and equipment and intangible assets; gains and losses on employee benefit plans; gains and losses related to foreign currency translations; and gains and losses on available-for-sale financial assets and hedging instruments.

Total comprehensive income can be reported in one of two formats: a single statement of comprehensive income that shows both profit or loss and other comprehensive income; or two separate statements: the statement of income and the statement of comprehensive income. A separate statement of changes in equity is also required that presents total comprehensive income as well as changes from profit or loss, other comprehensive income and transactions with owners.

A major issue related to profit or loss is appropriate revenue recognition. IFRS provides separate recognition criteria for goods, services, and interest, royalties and dividends. Revenue is measured at fair value of the consideration received or receivable. Profit or loss is also affected by the appropriate matching of tax expense. Because tax authorities often base the payment of taxes based on cash receipts or disbursements, a deferred tax asset must be recognized when taxes are paid in advance of the recognition of the related tax expense, and a deferred tax liability is created when taxes are paid after recognition of tax expense.

Finally, this chapter described four income-related ratios. The gross profit and profit margin ratios are both profitability related. The gross profit ratio measures gross profit as a percentage of net sales, while the profit margin ratio measures profit as a percentage of net sales. Return on assets measures the amount of profit as a percentage of average total assets. The times interest earned ratio calculates a multiple of pre-interest, pre-tax profit divided by interest expense as a solvency measure.

Summary
LEARNING OUTCOME 1
Equity Change Transactions Explained
Equity is affected by four types of transactions. First, contributed capital is changed when owners invest additional capital or shares are repurchased by the business entity. Second, the retained earnings reserve is increased or decreased by profit or loss, respectively. Third, accumulated earnings can be distributed to shareholders as dividends, which reduce the retained earnings. And finally, changes to reserves can be recognized directly in equity and reported as other comprehensive income on the statement of comprehensive income.

LEARNING OUTCOME 2
Statement of Comprehensive Income Explained
The statement of comprehensive income has two major elements: profit or loss and other comprehensive income. If a gain or loss is not reported in other comprehensive income, then by default it would be

reported in profit or loss. Under IFRS, a business can use one of two approaches to report total comprehensive income. It can present a single statement of comprehensive income or it can present two statements: a statement of income and a statement of other comprehensive income. In this textbook, we have used the single statement presentation.

LEARNING OUTCOME 3
Revenue Recognition Explained

Revenue can be earned on goods, services or from interest, royalties and dividends. Revenue on the sale of goods is earned when ownership is transferred to the buyer and the business no longer has control over the goods sold. In addition, the amount of revenues and associated cost must be able to be measured reliably and it must be probable that the economic benefits from the sale will flow to the business. One issue is how to judge when ownership has been transferred to the buyer. That often depends on how goods are shipped. When shipped FOB shipping point, ownership transfers when the carrier takes delivery of the goods. FOB destination means that ownership transfers when the goods are delivered to the buyer.

Revenue for services rendered is recognized based on stage of completion. However, to recognize any revenue related to the service, the business must be able to measure the revenue and associated costs reliably, and the economic benefits from the service must have a probability of flowing to the business. Finally, revenue from interest, royalties and dividends is recognized when the business is entitled to the associated economic benefits and they can be reliably measured.

LEARNING OUTCOME 4
Expense Recognition Explained

Expenses are recognized for different reasons. First, expenses are recognized when costs can be matched to associated revenues. Second, expenses are recognized based on the systematic allocation of the depreciable property, plant and equipment and amortizable intangible assets. Third, any expenditure that has no future benefit is expensed. And finally, if a liability is incurred without recognizing an associated asset, that amount would be expensed.

LEARNING OUTCOME 5
Other Comprehensive Income Recognition Explained

Transactions are recorded in other comprehensive income for several specific reasons under IFRS. In this textbook we examine only one: the revaluation of assets. Others relate to employee benefits, translation of the financial statements of foreign operations and certain financial assets and liabilities.

When an item is recorded as other comprehensive income, we say that it is recognized directly in equity. A change in other comprehensive income is reported on the statement of comprehensive income and is not part of profit or loss. Nor is other comprehensive income 'closed' to retained earnings, as revenue and expenses are. Other comprehensive income changes are simply reported on the statement of comprehensive income, but are reserves in equity on the statement of financial position.

LEARNING OUTCOME 6
Statement of Changes in Equity Reporting Requirements Explained

The statement of changes in equity reports all items that change equity balances, including contributed capital and reserves. The statement of changes in equity reconciles each balance, showing the beginning amount and ending amount and what changes account for the difference.

LEARNING OUTCOME 7
Equity Changes Evaluated

The items reported on the statement of comprehensive income expand the ratios available for evaluating the business. The times interest ratio is a solvency ratio that helps external users judge the business's ability to pay interest on debt. The gross profit ratio measures the percentage of gross profit based on net sales to help evaluate profitability before operating expenses, taxes and finance expenses are deducted. Finally, the profit margin ratio helps evaluate how successful the business has been at producing profit as a percentage of net sales.

Key terms

FOB destination
FOB shipping point
Gross profit ratio
Profit margin ratio
Realizable value
Realization
Return on assets

Return on investment
Royalties
Sales tax
Times interest earned ratio
Total comprehensive income
Value added tax (VAT)

Terminology practice

For each of the following, insert the correct term from the list of key terms preceding this section. Each key term can be used more than once.

1. _____ are charges for the use of long-term assets such as patents, trademarks and software.
2. The _____ is calculated by dividing gross profit by net sales.
3. _____ is the amount of cash or cash equivalent that could currently be obtained by selling an asset in an orderly disposal.
4. _____ is the total of profit or loss and other comprehensive income.
5. The _____ is calculated by dividing profit + interest expense + tax expense by interest expense.
6. _____ is payment received for earnings on amounts owed to the business entity.
7. A _____ is a tax assessed on the value of goods and services at each stage of distribution.
8. _____ and _____ refer to the point which the buyer assumes responsibility for the goods being shipped.

9. _____ is the income received from profit distributions from a company owned by the business entity.

10. _____ occurs when a transaction has been completed or consummated.

11. The _____ is calculated by dividing profit by net sales.

12. A _____ is a tax levied on the final sales price of goods or services.

13. _____ is calculated by dividing profit by average total assets.

14. _____ is calculated by dividing average noncurrent liabilities plus equity into profits plus after tax interest expense.

Comprehensive Application Problems

The following problems bring together lessons learned in Part I and II.

1. Gareth Carson Corporation has been in business since 1 May 2010. The company has prepared the draft statement of income shown below and has asked you to check if it is correct.

Draft Statement of Income as at 30 April 2011		
Sales		$97 600
Purchases	$46 840	
Rent	15 000	
Electricity	4 800	
Telephone	2 750	
Returns inward	954	
Carriage and delivery	1 846	
Wages	31 580	
Other expenses	839	
	104 609	
Trade discounts on purchases	(2 423)	103 086
Loss for year		(5 486)

Additional information:

i. Closing inventory cost $6378. This includes damaged items that cost $1564. These could be repaired for $375 and then sold for $1820.

ii. The figure for rent is the total paid in the year to 30 April 2011. Five equal payments were made for the three-month periods commencing on 1 May 2010, 1 August 2010, 1 November 2010, 1 February 2011 and 1 May 2011.

iii. Carriage and delivery comprise $1428 for carriage on goods received and $418 for delivering goods to customers.

iv. The charge for wages is made up of $28 000 paid to Gareth and $3580 paid to a part-time employee.

Required: Prepare Gareth's corrected statement of income for the year to 30 April 2011, showing both gross profit and net profit. [ACCA adapted]

2. Airn Enterprises Ltd does not keep a full set of accounting records. An analysis of the company's cash transactions for the year ended 30 June 2010 is given below:

	Reference to Notes	Receipts	Payments
Overdraft, 1 July 2009			$34 200
Cash banked	1	$418 200	
Proceeds of sale of old motor van	2, 3	4 500	
Payments for purchases			316 300
New motor van purchased 1 January 2010	3		22 000
Rent and general expenses			47 400
Dividends			80 400
Overdraft, 30 June 2010		77 600	
		500 300	500 300

Airn's other assets and liabilities at the beginning and the end of the year ended 30 June 2010 were:

		30 June	
	Reference to Notes	2010	2009
Shop fittings (cost $45 000)		to be calculated	$35 000
Motor van (cost $18 000)	2, 3	Sold	4 000
New motor van	3	22 000	–
Trade receivables		48 600	44 700
Trade payables		24 200	19 600
Inventories		63 200	58 900
Owing for rent and general expenses		13 000	12 500

Notes:
(1) Before banking the cash received from customers, Airn made the following payments:

Wages	$74 000
Purchases for cash	13 700
General expenses	7 400
	$95 100

(2) The motor van held at 30 June 2009 was sold during the year.

(3) Airn's depreciation policy is to charge depreciation on the straight-line basis as follows, assuming no residual value:

| Motor van | 20% per year |
| Shop fittings | 10% per year |

No depreciation is charged in the year of sale of assets, but there is a full year's depreciation in the year of purchase. [ACCA adapted]

Required: Prepare Airn's statement of income for the year ended 30 June 2010. [ACCA adapted]

3. The draft financial statements of Rampion, a limited liability company, for the year ended 31 December 2010 included the following figures:

Profit	$684 000
Closing inventory	$116 800
Trade receivables	$248 000
Allowance for receivables	$10 000

No adjustments have yet been made for the following matters:

i. The company's inventory count was carried out on 3 January 2011, leading to the figure shown above. Sales between the close of business on 31 December 2010 and the inventory count totalled $36 000. There were no deliveries from suppliers for that period. The company fixes selling prices to produce a 40% gross profit on sales. The $36 000 sales were included in the sales records of January 2011.

ii. $10 000 of goods supplied on sale or return terms in December 2010 have been included as sales and receivables. They had a cost of $6000. On 10 January 2011 the customer returned the goods in good condition.

iii. Goods included in inventory at cost $18 000 were sold in January 2011 for $13 500. Selling expenses were $500.

iv. $8000 of trade receivables are to be written off.

v. The allowance for receivables is to be adjusted to the equivalent of 5% of the trade receivables after allowing for the above matters, based on past experience.

Required:

(a) Prepare a statement showing the effect of the adjustments on the company's net profit for the year ended 31 December 2010.

(b) Show how the adjustments affected closing inventory and receivables (showing separately the deduction of the allowance for receivables). [ACCA adapted]

4. You have been provided with the following trial balance as of 31 May 2009 for a limited liability company called Sondaw.

	DR $'000	CR $'000
Cash in bank	50	
Inventories at 1 June 2008	1 200	
General expenses	600	
Heating and lighting	90	
Marketing and advertising expenses	248	

Wages	490	
Buildings at cost	5 000	
Motor vehicles at cost	160	
Plant and equipment at cost	700	
Retained earnings at 1 June 2008		280
Trade receivables	438	
Purchases	2 200	
Loan note interest paid	30	
5% loan note		600
Revenue		5 876
Discounts received		150
Trade payables		500
$1 ordinary shares		1 500
Accumulated depreciation at 1 June 2008		
Buildings		2 000
Motor vehicles		60
Plant and equipment		240
	11 206	11 206

The following notes are relevant:

i. Inventories at 31 May 2009 were valued at $800 000.

ii. Marketing and advertising expenses include $6000 paid in advance for a marketing campaign that will begin in June 2009. Marketing and advertising expenses should be allocated to administrative expenses.

iii. There are wages outstanding of $10 000 for the year ended 31 May 2009.

iv. A customer ceased trading owing the company $38 000; the debt is not expected to be recovered.

v. An allowance for doubtful debts is to be established amounting to 5% of trade receivables.

vi. Depreciation is to be provided for as follows:

    a. Buildings at 5% per annum on their original cost, allocated 50% to cost of sales, 20% to distribution costs and 30% to administrative expenses.

    b. Motor vehicles at 25% per annum of their written-down value, allocated to distribution costs.

    c. Plant and equipment at 20% per annum of their written-down value, allocated to cost of sales.

vii. No dividends have been paid or declared.

viii. Income tax of $250 000 is to be provided for the year.

ix. The audit fee is estimated to be $20 000.

x. The expenses listed below should be apportioned as follows:

	Cost of Sales	Distribution Costs	Administrative Expenses
General expenses	10%	40%	50%
Heating and lighting	50%	30%	20%
Wages and salaries	60%	30%	10%

Required:

  (a) Prepare the following financial statements for the year ended 31 May 2009: a statement of income and a statement of financial position.

  (b) Briefly explain the purpose of providing depreciation and identify the factors to be taken into account when deciding on which depreciation method to use. [ACCA adapted]

5. The draft statement of financial position shown below has been prepared for Shuswap, a limited liability company, as at 31 December 2009.

	$000		
	Cost	Accumulated Depreciation	Net Book Value
Assets			
Noncurrent assets			
Land and buildings	9 000	1 000	8 000
Plant and equipment	21 000	9 000	12 000
	30 000	10 000	20 000
Current assets			
Inventories			3 000
Receivables-Net allowance			2 600
Cash at bank			1 900
Total assets			27 500
Equity and liabilities			
Capital and reserves			
Issued share capital			11 000
(ordinary shares of 50c each)			
Retained earnings			12 400
Noncurrent liabilities			
Loan notes (redeemable 2010)			2 000
Current liabilities			
Trade payables			2 100
			27 500

The following further information is available:

  i. The land and buildings were revalued to $12 000 000 at 31 December 2009.

  ii. Trade receivables totaling $200 000 are to be written off.

  iii. During the year there was a contra settlement of $106 000 in which an amount due to a supplier was set off against the amount due from the same company for goods sold to it. No entry has yet been made to record the set-off.

iv. Some inventories items included in the draft statement of financial position at cost $500 000 were sold after the statement of financial position date for $400 000, with selling expense of $40 000.

v. The proceeds of issue of 4 000 000 50c shares at $1.10 per share, credited have not been recorded.

vi. A plant was sold for $400 000 on 1 January 2009 with a net book value at the date of sale of $700 000, which had originally cost $1 400 000. No entries have been made for the disposal of the plant except for depreciation which has been charged at 25% (straight-line basis) in preparing the draft statement of financial position. The depreciation for the year relating to the plant sold should be adjusted in full.

Required: Prepare the company's statement of financial position as at 31 December 2009. Details of noncurrent assets, adjusted appropriately, should appear as they are presented in the question. [ACCA adapted]

6. The trial balance for Adnett, a limited liability company, at 31 May 2011 was as follows:

	DR $'000	CR $'000
Revenue		3 500
Discounts received		80
Discounts allowed	70	
Bank balance	147	
Buildings at cost	1 040	
Buildings, accumulated depreciation at 1 June 2010		160
Plant at cost	1 200	
Plant, accumulated depreciation at 1 June 2010		400
Land at cost	345	
Purchases	2 170	
Returns inwards	15	
Returns outwards		17
Heating and lighting	270	
Administrative expenses	60	
Trade payables		1 030
Trade receivables	700	
Carriage inwards	105	
Wages and salaries	250	
10% loan notes		580
General reserve		35
Allowance for doubtful debts at 1 June 2010		30
Director's remuneration	60	
Retained earnings at 1 June 2010		115

(Continued)

	DR $'000	CR $'000
$1 ordinary shares		800
Inventories at 1 June 2010	515	
Share premium account		200
	6 947	6 947

Additional information as at 31 May 2011:

  (i)   Closing inventories has been counted and is valued at $560 000.
 (ii)   There are wages and salaries to be paid of $42 000.
(iii)   Loan note interest has not been paid during the year.
 (iv)   Plant is depreciated at 25% per annum using the reducing balance method. The entire charge is to be allocated to cost of sales.
  (v)   Buildings are depreciated at 5% per annum on their original cost, allocated 25% to cost of sales, 50% to distribution costs and 25% to administrative expenses.
 (vi)   On 1 August 2010 Adnett purchased and absorbed the net assets of another business. Adnett paid $85 000 for goodwill and $35 000 for the business's inventories. The purchase was paid for by the issue of 100 000 ordinary shares. This transaction has not yet been recorded in the books of Adnett. At 31 March 2011 the fair value of goodwill was $68 000.
(vii)   During May 2011 a bonus (or scrip) issue of one for five was made to ordinary shareholders. This has not been entered into the books. The share premium account is to be used for this purpose.
(viii) No dividends have been paid or declared.
 (ix)   The directors have agreed to a transfer of $35 000 to the general reserve from profits for the period.
  (x)   Tax has been calculated as $70 000 for the year.
 (xi)   The expenses listed below should be apportioned as indicated:

	Cost of Sales	Distribution Costs	Administrative Expenses
Discounts allowed and received	–	–	100%
Heating and lighting	40%	20%	40%
Wages and salaries	50%	25%	25%
Goodwill impairment	–	–	100%

Required:

(a) Prepare the following financial statements for Adnett:

  (i) the statement of income for the year ended 31 May 2011; and
 (ii) the statement of financial position as at 31 May 2011.

Notes to the financial statements are not required.

(b) Briefly explain the accounting treatment for purchased goodwill. [ACCA adapted]

7. At 1 July 2010 the statement of financial position of Yeung a limited liability company, contained the following items:

	$m
Issued share capital – ordinary shares of 50c	100
Share premium account	140
Revaluation reserve	60
Accumulated profits	120
	420

During the year ended 30 June 2011 the following events took place:

(i) An error in calculating the inventory at 30 June 2003 was discovered. The effect of the error was a reduction in the inventory at that date from $30m to $24m.

(ii) On 1 July 2010 the company issued 200m ordinary shares, ranking equally with those already in issue, at $1.40 per share.

(iii) Some land held by the company as a noncurrent asset was sold for $100m. The land had originally cost $25m and was revalued to $85m in 2009, giving rise to the revaluation reserve of $60m shown above.

(iv) The company's draft pre-tax profit for the year ended 30 June 2011 was $40m. In calculating this figure the opening inventory was taken as $30m, and $15m was included as the profit on the sale of the land. (See items (i) and (iii) above.)

(v) Dividends totalling 2c per share were paid in the year on the enlarged capital.

Required: Prepare the company's statement of changes in equity for the year ended 30 June 2011. [ACCA adapted]

8. The following information has been extracted from the books of Tonson, a limited liability company, as at 31 October 2011. [ACCA adapted]

	DR $'000	CR $'000
Cash	15	
Insurance	75	
Inventories at 1 November 2010	350	
General expenses	60	
Energy expenses	66	
Marketing expenses	50	
Wages and salaries	675	
Discounts received		50
Share premium account		200
Retained earnings at 1 November 2010		315
Allowance for receivables at 1 November 2010		40
Sales revenue		5 780
Telephone expenses	80	
Property expenses	100	

(Continued)

	DR $'000	CR $'000
Bank		94
Returns inward	95	
Trade payables		290
Loan note interest	33	
Trade receivables	900	
Purchases	3 570	
7% loan notes		470
Bad debts	150	
$1 ordinary shares		1 800
Accumulated depreciation at 1 November 2010		
Buildings		360
Motor vehicles		80
Furniture and equipment		420
Land at cost	740	
Buildings at cost	1 500	
Motor vehicles at cost	240	
Furniture and equipment at cost	1 200	
	9 899	9 899

You have also been provided with the following information:

i. Inventories at 31 October 2011 were valued at $275 000 based on original cost. However, $45 000 of these inventories has been in the warehouse for over two years and the directors have agreed to sell it in November 2011 for a cash price of $20 000.

ii. The marketing expenses include $5000 that relates to November 2011.

iii. Based on past experience the allowance for receivables is to be increased to 5% of trade receivables.

iv. There are wages and salaries outstanding of $40 000 for the year ended 31 October 2011.

v. Buildings are depreciated at 5% of cost. At 31 October 2011 the buildings were professionally valued at $1 800 000 and the directors wish this valuation to be incorporated into the accounts.

vi. Depreciation is to be charged as follows:
   a. Motor vehicles at 20% of written-down value.
   b. Furniture and equipment at 20% of cost.

vii. No dividends have been paid or declared.

viii. Tax of $150 000 is to be provided for the year.

ix. During October 2011 a bonus (or scrip) issue of one for ten was made to ordinary shareholders. This has not been entered into the books. The share premium account was used for this purpose.

Required:

Prepare the following statements for internal use: (a) the statement of income for the year ended 31 October 2011, and (b) the statement of financial position as at 31 October 2011.

Case Analysis
BOTSWANA WILD SAFARIS LLC

Botswana Wild Safaris LLC was introduced in Chapter 7. In this chapter we will continue the case by focusing on changes in equity. Recall that Tony Washford had purchased the company from Gerhardt Perst on 1 January 2009. Use the information presented for Botswana Wild Safaris from Chapters 7, 8 and 9 in addition to the information presented below to complete the requirements of the case.

Revenues and expenses – other than those covered in Chapters 7, 8 and 9 for 2009, 2010 and 2011 – are shown below.

	31 Dec. 2009	31 Dec. 2010	31 Dec. 2011
Revenues	800 000	1 110 000	1 460 000
Expenses	550 000	600 000	790 000

REQUIRED:

Construct the statements of comprehensive income and the statement of changes in equity for Botswana Wild Safaris for the three reporting dates.

End notes

1. Schilit, Howard (2002) *Financial Shenanigans: How to Detect Accounting Gimmicks and Fraud in Financial Reports*, New York: McGraw-Hill.

Cash flows

11

LEARNING OUTCOMES

At the completion of this chapter, you should be able to:

1. Describe how cash flows relate to the business life cycle.
2. Explain how cash flows differ from profit or loss.
3. Explain the sources and uses of cash and cash equivalents.
4. Construct a statement of cash flows using the indirect and direct methods.
5. Calculate cash flow related ratios.

In 2008, in the midst of the worst financial crisis in decades, major auto manufacturers the world over experienced significant decreases in sales. In Detroit, home of the three large American auto manufacturers, the situation was far worse. These auto makers, which had dominated global auto manufacturing, were now struggling for survival. The largest, General Motors, lost $39 billion in 2007 and the situation continued to deteriorate in 2008.

In December 2008, the United States government agreed to provide General Motors and Chrysler – two of America's three largest auto makers – with a $17.4 billion bailout.[1] The assistance was given only after a long debate about whether the American government should rescue the auto manufacturers or let them sort their own problems out. Some argued that the companies were poorly managed and should be allowed to fail if they could not succeed on their own.[2] Other people believed that millions of jobs were at risk if these companies failed and that dealers who sold autos, banks, suppliers and many others would suffer financial loss if General Motors, Chrysler and Ford were unable to pay their obligations.

Even after the bailout, the problem worsened. In 2008, General Motors' sales dropped by 22.7%[3] and the company reported a second huge $30.9 billion loss – the second worst in its 100-year history after the largest in 2007.[4] Within two years, the company had reported $70 billion in losses. The company informed the US government that it may need another $16.6 billion in assistance to remain in business.

While these massive losses were shocking, the real problem for the Detroit auto makers was the shortage of cash. At the end of 2008, General Motors' management estimated that the company needed $11 billion to

$14 billion in cash to continue operations. But the company's cash, marketable securities and readily available assets only amounted to $14 billion.[5] In the previous year, the company had used $19 billion more in cash than it had generated through operations. In other words, if the company continued to lose cash on its operations, its cash cushion would be depleted.

A company must be profitable over the long term in order to survive. Losses are not welcome news, *but a company can survive losses for a period of time* as long as it is able to obtain the cash needed to continue operations. That cash does not necessarily need to come from the sale of goods and services produced by the company – its operating activities. When a company initially begins, it often uses more cash than it generates from operations and therefore must obtain cash by increasing the investment from owners or through borrowings. A successful company may on occasion encounter difficulties and find that operations are not generating enough cash, and may also have to obtain cash by increasing the investment from owners or through borrowings. However, whether a company is new or an established company suffering a temporary setback, over the long run it must be able to generate cash from operations or it will not be able to survive.

Having access to cash is also important in some cases if a business wishes to take advantage of opportunities. For a retailer, this may include buying sufficient merchandise to have on hand for the forthcoming holiday season. If a company is expanding rapidly, it may outlay cash expenditures to develop new products or marketing channels in a new region, or a business may wish to buy a competing company in order to expand its operations. Having sufficient cash or access to cash to take advantage of opportunities would therefore be of interest to investors and other external users.

A complete picture of a company's financial position not only involves understanding its financial position, including what resources it has available and its profitability, but also its cash position. The cash position refers to what cash is available for immediate use, how cash was generated over the reporting period and what uses were made of the cash. Thus, the statement of cash flows, when used with the other three financial statements, provides information that allows users to evaluate:

- The ability of the business to generate cash flows to adapt to changing circumstances and opportunities.
- Changes in the net assets of the business.
- The financial structure of the business in terms of liquidity and solvency.

The statement of cash flows has another advantage. It allows users to compare the financial results of different entities in a way that eliminates the effects of different accounting treatments. For example, the use of the straight-line method to calculate depreciation expense on equipment versus diminishing balance method will cause profit to be different; the use of the FIFO method of determining cost of goods sold will cause profit to be different than if the average cost method is used. However, the choices of straight-line versus diminishing balance and FIFO versus average cost method do not affect cash flow.

LEARNING OUTCOME 1
DESCRIBE HOW CASH FLOWS RELATE TO BUSINESS LIFE CYCLE PHASES

Why are cash flows so important? The simple answer is that no business can survive for long without a healthy cash flow. However, over its business life cycle, businesses often experience periods when the amount of cash needed to operate the business exceeds the amount of cash the business is generating from operations. Or a business may be investing in future growth by building new research and manufacturing facilities that have not yet begun generating economic benefits. This is especially true of new businesses that are in their 'start-up' phase.

The business life cycle has four phases: start-up, growth, expansion and maturity, as illustrated in Figure 11.1.

FIGURE 11.1 BUSINESS LIFE CYCLE PHASES

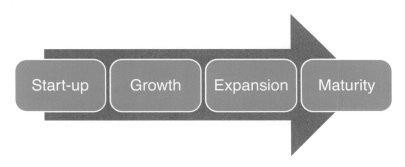

In the start-up phase or entrepreneurial phase, a business is just beginning operations. Costs typically exceed sales revenue. In fact, some businesses may have several years in which they earn no revenue. During this period, they may be undertaking research and development to produce a commercially viable product or service. Once they begin to generate sales, a further period may be required before cash receipts from sales exceed cash disbursements for costs. What does this mean for cash flows? Operating activities and investing activities will be using cash, while financing activities – the sale of share capital to investors and borrowing funds – may be the only source of cash.

In the growth phase, the business is beginning to produce and market the product or service. Although it may be selling products or services, the volume may not be enough to offset costs, which may include acquisition of production facilities, marketing to create brand awareness, and establishing a sales organization. Therefore, the pattern of cash flows is likely to be similar to in the start-up phase, with operating activities and investing activities using cash while financing activities provide cash.

The expansion phase is the turning point for cash flows. By this phase businesses have usually established a presence in the market place and sometimes have a positive cash flow from operating activities. However, cash is usually still needed from outside sources to expand the business. As a result, operating activities and financing activities may be sources of cash and investing activities a use of cash as the company continues to invest in further research and development, new equipment, marketing and its sales organization.

In the maturity phase, the business has reached the point where its infrastructure – property, plant and equipment and other assets – is fully developed. The company continues to make investments to replace and upgrade equipment. It also continues to innovate and introduce new products and services as market-place opportunities evolve. However, the cash devoted to these activities is often provided mostly by operating activities. Investing activities may continue to use cash as new investments are made, and financing activities may be a source or use depending on specifics of the company's financial structure.

These typical cash flow patterns are illustrated in Figure 11.2.

FIGURE 11.2 CASH FLOW PATTERNS BY BUSINESS LIFE CYCLE PHASE

Activity	Start-up Phase	Growth Phase	Expansion Phase	Maturity Phase
Operating activities	Use	Use	Source	Source
Investing activities	Use	Use	Use	Source or use
Financing activities	Source	Source	Source	Source or use

Remember, however, that these cash flow patterns relate to the business life cycle only in a general sense. Companies can experience different cash flow patterns depending on their specific circumstances. A company in a growth phase may find that operating activities quickly become a source of cash, while a mature-phase business experiences a market downturn so that its operating activities are cash flow negative.

ON YOUR OWN

LEARNING OUTCOME REVIEW
1. What are the four phases of the business life cycle?
2. How does each phase of the business life cycle typically affect cash flows from operating activities, investing activities and financing activities?

LEARNING OUTCOME 2
EXPLAIN HOW CASH FLOWS DIFFER FROM PROFIT OR LOSS

Recall that cash flows are inflows and outflows of cash and cash equivalents, also referred to as sources and uses, respectively.

Cash flows are reported by the statement of cash flows and differ from profit or loss, which is reported by the statement of comprehensive income. The reason they are different, we can recall from Chapter 5, Accrual and Closing, is that the revenue is recognized in the period in which the sale takes place, not the period in which cash is collected. And expenses are recognized in the period in which they are incurred, not the period in which a disbursement of cash is made.

Cash flows differ from profit or loss for two other reasons. One is that different companies, even within the same industry, may face different business circumstances. This is illustrated by Figure 11.3, which presents a cash flow comparison of five of the largest international airlines. The first line, which is highlighted, shows the airlines' profits for 2007, followed by a comparison of cash flows showing operating, investing and financing activities.

Notice in Figure 11.3 that the pattern differs somewhat between the airlines. Emirates Airline earned €558 million in profit for 2007, and yet it generated €1016 million in cash from operating activities. In fact, all the airlines generated significantly more cash from operating activities compared to profit. The question is what did they do with this cash?

We can see that Emirates Airline used €837 million for investing activities, mostly for the purchase of new equipment. In fact, Emirates used almost 2.5 times as much for investing activities as the next airline. Compare this to Singapore Airlines, which earned almost twice as much profit as Emirates, yet Emirates used over six times as much cash for investing activities.

Finally, compare this to American Airlines, which generated 3.84 times the cash from operating activities as profit, compared to Emirates, which generated only 1.82 times as much. Yet American Airlines used only 12% as much cash as its operating activities for investing activities, and 87% as much for financing activities, mostly to pay long-term debt. Emirates, on the other hand, spent 82% as much cash as it generated from operating activities for investing activities while the use of cash for financing activities was minimal.

FIGURE 11.3 COMPARISON OF PROFIT AND CASH FLOWS FOR MAJOR AIRLINES

€ Euros Millions	American Airlines	British Airways	Emirates Airline	Japan Airlines	Singapore Airlines
Profit (loss)	326	304	558	312	1 039
Net cash flow from (used by) operating activities	1 251	756	1 016	766	1 494
Net cash flow from (used by) investing activities	(151)	36	(837)	(337)	(131)
Net cash flow from (used by) financing activities	(1 083)	(461)	(35)	(318)	(385)
Net increase (decrease) in cash and cash equivalents	17	331	144	114	977
Net foreign exchange difference	–	(16)	(23)	2	(55)
Cash and cash equivalents – beginning balance	78	298	1 279	1 034	1 483
Cash and cash equivalents – ending balance	96	713	1 423	1 148	2 405

Note: Currencies were converted to Euros on 11 June 2008 using the following factors: American Airlines (.6467), Emirates Airline (.1763), Japan Airlines (.0060) and Singapore Airlines (.4721).

LEARNING OUTCOME 3
EXPLAIN THE SOURCES AND USES OF CASH AND CASH EQUIVALENTS

3.1 What is excluded from cash flows?

3.2 Can cash flows be offset?

3.3 What are the three sources and uses of cash reported in the statement of cash flows?

3.4 How are noncash transactions reported in the statement of cash flows?

3.1 What is excluded from cash flows?

Movements between components of cash and cash equivalents are excluded from the statement of cash flows, and therefore would not appear in one of the cash flow categories. The reason is that the investment of excess cash into a cash equivalent, and the conversion of a cash equivalent into cash, is part of normal cash management activities and is therefore not regarded as a source or use. For example, a company has excess cash at the end of the month, and the chief financial officer invests in corporate paper that matures within 60 days.

Normally, when an investment has a maturity date within three months of the date of acquisition, it would qualify as a cash equivalent, even though equity investments do not generally qualify as cash equivalents. Bank overdrafts are typically included as a normal cash management activity and thus also are not reported in one of the three cash flow categories. Otherwise, a bank or other borrowing would be included in financing activities.

3.2 Can cash flows be offset?

Cash inflows and outflows are not generally offset against one another and reported on a net basis.

> A business owes money to a second business on trade accounts payable, and at the same time, the second company owes money to the first business on trade accounts receivable. The two amounts would be reported separately, they would not be offset and reported on a net basis.

3.3 What are the three sources and uses of cash reported in the statement of cash flows?

Recall that three sources and uses of cash flows are reported in the statement of cash flows: operating activities, investing activities and financing activities. These are graphically illustrated in Figure 11.4.

FIGURE 11.4 THREE SOURCES AND USES OF CASH

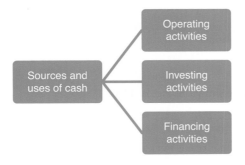

FIGURE 11.5 CASH INFLOWS AND OUTFLOWS FROM OPERATING ACTIVITIES

Transactions that are classified as operating activities are the same as those that affect profit or loss on the statement of comprehensive income. However, those transactions must be converted from an accrual basis, used for measuring profit or loss, to a cash basis for the statement of cash flows. Examples of cash inflows and outflows from operating activities include those shown in Figure 11.5.

Interest and dividends are usually included as part of operating activities. However, they can also be classified as part of financing activities, since they are considered to be a cost of obtaining financial resources or a return on investment.

IFRS 'Investing activities are the acquisition and disposal of long-term assets and other investments not included in cash equivalents.'

Examples of investing activities include those shown in Figure 11.6.

IFRS 'Financing activities are activities that result in changes in the size and composition of the contributed equity and borrowings of the entity.'

Examples of financing activities include those in Figure 11.7.

FIGURE 11.6 INVESTING ACTIVITIES

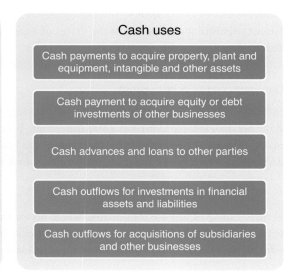

Cash sources	Cash uses
Cash receipts from the sale of property, plant and equipment, intangible and other assets	Cash payments to acquire property, plant and equipment, intangible and other assets
Cash receipts from the sale of equity or debt investments of other businesses	Cash payment to acquire equity or debt investments of other businesses
Cash receipts from the payment of advances and loans from other parties	Cash advances and loans to other parties
Cash inflows for investments in financial assets and liabilties	Cash outflows for investments in financial assets and liabilities
Cash inflows from the disposal of subsidiaries or other businesses	Cash outflows for acquisitions of subsidiaries and other businesses

FIGURE 11.7 FINANCING ACTIVITIES

Cash sources	Cash uses
Cash proceeds from the sale of the business's shares	Cash payments to acquire the business's own shares
Cash proceeds from short-term and long-term borrowings	Cash repayments of amounts borrowed

3.4 How are noncash transactions reported in the statement of cash flows?

Some financing and investing activities do not require the use of cash or cash equivalents and are therefore excluded from sources and uses reported on the face of the statement of cash flows. Examples include:

• The acquisition of assets by assuming a related liability.

> Dayyani Resources Ltd acquired a computer system from Rommy Services AB by assuming the outstanding debt owed by Rommy against the system owed by Rommy.

- The acquisition of another company by issuing additional shares in the business.

> Banks Corporation acquires all of the shares of Masi SpA by issuing its own shares to Masi's shareholders.

- The conversion of debt to equity.

> Mady Services Inc. currently has 1500 convertible bonds outstanding. The bonds can be exchanged for 10 ordinary shares each at the discretion of the bondholders. The bondholders elect to convert their bonds, which are then exchanged for the ordinary shares.

These three examples involve transactions where no exchange of cash or cash equivalents occurred. However, noncash transactions should be *disclosed elsewhere in the financial statements in a way that provides all the relevant information about these investing and financing activities.*

ON YOUR OWN

LEARNING OUTCOME REVIEW

1. What are operating activities as reported on the statement of cash flows? What are investing activities? What are financing activities?
2. What are examples of operating activities? What are examples of investing activities? What are examples of financing activities?
3. What is the difference between an investing activity and a financing activity?
4. Why are movements between cash and cash equivalents excluded from the statement of cash flows?
5. What is the rule of thumb in terms of the number of months for classifying an investment as a cash equivalent? If an investment has a maturity that does not meet this rule-of-thumb test, then how is it classified?
6. What are the two major exceptions for not reporting cash flows on a net basis? Why do you think that cash flows are generally not reported on a cash basis?
7. What options are available to report interest and dividends in the statement of cash flows?
8. What are examples of noncash transactions?

LEARNING OUTCOME PRACTICE

1. Borrowing a loan from a bank would be classified as which of the following?
   a. Operating activity
   b. Investing activity

    c.   Financing activity

    d.   None of the above

2. Cash used to purchase equipment would be classified as which of the following?

    a.   Operating activity

    b.   Investing activity

    c.   Financing activity

    d.   None of the above

3. Cash payments to acquire the business's own shares would be classified as which of the following?

    a.   Operating activity

    b.   Investing activity

    c.   Financing activity

    d.   None of the above

4. Cash flows from acquisitions and disposals of subsidiaries and other businesses would be classified as which of the following?

    a.   Operating activity

    b.   Investing activity

    c.   Financing activity

    d.   None of the above

5. Cash inflows and outflows related to income taxes would be classified as which of the following?

    a.   Operating activity

    b.   Investing activity

    c.   Financing activity

    d.   None of the above

6. Cash receipts from commissions earned would be classified as which of the following?

    a.   Operating activity

    b.   Investing activity

    c.   Financing activity

    d.   None of the above

7. Cash repayments of amounts borrowed would be classified as which of the following?

    a.   Operating activity

    b.   Investing activity

    c.   Financing activity

    d.   None of the above

8. Cash receipts from the sale of property, plant and equipment, intangible and other assets would be classified as which of the following?

    a.   Operating activity

    b.   Investing activity

    c.   Financing activity

    d.   None of the above

9. Cash payments to employees would be classified as which of the following?
   a. Operating activity
   b. Investing activity
   c. Financing activity
   d. None of the above

LEARNING OUTCOME 4
CONSTRUCT A STATEMENT OF CASH FLOWS USING THE INDIRECT AND DIRECT METHODS

4.1   How is the statement of cash flows constructed using the indirect method?

4.2   How is the statement of cash flows constructed using the direct method?

Two methods can be used to report cash flows: direct and indirect (see IFRS box).

IFRS   'An entity shall report cash flows from operating activities using either:

(a) the direct method, whereby major classes of gross cash receipts and gross cash payments are disclosed; or

(b) the indirect method, whereby profit or loss is adjusted for the effects of transactions of a noncash nature, any deferrals or accruals of past or future operating cash receipts or payments, and items of income or expense associated with investing or financing cash flows.'

The International Accounting Standards Board encourages use of the direct method, because the *direct method provides information that may be useful in estimating future cash flows and is not available under the indirect method*. However, in practice most businesses use the indirect method.

The choice between the two methods only affects *how cash flows from operating activities are calculated*. The amount of cash provided or used by operating activities will be the same under both methods. In addition, the general approach is the same: both adjust profit or loss for noncash revenue and noncash expenses. The calculation of cash inflows and outflows from investing and financing activities does not vary between the two methods.

The indirect method begins with profit or loss, which is then adjusted for the effects of any noncash transactions, deferrals or accruals of cash receipts or payments, and income or expense items related to investing or financing cash flows. The direct method reports cash flows by major classes of gross cash receipts and gross cash payments. In other words, sales and expenses are separately adjusted to a cash basis.

Unlike the statement of financial position and statement of comprehensive income, which are constructed from the adjusted trial balance, the statement of cash flows is created by comparing statements of financial position from the beginning of the period with that at the end of the period, and taking into account additional information, as illustrated by the following example, which has been adapted from an example provided by *IAS 7 Cash Flows*.

Washford & Monare Manufacturing Ltd reported the following results:

Washford & Monare Manufacturing Ltd Statement of Comprehensive Income for the Year Ended 31 December 2009 € Euros	
Sales	24 520
Cost of sales	(20 800)
Gross profit	3 720
Depreciation	(360)
Selling and administrative expenses	(728)
Interest expense	(320)
Gain on sale of equipment	400
Foreign exchange loss	(32)
Profit before tax	2 680
Income tax	(240)
Profit	2 440

Washford & Monare Manufacturing Ltd
Statement of Financial Position
At 31 December
€ Euros

	2009	2008	Change
Assets			
Cash and cash equivalents	184	128	56
Trade accounts receivable	1 020	960	60
Inventories	800	1 560	(760)

(*Continued*)

Washford & Monare Manufacturing Ltd			
Statement of Financial Position			
At 31 December			
€ Euros			
	2009	2008	Change
Investments	2 500	2 000	500
Property, plant and equipment at cost	2 984	1 528	1 456
Accumulated depreciation	(1 160)	(848)	312
Total assets	6 328	5 328	1 000
Liabilities			
Trade accounts payable	200	1 512	(1 312)
Interest payable	184	80	104
Income tax payable	320	800	(480)
Long-term debt	1 840	832	1 008
Total liabilities	2 544	3 224	(670)
Shareholders' equity			
Share capital	1 200	1 000	200
Retained earnings	2 584	1 104	1 480
Total shareholders' equity	3 784	2 104	1 680
Total liabilities and shareholders' equity	6 328	5 328	1 000

Other information for 2009 is as follows:

1. Dividends paid were €960.
2. Plant with an original cost of €64 and accumulated depreciation of €36 was sold for €16.
3. €200 was raised from share capital and a net amount of €384 in cash was paid on long-term borrowings.
4. Property, plant and equipment were acquired for a total cost of €1000 in 2009, of which €720 was by finance leases. Cash payments of €280 were made related to purchases of property, plant and equipment.
5. Investments were sold during the period for €700 in cash, and others acquired for €1200 for an increase of €500.

We can see in the statement of financial position that a column (far right) has been included that calculates the increase or decrease between the comparative information for 2008 and 2009. Notice that cash and cash equivalents have increased by €56 million from €128 million to €184 million. This difference is the amount that the statement of cash flows must explain.

4.1 How is the statement of cash flows constructed using the indirect method?

The major difference between the indirect method and the direct method is how cash from (used by) operating activities is presented. The following is a step-wise explanation of how the calculations are made for the indirect method. Step 1 explains how operating activities are derived and Steps 2 and 3 illustrate the calculations for investing activities and financing activities, respectively.

STEP 1: OPERATING ACTIVITIES

The indirect method begins with profit and loss from the statement of comprehensive income, and then makes adjustments to convert accrual basis amounts to a cash basis for changes in inventories, receivables and payables; noncash items such as depreciation, deferred taxes, unrealized foreign currency gains and losses and provisions; and other items for which effects are related to investing or financing cash flows. *Changes in other comprehensive income reported on the statement of comprehensive income are not included.* These figures come from the changes column in the statement of financial position.

Changes in Inventories, Receivables and Payables

We can see that the first change following cash and cash equivalents is trade receivables. In order to convert to cash, we deduct any increases in trade receivables, and add any decrease. The calculation would be as follows:

Washford & Monare Manufacturing Ltd Statement of Cash Flows for the Period Ended 31 December 2009 € Euros (millions)		
Cash flows from operating activities		
Profit	2680	
Adjustments for:		
Decrease in inventories	760	
Increase in trade accounts receivable	(60)	
Decrease in trade accounts payable	(1 312)	
Increase in interest payable	104	
Decrease in tax payable	480	

These adjustments are highlighted in the schedule shown above. Notice that a decrease in inventories results in an increase in cash. The reason is that cash is tied up in inventory. In other words, the higher the level of inventory, the more cash is decreased. Thus, when inventories decrease, as in this example, the amount of cash is increased. The same relationship applies for trade receivables. In this case trade receivables increased, which means that the amount of cash is decreased. Think of it this way: The customers still have possession of the company's cash. When the amount they owe (trade accounts receivable) increases, the amount of cash decreases. When customers pay, cash increases.

Both inventories and trade accounts receivable are assets, and thus the effect on cash is the same. However, trade accounts payable are a liability, and therefore the effect is the opposite. In this example, trade accounts payable decrease by €1312 million. Trade accounts payable represent an obligation to pay, and therefore in order to reduce that obligation, the business must pay cash; in other words, reduce the amount of cash. If trade accounts payable increase, then the effect would be to increase the amount of cash.

Interest payable and income tax payable are analysed in the same way as trade accounts payable. In this case, interest payable increased by €104 million, which means that it is a source of cash. In other words, cash increased for the period because the obligation has not yet been paid. However, income tax payable decreased, and like trade accounts payable that also decreased, this decreased cash.

Noncash Items such as Depreciation, Deferred Taxes, Unrealized Foreign Currency Gains and Losses and Provisions

The second group of adjustments relate to noncash items on the statement of comprehensive income. Depreciation is perhaps the most common example, and we can see by examining the statement of comprehensive income that depreciation is €360 million. This would be added back to profit.

The next item is a foreign exchange loss. This loss was recognized because cash and cash equivalents denominated in a foreign currency were translated at the spot rate on the reporting date. The gain or loss is not realized in the sense that a cash inflow or outflow results, but only recognized. Thus, in this example, the loss is a noncash reduction of profit, and therefore must be added back to profit in order to convert to a cash basis.

Washford & Monare Manufacturing Ltd Statement of Cash Flows for the Period Ended 31 December 2009 € Euros (millions)		
Cash flows from operating activities		
Profit		2 680
Adjustments for:		
Decrease in inventories	760	
Increase in trade accounts receivable	(60)	
Decrease in trade accounts payable	(1 312)	
Increase in interest payable	104	
Depreciation	360	
Foreign exchange loss	32	

Other Items for Which Effects are Related to Investing or Financing Cash Flows

The last adjustment to convert profit to a cash basis is the gain on the sale of equipment. This gain increased profit when it was recognized. However, the gain is not a cash inflow but is accounting profit, which is the difference between the consideration received for the equipment and its carrying amount. Any cash received from the sale of the equipment will be included in the investing section and, therefore, a gain or loss is removed from the operating activities section.

Washford & Monare Manufacturing Ltd Statement of Cash Flows for the Period Ended 31 December 2009 € Euros (millions)		
Cash flows from operating activities		
Profit	2 680	
Adjustments for:		
Decrease in inventories	760	
Increase in trade accounts receivable	(60)	
Decrease in trade accounts payable	(1 312)	
Increase in interest payable	104	
Depreciation	360	
Foreign exchange loss	32	
Gain on sale of equipment	(400)	
Cash provided by operating activities		2 164

STEP 2: INVESTING ACTIVITIES

In order to calculate cash from or used by investing activities, we return to the statement of financial position and again examine the right-hand column, which shows changes between the amounts for 2008 and 2009. However, in this case we want to consider changes to long-term assets.

Washford & Monare Manufacturing Ltd Statement of Cash Flows for the Period Ended 31 December 2009 € Euros (millions)		
Cash flows from operating activities		
Profit	2 680	
Adjustments for:		
Decrease in inventories	760	
Increase in trade receivables	(60)	
Decrease in trade payables	(1 312)	
Increase in interest payable	104	
Depreciation	360	
Foreign exchange loss	32	
Gain on sale of equipment	(400)	
Cash provided by operating activities		2 164

(Continued)

Washford & Monare Manufacturing Ltd Statement of Cash Flows for the Period Ended 31 December 2009 € Euros (millions)		
Cash flows from investing activities		
Purchase of property, plant and equipment – Note 2	(280)	
Proceeds from sale of equipment	16	
Purchase of investments	(1 200)	
Sale of investments	500	
Net cash used in investing activities		(964)

We know from the fourth note in the example that the business acquired €1000 million of property, plant and equipment, of which €280 million was paid in cash (the remainder of €720 million was a finance lease). Thus the €280 million was a use of cash for investing activities. The second note indicates that plant that originally cost €64 million with accumulated depreciation of €36 million was sold for €16 million, thus the €16 million is a source of cash under investing activities. Thus, the difference between the €280 million and €16 million is €264 million, which is a net use of cash from investing activities.

STEP 3: FINANCING ACTIVITIES

In this example, three items relate to financing activities, as shown highlighted in the schedule below.

The first item is proceeds from the issuance of share capital for €200 million, which we know from note 3 as well as the fact that share capital increased by €200 million, which is the difference between the 2008 and 2009 amounts. The second item represents net payment on long-term borrowings of €384 million, which were a use of cash. The final item under cash flows from financing activities is dividends paid of €960 million, which also use cash. When these three items are netted together, the net cash used in financing activities is €1144 million.

Washford & Monare Manufacturing Ltd Statement of Cash Flows for the Period Ended 31 December 2009 € Euros (millions)		
Cash flows from operating activities		
Profit	2 680	
Adjustments for:		
Decrease in inventories	760	
Increase in trade receivables	(60)	

Decrease in trade payables	(1 312)	
Increase in interest payable	104	
Depreciation	360	
Foreign exchange loss	32	
Gain on sale of equipment	(400)	
Cash provided by operating activities		2 164
Cash flows from investing activities		
Purchase of property, plant and equipment – Note 2	(280)	
Proceeds from sale of equipment	<u>16</u>	
Purchase of investments	(1 200)	
Sale of investments	<u>500</u>	
Net cash used in investing activities		(964)
Cash flows from financing activities		
Proceeds from issuance of share capital	200	
Payments on long-term borrowings – net	(384)	
Dividends paid	(960)	
Net cash used in financing activities		<u>(1 144)</u>

We are now ready to complete the statement of cash flows for Washford & Monare under the indirect method, as shown in the schedule below.

Washford & Monare Manufacturing Ltd Statement of Cash Flows for the Period Ended 31 December 2009 € Euros (millions)		
Cash flows from operating activities		
Profit	2 680	
Adjustments for:		
Decrease in inventories	760	
Increase in trade receivables	(60)	
Decrease in trade payables	(1 312)	
Increase in interest payable	104	
Depreciation	360	
Foreign exchange loss	32	
Gain on sale of equipment	(400)	
Cash provided by operating activities		2 164

(Continued)

Washford & Monare Manufacturing Ltd Statement of Cash Flows for the Period Ended 31 December 2009 € Euros (millions)		
Cash flows from investing activities		
Purchase of property, plant and equipment – Note 2	(280)	
Proceeds from sale of equipment	<u>16</u>	
Purchase of investments	(1 200)	
Sale of investments	<u>500</u>	
Net cash used in investing activities		(964)
Cash flows from financing activities		
Proceeds from issuance of share capital	200	
Payments on long-term borrowings – net	(384)	
Dividends paid	(960)	
Net cash used in financing activities		<u>(1 144)</u>
Net increase in cash and cash equivalents		56
Cash and cash equivalents at beginning of 2009		<u>**128**</u>
Cash and cash equivalents at end of 2009		<u>**184**</u>

The net change in cash and cash equivalents is calculated by adding cash provided by operating activities and deducting net cash used in investing activities and net cash used in financing activities. The result is €56 million, which is a net increase in cash and cash equivalents. This amount is then added to the beginning cash and cash equivalents amount of €128 million from the 2008 statement of financial position, to equal the cash and cash equivalents amount on the 2008 statement of financial position.

4.2 How is the statement of cash flows constructed using the direct method?

Under the direct method, only the operating activities section of the statement of cash flows is presented differently to under the indirect method. The investing activities and financing sections are the same.

For operating activities, the major categories of gross cash receipts and gross cash payments are calculated and disclosed. Information to calculate cash flows under the direct method can normally be obtained through either the accounting records of the business or by adjusting sales, cost of sales and other items in the statement of comprehensive income for changes in inventories, receivables and payables; other noncash items; and other items for which effects are related to investing or financing cash flows.

Making the adjustments is most easily accomplished by following the statement of comprehensive income format to convert sales, costs including cost of sales and operating expenses, financing expense and income tax expense.

CASH RECEIPTS FROM CUSTOMERS

Sales are converted to a cash basis by adjusting for the change in the trade accounts receivable balance between the comparable periods. We can see for the Washford & Monare example that trade accounts receivable increased by €56 million from €960 million in 2008 to €1020 million in 2009. The formula for the conversion is as follows:

Sales	€24 520
Deduct: Increase in trade accounts receivable	60
Cash receipts from sales	**€24 460**

The cash receipts from sales amount of €24 460 is shown as a line item in the statement of cash flows.

CASH PAID TO SUPPLIERS AND EMPLOYEES

Costs, including those related to both suppliers and employees, are then converted to a cash basis by adjusting for the change in trade payables and any amounts owing to employees. For the Washford & Monare example, trade receivables increased by €56 million from €960 million in 2008 to €1020 million in 2009. The formula for the conversion is as follows:

Cost of sales	(€20 800)
Selling and administrative expenses	(728)
Total expenses for period	(21 528)
Deduct: Decrease in trade accounts payable	(1 312)
Add: Decrease in inventories	760
Cash payments suppliers and employees	**€22 080**

The cash payments related to expenses amount of €22 080 is shown as a line item in the statement of cash flows. When these cash receipts from sales and cash payments to suppliers and employees are combined along with interest paid and income taxes paid, these would appear on the statement of cash flows – under the direct method – as follows.

Washford & Monare Manufacturing Ltd Statement of Cash Flows for the Period Ended 31 December 2009 € Euros (millions)		
Cash flows from operating activities		
Cash receipts from customers	24 460	
Cash paid to suppliers and employees	(22 080)	
Cash generated from operations	2 040	
Interest paid	(216)	
Income taxes paid	(720)	
Net cash from operating activities		2 164

(Continued)

Washford & Monare Manufacturing Ltd Statement of Cash Flows for the Period Ended 31 December 2009 € Euros (millions)		
Cash flows from investing activities		
Purchase of property, plant and equipment	(280)	
Proceeds from sale of equipment	16	
Purchase of investments	(1 200)	
Sale of investments	500	
Net cash used in investing activities		(964)
Cash flows from financing activities		
Proceeds from issuance of share capital	200	
Payments on long-term borrowings – net	(384)	
Dividends paid	(960)	
Net cash used in financing activities		(1 144)
Net increase in cash and cash equivalents		56
Cash and cash equivalents at beginning of 2009		128
Cash and cash equivalents at end of 2009		184

Again, notice that only the operating activities section changes. The investing activities and financing activities sections are the same.

ON YOUR OWN

LEARNING OUTCOMES REVIEW

1. What are the two methods for calculating the operating activities section of the statement of cash flows?
2. What is the approach used by the direct method? What is the approach used by the indirect method?
3. What three types of adjustments are made to profit or loss in the operating activities section under the indirect method?

LEARNING OUTCOMES PRACTICE

1. Which of the following would increase the amount of cash generated by operating activities under the indirect method?
   - i. Trade receivables increase by €120 000 during the period.
   - ii. Trade payables increase by €80 000 during the period.
   - iii. Inventories increase by €200 000 during the period.
       - a. i and ii only
       - b. ii only
       - c. ii and iii only
       - d. iii only

2. By how much does cash generated by operating activities under the indirect method increase or decrease when the effects of all the following items are considered?

   i. Trade receivables increase by €120 000 during the period.

   ii. Trade payables increase by €80 000 during the period.

   iii. Inventories increase by €200 000 during the period.

     a. €240 000 increase

     b. €240 000 decrease

     c. No increase or decrease

     d. €160 000 increase

3. By how much does cash generated by operating activities under the indirect method increase or decrease when the effects of all the following items are considered?

   i. Loss on a sale of equipment for €14 000 during the period.

   ii. Trade receivables decrease by €8 000 during the period.

   iii. Depreciation for the period was €43 000.

     a. €37 000 increase

     b. €65 000 increase

     c. €21 000 decrease

     d. €49 000 decrease

LEARNING OUTCOME 5
CALCULATE CASH FLOW RELATED RATIOS

5.1 What is the current cash debt coverage ratio?

5.2 What is the cash debt coverage ratio?

5.3 What is free cash flow?

5.4 What is operating cash flow per share?

We can now add the final set of ratios. These four ratios are all related to what cash from operating activities can tell us with regard to the business's liquidity and solvency. Following is Washford & Monare's statement of financial position, and statement of cash flows constructed earlier in this chapter for use in demonstrating these ratios.

Washford & Monare Manufacturing Ltd Statement of Financial Position at 31 December 2009 € Euros		
	2009	**2008**
Assets		
Cash and cash equivalents	184	128
Trade accounts receivable	1 020	960
Inventories	800	1 560
Investments	2 500	2 000
Property, plant and equipment at cost	2 984	1 528
Accumulated depreciation	(1 160)	(848)
Total assets	6 328	5 328
Liabilities		
Trade accounts payable	200	1 512
Interest payable	184	80
Income tax payable	320	800
Total current liabilities	704	2 392
Long-term debt	1 840	832
Total liabilities	2 544	3 224
Shareholders' equity		
Share capital	1 200	1 000
Retained earnings	2 584	1 104
Total shareholders' equity	3 784	2 104
Total liabilities and shareholders' equity	6 328	5 328

Washford & Monare Manufacturing Ltd Statement of Cash Flows for the period ended 31 December 2009 € Euros		
Cash flows from operating activities		
Profit	2 680	
Adjustments for:		
Decrease in inventories	760	
Increase in trade receivables	(60)	
Decrease in trade payables	(1 312)	
Increase in interest payable	104	
Depreciation	360	
Foreign exchange loss	32	
Gain on sale of equipment	(400)	

Cash provided by operating activities		2 164
Cash flows from investing activities		
Purchase of property, plant and equipment – Note 2	(280)	
Proceeds from sale of equipment	16	
Purchase of investments	(1 200)	
Sale of investments	500	
Net cash used in investing activities		(964)
Cash flows from financing activities		
Proceeds from issuance of share capital	200	
Payments on long-term borrowings – net	(384)	
Dividends paid	(960)	
Net cash used in financing activities		(1 144)
Net increase in cash and cash equivalents		56
Cash and cash equivalents at beginning of 2009		**128**
Cash and cash equivalents at end of 2009		**184**

5.1 What is the current cash debt coverage ratio?

The current cash debt coverage ratio is related to liquidity. It tells us what the business's ability is to pay its current liabilities using cash from operating activities. The formula is as follows.

$$\text{Current cash debt coverage ratio} = \frac{\text{Cash from operating activities}}{\text{Average current liabilities}}$$

For Washford & Monare, average current liabilities must first be calculated, which is as follows:

$$\text{Average current liabilities} = \frac{\text{Beginning current liabilities} + \text{Ending current liabilities}}{2}$$

$$\text{Average current liabilities} = \frac{€2\,392 + €704}{2}$$

$$€1\,548 = \frac{€3096}{2}$$

The average current liabilities amount then becomes the denominator for the current cash debt coverage ratio:

$$\text{Current cash debt coverage ratio} = \frac{\text{Cash from operating activities}}{\text{Average current liabilities}}$$

$$\text{Current cash debt coverage ratio} = \frac{€2\,164}{€1\,548}$$

$$1.40 = \frac{€2\,164}{€1\,548}$$

The preceding calculation tells us that at the current rate of cash inflows from operating activities, Washford & Monare has 1.4 times the amount of cash needed to pay average current liabilities.

5.2 What is the cash debt coverage ratio?

The cash debt coverage ratio is a solvency ratio, since it examines the business's ability to pay average total liabilities. Since not all liabilities are due within 12 months, this would be a longer-term measure of the business's ability to pay its obligations.

$$\text{Cash debt coverage ratio} = \frac{\text{Cash from operating activities}}{\text{Average total liabilities}}$$

Average total liabilities are first calculated as follows:

$$\text{Average total liabilities} = \frac{\text{Beginning total liabilities} + \text{Ending total liabilities}}{2}$$

$$\text{Average total liabilities} = \frac{€3\ 224 + €2\ 544}{2}$$

$$€2\ 884 = \frac{€4496}{2}$$

Using the average total liabilities to calculate the cash debt coverage ratio, the result would be as follows:

$$\text{Cash debt coverage ratio} = \frac{\text{Cash from operating activities}}{\text{Average total liabilities}}$$

$$\text{Cash debt coverage ratio} = \frac{€2\ 164}{€2\ 884}$$

$$0.75 = \frac{€2\ 164}{€2\ 884}$$

The preceding calculation tells us that at the current rate of cash inflows from operating activities, Washford & Monare has 75% of the amount needed to pay its average total liabilities. Again, we cannot make a judgement about whether this is sufficient or not without knowing something about the industry average and perhaps what Washford & Monare's competitors have as their cash debt coverage ratio.

5.3 What is free cash flow?

Free cash flow is also a measure of solvency. Although it is not a ratio, free cash flow assesses the amount of cash that a business generates from operating activities after deducting capital expenditures and cash dividends. Why capital expenditures and cash dividends? The rationale is that these expenditures must be made in the ordinary course of business; capital expenditures are needed for normal reinvestment in capital assets and cash dividends are needed to reward shareholders for the use of their capital. For Washford & Monare, the calculation of free cash flow would be as follows:

Free cash flow = Cash provided from operating activities − Capital expenditures − Cash dividends

Free cash flow = €2 164 − €280 − €960

€924 = €2 164 − €280 − €960

We can see that the free cash flow is €924 for Washford & Monare.

5.4 What is operating cash flow per share?

A profitability measure, sometimes used by investors, is operating cash flow per share. It tells how much cash flow is available on a per share basis. The calculation for Washford & Monare, assuming that 1200 million ordinary shares are currently outstanding, would be as follows:

$$\text{Operating cash flow per share} = \frac{\text{Cash from operating activities}}{\text{Ordinary shares outstanding}}$$

$$\text{Operating cash flow per share} = \frac{€2\ 164\ 000\ 000}{€1\ 200\ 000\ 000}$$

$$€0.18 = \frac{€2\ 164\ 000\ 000}{€1\ 200\ 000\ 000}$$

ON YOUR OWN

LEARNING OUTCOME REVIEW

1. How is the current cash debt coverage ratio calculated? Is this a liquidity, solvency or profitability ratio?
2. How is the cash debt coverage ratio calculated? Is this a liquidity, solvency or profitability ratio?
3. How is free cash flow calculated? Is this a liquidity, solvency or profitability measure?
4. How is operating cash flow per share calculated? Is this a liquidity, solvency or profitability measure?

Conclusion

Healthy cash flows are required if a company is to survive and prosper over the long term. The statement of cash flows explains why the balance of cash and cash equivalents reported on the statement of financial position changed between the beginning and end of the reporting period. Sources and uses of cash are classified as either operating activities, investing activities or financing activities. Each of these classifications can be either a net source of cash or a net use of cash.

Summary
LEARNING OUTCOME 1
Cash Flows' Relationship to Business Life Cycle Described

A business goes through four phases in its life cycle: start-up, growth, expansion and maturity. In the earlier phases, a business will typically consume more cash than it generates from operating activities. This is especially true in the start-up phase, before development of the product or service has been completed. In addition, a new and growing business will normally consume cash for investing activities as it expands production, other facilities and marketing efforts. Thus, the most likely source of cash is financing activity. This includes increasing contributed capital by selling more shares and borrowings.

In the later phases of the business cycle, the business will typically become a 'cash cow', generating more cash from operating activities than it consumes. Thus operating activities become a source of cash. This cash may be used for investing activities such as the replacement of property, plant and equipment or for repaying borrowings or dividend distributions to owners.

The business life cycle is only a general description of the phases that a business may experience. Businesses, regardless of the phase they are in, may experience setbacks because of an economic downturn. They may also experience a rapid growth rate if their product or service is in high demand. These events, whether negative or positive, affect cash flow.

LEARNING OUTCOME 2
The Difference Between Cash Flows and Profit or Loss Explained

Profit or loss as reported on the statement of comprehensive income is accounted for on the accrual basis. That means that revenue is recognized in the reporting period in which it was earned. Costs are either matched to the revenue they generated or allocated to the reporting period through depreciation or amortization. Therefore, revenue and cost recognition occur based on which reporting period was affected rather than when cash is received or disbursed.

LEARNING OUTCOME 3
Sources and Uses of Cash Explained

Cash sources and uses are classified into operating activities, investing activities and financing activities. Operating activities are the principal revenue-producing activities of the entity and other activities that do not fall into the categories of investing activities or financing activities. Investing activities involve the acquisition and disposal of long-term assets and other investments that are not included in cash equivalents. Financing activities are activities that result in changes in the size and composition of the contributed equity and borrowings of the entity. Taken together, the net amounts of these activities explain the difference in the cash and cash equivalents balances at the beginning and the end of the reporting period.

LEARNING OUTCOME 4
Statement of Cash Flows Constructed

Two methods are used for constructing the statement of cash flows: direct and indirect. These two methods differ only in the manner in which net cash used or provided by operating activities is reported. The method of calculating sources and uses of cash in the investing activities and financing activities sections is the same under both methods.

Most companies use the indirect method. Under the indirect method, net cash used or provided by operating activities is calculated by adjusting profit or loss as reported on the statement of comprehensive income. The adjustments are for any noncash transactions, which include deferrals or accruals of past or future operating cash receipts or payments. These include, for example, changes in the amount of trade accounts receivable and trade accounts payable.

In the direct method, net cash used or provided by operating activities is reported by major classes of gross cash receipts and gross cash payments. For example, sales as reported on the statement of comprehensive income are converted to a cash basis by adjusting for changes in the trade accounts receivables balances, and expenses are converted to a cash basis by adjusting for changes in the trade accounts payable balances.

LEARNING OUTCOME 5
Cash Flows Evaluated

We discussed four ratios that help evaluate the cash position of the business. The current cash debt coverage ratio is calculated by dividing cash from operating activities by average current liabilities. This ratio measures the ability of the business to pay liabilities over the next 12 months from cash generated by operations without relying on cash from investing or financing activities. The cash debt coverage ratio is calculated by dividing cash from operating activities by average total liabilities. It measures the ability of the business to pay all debts from cash being generated by operations without relying on cash from investing or financing activities.

Free cash flow is calculated by subtracting capital expenditures and cash dividends from cash provided from operating activities. Free cash flow is a measure of the amount of cash that is not needed for the normal replacement of property, plant and equipment or for payment to shareholders for the use of their capital. Operating cash flow per share is calculated by dividing cash from operating activities by the number of ordinary shares outstanding. This provides the user of financial statements with an idea of how much cash is being generated from operations per share.

Key Terms

Business life cycle
Cash debt coverage ratio
Current cash debt coverage ratio
Direct method
Expansion phase
Free cash flow

Growth phase
Indirect method
Maturity phase
Operating cash flow per share
Start-up phase

Terminology practice

For each of the following, insert the correct term from the list of key terms preceding this section. Each key term can be used more than once.

1. The _____ is calculated by dividing cash from operating activities by average total liabilities.
2. In the _____ of the business life cycle, a business has reached the point where its infrastructure is fully developed, even though it may replace and upgrade assets and invest in new products and services as market-place opportunities evolve.
3. When the _____ of calculating cash flows from operating activities is used, major classes of gross receipts and gross cash payments are disclosed.
4. In the _____ of the business life cycle, a business has usually established a presence in the market place and may have a positive cash flow from operating activities.
5. The _____ is calculated by dividing cash from operating activities by average current liabilities.
6. A _____ describes the typical evolution of a business and has four phases: start-up, growth, expansion and maturity.
7. In the _____ of the business life cycle, a business is beginning to produce and market a product or service.
8. _____ is calculated by subtracting capital expenditures and cash dividends from cash provided from operating activities.
9. In the _____ of the business life cycle, a business is just beginning operations and costs typically exceed revenue.
10. When the _____ of calculating cash flows from operating activities is used, profit or loss is adjusted for the effects of transactions of a noncash nature, any deferrals or accruals of past or future operating cash receipts or payments, and items of income and expense associated with investing or financing cash flows.
11. _____ is calculated by dividing cash from operating activities by ordinary shares outstanding.

Application exercises

1. Calculate the missing amount in each of the four cash flows shown below. Each cash flow is independent.

Cash balance at beginning of reporting period	$10 000	???	$7 900	$6 340
Net cash provided by (used by) operating activities	(2 000)	8 500	???	12 100
Net cash provided by (used by) investing activities	(6 000)	(12 000)	1 300	(19 000)
Net cash provided by (used by) financing activities	13 000	(3 600)	(4 800)	???
Cash balance at end of reporting period	???	11 000	500	8 650

2. A business reports revenue of ¥300 700 000 for the year ended 31 December 2009. 60% was sold on credit. The trade accounts receivable balance at the beginning of 2009 was ¥65 000 000 and the ending balance was ¥184 000 000. How much cash was provided by sales?

3. In 2010, a business reports cost of goods sold of £1 350 000 in its statement of comprehensive income. Beginning inventories for the reporting period were £230 000 and the ending balance was £285 000. The beginning balance for trade accounts payable was $440 000 and the ending balance was $390 000. How much cash was paid to suppliers?

4. Financing expenses reported on the statement of comprehensive income for 2009 were €230 000. The interest payable balance at the beginning of the reporting period increased from €110 000 to €135 000 at the end of the reporting period. How much cash was paid for interest during the period?

5. At the beginning of the 2009 reporting period, Cathay Enterprises Ltd reported prepaid expenses of $900 000 and accrued liabilities of $150 000. At the end of the period, prepaid expenses and accrued liabilities were $790 000 and $185 000, respectively. Cathay also reported $2 500 000 of operating expenses during 2009, which included $310 000 in depreciation expense. How much cash was paid for operating expenses for the 2009 reporting period?

6. A business reports €400 000 in profit for the reporting year ended 31 December 2009. The beginning balances for trade accounts receivable were €15 000 and for trade accounts payable €7500. The ending balances were €12 500 and €9500 respectively. Depreciation expense on property, plant and equipment was €22 000 and amortization of intangibles was €1370. How much cash was provided by operating activities for the 2009 reporting period?

7. A company reports the following information for the year ended 31 December 2009:

Cash from operating activities	£135 000
Beginning current liabilities	20 000
Ending current liabilities	18 000
Beginning noncurrent liabilities	110 000
Ending noncurrent liabilities	95 000
Capital expenditures	30 000
Cash dividends paid	14 000
Ordinary shares outstanding	20 000

Compute the current cash debt coverage ratio, cash debt coverage ratio, free cash flow and operating cash flow per share.

8. Classify the following transactions as a source or use of cash under the appropriate activity:

	Operating Activity		Investing Activity		Financing Activity	
	Source	Use	Source	Use	Source	Use
Cash outflows for acquisitions of subsidiaries and other businesses						
Cash receipts from the payment of advances						
Cash proceeds from short-term and long-term borrowings						

(Continued)

	Operating Activity		Investing Activity		Financing Activity	
	Source	Use	Source	Use	Source	Use
Cash repayments of amounts borrowed						
Cash loans to other parties						
Cash inflows from the disposal of subsidiaries and other businesses						
Cash receipts from the sale of property, plant and equipment, intangible and other assets						
Cash payments to acquire equity or debt investments of other businesses						
Cash payments to suppliers for goods and services						
Cash outflows for investments in financial assets and liabilities						
Cash payments to acquire the business's own shares						
Income tax refunds						
Cash receipts from the sale of goods and services, royalties, fees, commissions and other revenue						
Cash receipts from the sale of equity or debt investments of other businesses						
Cash proceeds from the sale of the business's shares						
Cash payments to employees						
Cash payments to acquire property, plant and equipment, intangible and other assets						
Income tax payments						
Cash inflows for investment in financial assets and liabilities						

9. You have been given the following information relating to a limited liability company called Nobrie. This company is preparing its financial statements for the year ended 31 May 2009. [ACCA adapted]

Nobrie
Statement of Comprehensive Income for the Year Ended
31 May 2009 '000

Revenue	$ 66 600
Cost of sales	(13 785)
Gross profit	$ 52 815
Distribution costs	(7 530)
Administrative expenses	(2 516)
Profit from operations	$ 42 769
Investment income	146
Finance cost	(1 177)
Profit before tax	$ 41 738
Tax	(9 857)
Net profit for the period	$ 31 881

Nobrie
Statement of Financial Position at
31 May '000

	2009		2008	
Assets				
Noncurrent assets				
Cost		$ 144 844		$ 114 785
Accumulated depreciation		(27 433)		(26 319)
		117 411		88 466
Current assets				
Inventory	$ 24 931		$ 24 065	
Trade accounts receivable	18 922		13 238	
Cash	3 689	47 542	2 224	39 527
Total assets		$ 164 953		$ 127 993
Equity and liabilities				
Capital and reserves				
Ordinary share capital	$ 27 000		23 331	
Share premium	14 569		10 788	
Revaluation reserve	15 395		7 123	
Accumulated profits	59 944	116 908	28 063	69 305
Noncurrent liabilities				
6% loan note		17 824		24 068
Current liabilities				
Bank overdraft	5 533		6 973	
Trade accounts payable	16 699		20 324	

(*Continued*)

Nobrie
Statement of Financial Position at
31 May '000

	2009		2008	
Taxation	7 989	30 221	7 323	34 620
Total equity and liabilities		$ 164 953		$ 127 993

Additional information:

(i) During the year ended 31 May 2009, the company sold a piece of equipment for $3 053 000, realizing a profit of $1 540 000. There were no other disposals of noncurrent assets during the year.

(ii) Profit from operations is stated after charging depreciation of $5 862 000.

(iii) There were no amounts outstanding in respect of interest payable or receivable as at 31 May 2008 or 2009.

(iv) There were no dividends paid or declared during the year.

Required:

Prepare a statement of cash flows for Nobrie for the year ended 31 May 2009 using the indirect method.

10. The following information is available for Sioux, a limited liability company:

Statement of Financial Position at
December 31 $'000

	2010		2009	
Noncurrent assets				
Cost or valuation		11 000		8 000
Accumulated depreciation		(5 600)		(4 800)
Net book value		5 400		3 200
Current assets				
Inventories	3 400		3 800	
Receivables	3 800		2 900	
Cash at bank	400	7 600	100	6 800
		13 000		10 000
Equity and liabilities				
Capital and reserves				
Ordinary share capital	1 000		1 000	
Revaluation reserve	1 500		1 000	
Retained earnings	3 100	5 600	2 200	4 200
Noncurrent liabilities				
10% loan notes		3 000		2 000
Current liabilities				
Trade payables	3 700		3 200	
Income tax	700	4 400	600	3 800
		13 000		10 000

Summarized statement of comprehensive income for the year ended 31 December 2010:

	$000
Profit from operations	2650
Finance cost (loan note interest)	(300)
	2 350
Income tax expense	(700)
Net profit for the period	1 650

Notes:

i. During the year noncurrent assets that had cost $800 000, with a net book value of $350 000, were sold for $500 000.

ii. The revaluations surplus arose from the revaluation of some land that was not being depreciated.

iii. The 2009 income tax liability was settled at the amount provided for on 31 December 2009.

iv. The additional loan notes were issued on 1 January 2010. Interest was paid on 30 June 2010 and 31 December 2010.

v. Dividends paid during the year amounted to $750 000.

Required:

Prepare the company's statement of cash flows for the year ended 31 December 2010, using the indirect method. [ACCA adapted]

11. The following information has been extracted from the draft financial statements of Snowdrop, a limited liability company. [ACCA adapted]

Snowdrop
Statement of Financial Position at
31 May $000

	2011		2010	
Assets				
Noncurrent assets		4 600		2 700
Current assets				
Inventory	580		500	
Trade receivables	260		230	
Bank	100	940	170	900
Total assets		5 540		3 600
Equity and liabilities				
Capital and reserves				
Ordinary share capital		3 500		2 370
Share premium		300		150
Retained earnings		1 052		470
		4 852		2 990
Noncurrent liabilities				
10% loan note – redeemable 31 May 2011		0		100

(*Continued*)

Snowdrop
Statement of Financial Position at
31 May $000

	2011		2010	
Current liabilities				
Trade payables	450		365	
Taxation	180		145	
Bank overdraft	58	688	0	510
Total equity and liabilities		5 540		3 600

Additional information:

(i) The statement of comprehensive income for the year ended 31 May 2011 shows the following:

$000	
Operating profit	1 042
Interest payable	(10)
Profit before taxation	1 032
Taxation	(180)
Profit for financial year	852

(ii) During the year dividends paid were $270 000.

(iii) During the year noncurrent assets with a net book value of $200 000 were sold for $180 000.

Required:

(a) Prepare a statement of cash flows for Snowdrop for the year ended 31 May 2011 using the indirect method.

(b) Comment on the financial position of Snowdrop as shown by the statement of cash flows you have prepared.

12. You have been given the following information relating to H. Marathon, a limited liability company. The company is preparing a statement of cash flows for the year ended 31 October 2011. [ACCA adapted]

H. Marathon
Statement of Comprehensive Income for the Year Ended
31 October 2011 $000

Revenue	$54 577
Cost of sales	(27 128)
Gross profit	27 449
Distribution costs	(9 146)
Administrative expenses	(5 766)

Profit from operations	12 537
Interest received	101
Finance cost	(1 749)
Profit before tax	10 889
Taxation	(2 570)
Profit for the period	8 319

H. Marathon
Statement of Financial Position at
31 October $000

	2011	2010
Assets		
Noncurrent assets		
Cost	133 152	124 252
Accumulated depreciation	(30 978)	(25 629)
	102 174	98 623
Current assets		
Inventory	26 350	29 365
Trade receivables	13 214	16 446
Bank	3 153	3 036
	42 717	48 847
Total assets	144 891	147 470
Equity and liabilities		
Capital and reserves		
Ordinary share capital	23 576	21 082
Share premium	11 982	10 245
Revaluation reserve	12 554	6 029
Retained earnings	58 532	53 910
	106 644	91 266
Noncurrent liabilities		
7% loan notes	5 743	22 632
Current liabilities		
Bank overdraft	6 869	7 842
Trade payables	23 534	23 804
Taxation	2 101	1 926
	32 504	33 572
Total equity and liabilities	144 891	147 470

Additional information:
(i)   During the year dividends paid were $3 697 000.
(ii) There were no amounts outstanding in respect of interest payable or receivable as at either year end.
(iii) Operating profit is stated after charging depreciation of $6 784 000.

(iv) During the year, the company sold equipment for $5 667 000, realizing a profit of $1 806 000. This equipment had never been revalued, and there were no other disposals of noncurrent assets during the year.

(v) The only revaluation of noncurrent assets was that of a piece of freehold land.

Required:

(a) Prepare a statement of cash flows for H. Marathon for the year ended 31 October 2011 using the indirect method.

(b) Comment on the financial performance and position of H. Marathon as shown by the statement of cash flows you have prepared.

(c) Why is the statement of cash flows sometimes considered more useful than profit statements?

13. The summarized financial statements of Granada for 2009 and 2010 are given below:

Statement of Financial Position at
$000

	Notes	31 December 2010		31 December 2009	
Noncurrent assets: cost	1	3 400		2 100	
Less Accumulated depreciation		(720)	2 680	(550)	1 550
Current assets					
Inventory		600		400	
Receivables		1 500		1 700	
Cash		80	2 180	50	2 150
			4 860		3 700
Equity and liabilities					
Ordinary share capital			900		600
Share premium account		500		320	
Retained earnings	2	920	1 420	500	820
			2 320		1 420
Noncurrent liabilities					
10% loan notes			1 200		1 000
Current liabilities					
Bank overdraft		140		280	
Trade payables		900		800	
Current tax payable		300	1 340	200	1 280
			4 860		3 700

Notes

i. Noncurrent assets that had cost $200 000 with a written-down value of $60 000 were sold for $80 000 during the year.

ii. The increase in retained earnings is made up as follows:

	$000	$000
Opening balance		500
Operating profit	1 090	
Less: Finance costs paid	(120)	
Profit before taxation	970	
Income tax expense	(300)	
Dividends paid	(250)	
Retained profit for the year		420
Closing balance		920

Required:

Prepare a statement of cash flows for Granada for the year ended 31 December 2010. [ACCA adapted]

14. The statement of financial position of Joyce, a limited liability company, at 30 June 2010 and 2011 is as follows:

Statement of Financial Position at
$000

	Notes	30 June 2011		30 June 2010	
Noncurrent assets	1		148 000		130 000
Current assets					
Inventories		14 000		9 100	
Receivables		21 400		12 500	
Cash at bank		–	35 400	4 600	26 200
			183 400		156 200
Ordinary share capital			110 000		109 000
Share premium account			5 000		4 000
Revaluation reserve			14 000		2 000
Retained earnings	1		28 000		18 000
Total equity			157 000		133 000
Noncurrent liabilities					
8% loan notes	3		10 000		8 000
Current liabilities					
Payables		7 100		9 200	
Current tax payable	2	8 000		6 000	
Bank overdraft		1 300	16 400	–	15 200
			183 400		156 200

Notes:

i. $6 200 000 was paid during the year to settle the income tax liability at 30 June 2010.

ii. The additional loan notes were issued on 1 January 2011. All interest due was paid on 31 December 2010 and 30 June 2011.

iii. Dividends paid during the year totalled $4 000 000.

Required: Prepare a statement of cash flows for the company for the year ended 30 June 2011. [ACCA adapted]

Case Analysis
BOTSWANA WILD SAFARIS LLC

Botswana Wild Safaris LLC was introduced in Chapter 7. In this chapter we will continue the case by focusing on changes in equity. Recall that Tony Washford had purchased the company from Gerhardt Perst on 1 January 2009. Use the information presented for Botswana Wild Safaris from Chapters 7, 8, 9 and 10 to complete the requirements.

REQUIRED:

Construct the statements of cash flows for Botswana Wild Safaris for the three reporting dates.

End notes

1. 'Bush Aids Detroit, but Hard Choices Wait for Obama', *New York Times*, December 19, 2008.
2. 'Auto executives in spotlight as U.S. weighs bailout', *Reuters*, November 16, 2008.
3. 'As GM losses deepen, bankruptcy fears grow', *Detroit Free Press*, February 27, 2009.
4. 'GM's '08 loss its 2nd-worst ever', chicagotribune.com, February 27, 2009.
5. *Ibid.*

Evaluating Financial Statements

INTRODUCTION TO PART V

In Chapter 1, we learned about the financial accounting reporting system, which is presented in the following diagram:

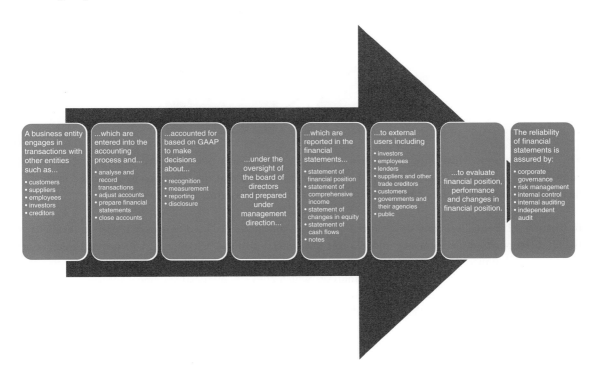

Recall that a business entity engages in transactions with customers, suppliers, employees, investors, creditors and other parties. The accounting process begins by analysing and recording these transactions, which are then summarized by account. At the end of the reporting period, adjustments are made to adjust the accounts to the accrual basis of accounting. Then the financial statements are prepared. Afterwards, temporary accounts are closed in preparation for the subsequent reporting period.

Decisions about how different transactions are to be recorded and reported in the financial statements are governed by generally accepted accounting principles, including accounting standards. In this textbook, we have relied on International Financial Reporting Standards. For each transaction, decisions are made about how the economic substance of the transaction is recognized, measured, reported and disclosed. Although management is responsible for accounting, the board of directors has the responsibility of overseeing the financial accounting reporting system.

A complete set of financial statements includes the statement of financial position, statement of comprehensive income, statement of changes in equity and statement of cash flows, as well as the accompanying notes. The objective of these financial statements is to report on the financial position, performance and changes in financial position. Financial statements are for the benefit of external users, who include investors, employees, lenders, suppliers, customers, governments and their regulatory agencies and the public.

Now, in Part V, we address two remaining questions – one in each of the last two chapters, shown in the diagram that follows.

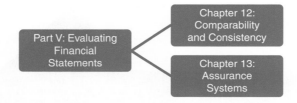

The first question is: How do we evaluate a company's performance over time and when compared to competitors? Second: How are financial statement users assured that the information contained in the financial statements presents a 'true and fair view' of the business's financial results?

In Chapter 12 we will see how the financial statements and notes are used by external users to evaluate the financial position, performance and changes in financial position. Chapter 12 will review three major evaluation techniques. The first is horizontal analysis, which examines the financial statements for trends – changes over time. The second is vertical analysis, which converts financial statement information to percentages. The value of vertical analysis is that it allows us to compare financial results between competitors of different size. Thus, vertical analysis is sometimes referred to as common size analysis.

The third evaluation technique is ratio analysis. We have already learned how to calculate ratios in Chapters 7 to 11. We will now see how they are used to provide additional information to evaluate changes over time further and to compare financial results between competitors.

Chapter 13 focuses on the question of how external users can be confident that the financial statements for a business entity are reliable and report a true and fair view of the economic substance of that business entity's transactions. In Chapter 13 we will address five assurance systems: corporate governance and especially the role of the board of directors; risk management; internal control; internal auditing; and independent audit. In addition, Chapter 13 discusses fraud and misrepresentation as these relate to financial statements.

Comparability and consistency

12

LEARNING OUTCOMES

By the end of this chapter you should be able to:

1. Explain how business entities are evaluated for consistency and comparability.
2. Apply horizontal analysis to the statement of comprehensive income.
3. Apply vertical analysis to the statement of comprehensive income.
4. Apply horizontal analysis to the statement of financial position.
5. Apply vertical analysis to the statement of financial position.
6. Analyse the liquidity of the reporting entity.
7. Analyse the solvency of the reporting entity.
8. Analyse the profitability of the reporting entity.

The preparation of the financial statements and their release to the public is really just the beginning. Once investors, creditors and other external users have access to the financial statements, a considerable amount of analysis and discussion follows about the success of the business entity, whether management is effectively managing the business, whether the business is realizing its potential for earnings and many other issues. Major financial newspapers and journals such as the *Financial Times*, the *Wall Street Journal* and *Forbes* magazine carry news stories about the financial results of major companies. In addition, these results are reported and commented on in other international, national and local media (see web links at the end of this chapter).

In fact, an entire industry of investment professionals – financial analysts and advisers – exists to follow the financial results of major companies, evaluate their performance and offer opinions and advice about whether to invest in the companies' debt and equity securities. For those investors who already hold securities of the company, they advise whether to dispose of those investments. In many cases, investment professionals specialize in a particular industry, type of security (equity, bonds or corporate notes) or region. Firms like Morgan Stanley, Merrill Lynch, Goldman Sachs and many others offer investment advice.

Institutional investors are also a major factor in evaluating the financial results of major companies. Institutional investors are organizations that pool significant sums of money and then invest in securities. Examples include commercial investment funds like Fidelity Investments in the US, F&C Investments in the UK and Shuaa Capital in Dubai. Malvern's Vanguard Group, one of the largest, managed over US$1 trillion at the beginning of 2008. Organizations responsible for investing retirement funds are institutional investors, one of the largest being CalPERS, the California Public Employees' Retirement System, which invests on behalf of 1.6 million people. Many of these funds, sometimes referred to as mutual funds, are also publicly traded. Insurance companies also qualify as institutional investors, since they manage large amounts of money accumulated by the payment of insurance premiums.

In fact, most individuals do not invest directly in debt and equity securities but in mutual funds, which in turn own these securities (see Figure 12.1). Pooling money in an investment fund rather than investing on one's own has many advantages. For example, risk is diversified so that poor performance by only one investment does not cause the entire fund to decline in value significantly; investment professionals make the decisions about which investments are added to and removed from the investment fund; and an individual can easily convert his or her investment to cash.

FIGURE 12.1 INSTITUTIONAL INVESTORS

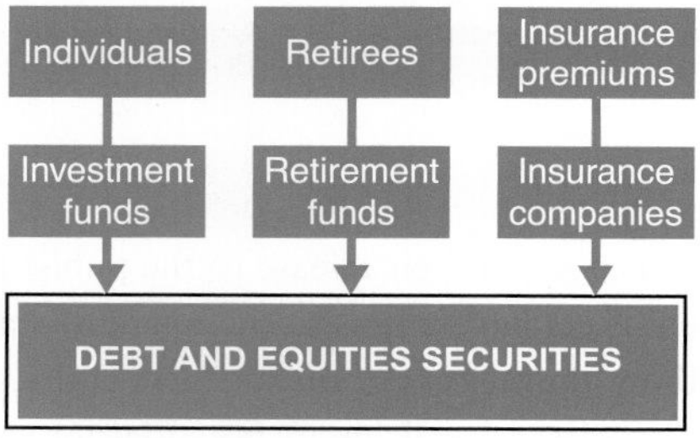

An active financial media and scruting by investment professionals mean that many people are interested in financial results and their opinions matter. If investment professionals take the view that a particular company is not performing satisfactorily, that may well cause the company to have to pay higher interest on debt and issue its shares for a lower amount. A positive evaluation of results often makes it easier for a company to obtain the investment capital it needs at a reasonable cost.

Institutional investors usually exercise the voting rights of the shares held in the investment fund, retirement fund or the insurance company's investment portfolio. This means that these professionals often have very large blocks of votes that they can use to elect members to the board and approve or disapprove policies put before the membership for vote. Boards of directors and managers of publicly traded companies are concerned, and rightfully so, about the relationship the company has with investment professionals, and in particular institutional investors.

Thus, the opinions of investment professionals about reported financial results matter a great deal. This is why PricewaterhouseCoopers, one of the largest international accounting firms, conducts surveys of investment professionals to learn more about their views on the usefulness of financial statements. According to a recent survey report: 'While there are many stakeholders who rely upon financial reports to underpin economic decisions, few are as dependent upon a cost-effective and relevant reporting model as the investment professional.'[1] Here are some excerpts from the PricewaterhouseCoopers report that explain some of the information that investment professionals seek:

> Equity specialists focus on building intrinsic valuation models, such as discounted cash flow and return on investment capital. [Investment professionals use these models to determine the value of a business, which is not necessarily the value of the business as determined by the price of its publicly traded shares.] They also want to perform market-based analysis, using ratios such as price/earnings. Fixed income specialists focus more on cash flows: how much cash will go out when, and what is the risk that incoming cash won't cover the outflows?

Survey Findings Related to the Statement of Income

Investors want to understand a company's operating performance. They want to be able to assess whether an increase in revenues or earnings is sustainable, whether it has come from organic or acquired growth, core or non-core operations, from unit volume gains or price rises. At present, many say that making such assessments is a greater challenge than it could, and should, be.

The current methodology [for revenue recognition] is considered overly complex; with many companies insufficiently clear about how accounting standards have been implemented. This makes it hard for investment professionals to be confident that they are comparing companies on an equitable basis.

Another common frustration relates to the breadth of the cost categories reported by companies. The survey respondents point out there is often insufficient detail: cost of goods sold may represent 90% of the total costs.

Historical Cost Versus Revaluation to Fair Market Value

Many respondents say that their ability to assess performance is increasingly muddled by revaluations of assets and liabilities. Although views are split on the merit or further cause of current values, there is a strong feeling that revaluations should not be allowed to obscure an understanding of underlying business performance.

Respondents generally welcome a current value for liquid financial assets and assets deemed to be 'investments' or 'available for sale'. However, the majority question the relevance of current value measures for assets used in the on-going operations of the business, for which historical cost is taken to be more appropriate.

Some survey participants made the point that current value would be a useful additional disclosure for certain operational assets – for example, a store purchased 50 years ago, for which the historical value probably bears no relation to current market value. However, for a number of reasons there is concern in the investment community about moving to a pure fair value model.

First, the respondents express the concern that their ability to assess managements' stewardship of the assets with which they are entrusted would be impeded if all assets and liabilities are restated. Second, they worry about the potential for subjectivity in valuations and ask whether management always provides reliable estimates of current value? And, finally, the respondents question whether introducing a pure fair value model would, in practice, deliver a favorable cost/benefit outcome for management. Their time might be better spent elsewhere.

Survey Findings Related to Cash Flows

Respondents are looking for more lines of information in the statement of cash flows and better notes to help them tie data between the income and statement of cash flows. They are also helping to ensure consistency in the way that cash is reported over time.

Thus, as a financial accountant, you are likely to have a large and enthusiastic audience of investment professionals eager to receive and evaluate the information you provide. But as you can see, not all those investment professionals will agree with what you report, nor in some cases will they agree with the manner in which you report the information. That is why professional judgement on your part will be critical.

LEARNING OUTCOME 1
EXPLAIN HOW BUSINESS ENTITIES ARE EVALUATED FOR CONSISTENCY AND COMPARABILITY

The two major tasks of comparative analysis are consistency and comparability. Recall from Chapter 2 that consistency refers to the use of the same set of accounting policies and procedures within an entity and between entities. This is important if we are to compare financial results over time, for example over the past three years. Recall also that comparability provides the ability for users to identify trends over time in a business entity's financial position and performance. Comparability is achieved through consistency, but also by the application of accounting standards in order to compare the performance of one business to others – especially competitors. Comparability also involves comparing financial results of a single business to the industry or other average.

As illustrated in Figure 12.2, we are interested in consistency and comparability to be able to compare a single company's performance over time or two or more companies' performance in a single time period. We can combine these to give a two-dimensional view that compares the results of multiple companies over multiple time periods.

FIGURE 12.2 CONSISTENCY AND COMPARABILITY

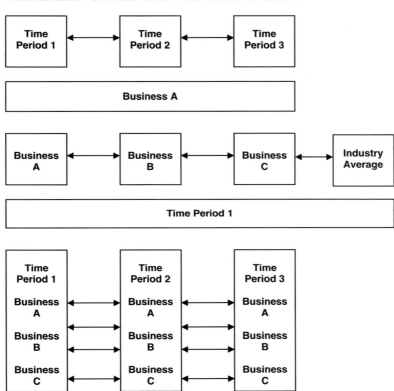

1.1 Evaluating performance

We compare the performance of companies over time using three methods that are covered in this chapter: horizontal analysis, vertical analysis and ratio analysis. Horizontal analysis examines each line item in the financial statements for changes over time by converting those changes to percentages. Vertical analysis calculates the percentage that a single line item (for example cost of goods sold) is of a total; for the statement of comprehensive income that total is sales revenue and total assets for the statement of financial position. We have already been introduced to basic ratio calculations in Chapters 7 to 11.

Following are excerpts from the financial statements of three major international airlines: British Airways, Emirates Airline and Lufthansa. These are presented here to demonstrate how horizontal analysis is performed. Notice that we only perform the analysis on those line items in profit or loss – and omit other comprehensive income. So the following examples will only include those items that would appear in profit or loss.

British Airways

The first statement of income is for British Airways, prepared on the basis of IFRS as adopted by the European Union.

FIGURE 12.3 BRITISH AIRWAYS

Group Consolidated Statement of Income for the Year Ended March 31, 2007		
£ million	**2007**	**2006**
Traffic revenue	7 263	6 924
Passenger	618	638
Cargo	7 881	7 562
Other revenue	611	651
Revenue	**8 492**	**8 213**
Employee costs	2 277	2 260
Depreciation, amortization and impairment	714	715
Aircraft operating lease costs	81	90
Fuel and oil costs	1 931	1 581
Engineering and other aircraft costs	414	441
Landing fees and en route charges	517	520
Handing charges, catering and other operating costs	930	915
Selling costs	436	438
Currency differences	18	(19)
Accommodation, ground equipment and IT costs	618	578
Total expenditure on operations before non-recurring items	**7 936**	**7 519**
Operating profit before non-recurring items	556	694
Credit arising on charges to pension scheme	396	
Provision for settlement of competition investigations	(350)	
Operating profit	**602**	**694**
Fuel derivative (losses)/gains	(12)	19
Finance costs	(168)	(214)
Finance income	129	92
Net financing expense relating to pensions	(19)	(18)
Retranslation credits/(charges) on currency borrowings	13	(12)
Profit on sale of property, plant and equipment and investments	47	27
Share of post-tax profits in associates accounted for using the equity method	5	28
Income relating to fixed asset investments	14	
Profit before tax	611	616
Tax	(173)	(152)
Profit after tax from continuing operations	438	464
(Loss)/profit from discontinued operations (after tax)	(134)	3
Profit after tax	**304**	**467**

Notice that revenues and expenses are classified by nature. We can also see that profit attributable to the parent and minority interest, which could have been presented in the notes, are presented on the face of the statement of income. The British Airways statement of income is notable because of the amount of detail that is presented on its face.

Emirates Airline

According to the notes that accompany Emirates Airline's 2007 financial statements:

BASIS OF PRESENTATION

The consolidated financial statements have been prepared in accordance with and comply with International Financial Reporting Standards (IFRS). The consolidated financial statements are prepared under the historical costs convention except for those assets and financial liabilities that are measured at fair value as stated in the accounting policies below.

Compare the British Airways statement of income to that of Emirates Airline, shown in Figure 12.4. Emirates Airline is itself a subsidiary of the Emirates Group, though the airline is itself a parent of other entities. This is why the statements of income are consolidated.

Notice also that information on the face of the statement of income is minimal. Whereas British Airways chose to include details of its revenue on the face of the statement of income, Emirates Airline included this information in an accompanying note, as in Figure 12.5.

FIGURE 12.4 EMIRATES AIRLINE

Consolidated Statement of Comprehensive Income for the Year Ended 31 March 2007			
	Notes	2007 AED '000	2006 AED '000
Revenue	4	28 642 701	22 307 539
Other operating income	5	530 420	350 451
Operating costs	6	(25 834 248)	(20 005 699)
Operating profit		**3 338 873**	**2 652 291**
Finance costs – net	7	(87 790)	(58 364)
Share of results in associated companies and joint ventures	11	75 225	55 007
Profit before income tax		**3 326 308**	**2 648 934**
Income tax expense	8	(162 581)	(87 608)
Profit for the year		**3 163 727**	**2 561 326**

FIGURE 12.5 EMIRATES AIRLINE NOTE 4, REVENUE

	2007 AED '000	2006 AED '000
Services		
Passenger	21 677 143	16 370 146
Cargo	5 046 888	4 178 223
Courier	263 485	277 297
Excess baggage	217 153	173 810
Destination and leisure	182 953	146 718
Hotel operations	91 467	79 754
Mail	65 992	47 515
Training	62 900	69 217
Licensed engineering income	15 558	15 897
	27 623 539	21 358 577
Sale of goods	1 019 162	948 962
	28 642 701	**22 307 539**

Also, Emirates Airline classifies expenses by function rather than nature. However, IAS 1 Presentation of Financial Statements also requires that if expenses are presented by function, a further disclosure should be made classifying expenses by nature because of the value of this for predicting future cash flows. Note 6 (shown in Figure 12.6) fulfils this requirement.

Lufthansa

Lufthansa's first note in its 2007 financial statements provides the basis for presentation:

NOTE 1, APPLICATION OF THE GERMAN COMMERCIAL CODE

The financial statements of Deutsche Lufthansa AG are drawn up in accordance with the rules and regulations of the German Commercial Code (HGB) and the German Stock Corporation Act (AktG).

In the interests of clearer presentation, certain items that are grouped together in the statement of financial position and the statement of income are shown and explained separately in the notes. Over and above the statutory classification system, the entry relating to aircraft is listed separately in order to improve the clarity of the financial statements.

FIGURE 12.6 EMIRATES AIRLINE NOTE 6, OPERATING COSTS

	2007 AED '000	2006 AED '000
Fuel and oil	7 525 311	6 445 152
Employee	4 024 328	3 187 108
Aircraft operating leases	2 909 181	2 312 168
Sales and marketing	2 907 483	2 195 381
Handling	1 751 697	1 406 250
In-flight catering and other operating costs	1 251 580	1 052 878
Depreciation	1 309 883	974 355
Overflying	947 168	765 349
Cost of goods sold	547 927	541 846
Landing and parking	534 754	436 904
Aircraft maintenance	499 630	373 401
Amortization	41 871	31 346
Corporate overheads	1 483 435	1 283 561
	25 834 248	**20 005 699**

The statements of income for 2007 and 2006 are shown in Figure 12.7.

Lufthansa also classifies expenses by nature, however details of the cost of materials and services are not provided with the same amount of detail as with British Airways and Japan Airlines. Like Emirates Airline, information about fuel costs, typically one of the two largest expenses for airlines, is in an accompanying note, which is shown in Figure 12.8.

What can we conclude from this comparison of statements of income from these three global airlines?

- Each business's statement of income was prepared under a different set of accounting standards. The statements of income look quite similar, but underlying the reported numbers are variations in accounting treatment. Thus, to be sure that we have achieved a valid comparison between companies, we would need to know more about how amounts were recognized, measured and presented.
- Some of the additional information needed can be obtained from the accompanying notes, although in some cases the external user may have to go to other sources to determine if the information is available at all. Once the information has been obtained, regardless of source, it must be formatted in a way that can be compared across companies. This essentially requires the investment analyst to recast the financial statements.

FIGURE 12.7 DEUTSCHE LUFTHANSA AG

Statement of Income for the Financial Year		
In €m	31.12.2007	31.12.2006
Traffic revenue	13 522	12 694
Other revenue	253	244
Total revenue	**13 775**	**12 938**
Other operating income	1 596	998
Cost of materials and services	−8 671	−8 286
Staff costs	−2 632	−2 652
Depreciation	−637	−438
Other operating expenses	−2 688	−2 552
Profit from operating activities	**+743**	**+8**
Income from subsidiaries and associated companies	+469	+705
Net interest	−31	−16
Write-down of investments and securities held as current assets	−11	−18
Financial result	**−489**	**+671**
Profit on ordinary activities before taxes	**+1 232**	**+679**
Taxes	−109	−156
Net profit for the year	**+1 123**	**+523**

FIGURE 12.8 LUFTHANSA NOTE 18, COST OF MATERIALS AND SERVICES

In €m	2007	2006
Aircraft fuel	2 888	2 767
Other costs of raw materials, supplies and goods purchased	69	65
Cost of services purchased	5 714	5 454
	8 671	8 286

- Each business's statement of income is presented in a different currency. Thus, given the financial statements in their 'raw' form, a complete comparison is impossible. If all statements were converted into a single currency, that would help somewhat. As we shall see in the following discussion, an easier way to make comparisons exists.

LEARNING OUTCOME 2
APPLY HORIZONTAL ANALYSIS TO THE STATEMENT
OF COMPREHENSIVE INCOME

2.1   How is horizontal analysis performed for one company over time?
    2.1.1   How is horizontal analysis performed using the base-period approach for a single company?
    2.1.2   How is horizontal analysis performed using the period-to-period approach for a single company?

2.2   How is horizontal analysis performed for multiple companies?
    2.2.1   How is horizontal analysis performed using the base-period approach for multiple companies?
    2.2.2   How is horizontal analysis performed using the period-to-period approach for multiple companies?

2.1 How is horizontal analysis performed for one company over time?

Horizontal analysis can be applied to a single company over time. Calculations can be made in two ways: using the base-period approach and using the period-to-period approach.

2.1.1 HOW IS HORIZONTAL ANALYSIS PERFORMED USING THE BASE-PERIOD APPROACH FOR A SINGLE COMPANY?

First, a horizontal analysis can be prepared using a base-period analysis in which one period is used as the base, and all other periods are calculated relative to that base. Figure 12.9 shows British Airways' statement of income for the last five years using a base-period approach.

In Figure 12.9, 2003 is the base year for all index calculations, which are done on a line item basis. For example, the base revenue figure is £7688 million for 2003, which is set equal to 100 as the index. This amount decreased to £7560 million in 2004, so when this is divided by the base amount of £7688 million, the index declines to 98 for 2004. The fact that the index is below 100 means that revenue has declined from the base period.

The index for 2005 is calculated in the same way. The 2005 revenue of £7813 million is divided by the base amount of £7688 million to yield 102. Since the index is over 100, revenue has increased when compared to the base period. Amounts for 2006 and 2007 are also calculated using the 2003 revenue figure as the base amount.

Over the five-year period covered by Figure 12.9, the index for revenue increased to 110, although the index for profit increased to 403, almost four times as much. The increase for EPS was only marginally less, at 381. When these indexes are graphed, as shown in Figure 12.10, the relationship becomes clearer. Although profitability retreated in 2007 when compared to 2006, the overall five-year result was much higher.

FIGURE 12.9 HORIZONTAL ANALYSIS FOR ONE COMPANY – BASE-PERIOD APPROACH

British Airways Group Consolidated Statement of Income										
	2007		2006		2005		2004		2003 Base Year	
	Index	£ million	Index	£ million	Index	£ million	Index	£ million	Index	£ million
Revenue	110	8 492	107	8 213	102	7 813	98	7 560	100	7 688
Operating profit	204	602	235	694	183	540	137	405	100	295
Share of operating profit in associates	13	5	72	28	105	41	149	58	100	39
Total operating profit including associates	182	607	216	722	174	581	139	463	100	334
Other income and charges	3,225	125	2,125	81	175	3	425	13	100	(4)
(Loss)/profit on sale of fixed assets and investments	78	47	45	27	(43)	(26)	(76)	(46)	100	60
Net interest payable	66	(168)	84	(214)	56	(143)	78	(200)	100	(255)
Profit before tax	453	611	456	616	307	415	170	230	100	135
Tax	346	(173)	304	(152)	298	(149)	170	(85)	100	(50)
Profit after tax	358	304	549	467	313	266	171	145	100	85
Minority interest	108	(14)	123	(16)	115	(15)	115	(15)	100	(13)
Profit for the year	403	290	626	451	349	251	181	130	100	72

2.1.2 HOW IS HORIZONTAL ANALYSIS PERFORMED USING THE PERIOD-TO-PERIOD APPROACH FOR A SINGLE COMPANY?

The second approach to horizontal analysis is to calculate the percentage change from year to year, as shown in Figure 12.11.

Period-to-period analysis uses the previous period as the base. In Figure 12.11, the percentage change for revenue between 2003 and 2004 is calculated by deducting 2004 revenue of £7688 million from 2004

FIGURE 12.10 CUMULATIVE CHANGE IN REVENUE, PROFIT AND EPS

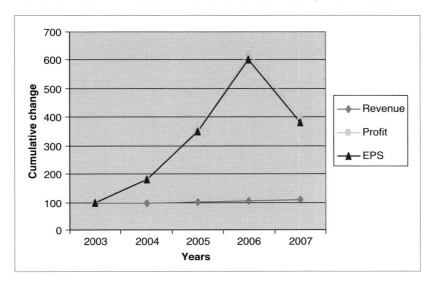

FIGURE 12.11 HORIZONTAL ANALYSIS FOR ONE COMPANY – PERIOD-TO-PERIOD APPROACH

		British Airways Group Consolidated Statement of Income							
	2007		2006		2005		2004		2003
	Percent change	£ million	Percent change	£ million	Percent change	£ million	Percent change	£ million	£ million
Revenue	3.4	8,492	5.1	8 213	3.3	7 813	(1.7)	7 560	7 688
Operating profit	(13.3)	602	28.5	694	33.3	540	37.3	405	295
Share of operating profit in associates	(82.1)	5	(31.7)	28	(29.3)	41	48.7	58	39
Total operating profit including associates	(15.9)	607	124.3	722	25.5	581	38.6	463	334
Other income and charges	54.3	125	2 700.0	81	(77.0)	3	425.0	13	(4)

(*Continued*)

FIGURE 12.11 (CONTINUED)

	British Airways Group Consolidated Statement of Income								
	2007		2006		2005		2004		2003
(Loss)/profit on sale of fixed assets and investments	74.1	47	203.8	27	(43.0)	(26)	(177.0)	(46)	60
Net interest payable	(21.5)	(168)	(49.7)	(214)	(28.5)	(143)	21.6	(200)	(255)
Profit before tax	(01)	611	48.4	616	80.4	415	70.4	230	135
Tax	13.8	(173)	2.0	(152)	75.3	(149)	70.0	(85)	(50)
Profit after tax	(34.9)	304	75.6	467	83.4	266	70.6	145	85
Minority interest	(12.5)	(14)	6.7	(16)	0.0	(15)	15.4	(15)	(13)
Profit for the year	(35.7)	290	79.7	451	93.1	251	80.6	130	72

revenue of £7560 million and then dividing the difference of negative £128 million by 2003 revenue to yield −1.7%, representing a marginal decline. When the calculation is made for 2005, the revenue for 2004 of £7560 million is deducted from the 2005 revenue of £7813 million for an increase of £253 million or 3.3%. For 2006 the base period is 2005, and for 2007 it is 2006.

FIGURE 12.12 RATE OF CHANGE IN REVENUE, PROFIT AND EPS

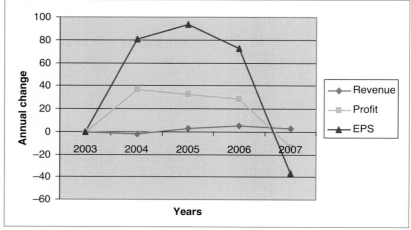

When the year-to-year changes in revenue, profit and EPS are plotted, as shown in Figure 12.12, quite a different pattern emerges. This graph depicts the rate of change over time, rather than the cumulative change since the beginning of the five-year sequence.

Despite a slight decrease between 2003 and 2005, British Airways has increased revenue each year. The rate of increase in profit and EPS was much higher between 2003 and 2004, although both slowed in 2005 then became negative in 2007.

2.2 How is horizontal analysis performed for multiple companies?

Horizontal analysis can also be used to compare multiple companies. For our example, we will compare British Airways, Emirates Airline and Lufthansa.

2.2.1 HOW IS HORIZONTAL ANALYSIS PERFORMED USING THE BASE-PERIOD APPROACH FOR MULTIPLE COMPANIES?

Figure 12.13 shows revenue and profit comparisons for all three international airline competitors using the base-period approach. Remember that different currencies were used in the financial statements. However,

FIGURE 12.13 HORIZONTAL ANALYSIS FOR MULTIPLE COMPANIES – BASE-PERIOD APPROACH

	Statement of Income – International Airlines									
	2007		2006		2005		2004		2003 Base Year	
	Index	million	Index	million	Index	million	Index	million	Index	million
Revenue										
British Airways £	110	8 492	107	8 213	102	7 813	98	7 560	100	7 688
Emirates Airline AED	307	28 643	239	22 308	189	17 620	138	12 855	100	9 342
Lufthansa €	86	13 775	81	12 938	113	18 065	106	16 965	100	15 957
Cohort average	168	–	142	–	135	–	114	–	100	–
Profit										
British Airways £	403	290	626	451	349	251	181	130	100	72
Emirates Airline AED	330	3 164	267	2 561	254	2 435	175	1 684	100	960
Lufthansa €	215	1 123	153	523	163	612	142	408	100	(978)
Cohort average	336	–	349	–	255	–	(134)	–	100	–

since the horizontal analysis creates an index, this currency difference no longer matters. The index provides the basis for comparison.

In Figure 12.13, 2003 is again our base period and all other years' indexes are calculated on that basis. If we examine indexes for 2007, we can see immediate differences. Emirates Airline's revenue more than tripled over the five-year period, while the others varied from a decrease to 86% of the 2003 level for Lufthansa to a 138% increase for British Airways. The average index for the cohort (all three companies) was 168% of the 2003 level. Indexes show that British Airways more than quadrupled and Emirates Airline more than tripled profit.

When we graph the indexes, relationships again become clearer. Figure 12.14a shows revenue growth by airline, with Emirates Airline noticeably outperforming the four other airlines.

FIGURE 12.14a REVENUE GROWTH

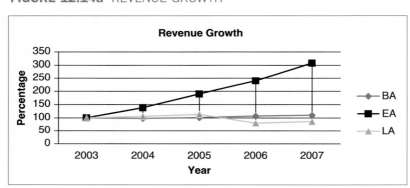

Figure 12.14b shows profit growth over the same five years.

FIGURE 12.14b PROFIT GROWTH

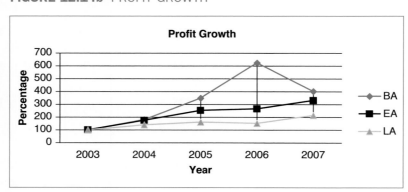

Figure 12.14b shows that profit growth for British Airways was the strongest despite the decrease between 2006 and 2007.

Finally, Figures 12.14c and 12.14d compare revenue and profit by company for British Airways and Emirates Airline.

FIGURE 12.14c BRITISH AIRWAYS

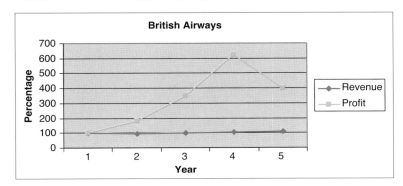

Figure 12.14c shows us that profit growth was far in excess of revenue growth. Later in this chapter when we apply ratio analysis, we will be able to determine more about this relationship.

FIGURE 12.14d EMIRATES AIRLINE

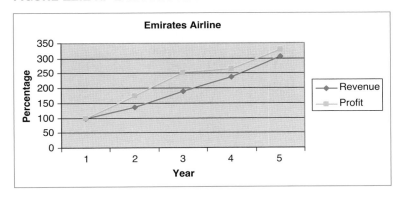

Figure 12.14d shows that Emirates Airline's profit growth was more closely matched with revenue growth, although it was slightly higher.

2.2.2 HOW IS HORIZONTAL ANALYSIS PERFORMED USING THE PERIOD-TO-PERIOD APPROACH FOR MULTIPLE COMPANIES?

The horizontal analysis comparing the three competitors could also be calculated using the period-to-period approach, as shown in Figure 12.15.

The period-to-period approach calculates the percentage increase or decrease from the previous period. For example, British Airways' revenues decreased by 7% between 2003 and 2004, and then increased by 3% from 2004 to 2005. Over the five-year period these percentages show the rate of increase or decrease. Figure 12.16 shows the rate of growth period to period for revenue for these three companies.

FIGURE 12.15 HORIZONTAL ANALYSIS FOR MULTIPLE COMPANIES – PERIOD-TO-PERIOD APPROACH

									2003 Base Year
Statement of Income – International Airlines									
	2007		2006		2005		2004		2003 Base Year
	%	million	%	million	%	million	%	million	million
Revenue									
British Airways £	3	8 492	5	8 213	3	7 813	(7)	7 560	7 688
Emirates Airline AED	28	28 643	27	22 308	37	17 620	38	12 855	9 342
Lufthansa €	6	13 775	(28)	12 938	6	18 065	6	16 965	15 957
Cohort average	12	–	1	–	15	–	12	–	–
Profit									
British Airways £	(36)	290	80	451	93	251	81	130	72
Emirates Airline AED	24	3 164	52	2 561	45	2 435	75	1 684	960
Lufthansa €	115	1 123	(15)	523	50	612	142	408	(978)
Cohort average	34	–	(39)	–	63	–	(99)	–	–

FIGURE 12.16 REVENUE GROWTH RATE

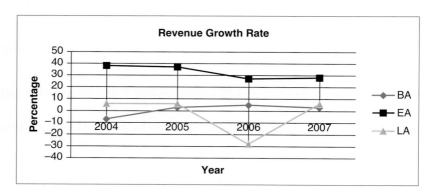

Figure 12.17 shows the growth rate for profits.

FIGURE 12.17 PROFIT GROWTH RATE

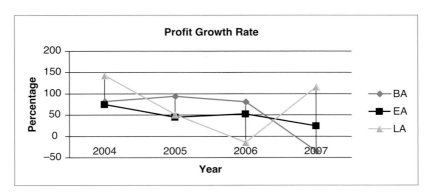

Figures 12.18a–c contrast revenue and profit for each company.

FIGURE 12.18a BRITISH AIRWAYS

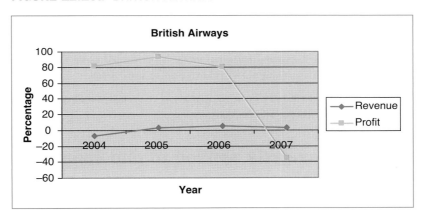

FIGURE 12.18b EMIRATES AIRLINE

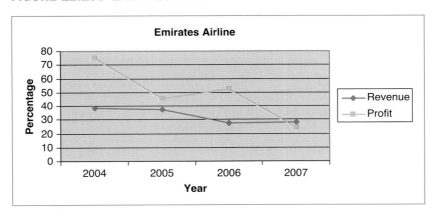

FIGURE 12.18c LUFTHANSA

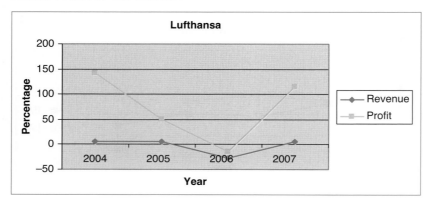

LEARNING OUTCOME 3
APPLY VERTICAL ANALYSIS TO THE STATEMENT
OF COMPREHENSIVE INCOME

3.1. What is the difference between horizontal analysis performed using the base period approach versus horizontal analysis using the period-to-period approach?

3.2. What is the advantage of using horizontal analysis to compare multiple companies of different size and which use different currencies?

3.1 How is vertical analysis applied to one company over multiple time periods?

A second method of analysing changes over time and performance between competitors is vertical analysis. In vertical analysis for the statement of income, total revenue (or net revenue) is the base and is thus set at 100%. All other line items in the statement of income are calculated as a *percentage of total revenue*, as the following brief example illustrates.

A company has the following statement of income for the years ending 31 December 2009 and 2010, with calculations for the vertical analysis shown in the right-hand column.

Statement of Income for the Years Ending 31 December				
	2010		**2009**	
Revenue	€1 200	100%	€1 000	100%
Cost of sales	516	43%	450	45%

Gross profit	684	57%	550	55%
Operating expenses	360	30%	300	30%
Profit	€384	32%	€250	25%

In the example above, profit has increased by 7% from 25% in 2009 to 32% in 2010. But why? We can see that revenue has risen from €1000 to €1200 between 2009 and 2010, but this does not tell us anything about the structure of the expenses. However, when we calculate the percentages using vertical analysis, we can see that the cost of sales has declined by 2% from 45% in 2009 to 43% in 2010. Operating expenses have not changed and are 30% of revenue for both years. Thus, improvement in profit is attributable to a relative decrease in the cost of sales.

Vertical analysis can be applied to one company to determine how expenses change *as a percentage of sales* over time, or it can be used to compare competitors. Figure 12.19 shows a base-period calculation for British Airways' statement of income from 2003 to 2007.

FIGURE 12.19 VERTICAL ANALYSIS FOR BRITISH AIRWAYS (2003–07)

British Airways Group Consolidated Statement of Income										
	2007		2006		2005		2004		2003	
	%	£ million	%	£ million	%	£ million	%	£ million	%	£ million
Revenue	100.0	8 492	100.0	8 213	100.0	7 813	100.0	7 560	100.0	7 688
Employee costs	26.8	2 277	27.5	2 260	29.1	2 273	28.9	2 180	27.4	2 107
Fuel and oil costs	22.7	1 931	19.2	1 581	14.4	1 128	12.2	922	11.0	842
Profit for the year	3.4	290	5.5	451	3.2	251	1.7	130	0.9	72

Only employee costs and fuel and oil costs (see shaded area) have been included in Figure 12.19, since these are typically an airline's biggest expenses. We can see that employee costs have remained more or less the same as a percentage of sales, actually decreasing by 0.6%. However, increasing fuel costs have caused fuel and oil costs to double as a percentage of sales over the five years. Yet with other reductions in expenses, management has increased profit after tax from 1.1% to 3.6%.

For contrast, Figure 12.20 shows a vertical analysis for Emirates Airline over the same period.

FIGURE 12.20 VERTICAL ANALYSIS FOR EMIRATES AIRLINE (2003–07)

Emirates Airline Consolidated Statement of Income									
	2007		2006		2005		2004		2003
	%	AED million	%	AED million	%	AED million	%	AED million	%	AED million
Revenue	100.0	28 643	100.0	22 308	100.0	17 620	100.0	12 855	100.0	9 342
Employee costs	14.0	4 024	14.3	3 187	15.3	2701	17.5	2254	18.7	1749
Fuel and oil costs	26.3	7 525	24.4	5 445	18.6	3279	12.7	1633	10.7	998
Profit after tax	11.0	3 164	11.4	2 561	13.8	2 435	13.1	1 684	10.3	960

When compared to British Airways, Emirate Airlines' fuel and oil costs as a percentage of revenues are actually higher, although its employee costs – historically the largest category for British Airways – are significantly less.

LEARNING OUTCOME 4
APPLY HORIZONTAL ANALYSIS TO THE STATEMENT OF FINANCIAL POSITION

4.1 How is horizontal analysis performed for one company over time?

    4.1.1 How is horizontal analysis performed using the base-period approach for a single company?

    4.1.2. How is horizontal analysis performed using the period-to-period approach for a single company?

4.2 How is horizontal analysis performed for multiple companies?

    4.2.1 How is horizontal analysis performed using the base-period approach for multiple companies?

    4.2.2 How is horizontal analysis performed using the period-to-period approach for multiple companies?

Evaluating financial position

Both horizontal and vertical analysis can also be useful for evaluating financial position. The following examples from our three airlines – British Airways, Emirates Airline, and Lufthansa – illustrate how horizontal and vertical analysis are applied to the statement of financial position.

4.1 How is horizontal analysis performed for one company over time?

Figure 12.21 shows the 2006 and 2007 statement of financial position for British Airways.

FIGURE 12.21 BRITISH AIRWAYS STATEMENT OF FINANCIAL POSITION

Group Consolidated Statement of Financial Position – at March 31		
£ million	2007	2006
Noncurrent assets		
Property, plant and equipment		
Fleet	6 153	6 606
Property	932	974
Equipment	272	302
	7 357	7 882
Goodwill	40	72
Landing rights	139	115
Software	33	46
	212	233
Investments in associates	125	131
Other investments	107	33
Employee benefit assets	116	137
Other financial assets	28	89
Total noncurrent assets	7 945	8 505
Noncurrent assets held for sale	8	3
Current assets and receivables		
Inventories	76	83
Trade receivables	654	685
Other current assets	346	458
Other current interest bearing deposits	1 642	2 042
Cash and cash equivalents	713	398
	3 431	3 666
Total assets	11 384	12 174
Shareholders' equity and liabilities		
Shareholders' equity		
Issued share capital	288	283
Share premium	933	888
Investment in own shares	(10)	
Other reserves	1 000	690

(Continued)

FIGURE 12.21 *(CONTINUED)*

Group Consolidated Statement of Financial Position – at March 31		
£ million	2007	2006
Total shareholders' equity	**2 211**	**1 861**
Minority interest	200	213
Total equity	**2 411**	**2 074**
Noncurrent liabilities		
Interest bearing long-term borrowings	2 929	3 602
Employee benefit obligations	1 142	1 803
Provisions for deferred tax	930	896
Other provisions	153	135
Other long-term liabilities	194	232
Total noncurrent liabilities	**5 348**	**6 668**
Current liabilities		
Current portion of long-term borrowings	417	479
Trade and other payables	2 744	2 822
Current tax payable	54	75
Short-term provisions	410	56
Total current liabilities	**3 625**	**3 432**
Total equity and liabilities	**11 384**	**12 174**

4.1.1 HOW IS HORIZONTAL ANALYSIS PERFORMED USING THE BASE-PERIOD APPROACH FOR A SINGLE COMPANY?

Figure 12.22 presents a horizontal analysis for British Airways for the period 2003 to 2007 using the base-period approach.

This preceding analysis shows that by 2007 British Airways had reduced its tangible assets to 78% of the 2003 level. In fact, throughout the five-year period, the percentage was continually reduced compared to the base year 2003.

4.1.2 HOW IS HORIZONTAL ANALYSIS PERFORMED USING THE PERIOD-TO-PERIOD APPROACH FOR A SINGLE COMPANY?

Figure 12.23 shows a horizontal analysis using the period-to-period approach for the same statement of financial position information.

What does this schedule tell us? We can see in 2006, for example, that the company made significant reductions in equipment and at the same time reduced both current liabilities and noncurrent liabilities.

FIGURE 12.22 HORIZONTAL ANALYSIS FOR BRITISH AIRWAYS – BASE-PERIOD APPROACH

	British Airways Group Consolidated Statement of Financial Position Horizontal Analysis – Base-Period Approach									
	2007		2006		2005		2004		2003 Base Year	
	Index	£ million	Index	£ million	Index	£ million	Index	£ million	Index	£ million
Noncurrent assets										
Intangible assets										
Goodwill	41	40	73	72	89	88	94	93	100	99
Landing rights and other	265	172	248	161	157	102	115	75	100	65
	129	212	142	233	116	190	102	168	100	164
Tangible assets										
Fleet	79	6 153	83	6 506	86	6 748	91	7 104	100	7 828
Property	76	932	80	974	79	959	85	1 042	100	1 219
Equipment	62	272	69	302	101	445	112	491	100	440
	78	7 357	83	7 882	86	8 152	91	8 637	100	9 487
Investments										
Investments in associates	27	125	28	131	26	120	109	501	100	461
Trade and other investments	784	251	809	259	94	30	94	30	100	32
Total noncurrent assets	78	7 945	84	8 505	82	8 302	92	9 367	100	10 144
Noncurrent assets held for sale	–	8	–	3	–	–	–	–	–	–
Current assets										
Inventories	87	76	95	83	97	84	87	76	100	87
Trade receivables and other current assets	101	1 000	116	1 143	109	1 078	103	1 019	100	986
Other current interest bearing deposits	115	1 642	143	2 042	112	1 604	112	1 606	100	1 430

(*Continued*)

FIGURE 12.22 (*CONTINUED*)

	British Airways Group Consolidated Statement of Financial Position Horizontal Analysis – Base-Period Approach									
	2007		**2006**		**2005**		**2004**		**2003** Base Year	
Cash and cash equivalents	321	713	179	398	35	78	29	64	100	222
Total current assets and receivables	126	3 431	135	3 666	104	2 844	101	2 765	100	2 725
TOTAL ASSETS	88	11 384	95	12 174	87	11 146	94	12 132	100	12 869
Capital and reserves										
Called up share capital	106	288	106	288	100	271	100	271	100	271
Reserves										
Share premium account	118	933	118	933	100	788	100	788	100	788
Investment in own shares	32	(10)	32	(10)	84	(26)	100	(31)	100	(31)
Other reserves	100	1 000	79	690	143	1 432	116	1 159	100	999
Total equity shareholders' funds	109	2 211	92	1 861	122	2 465		2 187	100	2 027
Minority interest	93	200	99	213	101	219	97	210	100	216
Total Equity	107	2 411	92	2 074	120	2 684	108	2 428	100	2 243
Noncurrent liabilities										
Interest bearing long term borrowings	102	4 071	82	5 405	66	4 346	84	5 486	100	6 553
Provision for deferred tax	88	930	84	896	117	1 243	107	1 137	100	1 062
Provisions for liabilities and charges	324	347	810	367	78	83	79	85	100	107

	2007 %	£ million	2006 %	£ million	2005 %	£ million	2004 %	£ million	2003 £ million
Total noncurrent liabilities	238	5 348	37	835	120	2 684	107	2 397	100	2 243
Current liabilities	125	3 625	118	3 432	103	2 980	103	2 996	100	2 904
Total Liabilities	174	8 973	83	4 267	110	5 664	105	5 393	100	5 147
TOTAL EQUITY AND LIABILITIES	88	11 384	95	12 174	87	11 146	94	12 132	100	12 869

FIGURE 12.23 HORIZONTAL ANALYSIS FOR BRITISH AIRWAYS – PERIOD-TO-PERIOD APPROACH

British Airways Group Consolidated Statement of Financial Position									
	2007		2006		2005		2004		2003
	%	£ million	%	£ million	%	£ million	%	£ million	£ million
Noncurrent assets									
Intangible assets									
Goodwill	(44)	40	(19)	72	(5)	88	(6)	93	99
Landing rights and other	7	172	59	161	36	102	15	75	65
	(9)	212	23	233	13	190	2	168	164
Tangible assets									
Fleet	(5)	6 153	(4)	6 506	(5)	6 748	(9)	7 104	7 828
Property	(4)	932	2	974	(8)	959	(15)	1 042	1 219
Equipment	(10)	272	(32)	302	(9)	445	12	491	440
	(7)	7 357	(3)	7 882	(6)	8 152	(9)	8 637	9 487
Investments									
Investments in associates	(5)	125	9	131	(76)	120	9	501	461
Trade and other investments	(3)	251	763	259	–	30	(6)	30	32

(*Continued*)

FIGURE 12.23 *(CONTINUED)*

British Airways Group Consolidated Statement of Financial Position									
	2007		**2006**		**2005**		**2004**		**2003**
Total noncurrent assets	(7)	7 945	2	8 505	(11)	8 302	(8)	9 367	10 144
Noncurrent assets held for sale	167	8	–	3	–	–	–	–	–
Current assets									
Inventories	(8)	76	(1)	83	11	84	(13)	76	87
Trade receivables and other current assets	(13)	1 000	(6)	1 143	6	1 078	(3)	1 019	986
Other current interest bearing deposits	(20)	1 642	27	2 042	–	1 604	12	1 606	1 430
Cash and cash equivalents	79	713	410	398	22	78	(71)	64	222
Total current assets and receivables	(6)	3 431	29	3 666	3	2 844	1	2 765	2 725
TOTAL ASSETS	(7)	11 384	9	12 174	(8)	11 146	(6)	12 132	12 869
Capital and reserves									
Called up share capital	–	288	6	288	–	271	–	271	271
Reserves									
Share premium account	–	933	18	933	–	788	–	788	788
Investment in own shares	–	(10)	(61)	(10)	16	(26)	–	(31)	(31)
Other reserves	45	1 000	(52)	690	(24)	1 432	16	1 159	999
Total equity shareholders' funds	19	2 211	(25)	1 861	13	2 465	8	2 187	2 027
Minority interest	(6)	200	3	213	4	219	(3)	210	216

	Index	million	Index	million	Index	million	Index	million	Index	million
Total Equity	16	2 411	(23)	2 074		2 684	8	2 428		2 243
Noncurrent liabilities										
Interest bearing long term borrowings	(25)	4 071	24	5 405	(21)	4 346	(16)	5 486		6 553
Provision for deferred tax	4	930	(28)	896	9	1 243	7	1 137		1 062
Provisions for liabilities and charges	(5)	347	342	367	2	83	(21)	85		107
Total noncurrent liabilities	540	5 348	(69)	835	12	2 684	7	2 397		2 243
Current liabilities	6	3 625	15	3 432	(1)	2 980	3	2 996		2 904
Total Liabilities	110	8 973	(25)	4 267	5	5 664	5	5 393		5 147
TOTAL EQUITY AND LIABILITIES	(7)	11 384	9	12 174	(8)	11 146	(6)	12 132		12 869

4.2 How is horizontal analysis performed for multiple companies?

Horizontal analysis can also be applied to the statement of financial position for multiple companies.

4.2.1 HOW IS HORIZONTAL ANALYSIS PERFORMED USING THE BASE-PERIOD APPROACH FOR MULTIPLE COMPANIES?

Figure 12.24 shows a horizontal analysis for British Airways and Emirates Airline using the base-period approach.

FIGURE 12.24 HORIZONTAL ANALYSIS FOR MULTIPLE COMPANIES – BASE-PERIOD APPROACH

	Statements of Financial Position									
	2007		2006		2005		2004		2003 Base Year	
	Index	million	Index	million	Index	million	Index	million	Index	million
Noncurrent assets British Airways £	78	7 945	84	8 505	82	8 302	92	9 367	100	10 144

(*Continued*)

FIGURE 12.24 (*CONTINUED*)

	Statements of Financial Position									
	2007		2006		2005		2004		2003 Base Year	
Emirates Airline AED	301	22 530	227	17 018	154	11 558	113	8 438	100	7 485
Cohort average	229	–	156	–	118	–	103	–	100	–
Current assets British Airways £	126	3 431	135	3 666	104	2 844	101	2 765	100	2 725
Emirates Airline AED	234	15 428	218	14 376	177	11 663	150	9 900	100	6 594
Cohort average	180	–	177	–	141	–	126	–	100	–
TOTAL ASSETS British Airways £	88	11 384	95	12 174	87	11 146	94	12 132	100	12 869
Emirates Airline AED	270	37 958	223	31 394	165	23 221	130	18 338	100	14 079
Cohort average	179	–	159	–	126	–	112	–	100	–
Total equity British Airways £	107	2 411	92	2 074	120	2 684	108	2 428	100	2 243
Emirates Airline AED	345	13 170	286	10 919	204	7 792	131	5 013	100	3 818
Cohort average	226	–	189	–	162	–	120	–	100	–
Noncurrent liabilities British Airways £	238	5 348	37	835	120	2 684	107	2 397	100	2 243
Emirates Airline AED	223	14 210	166	10 616	120	8 899	127	8 101	100	6 385
Cohort average	231	–	102	–	120	–	117	–	100	–
Current liabilities										

British Airways £	125	3 625	118	3 432	103	2 980	103	2 996	100	2 904
Emirates Airline AED	273	10 578	254	9 859	168	6 530	135	5 224	100	3 876
Cohort average	199	–	186	–	136	–	119	–	100	–
Total liabilities										
British Airways £	174	8 973	83	4 267	110	5 664	105	5 393	100	5 147
Emirates Airline AED	242	24 788	200	20 475	150	15 429	130	13 325	100	10 261
Cohort average	208	–	142	–	130	–	118	–	100	–
TOTAL EQUITY AND LIABILITIES										
British Airways £	88	11 384	95	12 174	87	11 146	94	12 132	100	12 869
Emirates Airline AED	270	37 958	223	31 394	165	23 221	130	18 338	100	14 079
Cohort average	179		159	–	126	–	112	–	100	–

Notice that this comparison allows us to compare changes in the airlines' assets, liabilities and equity from 2003 to 2007. We can see, for example, that Emirates Airline expanded its noncurrent assets more than three times, while British Airways reduced its asset bases somewhat to 78%. Should we take this change as a negative sign of the company's performance or is it a positive development? We cannot tell by simply examining these numbers. But we will be better able to answer these questions when we look at ratio analysis later in the chapter.

We can also see from Figure 12.24 that Emirates expanded its shareholders' equity by 345% compared to 2003, followed by Lufthansa and British Airways.

4.2.2 HOW IS HORIZONTAL ANALYSIS PERFORMED USING THE PERIOD-TO-PERIOD APPROACH FOR MULTIPLE COMPANIES?

Figure 12.25 also provides a horizontal analysis of the three international competitors, but in this case using the period-to-period approach.

FIGURE 12.25 HORIZONTAL ANALYSIS FOR MULTIPLE COMPANIES – PERIOD-TO-PERIOD APPROACH

	2007		2006		2005		2004		2003
Statement of Financial Position – International Airlines									
	%	million	%	million	%	million	%	million	million
Noncurrent assets									
British Airways £	(7)	7 945	2	8 505	(11)	8 302	(8)	9 367	10 144
Emirates Airline AED	32	22 530	47	17 018	37	11 558	13	8 438	7 485
Cohort average	13	–	25	–	13	–	3	–	–
Current assets									
British Airways £	(6)	3 431	29	3 666	3	2 844	1	2 765	2 725
Emirates Airline AED	7	15 428	23	14 376	18	11 663	50	9 900	6 594
Cohort average	1	–	26	–	11	–	26	–	–
TOTAL ASSETS									
British Airways £	(6)	11 384	9	12 174	(8)	11 146	(6)	12 132	12 869
Emirates Airline AED	21	37 958	35	31 394	27	23 221	30	18 338	14 079
Cohort average	8	–	22	–	10	–	12	–	–
Total Equity									
British Airways £	16	2 411	(23)	2 074	11	2 684	8	2 428	2 243
Emirates Airline AED	21	13 170	40	10 919	55	7 792	31	5 013	3 818
Cohort average	19	–	9	–	33	–	20	–	–
Noncurrent liabilities									
British Airways £	540	5 348	(69)	835	12	2 684	7	2 397	2 243

Emirates Airline AED	34	14 210	19	10 616	10	8 899	27	8 101	6 385
Cohort average	287	–	(25)	–	11	–	17	–	–
Current liabilities									
British Airways £	6	3 625	15	3 432	(1)	2 980	3	2 996	2 904
Emirates Airline AED	7	10 578	51	9 859	–	6 530	36	5 224	3 876
Cohort average	7	–	33	–	(1)	–	20	–	–
Total liabilities									
British Airways £	110	8 973	(25)	4 267	5	5 664	5	5 393	5 147
Emirates Airline AED	21	24 788	33	20 475	16	15 429	30	13 325	10 261
Cohort average	66	–	4	–	11	–	18	–	–
TOTAL EQUITY AND LIABILITIES									
British Airways £	(6)	11 384	9	12 174	(8)	11 146	(6)	12 132	12 869
Emirates Airline AED	21	37 958	35	31 394	27	23 221	30	18 338	14 079
Cohort average	8	–	22	–	10	–	12	–	–

LEARNING OUTCOME 5
APPLY VERTICAL ANALYSIS TO THE STATEMENT OF FINANCIAL POSITION

Figure 12.26 shows a vertical analysis for British Airways' statement of financial position for the years from 2003 to 2007. The base is total assets and total equity and liabilities.

Amounts in Figure 12.26 show that British Airways reduced its noncurrent assets from 78.8% of total assets to 69.8%. Notice also that equity increased from 17.4% of total assets in 2003 to 21.2% in 2007.

FIGURE 12.26 VERTICAL ANALYSIS OF BRITISH AIRWAYS' STATEMENT OF FINANCIAL POSITION (2003–07)

British Airways Group Consolidated Statement of Financial Position										
	2007		2006		2005		2004		2003 Base Year	
	%	£ million	%	£ million	%	£ million	%	£ million	%	£ million
Noncurrent assets										
Intangible assets										
Goodwill	0.4	40	0.6	72	0.8	88	0.8	93	0.8	99
Landing rights and other	1.5	172	1.3	161	0.6	102	0.6	75	0.5	65
	1.9	212	1.9	233	1.4	190	1.4	168	1.3	164
Tangible assets										
Fleet	54.0	6 153	53.4	6 506	60.5	6 748	58.6	7 104	60.8	7 828
Property	8.2	932	8.0	974	8.6	959	8.6	1 042	9.5	1 219
Equipment	2.4	272	2.5	302	4.0	445	4.1	491	3.4	440
	64.6	7 357	64.7	7 882	73.1	8 152	71.2	8 637	73.7	9 487
Investments										
Investments in associates	1.1	125	1.1	131	1.1	120	4.1	501	3.6	461
Trade and other investments	2.2	251	2.1	259	0.3	30	0.2	30	0.2	32
Total noncurrent assets	69.8	7 945	69.9	8 505	74.5	8 302	77.2	9 367	78.8	10 144
Noncurrent assets held for sale	–	8	–	3	–	–	–	–	–	–
Current assets										
Inventories	0.7	76	0.7	83	0.8	84	0.6	76	0.7	87
Trade receivables and other current assets	8.8	1 000	9.4	1 143	9.7	1 078	8.4	1 019	7.7	986
Other current interest bearing deposits	14.4	1 642	16.8	2 042	14.4	1 604	13.2	1 606	11.1	1 430
Cash and cash equivalents	6.3	713	3.3	398	0.7	78	0.5	64	1.7	222

Total current assets and receivables	30.1	3 431	30.1	3 666	25.5	2 844	22.8	2 765	21.2	2 725
TOTAL ASSETS	100.0	11 384	100.0	12 174	100.0	11 146	100.0	12 132	100.0	12 869
Capital and reserves										
Called up share capital	2.5	288	2.4	288	2.4	271	2.2	271	2.1	271
Reserves										
Share premium account	8.2	933	7.7	933	7.1	788	6.5	788	6.1	788
Investment in own shares	–	(10)	–	(10)	(0.2)	(26)	(0.3)	(31)	(0.2)	(31)
Other reserves	8.8	1 000	5.7	690	12.8	1 432	9.6	1 159	7.8	999
Total equity shareholders' funds	19.4	2 211	15.3	1 861	22.1	2 465	18.0	· 2 187	15.8	2 027
Minority interest	1.8	200	1.8	213	2.0	219	1.7	210	1.7	216
Total Equity	21.2	2 411	17.0	2 074	24.1	2 684	20.0	2 428	17.4	2 243
Noncurrent liabilities										
Interest bearing long term borrowings	35.8	4 071	44.4	5 405	40.0	4 346	45.2	5 486	50.9	6 553
Provision for deferred tax	8.2	930	7.4	896	11.2	1 243	9.4	1 137	8.3	1 062
Provisions for liabilities and charges	3.0	347	3.0	367	0.7	83	0.7	85	0.8	107
Total noncurrent liabilities	47.0	5 348	54.8	6 668	50.9	8 652	55.3	6 708	60.0	7 722
Current liabilities	31.8	3 625	28.2	3 432	26.7	2 980	24.7	2 996	22.6	2 904
Total Liabilities	78.8	8 973	83.0	10 100	77.6	5 672	80.0	9 704	83.6	10 626
TOTAL EQUITY AND LIABILITIES	100.0	11 384	100.0	12 174	100.0	11 146	100.0	12 132	100.00	12 869

LEARNING OUTCOME 6
ANALYSE THE LIQUIDITY OF THE REPORTING ENTITY

Throughout Parts III and IV, we introduced a number of ratios and calculations that related to liquidity, solvency and profitability. In the following, we will apply those ratios to our three international airlines.

6.1   Working capital

6.2   Current ratio

6.3   Acid-test ratio

6.4   Cash ratio

6.5   Receivables turnover ratio

6.6   Average collection period

6.7   Current cash debt coverage ratio

Recall that liquidity relates to the availability of cash in the near future to meet short-term financial commitments.

6.1 Working capital

Although not a ratio, working capital is the excess or deficiency of current assets compare to current liabilities.

$$\text{Working capital} = \text{Current assets} - \text{Current liabilities}$$

Calculations for the three airlines are as follows:

	British Airways	Emirates Airline	Lufthansa
	£ millions	**AED '000**	**€ millions**
2006	234	4 516 624	(196)
2007	(194)	4 849 880	(27)

Notice that each is calculated in a different currency. This makes the information difficult to compare, and all we can conclude from this is that British Airways' and Emirates Airline's working capital is positive.

However, we can take the same information – current assets and current liabilities – and calculate it as a current ratio, as follows.

6.2 Current ratio

The working capital ratio compares current assets with current liabilities using the following formula.

$$\text{Current ratio} = \frac{\text{Current assets}}{\text{Current liabilities}}$$

Following are the calculations of the current ratios for the three competitors for 2006 and 2007:

	British Airways	Emirates Airline	Lufthansa	Average
2006	1.07	1.46	0.97	1.2
2007	0.95	1.46	1.00	1.2

The current ratio provides useful information about liquidity. We can see in the last column to the right that the average for the three airlines (which we will use as a surrogate for the industry average) is 1.2. Thus, Emirates Airline is above the average and the others are below. Does this mean that Emirates Airline is better than British Airways and Lufthansa? We really don't know based on only this information. All we can say is that Emirates is *more liquid*. An investment professional might see this amount and conclude that Emirates is financially stronger, or wonder why Emirates has such a high current ratio compared to the other airlines.

6.3 Acid-test ratio

The acid-test ratio provides a stricter test to determine how well the current liabilities of the business could be met from more highly liquid current assets, which include cash and cash equivalents, trade receivables and marketable securities.

$$\text{Acid-test ratio} = \frac{\text{Cash and cash equivalents} + \text{trade receivables} + \text{marketable securities}}{\text{Current liabilities}}$$

Following are the calculations of the acid-test ratios for the three competitors for 2006 and 2007:

	British Airways	Emirates Airline	Lufthansa	Average
2006	1.05	1.37	0.85	1.01
2007	0.93	1.39	0.82	1.06

We have a similar result as with the current ratio: Emirates is well above the 2006 average, although British Airways is above as well. For 2007, only Emirates is above the average.

6.4 Cash ratio

The cash ratio is even more stringent that the acid-test ratio. The cash ratio uses only the most liquid current assets in the numerator:

$$\text{Cash ratio} = \frac{\text{Cash and cash equivalents} + \text{marketable securities}}{\text{Current liabilities}}$$

Following are the calculations of the cash ratios for the three competitors for 2006 and 2007:

	British Airways	Emirates Airline	Lufthansa	Average
2006	0.84	0.95	0.38	0.84
2007	0.57	0.88	0.44	0.66

The average cash ratio declined somewhat between 2006 and 2007. British Airways maintained a cash ratio near the average, and again, Emirates was above the average.

6.5 Receivables turnover ratio

Two liquidity ratios are related to trade receivables, which we examined in Chapter 8, Financial Assets and Liabilities. The first is the receivables turnover ratio:

$$\text{Receivables turnover ratio} = \frac{\text{Sales}}{\text{Average receivables}}$$

For the three airline competitors, we have the following calculations:

	British Airways	Emirates Airline	Lufthansa	Average
2007	12.7	14.1	7.0	10.3

The average receivables turnover ratio was 10.3, with British Airways and Emirates Airline exceeding this amount, while Lufthansa fell below.

6.6 Average collection period

The average collection period converts the receivables turnover ratio into the number of days before a receivable is collected:

$$\text{Average collection period} = \frac{365}{\text{Receivables turnover ratio}}$$

For the three airline competitors, we have the following calculations:

	British Airways	Emirates Airline	Lufthansa	Average
2007	28.7	25.9	52.1	38.1

The average collection period for all three airlines was 38.1 days. British Airways and Emirates Airline both fell below this amount, suggesting that their receivables collection, all else being equal, was faster. (This calculation is based on sales rather than net sales and therefore does not reflect the percentage of total sales that were cash versus credit sales.)

6.7 Current cash debt coverage ratio

Investors and others often want to know how much cash current operating activities are generating when compared to current liabilities. In other words, what is the ability of the business to pay its short-term debt without having to use current or noncurrent assets?

$$\text{Current cash debt coverage ratio} = \frac{\text{Cash from operating activities}}{\text{Average current liabilities}}$$

The calculations are as follows:

	British Airways	Emirates Airline	Lufthansa	Average
2007	0.30	0.56	0.35	0.41

What can we conclude from our comparison of these three competitors based on liquidity? The answer is that Emirates Airline is consistently more liquid than the other three companies, and British Airways and Lufthansa are less liquid.

LEARNING OUTCOME 7
ANALYSE THE SOVENCY OF THE REPORTING ENTITY

7.1   Debt ratio

7.2   Debt-to-equity ratio

7.3   Times interest earned ratio

7.4   Cash debt coverage ratio

7.5   Free cash flow

Recall that solvency relates to the availability of cash over the longer term to pay debts as they become due.

7.1 Debt ratio

The debt ratio measures the total amount of indebtedness of the business over its total assets:

$$\text{Debt ratio} = \frac{\text{Total liabilities}}{\text{Total assets}}$$

The calculations are as follows:

	British Airways	Emirates Airline	Lufthansa	Average
2006	0.83	0.65	0.75	0.94
2007	0.79	0.65	0.69	0.85

7.2 Debt-to-equity ratio

The debt-to-equity ratio compares total liabilities to total equity:

$$\text{Debt to equity ratio} = \frac{\text{Total liabilities}}{\text{Total equity}}$$

	British Airways	Emirates Airline	Lufthansa	Average
2006	4.90	1.90	2.97	3.5
2007	3.72	1.88	2.23	2.67

We can see from the comparison of the debt-to-equity ratios above that British Airways has a higher proportion of debt compared to equity than the other two airlines.

The debt to equity ratio is also refered to as the gearing ratio.

7.3 Times interest earned ratio

The times interest earned ratio is a solvency ratio because it examines the ability of the company to pay the interest expense on its debt. The pre-interest, pre-tax profit is divided by interest expense:

$$\text{Times interest earned ratio} = \frac{\text{Profit} + \text{interest expense} + \text{tax expense}}{\text{Interest expense}}$$

The calculations are as follows:

	British Airways	Emirates Airline	Lufthansa	Average
2006	3.89	46.4	3.44	14.2
2007	3.84	38.9	6.70	14.9

We can see that the average for the three competitors is between 14 and 15, yet significant variability exists between the individual companies. Emirates' profit before tax and interest is between 38 and 46 times the amount of interest expense that the company incurred.

7.4 Cash debt coverage ratio

The cash debt coverage ratio is similar to the current cash debt coverage ratio in that it measures the ability to pay debt from cash generated by operating activities. However, unlike the current cash debt coverage ratio, which is calculated using average current liabilities, making it a liquidity measure, the cash debt coverage ratio uses average total liabilities in the denominator. Thus, it addresses the business's ability to pay long-term as well as short-term debt from operating cash inflows.

$$\text{Cash debt coverage ratio} = \frac{\text{Cash from operating activities}}{\text{Average total liabilities}}$$

The competitors' ratios are calculated as follows:

	British Airways	Emirates Airline	Lufthansa	Average
2007	0.12	0.25	0.19	0.19

With an average of 0.19 for the three competitors, we can see that Emirates Airline generates above-average cash compared to its average total liabilities.

7.5 Free cash flow

Free cash flow calculates the amount of cash provided by operating activities after deducting both capital expenditures and cash dividends. Recall that the rationale for free cash flow is that it is the excess amount of cash over the amount reinvested in the business and compensation to owners for the use of their capital.

Free cash flow = Cash provided from operating activities − Capital expenditures − Cash dividends

Free cash flows for the three competitors are calculated as follows:

	British Airways	Emirates Airline	Lufthansa
	£ millions	AED '000	€ millions
2006	1 310	1 164 710	493
2007	691	719 866	927

In this case, since currencies differ, no meaningful comparison can be made. What we can conclude from our examination of solvency ratios is that Emirates Airline has less debt than its two counterparts. Thus, we must conclude that it is more solvent, all other factors being equal.

The third and final category of ratios that we cover in this textbook is those related to profitability and performance.

LEARNING OUTCOME 8
ANALYSE THE PROFITABILITY OF THE REPORTING ENTITY

8.1   Return on assets ratio
8.2   Return on investments ratio
8.3   Profit margin ratio

8.1 Return on assets ratio

The debt-to-equity ratio compares total liabilities to total equity.

$$\text{Return on assets} = \frac{\text{Profit}}{\text{Average total assets}}$$

The ratios are calculated as follows:

	British Airways	Emirates Airline	Lufthansa	Average
2007	2.6%	9.1%	8.4%	5.8%

For this group of airlines, the average return on assets was 5.8%. For 2007, we see that Emirates Airlines and Lufthansa were above this average.

8.2 Return on investment ratio

Return on investment, one of the major measures of business profitability, compares profit before interest to the total amount invested in the business, as represented by total noncurrent liabilities and equity.

$$\text{Return on investment} = \frac{\text{Profit} + \text{interest expense} (1 - \text{tax rate})}{\text{Average noncurrent liabilities} + \text{equity}}$$

Return on investment for the airlines is calculated as follows:

	British Airways	Emirates Airline	Lufthansa	Average
2007	5.1%	133.8%	15.3%	33.1%

Given the capital available to management, on a pre-interest basis the three airlines returned 33.1% on average, although this was influenced by the unusually large return of Emirates Airlines.

8.3 Profit margin ratio

The profit margin ratio calculates profit as a percentage of net sales. Thus, it takes into account all costs deducted from revenue.

$$\text{Profit margin ratio} = \frac{\text{Profit}}{\text{Net sales}}$$

The ratios for the airlines are calculated as follows:

	British Airways	Emirates Airline	Lufthansa	Average
2006	5.7%	11.5%	4.5%	6.3%
2007	3.6%	11.0%	7.9%	7.5%

The average profit margin for the three competitors rose from 6.3% to 7.5% between 2006 and 2007. Emirates and Lufthansa had profit margin ratios above the average in 2007.

Conclusion

The central task of financial accounting is the preparation of financial statements and notes in accordance with applicable generally accepted accounting principles. However, once available, the financial statements become the subject of intense scrutiny by external users; in particular investors, creditors and investment professionals. These users and others analyse the results presented in the financial statements to draw conclusions about whether to invest in the business or withdraw capital already invested in the business. The results of these analyses are also used to critique management performance, sometimes in an effort to persuade the board of directors and management that a different approach is needed. In some case, board members or management may be replaced. Three types of analyses are presented in this chapter as tools for evaluating financial position, performance and changes in financial position: horizontal analysis, vertical analysis and ratio analysis.

Summary
LEARNING OUTCOME 1
Consistency and Comparability Evaluation Explained

Users have two basic needs when evaluating financial statements. The first is the need to identify trends in financial position and performance over time. The second is to be able to compare the financial position and performance of different entities, especially when comparing competitors within an industry. These needs can be met only when financial information is comparable. The purpose of all three types of analysis – horizontal, vertical and ratio – is to make the information presented in financial statements comparable. In addition, financial statement information must be consistent, which means that the same set of accounting policies and procedures are used within an entity and between entities.

LEARNING OUTCOME 2
Horizontal Analysis of the Statement of Comprehensive Income Applied

Horizontal analysis compares the same financial information over time periods by calculating the percentage changes. Two basic approaches to horizontal analysis can be used. The first is a base-period approach, which compares the first period in a time series to each subsequent period. For example, a horizontal analysis of quarterly revenue would calculate second-quarter revenue as a percentage of *first*-quarter revenue, then third-quarter revenue as a percentage of *first*-quarter revenue, and finally fourth-quarter revenue as a percentage of *first*-quarter revenue. The period-to-period approach would calculate second-quarter revenue as a percentage of *first*-quarter revenue, then third-quarter revenue as a percentage of *second*-quarter revenue, and finally fourth-quarter revenue as a percentage of *third*-quarter revenue.

LEARNING OUTCOME 3
Vertical Analysis of the Statement of Comprehensive Income Applied

Vertical analysis has only one basic approach and is applied only to line items related to profit or loss on the statement of comprehensive income. Each line item is divided by total revenue. For example, cost of goods sold is divided by total revenue, sales expenses by total revenue and so forth. By converting each line item amount to a percentage (a base of 100), percentages can be compared for a company over time.

For example, we can see whether cost of goods sold has increased or decreased *as a percentage of total revenue*. Vertical analysis also allows the financial results of two or more companies of different size to be compared. Company A may have €2 332 000 in revenue and Company B €1 428 000 in revenue, with costs of goods sold of €863 000 and €497 000, respectively. Comparison of these two companies is difficult until we take the percentage of cost of goods sold to revenue – 37% and 35% respectively. This allows us easily to determine which company has the lower cost of goods sold.

LEARNING OUTCOME 4
Horizontal Analysis of the Statement of Financial Position Applied

Horizontal analysis can also be applied to the statement of financial position. This provides information about how asset, liability and equity categories change over time. Horizontal analysis can be applied to the statement of financial position using either the base-period or period-to-period approach.

LEARNING OUTCOME 5
Vertical Analysis of the Statement of Financial Position Applied

Vertical analysis can also be applied to the statement of financial position by dividing each line item amount by total assets. When evaluating competitors, for example, this would permit a comparison of the total amount of current assets. If Company A had total assets of €1 746 000 with current assets of €550 000 and Company B had total assets of €3 384 000 with current assets of €1 055 000, then we can see by dividing current assets by total assets that the percentages are 31.5% and 31.2% respectively. Thus, the companies are roughly comparable with respect to current assets.

LEARNING OUTCOME 6
Liquidity Analysed

The third evaluation technique is ratio analysis. A major task for ratio analysis is to determine the liquidity, solvency and profitability of the reporting entity. Liquidity refers to the availability of cash in the near future to meet short-term financial commitments. Short term normally refers to 12 months beyond the reporting date.

Working capital calculates the amount of current assets available to settle current liabilities. To be able to compare over time and between entities, a current ratio is calculated by dividing current assets by current liabilities. In order to determine liquidity over an even shorter time horizon of approximately three months, an acid-test ratio is calculated by dividing cash and cash equivalents, trade accounts receivable and marketable securities (all convertible to cash in the near term) by current liabilities. An even more rigorous test of liquidity is the cash ratio, which divides cash, cash equivalents and marketable securities (immediately convertible into cash) by current liabilities.

Cash is readily supplied to businesses when customers pay for purchases with cash. However, when customers purchase through trade accounts receivable, the receipt of cash is delayed. The receivables turnover ratio calculates sales as a percentage of trade accounts receivable, which provides an idea of the size of the receivable balance compared to sales. Thus, a larger receivables turnover ratio implies that less cash is absorbed by receivables. The receivables turnover ratio can then be divided into the number of days in a year to calculate the average collection period. This number provides an idea of how many days the company's cash is tied up in receivables before payment by the customer. A longer average collection period would mean that the company is less liquid. A shorter average collection period means the company is able to covert a sale into cash more quickly and is therefore more liquid.

Liquidity is also affected by whether operating activities are a source or a use of cash. When operating activities are a net use of cash, the shortfall must be made up through the use of cash and cash equivalents, from investing activities or financing activities. In this situation, the company is less liquid than if operating activities were a source of cash.

LEARNING OUTCOME 7
Solvency Analysed

Solvency measures the availability of cash over the longer term to pay debts as they become due. Longer term typically refers to time periods of more than 12 months after the reporting date. The debt ratio measures the debt load by dividing total liabilities by total assets. The debt-to-equity ratio is calculated by dividing total liabilities by total equity. The gearing ratio reverses this calculation and divides total equity by total liabilities.

The use of debt financing normally means that the business has an obligation to pay fixed interest charges. A company that uses equity rather than debt does not have this obligation. One issue in solvency is the ability of a company to service debt, which is measured in part by the times interest earned ratio. This is calculated by dividing profit plus interest plus tax expense by interest expense.

Solvency is also affected by whether or not operating activities are a net source of cash. The cash debt coverage ratio measures the ability of cash from operating activities to pay total liabilities. Free cash flow measures the amount of cash provided from operating activities after deducting capital expenditures and cash dividends.

LEARNING OUTCOME 8
Profitability Analysed

Profitability is evaluated using several different ratios. Return on assets divides profit by average total assets to determine how effectively those assets are being employed to generate profit. Return on investment measures profit before interest and taxes as a percentage of noncurrent liabilities and equities. The profit margin ratio is calculated by dividing profit by net sales.

REVIEW QUESTIONS

1. A company may choose to finance its activities mainly by equity capital, with low borrowings (low gearing) or by relying on high borrowings with relatively low equity capital (high gearing). [ACCA adapted]

    Required: Explain why a highly geared company is generally more risky from an investor's point of view than a company with low gearing.

2. Ratio analysis in general can be useful in comparing the performance of two companies, but it has its limitations. [ACCA adapted]

    Required: State and briefly explain three factors that can cause accounting ratios to be misleading when used for such a comparison.

Key terms

Base-period analysis
Common size analysis
Horizontal analysis
Institutional investors

Investment professionals
Period-to-period analysis
Trend analysis
Vertical analysis

Terminology review

For each of the following statements, insert the correct term from the preceding list of key terms. Each key term can be used more than once.

1. Horizontal analysis can be performed using either the _____ or the _____.
2. _____ attempts to identify patterns in information over time.
3. The _____ to horizontal analysis compares amounts for a line item in the current period with the amount for the same line item in the previous period.
4. _____ compares amounts on each line item on the statement of financial position and the statement of comprehensive income over time.
5. _____ include financial analysts, advisers and others who evaluate the financial position and performance of companies and offer opinions and advice about whether to invest in the companies' debt and equity securities.
6. _____ divides each line item on the statement of financial position by total assets and each line item on the statement of comprehensive income by revenue to calculate a percentage.

7. The _____ to horizontal analysis compares amounts for a line item in the current period to an amount for the same line item in a base period.

8. _____ converts financial amounts to ratios, which makes the information comparable for an entity over time and between entities.

9. _____ are organizations that pool significant sums of money to invest in debt and equity securities.

Application Exercises

1. You are presented with the following summarized accounts for F. Raser, a limited liability company.

F. Raser
Statement of Income for the Year
Ended 31 May 2011 $000

Revenue	160
Cost of sales	(100)
Gross profit	60
Distribution and administrative expenses	(35)
Profit from operations	25
Finance cost	(5)
Profit before tax	20
Tax expense	(10)
Net profit for the period	10

F. Raser
Statement of Financial Position as at
31 May 2011 $000

Assets		
Noncurrent assets		150
Current assets		
Inventory	45	
Trade receivables	25	
Cash and bank	5	75
Total assets		225
Equities and liabilities		
Capital and reserves		
$1 Ordinary shares		100
Reserves		30
		130
Noncurrent liabilities		
10% loan notes		50

Current liabilities		
Trade payables	30	
Taxation	10	
Dividends for the year	5	45
Total equity and liabilities		225

The ratio values for F. Raser for 2009 and 2010, as well as the current average ratio values for the industry sector in which F. Raser operates, are as follows:

Ratio	Historical data		Industry average
	2009	2010	2011
Return on assets (%)	16.2	14.7	16.2
Gross profit ratio (%)	30.4	34.7	32.3
Profit margin ratio (%)	19.3	17.7	17.3
Quick/acid-test ratio	1.5	1.1	1.5
Receivables collection period (days)	32.0	44.0	35.0
Earnings per share (cents)	18.0	13.0	15.0

Required:

(a) Calculate the following ratios for F. Raser for the year ended 31 May 2011. State clearly the formula used for each ratio.

  i. Return on assets

  ii. Gross profit ratio

  iii. Profit margin ratio

  iv. Acid-test ratio

  v. Receivables collection period

  vi. Earnings per share

(b) Using the additional information given and the ratios you calculated in part (a), write a brief report on the financial performance of F. Raser. Indicate in your report what additional information might be useful to help interpret the ratios. [ACCA adapted]

2. Aber and Cromby are two retail businesses trading in the leisurewear market. Your manager has asked you to review the performance of both businesses from the financial statements provided below.

Statement of Income for the Year Ended 31 October 2010 $000		
	Aber	Cromby
Revenue	5 500	7 200
Cost of sales	(4 400)	(5 040)
Gross profit	1 100	2 160
Expenses	(610)	(1 685)

Profit from operations	490		475	
Finance cost	(15)		(15)	
Profit before tax	475		460	
Income tax expense	(200)		(180)	
Net profit for the period	275		280	

Statement of Financial Position as at
31 October 2010 $000

	Aber		Cromby	
Assets				
Noncurrent assets		3 750		7 200
Current assets				
Inventory	125		360	
Trade receivables	500		190	
Cash	30	655	0	550
Total assets		4 405		7 750
Equity and liabilities				
Capital and reserves				
$1 Ordinary shares		3 000		7 000
Reserves		1 080		410
		4 080		7 410
Noncurrent liabilities				
Loan notes		75		110
Current liabilities				
Trade payables	200		205	
Overdraft	0		5	
Tax	50	250	20	230
Total equity and liabilities		4 405		7 750

Required:

    (a) Calculate the following ratios for both Aber and Cromby:

        i.   Gross profit ratio

        ii.   Return on assets

        iii.   Earnings per share

    (b) Comment on the performance of the businesses as indicated by each of the ratios you have calculated in part (a).

    (c) Explain the limitations of using ratios as a basis for analysing business performance. [ACCA adapted]

3. Two companies, Binky and Smokey, trade in the same market. Their financial statements for the year ended 31 October 2011 are summarized below:

Statement of Income for the Year
Ended 31 October 2011 $000

	Binky		Smokey	
Sales revenue		284		305
Cost of sales		(155)		(151)
Gross profit		129		154
Expenses				
Administrative	(24)		(37)	
Selling and distribution	(35)		(53)	
Depreciation	(9)		(12)	
Loan note interest	–	(68)	(5)	(107)
Net profit		61		47

Statement of Financial Position as at
31 October 2011 $000

	Binky		Smokey	
Assets				
Noncurrent assets				
At cost	320		515	
Accumulated depreciation	(75)	245	(96)	419
Current assets				
Inventory	91		293	
Receivables	46		75	
Bank	64	201	15	383
Total assets		446		802
Equity and liabilities				
Share capital and reserves				
Share capital		150		250
Retained earnings		108		177
10% loan note		–		50
Current liabilities		188		325
Total equity and liabilities		446		802

Required:
(a) Calculate the following ratios for Binky and Smokey:
   i.   Profitability ratios: Gross profit ratio, profit margin ratio and return on assets.
   ii. Liquidity ratios: Current ratio, acid-test ratio, receivables collection period.

(b) Compare and comment on the performance of companies as indicated by the ratios you have calculated in part (a). [ACCA adapted]

4. The statement of financial position of Hadrian, a limited liability company, as at 31 May 2009 is provided below, together with the comparative figures from the previous year.

Hadrian
Statement of Financial Position as at
31 May $000

		2009		2008
Assets				
Noncurrent assets		2 000		1 500
Current assets				
Inventory	340		230	
Trade receivables	270		150	
Bank	4	614	70	450
Total assets		2 614		1 950
Equity and liabilities				
Capital and reserves				
Ordinary share capital (shares of $1)		2 000		1 500
Share premium		100		50
Retained earnings		314		130
		2 414		1 680
Noncurrent liabilities				
10% loan note		–		60
Current liabilities				
Trade payables	120		150	
Taxation	80	200	60	210
Total equity and liabilities		2 614		1 950

Additional information:
(i)   Interest paid was $6000 during the year ended 31 May 2009.
(ii) There was no over- or underprovision of tax for the year ended 31 May 2008.
(iii) Dividends paid were $100 000 during the year ended 31 May 2009.
(iv) Depreciation of $132 000 was charged for the year ended 31 May 2009.
(v) Noncurrent assets with a net book value of $80 000 were sold at a profit of $20 000 during the year ended 31 May 2009.

Required:
(a) Calculate the profit before interest and tax of Hadrian for the year ended 31 May 2009.
(b) Prepare a statement of cash flows for Hadrian for the year ended 31 May 2009.

(c) Calculate the following ratio for 2009: return on assets, acid-test ratio, earnings per share and current ratio. [ACCA adapted]

5. The summarized financial statements of Renada, a limited liability company, at 31 October 2008 and 31 October 2009 are given below:

Statement of Financial Position
31 October

	Reference to Notes	2008		2009	
Noncurrent assets (net book value)	i, ii, iii		$1 000 000		$1 800 000
Current assets					
Inventories		600 000		1 600 000	
Receivables		1 270 000		1 800 000	
Cash		140 000	2 010 000	–	3 400 000
			3 010 000		5 200 000
Capital and reserves					
Ordinary share capital	iv		500 000		600 000
Share premium account	iv	420 000		820 000	
Revaluation reserve		–		300 000	
Accumulated profits		920 000	1 340 000	1 080 000	2 200 000
			1 840 000		2 800 000
Noncurrent liabilities					
6% loan note			800 000		1 900 000
Current liabilities					
Trade payables		200 000		280 000	
Taxation		170 000	370 000	220 000	500 000
			3 010 000		5 200 000

Statement of Income
31 October

	Reference to Notes	2008	2009
Sales revenue (all on credit)		$8 400 000	$9 000 000
Cost of sales	v	(6 300 000)	(7 200 000)
Gross profit		2 100 000	1 800 000
Operating expenses		(1 500 000)	(1 600 000)
Profit before tax		600 000	200 000
Income tax expense		(120 000)	(40 000)
Profit for the year		480 000	160 000

Notes:

    i. On 1 November 2008, office equipment that had a cost of $240 000, with a net book value of $80 000, was sold for $30 000.

    ii. The purchase of new noncurrent assets took place near the end of the year.

    iii. The depreciation charge for the year ended 31 October 2009 was $300 000.

    iv. The ordinary share issue was on 31 October 2009.

    v. Cost of sales was made up as follows:

	31 October	
	2008	2009
Opening inventory	$500 000	$600 000
Purchases	6 400 000	8 200 000
	6 900 000	8 800 000
Closing inventory	(600 000)	(1 600 000)
Cost of sales	6 300 000	7 200 000

Required:

  (a) Prepare a statement of cash flows for Renada for the year ended 31 October 2009.

  (b) Calculate in days for 2009 the following: days in inventory and average collection period.

6. Reactive is a publicly listed company that assembles domestic electrical goods, which it then sells to both wholesale and retail customers. Reactive's management was disappointed in the company's results for the year ended 31 March 2009. In an attempt to improve performance, the following measures were taken early in the year ended 31 March 2010:

- A national advertising campaign was undertaken.
- Rebates to all wholesale customers purchasing goods above set quantity levels were introduced.
- The assembly of certain lines ceased and was replaced by bought-in completed products. This allowed Reactive to dispose of surplus plant.

Reactive's summarized financial statements for the year ended 31 March 2010 are set out below:

Statement of Income	$ Million
Revenue (25% cash sales)	4 000
Cost of sales	(3 450)
Gross profit	550
Operating expenses	(370)
	180
Profit on disposal of plant (note i)	40
Finance charges	(20)
Profit before tax	200
Income tax expense	(50)
Profit for the period	150

Statement of financial position	$ million	$ million
Noncurrent assets		
Property, plant and equipment (note i)		550
Current assets		
Inventory	250	
Trade receivables	360	
Bank	nil	610
Total assets		1 160

Statement of Income		$ Million
Equity and liabilities		
Equity shares of 25 cents each		100
Retained earnings		380
		480
Noncurrent liabilities		
8% loan notes		200
Current liabilities		
Bank overdraft	10	
Trade payables	430	
Current tax payable	40	480
Total equity and liabilities		1 160

Below are ratios calculated for the year ended 31 March 2009.

Return on assets	28.1%
Gross profit margin	17%
Profit margin	6.3%
Current ratio	1.6:1
Average days in inventory	46 days
Trade receivables collection period	45 days
Dividend yield	3.75%
Earning per share	$0.39

Notes:
  i. Reactive received $120 million from the sale of plant that had a carrying amount of $80 million at the date of its sale.
  ii. The market price of Reactive's shares throughout the year averaged $3.75 each.
  iii. There were no issues or redemption of shares or loans during the year.

iv. Dividends paid during the year ended 31 March 2010 amounted to $90 000, maintaining the same dividend paid in the year ended 31 March 2009.

Required:

(a) Calculate ratios for the year ended 31 March 2010 for Reactive, equivalent to those provided above.

(b) Analyse the financial performance and position of Reactive for the year ended 31 March 2010 compared to the previous year. [ACCA adapted]

7. The financial statements of Egriff, a company limited by liability, for the years ended 31 May 2008 and 31 May 2009 are summarized below:

	Statement of Income for the Years Ended $ '000			
	31 May 2008		31 May 2009	
Revenue		20 000		26 000
Cost of sales		(15 400)		(21 050)
Gross profit		4 600		4 950
Expenses				
Administrative	(800)		(900)	
Selling and distribution	(1 550)		(1 565)	
Depreciation	(110)		(200)	
Loan note interest	–		(105)	
		(2 460)		(2 770)
Net profit		2 140		2 180

	Statement of Financial Position as at $ '000			
	31 May 2008		31 May 2009	
Noncurrent assets				
At cost	4 600		5 600	
Accumulated depreciation	(800)	3 800	(1 000)	4 600
Current assets				
Inventory	6 000		6 700	
Receivables	4 400		6 740	
Bank	120	10 520	960	14 400
		14 320		19 000

Capital and reserves				
Issued share capital		8 000		8 000
Accumulated profit		3 120		5 300
		11 120		13 300
Noncurrent liabilities				
7% loan notes		–		1 500
Current liabilities		3 200		4 200
		14 320		19 000

Additional information:

During 2008 Egriff issued loan notes of $1 500 000 at 7% per annum to fund the expansion of the business. The additional cash was received on 1 June 2008.

Required:

(a) Calculate the following ratios for Egriff for both years:
   1. Gross profit ratio
   2. Profit margin ratio
   3. Return on assets
   4. Inventory turnover
   5. Acid-test ratio
   6. Receivables collection period

(b) Comment on the success of the business expansion as indicated by the ratios you have calculated in part (a).

(c) Briefly explain the factors that Egriff should consider in deciding whether to raise finance by issuing loan notes rather than issuing more shares. [ACCA adapted]

8. Nicola is thinking of investing in a limited liability company called Tressven. She has asked for your help to calculate some of the ratios she needs to decide whether or not to invest. She has given you the summarized financial statements of Tressven, which are shown below:

Tressven
Statement of Income for the Year Ended
31 October 2009 $ '000

Sales revenue	23 420
Cost of sales	(8 245)
Gross profit	15 175
Expenses	(2 460)
Profit from operations	12 715
Finance cost	(50)
Profit before tax	12 665
Income tax expense	(1 515)
Net profit for the period	11 150

Tressven
Statement of Financial Position as at
31 October 2009 $ '000

Assets		
Noncurrent assets		31 000
Current assets		
Inventory	1 450	
Trade receivables	2 500	
Cash	50	4 000
Total assets		35 000
Equity and liabilities		
Capital and reserves		
$0.50 Ordinary shares		25 000
Reserves		7 520
		32 520
Current liabilities		
Trade payables	860	
Tax	620	1 480
Loan notes		1 000
Total equity and liabilities		35 000

Additional information:
  i. During the year Tressven paid dividends of $10 million.
 ii. The market share price for Tressven is $1.50.
iii. Tressven's main competitor is a company called Hilladay, which has the following ratios:

Dividend per share	10 cents
Dividend cover	5 times
Earnings per share (EPS)	20 cents
Price–earnings ratio	13.4
Debt-to-equity ratio	15%
Interest cover	100 times

Required:
  (a) Calculate the following ratios for Tressven:
    1. Dividend per share
    2. Dividend yield ratio
    3. Earnings per share (EPS)

4. Price–earnings ratio (PE ratio)
5. Debt-to-equity ratio

(b) Analyze the financial performance of Tressven compared to Hilladay. [ACCA adapted]

DAIRY FARM INTERNATIONAL HOLDINGS LIMITED: ANALYSING AN ANNUAL REPORT

Dairy Farm International Holdings Limited (Dairy Farm) was described in its annual report as a 'leading pan Asian retailer'. The company and its associates operate more than 3000 outlets, including supermarkets, hypermarkets, health and beauty stores, convenience stores, home furnishings stores and restaurants. Dairy Farm employs approximately 60 000 people with sales in excess of US$5 billion. Similar to most public companies around the world, it issues an annual report. Dairy Farm's annual report is the focus of this case and will be used to introduce the calculation and application of financial statement ratios.

The focus of this exercise is the financial analysis of Dairy Farm's statutory financial statements and the use of ratio analysis; however, the annual report provides additional useful data about the company and its financial position and performance. This additional financial data should be reconcilable with the statutory financial statements. In this case, we are analysing a two-year period; any analysis of Dairy Farm should be both longitudinal and comparative.

In order to initiate a discussion of international financial reporting and allow for some degree of comparison, data from two other companies have been included (see Figure 12.27). The two companies selected are the very successful British giant Tesco plc and a Canadian food retailer, Sobeys Inc.

These companies were chosen for a number of reasons. As Tesco enters and expands in the Asian markets, Dairy Farm will need to compete with Tesco. It might be interesting to consider the implications of Tesco's Asian entry for Dairy Farm. What kind of challenge might Dairy farm face with Tesco competing in its markets? In Canada, Sobeys is attempting to survive against larger rivals, including Wal-Mart and Loblaws. This position is perhaps similar to what Dairy Farm will face as Tesco and other multinationals expand to Asia. How prepared are the domestic companies for global reality? Figures 12.28 and 12.29 provide analysis in the form of common-size financial statements and ratio analysis. These will be used to compare with your analysis of Dairy Farm.

RATIO ANALYSIS

It is necessary to access Dairy Farm's 2006 annual report. Like most public companies, the annual report can be retrieved over the Internet, either directly through the company's website, www.dairyfarmgroup.com, or through an organization that accumulates and makes annual reports available, such as in this case www.irasia.com.

For this exercise, let us begin our analysis with the calculation and interpretation of some selected ratios. If we were to be more sophisticated and use our knowledge of corporate financial reporting, our first step would be to review the statements and make any desired adjustments prior to calculating the ratios. For example, Dairy Farm makes extensive use of operating leases that an analyst might consider to be a form of 'off-statement of financial position' financing, which should be treated as part of the company's long-term debt. In that case, an analyst might estimate a present value equivalent and add it to the company's debt structure. In this introductory note, take the financial statements at their face value; however, be aware of this limitation when drawing any conclusions from the data ratios for both Tesco and Sobeys, which can be found in Figure 12.29.

Calculate the following ratios for Dairy Farms for the last two years, 2005 and 2006. As mentioned earlier, it is unlikely that an analysis would span only two years' data; however, the objective of this exercise is to introduce the process of using the data in the annual report, not to reach final conclusions about the company's financial position or performance.

	2006	2005
Liquidity		
Current ratio		
Acid-test ratio		
Cash flow from operations		
Average receivables collection period		
Average number of days in inventory		
Solvency/leverage		
Total debt to total assets		
Total debt to total capital		
Long-term debt to equity		
Operating cash flow to debt		
Asset management		
Capital assets turnover		
Total assets turnover		
Profitability		
Gross margin		
Operating profit margin		
Net profit margin		
Return on total assets		

Return to investors
  Earnings per share
  Price–earnings ratio
  Dividend yield

After completing the calculations, what initial observations can you draw from these data? Have any significant year-to-year changes occurred? Do any of the ratios indicate good news or bad news? What explanation might account for your observations? Are the ratios consistent with your prior assumptions about the company? Keep in mind that ratios are rarely answers themselves but often point to areas that need further analysis.

COMMON-SIZE FINANCIAL STATEMENTS

Calculate Dairy Farm's common-size financial statements for 2005 and 2006 using the following groupings:

	2006	2005
Current assets		
Cash and investments		
Accounts receivable		
Inventory		
Other current assets		
Total current assets		
Fixed assets		
Intangible assets		
Other fixed assets		
Total assets	**100%**	**100%**
Current liabilities		
Accounts payable		
Short-term debt		
Other current liabilities		
Total current liabilities		
Long-term debt		
Deferred income taxes		
Other liabilities		
Total liabilities		

Shareholders' equity
Minority interests
Total shareholders' equity

Total liabilities and shareholders' equity	**100%**	**100%**

COMMON-SIZE STATEMENT OF INCOMES

	2006	2005
Sales	100%	100%
Cost of sales		
Gross margin		
Other operating income		
Subtotal		
Costs and expenses		
Selling, general and administrative expenses		
Total operating expenses		
Operating income		
Interest expense		
Other income		
Income before taxes		
Income taxes		
Net earnings		
Gains (losses) from discontinued operations		
Profit attributable to equity holders		
Minority interests		
Dividends paid		

As a result of this analysis, what additional observations can you make about Dairy Farm?

Before using the comparative data from Tesco and Sobeys, based on the ratio analysis and the common-size financial statement data of Dairy Farm up to this point, assess Dairy Farm's position and performance. How do you assess its future?

COMPARISON WITH TESCO AND SOBEYS

Tesco, with group sales of more than £43 billion, operates internationally and in a variety of retailing markets, including both food and nonfood products, as well as other services, such as telecom and financial services. Tesco discloses sales in Asia as £4.7 billion. Sobeys, with sales of almost Canadian $13 billion, operates only in Canada. It states that its strategy 'is to differentiate ourselves from the competition by sustaining our focus on food'. However, Sobeys operates a chain of drug stores in one area of Canada. It has chosen the strategy of a focus on food and service in the face of significant competition from larger and more diverse retailers, both Canadian and multinational companies, such as Loblaw and Wal-Mart. In early 2007, Sobeys initiated a process to change from a public company to a private company.

Again, recognizing the limitations of the data and the extent of our analysis, use the additional data provided to compare the three companies. They might be compared on a number of dimensions, including size.

How do their statements of financial position differ? How do their position and performance ratios differ? Can you suggest any possible explanations for the significant differences? Do these comparisons change how you might have assessed Dairy Farm earlier?

DAIRY FARM'S ANNUAL REPORT

Annual reports provide both qualitative and quantitative data and, as was mentioned earlier, are used as important communication tools by most public companies. What is your assessment of Dairy Farm's total annual report? List both your positive and negative observations from a review of the whole annual report. Are the data and the statutory financial statements consistent with what the company says about itself in the rest of the annual report?

Dairy Farm is a Bermuda-based company listed on the London Stock Exchange with secondary listings on the Bermuda and Singapore stock exchanges. Tesco, a UK-based company, is listed on the London Stock Exchange and has a level 1 OTC American Depository Receipt (ADR) programme in the United States. Sobeys operates only in Canada and is listed on the Toronto Stock Exchange. Did the international differences have any effect on your ability to compare the three companies? Explain with examples.

FIGURE 12.27 CONDENSED FINANCIAL STATEMENTS FOR TESCO

	Tesco Statement of Financial Position as at	
	25 Feb. 2006 (£ MM)	26 Feb. 2005 (£ MM)
Net operating assets		
Intangible assets	1 525.0	1 408.0
Other fixed assets	17 119.0	15 523.0
Noncurrent assets	18 644.0	16 931.0

(*Continued*)

FIGURE 12.27 (*CONTINUED*)

	Tesco Statement of Financial Position as at	
	25 Feb. 2006 (£ MM)	26 Feb. 2005 (£ MM)
Stocks	1 464.0	1 309.0
Debtors and prepayments	892.0	769.0
Other current assets	70.0	0.0
Bank balances	1 325.0	1 146.0
	3 751.0	3 224.0
Noncurrent assets classified as held for sale	168.0	0.0
Current assets	3 919.0	3 224.0
Creditors and accruals	(5 083.0)	(4 974.0)
Current borrowings	(1 885.0)	(482.0)
Current tax liabilities	(462.0)	(221.0)
Other current liabilities	(2.0)	(3.0)
	(7 432.0)	(5 680.0)
Liabilities directly associated with noncurrent assets classified as held for sale	(86.0)	0.0
Current liabilities	(7 518.0)	(5 680.0)
Net current liabilities	(3 599.0)	2 456.0)
Long-term borrowings	(3 742.0)	(4 563.0)
Deferred tax liabilities	(320.0)	(496.0)
Other noncurrent liabilities	(1 539.0)	(762.0)
	9 444.0	8 654.0
Total equity		
Share capital	395.0	369.0
Share premium and capital reserves	3 988.0	3 704.0
Revenue and other reserves	4 997.0	4 510.0
Shareholders' funds	9 380.0	8 603.0
Minority interests	64.0	51.0
	9 444.0	8 654.0
Sales	39 454.0	33 866.0
Cost of sales	36 426.0	31 231.0
Gross margin	3 028.0	2 635.0
Other operating income	77.0	49.0
Subtotal	3 105.0	2 684.0

Costs and expenses		
Selling, general and administrative expenses	825.0	732.0
Total operating expenses	825.0	732.0
Operating income	2 280.0	1 952.0
Interest expense	241.0	235.0
Other income	196.0	177.0
Income before taxes	2 235.0	1 894.0
Income taxes	649.0	541.0
Net earnings	1 586.0	1 353.0
Gain (losses) from discontinued operations	(10.0)	(6.0)
Profit attributable to equity holders	1 570.0	1 344.0
Minority interests	6.0	3.0
	1 576.0	1 347.0
Dividends paid	441.0	448.0
Fiscal year-end stock price	3.36	3.07
Weighted average shares (millions)		
For basic earnings per share	7 823.0	7 707.0
For diluted earnings per share	7 932.0	7 804.0
Basic earnings per share ($)	0.20	0.17
Diluted earnings per share ($)	0.20	0.17
Cash flow from operations	2 619.0	2 176.0
Cash flow from investing activities	(1 962.0)	(1 501.0)
Cash flow from financing activities	(492.0)	(651.0)
Net cash flow	165.0	24.0
Cash and cash equivalents at beginning of FY	1 146.0	1 100.0
Effect of exchange rate changes	16.0	22.0
Cash and cash equivalents at end of FY	1 327.0	1 146.0
Current assets		
Cash and investments	332.1	272.8
Accounts receivable	208.2	199.8
Inventory	626.8	588.6
Other current assets	67.6	80.8
Total current assets	1 234.7	1 142.0
Fixed assets		
Intangible assets	21.5	24.3
Other fixed assets	2 482.4	2 279.5
Total assets	3 738.6	3 445.8

(Continued)

FIGURE 12.27 (*CONTINUED*)

	Tesco Statement of Financial Position as at	
	25 Feb. 2006 (£ MM)	26 Feb. 2005 (£ MM)
Current liabilities		
Accounts payable	1 158.8	1 083.3
Other current liabilities	71.1	247.3
Total current liabilities	1 229.9	1 330.6
Long-term debt	465.0	272.9
Deferred income taxes	44.1	33.1
Other liabilities	120.1	107.5
Total liabilities	1 859.1	1 734.1
Shareholders' equity	1 834.3	1 682.1
Minority interests	45.2	29.6
Total shareholders' equity	1 879.5	1 711.7
Total liabilities and shareholders' equity	3 738.6	3 445.8
Sales	12 853.3	12 189.4
Costs and expense		
Selling, general and administrative expenses	12 521.7	11 866.8
Total operating expenses	12 521.7	11 866.8
Operating income	331.6	322.6
Interest expense	34.9	37.9
Income before taxes	296.7	284.7
Income taxes	100.1	98.0
Net earnings	196.6	186.7
Profit attributable to equity holders	189.4	186.7
Minority interests	7.2	0.0
	196.6	186.7
Dividends	35.6	32.8
Fiscal year end stock price	38.80	37.20
Weighted average shares (millions)		
For basic earnings per share	64.7	64.9
For diluted earnings per share	65.4	65.5
Basic earnings per share ($)	2.93	2.88
Diluted earnings per share ($)	2.90	2.85

Cash flow from operations	495.3	438.0
Cash flow from investing activities	(409.6)	(295.7)
Cash flow from financing activities	(26.4)	(67.0)
Net cash flow	59.3	75.3
Initial impact of variable interest entities		32.9
Cash and cash equivalents at beginning of FY	272.8	164.6
Effect of exchange rate changes	0.0	0.0
Cash and cash equivalents at end of FY	332.1	272.8

FIGURE 12.28 COMMON-SIZE FINANCIAL STATEMENTS

Common Size-Statement of Financial Position				
	Tesco 25 Feb. 2006	Tesco 26 Feb. 2005	Sobeys 6 May 2006	Sobeys 7 May 2005
Current assets				
Cash and investments	5.9%	5.7%	8.9%	7.95
Accounts receivable	4.0%	3.8%	5.6%	5.8%
Inventory	6.5%	6.5%	16.8%	17.1%
Other current assets	1.1%	0.0%	1.8%	2.3%
Total current assets	17.4%	16.0%	33.0%	33.1%
Fixed assets				
Intangible assets	6.8%	7.0%	0.6%	0.7%
Other fixed assets	75.9%	77.0%	66.4%	66.2%
Total assets	100.0%	100.0%	100.0%	100.0%
Current liabilities				
Accounts payable	22.5%	24.7%	31.0%	31.4%
Short-term debt	8.4%	2.4%	0.0%	0.0%
Other current liabilities	2.4%	1.1%	1.9%	7.2%
Total current liabilities	33.3%	28.2%	32.9%	38.6%
Long-term debt	16.6%	22.65	12.4%	7.6%
Deferred income taxes	1.4%	2.5%	1.2%	1.0%
Other liabilities	6.8%	2.8%	3.2%	3.1%
Total liabilities	58.1%	57.1%	49.7%	50.3%
Shareholders' equity	41.6%	42.7%	49.1%	48.8%
Minority interests	0.3%	0.3%	1.2%	0.9%
Total shareholders' equity	41.9%	42.9%	50.3%	49.7%

(*Continued*)

FIGURE 12.28 *(CONTINUED)*

	Common Size-Statement of Financial Position			
	Tesco 25 Feb. 2006	Tesco 26 Feb. 2005	Sobeys 6 May 2006	Sobeys 7 May 2005
Total liabilities and shareholders' equity	100.0%	100.0%	100.0%	100.0%
Sales	100.0%	100.0%	100.0%	100.0%
Cost of sales	92.3%	92.2%		
Gross margin	7.7%	7.8%		
Other operating income	0.2%	0.1%		
Subtotal	7.9%	7.9%		
Costs and expenses				
Selling, general and administrative expenses	2.1%	2.2%	97.4%	97.4%
Total operating expenses	2.1%	2.2%	97.4%	97.4%
Operating income	5.85	5.8%	2.6%	2.6%
Interest expense	0.6%	0.7%	0.3%	0.3%
Other income	0.5%	0.55	0.0%	0.0%
Income before taxes	5.7%	5.6%	2.3%	2.3%
Income taxes	1.6%	1.6%	0.8%	0.8%
Net earnings	4.0%	4.0%	1.5%	1.5%
Gain (losses) from discontinued operations	0.0%	0.0%	0.0%	0.0%
Profit attributable to equity holders	4.0%	4.0%	1.5%	1.5%
Minority interests	0.0%	0.0%	0.1%	0.0%
	4.0%	4.0%	1.5%	1.5%
Dividends paid	1.1%	1.3%	0.3%	0.35

FIGURE 12.29 RATIO ANALYSIS

	Tesco 25 Feb. 2006	Tesco 26 Feb. 2005	Sobeys 6 May 2006	Sobeys 7 May 2005
Liquidity				
Current ratio	0.52	0.57	1.00	0.86
Quick ratio	0.42	0.47	0.44	0.36
Cash flow from operations	0.35	0.38	0.40	0.33
Average receivable collection period	7.68	8.60	5.79	7.07

Average number of days in inventory	13.89	15.30		
Average number of days payable	50.39	43.29		
Solvency/Leverage				
Total debt to total assets	0.25	0.25	0.12	0.08
Total debt to total capital	0.37	0.37	0.20	0.13
Long-term debt to equity	0.40	0.53	0.25	0.15
Fixed charge coverage	10.27	9.06	9.50	8.51
Operating cash flow to debt	0.47	0.43	1.07	1.67
Asset management				
Capital assets turnover	2.22	2.10	5.35	5.25
Total assets turnover	1.85	1.75	3.58	3.63
Profitability				
Gross margin	7.7%	7.8%		
Operating profit margin	5.8%	5.8%	2.3%	2.3%
Net profit margin	4.0%	4.0%	1.5%	1.5%
Return on total assets	8.2%	7.9%	6.1%	6.3%
Return on equity	17.6%	16.3%	10.9%	11.4%
Return to investors				
Earnings per share	0.20	0.17	2.90	2.85
Price–earnings ratio	17.0	17.8	13.4	13.1
Dividend yield	1.66%	1.87%	1.405	1.35%
Modified Du Pont Formula				
Asset turnover	1.85	1.75	3.58	3.63
Net profit margins	0.04	0.04	0.02	0.02
Financial leverage	2.38	2.33	2.00	2.05
Return on equity	0.18	0.16	0.11	0.11

End note

1. *Corporate Reporting: Is It What Investment Professionals Expect?*, PricewaterhouseCoopers, November 2007.

Web links

- *Financial Times* – www.ft.com
- *Wall Street Journal* – www.wsj.com
- Forbes – www.forbes.com

Assurance systems | 13

LEARNING OUTCOMES

At the completion of this chapter, you should be able to:

1. Define assurance and list the five major components.
2. Explain corporate governance and how an effective board should be structured and function.
3. Define risk management and explain how risk management provides assurance for financial statements.
4. Define internal control and explain the principles and limitations of internal control.
5. Define internal auditing and explains its role in providing assurance for financial statements.
6. Define independent auditing and explain its role in providing assurance for financial statements.
7. Explain why fraud auditing and forensic accounting have become part of independent auditing.

Fraud and corporate scandals are problems the world over; no business is immune to financial abuses or unscrupulous managers and employees, or even customers and suppliers – or people who simply make unwise decisions that damage the business. History has provided ample examples of commercial fraud and abuse, although one American company, Enron, has become an iconic case in recent years because of the magnitude of its losses, the negative publicity generated, and the number of parties that were adversely affected.

When Enron filed for bankruptcy in 2001, as we saw in Chapter 2, the company was the seventh largest in the United States measured by revenue and had worldwide operations with 25 000 employees. It was revered as a highly innovative energy trader, lauded by *Fortune* magazine as one of the most admired American companies.

But Enron's management was under pressure to continue reporting growth in profits to maintain its share price. This led to 'aggressive' accounting practices for energy contracts, which reported income and asset values based on questionable estimates. The company also engaged in transactions that masked the existence of certain problems with assets and liabilities on its statement of financial position.

By 2000, Enron was having a number of problems, including on a power project that it was developing in India. Other ventures were losing money as well. In mid-2001, Jeffrey Skilling, who had become chief executive officer only six months earlier, resigned, fuelling investors' concerns that the company was in trouble. Some employees began to express their doubts about certain company practices. As a result, Enron's stock price continued to decline.

Worried bankers began to withdraw credit, eventually precipitating a liquidity crisis for the company since it did not have the cash it required to operate. No longer able to function, Enron filed for bankruptcy, costing investors, employees and others billions of dollars and creating a crisis of confidence in its management. In addition, Arthur Andersen, the company's independent auditor and one of the world's largest and most respected audit firms, collapsed amid allegations that it had contributed to the eventual failure of Enron.

The scandal forced the US government to act aggressively to curb abuses, and it did so by passing the Sarbanes–Oxley Act (2002). This law mandated a number of changes to improve the regulation of corporate governance, internal control and independent audits. Other nations, because of their own debacles and partly because of the impetus provided by high-profile US scandals like Enron, passed similar laws to strengthen protection for investors and others. Although these assurance mechanisms have been in place for a long time, laws like Sarbanes–Oxley increased the awareness that they are more important than ever.

Since they were enacted, these laws have sparked complaints from managers and others that compliance is too expensive and takes too much time away from managing the business. But every cloud has its silver lining, and some executives and others believe that these laws have real benefits. For example, as companies take measures to comply, costs are lowered and complexity reduced. Better corporate governance and internal control have improved businesses as well. In this sense, these regulatory changes have been a welcome contribution because they encourage effective management practices.

LEARNING OUTCOME 1
DEFINE ASSURANCE AND LIST THE FIVE MAJOR COMPONENTS

1.1   Define corporate governance.

1.2   Define risk management.

1.3   Define internal control.

1.4   Define audit and independant audit. What is the difference between these two types of audits?

1.1 What is assurance?

The term assurance, as used in accounting and auditing, refers to assurances given as to whether financial statements provide a true and fair view of financial position, performance and changes in financial position. In other words, assurance addresses the question of how investors and others know that the financial statements are reliable. More broadly, assurance also deals with whether assets entrusted to management are being safeguarded, whether management is recognizing and responding appropriately to risks faced by the business, and whether the business is being managed in an efficient and effective manner. Assurance is comprised of five interrelated components:

1. Corporate governance includes the organizational culture, policies and procedures that determine how the entity is directed, administered and controlled, as overseen by the business's board of directors.
2. Risk management refers to processes that 'identify, assess, manage, and control potential events or situations, to provide reasonable assurance regarding the achievement of the organization's objectives' (www.theiiaa.org). In other words, risk management focuses on events and situations that threaten the ability of the business to achieve its objectives.
3. Internal control is the system of policies and procedures within the business that facilitates efficient and effective operations that allow a company to respond to significant risks; safeguards assets; ensures the quality of internal and external reporting; and monitors compliance with laws, regulations and internal business policies.
4. An internal audit uses a systematic and disciplined approach to evaluate and review the effectiveness of risk management, the internal control system and corporate governance processes.
5. An independent audit is carried out by external accounting and auditing specialists, who perform tests and other procedures on the business to enable them to express an opinion about whether the financial statements of the business have been prepared, in all material respects, in accordance with applicable accounting standards.

These five assurance systems work together to form the safety net that investors and others rely on, as illustrated in Figure 13.1.

FIGURE 13.1 ASSURANCE SYSTEMS

We will examine each of these assurance systems in turn.

LEARNING OUTCOME 2
EXPLAIN CORPORATE GOVERNANCE AND HOW AN EFFECTIVE BOARD SHOULD BE STRUCTURED AND FUNCTION

2.1 What is corporate governance?
    2.1.1 How are boards structured?
    2.1.2 What committees does a board typically have?

2.1 What is corporate governance?

The ultimate responsibility for corporate governance belongs to the board of directors, which represents the shareholders' interests. Boards generally have three responsibilities: 1) shaping the strategy of the business; 2) monitoring management; and 3) ensuring accountability.

Directors are also fiduciaries. A fiduciary represents the principals (the owners), which is the highest standard of care imposed under law. Essentially, a fiduciary must put the principal's interest ahead of his or her own welfare. Figure 13.2 is a report on corporate governance from British Airways' 2006–07 annual report, which provides a description of the roles and responsibilities of the board and how it discharges its obligations.

FIGURE 13.2 CORPORATE GOVERNANCE, BRITISH AIRWAYS' 2006–07 ANNUAL REPORT

The Company is committed to high standards of corporate governance. The Board is accountable to the Company's shareholders for good corporate governance. The Company has complied throughout the year with the code of best practice set out in Section 1 of the Combined Code (issued in June 2006) appended to the Listing Rules of the Financial Services Authority (the 'Combined Code').

The role of the Board is to provide entrepreneurial leadership of the Company within a framework of prudent and effective controls, which enables risk to be assessed and managed. The Board sets the Company's strategic aims, ensures that the necessary financial and human resources are in place for the Company to meet its objectives and reviews management performance. The Board sets the Company's values and standards and ensures that its obligations to its shareholders and others are understood and met.

The Board of the Company routinely meets eight times a year and additionally when necessary to consider all matters relating to the overall control, business performance and strategy of the Company, and for these purposes the Board has drawn up a schedule of matters reserved for Board decision. Broadly, the Board has reserved to itself major strategic and financial decisions, including investment and divestment decision, approval of significant alliance or code-share partnerships and capital commitments of greater than £10 million. The Board has also drawn up a schedule of matters which must be reported to it. These schedules are reviewed at least annually.

The Board is led by the Chairman and the executive management of the Company is led by the Chief Executive. Of the 11 members serving at the year end, excluding the Chairman, two were executive directors and eight were non-executive directors. The eight non-executive directors are drawn from a diversity of business and other backgrounds, bringing a broad range of views and experiences to Board deliberations. The Board has included seven or more fully independent non-executive directors throughout the year under review. Although they are eligible for non-contractual travel concessions in addition to their fees, this is not considered to affect their independence.

All directors receive regular information about the Company so that they are equipped to play as full a part as possible in Board meetings. Papers for Board and Committee Meetings are typically distributed in the week prior to the relevant meeting. All Board members have access to the Company Secretary for any further information they require. In addition, the Secretary ensures that the Board members receive an appropriate induction and further training as necessary. Non-executive directors are encouraged to visit the Company's operations and to speak to customers and employees. They are also encouraged to attend the annual investor day to meet major shareholders. Independent professional advice would be available to directors in appropriate circumstances, at the Company's expense. All directors are required to submit themselves for re-election every three years. New directors are appointed to the Board on the recommendation of the Nominations Committee whose terms of reference are available at bashares.com.

During the financial year under review, a performance evaluation of the Board was undertaken through a questionnaire and one-to-one interviews by the Secretary. The results of this exercise were presented to, and considered by, the Board. The Chairman and non-executive members typically meet without any executives present on at least two occasions during each financial year. At least once a year, the non-executive members of the Board meet under the chairmanship of the senior independent director to review the performance of the Chairman, taking account of the views of the executive directors.

2.1.1 HOW ARE BOARDS STRUCTURED?

Boards comprise both inside directors and nonexecutive directors. In addition to serving on the board, an inside director also holds a position as an executive or manager within the business. A nonexecutive director serving on the board is not part of the executive or management team. Nonexecutive directors add strength to the business's corporate governance because of their independence from management and their willingness to voice dissenting opinions about management actions. They also have skills that may otherwise be absent from the board, which they can bring to bear on the oversight of the company. Nonexecutive directors are frequently recruited from the ranks of executives from other companies, academics, attorneys, former government employees and others who can bring necessary experience and contacts to bear on the board's duties.

Boards can be either unitary or multilevel. A unitary board means that both nonexecutive directors and executive directors serve on a single board that discharges all board obligations. Unitary boards are favoured in both the UK and US.

A multilevel board (see box) means that more than one board exists within the business, an approach preferred in continental Europe and Japan. One board may represent the interests of shareholders and employees. The second may be composed only of executive directors and focus on management concerns. Some Japanese companies use a three-tier system: one board focuses on strategic policy issues, another on management issues, and the third has a primarily symbolic role.

MULTILEVEL BOARDS

Some countries use a multilevel board structure that involves two or more boards with different functions. Lufthansa is one example. The company's website describes its two boards as follows.

SUPERVISORY BOARD

The Lufthansa Supervisory Board, representing both shareholders and employees, consists of 20 members with voting rights. The ten shareholder representatives are elected by the Annual General Meeting, the employee representatives by the Lufthansa Group. The term of office of the present Supervisory Board began on June 18, 2003 at the end of the Annual General Meeting and expires at the close of the Annual General Meeting 2008. Alongside the mandatory arbitration committee pursuant to §27 para. 3 of the Co-Determination Act, the Supervisory Board appoints from its members two other committees: The managing committee is responsible for the contracts of Executive Board members and other personal matters of the Executive Board and officers of the company; the audit committee for issues related to reporting, the year-end audit and risk management.

EXECUTIVE BOARD

The Executive Board defines the Group's strategic direction in coordination with the Supervisory Board and is responsible for implementing it in pursuance of growing and sustainable company value. The Executive Board is additionally charged with monitoring the Group's compliance with legal requirements and instituting risk management and appropriate controls. Corporate statutes determine the remits or duties of Executive Board members and cooperation between them.

Although many sources are available that provide guidance about effective board functioning, a representative example is the Combined Code on Corporate Governance.[1] The box shows its main and supporting principles.

COMBINED CODE ON CORPORATE GOVERNANCE

THE BOARD

Every company should be headed by an effective board, which is collectively responsible for the success of the company.

The board's role is to provide entrepreneurial leadership of the company within a framework of prudent and effective controls which enables risk to be assessed and managed. The board should set the company's strategic aims, ensure that the necessary financial and human resources are in place for the company to meet its objectives and review management performance. The board should set the company's values and standards and ensure that its obligations to its shareholders and others are understood and met.

All directors must take decisions objectively in the interests of the company.

As part of their role as members of a unitary board, non-executive directors should constructively challenge and help develop proposals on strategy. Non-executive directors should scrutinise the performance of management in meeting agreed goals and objectives and monitor the reporting of performance. They should satisfy themselves on the integrity of financial information and that financial controls and systems of risk management are robust and defensible. They are responsible for determining appropriate levels of remuneration of executive directors and have a prime role in appointing, and where necessary removing, executive directors, and in succession planning.

CHAIRMAN AND CHIEF EXECUTIVE

There should be a clear division of responsibilities at the head of the company between the running of the board and the executive responsibility for the running of the company's business. No one individual should have unfettered powers of decision.

The chairman is responsible for leadership of the board, ensuring its effectiveness on all aspects of its role and setting its agenda. The chairman is also responsible for ensuring that the directors receive accurate, timely and clear information. The chairman should ensure effective communication with shareholders. The chairman should also facilitate the effective contribution of non-executive directors in particular and ensure constructive relations between executive and non-executive directors.

BOARD BALANCE AND INDEPENDENCE

The board should include a balance of executive and nonexecutive directors (and in particular independent nonexecutive directors) such that no individual or small group of individuals can dominate the board's decision taking.

The board should not be so large as to be unwieldy. The board should be of sufficient size that the balance of skills and experience is appropriate for the requirements of the business and that changes to the board's composition can be managed without undue disruption.

To ensure that power and information are not concentrated in one or two individuals, there should be a strong presence on the board of both executive and non-executive directors.

The value of ensuring that committee membership is refreshed and that undue reliance is not placed on particular individuals should be taken into account in deciding chairmanship and membership of committees.

No one other than the committee chairman and members is entitled to be present at a meeting of the nomination, audit or remuneration committee, but others may attend at the invitation of the committee.

APPOINTMENTS TO THE BOARD

There should be a formal, rigorous and transparent procedure for the appointment of new directors to the board.

Appointments to the board should be made on merit and against objective criteria. Care should be taken to ensure that appointees have enough time available to devote to the job. This is particularly important in the case of chairmanships.

The board should satisfy itself that plans are in place for orderly succession for appointments to the board and to senior management, so as to maintain an appropriate balance of skills and experience within the company and on the board.

INFORMATION AND PROFESSIONAL DEVELOPMENT

The board should be supplied in a timely manner with information in a form and of a quality appropriate to enable it to discharge its duties. All directors should receive induction on joining the board and should regularly update and refresh their skills and knowledge.

The chairman is responsible for ensuring that the directors receive accurate, timely and clear information. Management has an obligation to provide such information but directors should seek clarification or amplification where necessary.

The chairman should ensure that the directors continually update their skills and the knowledge and familiarity with the company required to fulfil their role both on the board and on board committees. The company should provide the necessary resources for developing and updating its directors' knowledge and capabilities.

Under the direction of the chairman, the company secretary's responsibilities include ensuring good information flows within the board and its committees and between senior management and non-executive directors, as well as facilitating induction and assisting with professional development as required. The company secretary should be responsible for advising the board through the chairman on all governance matters.

PERFORMANCE EVALUATION

The board should undertake a formal and rigorous annual evaluation of its own performance and that of its committees and individual directors.

Individual evaluation should aim to show whether each director continues to contribute effectively and to demonstrate commitment to the role (including commitment of time for board and committee meetings and any other duties). The chairman should act on the results of the performance evaluation by recognising the strengths and addressing the weaknesses of the board and, where appropriate, proposing new members be appointed to the board or seeking the resignation of directors.

REMUNERATION

Levels of remuneration should be sufficient to attract, retain and motivate directors of the quality required to run the company successfully, but a company should avoid paying more than is necessary for this purpose. A significant proportion of executive directors' remuneration should be structured to link rewards to corporate and individual performance.

The remuneration committee should judge where to position their company relative to other companies. But they should use such comparisons with caution, in view of the risk of an upward ratchet of remuneration levels with no corresponding improvement in performance. They should also be sensitive to pay and employment conditions elsewhere in the group, especially when determining annual salary increases.

PROCEDURE

There should be a formal and transparent procedure for developing policy on executive remuneration and for fixing the remuneration packages of individual directors. No director should be involved in deciding his or her own remuneration.

The remuneration committee should consult the chairman and/or chief executive about their proposals relating to the remuneration of other executive directors. The remuneration committee should also be responsible for appointing any consultants in respect of executive director remuneration. Where executive directors or senior management are involved in advising or supporting the remuneration committee, care should be taken to recognise and avoid conflicts of interest.

The chairman of the board should ensure that the company maintains contact as required with its principal shareholders about remuneration in the same way as for other matters.

FINANCIAL REPORTING

The board should present a balanced and understandable assessment of the company's position and prospects.

> The board's responsibility to present a balanced and understandable assessment extends to interim and other price-sensitive public reports and reports to regulators as well as to information required to be presented by statutory requirements.

INTERNAL CONTROL

The board should maintain a sound system of internal control to safeguard shareholders' investment and the company's assets.

AUDIT COMMITTEE AND AUDITORS

The board should establish formal and transparent arrangements for considering how they should apply the financial reporting and internal control principles and for maintaining an appropriate relationship with the company's auditors.

DIALOGUE WITH INSTITUTIONAL SHAREHOLDERS

There should be a dialogue with shareholders based on the mutual understanding of objectives. The board as a whole has responsibility for ensuring that a satisfactory dialogue with shareholders takes place.

> Whilst recognising that most shareholder contact is with the chief executive and finance director, the chairman (and the senior independent director and other directors as appropriate) should maintain sufficient contact with major shareholders to understand their issues and concerns.

> The board should keep in touch with shareholder opinion in whatever ways are most practical and efficient.

ANNUAL GENERAL MEETING

The board should use the annual general meeting to communicate with investors and to encourage their participation.

DIALOGUE WITH COMPANIES

Institutional shareholders should enter into a dialogue with companies based on the mutual understanding of objectives.

> Institutional shareholders should apply the principles set out in the Institutional Shareholders' Committee's 'The Responsibilities of Institutional Shareholders and Agents – Statement of Principles', which should be reflected in fund manager contracts.

EVALUATION OF GOVERNANCE DISCLOSURES

When evaluating companies' governance arrangements, particularly those relating to board structure and composition, institutional shareholders should give due weight to all relevant factors drawn to their attention.

Institutional shareholders should consider carefully explanations given for departure from this Code and make reasoned judgments in each case. They should give an explanation to the company, in writing where appropriate, and be prepared to enter a dialogue if they do not accept the company's position. They should avoid a box-ticking approach to assessing a company's corporate governance. They should bear in mind in particular the size and complexity of the company and the nature of the risks and challenges it faces.

SHAREHOLDER VOTING

Institutional shareholders have a responsibility to make considered use of their votes.

Institutional shareholders should take steps to ensure their voting intentions are being translated into practice.

Institutional shareholders should, on request, make available to their clients information on the proportion of resolutions on which votes were cast and non-discretionary proxies lodged.

Major shareholders should attend annual general meetings where appropriate and practicable. Companies and registrars should facilitate this.

2.1.2 WHAT COMMITTEES DOES A BOARD TYPICALLY HAVE?

Boards accomplish much of their work through committees. Typical committees include an audit committee, nominations committee, remuneration committee and risk management committee, although boards often have other committees as well. Figure 13.3 shows typical board committees.

The audit committee, which is usually comprised of nonexecutive directors, oversees financial reporting and the external and internal auditors. This usually includes recommending the appointment or removal of an independent auditor. The audit committee may also review nonaudit work performed by the independent

FIGURE 13.3 TYPICAL BOARD COMMITTEES

auditors. Excerpts that address the structure and the key duties of the audit committee as discussed in British Airways' 2006–07 annual report are shown in Figure 13.4.

FIGURE 13.4 REPORT OF THE AUDIT COMMITTEE, BRITISH AIRWAYS'
2006–07 ANNUAL REPORT

The Committee consists solely of independent non-executive directors.

The Audit Committee is responsible for exercising the full powers and authority of the Board in accounting and financial reporting matters.

The key duties of the Committee include:

- To monitor the integrity of the Company's financial statements prior to their submission to the Board and any formal announcements relating to the Company's financial performance.
- To review the Company's financial statements to ensure that its accounting policies are the most appropriate to the Company's circumstances and that its financial reporting presents a balanced and understandable assessment of the Company's positions and prospects.
- To keep under review the Company's system of internal control, including compliance with the Company's codes of conduct and the scope and results of the work of internal audit and of external audit, together with the independence and objectivity of the auditors.
- To oversee the performance, as well the objectivity and independence, of the external auditor, which it does by requiring reports from the auditor, a requirement to pre-approve fees for non-audit work and by ensuring that fees for non-audit work remain lower than those for audit work.
- Responsibility for the oversight of the Company's policy on whistle-blowers and the risk management process.

Items reviewed during the year include:

- *Financial reporting:* The Committee reviewed the draft annual and interim reports before recommending their publication to the Board. The Committee discussed with the Chief Executive, Chief Financial Officer and external auditors the significant accounting policies, estimates and judgments applied in preparing these reports.
- *Internal controls:* The Committee has an ongoing process for reviewing the effectiveness of the system of internal controls. During the year it considered reports from the Head of Internal Control summarizing the work planned and undertaken, recommending improvements and describing actions taken by management. The Committee also sought the views of the external auditors in making its assessment.
- *Internal audit:* The Committee evaluated the performance of internal audit from the quality of reports and recommendations from the Head of Internal Control.

- *Risk group:* The Committee reviewed the reports produced by the risk management process during the year and recommended that there should be an annual half day risk management workshop carried out by the Board.
- *Whistle blowing:* The Committee reviewed the Group's procedures for staff to raise concerns in confidence about possible financial misreporting and other misconduct. The Company has established procedures which encourage staff members to raise concerns with their line managers, with the Secretary or through a confidential helpline run by Safecall, an independent call bureau, whose reports are immediately forwarded to the Secretary.
- *Reappointment of external auditors:* In appropriate circumstances the Committee may make recommendations to the Board, to be put to shareholders for the approval at the annual general meeting, in relation to the appointment, reappointment or removal of the Company's external auditors.

Auditor Independence

The Committee reviews the work undertaken by the external auditor and assesses annually its independence and objectivity taking into account relevant British and American professional and regulatory requirements and the relationship with the auditor as a whole, including provision of any non-audit services. The Committee monitors the auditor's compliance with relevant regulatory, ethical and professional guidance on the rotation of partners, as well as assessing annually their qualifications, expertise, resources and the effectiveness of the audit process which shall include a report from the external auditor on its own internal quality procedures.

The nominations committee identifies candidates to serve on the board and advises the board about directors who may need to be removed. The nominations committee may also conduct performance evaluations of board members. Figure 13.5 shows an excerpt from the Report of the Nominations Committee in the 2006–07 annual report of British Airways.

FIGURE 13.5 REPORT OF THE NOMINATIONS COMMITTEE, BRITISH AIRWAYS' 2006–07 ANNUAL REPORT

The Nominations Committee meets at least once a year, and additionally if required, to consider the balance of the Board's membership, to identify any additional skills or experience which might enhance the Board's performance, and to interview candidates and recommend appointments to or, where necessary, removals from, the Board. The Committee also reviews the performance of any director seeking re-election at the forthcoming annual general meeting.

The remuneration committee concerns itself with compensation for the board and top management. Figure 13.6 shows an excerpt from the Report of the Remuneration Committee in the 2006–07 annual report of British Airways.

FIGURE 13.6 REPORT OF THE REMUNERATION COMMITTEE, BRITISH AIRWAYS'
2006–07 ANNUAL REPORT

The Company's Remuneration Committee determines on behalf of the Board, within the agreed terms of reference, the overall remuneration packages for the executive directors, the members of the Leadership Team, the Chairman and the Company Secretary. Its members are all independent non-executive directors of the Company, none of whom has any personal financial interest, other than as a shareholder, in the matters to be decided.

The Company currently participates in four main salary survey sources – run by Hay, Monks (PWC), New Bridge Street Consultants and Towers Perrin. Data is extracted from each of these in determining the Company's approach to base pay market rates, and identifying competitive market practice in respect of the other remuneration elements. The Remuneration Committee is cognizant of the risk of an upward ratchet of remuneration that can result from the use of pay surveys.

Some companies also have a standing risk management committee, which is responsible for identifying, assessing and controlling risk. When no autonomous risk management committee exists, these duties are often assigned to the audit committee. One difference is that while the audit committee is usually staffed with nonexecutive directors, risk management committees are comprised of executive directors unless other skills and experience are needed.

Another difference is that audit committees focus on financial matters and as a result are more concerned with financial risk. As the role of risk management broadens to include nonfinancial considerations, so some companies find that a separate committee is desirable. An additional role for the risk management committee is to spearhead changes with respect to both risk management practices.

Committee responsibilities can include the following:

- Recommending to the full board any changes in risk management strategy and policy.
- Providing leadership in risk assessment and monitoring.
- Assessing the effectiveness of risk management systems.
- Reviewing reports on emerging risks and providing early warning on significant new risks to the full board.
- Reviewing internal control and internal audit function effectiveness in relation to the entity's risk profile.

The slate of board committees is dependent on the business's needs. For example, British Airways also has a standing Safety Review Committee. In addition, boards will sometimes create ad hoc committees to deal with special issues, disbanding the committee when its task is complete.

ON YOUR OWN

LEARNING OUTCOME REVIEW

1. What is an assurance system? What are the five assurance systems?
2. Define corporate governance. Who is ultimately responsible for corporate governance?
3. What is risk management?
4. Define internal control.
5. What is the difference between an internal audit and an independent audit?
6. What is a fiduciary? What is a principal?
7. Explain the difference between an inside director and a nonexecutive director.
8. Why are nonexecutive directors thought to add strength to the board of directors?
9. Describe the difference between a unitary board and a multilevel board.

According to the Combined Code on Corporate Governance:

10. How should the duties of the chairman and the chief executive officer be structured?
11. How should the board be balanced and achieve independence?
12. How should appointments to the board be made?
13. What responsibilities does the chairman have with respect to providing information and professional development opportunities to the board?
14. What performance evaluations should be made of the board?
15. How should remuneration of board members be handled?
16. What should the board's response be for financial reporting, internal control and dialogues with shareholders and institutional investors?
17. What are the main committees common to most boards? What are their functions?

LEARNING OUTCOME 3
DEFINE RISK MANAGEMENT AND EXPLAIN HOW RISK MANAGEMENT PROVIDES ASSURANCES FOR FINANCIAL STATEMENTS

In recent years, risk management has received heightened attention. Globalization has exposed many businesses to risks that they had never previously confronted, or with which they had had only modest experience. Examples include exposure to changes in foreign currency exchange rates and ownership of overseas assets. On the other hand, risk management practices such as hedging (see Chapter 8, Financial Assets and Liabilities) made risk more manageable. In recent years, these and other developments have shifted the focus of many companies to enterprise-wide risk management.

INSTITUTE OF INTERNAL AUDITORS

Risk is the 'possibility of an event occurring that will have an impact on the achievement of objectives. Risk is measured in terms of impact and likelihood.'

Source: www.theiia.org

Risks fall into a wide variety of categories, including financial, operational and political. When it comes to making key decisions about global investments, political considerations can be just as important as economic ones, as a report from PricewaterhouseCoopers notes: 'Elements that make emerging markets so attractive – including pent-up demand in a country opening itself up to foreign trade, investment, and cultural influence – also contribute to potential economic instability in those markets.'[2]

The risks faced by a business are largely a question of judgement. For example, British Airways management's assessment of risks and uncertainties from the 2006–07 annual report is shown in Figure 13.7.

FIGURE 13.7 PRINCIPAL RISKS AND UNCERTAINTIES, BRITISH AIRWAYS' 2006–07 ANNUAL REPORT

The operational complexities inherent in the Company's business, together with the highly regulated and commercially competitive environment of the airline industry, drive a number of risks for the Group. Many of these risks, though mitigated to a certain degree, remain outside the Group's control. For example, the effects of changes in governmental regulation, acts of terrorism and the availability or otherwise of financing.

The Company has invested a significant amount of time during the financial year 2007 in identifying, with an assessment of their likelihood and impact, the principal risks within its business. In no particular order, these risks have been identified as follows:

Government Intervention

The airline industry is becoming increasingly regulated, both directly and indirectly. The scope of such regulation ranges from infrastructure issues relating to slot capacity and route flying rights, through to new environmental and security requirements. The Company's ability to both comply with, and influence any changes in, these regulations is key to maintaining its operational and financial performance.

Competition

The markets in which the Group operates are highly competitive. The Group faces competition from other airlines on its routes, as well as from indirect flights, charter services and from other modes of transport. Some competitors have cost structures that are lower than the Group's or have other competitive advantages. Fare discounting by competitors has historically had a negative effect on the Group's results because the Group is generally required to respond to competitors' fares to maintain passenger traffic. Although lower cost 'no frills' competition has been prevalent for a number of years in the shorthaul market, more recently the longhaul market has seen the emergence of a significant number of new entrants in both the low cost and premium ends of the market.

Open Skies

Further to the agreement reached on Open Skies, the Company must ensure that it responds in a timely manner with any necessary changes to the structure of its operations to avoid a significant impact on its business performance.

Industrial Relations

The Group has a large unionised workforce. Collective bargaining takes place on a regular basis and a breakdown in the bargaining process could disrupt operations and adversely affect business performance.

The Company's continued drive to reduce its employment costs, through increased productivity and competitive wage awards, increases the risk in this area.

Brand Reputation

The Company's brand is of significant commercial value. Erosion of the brand, through either a single event, or series of events, could adversely impact the Company's leadership position with its customers and ultimately impact its revenue and profitability and future long term growth.

Pandemics

Epidemics (e.g. SARS) and pandemics, as well as other health risks, may occur and would be beyond the Group's control. Health concerns are one of the factors that can adversely affect demand for air travel. For example, in the Spring of 2003, an outbreak of SARS caused concerns among many travellers about the spread of disease and related health issues. This resulted in a decline in demand for certain of the Group's routes, most notably those to/from the Far East.

Transition to Terminal 5

In 2008, the Company expects to move the majority of its Heathrow operations into Terminal 5. The construction of Terminal 5 is one of the largest construction projects in Europe. This project and the planned move bring with them significant risks and challenges, including infrastructure risk, risks associated with migration and risks associated with starting operations in a new facility with new working practices.

Safety Incident

The safety and security of the Group's customers and employees are fundamental values of the Group. Failure to prevent a major safety or security incident would adversely impact both the Group's operations and financial performance.

Capital Investment

A wrong decision in respect of the Company's planned fleet growth, in terms of timing, aircraft numbers or fleet type, could have a material impact on the Group's future performance.

(Continued)

FIGURE 13.7 *(CONTINUED)*

Financial Commitments

The Group carries substantial debt, which needs to be repaid or refinanced. The Group's ability to finance both its ongoing operations and future fleet growth plans may be affected by various factors including financial market conditions. Most of the Company's debt is asset-related, reflecting the attractiveness of aircraft as security to lenders and other financiers. However, there can be no assurance that aircraft will continue to provide attractive security for lenders.

Adequate control over risk means that there is reasonable assurance that the business's risk is managed effectively, and that the business's goals and objectives are achieved efficiently and effectively. Any risk that remains once actions have been taken to reduce the likelihood of an adverse event is residual risk. Risk appetite refers to a broader statement about the level of tolerance for risk within the entity, while the term risk tolerance refers more to specific levels of acceptable risk around specific objectives. Management may set tolerances with respect to risk.

Figure 13.8 describes the risk management approach used by British Airways.

FIGURE 13.8 RISK MANAGEMENT APPROACH, BRITISH AIRWAYS' 2006–07 ANNUAL REPORT

The Company has put in place a structure and process to facilitate identification, assessment and management of risks. This process has been in place throughout the year to which these statements apply and up to the date of their approval.

Each of the Leadership Team directors has appointed a senior member of their team as a Risk Leader to coordinate the risk management activity for the directorate and to record the risks in the corporate risk register. The ten Risk Leaders, who report to the Risk Group, meet quarterly under the chairmanship of the Head of Risk Management to discuss the management of risk, in particular those risks that may have an impact in more than one directorate. The Risk Leaders also highlight to the Risk Group any changes to risks.

The Risk Group consists of the Leadership Team and the Heads of Internal Control and Risk Management. Meeting quarterly, it reviews the Company's key risks contained in the corporate risk register and ensures that all new and emerging risks are appropriately evaluated and any further actions identified. The Risk Group also provides policy and guidance to the Risk Leaders. The management of each major area of corporate risk is subject to review by an appropriate 'assurance body'. This includes a review of controls in place to mitigate the risks and the further actions being taken by management. The Risk Group reports bi-annually to the Audit Committee and the Board to assist them in the management of risk in accordance with the revised guidance for Directors on the Combined Code (October 2005).

Although risk management is evolving to become enterprise wide, practices still remain fragmented in some companies (see box).

THE EVOLVING ROLE OF RISK MANAGEMENT

In 2006, PricewaterhouseCoopers selected survey responses from 717 audit managers, 59% of which came from companies with more than $1 billion in revenue.[3] Some of its conclusions are as follows:

> Despite the increased emphasis on ERM (enterprise risk management) that has permeated the corporate sector in recent years, the 2007 State of the Profession survey reflects considerable volatility and uncertainty with respect to the roles and responsibilities of internal audit in the risk management arena.
>
> The survey also reveals a decided lack of consistency in the way risk management is practiced within major companies, specifically how internal audit functions assess risks and take part in risk management processes. At some companies, internal audit oversees risk management; at other organizations, other functions are responsible for risk management or there is no formal risk management oversight whatsoever.
>
> As a result of such inconsistency, the implementation of risk management at many organizations is immature at best and chaotic at worst. This is particularly true at companies where more than one function conducts risk management activities and where the risk assessments do not align strongly with corporate priorities or with each other. One third of responding companies conduct multiple enterprise-wide risk assessments, and of this group, only 20% consider their multiple risk assessments to be well aligned. Our experience indicates that multiple risk assessments that are not aligned effectively can be confusing for audit committees and the board.

One result is that the amount of confidence that internal audit managers have in risk assessments in various areas varies:

> In the areas of finance, compliance, and operations – sectors that might be characterized as traditional areas of focus for internal audit – respondents expressed high degrees of confidence, but they were significantly less confident when dealing with risk assessments in the areas of technology, fraud, and strategic or business risks. The specific responses, by area, were as follows:
>
> - Finance – 64% very confident; 33% somewhat confident; 3% not confident
> - Compliance – 49% very confident; 46% somewhat confident; 5% not confident
> - Operations – 43% very confident; 49% somewhat confident; 8% not confident
> - Technology – 33% very confident; 50% somewhat confident; 17% not confident
> - Fraud – 29% very confident; 63% somewhat confident; 8% not confident
> - Strategic/business – 20% very confident; 50% somewhat confident; 30% not confident

ON YOUR OWN

LEARNING OUTCOME REVIEW

1. Define risk. What are examples of risks experienced by global businesses?
2. What is adequate control over risk?
3. What is residual risk? What is risk appetite? What is risk tolerance?
4. What are examples of uncertainty as related to the financial statements?

LEARNING OUTCOME 4
DEFINE INTERNAL CONTROL AND EXPLAIN THE PRINCIPLES AND LIMITATIONS OF INTERNAL CONTROL

4.1 What are the principles of internal control?
    4.1.1 Assignment of responsibility
    4.1.2 Segregation of duties
    4.1.3 Documentation
    4.1.4 Physical controls
    4.1.5 Independent verification

4.2 What is the Treadway Commission?

4.3 What is the Turnbull Guidance?

4.4 What are the limitations of internal control?

Recall that a system of internal control comprises the policies and procedures within the business that facilitate efficient and effective operations that allow the company to respond to significant risks; safeguard assets; ensure the quality of internal and external reporting; and monitor compliance with laws, regulations and internal business policies. In other words, the internal control system exists to provide feedback so that management can determine whether business processes are functioning properly and as intended, and to implement corrective actions when they are not.

4.1 What are the principles of internal control?

Internal control systems are usually evaluated in terms of being strong or weak. What makes an internal control system strong? Several general principles are applied to make this assessment, as follows.

4.1.1 ASSIGNMENT OF RESPONSIBILITY

Strong internal control requires that responsibilities be assigned to specific individuals for accountability. For example, a purchase of less than €1000 may be approved by a departmental manager, while purchases between €1000 and €10 000 require a divisional manager's approval, with any amount above that needing a vice-president's signature. Another example would be an employee who is responsible for purchasing supplies who would be held accountable for overspending the supplies budget. The ability to assign responsibility depends in part on the existence of an organizational structure that facilitates the accomplishment of management's goals and objectives.

4.1.2 SEGREGATION OF DUTIES

When one individual performs related activities, opportunities exist for that individual to conceal instances where he or she commits errors or perpetrates fraud. For example, a person who processes cash payments from customers should not also approve sales allowances or write off uncollectible debts. With segregation of duties, employees would have to engage in collusion, actions by two or more people, to circumvent the system of internal controls.

Although duties must be assigned on a case-by-case basis to ensure that they are properly segregated, generally the responsibility for executing a transaction (for example ordering supplies) is assigned to individuals or departments other than those who eventually have custody of the asset. In fact, different steps in the execution of the transaction – approval, selection of vendor, ordering, payment and record keeping – should be segregated. Even within the accounting department, maintenance of records on cash payments, for example, should be kept separate from record keeping on the asset itself.

4.1.3 DOCUMENTATION

Documentation, which strengthens internal control, serves two major purposes: documentation of policies and procedures sets the standard for operating the business; and documentation provides evidence of transactions' validity.

- *Policies and procedures.* Companies maintain detailed descriptions of policies and procedures, which serve as a point of reference for all employees' actions and training. In addition, companies document how automated systems should perform and how employees should execute their duties. Job descriptions, which detail the required qualifications and responsibilities of an employee, are one example of this type of documentation.
- *Transactions' validity.* The second form of documentation ensures that companies have the appropriate documents to verify the validity of transactions. For example, if a company pays a supplier €500 for maintenance materials, an invoice from the vendor should be on record that shows that the payment received the appropriate approvals before it was paid, and also information on when and how the invoice was paid. This document would be traceable through the accounting system through the audit trail, as discussed in Chapter 6, Accounting Information Systems.

4.1.4 PHYSICAL CONTROLS

A broad range of physical controls exists to limit access to the business's assets, including its accounting and other records. Examples include locks on facilities, electronic screening devices to determine whether individuals have authorized access to information, shredders to destroy discarded documents and safes for keeping cash and valuable inventories like jewellery.

4.1.5 INDEPENDENT VERIFICATION

Another internal control principle is the independent verification of information prepared by employees. This usually takes the form of having someone from another function within the company review the material to ensure that it is accurate. This is sometimes done on an ongoing and in other cases a surprise basis.

These five internal control principles are illustrated in Figure 13.9.

FIGURE 13.9 FIVE INTERNAL CONTROL PRINCIPLES

Efforts to improve internal control practices have been undertaken by two notable organizations: the Committee of Sponsoring Organizations of the Treadway Commission (COSO) and the Turnbull Guidance.

4.2 What is the Treadway Commission?

In the mid-1980s, the Committee of Sponsoring Organizations of the Treadway Commission (COSO; www.coso.org) was created in the US as a private-sector initiative to study fraudulent financial reporting and recommend improvements. This resulted in the COSO Internal Control Framework, which provides a definition of internal control and establishes criteria that companies can use to evaluate their internal control systems. The COSO Framework was in recent years broadened into the Enterprise Risk Management – Integrated Framework, which identifies eight interrelated components for describing and analysing internal control systems, as shown in Figure 13.10.

4.3 What is the Turnbull Guidance?

The Turnbull Guidance[4] was issued in the United Kingdom in 1999, and in 2004 was revised by the Turnbull Review Group. The Group studied the effectiveness of the original report and concluded that substantial improvements had been achieved in internal control using the Turnbull Guidance's principles-based approach,

FIGURE 13.10 ENTERPRISE RISK MANAGEMENT – INTEGRATED FRAMEWORK

Internal environment – This sets the tone in an organization for how risk is viewed including management's risk management philosophy and risk appetite, integrity, and ethical values.

Risk response – Management selects a response to specific risks which could include avoidance, acceptance, reduction or risk sharing. The response should be aligned with the entity's risk tolerance and risk appetite.

Objective setting–This is the process of setting objectives consistent with the business's mission and risk appetite.

Monitoring–This is the ongoing process of assessing the quality of the business and internal control system's performance, and reporting the results to the appropriate parties.

Event identification–This involves the identification of events that may affect achievement of the business's objectives including distinguishing between those events that represent opportunities and those which pose risks.

Information and communication – Effective communication includes reports on operational, financial and compliance-related activities that make it possible to operate and control the business.

Risk assessment–This includes the identification and analysis of risks including their likehood.

Control activities–These include policies and procedures to ensure that management directives are carried out as intended. Examples include approval, authorization, verifications, reconciliation, review of operating performance, asset security and segregation of duties.

and that 'the companies which have derived the most benefit from application of the guidance were those whose boards saw embedded risk management and internal control as an integral part of running the business'.[5]

The Revised Turnbull Guidance notes that the board of directors is responsible for the system of internal control and should regularly seek assurances that the internal control system is functioning effectively. The board should also ensure that the internal control system is effectively managing those risks that it has approved. Thus, the board should consider the nature and extent of risks faced by the business: which risks are acceptable, the likelihood of the risk materializing and the business's ability to mitigate that risk if it does occur, and the cost of particular controls weighted against the benefit of managing the related risks.

Management's role is to implement board policies on risk and control. That includes identifying and evaluating risks for consideration by the board, and developing and operating an appropriate internal control system to implement the board's policies. All employees have some responsibility for internal control, which means that they must have the knowledge, skills, information and authority to implement and operate an internal control system.

The internal control system reflects the control environment, which includes control activities; information and communications processes; and ongoing monitoring of the effectiveness of the internal control system. The internal control system should be 'embedded in the operations of the company and form part of its culture', be capable of responding quickly to evolving risks and include procedures for reporting significant control failings and corrective actions or weaknesses to the appropriate levels of management.

The Revised Turnbull Guidance notes that while effective internal control can reduce but not eliminate poor decision making, companies also face the consequences of human error, situations in which employees and others circumvent control processes, management overriding controls and unforeseeable circumstances. The Guidance concludes:

> A sound system of internal control therefore provides reasonable, but not absolute, assurance that a company will not be hindered in achieving its business objectives, or in the orderly and legitimate conduct of its business, by circumstances which may reasonably be foreseen. A system of internal control cannot, however, provide protection with certainty against a company failing to meet its business objectives or all material errors, losses, fraud, or breaches of law or regulations.[6]

The Revised Turnbull Guidance also outlines responsibilities for reviewing the effectiveness of internal control, which is the board's responsibility. Boards have options about how they might fulfil this task, but the Guidance makes clear that the board should take responsibility for disclosures on internal control in the annual report and accounts.

The board should regularly receive and review reports on internal control, and conduct an annual assessment for the purposes of making its public statement on internal control. The annual assessment should consider significant risks; an assessment of how they were identified, evaluated and managed; the effectiveness of the internal control system in managing the risks in a prompt fashion; and whether more extensive monitoring is needed.

For purposes of making its annual statement, the board should review changes in significant risks since the last annual statement, including the ability of the business to respond; the scope and quality of management's ongoing monitoring of risk and the internal control system, including the internal audit function; the frequency and extent of communications of monitoring results; the incidence of internal control failings and weaknesses; and the effectiveness of the company's public reporting process.

Figure 13.11 shows British Airways' discussion of internal control offered to users in the company's 2006–07 annual report.

FIGURE 13.11 INTERNAL CONTROL, BRITISH AIRWAYS' 2006–07 ANNUAL REPORT

The directors are responsible for the Company's system of internal control, including internal financial control, which is designed to provide reasonable, but not absolute, assurance regarding: (a) the safeguarding of assets against unauthorized use or disposition, and (b) the maintenance of proper accounting records and the reliability of financial information used with the business or for publication.

The Company has a Statement of Business Principles applicable to all employees. The Company also has a Code of Business Conduct and Ethics which applies to all employees. These are two of a number of Standing Instructions to employees of the Group designed to enhance internal control. Along with the Finance Standing Instructions, these are regularly updated and made available to staff through the Company's intranet. Following the Company's decision to de-list from the NYSE, the Statement of Business Principles and the Code of Business Conduct and Ethics will be combined into a crisper, more effective statement.

A clear organizational structure exists detailing lines of authority and control responsibilities. The professionalism and competence of staff is maintained both through rigorous recruitment policies and a performance appraisal system which establishes targets, reinforces accountability and control consciousness, and identifies appropriate training requirements. Action plans are prepared and implemented to ensure that staff develop and maintain the required skills to fulfill their responsibilities, and that the Company can meet its future management requirements.

Information systems are developed to support the Company's long-term objectives and are managed by a professionally staffed Information Management department. Appropriate policies and procedures are in place covering all significant areas of the business. During the year under review, the Company has worked to enhance controls in relation to IT risks.

The business agenda is determined by the business plan which represents the operational and financial evaluation of the corporate strategy, setting out the agreed targets for financial return and service standards, identifying and prioritizing improvement opportunities to deliver those targets, and the agreed capital and manpower requirements. The business planning process confirms that the targeted results can be achieved, satisfies departments that their plans are robust and establishes performance indicators against which departments can be evaluated. The business plan is approved by the Board on an annual basis.

(Continued)

FIGURE 13.11 (*CONTINUED*)

A comprehensive management accounting system is in place providing financial and operational performance measurement indicators to management. Detailed management accounts are prepared monthly to cover each major area of the business. Variances from plan are analysed, explained and acted on in a timely manner. As well as regular Board discussions, monthly meetings are held by the Leadership Team to discuss performance with specific projects being discussed as and when required. Throughout the year under review, both the Capital Investment Committee (including the External Spend Group) and the Manpower Control Group were instrumental in maintaining tight control of capital expenditure, external expenditure and headcount.

Business controls are reviewed on an on-going basis by the internal audit function which operates internationally and to a programme based on risk assessment. The department is managed by professionally qualified personnel with experience gained from both inside and outside the industry. The department includes dedicated resources for regular audits of major projects, arrangements with third parties (suppliers, agents, partners), IT controls, and internal departments and processes. An annual audit plan for the calendar year 2007, which provides assurance over key business processes and commercial and financial risks facing the Company, was approved by the Audit Committee in November 2006.

The Audit Committee considers significant control matters raised by management and both the internal and external auditors and reports its findings to the Board. Where weaknesses are identified, the Audit Committee ensures that appropriate action is taken by management.

The directors have reviewed the effectiveness of the Company's internal control system considering the processes set out above and make this statement pursuant to the revised guidance for directors issued in October, 2005.

Figure 13.12 contains extracts from the section on assessing the effectiveness of the company's risk and control processes from the Revised Turnbull Guidance.

FIGURE 13.12 INTERNAL CONTROL: REVISED GUIDANCE FOR DIRECTORS ON THE COMBINED CODE, FINANCIAL REPORTING COUNCIL, OCTOBER 2005

Some questions which the board may wish to consider and discuss with management when regularly reviewing reports on internal control and when carrying out its annual assessment are set out below. The questions are not intended to be exhaustive and will need to be tailored to the particular circumstances of the company.

Risk assessment
- Does the company have clear objectives and have they been communicated so as to provide effective direction to employees on risk and control issues? For example, do objectives and related plans include measurable performance targets and indicators?

- Are the significant internal and external operations, financial, compliance and other risks identified and assessed on an ongoing basis?
- Is there a clear understanding by management and others within the company of what risks are acceptable to the board?

Control environment and control activities
- Does the board have clear strategies for dealing with the significant risks that have been identified? Is there a policy on how to manage these risks?
- Do the company's culture, code of conduct, human resources policies and performance reward systems support the business objectives and risk management and internal control system?
- Does senior management demonstrate, through its actions as well as its policies, the necessary commitment to competence, integrity and fostering a climate of trust within the company?
- Are authority, responsibility and accountability defined clearly such that decisions are made and actions taken by the appropriate people? Are the decisions and actions of different parts of the company appropriately coordinated?
- Does the company communicate to its employees what is expected of them and the scope of their freedom to act? This may apply to areas such as customer relations, service levels for both internal and outsourced activities; health, safety and environmental protection; security of tangible and intangible assets; business continuity issues; expenditure matters; accounting; and financial and other reporting.
- Do people in the company (and in its providers of outsourced services) have the knowledge, skills and tools to support the achievement of the company's objectives and to manage effectively risks to their achievement?
- How are processes/controls adjusted to reflect new or changing risks, or operational deficiencies?

Information and communication
- Do management and the board receive timely, relevant and reliable reports on progress against business objectives and the related risks that provide them with the information, from inside and outside the company, needed for decision-making and management review purposes? This could include performance reports and indicators of change, together with qualitative information such as on customer satisfaction, employee attitudes etc.
- Are information needs and related information systems reassessed as objectives and related risks change or as reporting deficiencies are identified?
- Are periodic reporting procedures, including half-yearly and annual reporting, effective in communicating a balanced and understandable account of the company's position and prospects?
- Are there established channels of communication for individuals to report suspected breaches of law or regulations or other improprieties?

Monitoring
- Are there ongoing processes embedded within the company's overall business operations, and addressed by senior management, which monitor the effective application of the policies, processes and activities related to internal control and risk management? (Such processes may include control

(Continued)

FIGURE 13.12 *(CONTINUED)*

self-assessment, confirmation by personnel of compliance with policies and codes of conduct, internal audit reviews or other management reviews).

- Do these processes monitor the company's ability to re-evaluate risks and adjust controls effectively in response to changes in its objectives, its business, and its external environment?
- Are there effective follow-up procedures to ensure that appropriate change or action occurs in response to changes in risk and control assessments?
- Is there appropriate communication to the board (or board committees) on the effectiveness of the ongoing monitoring processes on risk and control matters? This should include reporting any significant failings or weaknesses on a timely basis.
- Are there specific arrangements for management monitoring and reporting to the board on risk and control matters of particular importance? These could include, for example, actual or suspected fraud and other illegal or irregular acts, or matters that could adversely affect the company's reputation or financial position.

4.4 What are the limitations of internal control?

Internal controls provide reasonable assurance regarding achievement of the business's objectives, but cannot provide a guarantee. The inherent limitations of internal control systems are explained by several factors:

- *Cost versus benefit:* Internal control systems cannot be cost-effectively constructed to guard against all risks. The benefit of having internal controls in place for a particular risk should exceed the cost of having a particular control that addresses that risk.
- *Errors in judgement:* Internal control systems cannot overcome errors in judgement, especially in areas where risks to the business entity are rapidly evolving.
- *Management interference:* Since management is responsible for the development and maintenance of internal control systems, and supervises employees responsible for its operation, then management overrides are a danger, and in fact have figured prominently in some major internal control system failures.
- *Employee collusion:* A major threat to the effectiveness of internal control is when employees work together to circumvent the system in order to commit fraud or conceal irregularities.
- *Malfunctions:* Internal control systems have limitations in their design capabilities and therefore may not adequately address a specific risk.

ON YOUR OWN

LEARNING OUTCOME REVIEW

1. What are the five general principles of internal control?
2. List the eight components for describing and analysing internal control systems based on COSO's Enterprise Risk Management – Integrated Framework.
3. According to the Turnbull Guidance, which companies derive the most benefit from application of the Guidance?

4. What is the control environment?
5. According to the Turnbull Guidance, what should be contained in the annual statement made by the board?
6. What are the limitations of internal control?

LEARNING OUTCOME 5
DEFINE INTERNAL AUDITING AND EXPLAIN ITS ROLE IN PROVIDING ASSURANCE FOR FINANCIAL STATEMENTS

Internal audit departments are often led by the chief audit executive, who is the most senior person in the business responsible for internal audit activities. Internal audit services are often performed by an in-house department and sometimes by contracting these services to an external service provider, in which case the chief audit executive would oversee the relationship with the outside service provider. External service providers have specialized knowledge, skills and experience in a particular discipline.

INSTITUTE OF INTERNAL AUDITORS

'Internal auditing is an independent, objective assurance and consulting activity designed to add value and improve an organization's operations. It helps an organization to accomplish its objectives by bringing a systematic, disciplined approach to evaluate and improve the effectiveness of risk management, control and governance processes.'

Source: www.theiia.org

INTERNAL AUDIT ENGAGEMENTS

Internal audit activities are organized as engagements. An engagement may focus on any one of a number of different tasks, such as an internal audit, fraud examination or consultancy. These may include assurance services, which are objective examinations of evidence to provide an assessment on risk management, control or governance processes within the business, including financial, performance, compliance, system security and due diligence engagements. Compliance refers to an engagement that evaluates whether the business is conforming to policies, plans, procedures, laws, regulations, contracts and other requirements. An engagement may involve consulting services, which advise business units on adding value and improving governance, risk management and control processes.

Figure 13.13 shows selected portions of the International Standards for the Professional Practice of Internal Auditing promulgated by the Institute of Internal Auditors (www.theiia.org), which are widely accepted and used by many large, multinational companies.

FIGURE 13.13 INTERNATIONAL STANDARDS FOR THE PROFESSIONAL PRACTICE OF INTERNAL AUDITING (EXCERPTED)

Reporting to the Board and Senior Management

The chief audit executive should report periodically to the board and senior management on the internal audit activity's purpose, authority, responsibility, and performance relative to its plan. Reporting should also include significant risk exposures and control issues, corporate governance issues, and other matters needed or requested by the board and senior management.

Nature of Work

The internal audit activity should evaluate and contribute to the improvement of risk management, control, and governance processes using a systematic and disciplined approach.

Risk Management

The internal audit activity should evaluate risk exposures relating to the organization's governance, operations, and information systems regarding the

- Reliability and integrity of financial and operational information.
- Effectiveness and efficiency of operations.
- Safeguarding of assets.
- Compliance with laws, regulations, and contracts.

Control

The internal audit activity should assist the organization in maintaining effective controls by evaluating their effectiveness and efficiency and by promoting continuous improvement. Based on the results of the risk assessment, the internal audit activity should evaluate the adequacy and effectiveness of controls encompassing the organization's governance, operations, and information systems. This should include:

- Reliability and integrity of financial and operational information.
- Effectiveness and efficiency of operations.
- Safeguarding of assets.
- Compliance with laws, regulations, and contracts.

Governance

The internal audit activity should assess and make appropriate recommendations for improving the governance process in its accomplishment of the following objectives:

- Promoting appropriate ethics and values within the organization.
- Ensuring effective organizational performance management and accountability.
- Effectively communicating risk and control information to appropriate areas of the organization.
- Effectively coordinating the activities of and communicating information among the board, external and internal auditors and management.

Source: Copyright 2004 by The Institute of Internal Auditors, Inc., 247 Maitland Avenue, Altamonte Springs, Florida 32710-4201 U.S.A. Reprinted with permission.

In the past, internal audits were typically conducted on an annual cycle. Each year a risk assessment was carried out and an annual audit plan was created, which was then implemented over the year. Resources were assigned well in advance and the audit schedule throughout the year was seldom changed except in a crisis situation. The process therefore followed a predictable schedule and resulting reports were issued only after reviews by several management layers. In some companies internal audit no longer follows such a predictable trail and some surprise audits are conducted.

ON YOUR OWN

LEARNING OUTCOME REVIEW

1. Define internal auditing
2. What are assurance services?
3. What are compliance services?
4. What are consulting services?

LEARNING OUTCOME PRACTICE

1. To whom is the internal auditor primarily responsible?
   a. The directors of the company
   b. The company as a separate entity
   c. The shareholders of the company
   d. The employees of the company
   ACCA adapted

LEARNING OUTCOME 6
DEFINE INDEPENDENT AUDITING AND EXPLAIN ITS ROLE IN PROVIDING ASSURANCE FOR FINANCIAL STATEMENTS

6.1   Who conducts independent audits?

6.2   What qualifications must independent auditors have?

6.3   What is an audit engagement?

6.4   What is an audit report?

6.1 Who conducts independent audits?

Independent audits are conducted by outside service firms of independent auditors, sometimes referred to as registered auditors, external auditors or public accountants. Qualified individuals can also perform independent audits. Some audit firms have become business powerhouses themselves. Figure 13.14 lists the four largest international and best-known audit firms along with their annual revenues and estimated number of employees, and website addresses.

FIGURE 13.14 THE FOUR LARGEST GLOBAL AUDIT FIRMS

Rank	Firm	Revenue € Euros Billions	Approximate Number of Employees	Website
1	PricewaterhouseCoopers	16.0	160 000	www.pwc.com
2	Deloitte Touche Tohmatsu	14.7	150 000	www.deloitte.com
3	Ernst & Young	13.4	130 000	www.ey.com
4	KPMG	12.8	120 000	www.kpmg.com

6.2 What qualifications must independent auditors have?

In many nations, laws govern the qualifications and credentials that an independent auditor must have in order to legally perform audit services. These credentials are typically earned through some combination of education, qualification papers or examinations, experience and in some cases evidence of social and ethical responsibility. An example of the requirements set forth by one of these – the Association of Chartered Certified Accountants (ACCA), which has 115 000 members – is shown in the box.

ACCA PROFESSIONAL CERTIFICATION

Applicants for the ACCA Professional Certification are required to have two A levels and three GCSEs in five different subjects including Maths and English, or the equivalent. Separate admission standards are available for 'mature' students over 21 years of age. An applicant does not have to be university educated, however graduates of universities with programmes approved by the ACCA can waive up to nine of the exams within the Fundamentals Level.

OBJECTIVE OF ACCA EXAM SYLLABUS

The overall aim of the exam syllabus is to provide the core accounting knowledge, skills and appropriate professional values in order for affiliates to work in any employment sector. After completing the professional exams, affiliates should be capable of:

- Preparing and analysing financial accounts and reports, and giving appropriate professional advice
- Preparing and analysing management accounting reports, measuring, assessing and managing performance – giving appropriate professional advice
- Understanding the implications for – and constraints on – accountants and managers imposed by corporate and business law

- Preparing tax computations and giving professional advice on a range of taxation issues in regard to personal and corporate taxation
- Recognizing the role of internal and external auditing with respect to financial review, control, accountability and assurance
- Applying financial management theory and techniques in the interests of sustainable and responsible value creation, and giving appropriate professional advice on financing, investment and distribution
- Managing the strategic direction of an organization and supporting business strategy through implementing business process change by applying appropriate project, systems and people management techniques and theories
- Appreciating that an accountant must embrace and adhere to a set of professional values and behave within an ethical framework, showing responsibility to stakeholders through operating within an effective system of governance, internal control and risk management.

The ACCA Qualification contains 14 papers or exams. These are divided into two categories:

FUNDAMENTALS

Students must successfully complete nine Fundamentals papers. If the student has a relevant accounting degree from an institution accredited by the ACCA, then some or all of these papers are waived. The Fundamentals papers are divided into two categories:

<u>Knowledge module</u>
  F1 Accountant in Business
  F2 Management Accounting
  F3 Financial Accounting
<u>Skills module</u>
  F4 Corporate and Business Law
  F5 Performance Management
  F6 Taxation
  F7 Financial Reporting
  F8 Audit and Assurance
  F9 Financial Management

PROFESSIONAL

After completing the Fundamentals papers, the applicant must pass five Professional level papers. All three Essentials papers (see below) are required, and two of the Options must be successfully completed.

<u>Essentials module</u>
  P1 Professional Accountant
  P2 Corporate Reporting
  P3 Business Analysis

<u>Options module</u>
> P4 Advanced Financial Management
> P5 Advanced Performance Management
> P6 Advanced Taxation
> P7 Advanced Audit and Assurance

All these papers, according to the ACCA, have been set at an intellectual level expected of a student taking a master's degree.

Exams can be taken in a paper- or computer-based format. Knowledge exams are two hours long and all others are 3 hours and 15 minutes including reading time. Assessment methods include short answer questions, computational exercises, essays, scenarios and case studies. The modules – Knowledge, Skills, Essentials and Options – must be passed in the order shown. Candidates can take up to four papers in one sitting. The ACCA usually offers paper sittings over eight days twice per year (June and December).

PRACTICAL EXPERIENCE REQUIREMENT

In addition, to be awarded the ACCA Qualification, the candidate must have three years of practical experience. The candidate also has a practical experience requirement (PER) which is satisfied by meeting performance objectives in the workplace, overseen and agreed by a workplace mentor. The candidate does this by responding to a set of 'challenge questions', which are similar to those that might be expected in a performance review, interview or appraisal. An annual report is filed documenting progress towards the objectives. These are aligned with the papers and include the following:

ESSENTIALS

All nine objectives must be met

Professionalism, ethics and governance

1 Demonstrate the application of professional ethics, values and judgement
2 Contribute to the effective governance of an organization
3 Raise awareness of non-financial risk

Personal effectiveness

4 Manage self
5 Communicate effectively
6 Use information and communications technology

Business management

7 Manage on-going activities in your area of responsibility
8 Improve departmental performance
9 Manage an assignment

OPTIONS

Any four of the following objectives must be met.

Financial accounting and reporting

10 Prepare financial statements for external purposes

11 Interpret financial transactions and financial statements

Performance measurement and management accounting

12 Prepare financial information for management

13 Contribute to budget planning and production

14 Monitor and control budgets

Finance and financial management

15 Evaluate potential business/investment opportunities and the required finance options

16 Manage cash using active cash management and treasury systems

Audit and assurance

17 Prepare for and collect evidence for audit

18 Evaluate and report on audit

Taxation

19 Evaluate and compute taxes payable

20 Assist with tax planning

Passing all required exams and satisfying the practical experience requirement entitles the candidate to become a member of the Association of Chartered Certified Accountants.

6.3 What is an audit engagement?

An audit engagement involves work by independent auditors to evaluate the system of internal control and review accounting policies and procedures. The purpose is to provide a professional opinion about whether the financial statements provide a true and fair view of the business's financial position and performance in accordance with the relevant accounting standards. The audit engagement consists of four major phases:

1. Planning the audit, which establishes the objectives of the audit and what resources will be needed to achieve those objectives.
2. Evaluating the system of internal control to determine its strengths and weaknesses. This evaluation results in a decision about the nature, extent and timing of substantive testing.

3. Performing substantive tests, which involve collecting evidence about the validity of transactions and other events to verify financial information. For example, inventories are physically counted to ensure that accounting records accurately reflect the amount of inventories on hand.

4. An audit report is then prepared and presented to the client, which includes the auditor's opinion about whether the company's financial statements present a true and fair view of the company's financial position in all material respects. The auditor must provide one of four opinions (see box) based on the outcome of the independent audit.

6.4 What is an audit report?

An audit report contains the opinion of the independent auditors (see box). The opinion, if favourable, provides *reasonable assurance* to financial statement users that no material misstatement of financial results has occurred. However, the audit report does not provide absolute assurance.

AUDIT OPINIONS

1. *Unqualified opinion.* An unqualified opinion is given when the audit reports states that the client's financial statements provide a true and fair view in all material respects.

2. *Qualified opinion.* This opinion is given when the financial statements provide a true and fair view of the financial results of the business 'except for' one or more qualifications.

3. *Adverse opinion.* When the auditor concludes that the financial statements do not present a true and fair view, an adverse opinion is appropriate.

4. *Disclaimer of opinion.* The auditor is unable to provide an opinion because the audit engagement could not be completed or another factor made providing any opinion impossible.

In practice, any opinion other than an unqualified opinion would cast grave doubts on the business. Thus management and the board usually devote considerable effort to the relationship with the independent auditor and will take the necessary steps to ensure that the business meets accounting standards in a manner that is acceptable to the independent auditor.

Publicly traded companies are required to have annual independent audits by law in most countries and according to the regulations of the listing exchanges. In addition, privately held companies that seek major loans are often required by banks and other creditors to have independent audits. These audits are usually expensive and are thus obtained on a need-only basis.

EXCERPT FROM THE UK COMPANIES ACT 1985

AUDITORS' REPORT

(1) A company's auditors shall make a report to the company's members on all annual accounts of the company of which copies are to be laid before the company in general meeting during their tenure of office.

(2) The auditors' report shall state whether in the auditors' opinion the annual accounts have been properly prepared in accordance with this Act, and in particular whether a true and fair view is given—(a) in the case of an individual statement of financial position, of the state of affairs of the company as at the end of the financial year, (b) in the case of an individual profit and loss account, of the profit or loss of the company for the financial year, (c) in the case of group accounts, of the state of affairs as at the end of the financial year, and the profit or loss for the financial year, of the undertakings included in the consolidation as a whole, so far as concerns members of the company.

(3) The auditors shall consider whether the information given in the directors' report for the financial year for which the annual accounts are prepared is consistent with those accounts; and if they are of opinion that it is not they shall state that fact in their report.

SIGNATURE OF AUDITORS' REPORT

(1) The auditors' report shall state the names of the auditors and be signed by them.

(2) Every copy of the auditors' report which is laid before the company in general meeting, or which is otherwise circulated, published or issued, shall state the name of the auditors.

(3) The copy of the auditors' report which is delivered to the registrar shall state the names of the auditors and be signed by them.

(4) If a copy of the auditors' report (a) is laid before the company, or otherwise circulated, published or issued, without the required statement of the auditors' names, or (b) is delivered to the registrar without the required statement of the auditors' names or without being signed as required by this section, the company and every officer of it who is in default is guilty of an offence and liable to a fine.

(5) References in this section to signature by the auditors are, where the office of auditor is held by a body corporate or partnership, to signature in the name of the body corporate or partnership by a person authorised to sign on its behalf.

DUTIES OF AUDITORS

(1) A company's auditors shall, in preparing their report, carry out such investigations as will enable them to form an opinion as to (a) whether proper accounting records have been kept by the company and proper returns adequate for their audit have been received from branches not visited by them, and (b) whether the company's individual accounts are in agreement with the accounting records and returns.

(2) If the auditors are of opinion that proper accounting records have not been kept, or that proper returns adequate for their audit have not been received from branches not visited by them, or if the company's individual accounts are not in agreement with the accounting records and returns, the auditors shall state that fact in their report.

(3) If the auditors fail to obtain all the information and explanations which, to the best of their knowledge and belief, are necessary for the purposes of their audit, they shall state that fact in their report.

(4) If the requirements of Schedule 6 (disclosure of information: emoluments and other benefits of directors and others) are not complied with in the annual accounts, the auditors shall include in their report, so far as they are reasonably able to do so, a statement giving the required particulars.

Figure 13.15 presents an excerpt from British Airways' annual report that includes the fully independent auditor's report from Ernst & Young for the 2006–07 financial statements.

FIGURE 13.15 INDEPENDENT AUDITOR'S REPORT TO THE MEMBERS OF THE BRITISH AIRWAYS PLC

We have audited the Group and parent company financial statements (the 'financial statements') of British Airways Plc for the year ended March 31, 2007 which comprise the Group Statement of income, the Group and Parent Company Statement of financial positions, the Group and Parent Company Statement of cash flows, the Group and Parent Company Statement of Change in Shareholders' Equity and the related notes 1 to 35. These financial statements have been prepared under the accounting policies set out therein. We have also audited the information in the Directors' Remuneration Report that is described as having been audited.

The report is made solely to the Company's members, as a body, in accordance with Section 235 of the Companies Act 1985. Our audit work has been undertaken so that we might state to the Company's members those matters we are required to state to them in an auditor's report and for no other purpose. To the fullest extent permitted by law, we do not accept or assume responsibility to anyone other than the Company and the Company's members as a body, for our audit work, for this report, or for the opinions we have formed.

Respective Responsibilities of Directors and Auditors
The directors are responsible for preparing the Annual Report, the Directors' Remuneration Report and the financial statements in accordance with applicable United Kingdom law and IFRS as adopted by the European Union as set out in the Statement of Directors' Responsibilities.

Our responsibility is to audit the financial statements and the part of the Directors' Remuneration Report to be audited in accordance with relevant legal and regulatory requirements and International Standards on Auditing (UK and Ireland).

We report to you our opinion as to whether the financial statements give us a true and fair view, the financial statements and the part of the Director's Remuneration Report to be audited have been properly prepared in accordance with the Companies Act 1985 and Article 4 of the IAS Regulation and that the information given in the Directors' Report and Business Review is consistent with the financial statements.

We also report to you if, in our opinion, the Company has not kept proper accounting records, if we have not received all the information and explanations we require for our audit, or if information specified by law regarding directors' remuneration and other transactions is not disclosed.

We review whether the Corporate Governance Statement reflects the Company's compliance with the nine provisions of the 2006 FRC Combined Code specified for our review by the Listing Rules of the Financial Services Authority, and we report if it does not. We are not required to consider whether the Board's statements on internal control cover all risks and controls, or form an opinion on the effectiveness of the Group's corporate governance procedures or its risk and control procedures.

We read other information contained in the Annual Report and consider whether it is consistent with the audited financial statements. The other information comprises only the Directors' Report and Business Review, the unaudited part of the Directors' Remuneration Report, the Chairman's Statement, the Chief Executive's Statement and the Corporate Governance Statement. We consider the implications for our report if we become aware of any apparent misstatements or material inconsistencies with the financial statements. Our responsibilities do not extend to any other information.

Basis of Audit Opinion

We conducted our audit in accordance with International Standards on Auditing (UK and Ireland) issued by the Auditing Practices Board. An audit includes examination, on a test basis, of evidence relevant to the amounts and disclosures in the financial statements and the part of the Director's Remuneration Report to be audited. It also includes an assessment of the significant estimates and judgments made by the directors in the preparation of the financial statements, and of whether the accounting policies are appropriate to the Group's and Company's circumstances, consistently applied and adequately disclosed.

We planned and performed our audit so as to obtain all the information and explanations which we considered necessary in order to provide us with sufficient evidence to give reasonable assurance that the financial statements and the part of the Directors' Remuneration Report to be audited are free from material misstatement, whether caused by fraud or other irregularity of error. In forming our opinion we also evaluated the overall adequacy of the presentation of information in the financial statements and part of the Directors' Remuneration Report to be audited.

Opinion

In our opinion:

- the Group financial statements give a true and fair view, in accordance with IFRS as adopted by the European Union, of the state of the group's affairs as at March 31, 2007 and of its profit for the year then ended;
- the Parent company financial statements give a true and fair view, in accordance with IFRS as adopted by the European Union as applied in accordance with the provisions of the Companies Act of 1985, of the state of the parent company's affairs as at March 31, 2007;
- the financial statements and part of the Directors' Remuneration Report to be audited have been properly prepared in accordance with the Companies Act 1985 and Article 4 of the IAS Regulation; and

(Continued)

FIGURE 13.15 *(CONTINUED)*

- the information given in the directors' report and business review is consistent with the financial statements.

  Ernst & Young LLP
  Registered auditor
  London
  May 17, 2007

ON YOUR OWN

LEARNING OUTCOME REVIEW

1. Who conducts independent audits?
2. What is the difference between an internal audit and an independent audit?
3. What are the general requirements to become an independent auditor?
4. What does an independent auditor do?
5. What are the four types of opinions that an independent auditor can give?

LEARNING OUTCOME 7
EXPLAIN WHY FRAUD AUDITING AND FORENSIC ACCOUNTING HAVE BECOME PART OF INDEPENDENT AUDITING

Businesses are subject to many types of fraud. This includes, for example, fraud by managers who misrepresent financial results, employees who steal from employers, vendors who overcharge for goods or services, and others. Though the legal definition varies between jurisdictions, fraud is a false representation intentionally made in order to gain a material advantage. An unintentional act is an error, not fraud. Although fraud has always been a problem for businesses, the high-profile corporate scandals discussed at the beginning of this chapter – especially those where management was the primary perpetrator – have resulted in a broader recognition that risks associated with fraud need to be directly managed.

A perpetrator is the party who commits the fraud. Fraud generally occurs when three conditions are present. First, the perpetrator is under some pressure or has some incentive to commit fraud. Second, the opportunity must be present in the form of weak internal controls or the ability for management to override the controls. Third, individuals are able to rationalize the fraud by saying, for example, that they receive unfair compensation or that upper management condones unethical conduct and encourages any action that benefits the company financially.

In the past, auditors were charged with reporting incidents of fraud when they were encountered, however they were under no obligation to discover fraud. Now, awareness of the possibility of fraud is a larger factor in audits, although the focus is on conducting audits to obtain reasonable assurance about whether the financial statements are free of material misstatement, whether caused by error or fraud. The two types of misstatements are:

- Fraudulent financial reporting: Misstatement or omission of amounts or disclosures that cause financial statements to fail to conform to applicable accounting standards.
- Misappropriation of assets: The effect of a theft of a business's assets that causes the financial statements not to conform to applicable accounting standards.

In order to discover fraud, auditors in some jurisdictions are encouraged to exercise professional scepticism. For example, 'The auditor should conduct the engagement with a mindset that recognizes the possibility that a material misstatement due to fraud could be present, regardless of any past experience with the entity and regardless of the auditor's belief about management's honesty and integrity' (SAS 99).

At the beginning of engagements, audit teams should also discuss how and where material misstatement due to fraud might be most likely to occur, and how management could perpetrate and conceal fraudulent reporting. In addition, audit teams should obtain the information needed to identify the risks of material misstatements due to fraud and identify fraud risk factors. These would include pressures to perpetrate fraud, opportunities to commit fraud and attitudes that rationalize fraudulent actions, as previously discussed.

In recent years, much effort has been devoted to fraud prevention measures. In general these can be grouped into three categories:

- Creating and maintaining a culture of honesty and high ethics.
- Evaluating the risk of fraud and implementing the processes, procedures and controls needed to mitigate risks and reduce the opportunities for fraud.
- Developing an appropriate oversight process.

Figure 13.16 shows excerpts from recommended measures to improve the antifraud environment in businesses.

FIGURE 13.16 MEASURES TO IMPROVE THE ANTIFRAUD ENVIRONMENT

CREATING A CULTURE OF HONESTY AND HIGH ETHICS

Setting the Tone at the Top
In many cases, particularly in larger organizations, it is necessary for management to both behave ethically and openly communicate its expectations for ethical behavior because most employees are not in a position to observe management's actions. Management must show employees through its words and actions that dishonest or unethical behavior will not be tolerated, even if the result of the action

(Continued)

FIGURE 13.16 *(CONTINUED)*

benefits the entity. Moreover, it should be evident that all employees will be treated equally, regardless of their position.

Creating a Positive Workplace Environment

Research results indicate that wrongdoing occurs less frequently when employees have positive feelings about an entity than when they feel abused, threatened, or ignored. Without a positive workplace environment, there are more opportunities for poor employee morale, which can affect an employee's attitude about committing fraud against an entity. Factors that detract from a positive work environment and may increase the risk of fraud include:

- Top management that does not seem to care about or reward appropriate behavior
- Negative feedback and lack of recognition for job performance
- Perceived inequities in the organization
- Autocratic rather than participative management
- Low organizational loyalty or feelings of ownership
- Unreasonable budget expectations or other financial targets
- Fear of delivering 'bad news' to supervisors and/or management
- Less-than-competitive compensation
- Poor training and promotion opportunities
- Lack of clear organizational responsibilities
- Poor communication practices or methods within the organization

Mitigating factors that help create a positive work environment and reduce the risk of fraud may include:

- Recognition and reward systems that are in tandem with goals and results
- Equal employment opportunities
- Team-oriented, collaborative decision-making policies
- Professionally administered compensation programs
- Professionally administered training programs and an organizational priority of career development

Hiring and Promoting Appropriate Employees

If an entity is to be successful in preventing fraud, it must have effective policies that minimize the chance of hiring or promoting individuals with low levels of honesty, especially for positions of trust. Proactive hiring and promotion procedures may include:

- Conducting background investigations on individuals being considered for employment or for promotion to a position of trust
- Thoroughly checking a candidate's education, employment history, and personal references
- Periodic training of all employees about the entity's values and code of conduct

- Incorporating into regular performance reviews an evaluation of how each individual has contributed to creating an appropriate workplace environment in line with the entity's values and code of conduct
- Continuous objective evaluation of compliance with the entity's values and code of conduct, with violations being addressed immediately

Training

New employees should be trained at the time of hiring about the entity's values and its code of conduct. This training should explicitly cover expectations of all employees regarding (1) their duty to communicate certain matters; (2) a list of the types of matters, including actual or suspected fraud, to be communicated with specific examples; and (3) information on how to communicate those matters.

In addition to training at the time of hiring, employees should receive refresher training periodically thereafter.

Confirmation

Management needs to clearly articulate that all employees will be held accountable to act within the entity's code of conduct.

Requiring periodic confirmation by employees of their responsibilities will not only reinforce the policy but may also deter individuals from committing fraud and other violations and might identify problems before they become significant.

Discipline

The way an entity reacts to incidents of alleged or suspected fraud will send a strong deterrent message throughout the entity, helping to reduce the number of future occurrences. The following actions should be taken in response to an alleged incident of fraud:

- A thorough investigation of the incident should be conducted.
- Appropriate and consistent actions should be taken against violators.
- Relevant controls should be assessed and improved.
- Communication and training should occur to reinforce the entity's values, code of conduct, and expectations.

EVALUATING ANTIFRAUD PROCESSES AND CONTROLS

Neither fraudulent financial reporting nor misappropriation of assets can occur without a perceived opportunity to commit and conceal the act. Organizations should be proactive in reducing fraud opportunities by (1) identifying and measuring fraud risks, (2) taking steps to mitigate identified risks, and (3) implementing and monitoring appropriate preventative and detective internal controls and other deterrent measures.

(*Continued*)

FIGURE 13.16 *(CONTINUED)*

Identifying and Measuring Fraud Risks

Management has the primary responsibility for establishing and monitoring all aspects of the entity's fraud risk-assessment and prevention activities. Fraud risks often are considered as part of an enterprise-wide risk assessment program, though they may be addressed separately. The fraud risk-assessment process should consider the vulnerability of the entity to fraudulent activity (fraudulent financial reporting, misappropriation of assets, and corruption) and whether any of those exposures could result in a material misstatement of the financial statements or material loss to the organization. Identifying fraud risks, organizations should consider organizational, industry, and country-specific characteristics that influence the risk of fraud.

Mitigating Fraud Risks

It may be possible to reduce or eliminate certain fraud risks by making changes to the entity's activities and processes. An entity may choose to sell certain segments of its operations, cease doing business in certain locations, or reorganize its business processes to eliminate unacceptable risks.

Implementing and Monitoring Appropriate Internal Controls

Some risks are inherent in the environment of the entity, but most can be addressed with an appropriate system of internal control. Once fraud risk assessment has taken place, the entity can identify the processes, controls, and other procedures that are needed to mitigate the identified risks.

In particular, management should evaluate whether appropriate internal controls have been implemented in any areas management has identified as posing a higher risk of fraudulent activity, as well as controls over the entity's financial reporting process. Because fraudulent financial reporting may begin in an interim period, management also should evaluate the appropriateness of internal controls over interim financial reporting.

DEVELOPING AN APPROPRIATE OVERSIGHT PROCESS

Oversight can take many forms and can be performed by many within and outside the entity, under the overall oversight of the audit committee (or board of directors where no audit committee exists).

Audit Committee or Board of Directors

The audit committee (or board of directors where no audit committee exists) should evaluate management's identification of fraud risks, implementation of antifraud measures, and creation of the appropriate 'tone at the top.'

Management

Management is responsible for overseeing the activities carried out by employees, and typically does so by implementing and monitoring processes, and controls. However, management also may initiate, participate in, or direct the commission and concealment of a fraudulent act. Accordingly, the audit committee (or the board of directors where no audit committee exists) has the responsibility to oversee the activities of senior management and to consider the risk of fraudulent financial reporting involving the override of internal controls or collusion.

Internal Auditors

Internal audits can be both a detection and a deterrence measure. Internal auditors can assist in the deterrence of fraud by examining and evaluating the adequacy and effectiveness of the system of internal control, commensurate with the extent of the potential exposure or risk in various segments of the organization's operations. In carrying out this responsibility, internal auditors should, for example, determine whether:

- The organizational environment fosters control consciousness.
- Realistic organizational goals and objectives are met.
- Written policies (for example, a code of conduct) exist that describe prohibited activities and the action required whenever violations are discovered.
- Appropriate authorization policies for transactions are established and maintained.
- Policies, practices, procedures, reports, and other mechanisms are developed to monitor activities and safeguard assets, particularly in high-risk areas.
- Communication channels provide management with adequate and reliable information.
- Recommendations need to be made for establishment or enhancement of cost-effective controls to help deter fraud.

Independent Auditors

Independent auditors can assist management and the board of directors (or audit committee) by providing an assessment of the entity's process for identifying, assessing, and responding to the risks of fraud.

Certified Fraud Examiners

Certified fraud examiners may assist the audit committee and board of directors with aspects of the oversight process either directly or as part of a team of internal auditors or independent auditors. Certified fraud examiners can provide extensive knowledge and experience about fraud that may not be available within a corporation.

Source: Excerpted from SAS 99, AU Section 316 Consideration of Fraud in a Financial Statement Audit, American Institute of Certified Public Accountings, Inc. 2002.

ON YOUR OWN

LEARNING OUTCOME REVIEW

1. Define fraud.
2. What three conditions are normally present when fraud is committed?
3. What is the term for a person who commits a fraud?

4. What two types of misstatements could occur in financial statements?
5. What is the auditor's responsibility in terms of discovery of fraud?
6. What are the three general categories of fraud prevention?
7. What steps can a business take to create a culture of honesty and high ethics?
8. What steps can a business take to evaluate antifraud processes and controls?
9. What steps can a business take to develop an appropriate oversight process?

Conclusion

Some 500 years ago, Fra Luca Bartolomeo de Pacioli created his ingenious system of double-entry accounting using manual journals and ledgers with all transactions scribbled by hand using quill pens. Now massive computer systems record trillions of transactions at lightning speed worldwide each day, often without human intervention, although still using the venerable old monk's debit and credit system. The modest process of keeping tabs on a business's financial results is now the nexus of an enterprise-wide system of automated processes that span the width and breadth of today's global business. Accounting systems do not so much keep tabs on the business's financial position, but rather continuously monitor its pulse.

What Fra Luca would not recognize is the complex systems of laws, regulations and accounting standards that have come about over the last half century, largely as a result of the rise of the modern limited liability company, and the need to regulate its growing power in business as well as its impact on the public at large. Even more recently accounting standards have been influenced by globalization, which gave rise to the International Financial Reporting Standards that we have explored in this book.

Globalization continues to expand the scope and power of large multinational businesses as well as the capital markets – both debt and equity – from which they draw their capital. Thus the stakes are high. More than ever, external users need financial information that allows them to understand and evaluate the financial position, performance and changes in financial position of the business. It falls to financial accounting, at least in part, to maintain the balance between those who manage the business as fiduciaries and the shareholders who own or otherwise have a stake in the business. Thus, we are likely to see further developments in international accounting standards as the global market economy continues to evolve.

In Part I, we were introduced to the financial statements – statement of financial position, statement of income, statement of changes in equity and the statement of cash flows – and the notes. An examination of the complete financial statements for Emirates Airline allowed us to see how the financial statements appear in practice.

Part II explained how the accounting information system accumulates and summarizes transactions and creates the financial statements. This includes the requirement that the information be adjusted under the accrual basis of accounting to reflect financial information in the appropriate time period. Part II also explored how accounting systems relate to other business systems like sales, purchases, product conversion, human resource management and asset management. We were also introduced to the role of accounting standards, specifically International Financial Reporting Standards (IFRS).

Part III explored how financial position is reported. The statement of financial position contains three elements: assets, liabilities and equity. Assets can be tangible, as in the case of inventories or property, plant and equipment, or intangible. Assets and liabilities can also be financial, as with trade receivables and payables, notes, bonds, equity and more sophisticated financial instruments like derivatives. The central issues for both assets and liabilities are what items should be recognized, how the asset or liability is measured, how it should be presented in the financial statements and what related information should be disclosed.

Part III discussed equity, which represents the residual interest of the shareholders, the owners of the business. Equity has two major components: contributed capital and reserves, which most commonly include retained earnings. Contributed capital comprises ordinary and preference shares, each of which bestows different rights on the shareholders.

Part IV examined the factors that change financial position. Three factors change equity. Contributed capital is increased when shares are issued to investors and decreased when the company purchases its own shares. Reserves are increased in two ways. First, profit or loss increases or decreases the retained earnings, respectively, while dividends decrease the retained earnings reserve. Second, changes can be recognized directly in equity, one example being the revaluation of equipment to fair value that exceeds the carrying amount of the asset.

Part IV also examined the activities that cause the cash and cash equivalents position of the business to change. These activities fall into three categories: operating, investing and financing. Each can simultaneously have both cash inflows and cash outflows. The statement of cash flows offers important clues about whether the business's cash flow pattern is appropriate for its current stage in the life cycle. No business can be sustained without liquidity and solvency.

Part V began by exploring requirements related to the presentation of financial statements. Specifically, a parent must present consolidated financial statements that report results for both itself and its subsidiaries as a single economic entity, with the minority interest's share of income and equity shown separately. Both consolidated and separate businesses must also report segment information that reports results by major geographic area, product and service, or customer. A company may also present interim financial statements for a period of less than one year.

Throughout Parts III to V, we have also examined the insights into the information reported by the financial statements offered by ratio analysis. Ratios are powerful and commonly used tools for understanding the liquidity, solvency and profitability of a single business over time (consistency) and between businesses (comparability). Horizontal and vertical analyses also provide insights into trends.

And finally, in this chapter we have examined the five assurance systems that give external users confidence that the financial statements provide a true and fair view of the financial position, performance and changes to financial position of the business. These include corporate governance, risk management, the system of internal control, internal auditing and independent auditing.

Taken together, the accounting information system in tandem with accounting standards and the assurance systems that provide confidence in financial reports allow the external users served by the financial accounting profession to make the decisions they need to make; for example, whether to hold or sell their investment in the entity or whether to reappoint or replace the management.

Summary

LEARNING OUTCOME 1
Assurance Defined

Assurance refers to the degree of certainty that the financial statements provide a true and fair view of the financial results of the reporting entity. Five major assurance systems function together to provide reasonable assurances: corporate governance, risk management, internal control, internal auditing and independent auditing.

LEARNING OUTCOME 2
Governance Explained

Corporate governance begins and ends with the board of directors, who are fiduciaries of the shareholders. Board members are expected to represent the interests of the shareholders over their personal interest in order to avoid conflicts of interest. Boards usually have both inside directors and nonexecutive directors; nonexecutive directors bring valued skills and an independent perspective. A business can have a unitary board, in which all powers are vested in a single board, or a multilevel board structure. In the latter, a business may have two or three boards to deal with issues like strategic policy, management issues and other issues.

Much of the board's work is done in committees. Most boards have an audit committee that is responsible for financial reporting, including oversight of both the independent and internal auditors. A nominations committee oversees board issues like recruiting new board members and board member performance reviews. The remuneration committee deals with compensation for board members and senior managers. Increasingly, boards are forming risk management committees to oversee the process of identifying, assessing and controlling risk in the company.

LEARNING OUTCOME 3
Risk Management Explained

All businesses face risk, which is the possibility that events will occur that prevent the business from achieving its objectives. Thus, in order for shareholders and other stakeholders to be protected, risk must be efficiently managed. This becomes more difficult when the business operates globally. Risk management is the process that identifies risks, assesses their likely impact and then effectively manages the level of risk. Different companies will have different risk appetites and thus manage risks differently. For a specific risk, a business must decide how much risk can or will be tolerated. Not all risks can or will be eliminated.

LEARNING OUTCOME 4
Internal Control Defined

A major element of assurance is the strength of the internal control system, which comprises the policies and procedures within the business that facilitate efficient and effective operations that allow the company to respond to significant risks; safeguard assets; ensure the quality of internal and external reporting; and monitor compliance with laws, regulations and internal business policies. A weak internal control system creates a higher level of risk and opportunity for error, fraud and misrepresentation.

A strong system of internal control is based on several control principles, including the assignment of responsibility; segregation of duties to prevent collusion between employees; documentation of policies, procedures and transactions; controls related to the safeguarding of physical assets, including cash; and independent verification of information. Guidance on internal control effectiveness is available through the Treadway Commission and the Turnbull Guidance.

LEARNING OUTCOME 5
Internal Auditing Defined

Internal auditing is a systematic and disciplined approach for evaluating and improving the effectiveness of risk management, control and governance. This includes, for example, ensuring that financial and operational information is reported reliably and with integrity; that assets are being safeguarded; that the company is complying with applicable laws, regulations and contracts; and so forth. Most large companies have in-house internal audit departments that conduct internal audits. Some companies will hire outside professionals to conduct an internal audit.

LEARNING OUTCOME 6
Independent Auditing Defined

Independent audits are conducted by professional auditors. Auditors typically have professional credentials that identify them as a chartered accountant or certified public accountant and legally qualify them to render an opinion about the financial results of businesses. In an independent audit engagement, the auditors first review the system of internal controls (see Learning Outcome 4) to assess its strength and collect evidence about whether transactions have been properly accounted for. From the results of this audit, an opinion is formed about whether the financial statements present a true and fair view of the reporting entity's financial results in accordance with applicable accounting standards.

LEARNING OUTCOME 7
Fraud Auditing and Forensic Accounting Explained

Unfortunately, fraud is a frequent occurrence in business. Fraud is a misrepresentation intentionally made to gain a material advantage, as compared to an error, which is unintentional. Although jurisdictions differ, the perpetrator must have damaged his or her victim who relied on the fraudulent information. The role of fraud auditing and forensic accounting is to gather evidence of fraud for the legal system.

From an accounting perspective, fraud is relevant if it causes the financial statements of the reporting entity not to conform to applicable accounting standards. This can occur because of fraudulent financial reporting, which intentionally misstates or omits amounts or disclosures, or because of misappropriation of assets, which is the theft of business assets.

REVIEW QUESTIONS

1. Explain why assurance systems are regarded as part of the overall financial accounting reporting system.
2. What are the five assurance systems?
3. Why is the board of directors important in providing assurance to shareholders and other users? What is the responsibility of the board?
4. What are the consequences if the board fails to perform its fiduciary duties?
5. If risk is not managed appropriately, why would that cast doubts on the reliability of the financial statements?
6. What would be your concerns about a company that has no nonexecutive directors on the board?
7. Which do you think would be more effective at corporate governance – a unitary or multilevel board? Explain the reasons for your answer.
8. Why do you think the use of committees like the audit committee, nominations committee, remuneration committee and risk management committee is an effective way for boards to get their work done?
9. Why is potential collusion between employees a problem? How do the various principles of internal control contribute to preventing collusion?
10. Describe the eight factors in the integrated framework for Enterprise Risk Management from the Treadway Commission.
11. What are the similarities and differences between the Treadway Commission's Enterprise Risk Management Framework and the Turnbull Guidance?
12. What are the limitations of internal control? How do you think these limitations can be overcome?
13. Compare and contrast the purposes, activities and objectives of an internal audit versus an independent audit.
14. What opinions can be given by an independent auditor?
15. Why do accountants confine their concern about fraud to fraudulent financial reporting and misappropriation of assets that cause the financial statements not to conform to applicable accounting standards?

Key terms

Adequate control over risk	External auditors
Assurance services	Fiduciary
Audit committee	Fraud
Audit engagement	Fraudulent financial reporting
Audit report	Independent auditors
Compliance	Inside director
Consulting services	Internal audit
Corporate governance	Internal auditing
Engagement	Internal control

Misappropriation of assets
Multilevel board
Nominations committee
Nonexecutive director
Perpetrator
Registered auditors
Remuneration committee

Residual risk
Risk
Risk appetite
Risk management
Risk management committee
Risk tolerance
Unitary board

Terminology review

For each of the following statements, insert the correct term from the list of key terms. Each term can be used more than once.

1. A(n) _____ represents the principals (owners) of a business.
2. _____ refers to the processes that identify, assess, manage and control potential events or situations, to provide reasonable assurance regarding the achievement of the organization's objectives.
3. A(n) _____ means that both inside directors and nonexecutive directors serve on a single board that discharges all board obligations.
4. _____ is the risk that remains once actions have been taken to reduce the likelihood of an adverse event.
5. A(n) _____ is a committee of the board, usually comprised of nonexecutive directors who oversee financial reporting and both the external and internal auditors.
6. A(n) _____ holds a position as an executive or manager within the business as well as being a member of the board.
7. _____ are objective examinations of evidence to provide an assessment on risk management, control or governance processes within the business, including financial, performance, compliance, system security and due diligence engagements.
8. _____ is the system of policies and procedures within the business that facilitates efficient and effective operations that allow a company to respond to significant risks; safeguards assets; ensures the quality of internal and external reporting; and monitors compliance with laws, regulations and internal business policies.
9. _____ is the possibility of an event occurring that will have an impact on the achievement of objectives and measured in terms of impact and likelihood.
10. A(n) _____ is a party who commits fraud.
11. A(n) _____ is a systematic and disciplined approach to evaluate and review the effectiveness of risk management, the internal control system and corporate governance processes.
12. _____ includes the organizational culture, policies and procedures that determine how an entity is directed, administered and controlled, as overseen by the business's board of directors.
13. _____ refers to levels of acceptable risk around specific objectives.
14. _____ is an independent, objective assurance and consulting activity designed to add value and improve an organization's operations. It helps an organization to accomplish its objectives by

bringing a systematic, disciplined approach to evaluate and improve the effectiveness of risk management, control and governance processes.

15. _____ involve advising business units on adding value and improving governance, risk management and control processes.

16. _____ is the effect of a theft of a business's assets that causes the financial statements not to conform to applicable accounting standards.

17. A(n) _____ is conducted by external accounting and auditing specialists who perform tests and other procedures on the business to enable them to express an opinion about whether the financial statements of the business have been prepared, in all material respects, in accordance with applicable accounting standards.

18. _____ means that there is reasonable assurance that the business's risk is managed efficiently.

19. A(n) _____ means that more than one board exists within the business.

20. _____ , also known as _____ or _____ , are professionally qualified individuals or firms who can perform independent audits and render an opinion regarding the financial statements.

21. _____ involves misstatement or omission of amounts or disclosures that cause financial statements not to conform to applicable accounting standards.

22. A(n) _____ serves on the board of directors but is not an executive or manager of the business entity.

23. A(n) _____ is a committee of the board that advises the board about candidates for the board, removal of existing directors and conducts performance evaluations of board members.

24. _____ is the level of tolerance for risk within an entity.

25. A(n) _____ is the formal report to the board of directors that contains the opinion of the independent auditors about whether the financial statements, in all material respects, present a true and fair view of the financial results of the business in accordance with applicable accounting standards.

26. _____ provide advice to business units on adding value and improving governance, risk management and control processes.

27. _____ refers to an engagement that evaluates whether the business is conforming to policies, plans, procedures, laws, regulations, controls and other requirements.

Application cases

1. Chemco is a well-established listed European chemical company involved in research into, and the production of, a range of chemicals used in industries such as agrochemicals, oil and gas, paint, plastics and building materials. A strategic priority recognised by the Chemco board some time ago was to increase its international presence as a means of gaining international market share and servicing its increasingly geographically dispersed customer base.

The Chemco board, which operated as a unitary structure, identified JPX Industries LLC as a possible acquisition target because of its good product 'fit' with Chemco and the fact that its geographical coverage would significantly strengthen Chemco's internationalization strategy. Based outside Europe in a region of growth in the chemical industry, JPX was seen by analysts as a good opportunity for

Chemco, especially as JPX's recent flotation had provided potential access to a controlling shareholding through the regional stock market where JPX operated.

When the board of Chemco met to discuss the proposed acquisition of JPX, a number of issues were tabled for discussion. Bill White, Chemco's chief executive, had overseen the research process that had identified JPX as a potential acquisition target. He was driving the process and wanted the Chemco board of directors to approve the next move, which was to begin the valuation process with a view to making an offer to JPX's shareholders. Bill said that the strategic benefits of this acquisition lay in increasing overseas market share and gaining economies of scale. While Chemco was a public company, JPX had been family owned and operated for most of its 35-year history.

75% of JPX's share capital was sold on its own country's stock exchange two years ago, but Leena Sharif, Chemco's company secretary, suggested that the corporate governance requirements in JPX's country were not as rigorous as in many parts of the world. She also suggested that the family business culture was still present in JPX and pointed out that it operated a two-tier board, with members of the family on the upper tier.

At the last annual general meeting, observers noticed that the JPX board, mainly consisting of family members, had 'dominated discussions' and had discouraged the expression of views from the company's external shareholders. JPX had no nonexecutive directors and none of the board committee structure that many listed companies like Chemco had in place. Bill reported that although JPX's department heads were all directors, they were not invited to attend board meetings when strategy and management monitoring issues were being discussed. They were, he said, treated more like middle management by the upper tier of the JPX board and important views may not be being heard when devising strategy.

Leena suggested that these features made the JPX board's upper tier less externally accountable and less likely to take advice when making decisions. She said that board accountability was fundamental to public trust and that JPX's board might do well to recognize this, especially if the acquisition were to go ahead. Chemco's finance director, Susan Brown, advised caution over the whole acquisition proposal. She saw it as being very risky. In addition to the uncertainties over exposure to foreign markets, she believed that Chemco would also have difficulties with integrating JPX into the Chemco culture and structure. While Chemco was fully compliant with corporate governance best practice, the country in which JPX was based had few corporate governance requirements.

Manprit Randhawa, Chemco's operations director, asked Bill if he knew anything about JPX's risk exposure. Manprit suggested that the acquisition of JPX might expose Chemco to a number of risks that could not only affect the success of the proposed acquisition but also, potentially, Chemco itself. Bill replied that he would look at the risks in more detail if the Chemco board agreed to take the proposal forward to its next stage.

Finance director Susan Brown had obtained the most recent annual report for JPX and highlighted what she considered to be an interesting, but unexplained, comment about 'negative local environmental impact' in its accounts. She asked chief executive Bill White if he could find out what the comment meant and whether JPX had any plans to make provision for any environmental impact.

Bill White was able to report, based on his previous dealings with JPX, that it did not produce any voluntary environmental reporting. The Chemco board broadly supported the idea of environmental reporting, although company secretary Leena Sharif recently told Bill White that she was unaware of the meaning of the terms 'environmental footprint' and 'environmental reporting' and so could not say whether she was supportive or not. It was agreed, however, that relevant information on JPX's environmental performance and risk would be necessary if the acquisition went ahead.

Required:

(a) Evaluate JPX's current corporate governance arrangements and explain why they are likely to be considered inadequate by the Chemco board.

(b) Manprit suggested that the acquisition of JPX might expose Chemco to a number of risks. Illustrating from the case as required, identify the risks that Chemco might incur in acquiring JPX and explain how risk can be assessed.

(c) Construct the case for JPX adopting a unitary board structure after the proposed acquisition. Your answer should include an explanation of the advantages of unitary boards and a convincing case *for* the JPX board changing to a unitary structure.

(d) Explain the role of nonexecutive directors (NEDs) and assess the specific contributions that NEDs could make to improve the governance of the JPX board. [ACCA adapted]

2. In a recent case, it emerged that Frank Finn, a sales director at ABC Co., had been awarded a substantial over-inflation annual basic pay award with no apparent link to performance. When a major institutional shareholder, Swanland Investments, looked into the issue, it emerged that Mr Finn had a cross-directorship with Joe Ng, an executive director of DEF Co. Mr Ng was a nonexecutive director of ABC and chairman of its remunerations committee.

Swanland Investments argued at the annual general meeting that there was 'a problem with the independence' of Mr Ng and, further, that Mr Finn's remuneration package as a sales director was considered to be poorly aligned to Swanland's interests because it was too much weighted by basic pay and contained inadequate levels of incentive. Swanland Investments proposed that the composition of Mr Finn's remuneration package be reconsidered by the remunerations committee and that Mr Ng should not be present during the discussion.

Another of the larger institutional shareholders, Hanoi House, objected to this, proposing instead that Mr Ng and Mr Finn both resign from their respective nonexecutive directorships as there was 'clear evidence of malpractice'. Swanland considered this too radical a step, as Mr Ng's input was, in its opinion, valuable on ABC's board.

Required:

(a) Explain the role of a remunerations committee and how the cross-directorship might undermine these roles at ABC Co.

(b) Swanland Investments believed Mr Finn's remunerations package to be 'poorly aligned' to its interests. With reference to the different components of a director's remunerations package, explain how Mr Finn's remuneration might be more aligned to shareholders' interests at ABC Co.

(c) Evaluate the proposal from Hanoi House that both Mr Ng and Mr Finn be required to resign from their respective nonexecutive positions. [ACCA adapted]

3. As part of a review of its internal control systems, the board of FF Co., a large textiles company, has sought your advice as a senior accountant in the company.

   FF's stated objective has always been to adopt the highest standards of internal control because it believes that by doing so it will not only provide shareholders with confidence in its governance, but also enhance its overall reputation with all stakeholders.

   However, FF's reputation for internal control has been damaged somewhat by a qualified audit statement last year (over issues of compliance with financial reporting standards) and an unfortunate internal incident the year before that. This incident concerned an employee, Miss Osula, expressing concern about the compliance of one of the company's products with an international standard on fire safety. She raised the issue with her immediate manager but he said, according to Miss Osula, that it wasn't his job to report her concerns to senior management. When she failed to obtain a response herself from senior management, she decided to report the lack of compliance to the press. This embarrassed the company and led to a substantial deterioration in FF's reputation.

   The specifics of the above case concerned a fabric produced by FF Co., which, in order to comply with an international fire safety standard, was required to resist fire for ten minutes when in contact with a direct flame. According to Miss Osula, who was a member of the quality control staff, FF was allowing material rated at only five minutes' fire resistance to be sold labelled as ten minute rated. In her statement to the press, Miss Osula said that there was a culture of carelessness in FF and that this was only one example of the way the company approached issues such as international fire safety standards.

   Required:
   (a) Describe how the internal control systems at FF Co. differ from a 'sound' system of internal control, such as that set out in the Turnbull guidance.
   (b) Explain, with reference to FF as appropriate, the ethical responsibilities of a professional accountant both as an employee and as a professional (see Chapter 2). [ACCA adapted]

4. Sonia Tan, a fund manager at institutional investor Sentosa House, was reviewing the annual report of one of the major companies in her portfolio. The company, Eastern Products, had recently undergone a number of board changes as a result of a lack of confidence in its management from its major institutional investors, of which Sentosa House was one.

   The problems started two years ago when a new chairman at Eastern Products, Thomas Hoo, started to pursue what the institutional investors regarded as very risky strategies, while at the same time failing to comply with a stock market requirement for the number of nonexecutive directors on the board. Sonia contacted Eastern's investor relations department to ask why it still was not in compliance with the requirements relating to nonexecutive directors. She was told that because Eastern was listed in a principles-based jurisdiction, the requirement was not compulsory. It was simply that Eastern chose not to comply with that particular requirement.

When Sonia asked how its board committees could be made up of an insufficient number of nonexecutive directors, the investor relations manager said that he didn't know and that Sonia should contact the chairman directly. She was also told that there was no longer a risk committee because the chairman saw no need for one. Sonia telephoned Thomas Hoo, the chairman of Eastern Products. She began by reminding him that Sentosa House was one of Eastern's main shareholders and currently owned 13% of the company. She went on to explain that she had concerns over the governance of Eastern Products and that she would like Thomas to explain his noncompliance with some of the stock market's requirements and also why he was pursuing strategies viewed by many investors as very risky.

Thomas reminded Sonia that Eastern had outperformed its sector in terms of earnings per share in both years since he had become chairman and that rather than question him, she should trust him to run the company as he saw fit. He thanked Sentosa House for its support and hung up.

Required:
(a) Explain what an 'agency cost' is and discuss the problems that might increase agency costs for Sentosa House in the case of Eastern Products.
(b) Describe, with reference to the case, the conditions under which it might be appropriate for an institutional investor to intervene in a company whose shares it holds.
(c) Evaluate the contribution that a risk committee made up of nonexecutive directors could make to Sonia's confidence in the management of Eastern Products.
(d) Assess the opinion given to Sonia that because Eastern Products was listed in a principles-based jurisdiction, compliance with the stock market's rules was 'not compulsory'. [ACCA adapted]

5. The board of Franks & Fisher, a large manufacturing company, decided to set up an internal control and audit function. The proposal was to appoint an internal auditor at mid-management level and also to establish a board-level audit committee made up mainly of nonexecutive directors.

The initiative to do so was driven by a recent period of rapid growth. The company had taken on many more activities as a result of growth in its product range. The board decided that the increased size and complexity of its operations had led to the need for greater control over internal activities and that creating an internal audit function was a good way forward.

The need was highlighted by a recent event where internal quality standards were not enforced, resulting in the stoppage of a production line for several hours. The production director angrily described the stoppage as 'entirely avoidable' and the finance director, Jason Kumas, said that the stoppage had been very costly. Mr Kumas said that there were problems with internal control in a number of areas of the company's operations and that there was a great need for internal audit.

He said that as the head of the company's accounting and finance function, the new internal auditor should report to him. The reasons for this, he said, were because as an accountant, he was already familiar with auditing procedure and the fact that he already had information on budgets and other 'control' information that the internal auditor would need.

It was decided that the new internal auditor needed to be a person of some experience and with enough personality not to be intimidated nor diverted by other department heads who might find the internal audits an inconvenience. One debate the board had was whether it would be better to recruit to the position from inside or outside the company.

A second argument was over the limits of authority that the internal auditor might be given. It was pointed out that while the board considered the role of internal auditor to be very important, it didn't want it to interfere with the activities of other departments to the point where their operational effectiveness was reduced.

Required:
(a) Explain, with reference to the case, the factors that are typically considered when deciding to establish internal audit in an organization.
(b) Construct the argument in favour of appointing the new internal auditor from outside the company rather than promoting internally.
(c) Critically evaluate Mr Kumas's belief that the internal auditor should report to him as finance director.
(d) Define 'objectivity' and describe characteristics that might demonstrate an internal auditor's professional objectivity. [ACCA adapted]

End notes

1. For further information on the Combined Code on Corporate Governance (June 2006), visit www.frc.org.uk or call +44 (0)20 7492 2300. To obtain copies of the Combined Code free of charge, visit www.frcpublications.com.
2. *Internal Audit 2012: A Study Examining the Future of Internal Auditing and the Potential Decline of a Controls-Centric Approach*, PricewaterhouseCoopers, www.pwc.com/internalaudit.
3. *PricewaterhouseCoopers 2007 State of the Internal Audit Profession Study: Pressures Build for Continual Focus on Risk*, PricewaterhouseCoopers, www.pwc.com/internalaudit.
4. *Internal Control: Guidance for Directors on the Combined Code*, Financial Reporting Council (www.frc.org).
5. *Internal Control: Revised Guidance for Directors on the Combined Code, October 2005*, Financial Reporting Council (www.frc.org).
6. *Ibid.*, §23.

Glossary

Accounting equation – Assets = Equity + Liabilities. Also **balance sheet equation.**

Accounting policies – Specific policies chosen by management to be applied when preparing the entity's financial statements.

Accounting process – the method by which financial information is recorded and then classified into accounts from which the financial statements are prepared.

Accounting standards – The laws, regulations and rules that govern financial reporting. Sources include governments, regulatory agencies and accounting industry organizations.

Accrue – To record at transaction for which cash has not been received or paid but which must be recognized in the current reporting period.

Accrual – The process of recording a journal entry that accrues an item.

Accrual basis – The effects of transactions and other events are recognized when they occur, and not when cash or its equivalent is received or paid.

Accumulated depreciation – The total of all depreciation expense which has been accumulated over the useful life of a depreciable asset.

Acid-test ratio – A liquidity ratio calculated by dividing cash and cash equivalents + trade accounts receivable + marketable securities by current liabilities.

Adequate control over risk – Reasonable assurance that the business' s risk in managed efficiently.

Adjusted trial balance – The trial balance that is generated after adjusting entries are recorded and from which the financial statements are prepared.

Adjusting entries – Journal entries made at the end of the accounting period to classify revenue or expense into the appropriate reporting period.

Administrative expenses – Operating expenses related to the general administrative of the business.

Aged receivables method – A method to estimate the amount of uncollectible trade accounts receivable based on the age of the amount owed.

Allotment – The process by which the board grants a right to receive shares, often subject to the vote of the membership.

Allowance method – A method to account for uncollectible trade accounts receivable. Under the allowance method, a contra account (allowance for uncollectible accounts) is maintained based on an estimate of the amount of receivables likely to be uncollectible. The actual write-off is taken against the allowance account and does not affect net income in that period.

Annual meeting – see **general shareholders' meeting.**

Annual report – The annual document that is published by companies reporting on the results and the status of the business. The annual report often includes the financial statements.

Applied ethics – Ethical theory as it is applied to real world situations.

Assets – Resources that are is expected to have economic benefit to the business entity in the future.

Asset register – a listing of the assets with information like the asset's identity (serial number, location or description), original cost and date of purchase.

Assurance services – Objective examinations of evidence to provide an assessment on risk management, control or governance processes within the business, including financial, performance, compliance, system security and due diligence engagements.

Audit – A set of procedures performed to determine the validity and reliability of the business's financial information. See also **independent audit** and **internal audit**.

Audit committee – A board committee usually comprised of nonexecutive directors, that oversees the company's financial reporting and the external and internal auditors.

Audit trail – A system of cross-referencing documents, journal entries, ledger accounts and other records so that a particular account balance can be traced to the source documents that gave rise to the transactions that affected that account.

Audit report – A formal report to the board of directors that contains the opinion of the independent auditors about whether the financial statements, in all material respects, present a true and fair view of the financial results of the business in accordance with applicable accounting standards.

Audit engagement – An audit conducted by an external accounting and auditing specialist who perform tests and other procedures on the business to enable them to express an opinion about whether the financial statements of the business have been prepared, in all material respects, in accordance with applicable accounting standards.

Authorized shares – Shares of capital stock that have been approved by the jurisdiction in which a corporation or other legal entity was chartered.

Available-for-sale financial assets – Financial assets which are either designated as available for sale or are not classified as (a) loans and receivables, (b) held-to-maturity investments, or (c) financial assets at fair value through profit or loss.

AVCO – See **average cost method**.

Average collection period – A liquidity ratio related to trade accounts receivable calculated by diving the number of days in the year by the receivables turnover ratio.

Average cost method – A cost flow assumption that allocates the average cost of goods available to both cost of goods sold and ending inventories.

Balance between benefits and cost – The benefits of reporting information should justify the costs associated with providing and using it.

Balance between qualitative characteristics – When a trade-off between qualitative characteristics is necessary.

Balance sheet equation – See **accounting equation**.

Bank overdraft – A situation in which a bank balance has been overdrawn and is thus negative.

Bank statement – A document issued by a bank that shows all activity on the depositor's bank account for some specified period of time.

Bankruptcy – A legal procedure that provides protection from creditors while a business is reorganized or liquidated.

Barter transaction – An exchange that does not involve money.

Base period analysis – An approach to horizontal analysis that compares amounts for each line item in the current period to an amount for the same line item in a base period.

Bond – A debt instrument in which a borrower, also known as the issuer, promises to repay an amount of money over times plus interest or coupon rate.

Bonus issue – See scrip issue.

Book value – See **carrying amount**.

Book value per share – A ratio calculated by dividing equity – preference shares amount by ordinary shares outstanding.

Borrowing costs – Interest and other costs that an entity incurs to borrow funds.

Bourse – See **equity securities market**.

Business ethics – How ethical theories and principles are applied to the business environment.

Business life cycle – The typical evolution of a business which has four phases: start-up, growth, expansion and maturity.

Callable bond – A bond that grants the issuer the right to purchase the bond from the investor at a certain price.

Capital – See **contributed capital**.

Capital assets – See **property, plant and equipment** and depreciable assets.

Capital appreciation – The increase in the real value of shares.

Capital expenditure – When a cost is included as part of a tangible or intangible asset.

Carriage-inwards costs (also **transportation-in** or **freight-in costs**) – Costs to bring goods to the current location.

Carriage-outwards costs (also **transportation-out** or **freight-out costs**) – Costs referring to the shipment of goods to customers.

Carrying amount – The cost of a depreciable asset less accumulated depreciation and accumulated impairment losses. See also book value and net book value.

Cash – Currency and demand deposits.

Cash debt coverage ratio – A liquidity ratio calculated by dividing cash from operating activities by average total liabilities.

Cash disbursements journal – A special journal that records similar transactions in which cash is always credited.

Cash equivalents – Financial investments that are readily convertible to a known amount of cash and are subject to an insignificant risk of change in value.

Cash flow statement – One of the four basic financial statements. This statement shows the sources and uses of cash from operational, investing and financing activities, and reconciles the cash balance at the beginning of the accounting period to the cash balance.

Cash flows – Inflows and outflows of cash to the business. Also sources and uses of cash.

Cash receipts journal – A special journal that records similar transactions in which cash is always debited.

Cash ratio – A liquidity ratio calculated by dividing cash and cash equivalents + marketable securities by current liabilities.

Chart of accounts – A listing of all authorized account titles.

Charter – An internal document, although sometimes filed with the government authority, which determines how a share-based business will be governed.

Closely held – See **privately held**.

Closing entries – Journal entries that remove the balances in temporary accounts (revenue, expenses and dividends) into the permanent retained earnings account.

Codes of conduct – Rules established by employers and professional organizations to provide guidance for appropriate ethical behavior. See also ethical codes.

Common share – See ordinary shares

Common stock – See **ordinary shares**.

Comparability – The ability for users to identify trends over time in a business entity's financial position and performance; and to identify trends between the financial statements of different entities to evaluate their relative financial positions, performance and changes in financial position.

Compensating balance – A minimum balance that must be kept on hand at all times as part of a loan agreement with a commercial lender.

Completeness – Information is complete when its omission can cause information to be false or misleading.

Compliance – Conformance with policies, plans, procedures, laws, regulations, contracts and other requirements.

Convertible feature – The right to convert bonds or preference shares into ordinary shares.

Consignment sales – A system by which a good is sold by a retailer, but that good is not owned by the retailer. Ownership remains with the original seller until such time that the good is sold.

Consistency – The use of the same set of accounting policies and procedures either from period to period within an entity, and between entities.

Consolidated financial statements – Financial statements of a group presented as those of a single economic entity.

Consulting services – Advisory or service activities intended to add value and improve governance, risk management and control processes.

Contra account – A contra account is appended to another account and is used to adjust that account's balance.

Contributed capital – The amount the owners have invested in the business. See also **paid-in capital** and **share capital**.

Control – The power to govern the financial and operating policies of an entity so as to obtain economic benefits from its activities.

Conversion cycle – That portion of accounting cycle that relates to the material, labour and other resource costs associated with manufacturing goods.

Corporate governance – The organizational culture, policies and procedures that determine how the entity is directed, administered and controlled.

Corporation – An entity that has legal status under the laws and regulations of a particular jurisdiction. A corporation can typically own assets in its own name, create debt obligations and engage in transactions, including legal proceedings, with other entities.

Cost – The amount of cash or cash equivalents paid or the fair value of the other consideration given to acquire an asset at the time of its acquisition or construction, or when applicable, the amount attributed to that asset when initially recognized.

Cost model – An asset recorded at cost and changed subsequently only for accumulated depreciation and accumulated impairment.

Cost of goods available – Calculated by adding inventories still on hand at the beginning of the reporting period to the purchases made in the current reporting period.

Cost of goods sold – The cost of sales for a merchandising or manufacturing company. See **cost of sales.**

Cost of sales – An expense that is related to a good or purchased and then sold during the reporting period.

Coupon rate – The stated interest on a bond.

Credit – Abbreviated **CR**. A credit represents what is given in a transaction.

Credit memo – Authorization for the customer's account to be credited when a customer has requested a return or allowance.

Cumulative preference dividend – All past preference dividends that have not been declared and therefore have not been paid must be satisfied before any dividends can be declared and paid to ordinary shareholders.

Current assets – Assets that the entity expects to realize, sell or consume within a normal operating cycle; holds for the primary purposes of trading; expects to realize within 12 months; or is cash (unless restricted from being exchanges or used to settle a liability within 12 months). Also **short-term assets.**

Current cash debt coverage ratio – A liquidity ratio calculated by dividing cash from operating activities by average current liabilities.

Current cost – The amount of cash or cash equivalents that would have to be paid if the same or an equivalent asset was currently acquired. The amount of cash or cash equivalents that would be required to currently settle an obligation.

Current liabilities – A liability that the entity expects to settle in its normal operating cycle; holds primarily for the purpose of trading; is due to be settled within 12 months; or the entity does not have an unconditional right to defer settlement of the liability for at least 12 months. Also **short-term liabilities**.

Current ratio – A liquidity ratio calculated by dividing current assets by current liabilities.

Current portion of non current borrowing – The amount owed within the next 12 months on a non current liability.

Customer purchase order – The source document for an order to purchase equipment placed by a customer.

Date of record – the date that determines which shareholders will receive a dividend, i.e. the shareholders on the date of record.

Day book – See **special journal**.

Days in inventory – A liquidity ratio calculated by dividing the number of days in the year by the inventories turnover ratio.

Debit – Abbreviated **DR**. A debit represents what is received in a transaction.

Debit memo – Authorization to debit an account as when the business returns an item to a supplier for credit (the debit memo reduces trade accounts payable).

Debt securities – Forms of debt that can be publicly traded, which include primarily bonds and commercial paper.

Debt ratio – A solvency ratio calculated by dividing total assets by total liabilities.

Debt to equity ratio – A solvency ratio calculated by dividing total liabilities by total equity.

Declaration date – The date on which the board of directors declares a dividend and it therefore becomes a legal obligation of the entity.

Declining balance method – See reducing balance method and **diminishing balance method**.

Demand deposit – An account from which funds normally held at a commercial bank can be withdrawn without prior notice.

Depreciable amount – the cost of an asset less its residual value.

Depreciable asset – see property plant and equipment or **capital assets**.

Depreciation – The systematic allocation of the depreciable amount of an asset over its useful life.

Development – The application of research findings and other knowledge to a plan or design of production of a new good or service prior to commercial production or use.

Diluted earnings per share – Diluted earnings per share is calculated by adjusting the denominator of the basic earnings per share calculation by assuming that all convertible instruments are converted, all options and warrants are exercised, and that ordinary shares are issued in compliance with any outstanding obligations.

Dilution – The effect that conversion of all convertible financial instruments would have on earnings per share.

Diminishing balance method (also reducing balance method or declining balance method) – Depreciation expense shifted to earlier time periods in an asset's useful life.

Direct labour – Those costs related to the conversion of materials into product in the statement of cash flows.

Direct material – Goods that go into manufacturing of the product itself.

Direct method – A method whereby major classes of gross cash receipts and gross cash payments are disclosed in the statement of cash flows.

Discount – The amount by which a bond or other financial instrument sells below its par or stated value.

Dividend income – Income to the business from dividends paid on shares of another entity owned by the business.

Dividend yield ratio – The amount of dividend paid to investors as a percentage of the share price.

Dividends – Distributions of profits to holders of equity instruments in proportion to their holdings of a particular class of stock.

DR – Abbreviation for **debit**.

Double-entry method – The method used in the accounting process whereby two sides of transactions are recorded: What's received and What's given.

Earnings per share – Calculated by dividing the profit or loss attributable to ordinary shareholders by the weighted average number of ordinary shares outstanding during the period. The profit and loss attributable to ordinary shares is the profit or loss from continuing operations less preference dividends, and adjustments arising from the settlement of preference shares and other similar effects of preference shares.

Engagement – A specific internal audit assignment or review activity such as an internal audit, fraud examination, consultancy or self-assessment review.

Equity – The difference between assets and liabilities. Equity represents the business owners' residual interest in the assets after all liabilities have been deducted.

Equity instrument – A contract that grants a residual interest in the assets of an entity after deducting all liabilities.

Equity securities – Forms of ownership shares that are publicly traded on capital markets, typically referred to as stock markets or bourses.

Equity securities market – A public market on which equity securities such as ordinary shares can be bought and sold. Also **stock market** or **bourse**.

Ethical codes – See codes of conduct

Expansion phase – A phase of the business life cycle in which a business has usually established a presence in the market lace and may have a positive cash flow from operating activities.

Expenditure – Any outlay of cash or other consideration.

Expenditures subsystem – The accounting subsystem related to the purchase of merchandise and supplies from suppliers for use in the business. The expenditure subsystem typically records the cost and the associated trade accounts payable, and transactions for the subsequent payment of the payables. Also **purchase subsystem**.

Expenses – Decreases in economic benefits during the period in the form of outflows or depletions of assets, or incurrence of liabilities that reduce equity (other than those related to contributed capital). See also expired cost.

Expired cost – See expenses.

Extended trial balance – A worksheet version of the adjusted trail balance used to prepare the financial statements.

External auditors – See independent auditors.

External users – Third-party stakeholders in a business, that commonly include investors and their representatives, employees, lenders, suppliers and other trade creditors, customers, governments and their agencies, and the public.

Face value – The nominal or stated value of a bond or note.

Fair value – The amount for which an asset could be exchanged, or a liability settled, between knowledgeable, willing parties in an arm's-length transaction.

Faithful representation – Information must be **prudent** and **complete** (see separate definitions for each term).

Fiduciary – A legal concept that imposes the highest standard of care under law. A fiduciary acts as an agent of the principal, and must put that principal's interests ahead of his own.

FIFO – See **first-in, first-out**.

Finance expense – Expenses associated with borrowing funds, also interest expense.

Financial accounting – One of the two major fields of accounting that recognizes, measures and reports information on the financial position, performance and changes in financial position of the business, primarily to external users.

Financial asset – An asset that is cash, a cash equivalent, an equity instrument of another entity, a contractual right to receive cash or another financial asset, or a contract that will be settled in the entity's own equity instruments.

Financial assets or liabilities at fair value through profit or loss – a financial asset or financial liability that is classified as held from trading or is upon initial recognition is designated by the entity as at fair value through profit and loss.

Financial liability – A liability that is a contractual obligation to deliver cash or another financial asset or a contract that will be settled in the entity's own equity instruments.

Financial position – The relationship of the assets, liabilities and equity of an entity, as reported in the statement of financial position.

Financing activities – One of the three categories of sources and uses on the cash flow statement. Financing activities relate to changes in the size and composition of contributed capital and borrowings.

Financing expense – The amount of interest and other finance costs paid for borrowing money. See also **interest expense**.

Finished goods – All items on which production has been completed and that are ready for sale.

First-in, first-out method – A method for allocating inventory costs to cost of sales and ending inventory. First-in, first-out allocates the oldest costs to cost of sales and the most recent costs to ending inventory.

Fixed assets – See **property, plant and equipment**.

Fixed assets cycle – An accounting cycle that relates to the acquisition and disposal of fixed assets, and their depreciation or amortization.

Fixed income securities – Bonds and corporate debt.

FOB Destination – A shipping term that means that title to goods transfers to the buyer when the goods are delivered to the buyer.

FOB Shipping Point – A shipping term that means that title to goods transfers to the buyer when the goods are delivered to the carrier by the seller for shipment.

Fraud – Deception for personal gain. Laws generally require that the deception must have been based on an intentionally made false representation. In addition, the victim must have suffered material damage after having acted on the representation made by the perpetrator.

Fraudulent financial reporting – Misstatement or omission of amounts or disclosures that cause financial statements not to conform to applicable accounting standards.

Free cash flow – A ratio calculated by subtracting capital expenditures and cash dividends from cash provided from operating activities.

Gain – Increases in economic benefits and as such no different in nature from revenue.

General ledger – A listing of all accounts with detail on entries that comprise each account's balance. Account information in the general ledger is sometimes detailed in a subsidiary ledger.

General-purpose financial statements – Financial statements that are intended to meet the needs of users who are not in a position to require an entity to prepare reports tailored to their particular information needs.

General shareholders' meeting (or annual meeting) – An annual gathering of members. General meetings provide members with an opportunity to hear management's views on business developments and financial results.

Going concern – The assumption that a business entity will continue operating without threat of liquidation in the foreseeable future.

Goodwill – An intangible asset that represents the future economic benefits that arise from assets acquired when one business buys another

Gross margin – See **gross profit**.

Gross pay – The amount to be paid to an employee for services rendered before payroll deductions are subtracted.

Gross profit – Revenue less cost of sales or cost of goods sold.

Gross profit ratio – A profitability ratio calculated by dividing gross profit by net sales.

Gross sales – Sales before adjustments are made to deduct sales discounts and sales returns and allowances to calculate net sales. The total of all sales.

Growth phase – A phase of the business life cycle in which a business is beginning to produce and market a product or service.

Group – A parent company and all its subsidiaries.

Held-for-trading – See financial assets or liabilities at fair value though profit or loss.

Held-to-maturity investments – Are financial assets with fixed or determinable payments and a fixed maturity that an entity has the positive intention and ability to hold to maturity.

Historical cost – An accounting measurement basis in which assets are recorded for an amount of cash or cash equivalents paid or the fair value of the consideration given to acquire them at the time of their acquisition. Liabilities are measured by the amount of proceeds received in exchange for the obligation or in some circumstances, at the amounts of cash or cash equivalents expected to be paid to satisfy the liability in the normal course of business.

Horizontal analysis – An analysis that compares amounts on each line item on the statement of financial position and the statement of comprehensive income over time.

Impairment – A situation in which the recoverable amount of an asset is less than its carrying amount.

Imprest petty cash – See **petty cash.**

Income – **See revenue.**

Income tax expense – See **tax expense.**

Independent auditor – A professional accountant who tests the company's policies and procedures (internal controls) and performs tests to ascertain the validity and reliability of the company's accounting information. Generally, the independent auditor provides an opinion about whether this information fairly presents the company's financial position also external auditors.

Indirect costs – See **overhead.**

Indirect labour – Labour costs that relate to manufacturing but are not directly associated with production.

Indirect materials – Materials costs that relate to manufacturing but are not directly associated with production.

Indirect method – A method of calculating cash flows that adjusts profit or loss for the effects of transactions of a noncash nature, any deferrals or accruals of past of future operating cash receipts or payments, and items of income and expense associated with investing or financing activities.

Initial public offering (IPO) – The shares of a business sold into a public equities market for the first time.

Inside directors – Members of the board of directors who also hold an executive or management position within the business entity.

Institutional investors – Organizations that pool significant sums of money to invest in debt and equity securities.

Intangible assets – An identifiable nonmonetary asset without physical substance.

Interest expense – See **finance expense.**

Interest income – Income that is earned on debt instruments issued by other business entities.

Internal audit – An audit performed internally within the company to test the company's policies and procedures (internal controls) and perform tests to ascertain the validity and reliability of the company's accounting information. See also **audit.**

Internal auditing – The process of performing an internal audit.

Internal control – The system of policies and procedures within the business that facilitates efficient and effective operations that allow a company to respond to significant risks; safeguards assets; ensures the quality of internal and external reporting; and monitors compliance with laws, regulations and internal business policies.

Internal users – Managers, other employees and members of the board of directors.

International Accounting Standards (IAS) – Accounting standards promulgated by the former International Accounting Standards Committee (IASC), and continued in effect under the International Accounting Standards Board (IASB).

International Accounting Standards Board (IASB) – A nonprofit organization that sets international accounting standards. See www.iasb.org.

International Financial Reporting Interpretations Committee (IFRIC) – A committee that handles situations where no authoritative guidance is available from the IASB.

International Financial Reporting Standard (IFRS) – International Financial Reporting Standards adopted by the International Accounting Standards Board (IASB), International Accounting Standards (IAS) adopted by the former International Accounting Standards Committee (IASC), and Interpretations by the International Financial Reporting Interpretations Committee (IFRIC) and the former Standing Interpretations Committee that operated under the IASC.

Inventories – Assets held for sale in the ordinary course of business; in the process of production for such sale; or in the form of materials or supplies to be consumed in the production process or in the rendering of services. Also **merchandise inventory** or **merchandise.**

Inventories turnover ratio – A liquidity ratio that divides sales by average inventories.

Investing activities – The acquisition and disposal of long-term assets and other investments not included in cash equivalents.

Investment in associates – An amount representing the ownership of part of another business over which the entity has significant influence.

Investment in own shares – See **treasury shares.**

Investment professionals – Financial analysts, advisers and others who evaluate the financial position and performance of companies and offer opinions and advice about whether to invest in the companies' debt and equity securities.

Investment property – Land or buildings, or both, held by the owner or a lessee under a finance lease to earn rentals or for capital appreciation, or both.

Invoice – A document sent by a seller to a buyer that contains billing information including the product or services provided, price to be paid by the buyer and the payment terms. An invoice is a sales invoice to the seller, and a purchase invoice to the buyer.

IOU – Informal script that indicates indebtedness.

Issued shares – That portion of authorized shares already issued and which is the total of outstanding shares plus treasury shares.

Issuer – The entity which sells debt or equity securities.

Loans and receivables – Financial assets with fixed or determinable payments that are not quoted in an active market.

IPO – See **initial public offering.**

Joint stock company – An alternative term for a limited liability company.

Journal – A chronological listing of journal entries. The journal is where journal entries are first recorded, thus journals are corrections referred to as the 'books of original entry'.

Journal entry – A method of coding information related to a transaction in a way that can be entered into and processed by an accounting system. Journal entries include the date of the transactions, account titles, the amount received (debit) and given (credit) in the transaction, and an explanation.

Ledger – The ledger contains the detail of all accounts in the accounting system.

Liabilities – Obligations of the business that are expected to be satisfied in the future.

Limited liability company – A legally autonomous entity under the laws and regulations of the jurisdiction in which it is registered or incorporated. A limited liability company can typically own assets, create debt obligations, enter into legal contracts, and engage in transactions on its own cognizance.

Liquidation – The process by which a business entity is brought to an end.

Liquidity – The availability of cash in the near future after taking account of financial commitments over this period.

Long term – More than one year.

Long-term assets – See **noncurrent assets.**

Long-term liabilities – See **noncurrent liabilities.**

Loss – An outflow of economic benefits not related to ordinary business activity, which is not expected to recur frequently.

Lower of cost and net realizable value – The method of determining whether inventories have declined below the carrying amount.

Managerial accounting – One of the two major fields of accounting that collects, organizes and reports financial information related to internal business decisions made by management.

Manufacturing overhead – See **overhead**.

Materiality – When the omission or misstatement of information could influence users' decisions that are based on the entity's financial reports.

Maturity date – The date on which the issuer must repay the principal on a bond or other financial liability.

Maturity phase – A phase of the business life cycle in which a business has reached the point where its infrastructure is fully developed, even though it may replace and upgrade assets and invest in new products and services as marketplace opportunities evolve.

Measurement – The determination of what monetary amount will be recognized for a transaction.

Member – see **shareholder**.

Merchandise – See **inventory**.

Merchandise inventory – See **inventory**.

Minority interest – See **noncontrolling interest**.

Misappropriation of assets – The effect of a theft of a business's assets that causes the financial statements not to conform to applicable accounting standards.

Monetary unit assumption – The fact that accounting information is expressed in terms of money.

Mortgage – A form of debt for the purchase of real estate, whereby the real estate is pledged as security for the debt.

Multilevel board – More than one board existing within a business.

Net book value – See **carrying amount**.

Net income – See **profit or loss**.

Net pay – Gross pay less payroll deductions.

Net purchases – Calculated by subtracting purchase discounts and purchase returns and allowances from purchases.

Net realizable value – The estimated selling price less the estimated selling costs of completion and the estimated costs necessary to make the sale.

Net receivables – Gross trade accounts receivable less the allowance for uncollectible accounts.

Net sales – Gross sales less sales discounts, less sales returns and allowances.

Neutrality – Information with a freedom from bias so that it does not influence a decision or judgement in order to achieve a predetermined result or outcome.

Nominal accounts – See **temporary accounts**.

Nominal interest rate – See stated interest rate

Nominal value – See **par value**.

Nominations committee – A committee of a board of directors that identifies candidates to serve on the board and advises the board about directors who may need to be removed.

Noncontrolling interest – The equity in a subsidiary not attributable to the parent. See also **minority interest**.

Noncurrent assets – Assets that do not meet the definition for current assets. See **long-term assets**.

Noncurrent liabilities – Liabilities that do not meet the definition for current liabilities. See also **long-term assets**.

Nonexecutive director – Member of the board of directors who do not hold an executive or management position within the business entity.

Normal balance – The balance, whether debit or credit, that is typical for that account. The normal balance for any expense, asset or dividend account is a debit, and the normal balance for any revenue, liability or equity account is a credit. A normal debit account is increased by a debit and decreased by a credit, and vice versa.

Note – See promissory note

Notes – One element of a complete set of financial elements. Notes contains additional information or explanations of amounts that appear in the financial statement

Note payable – An obligation to pay a specified amount of money. See promissory note.

Note receivable – An obligation another entity has to pay the business a specified amount of money. See promissory note.

On account – Something purchased or sold on credit rather than using cash. Also **on credit**.

On credit – See **on account**.

Operating activities – The principal revenue-producing activities of an entity and other activities that are not investing or financing activities.

Operating cash flow per share – A liquidity ratio calculated by dividing cash from operating activities by ordinary shares outstanding.

Operating cycle – The time between the acquisition of assets for processing and their realization in cash or cash equivalents.

Operating expenses – Expenses that are not related to the good or service being produced and are either selling expenses or administrative expenses.

Operating income – See **operating profit**.

Operating profit – The profit from ordinary operations before other income and expenses, finance expense and tax expense are deducted. Also **operating income**.

Ordinary shares – An equity instrument that is subordinate to all other classes of equity instruments. See common shares and **common stock**.

Other comprehensive income – Income that is not recognized in profit or loss.

Outstanding shares – Issued shares less treasury shares.

Overhead – Manufacturing costs that have no direct association with a particular job. See indirect cost.

Paid-in capital – See **contributed capital**.

Par value – An amount per share designated when a share-based entity is registered.

Parent – An entity that has one or more subsidiaries.

Participating preference shares – A preference share that gives preference shareholders the right to receive a share of dividends beyond the preference dividend.

Partnership – An association of two or more persons or businesses as owners that conduct a business for profit.

Payables subsidiary ledger – The subsidiary ledger that provides detailed information on all trade accounts payable.

Payment date – The date on which a dividend is actually distributed to shareholders.

Payroll deductions – Amounts deducted from an employee's gross pay such as income taxes, union dues and health insurance.

Payroll subsidiary ledger – A subsidiary ledger that details all transactions for each employee.

Percentage of sales method – When a business relies on its past experience to predict the amount of current credit sales that will be uncollectible.

Performance – The relationship of the income and expenses of an entity as reported in the statement of comprehensive income.

Period to period analysis – Horizontal analysis that compares amounts for a line item in a current period with the amount for the same line item in the previous period.

Periodic inventory method – The cost of goods available is assigned to cost of goods sold and ending inventory at the end of the reporting period.

Permanent accounts – Balance sheet accounts are permanent; any account except revenue, expenses and dividends. See also **real accounts**.

Perpetrator – A party who commits fraud.

Perpetual inventory method – When inventory costs are updated continuously as sales and purchases of inventory occurs.

Petty cash – Cash that is kept on hand to pay small expenses. See **imprest petty cash**.

Post-closing trial balance – The trial balance that is generated after closing entries are recorded and after the financial statements are prepared.

Posting – The process of classifying debits and credits recorded in the journal into accounts in the ledger.

Pre-emptive rights – The legal rights of shareholders to have first refusal on new share issuances.

Preference shares – Shares that provide a stated dividend and which have a priority claim on assets over ordinary shares in a liquidation.

Preferred shares – See **preference shares**.

Premium – The amount by which a bond or other financial instrument sells above its par or stated value.

Prepaid expense – An asset created when cash is paid in advance for a future expense.

Present value – A current estimate of the present discounted value of the future net cash flows in the normal course of business.

Price–earnings ratio (also PE ratio or multiple) – the share price divided by earnings per share.

Primary market – The first time a specific share issue is sold to the public.

Principles-based standards – An approach to accounting standards that is based on the development of broad principles that can be applied with flexibility in different jurisdictions.

Privately held company – A company that is not publicly traded. See also **closely held**.

Profit – The amount by which revenue exceeds expenses.

Profit margin ratio – A profitability ratio calculated by dividing profit by net sales.

Profit or loss – Revenue less expenses.

Promissory note – A contractual obligation by one entity to pay money in the future for money borrowed in the past to another entity.

Property, plant and equipment – Tangible items held for use in the production of goods or services, rental to others or for administrative purposes, and expected to be used for more than one period. Also **capital assets** and **fixed assets**.

Provision – A liability that has either an uncertain timing or amount.

Prudence – The degree of caution exercised in judgments about uncertainties in reporting information.

Publicly traded – A company that is listed on a securities market.

Purchase discounts – Discounts offered by a supplier for timely payment.

Purchase journal – A special journal to record similar transactions to purchase goods and services.

Purchase requisition – An internal document representing a request for a purchase.

Purchase returns and allowances – Account records for when the business returns merchandise to a supplier or requests an allowance.

Purchase order – A document that approves a purchase requisition and is sent to the supplier for fulfillment.

Qualitative characteristic – An attribute that makes information provided in financial statements useful to users.

Real accounts – See **permanent accounts**.

Real value – The actual price of a share.

Realizable value – The amount of cash or cash equivalents that could currently be obtained by selling an asset in an orderly disposal.

Realization – When a transaction has been completed or consummated.

Rebates – A refund of a portion of the list price offered by the seller as an incentive to purchase an item.

Receivable subsidiary ledger – The subsidiary ledger that provides detailed information on all trade accounts receivable.

Receivables turnover ratio – A liquidity ratio calculated by dividing net credit sales by average receivables.

Receiving report – An internal report that documents the receipt of goods from a supplier.

Recognition – The process of incorporating into the financial statements an item that meets the definition of an element: asset, liability, equity, income or expense. In addition, it must be probable that the future economic benefit associated with the item flows to or from the entity, and the items cost or value must be able to be measured reliably.

Record – The process of entering a journal entry into the journal.

Reducing balance method – See **diminishing balance method** or declining balance method.

Register of members – See **shareholder register**.

Registered auditors – See independent auditors.

Relevance – Information that makes a difference to users' decisions either by helping them to evaluate the effects of past, present or future transactions or other events on future cash flows (predictive value), or to confirm or correct their previous evaluations (confirmatory value).

Reliability – Information that is free from material error and that faithfully represents what it purports to represent.

Remittance advice – A document accompanying a payment to advise the supplier what invoice or account is being paid.

Remuneration committee – A board committee that concerns itself with compensation for the board and top management.

Reporting date – The last day of the period for which the financial statements are issued.

Reporting entity – Any entity that has users who rely on its financial statements and notes as their major source of information.

Reporting period – The period covered by the financial statement which ends on the reporting date.

Research – Original and planned investigation undertaken to gain new scientific or technical knowledge and understanding.

Reserve – Equity other than contributed capital that has been designated for a specific purpose.

Residual risk – The risk that remains once actions have been taken to reduce the likelihood of an adverse event.

Residual value – The estimated amount that an entity would currently obtain from disposal of an asset, after deducting the estimated costs of disposal.

Restricted cash – An amount that has been set aside for a specific purpose.

Return on assets – A profitability ratio calculated by dividing profit by average total assets.

Return on investment – A profitability ratio calculated by dividing profit + after tax interest expense by average noncurrent liabilities + equity.

Revaluation model – An asset is adjusted to its fair value subsequent to its acquisition if the fair value can be reliably measured.

Revenue – The gross inflow of economic benefits during the period arising from the entity's ordinary activities that increase equity (other than increases related to contributed capital).

Revenue expenditure – A cost that is expensed.

Rights issue – When existing shareholders are allowed to purchase shares at a discounted price in proportion to their current shareholdings.

Risk – The possibility of an event occurring that will have an impact on the achievement of objectives and measured in terms of impact and likelihood.

Risk appetite – The level of tolerance for risk within an entity.

Risk management – Processes that identify, assess, manage and control potential events or situations, to provide reasonable assurance regarding the achievement of the organization's objectives.

Risk management committee – A board committee responsible for identifying, assessing and controlling risk.

Risk tolerance – Levels of acceptable risk around specific objectives.

Royalties – Charges for the use of long-term assets such as patents, trademarks and software.

Rules-based standards – An approach to accounting standards based on compliance with specific guidelines.

Sales discount – A reduction in the amount the customer is expected to pay because of timely payment by the customer.

Sales invoice – A bill to the customer that shows the date, what equipment was shipped, the quantity and the total amount owed to the company.

Sales order – A document that is the official record of a customer's order.

Sales returns and allowances – A contra account to the gross sales account that accumulates amounts related to merchandise that has been returned for credit by customers, or allowances that have been given to customers for damaged merchandise or other reasons.

Sales tax – A tax levied on the final sales price of goods and services.

Scrip issue (also bonus issue or share dividend) – When additional shares are issued to members in some proportion to their current shareholdings.

Secondary market – A public market that trades debt or equity instruments after they have been issued by the business.

Secured bond – Bonds that are backed up by a pledge of some asset such as real estate. The investor has a priority claim on the pledged asset in the event of liquidation.

Selling expenses – Operating expenses related to sales, marketing, advertising and distribution costs.

Serial bond – A bond on which the principle is paid in instalments over the term of the bond.

Shares – Evidence of ownership of a limited liability company. See also stocks.

Share-based entities – The general term for a business entity whose ownership is based on ownership shares.

Share capital – See **contributed capital.**

Share dividend – See scrip issue

Share premium – The amount shares were issued for above the par or nominal value.

Share price – The amount a share sells for. See real value.

Shareholder – An individual or an institution that owns shares. See also vendor.

Shareholder register – The official list of shareholders at any point in time.

Share options – Granting the right, but not the obligation, to buy at a reduced price.

Share split – An increase in the number of shares based on a ratio that is determined by the board of directors.

Short term – Less than one year.

Short-term assets – See **current assets.**

Short-term liabilities – See **current liabilities.**

Sole proprietor – The owner of a sole proprietorship.

Solvency – The availability of cash over the longer term to meet financial commitments as they fall due.

Sources and uses – See **cash flows.**

Source document – Either a hardcopy document or softcopy record that verifies information related to a transaction.

Special journal – Journals used to make entries that are similar, such as cash receipts or cash disbursements.

Specific identification – The cost for each separate inventory item can be identified and is therefore allocated to cost of saleswhen the sale is made.

Start-up phase – A phase of the business life cycle in which a business

Stated interest rate – The interest rate paid by the issuer based on the face or stated value. Also nominal interest rate.

Stated value – An amount set by the board of directors on each share that sets the legal capital of the share-based entity.

Statement – A document sent to a customer each month showing all amounts owing.

Stock – See shares.

Stock exchange – See **equity securities market.**

Straight-line method – The method of allocation an asset's cost over its useful life in equal amounts to each period.

Stock market – See **equity securities market.**

Subsidiary – A company owned in whole or part by a parent company.

Subsidiary ledger – A listing of all detail in a general ledger account.

Tax expense – Taxes paid to governments on income. See also **income tax expense.**

Temporary accounts –Temporary accounts include all revenue, expense and dividend accounts, which are closed at the end of the accounting period. See also **permanent accounts** also **nominal accounts.**

Term – The life of a bond.

Term bond – A bond on which the principal (the amount borrowed) is due on the maturity date.

Times interest earned ratio – A solvency ratio calculated by dividing profit + interest expense + tax expense by interest expense.

Time period assumption – Time can be divided into any intervals for reporting accounting information. The time period covered by a financial statement is included in the title. Typical time periods for accounting reports are yearly, quarterly and monthly. Also reporting period.

Timeliness – When information is available to users before it loses its capacity to influence decisions.

Total comprehensive income – Calculated by adding profit or loss to other comprehensive income.

Trade accounts payable – The amount the business owes to suppliers.

Trade accounts receivable – The amount a customer owes to the business for goods or services purchased.

Trade discounts – Reductions to list price provided by a seller as incentives to purchase an item.

Transaction – Any exchange of value between two economic entities, which can involve money, goods and services or promises.

Treasury shares – An entity's own shares that have been acquired and are being held by that same entity. Also **investment in own shares.**

Trend analysis – Analysis that attempts to identify patterns in information over time.

Trial balance – A listing of accounts that shows the net balance (debit or credit) in each account. The total amount of debits and credits is calculated at the end.

True and fair view – The concept that financial statements meet fairly; represents the economic substance, the financial position, performance and changes in financial position, regularities of the application of specific accounting standards.

Uncollectible accounts expense – An expense of the business related to trade accounts receivable balance that could not be collected from customers because of bankruptcy, financial distress or other reasons.

Understandability – Users of financial accounts are assumed to have a reasonable knowledge of business, economic activities and financial accounting, and will study the information with reasonable diligence to comprehend its meaning.

Unearned revenue – A liability that represents the business's obligation to deliver a product or service at some future time. Unearned revenue is recorded when payment has been received and before delivery has taken place.

Unitary board – Both nonexecutive directors and executive directors serving on a single board that discharges all board obligations. Unitary boards are favored in both the UK and the US.

Units-of-production method – A depreciation method which allocates the depreciable amount based on the expected use or output from the asset.

Unsecured bond – A bond that is sold on the cognizance of the issuer, with no claim against assets.

Useful life – The period of time which a depreciable asset is expected to be used by the business.

Value added tax – A tax assessed on the value added to goods and services. Part of the total price paid by the customer is actually a tax being collected for the government by the seller.

Vendor invoice – The source document from which the accounting department records the trade accounts payable using a **purchase journal.**

Vertical analysis – Analysis that divides each line item on the statement of financial position by total assets and each line item on the statement of comprehensive income by revenue to calculate a percentage.

Voucher – A written record of expenditure or disbursement, such as a cash receipt.

Work-in-process – Goods on which production has begun but not completed by the end of the reporting period.

Working capital – The difference between current assets and current liabilities .

Zero-interest bond – A bond that pays no interest.

Index

Note: Page references in **bold** refer to terms in the Glossary; those in *italics* refer to Figures and Tables